Praise for SQL Queries for Mere Mortals®

The good books show you how to do something. The great books enable you to think clearly about how you can do it. This book is the latter. To really maximize the potential of your database, thinking about data as a set is required and the authors' accessible writing really brings out the practical applications of SQL and the set-based thinking behind it.

— Ben Clothier, Lead Developer at IT Impact, Inc., co-author of *Professional Access 2013 Programming*, and Microsoft Access MVP

Unless you are working at a very advanced level, this is the only SQL book you will ever need. The author has taken the mystery out of complex queries and explained principles and techniques with such clarity that a "Mere Mortal" will indeed be empowered to perform the superhuman. Do not walk past this book!

— Graham Mandeno, Database Consultant

It's beyond brilliant! I have been working with SQL for a really long time, and the techniques presented in this book exposed some of the bad habits I picked up over the years in my learning process. I wish I had learned these techniques a long time ago and saved myself all the headaches of learning SQL the hard way. Who said you can't teach old dogs new tricks?

— Leo (theDBguy), Utter Access Moderator and Microsoft Access MVP

I learned SQL primarily from the first and second editions of this book…Starting from how to design your tables so that SQL can be effective (a common problem for database beginners), and then continuing through the various aspects of SQL construction and capabilities, the reader can become a moderate expert upon completing the book and its samples. Learning how to convert a question in English into a meaningful SQL statement will greatly facilitate your mastery of the language. Numerous examples from real life will help you visualize how to use SQL to answer the questions about the data in your database. Just one of the "watch out for this trap" items will save you more than the cost of the book when you avoid that problem when writing your queries. I highly recommend this book if you want to tap the full potential of your database.

— Kenneth D. Snell, Ph.D., Database Designer/Programmer

I don't think they do this in public schools anymore, and it is a shame, but do you remember in the seventh and eighth grades when you learned to diagram a sentence? Those of you who do may no longer remember how you did it, but all of you do write better sentences because of it. John Viescas must have remembered because he takes everyday English queries and literally translates them into SQL. This is an important book for all database designers. It takes the complexity of mathematical set theory and of first order predicate logic, as outlined in E. F. Codd's original treatise on relational database design, and makes it easy for anyone to understand. If you want an elementary-through intermediate-level course on SQL, this is the one book that is a requirement, no matter how many others you buy.

— Arvin Meyer, MCP, MVP

SQL Queries for Mere Mortals, provides a step-by-step, easy-to-read introduction to writing SQL queries. It includes hundreds of examples with detailed explanations. This book provides the tools you need to understand, modify, and create SQL queries.

— Keith W. Hare, Convenor, ISO/IEC JTC1 SC32 WG3, the International SQL Standards Committee

Even in this day of wizards and code generators, successful database developers still require a sound knowledge of Structured Query Language (SQL, the standard language for communicating with most database systems). In this book, John does a marvelous job of making what's usually a dry and difficult subject come alive, presenting the material with humor in a logical manner, with plenty of relevant examples. I would say that this book should feature prominently in the collection on the bookshelf of all serious developers, except that I'm sure it'll get so much use that it won't spend much time on the shelf!

— Doug Steele, Microsoft Access Developer and author

I highly recommend *SQL Queries for Mere Mortals* to anyone working with data. John makes it easy to learn one of the most critical aspects of working with data: creating queries. Queries are the primary tool for selecting, sorting, and reporting data. They can compensate for table structure, new reporting requirements, and incorporate new data sources. *SQL Queries for Mere Mortals* uses clear, easy to understand discussions and examples to take readers through the basics and into complex problems. From novice to expert, you will find this book to be an invaluable reference as you can apply the concepts to a myriad of scenarios, regardless of the program.

— Teresa Hennig, Microsoft MVP-Access, and lead author of several Access books, including *Professional Access 2013 Programming* (Wrox)

SQL Queries *for* Mere Mortals®

Fourth Edition

A Hands-On Guide to Data Manipulation in SQL

John L. Viescas

♦♦ Addison-Wesley

Boston • Columbus • Indianapolis • New York • San Francisco • Amsterdam
Cape Town • Dubai • London • Madrid • Milan • Munich • Paris • Montreal • Toronto
Delhi • Mexico City • São Paulo • Sydney • Hong Kong • Seoul • Singapore • Taipei • Tokyo

For information about buying this title in bulk quantities, or for special sales opportunities (which may include electronic versions; custom cover designs; and content particular to your business, training goals, marketing focus, or branding interests), please contact our corporate sales department at corpsales@pearsoned.com or (800) 382-3419.

For government sales inquiries, please contact governmentsales@pearsoned.com.

For questions about sales outside the U.S., please contact intlcs@pearson.com.

Visit us on the Web: informit.com/aw

Library of Congress Control Number: 2017964124

Copyright © 2018 John L. Viescas

Pearson Education, Inc.

ISBN-13: 978-0-134-85833-3
ISBN-10: 0-134-85833-6

1   18

Editor-in-Chief: Mark Taub

Acquisitions Editor: Trina Macdonald

Development Editor: Rick Kughen

Managing Editor: Sandra Schroeder

Senior Project Editor: Lori Lyons

Production Manager: Dhayanidhi Karunanidhi

Copy Editor: Rick Kughen

Indexer: Lisa Stumpf

Proofreader: Abigail Manheim

Technical Reviewer: Douglas J. Steele

Cover Designer: Chuti Prasertsith

Compositor: codemantra

Contents at a Glance

Contents

Foreword

In the 30 years since the database language SQL was adopted as an international standard, and the 30 years since SQL database products appeared on the market, SQL has become the predominant language for storing, modifying, retrieving, and deleting data. Today, a significant portion of the world's data—and the world's economy—is tracked using SQL databases.

SQL is everywhere because it is a very powerful tool for manipulating data. It is in high-performance transaction processing systems. It is behind Web interfaces. I've even found SQL in network monitoring tools and spam firewalls.

Today, SQL can be executed directly, embedded in programming languages, and accessed through call interfaces. It is hidden inside GUI development tools, code generators, and report writers. However visible or hidden, the underlying queries are SQL. Therefore, to understand existing applications and to create new ones, you need to understand SQL.

SQL Queries for Mere Mortals, Fourth Edition, provides a step-by-step, easy-to-read introduction to writing SQL queries. It includes hundreds of examples with detailed explanations. This book provides the tools you need to understand, modify, and create SQL queries.

As a database consultant and a participant in both the U.S. and international SQL standards committees, I spend a lot of time working with SQL. So, it is with a certain amount of authority that I state, "The authors of this book not only understand SQL, they also understand how to explain it." Both qualities make this book a valuable resource.

—Keith W. Hare, Senior Consultant,
JCC Consulting, Inc. Vice Chair, INCITS DM32.2
—the USA SQL Standards Committee; Convenor, ISO/IEC JTC1 SC32 WG3
—the International SQL Standards Committee

Preface

*"Language is by its very nature a communal thing;
that is, it expresses never the exact thing
but a compromise—that which is common
to you, me, and everybody."*
—THOMAS ERNEST HULME, SPECULATIONS

Learning how to retrieve information from or manipulate information in a database is commonly a perplexing exercise. However, it can be a relatively easy task as long as you understand the question you're asking or the change you're trying to make to the database. After you understand the problem, you can translate it into the language used by any database system, which in most cases is Structured Query Language (SQL). You have to translate your request into an SQL statement so that your database system knows what information you want to retrieve or change. SQL provides the means for you and your database system to communicate.

Throughout my many years as a database consultant, I've found that the number of people who merely need to retrieve information from a database or perform simple data modifications in a database far outnumber those who are charged with the task of creating programs and applications for a database. Unfortunately, no books focus solely on this subject, particularly from a "mere mortals" viewpoint. There are numerous good books on SQL, to be sure, but most are targeted to database programming and development.

With this in mind, I decided it was time to write a book that would help people learn how to query a database properly and effectively. I, along with my good friend, Michael J. Hernandez, produced the first edition of this book in 2000. We created a second edition in 2008 that introduced basic ways to change data in your database using SQL. With the third edition in 2014, we stepped lightly into the realm of tougher problems—the sorts of problems that make the heads of even experienced users spin around three times. In this fourth edition, I expand your knowledge of tougher problems by covering Window functions and

Grouping Sets. The result of my effort is in your hands. This book is unique among SQL books in that it focuses on SQL with little regard to any one specific database system implementation. This fourth edition includes dozens of new examples, and I included versions of the sample databases using Microsoft Office Access, Microsoft SQL Server, and the popular open-source MySQL and PostgreSQL database systems. When you finish reading this book, you'll have the skills you need to retrieve or modify any information you require.

Acknowledgments

Writing a book such as this is always a cooperative effort. There are always editors, colleagues, friends, and relatives willing to lend their support and provide valuable advice when I need it the most. These people continually provide me with encouragement, help me to remain focused, and motivate me to see this project through to the end.

First and foremost, I want to thank my acquisitions editor, Trina MacDonald, for helping me get signed up to produce this fourth edition. Thanks also to Developmental Editor, Rick Kughen, for shepherding me along the way. And I can't forget the production staff—they're a great team! Next, I'd like to acknowledge my technical editor, Doug Steele. I also had help from one of my database friends, Ben Clothier. Thanks once again to all of you for your time and input and for helping me to make this a solid treatise on SQL queries.

Finally, another very special thanks to Keith Hare for providing the Foreword. As the Convenor of the International SQL Standards Committee, Keith is an SQL expert par excellence. I have a lot of respect for Keith's knowledge and expertise on the subject, and I'm pleased to have his thoughts and comments at the beginning of my book.

About the Author

John L. Viescas is an independent database consultant with more than 50 years of experience. He began his career as a systems analyst, designing large database applications for IBM mainframe systems. He spent 6 years at Applied Data Research in Dallas, Texas, where he directed a staff of more than 30 people and was responsible for research, product development, and customer support of database products for IBM mainframe computers. While working at Applied Data Research, John completed a degree in business finance at the University of Texas at Dallas, graduating cum laude.

John joined Tandem Computers, Inc., in 1988, where he was responsible for the development and implementation of database marketing programs in Tandem's U.S. Western Sales region. He developed and delivered technical seminars on Tandem's relational database management system, NonStop SQL. John wrote his first book, *A Quick Reference Guide to SQL* (Microsoft Press, 1989), as a research project to document the similarities in the syntax among the ANSI-86 SQL standard, IBM's DB2, Microsoft's SQL Server, Oracle Corporation's Oracle, and Tandem's NonStop SQL. He wrote the first edition of *Running Microsoft Access* (Microsoft Press, 1992) while on sabbatical from Tandem. He has since written four editions of *Running*, three editions of *Microsoft Office Access Inside Out* (Microsoft Press, 2003, 2007, and 2010—the successor to the *Running* series), *Building Microsoft Access Applications* (Microsoft Press, 2005), and *Effective SQL* (Addison-Wesley, 2017).

John formed his own company in 1993. He provides information systems management consulting for a variety of small to large businesses around the world, with a specialty in the Microsoft Access and SQL Server database management products. He maintains offices in Nashua, New Hampshire, and Paris, France. He was recognized as a "Most Valuable Professional" (MVP) from 1993 to 2015 by Microsoft Product Support Services for his assistance with technical questions on public support forums. He set a landmark 20 consecutive years as an MVP in 2013.

You can visit John's Web site at www.viescas.com or contact him by e-mail at john@viescas.com.

Reader Services

Register your copy of *SQL Queries for Mere Mortals* on the InformIT site for convenient access to updates and corrections as they become available. To start the registration process, go to informit.com/register and log in or create an account. Enter the product ISBN **9780134858333** and click Submit. Look on the Registered Products tab for an Access Bonus Content link next to this product, and follow that link to access any available bonus materials. If you would like to be notified of exclusive offers on new editions and updates, please check the box to receive email from us.

Introduction

"I presume you're mortal, and may err."
—James Shirley, *The Lady of Pleasure*

If you've used a computer more than casually, you have probably used Structured Query Language or SQL—perhaps without even knowing it. SQL is *the* standard language for communicating with most database systems. Any time you import data into a spreadsheet or perform a merge into a word processing program, you're most likely using SQL in some form or another. Every time you go online to an e-commerce site on the Web and place an order for a book, a recording, a movie, or any of the dozens of other products you can order, there's a very high probability that the code behind the web page you're using is accessing its databases with SQL. If you need to get information from a database system that uses SQL, you can enhance your understanding of the language by reading this book.

Are You a Mere Mortal?

You might ask, "Who is a *mere mortal*? Me?" The answer is not simple. When I started to write this book, I thought was an expert in the database language called SQL. Along the way, I discovered I am a mere mortal, too, in several areas. I understood a few specific implementations of SQL very well, but I unraveled many of the complex intricacies of the language as I studied how it is used in many commercial products. So, if you fit any of the following descriptions, you're a mere mortal, too!

- If you use computer applications that let you access information from a database system, you're probably a mere mortal. The first time you don't get the information you expected using the query tools built into your application, you'll need to explore the underlying SQL statements to find out why.

- If you have recently discovered one of the many available desktop database applications but are struggling with defining and querying the data you need, you're a mere mortal.

- If you're a database programmer who needs to "think outside of the box" to solve some complex problems, you're a mere mortal.

- If you're a database guru in one product but are now faced with integrating the data from your existing system into another system that supports SQL, you're a mere mortal.

In short, *anyone* who has to use a database system that supports SQL can use this book. As a beginning database user who has just discovered that the data you need can be fetched using SQL, you will find that this book teaches you all the basics and more. For an expert user who is suddenly faced with solving complex problems or integrating multiple systems that support SQL, this book will provide insights into leveraging the complex abilities of the SQL database language.

About This Book

Everything you read in this book is based on the current International Organization for Standardization (ISO) Standard for the SQL database language – SQL/Foundation (document ISO/IEC 9075-2:2016), as currently implemented in most of the popular commercial database systems. The ISO document was also adopted by the American National Standards Institute (ANSI), so this is truly an international standard. The SQL you'll learn here *is not* specific to any particular software product.

As you'll learn in more detail in Chapter 3, "A Concise History of SQL," the SQL Standard defines both more and less than you'll find implemented in most commercial database products. Most database vendors have yet to implement many of the more advanced features, but most do support the core of the standard.

I researched a wide range of popular products to make sure that you can use what I'm teaching in this book. Where I found parts of the core of the language not supported by some major products, I warn you in the text and show you alternate ways to state your database requests in standard SQL. When I found significant parts of the SQL Standard supported by only a few vendors, I introduced you to the syntax and then suggested alternatives.

I have organized this book into six major sections:

- Part I, "Relational Databases and SQL," explains how modern database systems are based on a rigorous mathematical model and provides a brief history of the database query language that has evolved into what is known as SQL. I also discuss some simple rules that you can use to make sure your database design is sound.

- Part II, "SQL Basics," introduces you to using the SELECT statement, creating expressions, and sorting information with an ORDER BY clause. You'll also learn how to filter data by using a WHERE clause.

- Part III, "Working with Multiple Tables," shows you how to formulate queries that draw data from more than one table. Here I show you how to link tables in a query using the INNER JOIN, OUTER JOIN, and UNION operators, and how to work with subqueries.

- Part IV, "Summarizing and Grouping Data," discusses how to obtain summary information and group and filter summarized data. Here is where you'll learn about the GROUP BY and HAVING clauses.

- Part V, "Modifying Sets of Data," explains how to write queries that modify a set of rows in your tables. In the chapters in this section, you'll learn how to use the UPDATE, INSERT, and DELETE statements.

- Part VI, "Introduction to Solving Tough Problems," dips your toes into more complex problems. In the chapters in this section, you'll expand your horizons to include solving complex "NOT" and "AND" problems (multiple conditions on one table), performing logical evaluations with CASE, and thinking "outside the box" using "unlinked" tables (Cartesian Products). You'll also learn how to use additional keywords in GROUP BY to create subtotals and roll-ups and to partition your output data into subsets.

At the end of the book in the appendices, you'll find syntax diagrams for all the SQL elements you've learned, layouts of the sample databases, a list of date and time manipulation functions implemented in six of the major database systems, and book recommendations to further your study of SQL. You can download the five sample databases for the four database systems (Microsoft Access, Microsoft SQL Server, MySQL, and PostgreSQL) from www.informit.com/title/9780134858333 and clicking the Downloads tab.

What This Book Is Not

Although this book is based on the 2016 SQL Standard that was current at the time of this writing, it does not cover every aspect of the standard. In truth, many features in the 2016 SQL Standard won't be implemented for many years—if at all—in the major database system implementations. The fundamental purpose of this book is to give you a solid grounding in writing queries in SQL. Throughout the book, you'll find me recommending that you "consult your database documentation" for how a specific feature might or might not work. That's not to say I covered only the lowest common denominator for any feature among the major database systems. I do try to caution you when some systems implement a feature differently or not at all.

You'll find it difficult to create other than simple queries using a single table if your database design is flawed. I included a chapter on database design to help you identify when you will have problems, but that one chapter includes only the basic principles. A thorough discussion of database design principles and how to implement a design in a specific database system is beyond the scope of this book.

This book is also not about how to solve a problem in the most efficient way. As you work through many of the later chapters, you'll find I suggest more than one way to solve a particular problem. In some cases where writing a query in a particular way is likely to have performance problems on any system, I try to warn you about it. But each database system has its own strengths and weaknesses. After you learn the basics, you'll be ready to move on to digging into the particular database system you use to learn how to formulate your query solutions so that they run in a more optimal manner.

How to Use This Book

I have designed the chapters in this book to be read in sequence. Each succeeding chapter builds on concepts taught in earlier chapters. However, you can jump into the middle of the book without getting lost. For example, if you are already familiar with the basic clauses in a SELECT statement and want to learn more about JOINs, you can jump right in to Chapters 7, "Thinking in Sets," 8, "INNER JOINs," and 9, "OUTER JOINs."

At the end of many of the chapters, you'll find an extensive set of "Sample Statements," their solutions, and sample result sets. I recommend that you study several of the samples to gain a better understanding of the techniques involved and then try working out some of the later "Problems for You to Solve" yourself without looking at the solutions I propose.

Note that where a particular query returns dozens of rows in the result set, I show you only the first few rows to give you an idea of how the answer should look. You might not see the same result on your system, however, because each database system that supports SQL has its own optimizer that figures out the fastest way to solve the query. Also, the first few rows you see returned by your database system might not exactly match the first few that I show you unless the query contains an ORDER BY clause that requires the rows to be returned in a specific sequence.

I've also included a complete set of problems for you to solve on your own, which you'll find at the end of most chapters. This gives you the opportunity to really practice what you've just learned in the chapter. Don't worry—the solutions are included in the sample databases that you can download from the book's website. I've also included hints on those problems that might be a little tricky.

After you have worked your way through the entire book, you'll find the complete SQL diagrams in Appendix A, "SQL Standard Diagrams," to be an invaluable reference for all the SQL techniques I showed you. You will also be able to use the sample database layouts in Appendix B, "Schema for the Sample Databases," to help you design your own databases.

Reading the Diagrams Used in This Book

The numerous diagrams throughout the book illustrate the proper syntax for the statements, terms, and phrases you'll use when you work with SQL. Each diagram provides a clear picture of the overall construction of the SQL element currently being discussed. You can also use any of these diagrams as templates to create your own SQL statements or to help you acquire a clearer understanding of a specific example.

All the diagrams are built from a set of core elements and can be divided into two categories: *statements* and *defined terms.* A statement is always a major SQL operation, such as the SELECT statement I discuss in this book, while a defined term is always a component used to build part of a statement, such as a *value expression*, a *search condition*, or a *predicate.* (Don't worry—I'll explain all these terms later in the book.) The only difference between a syntax diagram for a statement and a syntax diagram for a defined term is the manner in which the main syntax line begins and ends. I designed the diagrams with these differences so that you can clearly see whether you're looking at the diagram for an entire statement or a diagram for a term that you might use within a statement. Figure I-1 shows the beginning and end points for both diagram categories. Aside from this difference, the diagrams are built from the same elements. Figure I-2 shows an example of each type of syntax diagram and is followed by a brief explanation of each diagram element.

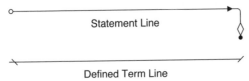

Figure I-1 *Syntax line end points for statements and defined terms*

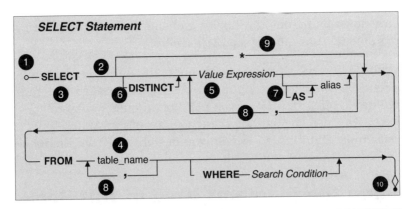

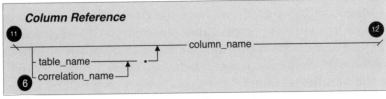

Figure I-2 *Sample statement and defined term diagrams*

1. ***Statement start point**—*denotes the beginning of the main syntax line for a statement. Any element that appears *directly on* the main syntax line is a *required element,* and any element that appears *below* it is an *optional element.*

2. ***Main syntax line**—*determines the order of all required and optional elements for the statement or defined term. Follow this line from left to right (or in the direction of the arrows) to build the syntax for the statement or defined term.

3. ***Keyword(s)**—*indicates a major word in SQL grammar that is a required part of the syntax for a statement or defined term. In a diagram, keywords are formatted in capital letters and bold font. (You don't have to worry about typing a keyword in capital letters when you actually write the statement in your database program, but it does make the statement easier to read.)

4. ***Literal entry**—*specifies the name of a value you explicitly supply to the statement. A literal entry is represented by a word or phrase that indicates the type of value you need to supply. Literal entries in a diagram are formatted in all lowercase letters.

5. ***Defined term**—*denotes a word or phrase that represents some operation that returns a final value to be used in this statement. I'll explain and diagram every defined term you need to know as you work through the book. Defined terms are always formatted in italic letters.

6. ***Optional element**—*indicates any element or group of elements that appears below the main syntax line. An optional element can be a statement, keyword, defined term, or literal value and, for purposes of clarity, appears on its own line. In some cases, you can specify a set of values for a given option, with each value separated by a comma (see number 8). Also, several optional elements have a set of sub-optional elements (see number 7). In general, you read the syntax line for an optional element from left to right, in the same manner that you read the main syntax line. Always follow the directional arrows and you'll be in good shape. Note that some options allow you to specify multiple values or choices, so the arrow will flow from right to left. After you've entered all the items you need, however, the flow will return to normal from left to right. Fortunately, all optional elements work the same way. After I show you how to use an optional element later in the book, you'll know how to use any other optional element you encounter in a syntax diagram.

7. *Sub-optional element*—denotes any element or group of elements that appears below an optional element. Sub-optional elements allow you to fine-tune your statements so that you can work with more complex problems.

8. *Option list separator*—indicates that you can specify more than one value for this option and that each value must be separated with a comma.

9. *Alternate option*—denotes a keyword or defined term that can be used as an alternative to one or more optional elements. The syntax line for an alternate option bypasses the syntax lines of the optional elements it is meant to replace.

10. *Statement end point*—denotes the end of the main syntax line for a statement.

11. *Defined term start point*—denotes the beginning of the main syntax line for a defined term.

12. *Defined term end point*—denotes the end of the main syntax line for a defined term.

Now that you're familiar with these elements, you'll be able to read all the syntax diagrams in the book. And on those occasions when a diagram requires further explanation, I provide you with the information you need to read the diagram clearly and easily. To help you better understand how the diagrams work, here's a sample SELECT statement that I built using Figure I-2.

```
SELECT FirstName, LastName, City, DOB AS DateOfBirth
FROM Students
WHERE City = 'El Paso'
```

This SELECT statement retrieves four columns from the Students table, as I've indicated in the SELECT and FROM clauses. As you follow the main syntax line from left to right, you see that you have to indicate at least one *value expression*. A value expression can be a column name, an expression created using column names, or simply a constant (literal) value that you want to display. You can indicate as many columns as you need with the value expression's *option list separator* (a comma). This is how I was able to use four column names from the Students table. I was concerned that some people viewing the information returned by this SELECT statement might not know what DOB means, so I assigned an *alias* to the DOB column with the value expression's AS sub-option. Finally, I used the WHERE clause to make certain the SELECT statement shows only those students who live in El Paso. (If this doesn't quite make sense to you just now, there's no cause for alarm. You'll learn all this in great detail throughout the remainder of the book.)

You'll find a full set of syntax diagrams in Appendix A. They show the complete and proper syntax for all the statements and defined terms that I discuss in the book. If you happen to refer to these diagrams as you work through each chapter, you'll notice a slight disparity between some of the diagrams in a given chapter and the corresponding diagrams in the appendix. The diagrams in the chapters are just simplified versions of the diagrams in the appendix. These simplified versions allow me to explain complex statements and defined terms more easily and give me the ability to focus on particular elements as needed. But don't worry—all the diagrams in the appendix will make perfect sense after you work through the material in the book.

Sample Databases Used in This Book

On the book website at www.informit.com/title/9780134858333 you'll find a downloadable file on the Downloads tab containing nine sample databases that I use for the example queries throughout the book. I've also included diagrams of the database structures in Appendix B.

1. **Sales Orders.** This is a typical order entry database for a store that sells bicycles and accessories. (Every database book needs at least one order entry example, right?)

2. **Entertainment Agency.** I structured this database to manage entertainers, agents, customers, and bookings. You would use a similar design to handle event bookings or hotel reservations.

3. **School Scheduling.** You might use this database design to register students at a high school or community college. This database tracks not only class registrations but also which instructors are assigned to each class and what grades the students received.

4. **Bowling League.** This database tracks bowling teams, team members, the matches they played, and the results.

5. **Recipes.** You can use this database to save and manage all your favorite recipes. I even added a few that you might want to try.

In the sample files, you can find all five of the sample databases in four different formats:

- Because of the great popularity of the Microsoft Office Access desktop database, I created one set of databases (.accdb file extension) using Microsoft Access 2007 (Version 12.0) format. I chose the Version 12 format of this product because it closely supports the current ISO/IEC SQL Standard, and you can open database files in this format using Access 2007, 2010, 2013, and later. You can find these files in the MSAccess subfolder. (I tested all the sample queries using Microsoft Access 2016.)

- The second format consists of database files (.mdf file extension) created using Microsoft SQL Server 2016 Express Edition. You can find these files in the MSSQLServer folder, and you can attach these files to a Microsoft SQL Server 2016 or later server. I have also included SQL command files (.sql file extension) that you can use to create the samples on a Microsoft SQL Server from scratch. You can find these files in the SQLScripts subfolder. You can obtain a free copy of Microsoft SQL Server 2016 Express Edition at www.microsoft.com/en-us/sql-server/sql-server-editions-express.

- I created the third set of databases using the popular open-source MySQL version 5.7.18 Community Edition database system. You can use the scripts (.sql file extension) that you will find in the SQLScripts subfolder to create the database structure, load the data, and create the sample views and stored procedures in your own MySQL data folder. You can obtain a free copy of the community edition of the MySQL database system at www.mysql.com/.

- The fourth set of databases uses the popular PostgreSQL version 9.6.3. As with MySQL, you can use the scripts (.sql file extension) that you will find in the SQLScripts subfolder to create the database structure, load the data, and create the sample views and functions. You can obtain a free copy of PostgreSQL at www.postresql.org.

To install the sample files, see the file ReadMe.txt included in the files you can download from www.informit.com/title/9780134858333

❖ **Note** Although I was very careful to use the most common and simplest syntax for the CREATE TABLE, CREATE INDEX, CREATE CONSTRAINT, and INSERT commands in the sample SQL scripts, you (or your database administrator) might need to modify these files slightly to work with your database system. If you're working with a database system on a remote server, you might need to gain permission from your database administrator to build the samples from the SQL commands that I supplied.

For the chapters in Parts II, III, IV, and VI that focus on the SELECT statement, you'll find all the example statements and solutions in the "example" version of each sample database (for example, SalesOrdersExample, Entertainment-AgencyExample). Because the examples in Part V modify the sample data, I created "modify" versions of each of the sample databases (for example, Sales-OrdersModify, EntertainmentAgencyModify). The sample databases for Part V also include additional columns and tables not found in the SELECT examples that enable me to demonstrate certain features of UPDATE, INSERT, and DELETE queries.

❖ **Caution** Throughout the book, I use ISO-Standard SQL when I explain concepts and show you sample statements. In many cases, I was able to use this SQL directly to create the sample Views, Functions, or Stored Procedures that you'll find in the sample databases. However, in many cases I had to modify the sample SQL so that it would work correctly with the target database system. For example, to create date expressions or calculations, I chose to use the appropriate function supported by the target database system. (For a list of all date and time functions supported by six of the major database systems, see Appendix C, "Date and Time Types, Operations, and Functions.")

Also, although I used scripts that closely match the original samples in the book, Microsoft SQL Server, MySQL, and PostgreSQL will modify the original SQL to "optimize" it before saving the view, function, or stored procedure. If you use Design in SQL Server Management Studio or Alter in MySQL Workbench or PostgreSQL pgAdmin to edit the view or procedure, what you see saved in the database might differ considerably from the script I used to define the view or procedure. When in doubt, always refer to the companion script file to see the SQL that I used.

"Follow the Yellow Brick Road"

—MUNCHKIN TO DOROTHY IN *THE WIZARD OF OZ*

Now that you've read through the Introduction, you're ready to start learning SQL, right? Well, maybe. At this point, you're still in the house, it's still being tossed about by the tornado, and you haven't left Kansas.

Before you make that jump to Chapter 4, "Creating a Sample Query," take my advice and read through the first three chapters. Chapter 1, "What Is Relational?," will give you an idea of how the relational database was conceived and how it has grown to be the most widely used type of database in the industry today. I hope this will give you some amount of insight into the database system you're currently using. In Chapter 2, "Ensuring Your Database Structure Is Sound," you'll learn how to fine-tune your data structures so that your data is reliable and, above all, accurate. You're going to have a tough time working with some of the SQL statements if you have poorly designed data structures, so I suggest you read this chapter carefully.

Chapter 3, "A Concise History of SQL," is literally the beginning of the "yellow brick road." Here you'll learn the origins of SQL and how it evolved into its current form. You'll also learn about some of the people and companies who helped pioneer the language and why there are so many varieties of SQL. Finally, you'll learn how SQL came to be a national and international standard and what the outlook for SQL will be in the years to come.

After you've read these chapters, consider yourself well on your way to Oz. Just follow the road I've laid out through each of the remaining chapters. When you've finished the book, you'll find that you've found the wizard—and he is you.

Part I

Relational Databases and SQL

What Is Relational?

"Knowledge is the small part of ignorance that we arrange and classify."
—Ambrose Bierce

Topics Covered in This Chapter

Types of Databases

A Brief History of the Relational Model

Anatomy of a Relational Database

What's in It for You?

Summary

Before jumping right into SQL, you should understand the logic behind the structure of the databases that SQL supports. In this chapter, you'll learn why the relational database was invented, how it is constructed, and why you should use it. This information provides the foundation you need to understand what SQL really is all about and will eventually help to clarify how you can leverage SQL to your best advantage.

Types of Databases

What is a database? As you probably know, a database is an organized collection of data used to model some type of organization or organizational process. It really doesn't matter whether you're using paper or an application program to collect and store the data. You have a database as long as you're collecting and storing data in some organized manner for a specific purpose. Throughout the remainder of this discussion, I'll assume that you're using an application program to collect and maintain your data.

Generally, two types of databases are used in database management: *operational databases* and *analytical databases.*

Operational databases are the backbone of many companies, organizations, and institutions throughout the world today. This type of database is primarily used to collect, modify, and maintain data on a day-to-day basis. The type of data stored is *dynamic*, meaning that it changes constantly and always reflects up-to-the-minute information. Organizations such as retail stores, manufacturing companies, hospitals and clinics, and publishing houses use operational databases because their data is in a constant state of flux.

In contrast, an analytical database stores and tracks historical and time-dependent data. It is a valuable asset for tracking trends, viewing statistical data over a long period, or making tactical or strategic business projections. The type of data stored is *static*, meaning that the data is never (or very rarely) modified, although new data might often be added. The information gleaned from an analytical database reflects a point-in-time snapshot of the data and is usually not up to date. Chemical labs, geological companies, and marketing analysis firms are examples of organizations that use analytical databases. Note that the data found in analytical databases is usually gleaned from an operational database. For example, sales history each month might be summarized and saved in an analytical database.

A Brief History of the Relational Model

Several types of database models exist. Some, such as hierarchical and network, are used only on legacy systems, while others, such as relational, have gained wide acceptance. You might also encounter discussions in other books about object, object-relational, or online analytical processing (OLAP) models. In fact, there are extensions defined in the SQL Standard that support these models, and some commercial database systems have implemented some of these extensions. For my purposes, however, I will focus strictly on the relational model and the core of the international SQL Standard.

In the Beginning . . .

The relational database was first conceived in 1969 and has arguably become the most widely used database model in database management today. The father of the relational model, Dr. Edgar F. Codd (1923–2003), was an IBM research scientist in the late 1960s and was at that time looking into new ways to handle large amounts of data. His dissatisfaction with database models and database products of the time led him to begin thinking of ways to apply the disciplines and structures of mathematics to solve the myriad problems he had been encountering. A mathematician by profession, he strongly believed that he could apply specific branches of mathematics to solve problems such as data redundancy, weak data integrity, and a database structure's overdependence on its physical implementation.

Dr. Codd formally presented his new relational model in a landmark work titled "A Relational Model of Data for Large Shared Databanks" in June 1970.[1] He based his new model on two branches of mathematics—set theory and first-order predicate logic. Indeed, the name of the model itself is derived from the term *relation*, which is part of set theory. (A widely held misconception is that the relational model derives its name from the fact that tables within a relational database can be related to one another. However, the term relation in the model is used to describe what most relational database systems call a table. Now that you know the truth, you'll have a peaceful, restful sleep tonight!) Fortunately, you don't need to know the details of set theory or first-order predicate logic to design and use a relational database. If you use a good database design methodology—such as the one presented in Mike Hernandez's *Database Design for Mere Mortals,* Third Edition (Addison-Wesley, 2013)—you can develop a sound and effective database structure that you can confidently use to collect and maintain any data. (Well, OK, you *do* need to understand a little bit about predicates and set theory to solve more complex problems. I cover the essentials that you need to know about predicates—really a fancy name for a filter—in Chapter 6, "Filtering Your Data," and the basics of set theory in Chapter 7, "Thinking in Sets.")

Relational Database Systems

A *relational database management system* (RDBMS) is a software application program you use to create, maintain, modify, and manipulate a relational database. Many RDBMS programs also provide the tools you need to create end-user applications that interact with the data stored

---

1. *Communications of the ACM,* June 1970, 377–87.

in the database. RDBMS programs have continually evolved since their first appearance, and they continue to become more full-featured and powerful as advances occur in hardware technology and operating environments.

In the earliest days of the relational database, RDBMSs were written for use on mainframe computers. Two RDBMS programs prevalent in the early 1970s were System R, developed by IBM at its San Jose Research Laboratory in California, and Interactive Graphics Retrieval System (INGRES), developed at the University of California at Berkeley. These two programs contributed greatly to the general appreciation of the relational model.

As the benefits of the relational database became more widely known, many companies decided to make a slow move from hierarchical and network database models to the relational database model, thus creating a need for more and better mainframe RDBMS programs. The 1980s saw the development of various commercial RDBMSs for mainframe computers by companies such as Oracle and IBM.

The early to mid-1980s saw the rise of the personal computer, and with it, the development of PC-based RDBMS programs. Some of the early entries in this category, from companies such as Ashton-Tate and Fox Software, were nothing more than elementary file-based database-management systems. True PC-based RDBMS programs began to emerge with products developed by companies such as Microrim and Ansa Software. These companies helped to spread the idea and potential of database management from the mainframe-dominated domain of information systems departments to the desktop of the common end user.

The need to share data became apparent as more and more users worked with databases throughout the late 1980s and early 1990s. The concept of a centrally located database that could be made available to multiple users seemed a very promising idea. This would certainly make data management and database security much easier to implement. Database vendors such as Microsoft and Oracle responded to this need by developing *client/server* RDBMS programs.

The manner in which databases are used evolved immensely over the years, and many organizations began to realize that a lot of useful information could be gathered from data they stored in various relational and nonrelational databases. This prompted them to question whether there was a way to mine the data for useful analytical information that they could then use to make critical business decisions.

Furthermore, they wondered whether they could consolidate and integrate their data into a viable knowledgebase for their organizations. Indeed, these would be difficult questions to answer.

IBM proposed the idea of a *data warehouse*, which, as originally conceived, would enable organizations to access data stored in any number of nonrelational databases. It was unsuccessful in its first attempts at implementing data warehouses, primarily because of the complexities and performance problems associated with such a task. Only since the 1990s has the implementation of data warehouses become more viable and practical. William H. (Bill) Inmon, widely regarded as the father of the data warehouse, is a strong and vocal advocate of the technology and has been instrumental in its evolution. Data warehouses are now more commonplace as companies move to leverage the vast amounts of data they've stored in their databases over the years.

The Internet has had a significant impact on the way organizations use databases. Many companies and businesses use the Web to expand their consumer base, and much of the data they share with and gather from these consumers is stored in a database. Developers commonly use eXtensible Markup Language (XML) to assemble and consolidate data from various relational and nonrelational systems.

There has been a considerable effort by various vendors to get their clients to create databases and store data in the "cloud"; that is, a location that is completely apart from the client's location. The idea is that the client can access data from the cloud database via the Internet from anywhere at any time. As an example of using the "cloud" for database management, Microsoft's focus in the last several releases of Microsoft Access has been to migrate data from desktop devices to cloud servers. Given the broad emergence and use of connected devices within the past several years (as of this writing), it will be interesting to see how database management systems evolve within this type of environment.

Anatomy of a Relational Database

According to the relational model, data in a relational database is stored in *relations*, which are perceived by the user as tables. Each relation is composed of *tuples* (records or rows) and *attributes* (fields or columns). A relational database has several other characteristics, which are discussed in this section.

Tables

Tables are the main structures in the database. Each table always represents a single, specific subject. The logical order of rows and columns within a table is of absolutely no importance. Every table contains at least one column—known as a *primary key*—that uniquely identifies each of its rows. (In Figure 1-1, for example, CustomerID is the primary key of the Customers table.) In fact, data in a relational database can exist independent of the way it is physically stored in the computer because of these last two table characteristics. This is great news for users because they aren't required to know the physical location of a row in order to retrieve its data.

The subject that a given table represents can be either an *object* or an *event*. When the subject is an object, the table represents something that is tangible, such as a person, place, or thing. Regardless of its type, every object has characteristics that can be stored as data. You can then process this data in an almost infinite number of ways. Pilots, products, machines, students, buildings, and equipment are all examples of objects that can be represented by a table. Figure 1-1 illustrates one of the most common examples of this type of table.

Customers

CustomerID	FirstName	LastName	StreetAddress	City	State	ZipCode
1010	Angel	Kennedy	667 Red River Road	Austin	TX	78710
1011	Alaina	Hallmark	Route 2, Box 203B	Woodinville	WA	98072
1012	Liz	Keyser	13920 S.E. 40th Street	Bellevue	WA	98006
1013	Rachel	Patterson	2114 Longview Lane	San Diego	CA	92199
1014	Sam	Abolrous	611 Alpine Drive	Palm Springs	CA	92263
1015	Darren	Gehring	2601 Seaview Lane	Chico	CA	95926

Rows

COLUMNS

Figure 1-1 *A sample table*

When the subject of a table is an event, the table represents something that occurs at a given point in time and has characteristics you wish to record. These characteristics can be stored as data and then processed as information in the same manner as a table that represents some specific object. Examples of events you might need to record include judicial hearings, distributions of funds, lab test results, and geological surveys. In a sales orders database, an order can be considered both an object (the physical piece of paper representing an order) and an event (the shipment of the items ordered). Figure 1-2 shows an example of a table representing an event that we all have experienced at one time or another—a doctor's appointment.

Patient Visit

PatientID	VisitDate	VisitTime	Physician	BloodPressure	Temperature
92001	2006-05-01	10:30	Ehrlich	120 / 80	98.8
96105	2006-05-02	11:00	Hallmark	160 / 90	99.1
96203	2006-05-02	14:00	Hallmark	110 / 75	99.3
97002	2006-05-01	13:00	Hallmark	112 / 74	97.5
98003	2006-05-02	9:30	Fournier	120 / 82	98.6
99014	2006-05-02	9:30	Fournier	120 / 80	98.8

Figure 1-2 *A table representing events*

Columns

A column is the smallest structure in the database, and it represents a characteristic of the subject of the table to which it belongs. Columns are the structures that store data. You can retrieve the data in these columns and then present it as information in almost any configuration imaginable. Remember that the quality of the information you get from your data is in direct proportion to the amount of time you've dedicated to ensuring the structural integrity and data integrity of the columns themselves. There is just no way to underestimate the importance of columns.

Every column in a properly designed database contains one and only one value, and its name identifies the type of value it holds. This makes entering data into a column very intuitive. If you see columns with names such as FirstName, LastName, City, State, and ZipCode, you know exactly what type of value goes into each column. You'll also find it very easy to sort the data by state or to look for everyone whose last name is Viescas.

Rows

A row represents a unique instance of the subject of a table. It is composed of the entire set of columns in a table, regardless of whether or not the columns contain any values. Because of the manner in which a table is defined, each row is identified throughout the database by a unique value in the primary key column(s) of that row.

In Figure 1-1, for example, each row represents a unique customer within the table, and the CustomerID column identifies a given customer throughout the database. In turn, each row includes all the columns within the table, and each column describes some aspect of the customer represented by the row. Rows are a key factor in understanding table relationships because you need to know how a row in one table relates to other rows in another table.

Keys

Keys are special columns that play very specific roles within a table. The type of key determines its purpose within the table. Although a table might contain several types of keys, I will limit my discussion to the two most important ones: the *primary key* and the *foreign key*.

A primary key consists of one or more columns that uniquely identify each row within a table. (When a primary key is composed of two or more columns, it is known as a *composite primary key*.) The primary key is the most important for two reasons: Its *value* identifies *a specific row* throughout the entire database, and its *column* identifies *a given table* throughout the entire database. Primary keys also enforce table-level integrity and help establish relationships with other tables. Every table in your database should have a primary key.

The AgentID column in Figure 1-3 is a good example of a primary key because it uniquely identifies each agent within the Agents table and helps to guarantee table-level integrity by ensuring nonduplicate rows. It is also used to establish relationships between the Agents table and other tables in the database, such as the Entertainers table shown in the example.

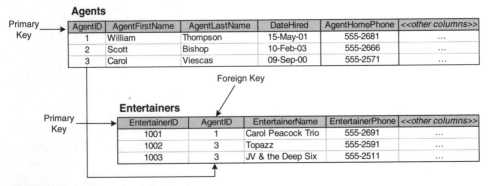

Figure 1-3 *Primary and foreign keys*

When you determine that a pair of tables has a relationship to each other, you typically establish the relationship by taking a copy of the primary key from the first table and inserting it into the second table, where it becomes a foreign key. (The term *foreign key* is derived from the fact that the second table already has a primary key of its own, and the primary key you are introducing from the first table is foreign to the second table.)

Figure 1-3 also shows a good example of a foreign key. In this example, AgentID is the primary key of the Agents table, and it is a foreign key in the Entertainers table. As you can see, the Entertainers table already has a primary key—EntertainerID. In this relationship, AgentID is the column that establishes the connection between Agents and Entertainers.

Foreign keys are important not only for the obvious reason that they help establish relationships between pairs of tables but also because they help ensure relationship-level integrity. This means that the rows in both tables will always be properly related because the values of a foreign key *must* be drawn from the values of the primary key to which it refers. Foreign keys also help you avoid the dreaded "orphaned rows," a classic example of which is an order row without an associated customer. If you don't know who placed the order, you can't process it, and you obviously can't invoice it. That'll throw off your quarterly sales!

Views

A view is a virtual table composed of columns from one or more tables in the database. The tables that comprise the view are known as *base tables*. The relational model refers to a view as virtual because it draws data from base tables rather than storing any data on its own. In fact, the only information about a view that is stored in the database is its structure.

Views enable you to see the information in your database from many different perspectives, thus providing great flexibility for working with data. You can create views in a variety of ways—they are especially useful when based on multiple related tables. For example, you can create a view that summarizes information such as the total number of hours worked by every carpenter within the downtown Seattle area. Or you can create a view that groups data by specific columns. An example of this type of view is displaying the total number of employees in each city within every state of a specified set of regions. Figure 1-4 presents an example of a typical view.

In many RDBMS programs, a view is commonly implemented and referred to as a *saved query* or, more simply, a *query*. In most cases, a query has all the characteristics of a view, so the only difference is that it is referred to by a different name. (I often wonder if someone in some marketing department had something to do with this.) It's important to note that some vendors refer to a query by its real name. Regardless of what it's called in your RDBMS program, you'll certainly use views in your database.

Customers

CustomerID	CustFirstName	CustLastName	CustPhone	<<other columns>>
10001	Doris	Hartwig	555-2671	...
10002	Deb	Waldal	555-2496	...
10003	Peter	Brehm	555-2501	...
<< more rows here >>				

Engagements

EngagementNumber	CustomerID	StartDate	EndDate	StartTime	<<other columns>>
3	10001	2016-09-10	2016-09-15	13:00	...
13	10003	2016-09-17	2016-09-20	20:00	...
14	10001	2016-09-24	2016-09-29	16:00	...
17	10002	2016-09-29	2016-10-02	18:00	...
<< more rows here >>					

Customer_Engagements *(view)*

EngagementNumber	CustFirstName	CustLastName	StartDate	EndDate
3	Doris	Hartwig	2016-09-10	2016-09-15
13	Peter	Brehm	2016-09-17	2016-09-20
14	Doris	Hartwig	2016-09-24	2016-09-29
17	Deb	Waldal	2016-09-29	2016-10-02
<< more rows here >>				

Figure 1-4 *A sample view*

Having said that, the name of this book is *SQL Queries for Mere Mortals*, but I'm really focused on teaching you how to build views. As you'll learn in Chapter 2, "Ensuring Your Database Structure Is Sound," the correct way to design a relational database is to break up your data so that you have one table per subject or event. Most of the time, however, you'll want to get information about related subjects or events—which customers placed what orders or what classes are taught by which instructors. To do that, you need to build a view, and you need to know SQL to do that.

Relationships

If rows in a given table can be associated in some way with rows in another table, the tables are said to have a relationship between them. The manner in which the relationship is established depends on the type of relationship. Three types of relationships can exist between a pair of tables: one-to-one, one-to-many, and many-to-many. Understanding relationships is crucial to understanding how views work and, by definition, how multi-table SQL queries are designed and used. (You'll learn more about this in Part III, "Working with Multiple Tables.")

One-to-One

A pair of tables has a one-to-one relationship when a single row in the first table is related to *only one* row in the second table, and a single row in the second table is related to *only one* row in the first table. In this type of relationship, one table is referred to as the *primary table*, and the other is referred to as the *secondary table*. You establish this relationship by taking the primary key of the primary table and inserting it into the secondary table, where it becomes a foreign key. This is a special type of relationship because in nearly all cases the foreign key also acts as the primary key of the secondary table.

Figure 1-5 shows an example of a typical one-to-one relationship in which Agents is the primary table and Compensation is the secondary table. The relationship between these tables is such that a single row in the Agents table can be related to only one row in the Compensation table, and a single row in the Compensation table can be related to only one row in the Agents table. Note that AgentID is indeed the primary key in both tables but also serves as a foreign key in the secondary table.

Agents

AgentID	AgentFirstName	AgentLastName	DateOfHire	AgentHomePhone	<<*other columns*>>
1	William	Thompson	1997-05-15	555-2681	...
2	Scott	Bishop	1998-02-05	555-2666	...
3	Carol	Viescas	1997-11-19	555-2571	...

Compensation

AgentID	Salary	CommissionRate	<<*other columns*>>
1	$35,000.00	4.00%	...
2	$27,000.00	4.00%	...
3	$30,000.00	5.00%	...

Figure 1-5 *An example of a one-to-one relationship*

The selection of the table that will play the primary role in this type of relationship depends on whether rows can exist in one table with no matching row in the other table. You cannot add rows to the secondary table in a one-to-one relationship unless a matching row already exists in the primary table. For example, a new agent might be hired, but the compensation is not decided yet. You need to be able to define the agent without requiring that a matching compensation row exists, so Agent becomes the primary table. Also, defining a compensation row for an employee who doesn't exist does not make sense, so clearly compensation is the secondary table. One-to-one relationships are not very common and are usually found in cases where a table has been split into two parts for confidentiality purposes.

One-to-Many

When a pair of tables has a one-to-many relationship, a single row in the first table can be related to *many* rows in the second table, but a single row in the second table can be related to *only one* row in the first table. This relationship is established by taking the primary key of the table on the "one" side and inserting it into the table on the "many" side, where it becomes a foreign key.

Figure 1-6 shows a typical one-to-many relationship. In this example, a single row in the Entertainers table can be related to *many* rows in the Engagements table, but a single row in the Engagements table can be related to *only one* row in the Entertainers table. As you probably have guessed, EntertainerID is a foreign key in the Engagements table.

Entertainers

EntertainerID	EntertainerName	EntertainerPhone	<<other columns>>
1001	Carol Peacock Trio	555-2691	...
1002	Topazz	555-2591	...
1003	JV & the Deep Six	555-2511	...

Engagements

EngagementID	EntertainerID	CustomerID	StartDate	EndDate	<<other columns>>
5	1003	10006	2007-09-11	2007-09-14	...
7	1002	10004	2007-09-11	2007-09-18	...
10	1003	10005	2007-09-17	2007-09-26	...
12	1001	10014	2007-09-18	2007-09-26	...

Figure 1-6 *An example of a one-to-many relationship*

Many-to-Many

A pair of tables is in a many-to-many relationship when a single row in the first table can be related to *many* rows in the second table, and a single row in the second table can be related to *many* rows in the first table. To establish this relationship properly, you must create what is known as a *linking table*. This table provides an easy way to associate rows from one table with those of the other and will help to ensure that you have no problems adding, deleting, or modifying any related data. You define a linking table by taking a copy of the primary key of each table in the relationship and using them to form the structure of the new table. These columns actually serve two distinct roles: Together they form the composite primary key of the linking table, and separately they each serve as a foreign key.

A many-to-many relationship that has not been properly established is said to be *unresolved*. Figure 1-7 shows a clear example of an unresolved many-to-many relationship. In this case, a single row in the Customers table can be related to *many* rows in the Entertainers table, *and* a single row in the Entertainers table can be related to *many* rows in the Customers table.

Customers

CustomerID	CustFirstName	CustLastName	CustPhone	*<<other columns>>*
10001	Doris	Hartwig	555-2671	...
10002	Deb	Waldal	555-2496	...
10003	Peter	Brehm	555-2501	...

Entertainers

EntertainerID	EntertainerName	EntertainerPhone	*<<other columns>>*
1001	Carol Peacock Trio	555-2691	...
1002	Topazz	555-2591	...
1003	JV & the Deep Six	555-2511	...

Figure 1-7 *An unresolved many-to-many relationship*

This relationship is unresolved because of the inherent problem with a many-to-many relationship. The issue is this: How do you easily associate rows from the first table with rows in the second table? To reframe the question regarding the tables shown in Figure 1-7, how do you associate a single customer with several entertainers or a specific entertainer with several customers? (If you are running an entertainment booking agency, you certainly hope that any one customer will book multiple entertainers over time and that any one entertainer has more than one customer!) Do you insert a few columns from the Customers table into the Entertainers table? Or do you add several columns from the Entertainers table to the Customers table? Either of these approaches is going to create some problems when you try to work with related data, not least of which regards data integrity. The solution to this dilemma is to create a linking table in the manner previously stated. By creating and using the linking table, you can properly resolve the many-to-many relationship. Figure 1-8 shows this solution in practice.

Customers

CustomerID	CustFirstName	CustLastName	CustPhone	<<other columns>>
10001	Doris	Hartwig	555-2671	...
10002	Deb	Waldal	555-2496	...
10003	Peter	Brehm	555-2501	...

Engagements ↓ **(linking table)**

EngagementID	CustomerID	EntertainerID	StartDate	<<other columns>>
43	10001	1001	2007-10-21	...
58	10001	1002	2007-12-01	...
62	10003	1005	2007-12-09	...
71	10002	1003	2007-12-22	...
125	10001	1003	2008-02-23	...

Entertainers

EntertainerID	EntertainerName	EntertainerPhone	<<other columns>>
1001	Carol Peacock Trio	555-2691	...
1002	Topazz	555-2591	...
1003	JV & the Deep Six	555-2511	...

Figure 1-8 *A properly resolved many-to-many relationship*

The linking table in Figure 1-8 was created by taking the CustomerID from the Customers table and the EntertainerID from the Entertainers table and using them as the basis for a new table. As with any other table in the database, the new linking table has its own name—Engagements. In fact, the Engagements table is a good example of a table that stores the information about an event. Entertainer 1003 (JV & the Deep Six) played an engagement for customer 10001 (Doris Hartwig) on February 23. And a linking table lets you store additional information about the link—like the date and perhaps the cost of the engagement. The real advantage of a linking table is that it allows you to associate any number of rows from both tables in the relationship. As the example shows, you can now easily associate a given customer with any number of entertainers or a specific entertainer with any number of customers.

As I stated earlier, understanding relationships will pay great dividends when you begin to work with multi-table SQL queries, so be sure to revisit this section when you begin working on Part III of this book.

What's in It for You?

Why should you be concerned with understanding relational databases? Why should you even care what kind of environment you're using to work with your data? And in addition to all this, what's really in it for you? Here's where the enlightenment starts and the fun begins.

The time you spend learning about relational databases is an investment, and it is to your distinct advantage to do so. You should develop a good working knowledge of the relational database because it's the most widely used data model in existence today. Forget what you read in the trades and what Harry over in the Information Technology Services department told you—a vast majority of the data being used by businesses and organizations is being collected, maintained, and manipulated in relational databases. Yes, there have been extensions to the model, the application programs that work with relational databases have been injected with object orientation, and relational databases have been thoroughly integrated into the Web and the cloud. But no matter how you slice it, dice it, and spice it, it's still a relational database! The relational database has been around for more than 40 years, it's still going strong, and it's not going be replaced anytime in the foreseeable future.

Nearly all commercial database management software used today is relational. (However, folks such as C. J. Date and Fabian Pascal might seriously question whether any commercial implementation is truly relational!) If you want to be gainfully employed in the database field, you'd better know how to design a relational database and how to implement it using one of the popular RDBMS programs. And now that so many companies and corporations depend on the Internet, the cloud, and connected services, you'd better have some Web development experience under your belt as well.

Having a good working knowledge of relational databases is helpful in many ways. For instance, the more you know about how relational databases are designed, the easier it will be for you to develop end-user applications for a given database. You'll also be surprised by how intuitive your RDBMS program will become because you'll understand why it provides the tools it does and how to use those tools to your best advantage. Your working knowledge will be a great asset as you learn how to use SQL because SQL is the standard language for creating, maintaining, and working with a relational database.

Where Do You Go from Here?

Now that you know the importance of learning about relational databases, you must understand that there is a difference between *database theory* and *database design*. Database theory involves the principles and rules that formulate the basis of the relational database model. It is what is learned in the hallowed halls of academia and then quickly dismissed in the dark dens of the real world. But theory is important, nonetheless, because it guarantees that the relational database is structurally sound and that all actions taken on the data in the database have predictable results. On the other hand, database design involves the structured, organized set of processes used to design a relational database. A good database design methodology will help you ensure the integrity, consistency, and accuracy of the data in the database and guarantee that any information you retrieve will be as accurate and up to date as possible.

If you want to design and create enterprise-wide databases, or develop web-based Internet commerce databases, or begin to delve into data warehousing, you should seriously think about studying database theory. This applies even if you're not going to explore any of these areas but are considering becoming a high-end database consultant. For the rest of you who are going to design and create relational databases on a variety of platforms (which, I believe, is the vast majority of the people reading this book), learning a good, solid database design methodology will serve you well. Always remember that designing a database is relatively easy, but *implementing* a database within a specific RDBMS program on a particular platform is another issue altogether. (Another story, another book, another time.)

There are a number of good database design books on the market. Some, such as Mike Hernandez's companion book *Database Design for Mere Mortals*, Third Edition (Addison-Wesley, 2013), deals only with database design methodologies. Others, such as C. J. Date's *An Introduction to Database Systems*, Eighth Edition (Addison-Wesley, 2003), mix both theory and design. (Be warned, though, that the books dealing with theory are not necessarily light reading.) After you decide in which direction you want to go, select and purchase the appropriate books, grab a double espresso (or your beverage of choice), and dig right in. After you become comfortable with relational databases in general, you'll find that you will need to study and become very familiar with SQL.

And that's why you're reading this book.

Summary

I began this chapter with a brief discussion of the different types of databases commonly found today. You learned that organizations working with dynamic data use operational databases, ensuring that the information retrieved is always as accurate and up-to-the-minute as possible. You also learned that organizations working with static data use analytical databases.

I then looked at a brief history of the relational database model. I explained that Dr. E. F. Codd created the model based on specific branches of mathematics and that the model has been in existence for nearly 50 years. Database software, as you now know, has been developed for various computing environments and has steadily grown in power, performance, and capability since the 1970s. From the mainframe to the desktop to the Web to connected services, RDBMS programs are the backbone of many organizations today.

Next, I looked at an anatomy of a relational database. I introduced you to its basic components and briefly explained their purpose. You learned about the three types of relationships and now understand their importance, not only regarding the database structure itself but also as they relate to your understanding of SQL.

Finally, I explained why it's to your advantage to learn about relational databases and how to design them. You now know that the relational database is the most common type of database in use today and that just about every database software program you're likely to encounter will be used to support a relational database. You now have some ideas of how to pursue your education on relational database theory and design a little further.

In the next chapter, you'll learn some techniques to fine-tune your existing database structures.

2

Ensuring Your Database Structure Is Sound

"We shape our buildings: thereafter, they shape us."
—Sir Winston Churchill

Topics Covered in This Chapter

Why Is This Chapter Here?

Why Worry about Sound Structures?

Fine-Tuning Columns

Fine-Tuning Tables

Establishing Solid Relationships

Is That All?

Summary

Most of you reading this book are probably working with an existing database structure implemented on your favorite (I hope) RDBMS program. It's hard for me to assume, at this point, whether or not you—or the person who developed the database—really had the necessary knowledge and skills or the time to design the database properly. Assuming the worst, you probably have a number of tables that could use some fine-tuning. Fortunately, you're about to learn some techniques that will help you get your database in shape and will ensure that you can easily retrieve the information you need from your tables.

Why Is this Chapter Here?

You might wonder why I'm discussing database design topics in this book and why they're included in a beginning chapter. The reason is simple: If you have a poorly designed database structure, many of the SQL statements you'll learn to build in the remainder of the book will be, at best, difficult to implement or, at worst, relatively useless. However, if you have a well-designed database structure, the skills you learn in this book will serve you well.

This chapter will not teach you the intricacies of database design, but it will help you get your database in relatively good shape. I highly recommend that you read through this chapter so that you can make certain your table structures are sound.

> ❖ **Note** It is important to understand that I am about to discuss the *logical* design of the database. I'm not teaching you how to create or implement a database in a database management system that supports SQL because, as I mentioned in the Introduction, these subjects are beyond the scope of this book.

Why Worry about Sound Structures?

If your database structure isn't sound, you'll have problems retrieving seemingly simple information from your database, it will be difficult to work with your data, and you'll cringe every time you need to add or delete columns in your tables. Other aspects of the database, such as data integrity, table relationships, and the ability to retrieve accurate information, are affected when you have poorly designed structures. These issues are just the tip of the iceberg. And it goes on! Make sure you have sound structures to avoid all this grief.

You can avoid many of these problems if you properly design your database from the beginning. Even if you've already designed your database, all is not lost. You can still apply the following techniques and gain the benefits of a sound structure. However, you must be aware that the quality of your final structures is in direct proportion to the amount of time you invest in fine-tuning them. The more care and patience you give to applying the techniques, the more you can guarantee your success.

Let's now turn to the first order of business in shaping up your structures: working with the columns.

Fine-Tuning Columns

Because columns are the most basic structures in a database, you must ensure that they are in tip-top shape before you begin fine-tuning the tables as a whole. Fixing the columns usually will eliminate some existing problems with a given table and help you avoid any potential problems that might have arisen.

What's in a Name? (Part One)

As you learned in the previous chapter, a column represents a characteristic of the subject of the table to which it belongs. If you give the column an appropriate name, you should be able to identify the characteristic it's supposed to represent. A name that is ambiguous, vague, or unclear is a sure sign of trouble and suggests that the purpose of the column has not been carefully thought out. Use the following checklist to test each of your column names:

- *Is the name descriptive and meaningful to your entire organization?* If users in several departments are going to work with this database, make certain you choose a name that is meaningful to everyone who accesses this column. Semantics is a funny thing, and if you use a word that has a different meaning to different groups of people, you're just inviting trouble.

- *Is the column name clear and unambiguous?* PhoneNumber is a column name that can be very misleading. What kind of phone number is this column supposed to represent? A home phone? A work phone? A cellular phone? Learn to be specific. If you need to record each of these types of phone numbers, then create HomePhone, WorkPhone, and CellPhone columns.

❖ **Note** An argument could be made that HomePhone, WorkPhone, and CellPhone are actually a repeating group that should be moved to a separate table that could hold multiple phone numbers for the related customer or employee. Such a table would also have a column to indicate the type of phone, and it would be possible for each related person or company to have an unlimited list of phone numbers. You'll see more about this when I discuss table structures in the next section.

In addition to making your column names clear and unambiguous, be sure that you don't use the same column name in several tables. Let's say you have three tables called Customers, Vendors, and Employees. No doubt you will have City and State columns in each of these tables, and the columns will have the same names in all three tables. There isn't a problem with this until you have to refer to one particular column. How do you distinguish between, say, the City column in the Vendors table, the City column in the Customers table, and the City column in the Employees table? The answer is simple: Add a short prefix to each of the column names. For example, use the name VendCity in the Vendors table, CustCity in the Customers table, and EmpCity in the Employees table. Now you can easily make a clear reference to any of these columns. (You can use this technique on any generic column such as FirstName, LastName, and Address.)

Here's the main thing to remember: Make sure that each column in your database has a unique name and that it appears only once in the entire database structure. The only exception to this rule is when a column is being used to establish a relationship between two tables.

❖ **Note** The degree to which you use prefixes within a table is a matter of style. When a table contains generic column names, some database designers will choose to prefix the generic names only, while others elect to prefix *all* of the column names within the table. Regardless of the prefix method you use, it is very important that you use it consistently throughout the database structure.

- *Did you use an acronym or abbreviation as a column name?* If you did, change it! Acronyms can be hard to decipher and are easily misunderstood. Imagine seeing a column named CAD_SW. How would you know what the column represents? Use abbreviations sparingly, and handle them with care. Use an abbreviation only if it supplements or positively enhances the column name. It shouldn't detract from the meaning of the column name.

- *Did you use a name that implicitly or explicitly identifies more than one characteristic?* These types of names are easy to spot because they typically use the words *and* or *or.* Column names that contain a back slash (\), a hyphen (-), or an ampersand (&) are dead giveaways as well. If you have columns with names such as Phone\Fax or Area or Location, review the data that they store and determine whether you need to deconstruct them into smaller, distinct columns.

❖ **Note** The SQL Standard defines a *regular identifier* as a name that must begin with a letter and can contain only letters, numbers, and the underscore character. Spaces *are not* allowed. It also defines a *delimited identifier* as a name—surrounded by double quotes—that must start with a letter and can contain letters, numbers, the underscore character, spaces, and a very specific set of special characters. I recommend that you use the regular identifier naming convention exclusively for your column names because many SQL implementations support only the regular identifier naming convention.

After using this checklist to revise your column names, you have one task left: Make certain you use the singular form of the column name. A column with a plural name such as Categories implies that it might contain two or more values for any given row, which is not a good idea. A column name is singular because it represents a single characteristic of the subject of the table to which it belongs. A table name, on the other hand, is plural because it represents a collection of similar objects or events. You can distinguish table names from column names quite easily when you use this naming convention.

❖ **Note** Although I recommended that you use the SQL Standard naming convention, keep in mind that the column names might change when you (or the database developer in charge of implementing the database) begin implementing the database into a specific RDBMS application. The names will need to conform to the naming convention that developers commonly use for the RDBMS.

Smoothing Out the Rough Edges

Now that you've straightened out the column names, let's focus on the structure of the column itself. You might be fairly sure that your columns are sound, but you can still do a few things to make certain they're built as efficiently as possible. Test your columns against the following checklist to determine whether or not your columns need a little more work:

- *Make sure the column represents a specific characteristic of the subject of the table.* The idea here is to determine whether the column truly belongs in the table. If it isn't germane to the table, remove it, or perhaps move it to another table. The only exceptions to this rule occur when the column is being used to establish a relationship between this table and other tables in the database or when it has been added to the table in support of some task required by a database application. For example, in the Classes table in Figure 2-1, the StaffLastName and Staff-FirstName columns are unnecessary because of the presence of the StaffID column. StaffID is being used to establish a relationship between the Classes table and the Staff table, and you can view data from both tables simultaneously by using a view or an SQL SELECT query. If you have unnecessary columns in your tables, you can either remove them completely or use them as the basis of a new table if they don't appear anywhere else in the database structure. (I'll show you how to do this later in this chapter.)

Staff

StaffID	StaffFirstName	StaffLastName	StaffStreetAddress	StaffCity	StaffState	<<other columns>>
98014	Peter	Brehm	722 Moss Bay Blvd.	Kirkland	WA	...
98019	Mariya	Sergienko	901 Pine Avenue	Portland	OR	...
98020	Jim	Glynn	13920 S.E. 40th Street	Bellevue	WA	...
98021	Tim	Smith	30301 166th Ave. N.E.	Seattle	WA	...
98022	Carol	Viescas	722 Moss Bay Blvd.	Kirkland	WA	...
98023	Alaina	Hallmark	Route 2, Box 203 B	Woodinville	WA	...

Classes

ClassID	Class	ClassroomID	StaffID	StaffLastName	StaffFirstName	<<other columns>>
1031	Art History	1231	98014	Brehm	Peter	...
1030	Art History	1231	98014	Brehm	Peter	...
2213	Biological Principles	1532	98021	Smith	Tim	...
2005	Chemistry	1515	98019	Sergienko	Mariya	...
2001	Chemistry	1519	98023	Hallmark	Alaina	...
1006	Drawing	1627	98020	Glynn	Jim	...
2907	Elementary Algebra	3445	98022	Viescas	Carol	...

Figure 2-1 *A table with unnecessary columns*

- *Make certain that the column contains only a single value.* A column that can potentially store several instances of the same type of value is known as a *multivalued* column. (A column that contains multiple phone numbers is an example of a multivalued column.) Likewise, a column that can potentially store two or more *distinct* values is known as a *multipart* column. (A column that contains both an item number and an item description is an example of a multipart column.) Multivalued and multipart columns can wreak havoc in your database, especially when you try to edit, delete, or sort the data. When you ensure that each column stores only a single value, you go a long way toward guaranteeing data integrity and accurate information. But for the time being, just try to identify any multivalued or multipart columns and make a note of them. You'll learn how to resolve them in the next section.

- *Make sure the column does not store the result of a calculation or concatenation.* Calculated columns are not allowed in a properly designed table. The issue here is the value of the calculated column itself. A column, unlike a cell in a spreadsheet, does not store an actual calculation. When the value of any part of the calculation changes, the result value stored in the column is not updated. The only ways to update the value are to do so manually or to write some procedural code that will do it automatically. Either way, it is incumbent on the user or you, the developer, to make certain the value is updated. The preferred way to work with a calculation, however, is to incorporate it into a SELECT statement. You'll learn the advantages of dealing with calculations in this manner when you get to Chapter 5, "Getting More Than Simple Columns."

- *Make certain the column appears only once in the entire database.* If you've made the common mistake of inserting the same column (for example, CompanyName) into several tables within the database, you're going to have a problem with inconsistent data. This occurs when you change the value of the column in one table and then you forget to make the same modification wherever else the same column appears. Avoid this problem entirely by ensuring that a column appears only once in the entire database structure. (The only exception to this rule is when you're using a column to establish a relationship between two tables.)

❖ **Note** The most recent versions of some commercially available database management systems allow you to define a column that is the result of a calculated expression. You can define calculated columns if your database system has this feature, but be aware that the database system requires additional resources to keep the calculated value current any time the value of one of the columns in the expression changes or you fetch a row containing a calculated column.

Resolving Multipart Columns

As I mentioned earlier, multipart and multivalued columns will wreak havoc with data integrity, so you need to resolve them to avoid any potential problems. Deciding which to resolve first is purely arbitrary, so I'll begin with multipart columns.

You'll know if you have a multipart column by answering some very simple questions: "Can I take the current value of this column and break it up into smaller, more distinct parts?" "Will I have problems extracting a specific piece of information because it is buried in a column containing other information?" If your answer to either question is "Yes," you have a multipart column. Figure 2-2 shows a poorly designed table with several multipart columns.

Customers

CustomerID	CustomerName	StreetAddress	PhoneNumber	<<other columns>>
1001	Suzanne Viescas	15127 NE 24th, #383, Redmond, WA 98052	425 555-2686	...
1002	William Thompson	122 Spring River Drive, Duvall, WA 98019	425 555-2681	...
1003	Gary Hallmark	Route 2, Box 203B, Auburn, WA 98002	253 555-2676	...
1004	Robert Brown	672 Lamont Ave, Houston, TX 77201	713 555-2491	...
1005	Dean McCrae	4110 Old Redmond Rd., Redmond, WA 98052	425 555-2506	...
1006	John Viescas	15127 NE 24rh, #383, Redmond, WA 98052	425 555-2511	...
1007	Mariya Sergienko	901 Pine Avenue, Portland, OR 97208	503 555-2526	...
1008	Neil Patterson	233 West Valley Hwy, San Diego, CA 92199	619 555-2541	...

MULTIPART COLUMNS

Figure 2-2 *A table with multipart columns*

The Customers table shown in the figure contains two multipart columns: CustomerName, and StreetAddress. There's also one column that is potentially multipart: PhoneNumber. How can you sort the data by last name or ZIP Code or search on state? You can't because these values are embedded in columns that contain other information. You can see that each column can be broken into smaller columns. For example, CustomerName can be broken into two distinct columns—CustFirstName and CustLastName. (Note that I'm using the naming convention discussed earlier in this chapter when I add the prefix Cust to the FirstName and LastName columns.) When you identify a multipart column in a table, determine how many parts there are to the value it stores, and then break the column into as many smaller columns as appropriate. Figure 2-3 shows how to resolve two of the multipart columns in the Customers table.

Customers

CustomerID	CustFirstName	CustLastName	CustAddress	CustCity	CustState	CustZipcode
1001	Suzanne	Viescas	15127 NE 24th, #383	Redmond	WA	98052
1002	William	Thompson	122 Spring River Drive	Duvall	WA	98019
1003	Gary	Hallmark	Route 2, Box 203B	Auburn	WA	98002
1004	Robert	Brown	672 Lamont Ave	Houston	TX	77201
1005	Dean	McCrae	4110 Old Redmond Rd.	Redmond	WA	98052
1006	John	Viescas	15127 NE 24th, #383	Redmond	WA	98052
1007	Mariya	Sergienko	901 Pine Avenue	Portland	OR	97208
1008	Neil	Patterson	233 West Valley Hwy	San Diego	CA	92199

Figure 2-3 *The resolution of the multipart columns in the Customers table*

> ❖ **Note** Along with breaking down CustomerName and StreetAddress, it might also be a good idea in a database storing phone numbers in North America to break PhoneNumber into two distinct columns—area code and the local phone number. In other countries, separating out the city code portion of the phone number might be useful. In truth, most business databases store a phone number as one column, but separating out the area or city code might be important for databases that analyze demographic data. Unfortunately, I couldn't demonstrate this in Figure 2-3 due to space limitations.

Sometimes you might have difficulty recognizing a multipart column. Take a look at the Instruments table shown in Figure 2-4. At first glance, there do not seem to be any multipart columns. On closer inspection, however, you will see that InstrumentID is actually a multipart column. The value stored in this column represents two distinct pieces of information: the category to which the instrument belongs—such as AMP (amplifier), GUIT (guitar), and MFX (multi-effects unit)—and its identification number. You should separate these two values and store them in their own columns to ensure data integrity. Imagine the difficulty of updating this column if the MFX category changed to MFU. You would have to write code to parse the value in this column, test for the existence of MFX, and then replace it with MFU if it does exist within the parsed value. It's not so much that you *couldn't* do this, but you'd definitely be working harder than necessary, and you shouldn't have to go through this at all if your database is properly designed. When you have columns such as the one in this example, break them into smaller columns so that you will have sound, efficient column structures.

Instruments

InstrumentID	Manufacturer	InstrumentDescription	<<*other columns*>>
GUIT2201	Fender	Fender Stratocaster	...
MFX3349	Zoom	Player 2100 Multi-Effects	...
AMP1001	Marshall	JCM 2000 Tube Super Lead	...
AMP5590	Crate	VC60 Pro Tube Amp	...
SFX2227	Dunlop	Cry Baby Wah-Wah	...
AMP2766	Fender	Twin Reverb Reissue	...

Figure 2-4 *An example of a subtle multipart column*

Resolving Multivalued Columns

Resolving multipart columns is not very hard at all, but resolving multivalued columns can be a little more difficult and will take some work. Fortunately, identifying a multivalued column is easy. Almost without exception, the data stored in this type of column contains some commas, semicolons, or other common separator characters. The separator characters are used to separate the various values within the column itself. Figure 2-5 shows an example of a multivalued column.

Pilots

PilotID	PilotFirstName	PilotLastName	HireDate	Certifications	<<*other columns*>>
25100	Sam	Alborous	1994-07-11	727, 737, 757, MD80	...
25101	Jim	Wilson	1994-05-01	737, 747, 757	...
25102	David	Smith	1994-09-11	757, MD80, DC9	...
25103	Kathryn	Patterson	1994-07-11	727, 737, 747, 757	...
25104	Michael	Hernandez	1994-05-01	737, 757, DC10	...
25105	Kendra	Bonnicksen	1994-09-11	757, MD80, DC9	...

Figure 2-5 *A table with a multivalued column*

In this example, each pilot is certified to fly any number of planes, and those certifications are stored in a single column called Certifications. The manner in which the data is stored in this column is very troublesome because you are bound to encounter the same type of data integrity problems associated with multipart columns. When you look at the data more closely, you'll see that it will be difficult for you to perform searches and sorts on this column in an SQL query. Before you can resolve this column in the appropriate manner, you must first understand the true relationship between a multivalued column and the table to which it is originally assigned.

The values in a multivalued column have a many-to-many relationship with every row in its parent table: One specific value in a multivalued column can be associated with any number of rows in the parent table, and a single row in the parent table can be associated with any number of values in the multivalued column. In Figure 2-5, for example, a specific aircraft in the Certifications column can be associated with any number of pilots, and a single pilot can be associated with any number of aircraft in the Certifications column. You resolve this many-to-many relationship as you would any other many-to-many relationship within the database—with a linking table.

You can create the linking table by using the multivalued column and a *copy* of the primary key column from the original table as the basis for the new table. Give the new linking table an appropriate name, and designate both columns as a composite primary key. (In this case, the combination of the values of both columns will uniquely identify each row within the new table.) Now you can associate the values of both columns in the linking table on a one-to-one basis. Figure 2-6 shows an example of this process using the Pilots table shown in Figure 2-5.

Contrast the entries for Sam Alborous (PilotID 25100) in both the old Pilots table and the new Pilot_Certifications table. The major advantage of the new linking table is that you can now associate *any* number of certifications with a single pilot. Asking certain types of questions is now much easier as well. For example, you can determine which pilots are certified to fly a Boeing 747 aircraft or retrieve a list of certifications for a specific pilot. You'll also find that you can sort the data in any order you wish, without any adverse effects.

Pilots

PilotID	PilotFirstName	PilotLastName	HireDate	<<other columns>>
25100	Sam	Alborous	1994-07-11	...
25101	Jim	Wilson	1994-05-01	...
25102	David	Smith	1994-09-11	...
25103	Kathryn	Patterson	1994-07-11	...
25104	Michael	Hernandez	1994-05-01	...
25105	Kendra	Bonnicksen	1994-09-11	...

Pilot_Certifications *(linking table)*

PilotID	CertificationID
25100	8102
25100	8103
25100	8105
25100	8106
25101	8103
25101	8104
25101	8105

Certifications

CertificationID	TypeofAircraft	<<other columns>>
8102	Boeing 727	...
8103	Boeing 737	...
8104	Boeing 747	...
8105	Boeing 757	...
8106	McDonnell Douglas MD80	...

Figure 2-6 *Resolving a multivalued column by using a linking table*

> ❖ **Note** Some database management systems—most notably Microsoft Office Access 2007 and later—allow you to explicitly define multivalued columns. The database system does this, however, by creating a hidden system table similar to the linking table shown in Figure 2-6. Frankly, I like to see and control my table designs, so I recommend that you create the correct data structures yourself rather than depend on a feature in your database system.

Your columns will be in good shape when you follow the procedures presented in this section. Now that you've refined the columns, let's turn to our second order of business and take a look at the table structures.

Fine-Tuning Tables

Tables serve as the basis for any SQL query you create. You'll soon find that poorly designed tables pose data integrity problems and are difficult to work with when you create multi-table SQL queries. As a result, you must make certain that your tables are structured as efficiently as possible so that you can easily retrieve the information you need.

What's in a Name? (Part Two)

In the section on columns, you learned how important it is for a column to have an appropriate name and why you should give serious thought to naming your columns. You'll soon learn that the same applies to tables as well. By definition, a table should represent a single subject. If it represents more than one subject, it should be divided into smaller tables. The name of the table must clearly identify the subject the table represents. You can be confident that the subject of the table has not been carefully thought out if a table name is ambiguous, vague, or unclear. Make sure your table names are sound by checking them against the following checklist:

- *Is the name unique and descriptive enough to be meaningful to your entire organization?* Giving your table a unique name ensures that each table in the database represents a different subject and that everyone in the organization will understand what the table represents. Defining a unique and descriptive name does take some work on your part, but it's well worth the effort in the long run.

- *Does the name accurately, clearly, and unambiguously identify the subject of the table?* When the table name is vague or ambiguous, you can bet that the table represents more than one subject. For example, Dates is a vague table name. It's hard to determine exactly what this table represents unless you have a description of the table at hand. Let's say this table appears in a database used by an entertainment agency. If you inspect this table closely, you'll probably find that it contains dates for client meetings and booking dates for the agency's stable of entertainers. This table clearly represents two subjects. You can resolve this issue by dividing the table into two new tables and give each table an appropriate name, such as Client_Meetings and Entertainer_Schedules.

- *Does the name contain words that convey physical characteristics?* Avoid using words such as *File, Record,* and *Table* in the table name because they introduce a level of confusion that you don't need. A table name that includes this type of word is very likely to represent more than one subject. Consider the name Employee_ Record. On the surface, there doesn't appear to be any problem with this name. When you think about what an employee record is supposed to represent, however, you'll realize that there are potential problems. The name contains a word that we're trying hard to avoid, and it potentially represents three subjects: employees, departments, and payroll. With this in mind, split the original table (Employee_Record) into three new tables, one for each of the three subjects.

- *Did you use an acronym or abbreviation as a table name?* If the answer to this question is "Yes," change the name right now! Abbreviations rarely convey the subject of the table, and acronyms are usually hard to decipher. Suppose your company database has a table named SC. How do you know what the table represents without knowing the meaning of the letters themselves? The fact is that you can't easily identify the subject of the table. What's more, you might find that the table means different things to different departments in the company. (Now, this is scary.) The folks in Personnel think it stands for Steering_Committees; the Information Systems staff believes it to be System_Configurations, and the people in Security insist that it represents Security_Codes. This example clearly illustrates why you should avoid using abbreviations and acronyms in a table name.

- *Did you use a name that implicitly or explicitly identifies more than one subject?* This is one of the most common mistakes you can make with a table name, and it is relatively easy to identify. This type of name typically contains the words *and* or *or* and characters such as the back slash (\), hyphen (-), or ampersand (&). Facility\ Building and Department or Branch are typical examples. When you name a table in this manner, you must clearly identify whether it truly represents more than one subject. If it does, deconstruct it into smaller tables, and then give the new tables appropriate names.

> ❖ **Note** Remember that the SQL Standard defines a *regular identifier* as a name that must begin with a letter and can contain only letters, numbers, and the underscore character. Spaces *are not* allowed. It also defines a *delimited identifier* as a name—surrounded with double quotes—that must start with a letter and can contain letters, numbers, the underscore character spaces, and a very specific set of special characters. I recommend that you use the regular identifier naming convention exclusively for your table names because many SQL implementations support only the regular identifier naming convention.

After you've finished revising your table names, you have one more task to perform: Check each table name again and make certain you used the plural form of the name. You use the plural form because a table stores a *collection of instances* of the subject of the table. For example, an Employees table stores the data for many employees, not just one employee. Using the plural form also helps you to distinguish a table name from a column name.

> ❖ **Note** The guideline for using a plural form for a table name is a particularly good one while you're working on the logical design of the database. It makes it very easy to differentiate table names from column names, especially when you're displaying them on a projection screen or when you've written them all across a whiteboard in a conference room.
>
> Keep in mind, however, that the table names might change when you (or the database developer in charge of implementing the database) begin implementing the database into a specific RDBMS application. The names will then need to conform to the naming convention that developers commonly use for the RDBMS.

Ensuring a Sound Structure

Let's focus on the table structures now that you've revised the table names. It's imperative that the tables are properly designed so that you can efficiently store data and retrieve accurate information. The time you spend ensuring your tables are well built will pay dividends when you need to create complex multi-table SQL queries. Use the following checklist to determine whether your table structures are sound:

- *Make sure the table represents a single subject.* Yes, I know, I've said this a number of times already, but I can't overemphasize this point. As long as you guarantee that each of your tables represents a single subject, you greatly reduce the risk of potential data integrity problems. Also, remember that the subject represented by the table can be an object or event. By "object" I mean something that is tangible, such as employees, vendors, machines, buildings, or departments, whereas an "event" is something that happens at a given point in time that has characteristics you want to record. The best example of an event that everyone can relate to is a doctor's appointment. Although you can't explicitly touch a doctor's appointment, it does have characteristics that you need to record, such as the appointment date, the appointment time, the patient's blood pressure, and the patient's temperature.

- *Make certain each table has a primary key.* You must assign a primary key to each table for two reasons. First, the primary key uniquely identifies each row within a table, and second, it is used in establishing table relationships. If you do not assign a primary key to each table, you will eventually have data integrity problems and problems with some types of multi-table SQL queries. You'll learn some tips on how to define a proper primary key later in this chapter.

- *Make sure the table does not contain any multipart or multivalued columns.* Theoretically, you should have resolved these issues when you refined the column structures. Nonetheless, it's still a good idea to review the columns one last time to ensure that you've completely removed every multipart or multivalued column.

- *Make sure there are no calculated columns in the table.* Although you might believe that your current table structures are free of calculated columns, you might have overlooked one or two during the column refinement process. This is a good time to take another look at the table structures and remove any calculated columns you might have missed.

- *Make certain the table is free of any unnecessary duplicate columns.* One of the hallmarks of a poorly designed table is the inclusion of duplicate columns from other tables. You might feel compelled to add duplicate columns to a table for one of two reasons: 1) to provide reference information or 2) to indicate multiple occurrences of a particular type of value. Remember that earlier I talked about HomePhone, WorkPhone, and CellPhone potentially being repeating or duplicate columns. These duplicate columns raise various difficulties when you work with the data and attempt to retrieve information from the table. Let's now take a look at how to deal with duplicate columns.

Resolving Unnecessary Duplicate Columns

Possibly the hardest part of ensuring well built structures is dealing with duplicate columns. Here are a couple of examples that demonstrate the proper way to resolve tables that contain duplicate columns.

Figure 2-7 illustrates an example of a table containing duplicate columns that supply reference information.

Staff

StaffID	StaffFirstName	StaffLastName	StaffStreetAddress	StaffCity	StaffState	<<other columns>>
98014	Peter	Brehm	722 Moss Bay Blvd.	Kirkland	WA	...
98019	Mariya	Serglenko	901 Pine Avenue	Portland	OR	...
98020	Jim	Glynn	13920 S.E. 40th Street	Bellevue	WA	...
98021	Tim	Smith	30301 166th Ave. N.E.	Seattle	WA	...
98022	Carol	Viescas	722 Moss Bay Blvd.	Kirkland	WA	...
98023	Alaina	Hallmark	Route 2, Box 203 B	Woodinville	WA	...

These columns are unnecessary

Classes

ClassID	Class	ClassroomID	StaffID	StaffLastName	StaffFirstName	<<other columns>>
1031	Art History	1231	98014	Brehm	Peter	...
1030	Art History	1231	98014	Brehm	Peter	...
2213	Biological Principles	1532	98021	Smith	Tim	...
2005	Chemistry	1515	98019	Sergienko	Mariya	...
2001	Chemistry	1519	98023	Hallmark	Alaina	...
1006	Drawing	1627	98020	Glynn	Jim	...
2907	Elementary Algebra	3445	98022	Viescas	Carol	...

Figure 2-7 *A table with duplicate columns added for reference information*

In this case, StaffLastName and StaffFirstName appear in the Classes table so that a person viewing the table can see the name of the instructor for a given class. These columns are unnecessary because of the one-to-many relationship that exists between the Classes and Staff tables. (A single staff member can teach any number of classes, but a single class is taught by one staff member.) StaffID establishes the relationship between these tables, and the relationship itself lets you view data from both tables simultaneously in an SQL query. With this in mind, you can confidently remove the StaffLastName and Staff-FirstName columns from the Classes table without any adverse effects. Figure 2-8 shows the revised Classes table structure.

Staff

StaffID	StaffFirstName	StaffLastName	StaffStreetAddress	StaffCity	StaffState	*<<other columns>>*
98014	Peter	Brehm	722 Moss Bay Blvd.	Kirkland	WA	...
98019	Mariya	Sergienko	901 Pine Avenue	Portland	OR	...
98020	Jim	Glynn	13920 S.E. 40th Street	Bellevue	WA	...
98021	Tim	Smith	30301- 166th Ave. N.E.	Seattle	WA	...
98022	Carol	Viescas	722 Moss Bay Blvd.	Kirkland	WA	...
98023	Alaina	Hallmark	Route 2, Box 203 B	Woodinville	WA	...

Classes

ClassID	Class	ClassroomID	StaffID	*<<other columns>>*
1031	Art History	1231	98014	...
1030	Art History	1231	98014	...
2213	Biological Principles	1532	98021	...
2005	Chemistry	1515	98019	...
2001	Chemistry	1519	98023	...
1006	Drawing	1627	98020	...
2907	Elementary Algebra	3445	98022	...

Figure 2-8 *Resolving the duplicate reference columns*

Keeping these unnecessary columns in the table automatically introduces a major problem with inconsistent data. You must ensure that the values of the StaffLastName and StaffFirstName columns in the Classes table always match their counterparts in the Staff table. For example, say a female staff member marries and decides to use her married name as her legal name from that day forward. Not only do you have to be

certain to make the appropriate change to her row in the Staff table, but
you must ensure that every occurrence of her name in the Classes table
changes as well. Again, it's possible to do this (at least, technically), but
you're working much harder than is necessary. Besides, one of the major
premises behind using a relational database is that you should enter a
piece of data only once in the entire database. (The only exception to this
rule is when you're using a column to establish a relationship between
two tables.) As always, the best course of action is to remove all duplicate columns from the tables in your database.

Figure 2-9 shows another clear example of a table containing duplicate
columns. This example illustrates how duplicate columns are mistakenly
used to indicate multiple occurrences of a particular type of value. In
this case, the three Committee columns are ostensibly used to show the
names of the committees in which the employee participates.

Employees

EmployeeID	EmpLastName	EmpFirstName	Committee1	Committee2	Committee3	*<<other columns>>*
7004	Gehring	Darren	Steering			...
7005	Kennedy	John	ISO 9000	Safety		...
7006	Thompson	Sarah	Safety	ISO 9000	Steering	...
7007	Wilson	Jim				...
7008	Seidel	Manuela	ISO 9000			...
7009	Smith	David	Steering	Safety	ISO 9000	...
7010	Patterson	Neil				...
7011	Viescas	Michael	ISO 9000	Steering	Safety	...

Figure 2-9 *A table with duplicate columns used to indicate multiple occurrences of
a particular type of value*

It's relatively easy to see why these duplicate columns will create problems. One problem concerns the actual number of Committee columns
in the table. What if a few employees end up belonging to four committees? For that matter, how can you tell exactly how many Committee
columns you're going to need? If it turns out that several employees participate in more than three committees, you'll need to add more Committee columns to the table.

A second problem pertains to retrieving information from the table.
How do you retrieve those employees who are currently in the ISO 9000
committee? It's not impossible, but you'll have difficulty retrieving this

information. You must execute three separate queries (or build a search condition that tests three separate columns) in order to answer the question accurately because you cannot be certain in which of the three Committee columns the value ISO 9000 is stored. Now you're expending more time and effort than is truly necessary.

A third problem concerns sorting the data. You cannot sort the data by committee in any practical fashion, and there's no way that you'll get the committee names to line up correctly in alphabetical order. Although these might seem like minor problems, they can be quite frustrating when you're trying to get an overall view of the data in some orderly manner.

If you study the Employees table in Figure 2-9 closely, you'll soon realize that there is a many-to-many relationship between the employees and committees to which they belong. A single employee can belong to any number of committees, and a single committee can be composed of any number of employees. You can, therefore, resolve these duplicate columns in the same manner that you would resolve any other many-to-many relationship—by creating a linking table. In the case of the Employees table, create the linking table by using a copy of the primary key (EmployeeID) and a single Committee column. Give the new table an appropriate name, such as Committee_Members, designate both the EmployeeID and Committee columns as a composite primary key, remove the Committee columns from the Employees table, and you're done. (You'll learn more about primary keys later in this chapter.) Figure 2-10 shows the revised Employees table and the new Committee_Members table.

Employees   **Committee_Members**

EmployeeID	EmpLastName	EmpFirstName	EmpCity	*<<other columns>>*	EmployeeID	Committee
7004	Gehring	Darren	Chico	...	7004	Steering
7005	Kennedy	John	Portland	...	7005	ISO 9000
7006	Thompson	Sarah	Lubbock	...	7005	Safety
7007	Wilson	Jim	Salem	...	7006	Safety
7008	Seidel	Manuela	Medford	...	7006	ISO 9000
7009	Smith	David	Fremont	...	7006	Steering
7010	Patterson	Neil	San Diego	...	7008	ISO 9000
7011	Viescas	Michael	Redmond	...	7009	Steering

Figure 2-10 *The revised Employees table and the new Committee_Members table*

You've resolved the duplicate columns that were in the original Employees table, but you're not quite finished yet. Keeping in mind that there is a many-to-many relationship between the employees and the committees to which they belong, you might very well ask, "Where is the Committees table?" There isn't one—yet! Chances are that a committee has some other characteristics that you need to record, such as the name of the room where the committee meets and the day of the month that the meeting is held. It would be a good idea for you to create a real Committees table that includes columns such as CommitteeID, CommitteeName, MeetingRoom, and MeetingDay. When you finish creating the new table, replace the Committee column in the Committee_Members table with the CommitteeID column from the new Committees table. The final structures appear in Figure 2-11.

Employees

EmployeeID	EmpLastName	EmpFirstName	EmpCity	<<*other columns*>>
7004	Gehring	Darren	Chico	...
7005	Kennedy	John	Portland	...
7006	Thompson	Sarah	Lubbock	...
7007	Wilson	Jim	Salem	...
7008	Seidel	Manuela	Medford	...
7009	Smith	David	Fremont	...
7010	Patterson	Neil	San Diego	...
7011	Viescas	Michael	Redmond	...

Committee_Members

EmployeeID	CommitteeID
7004	103
7005	104
7005	102
7006	102
7006	104
7006	103
7008	104
7009	103

Committees

CommitteeID	CommitteeName	MeetingRoom	MeetingDay
100	Budget	11-C	Tuesday
101	Christmas	9-F	Monday
102	Safety	12-B	Monday
103	Steering	12-D	Tuesday
104	ISO 9000	Main-South	Wednesday

Figure 2-11 *The final Employees, Committee_Members, and Committees structures*

You gain a real advantage by structuring the tables in this manner because you can now associate a single member with any number of committees or a single committee with any number of employees. You can then use an SQL query to view information from all three tables simultaneously.

Let's revisit the problem I mentioned earlier about multiple, though uniquely named, columns potentially being a set of duplicate columns. Consider the table shown in Figure 2-12.

Employees

EmployeeID	EmpLastName	EmpFirstName	EmpCity	EmpHomePhone	EmpWorkPhone	EmpCellPhone	<<*other columns*>>
7004	Gehring	Darren	Chico	555-1234	556-1234	889-1234	...
7005	Kennedy	John	Portland	555-2345	556-2345	889-2345	...
7006	Thompson	Sarah	Lubbock	555-3456	556-3456	889-3456	...
7007	Wilson	Jim	Salem	555-4567	556-4567		...
7008	Seidel	Manuela	Medford		556-5678	889-5678	...
7009	Smith	David	Fremont	555-5689	556-5689	889-6789	...
7010	Patterson	Neil	San Diego	555-7890	556-7890	889-7890	...
7011	Viescas	Michael	Redmond	555-4321	555-4321		...

Figure 2-12 *Repeating phone number columns in an Employees table*

What potential problems do you see? First, there's wasted space in the table when an employee doesn't have a particular type of phone. But there's an even bigger problem. Can you guess what it is? What do you do if an employee has two home phones or a fax line? What about key employees who not only have a personal cell phone but also are given a cell phone by the company? The solution is to create a separate Phone_Numbers table and relate it back to the Employees table as shown in Figure 2-13.

With this new design, I can store an unlimited set of phone numbers for each employee. If I need to store a new phone type, all I need to do is define a data value for the PhoneType column. And notice that there's no wasted storage space for a home phone number for employee 7008—there simply is no Home phone row for that employee. Notice also that each row in the Phone_Numbers table has a PhoneID with a unique value for each row. You'll learn more about the importance of uniquely identifying each row in the next section.

Employees

EmployeeID	EmpLastName	EmpFirstName	EmpCity	<<*other columns*>>
7004	Gehring	Darren	Chico	...
7005	Kennedy	John	Portland	...
7006	Thompson	Sarah	Lubbock	...
7007	Wilson	Jim	Salem	...
7008	Seidel	Manuela	Medford	...
7009	Smith	David	Fremont	...
7010	Patterson	Neil	San Diego	...
7011	Viescas	Michael	Redmond	...

Phone_Numbers

EmployeeID	PhoneID	PhoneType	PhoneNumber
7004	1	Home	555-1234
7005	2	Home	555-2345
7006	3	Home	555-3456
7007	4	Home	555-4567
7009	5	Home	555-5678
7010	6	Home	555-7890
7011	7	Home	555-4321
7004	8	Work	555-1234

Figure 2-13 *Solving the phone number problem with a separate related table*

You're now close to completing the process of fine-tuning your table structures. The last order of business is to make certain that each row within a table can be uniquely identified and that the table itself can be identified throughout the entire database.

Identification Is the Key

You learned in Chapter 1, "What Is Relational?" that the primary key is one of the most important keys in a table because it uniquely identifies each row within a table and officially identifies that table throughout the database. It also establishes a relationship between a pair of tables. You cannot underestimate the importance of the primary key—every table in your database must have one!

By definition, a primary key is a column or group of columns that uniquely identifies each row within a table. A primary key is known as a *simple primary key* (or just primary key for short) when it is composed of a single column. A primary key is known as a *composite primary key* when it is composed of two or more columns. Define a simple primary key when you can because it's more efficient and is much easier to use when establishing a table relationship. Use a composite primary key only when it's appropriate, such as when you're defining and creating a linking table.

You can use an existing column or a combination of columns as the primary key as long as they satisfy all the criteria in the following checklist. When the column or columns that you propose to use as the primary key do not conform to *all* the criteria, use a different column or define a new column to act as the primary key for the table. Take some time now and use this checklist to determine whether each primary key in your database is sound:

- *Do the columns uniquely identify each row in the table?* Each row in a table represents an instance of the subject of the table. A good primary key ensures that you have a means of accurately identifying or referencing each row in this table from other tables in the database. It also helps you to avoid having duplicate rows within the table.

- *Does this column or combination of columns contain unique values?* As long as the values of the primary key are unique, you have a means of ensuring that there are no duplicate rows in the table.

- *Will these columns ever contain unknown values?* This is a very important question because a primary key cannot contain unknown values. You should disqualify this column immediately if you think it has even the slightest possibility of containing unknown values.

- *Can the value of these columns ever be optional?* You cannot use this column as the primary key if the answer to this question is "Yes." If the value of the column can be optional, it implies that it might be unknown at some point. As you learned in the previous item, a primary key cannot contain unknown values.

- *Is this a multipart column?* It's a good idea to ask yourself this question, although you should have eliminated all your multipart columns by now. If you missed a multipart column earlier, resolve it now and try to use another column as the primary key, or use the new separate columns together as a composite primary key.

- *Can the value of these columns ever be modified?* The values of primary key columns should remain static. You should never change the value of a column in a primary key unless you have a truly compelling reason to do so. When the value of the column is subject to arbitrary changes, it is difficult for the column to remain in conformance with the other points in this checklist.

As I stated earlier, a column or combination of columns must pass all the points on this checklist with flying colors before it can be used as a primary key. In Figure 2-14, PilotID serves as the primary key of the Pilots table. But the question is this: Does PilotID conform to all the points on the previous checklist? The primary key is sound if it does, but if it doesn't, you must either modify it to conform to all the points on the checklist or select a different column as the primary key.

Pilots

PilotID	PilotFirstName	PilotLastName	HireDate	Position	PilotAreaCode	PilotPhone
25100	Sam	Alborous	1994-07-11	Captain	206	555-3982
25101	Jim	Wilson	1994-05-01	Captain	206	555-6657
25102	David	Smith	1994-09-11	FirstOfficer	915	555-1992
25103	Kathryn	Patterson	1994-07-11	Navigator	972	555-8832
25104	Michael	Hernandez	1994-05-01	Navigator	360	555-9901
25105	Kendra	Bonnicksen	1994-09-11	Captaln	206	555-1106

Figure 2-14 *Is PilotID a sound primary key?*

As a matter of fact, PilotID is a sound primary key because it does conform to all the points on the checklist. But what happens when you don't have a column that can act as a primary key? Take the Employees table in Figure 2-15, for example. Is there a column in this table that can act as a primary key?

It's very clear that this table doesn't contain a column (or group of columns) that can be used as a primary key. With the exception of EmpPhone, every column contains duplicate values. EmpZip, EmpAreaCode, and EmpPhone all contain unknown values. Although you might be tempted to use the combination of EmpLastName and EmpFirstName, there's no guarantee that you won't employ a new person who is also named Jim Wilson or David Smith. It's evident that there is no column you can use as the primary key for this table because the value of every column in the table is subject to arbitrary change.

Employees

EmpLastName	EmpFirstName	EmpCity	EmpState	EmpZip	EmpAreaCode	EmpPhone	HireDate
Gehring	Darren	Chico	CA	95926			1998-12-31
Kennedy	John	Portland	OR	97208	503	555-2621	1998-05-01
Thompson	Sarah	Redmond	WA	98052	425	555-2626	1998-09-11
Wilson	Jim	Salem	OR				1998-12-27
Seidel	Manuela	Medford	OR	97501	541	555-2641	1998-05-01
Smith	David	Fremont	CA	94538	510	555-2646	1998-09-11
Patterson	Neil	San Diego	CA	92199	619	555-2541	1998-05-01
Viescas	Michael	Redmond	WA	98052	425	555-2511	1998-09-11
Viescas	David	Portland	OR	97207	503	555-2633	1998-10-15

Figure 2-15 *Does this table have a primary key?*

What do you do now? You might be tempted to use some sort of national identity number associated with each employee—for example, a Social Security number in the U.S. or the Social Insurance number in Canada. Be aware that although it is rare, it is possible for two or more people to have the same number. When in doubt, the solution is to create an artificial primary key. This is an arbitrary column you define and add to the table for the sole purpose of using it as the table's primary key. The advantage of adding this arbitrary column is that you can ensure that it conforms to all the points on the checklist. After you've added the column to the table, designate it as the primary key, and you're done! That's all there is to it. Figure 2-16 shows the Employees table with an artificial primary key called EmployeeID.

Employees

EmployeeID	EmpLastName	EmpFirstName	EmpCity	EmpState	EmpZip	<<other columns>>
98001	Gehring	Darren	Chico	CA	95926	...
98002	Kennedy	John	Portland	OR	97208	...
98003	Thompson	Sarah	Redmond	WA	98052	...
98004	Wilson	Jim	Salem	OR		...
98005	Seidel	Manuela	Medford	OR	97501	...
98006	Smith	David	Fremont	CA	94538	...
98007	Patterson	Neil	SanDiego	CA	92199	...
98008	Viescas	Michael	Redmond	WA	98052	...
98009	Viescas	David	Portland	OR	97207	...

Figure 2-16 *The Employees table with the new artificial primary key*

> ❖ **Note** Although artificial primary keys are an easy way to solve the problem, they don't really guarantee that you won't get duplicate data in your table. For example, if someone adds a new row for a person named John Kennedy and provides a new unique artificial EmployeeID value, how do you know that this second John Kennedy isn't the same as the employee 98002 already in the table?
>
> The answer is to add a verification routine to your application code that checks for a potentially duplicate name and warns the user. In many database systems, you can write such validation code as something called a trigger that your database system automatically runs each time a row is changed, added, or deleted. However, discussing triggers is far beyond the scope of this book. Consult your database system documentation for details.

At this point, you've done everything you can to strengthen and fine-tune your table structures. Now I'll take a look at how you can ensure that all your table relationships are sound.

Establishing Solid Relationships

In Chapter 1, you learned that a relationship exists between a pair of tables if rows in the first table are in some way associated with rows in the second table. You also learned that the relationship itself can be designated as one of three types: one-to-one, one-to-many, and many-to-many. And you learned that each type of relationship is established in a specific manner. Let's review this for a moment.

> ❖ **Note** The diagram symbols shown in this section are part of the diagramming method presented in Mike Hernandez's book *Database Design for Mere Mortals*, Third Edition (Addison-Wesley, 2013). PK indicates a primary key column. FK indicates a foreign key column. CPK indicates a column that is part of a composite primary key.

- You establish a **one-to-one relationship** by taking the primary key from the primary table and inserting it into the subordinate table, where it becomes a foreign key. This is a special type of relationship because in many cases the foreign key will also act as the primary key of the subordinate table. Figure 2-17 shows how to diagram this relationship.

This line indicates that a single record in Employee_Confidential is related to *only* one row in Employees.

Employees				Employee_Confidential	
EmployeeID	PK			EmployeeID	PK

This line indicates that a single record in Employees is related to *only* one row in Employee_Confidential.

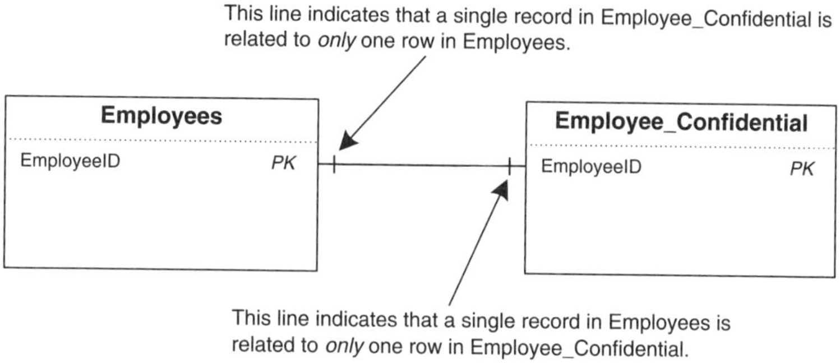

Figure 2-17 *Diagramming a one-to-one relationship*

- You establish a **one-to-many relationship** by taking the primary key of the table on the "one" side and inserting it into the table on the "many" side, where it becomes a foreign key. Figure 2-18 shows how to diagram this type of relationship.

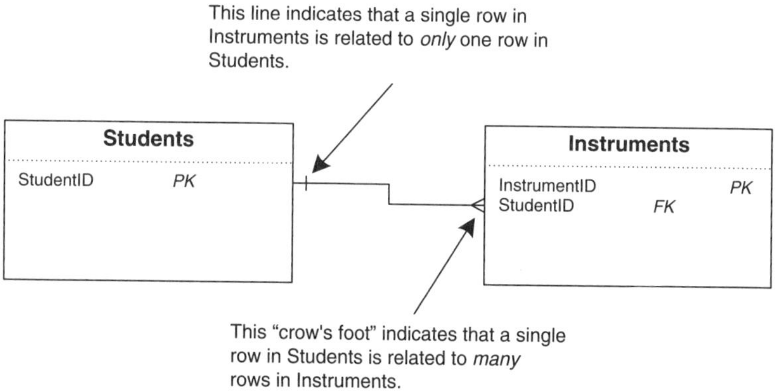

This line indicates that a single row in Instruments is related to *only* one row in Students.

Students				Instruments	
StudentID	PK			InstrumentID	PK
				StudentID	FK

This "crow's foot" indicates that a single row in Students is related to *many* rows in Instruments.

Figure 2-18 *Diagramming a one-to-many relationship*

- You establish a **many-to-many relationship** by creating a linking table. Define the linking table by taking a copy of the primary key of each table in the relationship and using them to form the structure of the new table. These columns commonly serve two distinct roles: Together, they form the composite primary key of the linking table; separately, they each serve as a foreign key. You would diagram this relationship as shown in Figure 2-19.

A many-to-many relationship is always resolved by using a *linking table*. In this example, Pilot_Certifications is the linking table. A single pilot can have any number of certifications, and a single certification can be associated with any number of pilots.

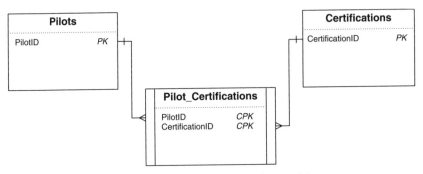

Figure 2-19 *Diagramming a many-to-many relationship*

In order to make certain that the relationships among the tables in your database are really solid, you must establish relationship characteristics for each relationship. The characteristics you're about to define indicate what will occur when you delete a row, the type of participation a table has within the relationship, and to what degree each table participates within the relationship.

It's important to note that the related columns that you use to link two tables must be the same data type. For example, you can link a primary key of Int (Integer) data type only to a foreign key that is also Int. You cannot link a number to character or date. The one exception to this rule involves primary keys that are automatically generated by your database system, known as AutoNumber, Identity, Serial, or Auto_Increment, depending on the database system. For each of these, there is an underlying numeric data type—Long Integer in Microsoft Access and Int in most others—so it's perfectly okay to link a primary key created this way to a column that is simply the underlying data type. So you can link an AutoNumber in Microsoft Access to a Number / Long Integer foreign key in a related table, or an Identity in Microsoft SQL Server to a column that is Int.

Before my discussion on relationship characteristics begins, I must make one point perfectly clear: I present the following characteristics within a generic and logical frame of reference. These characteristics are important because they allow you to enforce relationship integrity (referred to by some database systems as *referential integrity*). The manner in which you implement them, however, will vary from one database software program to another. You will have to study your database software's documentation to determine whether these characteristics are supported and, if so, how you can implement them.

Establishing a Deletion Rule

A *deletion rule* dictates what happens when a user makes a request to delete a row in the primary table of a one-to-one relationship or in the table on the "one" side of a one-to-many relationship. You can guard against orphaned rows by establishing this rule. (*Orphaned rows* are those rows in the subordinate table of a one-to-one relationship that don't have related rows in the primary table or rows in the table on the "many" side of a one-to-many relationship that don't have related rows in the table on the "one" side.)

You can set two types of deletion rules for a relationship: *restrict* and *cascade.*

- The **restrict deletion rule** does not allow you to delete the requested row when there are related rows in the subordinate table of a one-to-one relationship or in the table on the "many" side of a one-to-many relationship. You must delete any related rows *before* deleting the requested row. You'll use this type of deletion rule as a matter of course. In database systems that allow you to define relationship rules, this is usually the default and sometimes the only option.

- When the **cascade deletion rule** is in force, deleting the row on the "one" side of a relationship causes the system to automatically delete any related rows in the subordinate table of a one-to-one relationship or in the table on the "many" side of a one-to-many relationship. Use this rule very judiciously, or you might wind up deleting rows you really wanted to keep! Not all database systems support cascade deletion.

Regardless of the type of deletion rule you use, always examine your relationship very carefully to determine which type of rule is appropriate. You can use a very simple question to help you decide which type of rule to use. First, select a pair of tables, and then ask yourself the following question: "If a row in [name of primary or 'one' side table] is deleted, should related rows in [name of subordinate or 'many' side table] be deleted as well?"

This question is framed in a generic sense so that you can understand the premise behind it. To apply this question, substitute the phrases within the square brackets with table names. Your question will look something like this: "If a row in the Committees table is deleted, should related rows in the Committee_Members table be deleted as well?"

Use a restrict deletion rule if the answer to this question is "No." Otherwise, use the cascade deletion rule. In the end, the answer to this question greatly depends on how you use the data stored within the database. This is why you must study the relationship carefully and make certain you choose the right rule. Figure 2-20 shows how to diagram the deletion rule for this relationship. Note that you'll use (R) for a restricted deletion rule and (C) for a cascade deletion rule.

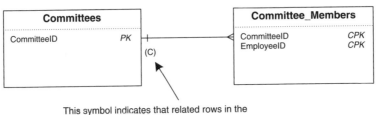

Figure 2-20 *Diagramming the deletion rule for the Committees and Committee_Members tables*

Setting the Type of Participation

When you establish a relationship between a pair of tables, each table participates in a particular manner. The *type of participation* assigned to a given table determines whether a row must exist in that table before you can enter a row into the other table. There are two types of participation:

- **Mandatory**—At least one row must exist in this table before you can enter any rows into the other table.

- **Optional**—There is no requirement for any rows to exist in this table before you enter any rows in the other table.

The type of participation you select for a pair of tables depends mostly on the business logic of your organization. For example, let's assume you work for a large company consisting of several departments. Let's also assume that you have an Employees table, a Departments table, and a Department_Employees table in the database you've created for your company. All relevant information about an employee is in the Employees table, and all relevant information about a department is in the Departments table. The Department_Employees table is a linking table that allows you to associate any number of departments with a given employee. Figure 2-21 shows these tables. (In this figure, I used simple arrows pointing to the "many" side of the relationship.)

Employees

EmployeeID	EmpLastName	EmpFirstName	EmpCity	<<other columns>>
7004	Gehring	Darren	Chico	...
7005	Kennedy	John	Portland	...
7006	Thompson	Sarah	Lubbock	...
7007	Wilson	Jim	Salem	...
7008	Seidel	Manuela	Medford	...
7009	Smith	David	Fremont	...
7010	Patterson	Neil	San Diego	...
7011	Viescas	Michael	Redmond	...

Department_Employees

EmployeeID	DepartmentID	Position
7004	1000	Head
7005	1000	Floater
7005	1001	Floater
7007	1001	Staff
7008	1001	Head
7009	1003	Floater
7010	1002	Head
7011	1004	Head

Departments

DepartmentID	DepartmentName	Floor
1000	Accounting	5
1001	Administration	5
1002	HumanResources	7
1003	InformationServices	6
1004	Legal	7

Figure 2-21 *The Employees, Departments, and Department_Employees tables*

In the last staff meeting, you were told to assign some of the staff to a new Research and Development department. Now here's the problem: You want to make certain you add the new department to the Departments table so that you can assign staff to that department in the Department_Employees table. This is where the type of participation characteristic comes into play. Set the type of participation for the Departments table to mandatory and the type of participation for the Department_Employees table to optional. By establishing these settings, you ensure that a department must exist in the Departments table before you can assign any employees to that department in the Department_Employees table.

As with the deletion rule, study each relationship carefully to determine the appropriate type of participation setting for each table in the relationship. You would diagram the type of participation as shown in Figure 2-22.

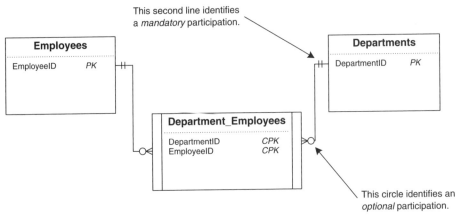

Figure 2-22 *Diagramming the type of participation for the Departments and Department_Employees tables*

Setting the Degree of Participation

Now that you've determined *how* each table will participate in the relationship, you must figure out *to what degree* each will participate. You do this by determining the minimum and maximum number of rows in one table that can be related to a single row in the other table. This process is known as identifying a table's *degree of participation*. The degree of participation for a given table is represented by two numbers that are separated with a comma and enclosed within parentheses. The first number indicates the minimum possible number of related rows, and the second number indicates the maximum possible number of related rows. For example, a degree of participation such as "(1,12)" indicates that the minimum number of rows that can be related is 1 and the maximum is 12.

The degree of participation you select for various tables in your database largely depends on how your organization views and uses the data. Let's say that you're a booking agent for a talent agency and that two of the tables in your database are Agents and Entertainers. Let's further assume that there is a one-to-many relationship between these tables— one row in the Agents table can be related to many rows in the Entertainers table, but a single row in the Entertainers table can be related to only one row in the Agents table. In this case, I've ensured (in a general sense) that an entertainer is assigned to only one agent. (I definitely avoid the possibility of the entertainer playing one agent against another. This is a good thing.)

In nearly all cases, the maximum number of rows on the "many" side of a relationship will be infinite. However, in some cases your business rules might dictate that you limit this participation. One example would be to limit the number of students who can enroll in a class. In this example, let's assume that the boss wants to ensure that all his agents have a fair shake at making good commissions and wants to keep the infighting between agents down to a bare minimum. So he sets a new policy stating that a single agent can represent a maximum of six entertainers. (Although he thinks it might not work in the long run, he wants to try it anyway.) In order to implement his new policy, he sets the degree of participation for both tables to the following:

Agents	(1,1)—An entertainer can be associated with one and only one agent.
Entertainers	(0,6)—Although an agent doesn't have to be associated with an entertainer at all, he or she cannot be associated with more than six entertainers at any given time.

Figure 2-23 shows how to diagram the degree of participation for these tables.

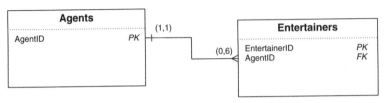

Figure 2-23 *Diagramming the degree of participation for the Agents and Entertainers tables*

After setting the degree of participation, you should decide how you want your database system to enforce the relationship. What you choose depends on the features provided by your database system. The simplest enforcement supported by most database systems is to restrict the values in the foreign key in the "many" table so that the user cannot enter a value that is not in the related "one" table. You can indicate this by placing the letter R in parentheses next to the relationship line pointing to the "one" table, as shown in Figure 2-24.

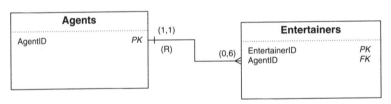

Figure 2-24 *A diagram of all the relationship characteristics for the Agents and Entertainers tables*

Some database systems allow you to define a rule that cascades (C) the key value from the "one" table to the "many" table if the user changes the value of the primary key in the "one" table. Essentially, the database system corrects the foreign key value in related rows in the "many" table when you change the value of the primary key in the "one" table. And some database systems provide a feature that automatically deletes (D) the rows in the "many" table when you delete a row in the "one" table. Check your database system documentation for details.

❖ **Note** To enforce degree of participation constraints, you'll have to define one or more triggers or constraints in your database definition (if your database system supports these features).

Is That All?

By using the techniques you learned in this chapter, you make the necessary beginning steps toward ensuring a fundamental level of data integrity in your database. The next step is to begin studying the manner in which your organization views and uses its data so that you can establish and impose business rules for your database. But to really get the most from your database, you should go back to the beginning and run it through a thorough database design process using a good design methodology. Unfortunately, these topics are beyond the scope of this book. However, you can learn a good design methodology from books such as *Database Design for Mere Mortals*, Third Edition (Addison-Wesley, 2013) by Michael J. Hernandez or *Database Systems: A Practical Approach to Design, Implementation, and Management*, Sixth Edition (Addison-Wesley, 2014) by Thomas Connolly and Carolyn Begg. The point to remember is this: The more solid your database structure, the easier it will be both to extract information from the data in the database and to build applications programs for it.

Summary

I opened this chapter with a short discussion on why you should be concerned with having sound structures in your database. You learned that poorly designed tables can cause numerous problems, not the least of which concern data integrity.

Next, I discussed fine-tuning the columns in each table. You learned that giving your columns good names is very important because it ensures that each name is meaningful and actually helps you to find hidden problems with the column structure itself. You now know how to fine-tune your column structures by ensuring they conform to a few simple rules. These rules deal with issues such as guaranteeing that each column represents a single characteristic of the table's subject, contains only a single value, and never stores a calculation. I also discussed the problems found in multipart and multivalued columns, and you learned how to resolve them properly.

Fine-tuning the tables was the next issue I addressed. You learned that the table names are just as important an issue as column names for many of the same reasons. You now know how to give your tables meaningful names and ensure that each table represents only a single subject. I then discussed a set of rules you can use to make certain each table structure is sound. Although some of the rules seemed to duplicate some of the efforts you made in fine-tuning your column structures, you learned that the rules used for fine-tuning the table structures actually add an extra level of insurance in making sure that the table structures are as absolutely sound as they can be.

The next subject I tackled was primary keys. You learned the importance of establishing a primary key for each table in your database. You now know that a primary key must conform to a specific set of characteristics and that the column that will act as the primary key of a table must be chosen very carefully. You also learned that you can create an artificial primary key if there is no column in the table that conforms to the complete set of characteristics for a primary key.

I closed this chapter with a discussion on establishing solid relationships. After reviewing the three types of relationships, you learned how to diagram each one. You then learned how to establish and diagram a deletion rule for the relationship. This rule is important because it helps you guard against orphaned rows. The last two topics I discussed were the type of participation and degree of participation for each table within the relationship. You learned that a table's participation can be mandatory or optional and that you can set a specific range for the number of related rows between each table.

In the next chapter, you'll learn a little bit about the history of SQL and how it evolved into the current version at press time, SQL:2016.

3

A Concise History of SQL

"There is only one religion, though there are many versions of it."
—GEORGE BERNARD SHAW, *PLAYS PLEASANT AND UNPLEASANT*

Topics Covered in This Chapter

The Origins of SQL

Early Vendor Implementations

". . . And Then There Was a Standard"

Evolution of the ANSI/ISO Standard

Commercial Implementations

What the Future Holds

Why Should You Learn SQL?

Which Version of SQL Does This Book Cover?

Summary

The telling of history always involves vague and ambiguous accounts of various incidents, political intrigue, and human foibles. The history of SQL is no different than that of any other subject in this sense. SQL has been around in one form or another since just after the dawn of the relational model, and there are several detailed accounts of its long and spotty existence. In this chapter, however, I take a close look at the origin, evolution, and future of this database language. I have two goals: first, to give you an idea of how SQL matured into the language used by a majority of relational database systems today, and second, to give you a sense of why it is important for you to learn how to use SQL.

The Origins of SQL

As you learned in Chapter 1, "What Is Relational?" Dr. E. F. Codd presented the relational database model to the world in 1970. Soon after this landmark moment, organizations such as universities and research laboratories began efforts to develop a language that could be used as the foundation to a database system that supported the relational model. Initial work led to the development of several languages in the mid- to early 1970s, and later efforts resulted in the development of SQL and the SQL-based databases in use today. But just where did SQL originate? How did it evolve? What is its future? For the answers to these questions, I must begin the story at IBM's Santa Teresa Research Laboratory in San Jose, California.

IBM began a major research project in the early 1970s called System/R. The goals of this project were to prove the viability of the relational model and to gain some experience in designing and implementing a relational database. The researchers' initial endeavors between 1974 and 1975 proved successful, and they managed to produce a minimal prototype of a relational database.

In addition to their efforts to develop a working relational database, researchers were also working to define a database language. The work performed at this laboratory is arguably the most commercially significant of the initial efforts to define such a language. In 1974, Dr. Donald Chamberlin and his colleagues developed Structured English Query Language (SEQUEL). The language allowed users to query a relational database using clearly defined English-style sentences. Dr. Chamberlin and his staff first implemented this new language in a prototype database called SEQUEL-XRM.

The initial feedback and success of SEQUEL-XRM encouraged Dr. Chamberlin and his staff to continue their research. They completely revised SEQUEL between 1976 and 1977 and named the new version SEQUEL/2. However, they subsequently had to change the name SEQUEL to SQL (Structured Query Language or SQL Query Language) for legal reasons—someone else had already used the acronym SEQUEL. To this day, many people still pronounce SQL as *sequel*, although the widely accepted "official" pronunciation is *es-cue-el*. SQL provided several new features, such as support for multi-table queries and shared data access by multiple users.

Soon after the emergence of SQL, IBM began a new and more ambitious project aimed at producing a prototype database that would further substantiate the feasibility of the relational model. They called the new prototype System R and based it on a large subset of SQL. After much of the initial development work was completed, IBM installed System R in a number of internal sites and selected client sites for testing and evaluation. Many changes were made to System R and SQL based on the experiences and feedback of users at these sites. IBM closed the project in 1979 and concluded that the relational model was indeed a viable database technology with commercial potential.

> ❖ **Note** One of the more important successes attributed to this project is the development of SQL. But SQL's roots are actually based in a research language called Specifying Queries As Relational Expressions (SQUARE). This language was developed in 1975 (predating the System R project) and was designed to implement relational algebra with English-style sentences.

You might well ask, "If IBM concluded that there was commercial potential, why did the company close the project?" I remember seeing a demonstration of System R in the late 1970s. It had lots of "wow" factor, but on the hardware technology available at the time, even a simple query took minutes to run. It clearly had potential, but it definitely needed better hardware and software to make the product appealing to businesses.

Early Vendor Implementations

The work done at the IBM research lab during the 1970s was followed with great interest in various technical journals, and the merits of the new relational model were briskly debated at database technology seminars. Toward the latter part of the decade, it became clear that IBM was keenly interested in and committed to developing products based on relational database technology and SQL. This, of course, led many vendors to speculate how soon IBM would roll out its first product. Some vendors had the good sense to start work on their own products as quickly as possible and not wait around for IBM to lead the market.

In 1977, Relational Software, Inc. was formed by a group of engineers in Menlo Park, California, to build a new relational database product based on SQL. They called their product Oracle. Relational Software shipped its product in 1979, beating IBM's first product to market by two years and providing the first commercially available relational database management system (RDBMS). One of Oracle's advantages was that it ran on Digital's VAX minicomputers instead of the more expensive IBM mainframes. Relational Software has since been renamed to Oracle Corporation and is one of the leading vendors of RDBMS software.

Meanwhile, Michael Stonebraker, Eugene Wong, and several other professors at the University of California's Berkeley computer laboratories were also researching relational database technology. Like the IBM team, they developed a prototype relational database and dubbed their product Ingres. Ingres included a database language called Query Language (QUEL), which, in comparison to SQL, was much more structured but made less use of English-like statements. Ingres was eventually converted to an SQL-based RDBMS when it became clear that SQL was emerging as the standard database language. Several professors left Berkeley in 1980 to form Relational Technology, Inc., and in 1981 they announced the first commercial version of Ingres. Relational Technology has gone through several transformations and is now part of Computer Associates International, Inc. Ingres (now owned and supported by a company called Actian) is still one of the leading database products in the industry today.

Now we come full circle back to IBM. IBM announced its own RDBMS called SQL/Data System (SQL/DS) in 1981 and began shipping it in 1982. In 1983, the company introduced a new version of SQL/DS for the VM/CMS operating system (one of several offered by IBM for their mainframe systems) and announced a new RDBMS product called Database 2 (DB2), which could be used on IBM mainframes using IBM's mainstream MVS operating system. First shipped in 1985, DB2 has become IBM's premiere RDBMS, and its technology has been incorporated into the entire IBM product line. By the way, IBM hasn't changed—it's still IBM.

During the course of more than 40 years, I've seen what began as research for the System R project become a force that impacts almost every level of business today and evolve into a multibillion-dollar industry.

". . . And Then There Was a Standard"

With the flurry of activity surrounding the development of database languages, you could easily wonder if anyone ever thought of standardization. Although the idea was tossed about among the database community, there was never any consensus or agreement as to who should set the standard or which dialect it should be based upon. So each vendor continued to develop and improve its own database product in the hope that it—and by extension, its dialect of SQL—would become the industry standard.

Customer feedback and demand drove many vendors to include certain elements in their SQL dialects, and in time an unofficial standard emerged. It was a small specification by today's standards, as it encompassed only those elements that were similar across the various SQL dialects. However, this specification (such as it was) did provide database customers with a core set of criteria by which to judge the various database programs on the market, and it also gave users a small set of knowledge that they could leverage from one database program to another.

In 1982, the American National Standards Institute (ANSI) responded to the growing need for an official relational database language standard by commissioning its X3 organization's database technical committee, X3H2, to develop a proposal for such a standard. X3 is one of many organizations overseen by ANSI. In turn, X3H2 is only one of many technical committees that report to X3. X3H2 was and continues to be composed of database industry experts and representatives from almost every major SQL-based database vendor. In the beginning, the committee reviewed and debated the advantages and disadvantages of various proposed languages and also began work on a standard based on QUEL, the database language for Ingres. But market forces and the increasing commitment to SQL by IBM induced the committee to base its proposal on SQL instead.

The X3H2 committee's proposed standard was largely based on IBM's DB2 SQL dialect. The committee worked on several versions of its standard over the next two years and even improved SQL to some extent. However, an unfortunate circumstance arose as a result of these improvements: This new standard became incompatible with existing major SQL dialects. X3H2 soon realized that the changes made to SQL did not significantly improve it enough to warrant the incompatibilities, so the committee reverted to the original version of the standard.

ANSI ratified X3H2's standard in 1986 as "ANSI X3.135-1986 Database Language SQL," which became commonly known as SQL/86. Although X3H2 made some minor revisions to its standard before ANSI adopted it, SQL/86 merely defined a minimal set of "least common denominator" requirements to which database vendors could conform. In essence, it conferred official status on the elements that were similar among the various SQL dialects and that had already been implemented by many database vendors. But the new standard finally provided a specific foundation from which the language and its implementations could be developed further.

The International Organization for Standardization (ISO) approved its own document (which corresponded exactly with ANSI SQL/86) as an international standard in 1987 and published it as "ISO 9075-1987 Database Language SQL." (Both standards are still often referred to as just SQL/86.) The international database vendor community could now work from the same standards as those vendors in the United States. Despite the fact that SQL gained the status of an official standard, the language was far from being complete.

Evolution of the ANSI/ISO Standard

SQL/86 was soon criticized in public reviews, by the government, and by industry pundits such as C. J. Date. Some of the problems cited by these critics included redundancy within the SQL syntax (there were several ways to define the same query), lack of support for certain relational operators, and lack of referential integrity. Although X3H2 knew of these problems even before SQL/86 was published, the committee decided that it was better to release a standard now (even though it still needed work) than to have no standard at all.

Both ISO and ANSI addressed the criticism pertaining to referential integrity by adopting refined versions of their standards. ISO published "ISO 9075:1989 Database Language SQL with Integrity Enhancements" in mid-1989, while ANSI adopted its "X3.135-1989 Database Language SQL with Integrity Enhancements," also often referred to as SQL/89, late that same year. But the ANSI committee's work for the year wasn't over just yet. X3H2 was still trying to address an important issue brought forth by the government.

Some government users complained that the specification explaining how to embed SQL within a conventional programming language was not an explicit component of the standard. (Although the specification was included, it was relegated to an appendix.) Their concern was that vendors might not support portable implementations of embedded SQL because there was no specific requirement within the standard for them to do so. X3H2 responded by developing a second standard that required conformance to the embedding specification, publishing it as "ANSI X3.168-1989 Database Language Embedded SQL." It's interesting to note that ISO chose not to publish a corresponding standard because of a lack of similar concern within the international community. This meant that ISO had no specification for embedding SQL within a programming language, a situation that would not change until ISO's publication of its SQL/92 Standard.

SQL/86 and SQL/89 were far from being complete standards—they lacked some of the most fundamental features needed for commercial database systems. For example, neither standard specified a way to make changes to the database structure (including within the database system itself) after it was defined. No one could modify or delete any structural components (such as tables or columns) or make any changes to the security of the database. For example, you could CREATE a table, but the standard included no definition of the DROP command to delete a table or the ALTER command to change it. Also, you could GRANT security access to a table, but the standard did not define the REVOKE command to allow removal of access authority. Ironically, these capabilities were provided by all commercial SQL-based databases. They were not included in either standard, however, because each vendor implemented them in different ways. Other features were widely implemented among many SQL-based databases but omitted from the standards. Once again, it was an issue of varied implementations.

By the time SQL/89 was completed, both ANSI and ISO were already working on major revisions to SQL that would make it a complete and robust language. The new version would be referred to as SQL/92 (what else?) and would include features that had already been widely implemented by most major database vendors. But one of the main objectives of both ANSI and ISO was to avoid defining a "least common denominator" standard yet again. As a result, they decided to both include features that had not yet gained wide acceptance and add new features that were substantially beyond those currently implemented.

ANSI and ISO published their new SQL Standards—"X3.135-1992 Database Language SQL" and "ISO/IEC 9075:1992 Database Language SQL," respectively—in October 1992. (Work on these documents was completed in late 1991, but some final fine-tuning took place during 1992.) The SQL/92 document is considerably larger than the one for SQL/89, but it's also much broader in scope. For example, it provides the means to modify the database structure after it has been defined, supports additional operations for manipulating character strings as well as dates and times, and defines additional security features. SQL/92 was a major step forward from any of its predecessors.

Fortunately, the standards committees anticipated this situation to some extent. To facilitate a smooth and gradual conformance to the new standard, ANSI and ISO defined SQL/92 on three levels:

Entry SQL	Similar to SQL/89, this level also includes features to make the transition from SQL/89 to SQL/92 easier as well as features that corrected errors in the SQL/89 Standard. The idea was that this level would be the easier to implement because most of its features had already been widely incorporated into existing products.
Intermediate SQL	This level encompasses most of the features in the new standard. Both committees' decisions to include certain features at this level were based on several factors. The overall objectives were to enhance the standard so that SQL better supported the concepts in the relational model and to redefine syntax that was ambiguous or unclear. It was an easy decision to include features that were already implemented in some way by one or more vendors and that met these objectives. Features demanded by users of SQL database systems were given high consideration as long as they met these objectives and were relatively easy for most vendors to implement. This level was meant to ensure that it would be reasonably possible for a given product to have as robust an implementation as possible.

FULL SQL

The entire SQL/92 specification is encompassed within this level. It obviously includes the more complex features that were omitted in the first two levels. This level includes features that, although considered important to meet customer demands or further "purify" the language, would be difficult for most vendors to implement immediately. Unfortunately, compliance with Full SQL was not yet a requirement, so it would be some time before we could expect database products to fully implement the standard.

Although many database vendors continued work on implementing the features in SQL/92, they also developed and implemented features of their own. The additions they made to the SQL Standard are known as *extensions*. For example, a vendor might provide more data types than the six specified in SQL/92. Although these extensions provide more functionality within a given product and allow vendors to differentiate themselves from one another, there are drawbacks. The main problem with adding extensions is that it caused each vendor's dialect of SQL to diverge further from the original standard. This, in turn, prevented database developers from creating portable applications that could be run using any SQL database.

Other SQL Standards

The ANSI/ISO SQL Standard is the most widely accepted standard to date. This means, of course, that other standards in existence also incorporate SQL in one form or another. These are some of the more significant alternate standards:

X/OPEN

A group of European vendors (collectively known as X/OPEN) developed a set of standards that would help establish a portable application environment based on UNIX. The ability to port an application from one computer system to another without changing it is an important issue in the European market. Although the X/OPEN members have adopted SQL as part of this set of standards, their version deviates from the ANSI/ISO Standard in several areas.

SAA
: IBM has always developed its own dialect of SQL, which the company incorporated into its Systems Application Architecture (SAA) specification. Integrating IBM's SQL dialect into the complete line of IBM database products was one of the goals of the SAA specification. Although this goal has never been achieved, SQL still plays an important role in unifying IBM's database products.

FIPS
: The National Institute of Standards and Technology (NIST) made SQL a Federal Information Processing Standard (FIPS) beginning in 1987. Originally published as "FIPS PUB 127," it specifies the level to which an RDBMS must conform to the ANSI/ISO Standard. Since then, all relational database products used by the U.S. government have been required to conform to the current FIPS publication.

ODBC
: In 1989, a group of database vendors formed the SQL Access group to address the problem of database interoperability. Although these vendors' first efforts were somewhat unsuccessful, they widened their focus to include a way to bind an SQL database to a user-interface language. The result of their efforts was the Call-Level Interface (CLI) specification published in 1992. That same year, Microsoft published its Open Database Connectivity (ODBC) specification, which was based on the CLI Standard. ODBC has since become the *de facto* means of accessing and sharing data among SQL databases that support it.

These standards continually evolved as newer versions of ANSI/ISO SQL were adopted, and they are sometimes independently developed as well.

In 1997, ANSI's X3 organization was renamed the National Committee for Information Technology Standards (NCITS), and the technical committee in charge of the SQL Standard was called ANSI NCITS-H2 and has more recently become INCITS DM32.2. Because of the rapidly growing complexity of the SQL Standard, the ANSI and ISO standards committees agreed to break the standard into twelve separate numbered parts and one addendum as they began to work on SQL3 (so named because it's the third major revision of the standard) so that work on each part could proceed in parallel. Since 1997, two additional parts have been defined.

Table 3-1 shows the name and description of each part of the SQL Standard, as well as the status of each part as of SQL:2016 (ISO/IEC 9075:2016).

Table 3-1 *Structure of the SQL Standard*

Name	Status	Description	Pages in SQL:2016
Part 1: Framework (SQL/Framework)	Completed in 1999 and updated in 2003, 2008, 2011, and 2016.	Describes each part of the standard and contains information common to all parts.	78
Part 2: Foundation (SQL/Foundation)	The core 1992 standard that has been updated in 1999, 2003, 2008, 2011, and 2016.	Defines the syntax and semantics of the data definition and data manipulation portions of the SQL language.	1,707
SQL/OLAP (Online Analytical Processing)	Merged with Foundation in 1999.	Describes the functions and operations used for analytical processing. (This is intended as an amendment to SQL/Foundation.)	
Part 3: Call-Level Interface (SQL/CLI)	Completed in 1995 and expanded in 1999, 2003, 2008, and 2016.	Developed by the SQL Access group, this part corresponds to Microsoft's ODBC specification.	391
Part 4: Persistent Stored Modules (SQL/PSM)	Completed in 1996. Stored routines and the CALL statement moved to Foundation in 1999. Remaining standard updated in 2003, 2011, and 2016.	Defines procedural language SQL statements that are useful in user-defined functions and procedures. (Support for stored procedures, stored functions, the CALL statement, and routine invocation was eventually moved to SQL/Foundation.)	188
Part 5: SQL/Bindings	Specification for embedding SQL moved to a separate part in 1999 and then was embedded in Foundation in 2003.	Specifies how SQL is embedded in non-object programming languages. This part will be merged into SQL/Foundation in the next version of SQL.	
Part 6: Transaction (XA Specialization)	Canceled in 1999.	SQL specialization of the X/OPEN XA specification.	

Name	Status	Description	Pages in SQL:2016
Part 7: SQL/ Temporal	Withdrawn in 2003.	Defines support for storage and retrieval of temporal data. There has been some difference of opinion on the requirements and details of Temporal, so work has stalled over the last several years.	
Part 8: SQL/ Objects Extended Objects	Merged into Foundation in 1999.	Defines how application-defined abstract data types are handled by the RDBMS.	
Part 9: Management of External Data (SQL/MED)	ISO version completed in 2003 and revised in 2008 and 2016.	Defines additional syntax and definitions to SQL/ Foundation that allow SQL to access non-SQL data sources (files).	471
Part 10: Object Language Bindings (SQL/OLB)	Completed in 1998 as an ANSI-only standard, revised in 1999 by ISO, and revised again in 2003, 2008, and 2016.	Specifies the syntax and semantics of embedding SQL in the Java programming language. This corresponds to another ANSI standard, SQLJ Part 0.	376
Part 11: Information and Definition Schemas (SQL/ Schemata)	Extraction from Foundation completed in 2003. Revised in 2008 and 2016.	Information and definition schemas.	327
Part 12: SQL/ Replication	Project started in 2000 but dropped in 2003 due to lack of progress.	Defines support and facilities for replicating an SQL database.	
Part 13: SQL Routines and Types Using the Java Programming Language (SQL/ JRT)	Completed in 1999 as an ANSI-only standard based on SQL/92. Revised as an international standard in 2003, 2008, and 2016.	Defines how Java code can be used within an SQL database.	151
Part 14: XML-Related Specifications (SQL/XML)	Completed in 2003 and expanded in 2006, 2008, 2011, and 2016.	Defines how XML can be used within an SQL database. This part is aligned with the W3C XQuery V1.1 specification.	444

Commercial Implementations

As you read earlier in this chapter, SQL first appeared in the mainframe environment. Products such as DB2, Ingres, and Oracle have been around since 1979 and have legitimized the use of SQL as the preferred method of working with relational databases. During the 1980s, relational databases hit the desktop on personal computers, and products such as R:BASE, dBase IV, and Super Base put the power of data in tables at the user's fingertips. However, it wasn't until the very late 1980s and early 1990s that SQL became the language of choice for desktop relational databases. The product that arguably broke the dam was Microsoft Access version 1 in 1992.

The early 1990s also heralded the advent of client/server computing, and RDBMS programs such as Microsoft SQL Server and Informix-SE have been designed to provide database services to users in numerous types of multi-user environments. Since 2000, there has been a concerted effort to make database information available via the Internet. Businesses have caught on to the idea of e-commerce, and those who haven't already established a Web presence are moving quickly to do so. As a result, database developers are demanding more powerful client/ server databases and newer versions of long-established mainframe RDBMS products that they can use to develop and maintain the databases needed for their Web sites. One response has been to migrate data to the "cloud" using servers shared over the Internet. Companies such as Amazon, Microsoft, and IBM have introduced popular cloud services. As one might expect, nearly all of these cloud servers use databases that support SQL.

I could attempt to list all the mainstream products that support SQL, but the list would go on for pages and pages. Suffice it to say that SQL in commercial database systems is here to stay.

What the Future Holds

When Mike Hernandez and I first wrote this book in 1999, the standards committees were just putting the finishing touches on SQL3, which had been a long time in coming. Since then, SQL:1999, SQL:2003, SQL:2008, SQL:2011, and SQL:2016 have been published. As of early 2017, both the ANSI and ISO committees are hard at work on a separate

SQL/MM—Multimedia standard that has its own five parts: Framework, Full Text, Spatial, Still Image, and Data Mining. Although the standards committees started out far behind the commercial implementations in 1986, it's fair to say that the SQL Standard long ago caught up with— and in many areas is now staying ahead of—features in available database systems.

Why Should You Learn SQL?

Learning SQL gives you the skills you need to retrieve information from any relational database. It also helps you understand the mechanisms behind the graphical query interfaces found in many RDBMS products. Understanding SQL helps you craft complex queries and provides the knowledge required to troubleshoot queries when problems occur.

Because SQL is found in a wide variety of RDBMS products, you can use your skills across a variety of platforms. For example, after you learn SQL in a product such as Microsoft Access, you can leverage your existing knowledge if your company decides to move to Microsoft SQL Server, Oracle Corporation's Oracle, or IBM's DB/2. You won't have to relearn SQL— you'll just have to learn the differences between the first dialect that you learn and the dialect used in another product. Imagine you learned English in the UK and the found out you needed to drop the letter "u" from certain words (favor instead of favour) when you moved to the US.

It bears repeating that SQL is here to stay. Many vendors have invested huge amounts of money, time, and research to incorporate SQL into their RDBMS products, and a vast number of businesses and organizations have built much of their information technology infrastructures on those products. As you have probably surmised by what you've learned in this chapter, SQL will continue to evolve to meet the changing demands and requirements of the marketplace.

Which Version of SQL Does this Book Cover?

Good question! Remember, this is a "Mere Mortals" book. The current standard is nearly 5,000 pages long, so there is no way I am going to try to teach you everything. What I strive to do in this book is give you a really solid grounding in the basics (as standardized in Framework and Foundation) that are supported by virtually every commercial implementation. I also provide sample databases and solutions to all the problems I pose using four of the most popular implementations: Microsoft Office Access 2016, Microsoft SQL Server 2016, MySQL version 5.7 Community Edition, and PostgreSQL version 9.6. If you were learning a language, think of it as covering the basic present, past, and future tenses. If you want to tackle the subjunctive, pluperfect, or progressive, you'll have to dig into more advanced books.

Summary

I began this chapter with a discussion on the origins of SQL. You learned that SQL is a relational database language that was created soon after the introduction of the relational model. I also explained that the early evolution of SQL was closely tied to the evolution of the relational model itself.

Next, I discussed the initial implementations of the relational model by various database vendors. You learned that the first relational databases were implemented on mainframe computers. You also learned how IBM and Oracle came to be big players in the database industry.

I then discussed the origin of the ANSI SQL Standard. You learned that there was an unofficial standard before ANSI decided to define an official one, and I discussed the ANSI X3H2 committee's initial work on the specification. I explained that although the new standard was basically a set of "least common denominator" features, it did provide a foundation from which the language could be further developed. You also learned that the ISO published its own standard, which corresponded exactly with the ANSI specification.

The evolution of the ANSI/ISO Standard was the next topic of discussion, and you learned that various people and organizations criticized the initial standards. I then discussed how ANSI/ISO responded to the criticisms by adopting several revisions to the standard. You learned how one version led to the next and how we arrived at the SQL/92 Standard. I explained how that standard defined various conformance levels that allowed vendors to implement the standard's features into their products as smoothly as possible. Next, I discussed the progress that the SQL Standard has made since 1992, and I took a quick look at the evolution of commercial SQL databases.

I closed the chapter with a short discussion on the future of SQL. You learned that SQL:2016 is a much more complex standard than SQL/92. I also explained why SQL will continue to be developed, gave you some good reasons for learning the language, and explained what parts of SQL I cover in this book.

Part II
SQL Basics

4

Creating a Simple Query

"Think like a wise man but communicate in the language of the people."
—William Butler Yeats

Topics Covered in This Chapter

Introducing SELECT

The SELECT Statement

A Quick Aside: Data versus Information

Translating Your Request into SQL

Eliminating Duplicate Rows

Sorting Information

Saving Your Work

Sample Statements

Summary

Problems for You to Solve

Now that you've learned a little bit about the history of SQL, it's time to jump right in and learn the language itself. As I mentioned in the Introduction, I'm going to spend most of this book covering the data manipulation portion of the language. So my initial focus will be on the true workhorse of SQL—the SELECT statement.

Introducing SELECT

Above all other keywords, SELECT truly lies at the heart of SQL. It is the cornerstone of the most powerful and complex statement within the language and the means by which you retrieve information from the tables in your database. You use SELECT in conjunction with other keywords and clauses to find and view information in an almost limitless number of ways. Nearly any question regarding who, what, where, when, or even what if and how many can be answered with SELECT. As long as you've designed your database properly and collected the appropriate data, you can get the answers you need to make sound decisions for your organization. As you'll discover when you get to Part V, "Modifying Sets of Data," you'll apply many of the techniques you learn about SELECT to create UPDATE, INSERT, and DELETE statements.

The SELECT operation in SQL can be broken down into three smaller operations, which I will refer to as the SELECT statement, the SELECT expression, and the SELECT query. (Breaking down the SELECT operation in this manner will make it far easier to understand and to appreciate its complexity.) Each of these operations provides its own set of keywords and clauses, providing you with the flexibility to create a final SQL statement that is appropriate for the question you want to pose to the database. As you'll learn in later chapters, you can even combine the operations in various ways to answer very complex questions.

In this chapter, I'll begin my discussion of the SELECT statement and take a brief look at the SELECT query. I'll then examine the SELECT statement in more detail as you work through to Chapter 5, "Getting More Than Simple Columns," and Chapter 6, "Filtering Your Data."

> ❖ **Note** In other books about relational databases, you'll sometimes see the word *relation* used for *table*, and you might encounter *tuple* or *record* for *row* and perhaps *attribute* or *field* for *column*. However, the SQL Standard specifically uses the terms *table*, *row*, and *column* to refer to these particular elements of a database structure. I'll stay consistent with the SQL Standard and use these latter three terms throughout the remainder of the book.

The SELECT Statement

The SELECT statement forms the basis of every question you pose to the database. When you create and execute a SELECT statement, you are querying the database. (I know it sounds a little obvious, but I want to make certain that everyone reading this starts from the same point of reference.) In fact, many RDBMS programs allow you to save a SELECT statement as a *query*, *view*, *function*, or *stored procedure*. Whenever someone says she is going to query the database, you know that she's going to execute some sort of SELECT statement. Depending on the RDBMS program, SELECT statements can be executed directly from a command line window, from an interactive Query by Example (QBE) grid, or from within a block of programming code. Regardless of how you choose to define and execute it, the syntax of the SELECT statement is always the same.

❖ **Note** Many database systems provide extensions to the SQL Standard to allow you to build complex programming statements (such as If...Then...Else) in functions and stored procedures, but the specific syntax is unique to each different product. It is far beyond the scope of this book to cover even one or two of these programming languages—such as Microsoft SQL Server's Transact-SQL or Oracle's PL/SQL. (I cover a basic form of If...Then...Else [CASE] defined in the SQL Standard in Chapter 19, "Condition Testing.") You'll still use the cornerstone SELECT statement when you build functions and stored procedures for your particular database system. Throughout this book, I'll use the term *view* to refer to a saved SQL statement even though you might embed your SQL statement in a function or procedure.

A SELECT statement is composed of several distinct keywords, known as *clauses*. You define a SELECT statement by using various configurations of these clauses to retrieve the information you require. Some of these clauses are required, although others are optional. Additionally, each clause has one or more keywords that represent required or optional values. These values are used by the clause to help retrieve the information requested by the SELECT statement as a whole. Figure 4-1 shows a diagram of the SELECT statement and its clauses.

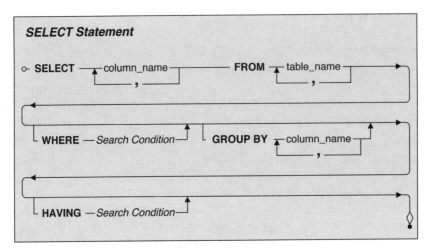

Figure 4-1 *A diagram of the SELECT statement*

> ❖ **Note** The syntax diagram in Figure 4-1 reflects a rudimentary
> SELECT statement. I'll continue to update and modify the diagram as
> I introduce and work with new keywords and clauses. So for those of
> you who might have some previous experience with SQL statements,
> just be patient and bear with me for the time being.

Here's a brief summary of the clauses in a SELECT statement.

- **SELECT**—This is the primary clause of the SELECT statement and
  is absolutely required. You use it to specify the columns you want
  in the result set of your query. The columns themselves are drawn
  from the table or view you specify in the FROM clause. (You can
  also draw them from several tables simultaneously, but I'll discuss
  this later in Part III, "Working with Multiple Tables.") You can also
  use in this clause aggregate functions, such as Sum(HoursWorked),
  or mathematical expressions, such as Quantity * Price.

- **FROM**—This is the second most important clause in the SELECT
  statement and is also required. You use the FROM clause to specify
  the tables or views from which to draw the columns you've listed in
  the SELECT clause. You can use this clause in more complex ways,
  but I'll discuss this in later chapters.

- **WHERE**—This is an optional clause that you use to filter the rows returned by the FROM clause. The WHERE keyword is followed by an expression, technically known as a *predicate*, that evaluates to true, false, or unknown. You can test the expression by using standard comparison operators, Boolean operators, or special operators. I'll discuss all the elements of the WHERE clause in Chapter 6.

- **GROUP BY**—When you use aggregate functions in the SELECT clause to produce summary information, you use the GROUP BY clause to divide the information into distinct groups. Your database system uses any column or list of columns following the GROUP BY keywords as grouping columns. The GROUP BY clause is optional, and I'll examine it further in Chapter 13, "Grouping Data."

- **HAVING**—The HAVING clause filters the result of aggregate functions in grouped information. It is similar to the WHERE clause in that the HAVING keyword is followed by an expression that evaluates to true, false, or unknown. You can test the expression by using standard comparison operators, Boolean operators, or special operators. HAVING is also an optional clause, and I'll take a closer look at it in Chapter 14, "Filtering Grouped Data."

You're going to work with a very basic SELECT statement at first, so I'll focus on the SELECT and FROM clauses. I'll add the other clauses, one by one, as you work through the other chapters to build more complex SELECT statements.

A Quick Aside: Data versus Information

Before you pose the first query to the database, one thing must be perfectly clear: There is a distinct difference between *data* and *information*. In essence, data is what you store in the database, and information is what you retrieve from the database. This distinction is important for you to understand because it helps you to keep things in proper perspective. Remember that a database is designed to provide meaningful information to someone within your organization. However, the information can be provided only if the appropriate data exists in the database and if the database itself has been structured in such a way to support that information. Let's examine these terms in more detail.

The values that you store in the database are data. Data is static in the sense that it remains in the same state until you modify it by some manual or automated process. Figure 4-2 shows some sample data.

Katherine Ehrlich 89931 Active 79915

Figure 4-2 *An example of basic data*

On the surface, this data is meaningless. For example, there is no easy way for you to determine what 89931 represents. Is it a ZIP Code? Is it a part number? Even if you know it represents a customer identification number, is it associated with Katherine Ehrlich? There's no way to know until the data is processed. After you process the data so that it is meaningful and useful when you work with it or view it, the data becomes information. Information is dynamic in that it constantly changes relative to the data stored in the database and also in its ability to be processed and presented in an unlimited number of ways. You can show information as the result of a SELECT statement, display it in a form on your computer screen, or print it on paper as a report. But the point to remember is that you must process your data in a manner that enables you to turn it into meaningful information.

Figure 4-3 shows the data from the previous example transformed into information on a customer screen. This illustrates how the data can be manipulated in such a way that it is now meaningful to anyone who views it.

Customer Information

Name (F/L): Katherine Ehrlich	ID #: 89931	
Address: 7402 Taxco Avenue	Status: Active	
City: El Paso	Phone: 555-9284	
State: TX ZIP: 79915	Fax: 554-0099	

Figure 4-3 *An example of data processed into information*

When you work with a SELECT statement, you use its clauses to manipulate *data*, but the statement itself returns *information*. Get the picture?

There's one last issue I need to address. When you execute a SELECT statement, it usually retrieves one or more rows of information—the exact number depends on how you construct the statement. These rows are collectively known as a *result set*, which is the term I use throughout the remainder of the book. This name makes perfect sense because you always work with sets of data whenever you use a relational database. (Remember that the relational model is based, in part, on set theory.) You can easily view the information in a result set and, in many cases, you can modify its data. But, once again, it all depends on how you construct your SELECT statement.

So let's get down to business and start using the SELECT statement.

Translating Your Request into SQL

When you request information from the database, it's usually in the form of a question or a statement that implies a question. For example, you might formulate statements such as these:

> *"Which cities do our customers live in?"*
>
> *"Show me a current list of our employees and their phone numbers."*
>
> *"What kind of classes do we currently offer?"*
>
> *"Give me the names of the folks on our staff and the dates they were hired."*

After you know what you want to ask, you can translate your request into a more formal statement. You compose the translation using this form:

```
Select <item> from the <source>
```

Start by looking at your request and replacing words or phrases such as *"list," "show me," "what," "which,"* and *"who"* with the word *"Select."* Next, identify any nouns in your request, and determine whether a given noun represents an item you want to see or the name of a table in which an item might be stored. If it's an item, use it as a replacement for <item> in the translation statement. If it's a table name, use it as a replacement for <source>. If you translate the first question listed earlier, your statement looks something like this:

```
Select city from the customers table
```

After you define your translation statement, you need to turn it into a full-fledged SELECT statement using the SQL syntax shown in Figure 4-4.

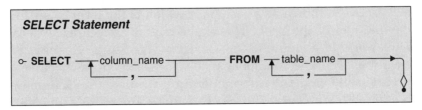

Figure 4-4 *The syntax of a simple SELECT statement*

The first step, however, is to clean up your translation statement. You do so by crossing out any word that is not a noun representing the name of a column or table or that is not a word specifically used in the SQL syntax. Here's how the translation statement looks during the process of cleaning it up:

```
Select city from the customers table
```

Remove the words you've crossed out, and you now have a complete SELECT statement.

```
SELECT City FROM Customers
```

You can use the three-step technique I just presented on any request you send to your database. In fact, I use this technique throughout most of the book, and I encourage you to use it while you're beginning to learn how to build these statements. However, you'll eventually merge these steps into one seamless operation as you get more accustomed to writing SELECT statements.

Remember that you'll work mostly with columns and tables when you're beginning to learn how to use SQL. The syntax diagram in Figure 4-4 reflects this fact by using column_name in the SELECT clause and table_name in the FROM clause. In the next chapter, you'll learn how to use other terms in these clauses to create more complex SELECT statements.

You probably noticed that the request I used in the previous example is relatively straightforward. It was easy to both redefine it as a translation statement and identify the column names that were present in the statement. But what if a request is not as straightforward and easy to translate, and it's difficult to identify the columns you need for the SELECT clause? The easiest course of action is to refine your request and make it more specific. For example, you can refine a request such as *"Show me the information on our clients"* by recasting it more clearly as *"List the name, city, and phone number for each of our clients."* If refining the request doesn't solve the problem, you still have two other options. Your first alternative is to determine whether the table specified in the FROM clause of the SELECT statement contains any column names that can help to clarify the request and thus make it easier to define a translation statement. Your second alternative is to examine the request more closely and determine whether a word or phrase it contains *implies* any column names. Whether you can use either or both alternatives depends on the request itself. Just remember that you do have techniques available when you find it difficult to define a translation statement. Let's look at an example of each technique and how you can apply it in a typical scenario.

To illustrate the first technique, let's say you're trying to translate the following request:

"I need the names and addresses of all our employees."

This looks like a straightforward request on the surface. But if you review this request again, you'll find one minor problem: Although you can determine the table you need (Employees) for the translation statement, there's nothing within the request that helps you identify the specific columns you need for the SELECT clause. Although the words *"names"* and *"addresses"* appear in the request, they are terms that are general in nature. You can solve this problem by reviewing the table you identified in the request and determining whether it contains any columns you can substitute for these terms. If so, use the column names in the translation statement. (You can opt to use generic versions of the column names in the translation statement if it will help you visualize the statement more clearly. However, you will need to use the actual column names in the SQL syntax.) In this case, look for column names in the Employees table shown in Figure 4-5 that could be used in place of the words *"names"* and *"addresses."*

```
┌─────────────────────────────────┐
│         EMPLOYEES               │
│·································│
│ EmployeeID          PK          │
│ EmpFirstName                    │
│ EmpLastName                     │
│ EmpStreetAddress                │
│ EmpCity                         │
│ EmpState                        │
│ EmpZipCode                      │
│ EmpAreaCode                     │
│ EmpPhoneNumber                  │
└─────────────────────────────────┘
```

Figure 4-5 *The structure of the Employees table*

To fully satisfy the need for "names" and "addresses," you will indeed use six columns from this table. EmpFirstName and EmpLastName will both replace "names" in the request, and EmpStreetAddress, EmpCity, Emp-State, and EmpZipCode will replace "addresses." Now, apply the entire translation process to the request, which I've repeated for your convenience. (I'll use generic forms of the column names for the translation statement and the actual column names in the SQL syntax.)

"I need the names and addresses of all our employees."

Translation	Select first name, last name, street address, city, state, and ZIP Code from the employees table
Clean Up	Select first name, last name, street address, city, state, ~~and~~ ZIP Code from ~~the~~ employees ~~table~~
SQL	SELECT EmpFirstName, EmpLastName, EmpStreetAddress, EmpCity, EmpState, EmpZipCode FROM Employees

❖ **Note** This example clearly illustrates how to use multiple columns in a SELECT clause. I'll discuss this technique in more detail later in this section.

The next example illustrates the second technique, which involves searching for implied columns within the request. Let's assume you're trying to put the following request through the translation process:

"What kind of classes do we currently offer?"

At first glance, it might seem difficult to define a translation statement from this request. The request doesn't indicate any column names, and without even one item to select, you can't create a complete translation statement. What do you do now? Take a closer look at each word in the request and determine whether there is one that *implies* a column name within the Classes table. Before you read any further, take a moment to study the request again. Can you find such a word?

In this case, the word "kind" might imply a column name in the Classes table. Why? Because a kind of class can also be thought of as a category of class. If there is a category column in the Classes table, then you have the column name you need to complete the translation statement and, by inference, the SELECT statement. Let's assume that there is a category column in the Classes table and take the request through the three-step process once again.

"What kind of classes do we currently offer?"

Translation	Select category from the classes table
Clean Up	Select category from ~~the~~ classes ~~table~~
SQL	SELECT Category FROM Classes

As the example shows, this technique involves using synonyms as replacements for certain words or phrases within the request. If you identify a word or phrase that might imply a column name, try to replace it with a synonym. The synonym you choose might indeed identify a column that exists in the database. However, if the first synonym that comes to mind doesn't work, try another. Continue this process until you either find a synonym that does identify a column name or until you're satisfied that neither the original word nor any of its synonyms represent a column name.

❖ **Note** Unless I indicate otherwise, all column names and table names used in the SQL syntax portion of the examples are drawn from the sample databases in Appendix B, "Schema for the Sample Databases." This convention applies to all examples for the remainder of the book.

Expanding the Field of Vision

You can retrieve multiple columns within a SELECT statement as easily as you can retrieve a single column. List the names of the columns you want to use in the SELECT clause, and separate each name in the list with a comma. In the syntax diagram shown in Figure 4-6, the option to use more than one column is indicated by a line that flows from right to left beneath column_name. The comma in the middle of the line denotes that you must insert a comma before the next column name you want to use in the SELECT clause.

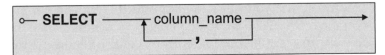

Figure 4-6 *The syntax for using multiple columns in a SELECT clause*

The option to use multiple columns in the SELECT statement provides you with the means to answer questions such as these:

"Show me a list of our employees and their phone numbers."

Translation	Select the last name, first name, and phone number of all our employees from the employees table
Clean Up	Select ~~the~~ last name, first name, ~~and~~ phone number ~~of all our employees~~ from ~~the~~ employees ~~table~~
SQL	SELECT EmpLastName, EmpFirstName, EmpPhoneNumber FROM Employees

"What are the names and prices of the products we carry, and under what category is each item listed?"

Translation	Select the name, price, and category of every product from the products table
Clean Up	Select ~~the~~ name, price, ~~and~~ category ~~of every product~~ from ~~the~~ products ~~table~~
SQL	SELECT ProductName, RetailPrice, Category FROM Products

You gain the advantage of seeing a wider spectrum of information when you work with several columns in a SELECT statement. Incidentally, the sequence of the columns in your SELECT clause is not important—you can list the columns in any order you want. This gives you the flexibility to view the same information in a variety of ways.

For example, let's say you're working with the table shown in Figure 4-7, and you're asked to pose the following request to the database:

> *"Show me a list of subjects, the category each belongs to, and the code we use in our catalog. But I'd like to see the name first, followed by the category, and then the code."*

SUBJECTS	
SubjectID	*PK*
CategoryID	*FK*
SubjectCode	
SubjectName	
SubjectDescription	

Figure 4-7 *The structure of the Subjects table*

You can still transform this request into an appropriate SELECT statement, even though the person making the request wants to see the columns in a specific order. Just list the column names in the order specified when you define the translation statement. Here's how the process looks when you transform this request into a SELECT statement:

Translation	Select the subject name, category ID, and subject code from the subjects table
Clean Up	Select ~~the~~ subject name, category ID, ~~and~~ subject code from ~~the~~ subjects ~~table~~
SQL	SELECT SubjectName, CategoryID, SubjectCode FROM Subjects

Using a Shortcut to Request All Columns

There is no limit to the number of columns you can specify in the SELECT clause—in fact, you can list all the columns from the source table.

The following example shows the SELECT statement you use to specify all the columns from the Subjects table in Figure 4-7:

SQL   SELECT SubjectID, CategoryID, SubjectCode,

                SubjectName, SubjectDescription

        FROM Subjects

When you specify all the columns from the source table, you'll have a lot of typing to do if the table contains a number of columns! Fortunately, the SQL Standard specifies the asterisk as a shortcut you can use to shorten the statement considerably. The syntax diagram in Figure 4-8 shows that you can use the asterisk as an alternative to a list of columns in the SELECT clause.

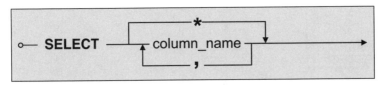

Figure 4-8 *The syntax for the asterisk shortcut*

Place the asterisk immediately after the SELECT clause when you want to specify all the columns from the source table in the FROM clause. For example, here's how the preceding SELECT statement looks when you use the shortcut:

SQL   SELECT *

        FROM Subjects

You'll certainly do less typing with this statement! However, one issue arises when you create SELECT statements in this manner: The asterisk represents all of the columns that *currently exist* in the source table, and adding or deleting columns affects what you see in the result set of the SELECT statement. (Oddly enough, the SQL Standard states that adding or deleting columns *should not* affect your result set.) This issue is important only if you must see the same columns in the result set consistently. Your database system will not warn you if columns have been deleted from the source table when you use the asterisk in the SELECT clause, but it will raise a warning when it can't find a column you *explicitly* specified. Although this does not pose a real problem for our purposes, it will be an important issue when you delve into the world of programming with SQL. My rule of thumb is this: Use the asterisk only when you need to create a "quick and dirty" query to see all the information in a given table. Otherwise, specify all the columns you need for the query. In the end, the query will return exactly the information you need and will be more self-documenting.

The examples we've seen so far are based on simple requests that require columns from only one table. You'll learn how to work with more complex requests that require columns from several tables in Part III.

Eliminating Duplicate Rows

When working with SELECT statements, you'll inevitably come across result sets with duplicate rows. There is no cause for alarm if you see such a result set. Use the DISTINCT keyword in your SELECT statement, and the result set will be free and clear of all duplicate rows. Figure 4-9 shows the syntax diagram for the DISTINCT keyword.

As the diagram illustrates, DISTINCT is an optional keyword that precedes the list of columns specified in the SELECT clause. The DISTINCT keyword asks your database system to evaluate the values of all the columns *as a single unit* on a row-by-row basis and eliminate any redundant rows it finds. The remaining unique rows are then returned to the result set. The following example shows what a difference the DISTINCT keyword can make under the appropriate circumstances.

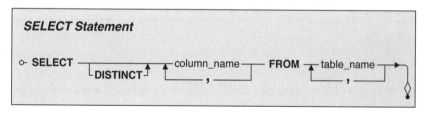

Figure 4-9 *The syntax for the DISTINCT keyword*

Let's say you're posing the following request to the database:

"Which cities are represented by our bowling league membership?"

The question seems easy enough, so you take it through the translation process.

Translation	Select city from the bowlers table
Clean Up	Select city from ~~the~~ bowlers ~~table~~
SQL	SELECT City FROM Bowlers

The problem is that the result set for this SELECT statement shows *every occurrence* of each city name found in the Bowlers table. For example, if there are 20 people from Bellevue, 7 people from Kent, and 14 people from Seattle, the result set displays 20 occurrences of Bellevue, 7 occurrences of Kent, and 14 occurrences of Seattle. Clearly, this redundant information is unnecessary. All you want to see is a *single* occurrence of each city name found in the Bowlers table. You resolve this problem by using the DISTINCT keyword in the SELECT statement to eliminate the redundant information.

Let's run the request through the translation process once again using the DISTINCT keyword. Note that I now include the word "distinct" in both the Translation step and the Clean Up step.

"Which cities are represented by our bowling league membership?"

Translation	Select the distinct city values from the bowlers table
Clean Up	Select ~~the~~ distinct city ~~values~~ from ~~the~~ bowlers ~~table~~
SQL	SELECT DISTINCT City FROM Bowlers

The result set for this SELECT statement displays exactly what you're looking for—a single occurrence of each distinct (or unique) city found in the Bowlers table.

You can use the DISTINCT keyword on multiple columns as well. Let's modify the previous example by requesting both the city and the state from the Bowlers table. The new SELECT statement looks like this:

```
SELECT DISTINCT City, State FROM Bowlers
```

This SELECT statement returns a result set that contains unique records and shows definite distinctions between cities with the same name. For example, it shows the distinction between "Portland, ME," "Portland, OR," "Hollywood, CA," and "Hollywood, FL." It's worthwhile to note that most database systems sort the output in the sequence in which you specify the columns, so you'll see these values in the sequence "Hollywood, CA," "Hollywood, FL," "Portland, ME," and "Portland, OR." However, the SQL Standard does not require the result to be sorted in this order. If you want to guarantee the sort sequence, read on to the next section to learn about the ORDER BY clause.

The DISTINCT keyword is a very useful tool under the right circumstances. Use it only when you really want to see unique rows in your result set.

> ❖ **Caution** For database systems that include a graphical interface, you can usually request that the result set of a query be displayed in an updatable grid of rows and columns. You can type a new value in a column on a row, and the database system updates the value stored in your table. (Your database system actually executes an UPDATE query on your behalf behind the scenes—you can read more about that in Chapter 15, "Updating Sets of Data.")
>
> However, in all database systems that I studied, when you include the DISTINCT keyword, the resulting set of rows cannot be updated. To be able to update a column in a row, your database system needs to be able to uniquely identify the specific row and column you want to change. When you use DISTINCT, the values you see in each row are the result of evaluating perhaps dozens of duplicate rows. If you try to update one of the columns, your database won't know which specific row to change. Your database system also doesn't know if perhaps you mean to change all the rows with the same duplicate value.

Sorting Information

At the beginning of this chapter, I said that the SELECT operation can be broken down into three smaller operations: the SELECT statement, the SELECT expression, and the SELECT query. I also stated that you can combine these operations in various ways to answer complex requests. However, you also need to combine these operations in order to sort the rows of a result set.

By definition, the rows of a result set returned by a SELECT statement are unordered. The sequence in which they appear is typically based on their physical position in the table. (The actual sequence is often determined dynamically by your database system based on how it decides to most efficiently satisfy your request.) The only way to sort the result set is to embed the SELECT statement within a SELECT query, as shown in Figure 4-10. I define a SELECT query as a SELECT statement with an ORDER BY clause. The ORDER BY clause of the SELECT query lets you specify the sequence of rows in the final result set. As you'll learn in later chapters, you can actually embed a SELECT statement within another SELECT statement or SELECT expression to answer very complex questions. However, the SELECT query cannot be embedded at any level.

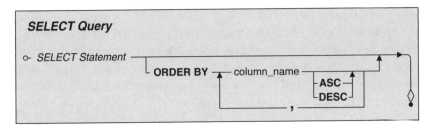

Figure 4-10 *The syntax diagram for the SELECT query*

❖ **Note** Throughout this book, I use the same terms you'll find in the SQL Standard or in common usage in most database systems. Earlier versions of the SQL Standard, however, defined the ORDER BY clause as part of a *cursor* (an object that you define inside an application program), as part of an *array* (a list of values that form a logical table such as a *subquery*, discussed in Chapter 11, "Subqueries"), or as part of a *scalar subquery* (a subquery that returns only one value). A complete discussion of cursors and arrays is beyond the scope of this book.

Because nearly all implementations of SQL allow you to include an ORDER BY clause at the end of a SELECT statement that you can save in a view, I invented the term *SELECT query* to describe this type of statement. This also allows me to discuss the concept of sorting the final output of a query for display online or for use in a report. The latest 2016 standard uses the term *<query specification>* for what I call a *SELECT statement* and the term *<query expression>* for the construct that I have called *SELECT query*. In this one case, I'll deviate (with your permission) from the names in the standard and use my terminology.

The ORDER BY clause allows you to sort the result set of the specified SELECT statement by one or more columns and also provides the option of specifying an ascending or descending sort order for each column. The only columns you can use in the ORDER BY clause are those that are currently listed in the SELECT clause. (Although this requirement is specified in the SQL Standard, some vendor implementations allow you to disregard it completely and include any column from any table in the FROM clause. However, I comply with this requirement in all the examples used throughout the book.) When you use two or more columns in an ORDER BY clause, separate each column with a comma. The SELECT query returns a final result set once the sort is complete.

❖ **Note** The ORDER BY clause *does not* affect the physical order of the rows in a table. If you do need to change the physical order of the rows, refer to your database software's documentation for the proper procedure.

First Things First: Collating Sequences

Before I look at some examples using the SELECT query, a brief word on collating sequences is in order. The manner in which the ORDER BY clause sorts the information depends on the collating sequence used by your database software. The collating sequence determines the order of precedence for every character listed in the current language character set specified by your operating system. For example, it identifies whether lowercase letters will be sorted before uppercase letters, or whether case will even matter. Check your database software's documentation, and perhaps consult your database administrator to determine the default collating sequence for your database. For more information on collating sequences, see the subsection "Comparing String Values: A Caution" in Chapter 6.

Let's Now Come to Order

With the availability of the ORDER BY clause, you can present the information you retrieve from the database in a more meaningful fashion. This applies to simple requests as well as complex ones. You can now rephrase your requests so that they also indicate sorting requirements. For example, a question such as *"What are the categories of classes we currently offer?"* can be restated as *"List the categories of classes we offer and show them in alphabetical order."*

Before beginning to work with the SELECT query, you need to adjust the way you define a translation statement. This involves adding a new section at the end of the translation statement to account for the new sorting requirements specified within the request. Use this new form to define the translation statement:

Select <item> from the <source> **and order by <column(s)>**

Now that your request will include phrases such as "sort the results by city," "show them in order by year," or "list them by last name and first name," study the request closely to determine which column or columns you need to use for sorting purposes. This is a simple exercise because most people use these types of phrases, and the columns needed for the sort are usually self-evident. After you identify the appropriate column or columns, use them as a replacement for <column(s)> in the translation statement. Let's take a look at a simple request to see how this works:

"List the categories of classes we offer and show them in alphabetical order."

Translation	Select category from the classes table and order by category
Clean Up	Select category from ~~the~~ classes ~~table and~~ order by category
SQL	SELECT Category FROM Classes ORDER BY Category

In this example, you can assume that Category will be used for the sort because it's the only column indicated in the request. You can also assume that the sort should be in ascending order because there's nothing in the request to indicate the contrary. This is a safe assumption. According to the SQL Standard, ascending order is automatically assumed if you don't specify a sort order. However, if you want to be absolutely explicit, insert ASC after Category in the ORDER BY clause.

In the following request, the column needed for the sort is more clearly defined:

"Show me a list of vendor names in ZIP Code order."

Translation	Select vendor name and ZIP Code from the vendors table and order by ZIP Code
Clean Up	Select vendor name ~~and~~ ZIP Code from ~~the~~ vendors ~~table and~~ order by ZIP Code
SQL	SELECT VendName, VendZipCode FROM Vendors ORDER BY VendZipCode

In general, most people will tell you if they want to see their information in descending order. When this situation arises and you need to display the result set in reverse order, insert the DESC keyword after the appropriate column in the ORDER BY clause. For example, here's how you would modify the SELECT statement in the previous example when you want to see the information sorted by ZIP Code in descending order:

SQL	SELECT VendName, VendZipCode FROM Vendors ORDER BY VendZipCode DESC

❖ **Note** If there is more than one vendor in a given ZIP Code, your database system determines the sort order of the vendor names unless you add that to the ORDER BY clause.

The next example illustrates a more complex request that requires a multicolumn sort. The only difference between this example and the previous two examples is that this example uses more columns in the ORDER BY clause. Note that the columns are separated with commas, which is in accordance with the syntax diagram shown earlier in Figure 4-10.

"Display the names of our employees, including their phone number and ID number, and list them by last name and first name."

Translation	Select last name, first name, phone number, and employee ID from the employees table and order by last name and first name
Clean Up	Select last name, first name, phone number, ~~and~~ employee ID from ~~the~~ employees ~~table and~~ order by last name ~~and~~ first name
SQL	SELECT EmpLastName, EmpFirstName, EmpPhoneNumber, EmployeeID FROM Employees ORDER BY EmpLastName, EmpFirstName

One of the interesting things you can do with the columns in an ORDER BY clause is to specify a different sort order for each column. In the previous example, you can specify a descending sort for the column containing the last name and an ascending sort for the column containing the first name. Here's how the SELECT statement looks when you make the appropriate modifications:

SQL	SELECT EmpLastName, EmpFirstName, EmpPhoneNumber, EmployeeID FROM Employees ORDER BY EmpLastName DESC, EmpFirstName ASC

Although you don't need to use the ASC keyword explicitly, the statement is more self-documenting if you include it.

The previous example brings an interesting question to mind: Is any importance placed on the sequence of the columns in the ORDER BY clause? The answer is *"Yes!"* The sequence is important because your database system will evaluate the columns in the ORDER BY clause from left to right. Also, the importance of the sequence grows in direct proportion to the number of columns you use. Always sequence the columns in the ORDER BY clause properly so that the result sorts in the appropriate order.

❖ **Note** The database products from Microsoft (Microsoft Office Access and Microsoft SQL Server) include an interesting extension that allows you to request a subset of rows based on your ORDER BY clause by using the TOP keyword in the SELECT clause. For example, you can find out the five most expensive products in the Sales Orders database by requesting:

```
SELECT TOP 5 ProductName, RetailPrice
    FROM Products
    ORDER BY RetailPrice DESC
```

The database sorts all the rows from the Products table descending by price and then returns the top five rows. Both database systems also allow you to specify the number of rows returned as a percentage of all the rows. For example, you can find out the top 10 percent of products by price by requesting:

```
SELECT TOP 10 PERCENT ProductName, RetailPrice
    FROM Products
    ORDER BY RetailPrice DESC
```

In fact, if you want to specify ORDER BY in a view, SQL Server requires that you include the TOP keyword. If you want all rows, you must specify TOP 100 PERCENT. For this reason, you'll see that all the sample views in SQL Server that include an ORDER BY clause also specify TOP 100 PERCENT. There is no such restriction in Microsoft Access.

Saving Your Work

Save your SELECT statements—every major database software program provides a way for you to save them! Saving your statements eliminates the need to recreate them every time you want to make the same request to the database. When you save your SELECT statement, assign a meaningful name that will help you remember what type of information the statement provides. And if your database software allows you to do so, write a concise description of the statement's purpose. The value of the description will become quite clear when you haven't seen a particular SELECT statement for some time and you need to remember why you constructed it in the first place.

A saved SELECT statement is categorized as a query in some database programs and as a view, function, or stored procedure in others. Regardless of its designation, every database program provides you with a means to execute, or run, the saved statement and work with its result set.

> ❖ **Note** For the remainder of this discussion, I'll use the word *query* to represent the saved SELECT statement and *execute* to represent the method used to work with it.

Two common methods are used to execute a query. The first is an interactive device (such as a command on a toolbar or query grid), and the second is a block of programming code. You'll use the first method quite extensively. There's no need to worry about the second method until you begin working with your database software's programming language. Although it's my job to teach you how to create and use SQL statements, it's your job to learn how to create, save, and execute them in your database software program.

> ❖ **Note** You'll find all the sample statements and problems saved in the sample databases for Microsoft Access (queries), Microsoft SQL Server (views), MySQL (views), and PostgreSQL (views).
>
> Unlike most database systems, SQL Server has a small quirk about using ORDER BY in views. Although you can certainly save a query with an ORDER BY clause as a view, SQL Server ignores the ORDER BY if you call the view from a program, another view, or from a command line utility. As a result, sample queries saved in SQL Server that include ORDER BY will not be returned in the sequence specified in the query. You must either open the view in the designer tool and execute it from there or call the view with an additional ORDER BY clause, as in SELECT * FROM <view name> ORDER BY <original ORDER by specification>.

Sample Statements

Now that I've covered the basic characteristics of the SELECT statement and SELECT query, let's take a look at some examples of how these operations are applied in different scenarios. These examples encompass each of the sample databases, and they illustrate the use of the SELECT statement, the SELECT query, and the two supplemental techniques used to establish columns for the translation statement. I've also included sample result sets that would be returned by these operations and placed them immediately after the SQL syntax line. The name that appears immediately above a result set has a twofold purpose: It identifies the result set itself, and it is also the name that I assigned to the SQL statement in the example.

In case you're wondering why I assigned a name to each SQL statement, it's because I saved them! In fact, I've named and saved all the SQL statements that appear in the examples here and throughout the remainder of the book. Each is stored in the appropriate sample database (as indicated within the example), and I prefixed the names of the queries relevant to this chapter with "CH04." You can follow the instructions in the Introduction of this book to load the samples onto your computer. This gives you the opportunity to see these statements in action before you try your hand at writing them yourself.

> ❖ **Note** Just a reminder: All the column names and table names used in these examples are drawn from the sample database structures shown in Appendix B. Also keep in mind that for any query you run which does not have an ORDER BY clause, the sequence of rows returned is undefined. In most cases, the sequence of rows returned by any such query in any of my sample databases (Microsoft SQL Server, Microsoft Office Access, MySQL, or PostgreSQL) will not necessarily match the sequence of rows I show you in this book. If you use the SQL Scripts to load the samples into another database system, you will see the same number of rows and the same data in those rows, but the sequence might be different.

Sales Orders Database

"Show me the names of all our vendors."

Translation	Select the vendor name from the vendors table
Clean Up	Select ~~the~~ vendor name from ~~the~~ vendors ~~table~~
SQL	SELECT VendName FROM Vendors

CH04_Vendor_Names (10 Rows)

VendName
Shinoman, Incorporated
Viscount
Nikoma of America
ProFormance
Kona, Incorporated
Big Sky Mountain Bikes
Dog Ear
Sun Sports Suppliers
Lone Star Bike Supply
Armadillo Brand

"What are the names and prices of all the products we carry?"

Translation	Select product name, retail price from the products table
Clean Up	Select product name, retail price from ~~the~~ products ~~table~~
SQL	SELECT ProductName, RetailPrice FROM Products

CH04_Product_Price_List (40 Rows)

ProductName	Retail Price
Trek 9000 Mountain Bike	$1,200.00
Eagle FS-3 Mountain Bike	$1,800.00
Dog Ear Cyclecomputer	$75.00
Victoria Pro All Weather Tires	$54.95
Dog Ear Helmet Mount Mirrors	$7.45
Viscount Mountain Bike	$635.00
Viscount C-500 Wireless Bike Computer	$49.00
Kryptonite Advanced 2000 U-Lock	$50.00
Nikoma Lok-Tight U-Lock	$33.00
Viscount Microshell Helmet	$36.00

<< more rows here >>

"Which states do our customers come from?"

Translation	Select the distinct state values from the customers table
Clean Up	Select ~~the~~ distinct state ~~values~~ from ~~the~~ customers ~~table~~
SQL	SELECT DISTINCT CustState FROM Customers

CH04_Customer_States (4 Rows)

CustState
CA
OR
TX
WA

Entertainment Agency Database

"List all entertainers and the cities they're based in, and sort the results by city and name in ascending order."

Translation	Select city and stage name from the entertainers table and order by city and stage name
Clean Up	Select city ~~and~~ stage name from ~~the~~ entertainers ~~table~~ ~~and~~ order by city ~~and~~ stage name
SQL	SELECT EntCity, EntStageName FROM Entertainers ORDER BY EntCity ASC, EntStageName ASC

CH04_Entertainer_Locations (13 Rows)

EntCity	EntStageName
Auburn	Caroline Coie Cuartet
Auburn	Topazz
Bellevue	Jazz Persuasion
Bellevue	Jim Glynn
Bellevue	Susan McLain
Redmond	Carol Peacock Trio
Redmond	JV & the Deep Six
Seattle	Coldwater Cattle Company
Seattle	Country Feeling
Seattle	Julia Schnebly
<< more rows here >>	

"Give me a unique list of engagement dates. I'm not concerned with how many engagements there are per date."

Translation	Select the distinct start date values from the engagements table
Clean Up	Select ~~the~~ distinct start date ~~values~~ from ~~the~~ engagements ~~table~~
SQL	`SELECT DISTINCT StartDate` `FROM Engagements`

CH04_Engagement_Dates (64 Rows)

StartDate
2017-09-02
2017-09-11
2017-09-12
2017-09-16
2017-09-18
2017-09-19
2017-09-25
2017-09-30
2017-10-01
2017-10-02
<< more rows here >>

School Scheduling Database

"Can we view complete class information?"

Translation	Select all columns from the classes table
Clean Up	Select ~~all columns~~ * from ~~the~~ classes ~~table~~
SQL	`SELECT *` `FROM Classes`

CH04_Class_Information (132 Rows)

ClassID	SubjectID	ClassRoomID	Credits	StartDate	StartTime	Duration	<<other columns>>
1000	11	1231	5	2017-9-12	10:00	50	…
1002	12	1619	4	2017-9-11	15:30	110	…
1004	13	1627	4	2017-9-11	08:00	50	…
1006	13	1627	4	2017-9-11	09:00	110	…
1012	14	1627	4	2017-9-12	13:00	170	…
1020	15	3404	4	2017-9-12	13:00	110	…
1030	16	1231	5	2017-9-11	11:00	50	…
1031	16	1231	5	2017-9-11	14:00	50	…
1156	37	3443	5	2017-9-11	16:00	50	…
1162	37	3443	5	2017-9-11	09:00	80	…
			<< more rows here >>				

"Give me a list of the buildings on campus and the number of floors for each building. Sort the list by building in ascending order."

Translation	Select building name and number of floors from the buildings table, ordered by building name
Clean Up	Select building name ~~and~~ number of floors from ~~the~~ buildings ~~table,~~ ordered by building name
SQL	SELECT BuildingName, NumberOfFloors FROM Buildings ORDER BY BuildingName ASC

CH04_Building_List (6 Rows)

BuildingName	NumberOfFloors
Arts and Sciences	3
College Center	3
Instructional Building	3
Library	2
PE and Wellness	1
Technology Building	2

Bowling League Database

"Where are we holding our tournaments?"

Translation	Select the distinct tourney location values from the tournaments table
Clean Up	Select ~~the~~ distinct tourney location ~~values~~ from ~~the~~ tournaments ~~table~~
SQL	SELECT DISTINCT TourneyLocation FROM Tournaments

CH04_Tourney_Locations (7 Rows)

TourneyLocation
Acapulco Lanes
Bolero Lanes
Imperial Lanes
Red Rooster Lanes
Sports World Lanes
Thunderbird Lanes
Totem Lanes

"Give me a list of all tournament dates and locations. I need the dates in descending order and the locations in alphabetical order."

Translation	Select tourney date and location from the tournaments table and order by tourney date in descending order and location in ascending order
Clean Up	Select tourney date ~~and~~ location from ~~the~~ tournaments ~~table and~~ order by tourney date ~~in~~ descending ~~order and~~ location ~~in~~ ascending ~~order~~
SQL	SELECT TourneyDate, TourneyLocation FROM Tournaments ORDER BY TourneyDate DESC, TourneyLocation ASC

CH04_Tourney_Dates (20 Rows)

TourneyDate	TourneyLocation
2018-08-16	Totem Lanes
2018-08-09	Imperial Lanes
2018-08-02	Sports World Lanes
2018-07-26	Bolero Lanes
2018-07-19	Thunderbird Lanes
2018-07-12	Red Rooster Lanes
2017-12-04	Acapulco Lanes
2017-11-27	Totem Lanes
2017-11-20	Sports World Lanes
2017-11-13	Imperial Lanes
<< more rows here >>	

Recipes Database

"What types of recipes do we have, and what are the names of the recipes we have for each type? Can you sort the information by type and recipe name?"

Translation	Select recipe class ID and recipe title from the recipes table and order by recipe class ID and recipe title
Clean Up	Select recipe class ID ~~and~~ recipe title from ~~the~~ recipes ~~table and~~ order by recipe class ID ~~and~~ recipe title
SQL	SELECT RecipeClassID, RecipeTitle FROM Recipes ORDER BY RecipeClassID ASC, RecipeTitle ASC

CH04_Recipe_Classes_And_Titles (15 Rows)

RecipeClassID	RecipeTitle
1	Fettuccini Alfredo
1	Huachinango Veracruzana (Red Snapper, Veracruz style)
1	Irish Stew

RecipeClassID	RecipeTitle
1	Pollo Picoso
1	Roast Beef
1	Salmon Filets in Parchment Paper
1	Tourtière (French-Canadian Pork Pie)
2	Asparagus
2	Garlic Green Beans
3	Yorkshire Pudding
	<< more rows here >>

"Show me a list of unique recipe class IDs in the recipes table."

Translation	Select the distinct recipe class ID values from the recipes table
Clean Up	Select ~~the~~ distinct recipe class ID ~~values~~ from ~~the~~ recipes ~~table~~
SQL	SELECT DISTINCT RecipeClassID FROM Recipes

CH04_Recipe_Class_Ids (6 Rows)

RecipeClassID
1
2
3
4
5
6

Summary

In this chapter, I introduced the SELECT operation, and you learned that it is one of four data manipulation operations in SQL. (The others are UPDATE, INSERT, and DELETE, covered in Part V.) I also discussed how the SELECT operation can be divided into three smaller operations: the SELECT statement, the SELECT expression, and the SELECT query.

The discussion then turned to the SELECT statement, where you were introduced to its component clauses. I covered the fact that the SELECT and FROM clauses are the fundamental clauses required to retrieve information from the database and that the remaining clauses— WHERE, GROUP BY, and HAVING—are used to conditionally process and filter the information returned by the SELECT clause.

I briefly diverged into a discussion of the difference between data and information. You learned that the values stored in the database are data and that information is data that has been processed in a manner that makes it meaningful to the person viewing it. You also learned that the rows of information returned by a SELECT statement are known as a result set.

Retrieving information was the next topic of discussion, and I began by presenting the basic form of the SELECT statement. You learned how to build a proper SELECT statement by using a three-step technique that involves taking a request and translating it into proper SQL syntax. You also learned that you could use two or more columns in the SELECT clause to expand the scope of information you retrieve from your database. I followed this section with a quick look at the DISTINCT keyword, which you learned is the means for eliminating duplicate rows from a result set.

Next, I looked at the SELECT query and how it can be combined with a SELECT statement to sort the SELECT statement's result set. You learned that this is necessary because the SELECT query is the only SELECT operation that contains an ORDER BY clause. I went on to show that the ORDER BY clause is used to sort the information by one or more columns and that each column can have its own ascending or descending sort specification. A brief discussion on saving your SELECT statements followed, and you learned that you can save your statement as a query or a view for future use.

Finally, I presented a number of examples using various tables in the sample databases. The examples illustrated how the various concepts and techniques presented in this chapter are used in typical scenarios and applications. In the next chapter, I'll take a closer look at the SELECT clause and show you how to retrieve something besides information from a list of columns.

The following section presents a number of requests that you can work out on your own.

Problems for You to Solve

Below, I show you the request statement and the name of the solution query in the sample databases. If you want some practice, you can work out the SQL you need for each request and then check your answer with the query I saved in the samples. Don't worry if your syntax doesn't exactly match the syntax of the queries I saved—as long as your result set is the same.

Sales Orders Database

1. *"Show me all the information on our employees."*

   You can find the solution in CH04_Employee_Information (8 rows).

2. *"Show me a list of cities, in alphabetical order, where our vendors are located, and include the names of the vendors we work with in each city."*

   You can find the solution in CH04_Vendor_Locations (10 rows).

Entertainment Agency Database

1. *"Give me the names and phone numbers of all our agents, and list them in last name/first name order."*

   You can find the solution in CH04_Agent_Phone_List (9 rows).

2. *"Give me the information on all our engagements."*

   You can find the solution in CH04_Engagement_Information (111 rows).

3. *"List all engagements and their associated start dates. Sort
    the records by date in descending order and by engagement in
    ascending order."*

    You can find the solution in CH04_Scheduled_Engagements
    (111 rows).

School Scheduling Database

1. *"Show me a complete list of all the subjects we offer."*

    You can find the solution in CH04_Subject_List (56 rows).

2. *"What kinds of titles are associated with our faculty?"*

    You can find the solution in CH04_Faculty_Titles (3 rows).

3. *"List the names and phone numbers of all our staff, and sort them
    by last name and first name."*

    You can find the solution in CH04_Staff_Phone_List (27 rows).

Bowling League Database

1. *"List all of the teams in alphabetical order."*

    You can find the solution in CH04_Team_List (10 rows).

2. *"Show me all the bowling score information for each of our
    members."*

    You can find the solution in CH04_Bowler_Score_Information
    (1,344 rows).

3. *"Show me a list of bowlers and their addresses, and sort it in
    alphabetical order."*

    You can find the solution in CH04_Bowler_Names_Addresses
    (32 rows).

Recipes Database

1. *"Show me a list of all the ingredients we currently keep track of."*

    You can find the solution in CH04_Complete_Ingredient_List
    (79 rows).

2. *"Show me all the main recipe information, and sort it by the name of
    the recipe in alphabetical order."*

    You can find the solution in CH04_Main_Recipe_Information
    (15 rows).

5

Getting More Than Simple Columns

"Facts are stubborn things."
—Tobias Smollett *Gil Blas de Santillane*

Topics Covered in This Chapter

What Is an Expression?

What Type of Data Are You Trying to Express?

Changing Data Types: The CAST Function

Specifying Explicit Values

Types of Expressions

Using Expressions in a SELECT Clause

That "Nothing" Value: Null

Sample Statements

Summary

Problems for You to Solve

In Chapter 4, "Creating a Simple Query," you learned how to use a SELECT statement to retrieve information from one or more columns in a table. This technique is useful if you're posing only simple requests to the database for some basic facts. However, you'll need to expand your SQL vocabulary when you begin working with complex requests. In this chapter, I'll introduce you to the concept of an expression as a way to manipulate the data in your tables to calculate or generate new columns of information. Next, I'll discuss how the *type* of data stored in a column can have an important impact on your queries and the expressions you create. I'll take a brief detour to the CAST function, which you can use to actually change the type of data you include in your expressions. You'll learn to create a constant (or literal) value that you can use in creative ways in your queries. You'll learn to use literals and values from columns in your table to create expressions. You'll learn how to adjust the scope of information you retrieve with a SELECT statement by using *expressions* to manipulate the data from which the information is drawn. Finally, you'll explore the special Null value and learn how it can impact how you work with expressions that use columns from your tables.

What Is an Expression?

To get more than simple columns, you need to create an expression. An *expression* is some form of operation involving numbers, character strings, or dates and times. It can use values drawn from specific columns in a table, constant (literal) values, or a combination of both. I'll show you how to generate literal values later in this chapter. After your database completes the operation defined by the expression, the expression returns a value to the SQL statement for further processing. You can use expressions to broaden or narrow the scope of the information you retrieve from the database. Expressions are especially useful when you are asking "what if" questions. Here's a sample of the types of requests you can answer using expressions:

> "What is the total amount for each line item?"
>
> "Give me a mailing list of employees, last name first."
>
> "Show me the start time, end time, and duration for each class."
>
> "Show the difference between the handicap score and the raw score for each bowler."
>
> "What is the estimated per-hour rate for each engagement?"
>
> "What if we raised the prices of our products by 5 percent?"

As you'll learn as you work through this chapter, expressions are a very valuable technique to add to your knowledge of SQL. You can use expressions to "slice and dice" the plain-vanilla data in your columns to create more meaningful results in your queries. You'll also find that expressions are very useful when you move on to Chapter 6, "Filtering Your Data," and beyond. You'll use expressions to filter your data or to link data from related tables.

What Type of Data Are You Trying to Express?

The type of data used in an expression impacts the value the expression returns, so let's first look at some of the data types the SQL Standard provides. Every column in the database has an assigned *data type* that determines the kind of values the column can store. The data type also determines the operations that can be performed on the column's values. You need to understand the basic data types before you can begin to create literal values or combine columns and literals in an expression that is meaningful and that returns a proper value.

The SQL Standard defines seven general categories of types of data—character, national character, binary, numeric, Boolean, datetime, and interval. In turn, each category contains one or more uniquely named data types. Here's a brief look at each of these categories and their data types. (In the following list, I've broken the numeric category into two subcategories: exact numeric and approximate numeric.)

CHARACTER The character data type stores a fixed- or varying-length character string of one or more printable characters. The characters it accepts are usually based upon the American Standard Code for Information Interchange (ASCII) or the Extended Binary Coded Decimal Interchange Code (EBCDIC) character sets. A fixed-length character data type is known as CHARACTER or CHAR, and a varying-length character data type is known as CHARACTER VARYING, CHAR VARYING, or VARCHAR. You can define the length of data that you want to store in a character data type, but the maximum length that you can specify is defined by your database system. (This rule applies to the national character data types as well.) When the length of a character string exceeds a system-defined maximum (usually 255 or 1,024 characters), you must use a CHARACTER LARGE OBJECT, CHAR LARGE OBJECT, or CLOB data type. In many systems, the alias for CLOB is TEXT or MEMO.

NATIONAL CHARACTER
: The national character data type is the same as the character data type except that it draws its characters from ISO-defined foreign language character sets. NATIONAL CHARACTER, NATIONAL CHAR, and NCHAR are names used to refer to a fixed-length national character, and NATIONAL CHARACTER VARYING, NATIONAL CHAR VARYING, and NCHAR VARYING are names used to refer to a varying-length national character. When the length of a character string exceeds a system-defined maximum (usually 255 or 1,024 characters), you must use a NATIONAL CHARACTER LARGE OBJECT, NCHAR LARGE OBJECT, or NCLOB data type. In many systems, the alias for NCLOB is NTEXT.

BINARY
: Use the BINARY LARGE OBJECT (or BLOB) data type to store binary data such as images, sounds, videos, or complex embedded documents such as word processing files or spreadsheets. In many systems, the names used for this data type include BINARY, BIT, and BIT VARYING.

EXACT NUMERIC
: This data type stores whole numbers and numbers with decimal places. The precision (the number of significant digits) and the scale (the number of digits to the right of the decimal place) of an exact numeric can be user-defined and can only be equal to or less than the maximum limits allowed by the database system. NUMERIC, DECIMAL, DEC, SMALLINT, INTEGER, INT, and BIGINT are all names used to refer to this data type. One point you must remember is that the SQL Standard—as well as most database systems—defines a BIGINT as having a greater range of values than INTEGER, and INTEGER as having a greater range of values than a SMALLINT. Check your database system's documentation for the applicable ranges. Some systems also support a TINYINT data type that can hold a smaller range of values than SMALLINT.

APPROXIMATE NUMERIC	This data type stores numbers with decimal places and exponential numbers. Names used to refer to this data type include FLOAT, REAL, and DOUBLE PRECISION. The approximate numeric data types don't have a precision and scale per se, but the SQL Standard does allow a user-defined precision only for a FLOAT data type. Any scale associated with these data types is always defined by the database system. Note that the SQL Standard and most database systems define the range of values for a DOUBLE PRECISION data type to be greater than those of a REAL or FLOAT data type. Check your documentation for these ranges as well.
BOOLEAN	This data type stores true and false values, usually in a single binary bit. Some systems use BIT, INT, or TINYINT to store this data type.
DATETIME	Dates, times, and combinations of both are stored in this data type. The SQL Standard defines the date format as year-month-day and specifies time values as being based on a 24-hour clock. Although most database systems allow you to use the more common month/day/year or day/month/year date format and time values based on an A.M./P.M. clock, I use the date and time formats specified by the SQL Standard throughout the book. The three names used to refer to this data type are DATE, TIME, and TIMESTAMP. You can use the TIMESTAMP data type to store a combination of a date and time. Note that the names and usages for these data types vary depending on the database system you are using. Some systems store both date and time in the DATE data type, while others use TIMESTAMP or a data type called DATETIME. Consult your system documentation for details.
INTERVAL	This data type stores the quantity of time between two datetime values, expressed as either year, month; year/month; day, time; or day/time. Not all major database systems support the INTERVAL data type, so consult your system documentation for details.

Many database systems provide additional data types known as *extended data types* beyond those specified by the SQL Standard. (I listed a few of them in the previous list of data type categories.) Examples of extended data types include MONEY/CURRENCY and SERIAL/ROWID/AUTOINCREMENT/IDENTITY (for unique row identifiers).

Because our primary focus is on the *data manipulation* portion of SQL, you need be concerned only with the appropriate range of values for each data type your database system supports. This knowledge will help ensure that the expressions you define will execute properly, so be sure to familiarize yourself with the data types provided by your RDBMS program.

Changing Data Types: The CAST Function

You must be careful when you create an expression to make sure that the data types of the columns and literals are compatible with the operation you are requesting. For example, it doesn't make sense to try to add character data to a number. But if the character column or literal contains a number, you can use the CAST function to convert the value before trying to add another number. Figure 5-1 shows you the CAST function, which is supported in nearly all commercial database systems.

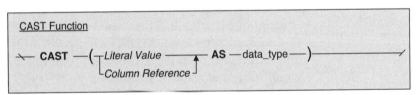

Figure 5-1 *The syntax diagram for the CAST function*

The CAST function converts a literal value or the value of a column into a specific data type. This helps to ensure that the data types of the values in the expression are *compatible*. By compatible I mean that all columns or literals in an expression are either characters, numbers, or datetime values. (As with any rule, there are exceptions that I'll mention later.) All the values you use in an expression must generally be compatible in order for the operation defined within the expression to work properly. Otherwise, your database system might raise an error message.

❖ **Note** Although most commercial database systems support the CAST function, some do not. Those systems that do not support CAST do have available a set of custom functions to achieve the same result. Consult your system documentation for details.

Converting a value in a column or a literal from one data type to another is a relatively intuitive and straightforward task. However, you'll have to keep the following restrictions in mind when you convert a value from its original data type to a different data type:

- Let's call this the "don't put a ten-pound sack in a five-pound box" rule. As mentioned earlier, you can define the maximum length of the data you want to store in a character data type. If you try to convert from one type of character field (for example, VARCHAR) to another character type (such as CHARACTER) and the data stored in the original column or literal is larger than the maximum length specified in the receiving data type, your database system will truncate the original character string. Your database system should also give you a warning that the truncation is about to occur.

- Let's call this the "don't put a square peg in a round hole" rule. You can convert a character column or literal to any other data type, but the character data in the source column or literal must be convertible to the target data type. For example, you can convert a five-character ZIP Code to a number, but you will encounter an error if your ZIP Code column contains Canadian or European postal codes that have letters. Note that the database system ignores any leading and/or trailing spaces when it converts a character column value to a numeric or datetime value. Also, most commercial systems support a wide range of character strings that are recognizable as date or time values. Consult your system documentation for details.

- This is the "ten-pound sack" rule, version 2. When you convert a numeric column's value to another numeric data type, the current contents of the convert-from column or literal had better fit in the target data type. For example, you will likely get an error if you attempt to convert a REAL value greater than 32,767 to a SMALLINT. Additionally, numbers to the right of the decimal place will be truncated or rounded as appropriate when you convert a number that has a decimal fraction to an INTEGER or SMALLINT. The amount of truncation or rounding is determined by the database system.

- But you can put "a square peg in a round hole" with certain limitations. When you convert the value of a numeric column to a character data type, one of three possible results will occur:

  1. It will convert successfully.

  2. Your system will pad it with blanks if its length is shorter than the defined length of the character column.

  3. The database system will raise an error if the character representation of the numeric value is longer than the defined length of the character column.

❖ **Note** Although the SQL Standard defines these restrictions, your database system might allow you some leeway when you convert a value from one data type to another. Some database systems provide automatic conversion for you without requiring you to use the CAST function. For example, some systems allow you to concatenate a number with text or to add text containing a number to another number without an explicit conversion. Refer to your database system's documentation for details.

It's important to note that this list does not constitute the entire set of restrictions defined by the SQL Standard. I listed only those restrictions that apply to the data types I use in this book. For a more in-depth discussion on data types and data conversion issues, please refer to any of the books listed in Appendix D, "Suggested Reading."

Keep the CAST function in mind as you work through the rest of this book. You'll see me use it whenever appropriate to make sure I'm working with compatible data types.

Specifying Explicit Values

The SQL Standard provides flexibility for enhancing the information returned from a SELECT statement by allowing the use of constant values such as character strings, numbers, dates, times, or a suitable combination of these items, in any valid expression used within a SELECT statement. The SQL Standard categorizes these types of values as *literal values* and specifies the manner in which they are defined.

Character String Literals

A *character string literal* is a sequence of individual characters enclosed in *single* quotes. Yes, I know that you are probably used to using double quotes to enclose character strings, but I'm presenting these concepts as the SQL Standard defines them. Figure 5-2 shows the diagram for a character string literal.

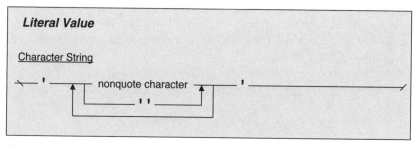

Figure 5-2 *The syntax diagram of a character string literal*

Here are a few examples of the types of character string literals you can define:

```
'This is a sample character string literal.'
'Here's yet another! '
'B-28'
'Seattle'
```

You probably noticed what seemed to be a double quote in both the diagram and the second line of the previous example. Actually, it's not a double quote but two consecutive single quotes with no space between them. The SQL Standard states that a single quote embedded within a character string is represented by two consecutive single quotes. The SQL Standard defines it this way so that your database system can distinguish between a single quote that defines the beginning or end of a character string literal and a quote that you want to be included within the literal. The following two lines illustrate how this works:

```
SQL           'The Vendor's name is:'
Displayed as  The Vendor's name is:
```

As I mentioned earlier, you can use character string literals to enhance the information returned by a SELECT statement. Although the information you see in a result set is usually easy to understand, it's very likely that the information can be made clearer. For example, if you execute the following SELECT statement, the result set displays only the vendor's Web site address and the vendor's name:

```
SQL          SELECT VendWebPage, VendName
             FROM Vendors
```

In some instances, you can enhance the clarity of the information by defining a character string that provides supplementary descriptive text and then adding it to the SELECT clause. Use this technique judiciously because the character string literal will appear in each row of the result set. Here's how you might modify the previous example with a character string literal:

```
SQL          SELECT VendWebPage, 'is the Web site for',
                VendName
             FROM Vendors
```

A row in the result set generated by this SELECT statement looks like this:

www.viescas.com	is the Web site for	John Viescas Consulting

This somewhat clarifies the information displayed by the result set by identifying the actual purpose of the web address. Although this is a simple example, it illustrates what you can do with character string literals. Later in this chapter, you'll see how you can use them in expressions.

❖ **Note** You'll find this technique especially useful when working with legacy databases that contain cryptic column names. However, you won't have to use this technique very often with your own databases if you follow the recommendations in Chapter 2, "Ensuring Your Database Structure Is Sound."

Numeric Literals

A *numeric literal* is another type of literal you can use within a SELECT statement. As the name implies, it consists of an optional sign and a number and can include a decimal place, the exponent symbol, and an exponential number. Figure 5-3 shows the diagram for a numeric literal.

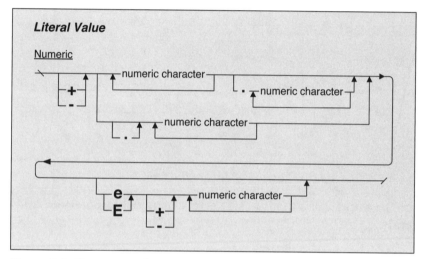

Figure 5-3 *The syntax diagram of a numeric literal*

Examples of numeric literals include the following:

```
427
-11.253
.554
0.3E-3
```

Numeric literals are most useful in expressions (for example, to multiply by or to add a fixed number value), so I'll postpone further discussion until later in this chapter.

Datetime Literals

You can supply specific dates and times for use within a SELECT statement by using *date literals*, *time literals*, and *timestamp literals*. The SQL Standard refers to these literals collectively as *datetime literals*. Defining these literals is a simple task, as Figure 5-4 shows.

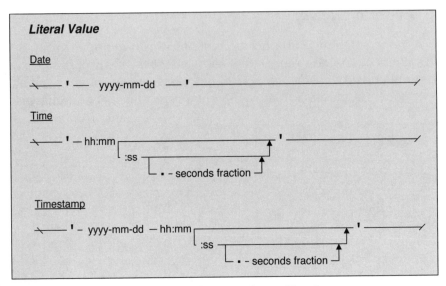

Figure 5-4 *The syntax diagram of date and time literals*

Bear in mind a few points, however, when using datetime and interval literals:

DATE   The format for a date literal is year-month-day, which is the format I follow throughout the book. However, many SQL databases allow the more common month/day/year format (United States) or day/month/year format (most non-U.S. countries). The SQL Standard also specifies that you include the DATE keyword before the literal, but nearly all commercial implementations allow you to simply specify the literal value surrounded by delimiter characters—usually single quotes. I found one case, the MySQL system, that requires you to specify a date literal in quotes and then to use the CAST function to convert the string to the DATE data type before you can use it in date calculations. Microsoft Office Access requires you to use a hashtag (#) character as the delimiter for DATE literals.

TIME   The hour format is based on a 24-hour clock. For example, 07:00 P.M. is represented as 19:00. The SQL Standard also specifies that you include the TIME keyword before the literal, but nearly all commercial implementations allow you to simply specify the literal value surrounded by delimiter characters—usually single quotes. I found one case, the MySQL system, that requires you to specify a time literal in quotes and then to use the CAST function to convert the string to the TIME data type before you can use it in time calculations. Microsoft Office Access requires you to use a hashtag (#) character as the delimiter for TIME literals.

TIMESTAMP   A timestamp literal is simply the combination of a date and a time separated by a single space. The rules for formatting the date and the time within a timestamp follow the individual rules for date and time. The SQL Standard also specifies that you include the TIMESTAMP keyword before the literal, but all commercial implementations that support the TIMESTAMP data type allow you to simply specify the literal value surrounded by delimiter characters—usually single quotes.

❖ **Note** In some systems, you can also define an *interval literal* to use in calculated expressions with datetime literals, but I won't be covering that type of literal in this book. See your system documentation for details.

You can find the diagrams for DATE, TIME, TIMESTAMP, and INTERVAL as defined by the SQL Standard in Appendix A, "SQL Standard Diagrams."

Here are some examples of datetime literals:

```
'2007-05-16'
'2016-11-22'
'21:00'
'03:30:25'
'2008-09-29 14:25:00'
```

Note that when using MySQL, you must explicitly convert any character literal containing a date or a time or a date and a time by using the CAST function. Here are some examples:

```
CAST('2016-11-22' AS DATE)
CAST('03:30:25' AS TIME)
CAST('2008-09-29 14:25:00' AS DATETIME)
```

As I noted previously, in order to follow the SQL Standard, you must precede each literal with a keyword indicating the desired value. Although the DATE and TIME keywords are defined in the SQL Standard as required components of date and time literals, respectively, most database systems rarely support these keywords in this particular context and require only the character string portion of the literal. Therefore, I'll refrain from using the keywords and instead use single quotes to delimit a date or time literal that appears in any example throughout the remainder of the book. I show you how to use dates and times in expressions later in this chapter. See Appendix A for more details on forming datetime literals that follow the SQL Standard.

Types of Expressions

You will generally use the following three types of expressions when working with SQL statements:

CONCATENATION	Combining two or more character columns or literals into a single character string
MATHEMATICAL	Adding, subtracting, multiplying, and dividing numeric columns or literals
DATE AND TIME ARITHMETIC	Applying addition or subtraction to dates and times

Concatenation

The SQL Standard defines two sequential vertical bars as the concatenation operator. You can concatenate two character items by placing a single item on either side of the concatenation operator. The result is a single string of characters that is a combination of both items. Figure 5-5 shows the syntax diagram for the concatenation expression.

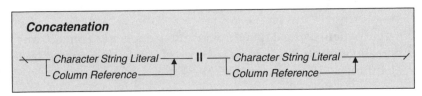

Figure 5-5 *The syntax diagram for the concatenation expression*

❖ **Note** Of the major database systems, I found that only IBM's DB2 and Informix, Oracle's Oracle, and PostgreSQL support the SQL Standard operator for concatenation. Microsoft Office Access supports & and + as concatenation operators, Microsoft SQL Server and Ingres support +, and in MySQL you must use the CONCAT function. In all the examples in the book, I use the SQL Standard || operator. In the sample databases on the website for the book, I use the appropriate operator for each database type (Microsoft Access, Microsoft SQL Server, MySQL, and PostgreSQL).

Here's a general idea of how the concatenation operation works:

Expression   ColumnOne || ColumnTwo
Result   **ContentsOfColumnOneContentsOfColumnTwo**

Let's start with the easiest example in the world: concatenating two character string literals, such as a first name and a last name:

Expression   'Mike' || 'Hernandez'
Result   **MikeHernandez**

There are two points to consider in this example: First, single quotes are required around each name because they are character string literals. Second, the first and last names are right next to each other. Although the operation combined them correctly, it might not be what you expected. The solution is to add a space between the names by inserting another character literal that contains a single space.

Expression   'Mike' || ' ' || 'Hernandez'
Result   **Mike Hernandez**

The previous example shows that you can concatenate additional character values by using more concatenation operators. There is no limit to the number of character values you can concatenate, but there is a limit to the length of the character string the concatenation operation returns. In general, the length of the character string returned by a concatenation operation can be no greater than the maximum length allowed for a varying-length character data type. Your database system might handle this issue slightly differently, so check your documentation for further details.

Concatenating two or more character strings makes perfect sense, but you can also concatenate the values of two or more character columns in the same fashion. For example, suppose you have two columns called CompanyName and City. You can create an expression that concatenates the value of each column by using the column names within the expression. Here's an example that concatenates the values of both columns with a character string:

Expression	CompanyName || ' is based in ' || City
Result	**DataTex Consulting Group is based in Seattle**

You don't need to surround CompanyName or City with single quotes because they are column references. (Remember column references from the previous chapter?) You can use a column reference in any type of expression, as you'll see in the examples throughout the remainder of the book.

Notice that all the concatenation examples so far concatenate characters with characters. I suppose you might be wondering if you need to do anything special to concatenate a number or a date. Most database systems give you some leeway in this matter. When the system sees you trying to concatenate a character column or literal with a number or a date, the system automatically casts the data type of the number or date for you so that the concatenation works with compatible data types.

But you shouldn't always depend on your database system to quietly do the conversion for you. To concatenate a character string literal or the value of a character column with a date literal or the value of a numeric or date column, use the CAST function to convert the numeric or date value to a character string. Here's an example of using CAST to convert the value of a date column called DateEntered:

Expression	EntStageName || ' was signed with our agency on ' || CAST(DateEntered as CHARACTER(10))
Result	**Modern Dance was signed with our agency on 1995-05-16**

❖ **Note** I specified an explicit length for the CHARACTER data type because the SQL Standard specifies that the absence of a length specification defaults to a length of 1. I found that most major implementations give you some leeway in this regard and generate a character string long enough to contain what you're converting. You can check your database documentation for details, but if you're in doubt, always specify an explicit length.

You should also use the CAST function to concatenate a numeric literal or the value of a numeric column to a character data type. In the next example, I use CAST to convert the value of a numeric column called RetailPrice:

Expression
```
ProductName || ' sells for ' ||
CAST(RetailPrice AS CHARACTER(8))
```
Result   **Trek 9000 Mountain Bike sells for 1200.00**

A concatenation expression can use character strings, datetime values, and numeric values simultaneously. The following example illustrates how you can use all three data types within the same expression:

Expression
```
'Order Number ' || CAST(OrderNumber AS
CHARACTER(2)) || ' was placed on ' ||
CAST(OrderDate AS CHARACTER(10))
```
Result   **Order Number 1 was placed on 2017-09-02**

❖ **Note** The SQL Standard defines a variety of functions that you can use to extract information from a column or calculate a value across a range of rows. I'll cover some of these in more detail in Chapter 12, "Simple Totals." Most commercial database systems also provide various functions to manipulate parts of strings or to format date, time, or currency values. Check your system documentation for details.

Now that I've shown how to concatenate data from various sources into a single character string, let's look at the different types of expressions you can create using numeric data.

Mathematical Expressions

The SQL Standard defines addition, subtraction, multiplication, and division as the operations you can perform on numeric data. The standard also defines common mathematical functions to calculate values such as absolute value, modulus, exponentiation, and logarithms. Here are the mathematical functions defined by the standard:

Function	Purpose
ABS(<numeric expression>)	Returns the absolute value of the expression
MOD(<dividend>, <divisor>)	Returns the remainder produced by dividing the dividend by the divisor
LN(<numeric expression>)	Returns the natural logarithm of the expression
EXP(<numeric expression>)	Returns the value of the natural logarithm raised to the power of the expression
POWER(<numeric base>, <numeric exponent>)	Returns the value of the base raised to the power of the exponent
SQRT(<numeric expression>)	Returns the square root of the expression
FLOOR(<numeric expression>)	Returns the largest integer less than or equal to the expression
CEIL(<numeric expression>) CEILING(<numeric expression>)	Returns the smallest integer greater than or equal to the expression
WIDTH_BUCKET(<numeric value>, <numeric lower bound>, <numeric upper bound>, <numeric bucket count>)	Divides the range between the lower bound and the upper bound into the number of equal "buckets" specified by the count and returns a number between 0 and the bucket count + 1 indicating where in the range the first argument resides

Most RDBMS programs provide these operations, as well as a wide array of scientific, trigonometric, statistical, and mathematical functions. In this book, however, I focus only on the four basic operations defined by the SQL Standard—addition, subtraction, multiplication, and division.

The order in which the four basic mathematical operations are performed—known as the *order of precedence*—is an important issue when you create mathematical expressions. The SQL Standard gives equal precedence to multiplication and division and specifies that they should be performed before any addition or subtraction. This is slightly contrary to the order of precedence you probably learned back in school, where multiplication is done before division, division before addition, and addition before subtraction, but it matches the order of precedence used in most modern programming languages. Mathematical expressions are evaluated from left to right. This could lead to some interesting results, depending on how you construct the expression! So, I strongly recommend that you make extensive use of parentheses in complex mathematical expressions to ensure that they evaluate properly.

If you remember how you created mathematical expressions back in school, then you already know how to create them in SQL. In essence, you use an optionally signed numeric value, a mathematical operator, and another optionally signed numeric value to create the expression. Figure 5-6 shows a diagram of this process.

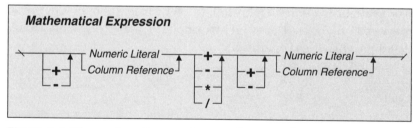

Figure 5-6 *The syntax diagram for a mathematical expression*

Here are some examples of mathematical expressions using numeric literal values, column references, and combinations of both:

```
25 + 35
-12 * 22
RetailPrice * QuantityOnHand
TotalScore / GamesBowled
RetailPrice - 2.50
TotalScore / 12
```

As mentioned earlier, you need to use parentheses to ensure that a complex mathematical expression evaluates properly. Here's a simple example of how you might use parentheses in such an expression:

```
Expression      (11 - 4) + (12 * 3)
Result          43
```

Pay close attention to the placement of parentheses in your expression because it affects the expression's resulting value. The two expressions in the following example illustrate this quite clearly. Although both expressions have the same numbers and operators, the placement of the parentheses is entirely different and causes the expressions to return completely different values.

```
Expression      (23 * 11) + 12
Result          265
Expression      23 * (11 + 12)
Result          529
```

It's easy to see why you need to be careful with parentheses, but don't let this stop you from using them. They are invaluable when working with complex expressions.

You can also use parentheses as a way to nest operations within an expression. When you use nested parenthetical operations, your database system evaluates them left to right and then in an "innermost to outermost" fashion. Here's an example of an expression that contains nested parenthetical operations:

```
Expression      (12 * (3 + 4)) - (24 / (10 + (6 - 4)))
Result          82
```

Executing the operations within the expression is not really as difficult as it seems. Here's the order in which your database system evaluates the expression:

(3 + 4) = **7**

(12 * 7) = **84**   *12 times the result of the first operation*

(6 − 4) = **2**

(10 + 2) = **12**   *10 plus the result of the third operation*

(24 / 12) = **2**   *24 divided by the result of the fourth operation*

84 − 2 = **82**   *84 minus the result of the second operation*

As you can see, the system proceeds left to right but must evaluate inner expressions when encountering an expression surrounded by parentheses. Effectively, (12 * (3 + 4)) and (24 / (10 + (6 − 4))) are on an equal level, so your system will completely evaluate the leftmost expression first, innermost to outermost. It then encounters the second expression surrounded by parentheses and evaluates that one innermost to outermost. The final operation subtracts from the result of the left expression the result of evaluating the right expression. (Does your head hurt yet? Mine does!)

Although I used numeric literals in the previous example, I could just as easily have used column references or a combination of numeric literals and column references as well. The key point to remember here is that you should plan and define your mathematical expressions carefully so that they return the results you seek. Use parentheses to clearly define the sequence in which you want operations to occur, and you'll get the result you expect.

When working with a mathematical expression, be sure that the values used in the expression are compatible. This is especially true of an expression that contains column references. You can use the CAST function for this purpose exactly as you did within a concatenation expression. For example, say you have a column called TotalLength based on an INTEGER data type that contains the whole number value 345, and a column called Distance based on a REAL data type that contains the value 138.65. To add the value of the Distance column to the value of the TotalLength column, you should use the CAST function to convert the Distance column's value into an INTEGER data type or the Total-Length column's value into a REAL data type, depending on whether you want the final result to be an INTEGER or a REAL data type. Assuming you're interested in adding only the integer values, you would accomplish this with the following expression:

Expression   TotalLength + CAST(Distance AS INTEGER)

Result   **483**

Not the answer you expected? Maybe you thought converting 138.65 to an integer would round the value up? Although the SQL Standard states that rounding during conversion using the CAST function depends on your database system, most systems truncate a value with decimal places when converting to an integer. So, I'm assuming my system also does that and thus added 345 to 138, not the rounded value 139.

If you forget to ensure the compatibility of the column values within an expression, your database system might raise an error message. If it does, it will probably cancel the execution of the operations within the expression as well. Most RDBMS systems handle such conversions automatically without warning you, but they usually convert all numbers to the most complex data type before evaluating the expression. In the previous example, your RDBMS would most likely convert TotalLength to REAL (the more complex of the two data types). Your system will use REAL because all INTEGER values can be contained within the REAL data type. However, this might not be what you wanted. Those RDBMS programs that do not perform this sort of automatic conversion are usually good about letting you know that it's a data type mismatch problem, so you'll know what you need to do to fix your expression.

As you just learned, creating mathematical expressions is a relatively easy task as long as you do a little planning and know how to use the CAST function to your advantage. In our last discussion for this section, I'll show you how to create expressions that add and subtract dates and times.

Date and Time Arithmetic

The SQL Standard defines addition and subtraction as the operations you can perform on dates and times. Contrary to what you might expect, many RDBMS programs differ in the way they implement these operations. Some database systems allow you to define these operations as you would in a mathematical expression, while others require you to use special built-in functions for these tasks. Refer to your database system's documentation for details on how your particular RDBMS handles these operations. In this book, I discuss date and time expressions only in general terms so that I can give you an idea of how these operations should work.

Date Expressions

Figure 5-7 shows the syntax for a date expression as defined by the SQL Standard. As you can see, creating the expression is simple enough—take one value and add it to or subtract it from a second value.

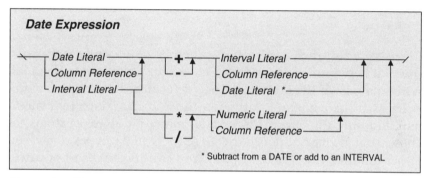

Figure 5-7 *The syntax diagram for a date expression*

The SQL Standard further defines the valid operations and their results as follows:

    DATE plus or minus INTERVAL yields DATE

    DATE minus DATE yields INTERVAL

    INTERVAL plus DATE yields DATE

    INTERVAL plus or minus INTERVAL yields INTERVAL

    INTERVAL times or divided by NUMBER yields INTERVAL

Note that in the SQL Standard you can subtract only a DATE from a DATE or add only a DATE to an INTERVAL.

When you use a column reference, make certain it is based on a DATE or INTERVAL data type, as appropriate. If the column is not an acceptable data type, you might have to use the CAST function to convert the value you are adding or subtracting. The SQL Standard explicitly specifies that you can perform these operations only using the indicated data types, but many database systems convert the column's data type for you automatically. Your RDBMS will ultimately determine whether the conversion is required, so check your documentation.

Although only a few commercial systems support the INTERVAL data type, many of them allow you to use an integer value (such as

SMALLINT or INT) to add to or subtract from a date value. You can think of this as adding and subtracting days. This allows you to answer questions such as *"What is the date nine days from now?"* and *"What was the date five days ago?"* Note also that some database systems allow you to add to or subtract from a datetime value using a fraction. For example, adding 3.5 to a datetime value in Microsoft Access adds three days and 12 hours.

When you subtract a date from another date, you are calculating the interval between the two dates. For example, you might need to subtract a hire date from the current date to determine how long an employee has been with the company. Although the SQL Standard indicates that you can add only an interval to a date, many database systems (especially those that do not support the INTERVAL data type) allow you to add either a number or a date anyway. You can use this sort of calculation to answer questions such as *"When is the employee's next review date?"*

> ❖ **Note** The SQL Standard defines a variety of functions that you can use to extract information from a column or calculate a value across a range of rows. I'll cover some of these in more detail in Chapter 12, "Simple Totals." Most commercial database systems also provide various functions to manipulate parts of strings or to format date, time, or currency values. Check your system documentation for details.

In this book, I'll show you simple calculations using dates and assume that you can at least add an integer number of days to a date value. I'll also assume that subtracting one date from another yields an integer number of days between the two dates. If you apply these simple concepts, you can create most of the date expressions that you'll need. Here are some examples of the types of date expressions you can define:

```
'2017-05-16' - 5
'2017-11-14' + 12
ReviewDate + 90
EstimateDate - DaysRequired
'2017-07-22' - '2017-06-13'
ShipDate - OrderDate
```

Time Expressions

You can create expressions using time values as well, and Figure 5-8 shows the syntax. Date and time expressions are very similar, and the same rules and restrictions that apply to a date expression also apply to a time expression.

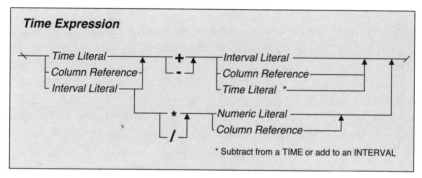

Figure 5-8 *The syntax diagram for a time expression*

The SQL Standard further defines the valid operations and their results as follows:

> TIME plus or minus INTERVAL yields TIME
>
> TIME minus TIME yields INTERVAL
>
> INTERVAL plus or minus INTERVAL yields INTERVAL
>
> INTERVAL times or divided by NUMBER yields INTERVAL

Note that in the SQL Standard you can subtract only a TIME from a TIME or add only a TIME to an INTERVAL.

All the same "gotchas" I noted for date expressions apply to time expressions. Also, for systems that support a combination DATETIME data type, the time portion of the value is stored as a fraction of a day accurate at least to seconds. When using systems that support datetime, you can also usually add or subtract a decimal fraction value to a datetime value. For example, 0.25 is 6 hours (one-fourth of a day). In this book, I'll assume that your system supports both adding and subtracting time literals or columns. I make no assumption about adding or subtracting decimal fractions. Again, check your documentation to find out what your system actually supports.

Given our assumptions, here are some general examples of time expressions:

```
'14:00' + '00:22'
'19:00' - '16:30'
StartTime + '00:19'
StopTime - StartTime
```

I said earlier that I would present date and time expressions only in general terms. My goal was to make sure that you understood date and time expressions conceptually and that you had a general idea of the types of expressions you should be able to create. Unfortunately, most database systems do not implement the SQL Standard's specification for time expressions exactly, and many only partially support the specification for the date expression. As I noted, however, all database systems provide one or more functions that allow you to work with dates and times. You can find a summary of these functions for six major implementations in Appendix C, "Date and Time Types, Operations, and Functions." I strongly recommend that you study your database system's documentation to learn what types of functions your system provides.

Now that you know how to create the various types of expressions, the next step is to learn how to use them.

> ❖ **See Also** Take a look at Appendix C for an overview of how six of the most popular database systems deal with dates and times. I list the data types and arithmetic operations supported along with a comprehensive list of date and time functions for each.

Using Expressions in a SELECT Clause

Knowing how to use expressions is arguably one of the most important concepts you'll learn in this book. You'll use expressions for a variety of purposes when working with SQL. For example, you would use an expression to

- Create a calculated column in a query

- Search for a specific column value

- Filter the rows in a result set

- Connect two tables in a JOIN operation

I'll show you how to do this (and more) as you work through the rest of the book. I begin by showing you how to use basic expressions in a SELECT clause.

> ❖ **Note** Throughout this chapter, I use the "Request/Translation/ Clean Up/SQL" technique introduced in Chapter 4.

You can use basic expressions in a SELECT clause to clarify information in a result set and to expand the result set's scope of information. For example, you can create expressions to concatenate first and last names, calculate the total price of a product, determine how long it took to complete a project, or specify a date for a patient's next appointment. Let's look at how you might use a concatenation expression, a mathematical expression, and a date expression in a SELECT clause. First, I'll work with the concatenation expression.

Working with a Concatenation Expression

Unlike mathematical and date expressions, you use concatenation expressions only to enhance the readability of the information contained in the result set of a SELECT statement. Suppose you are posing the following request:

"Show me a current list of our employees and their phone numbers."

When translating this request into a SELECT statement, you can improve the output of the result set somewhat by concatenating the first and last names into a single column. Here's one way you can translate this request:

Translation	Select the first name, last name, and phone number of all our employees from the employees table
Clean Up	Select ~~the~~ first name, last name, ~~and~~ phone number ~~of all our employees~~ from ~~the~~ employees ~~table~~

SQL	`SELECT EmpFirstName || ' ' || EmpLastName,`
	`    'Phone Number: ' || EmpPhoneNumber`
	`FROM Employees`

The result for one of the rows will look something like this:

Mary Thompson	Phone Number: 555-2516

You probably noticed that in addition to concatenating the first name column, a space, and the last name column, I also concatenated the character literal string "Phone Number: " with the phone number column. This example clearly shows that you can easily use more than one concatenation expression in a SELECT clause to enhance the readability of the information in the result set. Remember that you can also concatenate values with different data types by using the CAST function. For instance, I concatenate a character column value with a numeric column value in the next example:

"Show me a list of all our vendors and their identification numbers."

Translation	Select the vendor name and vendor ID from the vendors table
Clean Up	Select ~~the~~ vendor name ~~and~~ vendor ID from ~~the~~ vendors ~~table~~
SQL	SELECT 'The ID Number for ' || VendName || ' is ' || CAST(VendorID AS CHARACTER) FROM Vendors

Although the concatenation expression is a useful tool in a SELECT statement, it is one that you should use judiciously. When you use concatenation expressions containing long character string literals, keep in mind that the literals will appear in every row of the result set. You might end up cluttering the final result with repetitive information instead of enhancing it. Carefully consider your use of literals in concatenation expressions so that they work to your advantage.

Naming the Expression

When you use an expression in a SELECT clause, the result set includes a new column that displays the result of the operation defined in the expression. This new column is known as a calculated (or derived) column. For example, the result set for the following SELECT statement will contain three columns—two "real" columns and one calculated column:

```
SQL                    SELECT EmpFirstName || ' ' || EmpLastName,
                          EmpPhoneNumber, EmpCity
                       FROM Employees
```

The two real columns are, of course, EmpPhoneNumber and EmpCity, and the calculated column is derived from the concatenation expression at the beginning of the SELECT clause.

According to the SQL Standard, you can optionally provide a name for the new column by using the AS keyword. (In fact, you can assign a new name to any column using the AS clause.) Almost every database system, however, *requires* a name for a calculated column. Some database systems require you to provide the name explicitly, while others actually provide a generated name for you. Determine how your database system handles this before you work with the examples. If you plan to reference the result of the expression in your query, you should provide a name.

Figure 5-9 shows the syntax for naming an expression. You can use any valid character string literal (enclosed in single quotes) for the name. Some database systems relax this requirement when you're naming an expression and require quotes only when your column name includes embedded spaces. However, I strongly recommend that you not use spaces in your names because the spaces can be difficult to deal with in some database programming languages.

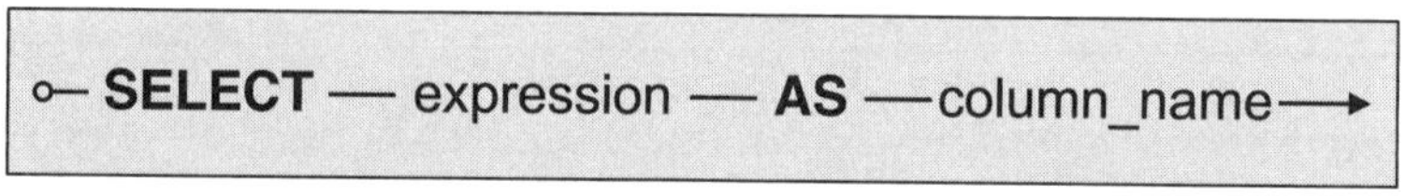

o— **SELECT** — expression — **AS** —column_name—→

Figure 5-9 *The syntax diagram for naming an expression*

Now I'll modify the SELECT statement in the previous example and supply a name for the concatenation expression:

```
SQL                    SELECT EmpFirstName || ' ' || EmpLastName AS
                          EmployeeName, EmpPhoneNumber, EmpCity
                       FROM Employees
```

The result set for this SELECT statement will now contain three columns called EmployeeName, EmpPhoneNumber, and EmpCity.

In addition to supplying a name for expressions, you can use the AS keyword to supply an alias for a real column name. Suppose you have a column called DOB and are concerned that some of your users might not be familiar with this abbreviation. You can eliminate any possible misinterpretation of the name by using an alias, as shown here:

SQL	SELECT EmpFirstName || ' ' || EmpLastName AS
	EmployeeName, DOB AS DateOfBirth
	FROM Employees

This SELECT statement produces a result set with two columns called EmployeeName and DateOfBirth. You've now effectively eliminated any possible confusion of the information displayed in the result set.

Providing names for your calculated columns has a minor effect on the translation process. For example, here's one possible version of the translation process for the previous example:

"Give me a list of employee names and their dates of birth."

Translation	Select first name and last name as employee name and DOB as date of birth from the employees table
Clean Up	Select first name ~~and~~ || ʻ ʼ || last name as EmployeeName ~~and~~ DOB as DateOfBirth from ~~the~~ employees ~~table~~
SQL	SELECT EmpFirstName || ' ' || EmpLastName
	AS EmployeeName, DOB AS DateOfBirth
	FROM Employees

After you become accustomed to using expressions, you won't need to state them quite as explicitly in your translation statements as I did here. You'll eventually be able to easily identify and define the expressions you need as you construct the SELECT statement itself.

❖ **Note** Throughout the remainder of the book, I provide names for all calculated columns within an SQL statement, as appropriate.

Working with a Mathematical Expression

Mathematical expressions are possibly the most versatile of the three types of expressions, and you'll probably use them quite often. For example, you can use a mathematical expression to calculate a line item total, determine the average score from a given set of tests, calculate the difference between two lab results, and estimate the total seating capacity of a building. The real trick is to make certain your expression works, and that is just a function of doing a little careful planning.

Here's an example of how you might use a mathematical expression in a SELECT statement:

> *"Display for each agent the agent name and projected income (salary plus commission), assuming each agent will sell $50,000 worth of bookings."*

Translation	Select first name and last name as agent name and salary plus 50000 times commission rate as projected income from the agents table
Clean Up	Select first name ~~and~~ || ` ` || last name as AgentName, ~~and~~ salary ~~plus~~ + 50000 ~~times~~ * commission rate as ProjectedIncome from ~~the~~ agents ~~table~~

SQL	SELECT AgtFirstName || ' ' || AgtLastName
	    AS AgentName,
	  Salary + (50000 * CommissionRate)
	    AS ProjectedIncome
	FROM Agents

Notice that I added parentheses to make it crystal clear that I expect the commission rate to be multiplied by 50,000 and then add the salary, not add 50,000 to the salary and then multiply by the commission rate. As the example shows, you're not limited to using a single type of expression in a SELECT statement. Rather, you can use a variety of expressions to retrieve the information you need in the result set. Here's another way you can write the previous SQL statement:

SQL	SELECT AgtFirstName || ' ' || AgtLastName
	    || ' has a projected income of ' ||
	    CAST(Salary + (50000 * CommissionRate)
	      AS CHARACTER) AS ProjectedIncome
	FROM Agents

The information you can provide by using mathematical expressions is virtually limitless, but you must properly plan your expressions and use the CAST function as appropriate.

Working with a Date Expression

Using a date expression is similar to using a mathematical expression in that you're simply adding or subtracting values. You can use date expressions for all sorts of tasks. For example, you can calculate an estimated ship date, project the number of days it will take to finish a project, or determine a follow-up appointment date for a patient. Here's an example of how you might use a date expression in a SELECT clause:

"How many days did it take to ship each order?"

Translation	Select the order number and ship date minus order date as days to ship from the orders table
Clean Up	Select ~~the~~ order number ~~and~~ ship date ~~minus~~ – order date as DaysToShip from ~~the~~ orders ~~table~~

SQL	SELECT OrderNumber,
	    CAST(ShipDate – OrderDate AS INTEGER)
	  AS DaysToShip
	FROM Orders

You can use time expressions in the same manner.

"What would be the start time for each class if we began each class ten minutes later than the current start time?"

Translation	Select the start time and start time plus 10 minutes as new start time from the classes table
Clean Up	Select ~~the~~ start time ~~and~~ start time ~~plus~~ + '00:10' ~~minutes~~ as NewStartTime from ~~the~~ classes ~~table~~
SQL	SELECT StartTime, StartTime + '00:10' AS NewStartTime FROM Classes

As I mentioned earlier, all database systems provide a function or set of functions for working with date values. I did want to give you an idea of how you might use dates and times in your SELECT statements, however, and I again recommend that you refer to your database system's documentation for details on the date and time functions your database system provides.

A Brief Digression: Value Expressions

You now know how to use column references, literal values, and expressions in a SELECT clause. You also know how to assign a name to a column reference or an expression. Now I'll show you how this all fits into the larger scheme of things.

The SQL Standard refers to a column reference, literal value, and expression collectively as a *value expression*. Figure 5-10 shows how to define a value expression.

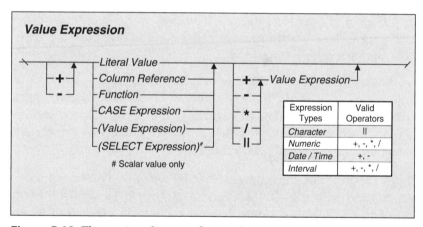

Figure 5-10 *The syntax diagram for a value expression*

Let's take a closer look at the components of a value expression:

- The syntax begins with an optional plus or minus sign. You use either of these signs when you want the value expression to return a signed numeric value. The value itself can be a numeric literal, the value of a numeric column, a call to a function that returns a numeric value (see our discussion of the CAST function earlier in this chapter), or the return value of a mathematical expression. You cannot use the plus or minus sign before an expression that returns a character or datetime data type.

- You can see that the first list in the figure also includes *(Value Expression)*. This means that you can use a complex value expression comprised of other value expressions that include concatenation or mathematical operators of their own. The parentheses force the database system to evaluate this value expression first. (Don't worry about *(SELECT Expression)* and *CASE Expression* just yet—I cover those in detail in Chapter 11, "Subqueries," and Chapter 19, "Condition Testing," respectively.)

- The next item in the syntax is a list of operators. As you can see in the inset box, the type of expression you use at the beginning of the syntax determines which operators you can select from this list.

- No, you're not seeing things: *Value Expression* does appear after the list of operators as well. The fact that you can use other value expressions within a value expression allows you to create very complex expressions.

By its very definition, a value expression returns a value that is used by some component of an SQL statement. The SQL Standard specifies the use of a value expression in a variety of statements and defined terms. No matter where you use it, you'll always define a value expression in the same manner as you've learned here.

I'll put this all into some perspective by showing you how a value expression is used in a SELECT statement. Figure 5-11 shows a modified version of the SELECT statement syntax diagram presented in Figure 4-9 in Chapter 4. This new syntax gives you the flexibility to use literals, column references, expressions, or any combination of these within a single SELECT statement. You can optionally name your value expressions with the AS keyword.

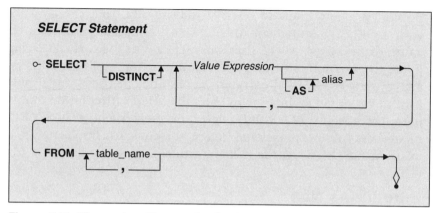

Figure 5-11 *The syntax diagram for the SELECT statement that includes a value expression*

Throughout the remainder of the book, I use the term *value expression* to refer to a column reference, a literal value, or an expression, as appropriate. In later chapters, I discuss how to use a value expression in other statements and show you a couple of other items that a value expression represents.

Now, back to our regularly scheduled program.

That "Nothing" Value: Null

As you know, a table consists of columns and rows. Each column represents a characteristic of the subject of the table, and each row represents a unique instance of the table's subject. You can also think of a row as one complete set of column values—each row contains exactly one value from each column in the table. Figure 5-12 shows an example of a typical table.

Customers

CustomerID	CustFirstName	CustLastName	CustStreetAddress	CustCity	CustCounty	CustState
1001	Suzanne	Viescas	15127 NE 24th, #383	Redmond	King	WA
1002	William	Thompson	122 Spring River Drive	Duvall	King	WA
1003	Gary	Hallmark	Route 2, Box 203B	Auburn	King	WA
1004	Robert	Brown	672 Lamont Ave	Houston		TX
1005	Dean	McCrae	4110 Old Redmond Rd.	Redmond		WA
1006	John	Viescas	15127 NE 24th, #383	Redmond	King	WA
1007	Mariya	Sergienko	901 Pine Avenue	Portland		OR
1008	Neil	Patterson	233 West Valley Hwy	San Diego	San Diego	CA

Figure 5-12 *A typical Customers table*

So far I've shown how to retrieve information from the data in a table with a SELECT statement and how to manipulate that data by using value expressions. All of this works just fine because I've continually made the assumption that each column in the table contains data. But as Figure 5-12 clearly illustrates, a column sometimes might not contain a value for a particular row in the table. Depending on how you use the data, the absence of a value might adversely affect your SELECT statements and value expressions. Before I discuss any implications, let's first examine how SQL regards missing values.

Introducing Null

In SQL, a *Null* represents a *missing* or an *unknown* value. You must understand from the outset that a Null *does not* represent a zero, a character string of one or more blank spaces, or a "zero-length" character string. The reasons are quite simple:

- A zero can have a very wide variety of meanings. It can represent the state of an account balance, the current number of available first-class ticket upgrades, or the current stock level of a particular product.

- Although a character string of one or more blank spaces is guaranteed to be meaningless to most of us, it is something that is definitely meaningful to SQL. A blank space is a valid character as far as SQL is concerned, and a character string composed of three blank spaces ('   ') is just as legitimate as a character string composed of several letters ('a character string').

- A zero-length string—two consecutive single quotes with no space in between ('')—can be meaningful under certain circumstances. In an employee table, for example, a zero-length string value in a column called MiddleInitial might represent the fact that a particular employee does not have a middle initial in her name. Note, however, that some implementations (notably Oracle) treat a zero-length string in a VARCHAR as Null.

A Null is quite useful when used for its stated purpose, and the Customers table in Figure 5-12 shows a clear example of this. In the Cust-County column, each blank cell represents a missing or unknown county name for the row in which it appears—a Null. In order to use Nulls correctly, you must understand why they occur in the first place.

Missing values are commonly the result of human error. Consider the row for Robert Brown, for example. If you're entering the data for Mr. Brown and you fail to ask him for the name of the county he lives in, that data is considered missing and is represented in the row as a Null. After you recognize the error, however, you can correct it by calling Mr. Brown and asking him for the county name.

Unknown values appear in a table for a variety of reasons. One reason might be that a specific value you need for a column is as yet undefined. For example, you might have a Categories table in a School Scheduling database that doesn't have a category for a new set of classes that you want to offer beginning in the fall session. Another reason a table might contain unknown values is that the values are truly unknown. Let's use the Customers table in Figure 5-12 once again and consider the row for Dean McCrae. Say that you're entering the data for Mr. McCrae, and you ask him for the name of the county he lives in. If neither of you knows the county that includes the city in which he lives, then the value for the county column in his row is truly unknown. This is represented in his row as a Null. Obviously, you can correct the problem after either of you determines the correct county name.

A column value might also be Null if none of its values apply to a particular row. Let's assume for a moment that you're working with an employee table that contains a Salary column and an HourlyRate column. The value for one of these two columns is always going to be Null because an employee cannot be paid both a fixed salary and an hourly rate.

It's important to note that there is a very slim difference between "does not apply" and "is not applicable." In the previous example, the value of one of the two columns literally does not apply. But let's assume you're working with a patient table that contains a column called HairColor and you're currently updating a row for an existing male patient. If that patient is bald, then the value for that column is definitely not applicable. Although you could just use a Null to represent a value that is not applicable, I recommend that you use a true value such as "N/A" or "Not Applicable." This will make the information clearer in the long run.

As you can see, whether you allow Nulls in a table depends on the manner in which you're using the data. Now that I've shown you the positive side of using Nulls, let's take a look at the negative implication of using Nulls.

The Problem with Nulls

The major drawback of Nulls is their adverse effect on mathematical operations. Any operation involving a Null evaluates to Null. This is logically reasonable—if a number is unknown, then the result of the operation is necessarily unknown. Note how a Null alters the outcome of the operation in the next example:

```
(25 * 3) + 4 = 79
(Null * 3) + 4 = Null
(25 * Null) + 4 = Null
(25 * 3) + Null = Null
```

The same result occurs when an operation involves columns containing Null values. For example, suppose you execute the following SELECT statement (the statement is just an example—it won't work as coded in the sample database) and it returns the result set shown in Figure 5-13.

```
SQL        SELECT ProductID, ProductDescription, Category,
                Price, QuantityOnHand, Price *
                QuantityOnHand AS TotalValue
           FROM Products
```

The operation represented by the TotalValue column is completed successfully as long as both the Price and QuantityOnHand columns have valid numeric values. Otherwise, TotalValue will contain a Null if either Price or QuantityOnHand contains a Null. The good news is that TotalValue will contain an appropriate value after you replace the Nulls in Price and QuantityOnHand with valid numeric values. You can avoid this problem completely by ensuring that the columns you use in a mathematical expression do not contain Null values.

ProductID	ProductDescription	Category	Price	QuantityOnHand	TotalValue
70001	Shur-Lok U-Lock	Accessories		12	
70002	SpeedRite Cyclecomputer		65.00	20	1,300.00
70003	SteelHead Microshell Helmet	Accessories	36.00	33	1,118.00
70004	SureStop 133-MB Brakes	Components	23.50	16	376.00
70005	Diablo ATM Mountain Bike	Bikes	1,200.00		
70006	UltraVision Helmet Mount Mirrors		7.45	10	74.50

Figure 5-13 *Nulls involved in a mathematical expression*

This is not the only time I'll be concerned with Nulls. In Chapter 12, we'll see how Nulls impact SELECT statements that summarize information.

Sample Statements

Now that you know how to use various types of value expressions in the SELECT clause of a SELECT statement, let's take a look, on the next few pages, at some examples using the tables from four of the sample databases. These examples illustrate the use of expressions to generate an output column.

I've also included sample result sets that would be returned by these operations and placed them immediately after the SQL syntax line. The name that appears immediately above a result set is the name I gave each query in the sample data on the companion website for the book, www.informit.com/title/9780134858333. I stored each query in the appropriate sample database (as indicated within the example) and prefixed the names of the queries relevant to this chapter with "CH05." You can follow the instructions in the Introduction of this book to load the samples onto your computer and try them.

> ❖ **Note** I've combined the Translation and Clean Up steps in the following examples so that you can begin to learn how to consolidate the process. Although you'll still work with all three steps during the body of any given chapter, you'll get a chance to work with the consolidated process in each "Sample Statements" section.

Sales Orders Database

"What is the inventory value of each product?"

Translation/ Clean Up	Select ~~the~~ product name, retail price ~~times~~ * quantity on hand as InventoryValue from ~~the~~ products ~~table~~

SQL	SELECT ProductName,
	    RetailPrice * QuantityOnHand AS
	    InventoryValue
	FROM Products

CH05_Product_Inventory_Value (40 Rows)

ProductName	InventoryValue
Trek 9000 Mountain Bike	$7,200.00
Eagle FS-3 Mountain Bike	$14,400.00
Dog Ear Cyclecomputer	$1,500.00
Victoria Pro All Weather Tires	$1,099.00
Dog Ear Helmet Mount Mirrors	$89.40
Viscount Mountain Bike	$3,175.00
Viscount C-500 Wireless Bike Computer	$1,470.00
Kryptonite Advanced 2000 U-Lock	$1,000.00
<< more rows here >>	

"How many days elapsed between the order date and the ship date for each order?"

Translation/ Clean Up	Select ~~the~~ order number, order date, ship date, ship date ~~minus~~ – order date as DaysElapsed from ~~the~~ orders ~~table~~

SQL	SELECT OrderNumber, OrderDate, ShipDate,
	    CAST(ShipDate – OrderDate AS INTEGER)
	    AS DaysElapsed
	FROM Orders

CH05_Shipping_Days_Analysis (944 Rows)

OrderNumber	OrderDate	ShipDate	DaysElapsed
1	2017-09-02	2017-09-05	3
2	2017-09-02	2017-09-04	2
3	2017-09-02	2017-09-05	3
4	2017-09-02	2017-09-04	2
5	2017-09-02	2017-09-02	0
6	2017-09-02	2017-09-06	4
7	2017-09-02	2017-09-05	3
8	2017-09-02	2017-09-02	0
9	2017-09-02	2017-09-05	3
10	2017-09-02	2017-09-05	3
<< more rows here >>			

Entertainment Agency Database

"How long is each engagement due to run?"

Translation/ Clean Up	Select ~~the~~ engagement number, end date ~~minus~~ – start date ~~plus one~~ + 1 as DueToRun from ~~the~~ engagements ~~table~~

SQL	SELECT EngagementNumber,
	      CAST(CAST(EndDate – StartDate
	        AS INTEGER) + 1 AS CHARACTER)
	      || ' day(s)' AS DueToRun
	FROM Engagements

CH05_Engagement_Lengths (111 Rows)

EngagementNumber	DueToRun
2	5 day(s)
3	6 day(s)
4	7 day(s)
5	4 day(s)

EngagementNumber	DueToRun
6	5 day(s)
7	8 day(s)
8	8 day(s)
9	11 day(s)
10	10 day(s)
11	2 day(s)
<< more rows here >>	

❖ **Note** You have to add "1" to the date expression in order to account for each date in the engagement. Otherwise, you'll get "0 day(s)" for an engagement that starts and ends on the same date. You can also see that I CAST the result of subtracting the two dates first as INTEGER (in MySQL, Signed Integer) so that I could add the value 1, then CAST the result of that to CHARACTER to ensure the concatenation works as expected.

"What is the net amount for each of our contracts?"

Translation/ Clean Up	Select ~~the~~ engagement number, contract price, contract price ~~times~~ * 0.12 as OurFee, contract price ~~minus~~ – (contract price ~~times~~ * 0.12) as NetAmount from ~~the~~ engagements ~~table~~
| SQL | ```
SELECT EngagementNumber, ContractPrice,
     ContractPrice * 0.12 AS OurFee, ContractPrice
     -(ContractPrice * 0.12)
   AS NetAmount
FROM Engagements
``` |

CH05_Net_Amount_Per_Contract (111 Rows)

EngagementNumber	ContractPrice	OurFee	NetAmount
2	$200.00	$24.00	$176.00
3	$590.00	$70.80	$519.20
4	$470.00	$56.40	$413.60
```

EngagementNumber	ContractPrice	OurFee	NetAmount
5	$1,130.00	$135.60	$994.40
6	$2,300.00	$276.00	$2,024.00
7	$770.00	$92.40	$677.60
8	$1,850.00	$222.00	$1,628.00
9	$1,370.00	$164.40	$1,205.60
10	$3,650.00	$438.00	$3,212.00
11	$950.00	$114.00	$836.00

<< more rows here >>

School Scheduling Database

"List how many complete years each staff member has been with the school as of October 1, 2017, and sort the result by last name and first name."

Translation/ Clean Up	Select last name || ', ' || ~~and~~ first name ~~concatenated with a comma~~ as Staff, date hired, ~~and~~ (('2017-10-01' ~~minus~~ – date hired) ~~divided by~~ / 365) as YearsWithSchool from ~~the~~ staff ~~table and sort~~ order by last name ~~and~~ first name
SQL	```SELECT StfLastName || ', ' || StfFirstName
AS Staff,
DateHired,
CAST(CAST('2017-10-01' – DateHired
AS INTEGER) / 365 AS INTEGER)
AS YearsWithSchool
FROM Staff
ORDER BY StfLastName, StfFirstName```

CH05_Length_Of_Service (27 Rows)

Staff	DateHired	YearsWithSchool
Alborous, Sam	1990-11-20	26
Black, Alastair	1996-12-11	20
Bonnicksen, Joyce	1994-03-02	23

Staff	DateHired	YearsWithSchool
Brehm, Peter	1994-07-16	23
Brown, Robert	1997-02-09	20
Coie, Caroline	1991-01-28	26
DeGrasse, Kirk	1996-03-02	21
Ehrlich, Katherine	1993-03-08	24
Glynn, Jim	1993-08-02	23
Hallmark, Alaina	1992-01-07	24

<< more rows here >>

❖ **Note** The objective is to calculate the number of *complete* years of service as of October 1, 2017. (Note that I used the CAST function to ensure that the string literal is treated as a date.) For example, if a staff member was hired on October 10, 2015, the answer should be 1, not 2. The expression in this SELECT statement is technically correct and works as expected, but it returns the wrong answer when there are any leap years between the hire date and October 1, 2017. Strangely enough, the SQL Standard does not define any functions for performing specialized date and time calculations. The Standard defines only basic subtraction of two dates/times, addition of a date/time and an interval, and multiplication or division by a number to yield an interval.

You can correct this problem by using the appropriate date arithmetic function provided by your database system. As mentioned earlier, most database systems provide their own methods of working with dates and times, and you can find a summary of date and time functions supported by six of the major database systems in Appendix C. But be careful! For example, both Microsoft SQL Server and Microsoft Office Access have a DateDiff function that lets you calculate the difference in years, but the answer returned is simply the difference between the year portion of the two dates. The number of years between December 31, 2016 and January 1, 2017 is 1! I'll show you a more precise way to answer this problem in Chapter 19 using CASE.

"Show me a list of staff members, their salaries, and a proposed 7 percent bonus for each staff member."

Translation/ Clean Up	Select ~~the~~ last name || ', ' || ~~and~~ first name as StaffMember, salary, ~~and~~ salary ~~times~~ * 0.07 as Bonus from ~~the~~ staff ~~table~~
SQL	SELECT StfLastName || ', ' || StfFirstName AS Staff, Salary, Salary * 0.07 AS Bonus FROM Staff

CH05_Proposed_Bonuses (27 Rows)

Staff	Salary	Bonus
Alborous, Sam	$60,000.00	$4,200.00
Black, Alastair	$60,000.00	$4,200.00
Bonnicksen, Joyce	$60,000.00	$4,200.00
Brehm, Peter	$60,000.00	$4,200.00
Brown, Robert	$49,000.00	$3,430.00
Coie, Caroline	$52,000.00	$3,640.00
DeGrasse, Kirk	$45,000.00	$3,150.00
Ehrlich, Katherine	$45,000.00	$3,150.00
Glynn, Jim	$45,000.00	$3,150.00
Hallmark, Alaina	$57,000.00	$3,900.00

<< more rows here >>

Bowling League Database

"Display a list of all bowlers and addresses formatted suitably for a mailing list, sorted by ZIP Code."

Translation/ Clean Up	Select first name || ' ' || ~~and~~ last name as FullName, BowlerAddress, city || ',' || state || ' ' || ~~and~~ ZIP Code as CityStateZip, BowlerZip from ~~the~~ bowlers ~~table and~~ order by ZIP Code

SQL	`SELECT BowlerFirstName || ' ' || BowlerLastName AS`
	`    FullName,`
	`  Bowlers.BowlerAddress,`
	`  BowlerCity || ', ' || BowlerState || ' ' ||`
	`  BowlerZip AS CityStateZip, BowlerZip`
	`FROM Bowlers`
	`ORDER BY BowlerZip`

CH05_Names_Address_For_Mailing (32 Rows)

FullName	BowlerAddress	CityStateZip	BowlerZip
Kathryn Patterson	16 Maple Lane	Auburn, WA 98002	98002
Rachel Patterson	16 Maple Lane	Auburn, WA 98002	98002
Ann Patterson	16 Maple Lane	Auburn, WA 98002	98002
Neil Patterson	16 Maple Lane	Auburn, WA 98002	98002
Megan Patterson	16 Maple Lane	Auburn, WA 98002	98002
Carol Viescas	16345 NE 32nd Street	Bellevue, WA 98004	98004
Sara Sheskey	17950 N 59th	Seattle, WA 98011	98011
Richard Sheskey	17950 N 59th	Seattle, WA 98011	98011
William Thompson	122 Spring Valley Drive	Duvall, WA 98019	98019
Mary Thompson	122 Spring Valley Drive	Duvall, WA 98019	98019

<< more rows here >>

❖ **Note** Notice that I included the BowlerZip column not only in the CityStateZip expression but also as a separate column. Remember that the SQL Standard enables you to sort only on columns that are included in the SELECT clause. Even though you don't need the

BowlerZip again to create your mailing list, you should include the column so that you can use it in the ORDER BY clause. Some database systems, notably Microsoft Office Access, do not impose this requirement, but remember that I'm strictly following the standard in every query I use as an example.

"What was the point spread between a bowler's handicap and raw score for each match and game played?"

Translation/ Clean Up	Select bowler ID, match ID, game number, handicap score, raw score, handicap score ~~minus~~ – raw score as PointDifference from ~~the~~ bowler scores ~~table and~~ order by bowler ID, match ID, game number
SQL	SELECT BowlerID, MatchID, GameNumber, HandiCapScore, RawScore, HandiCapScore – RawScore AS PointDifference FROM Bowler_Scores ORDER BY BowlerID, MatchID, GameNumber

CH05_Handicap_vs_RawScore (1344 Rows)

BowlerID	MatchID	GameNumber	HandiCapScore	RawScore	PointDifference
1	1	1	192	146	46
1	1	2	192	146	46
1	1	3	199	153	46
1	5	1	192	145	47
1	5	2	184	137	47
1	5	3	199	152	47
1	10	1	189	140	49
1	10	2	186	137	49
1	10	3	210	161	49

<< more rows here >>

Summary

I began the chapter with a brief overview of expressions. I then explained that you need to understand data types before you can build expressions, and I went on to discuss each of the major data types in some detail. I next showed you the CAST function and explained that you'll often use it to change the data type of a column or literal so that it's compatible with the type of expression you're trying to build. I then covered all the ways that you can introduce a constant value—a literal—into your expressions. I then introduced you to the concept of using an expression to broaden or narrow the scope of information you retrieve from the database. I also explained that an expression is some form of operation involving numbers, character strings, or dates and times.

I continued our discussion of expressions and provided a concise overview of each type of expression. I showed you how to concatenate strings of characters and how to concatenate strings with other types of data by using the CAST function. I then showed you how to create mathematical expressions, and I explained how the order of precedence affects a given mathematical operation. I closed this discussion with a look at date and time expressions. After showing you how the SQL Standard handles dates and times, I revealed that most database systems provide their own methods of working with dates and times.

I then proceeded to the subject of using expressions in a SELECT statement, and I showed you how to incorporate expressions in the SELECT clause. I then showed you how to use both literal values and columns within an expression, as well as how to name the column that holds the result value of the expression. Before ending this discussion, I took a brief digression and introduced you to the value expression. I revealed that the SQL Standard uses this term to refer to a column reference, literal value, and expression collectively and that you can use a value expression in various clauses of an SQL statement. (More on this in later chapters, of course!)

I closed this chapter with a discussion on Nulls. You learned that a Null represents a missing or an unknown value. I showed you how to use a Null properly and explained that it can be quite useful under the right circumstances. But I also discussed how Nulls adversely affect mathematical operations. You now know that a mathematical operation involving a Null value returns a Null value. I also showed you how Nulls can make the information in a result set inaccurate.

In the next chapter, I'll discuss the idea of retrieving a very specific set of information. I'll then show you how to use a WHERE clause to filter the information retrieved by a SELECT statement.

The following section presents a number of requests that you can work out on your own.

Problems for You to Solve

Below, I show you the request statement and the name of the solution query in the sample databases. If you want some practice, you can work out the SQL for each request and then check your answer with the query I saved in the samples. Don't worry if your syntax doesn't exactly match the syntax of the queries I saved—as long as your result set is the same.

Sales Orders Database

1. *"What if we adjusted each product price by reducing it 5 percent?"*

    You can find the solution in CH05_Adjusted_Wholesale_Prices (90 rows).

2. *"Show me a list of orders made by each customer in descending date order."*

    (Hint: You might need to order by more than one column for the information to display properly.)

    You can find the solution in CH05_Orders_By_Customer_And_Date (944 rows).

3. *"Compile a complete list of vendor names and addresses in vendor name order."*

    You can find the solution in CH05_Vendor_Addresses (10 rows).

Entertainment Agency Database

1. *"Give me the names of all our customers by city."*

    (Hint: You'll have to use an ORDER BY clause on one of the columns.)

    You can find the solution in CH05_Customers_By_City (15 rows).

2. *"List all entertainers and their Web sites."*

    You can find the solution in CH05_Entertainer_Web_Sites (13 rows).

3. *"Show the date of each agent's first six-month performance review."*

   (Hint: You'll need to use date arithmetic to answer this request. Be sure to refer to Appendix C.)

   You can find the solution in CH05_First_Performance_Review (9 rows).

School Scheduling Database

1. *"Give me a list of staff members, and show them in descending order of salary."*

   You can find the solution in CH05_Staff_List_By_Salary (27 rows).

2. *"Can you give me a staff member phone list?"*

   You can find the solution in CH05_Staff_Member_Phone_List (27 rows).

3. *"List the names of all our students, and order them by the cities they live in."*

   You can find the solution in CH05_Students_By_City (18 rows).

Bowling League Database

1. *"Show next year's tournament date for each tournament location."*

   (Hint: Add 364 days to get the same day of the week, and be sure to refer to Appendix C.)

   You can find the solution in CH05_Next_Years_Tourney_Dates (20 rows).

2. *"List the name and phone number for each member of the league."*

   You can find the solution in CH05_Phone_List (32 rows).

3. *"Give me a listing of each team's lineup."*

   (Hint: Base this query on the Bowlers table.)

   You can find the solution in CH05_Team_Lineups (32 rows).

Filtering Your Data

"I keep six honest-serving men (They taught me all I knew.) Their names are What and Why and When and How and Where and Who."

—RUDYARD KIPLING *"I KEEP SIX HONEST-SERVING MEN"*

Topics Covered in This Chapter

Refining What You See Using WHERE

Defining Search Conditions

Using Multiple Conditions

Nulls Revisited: A Cautionary Note

Expressing Conditions in Different Ways

Sample Statements

Summary

Problems for You to Solve

In the previous two chapters, I discussed the techniques you use to see all the information in a given table. I also discussed how to create and use expressions to broaden or narrow the scope of that information. In this chapter, I'll show you how to fine-tune what you retrieve by filtering the information using a WHERE clause.

Refining What You See Using WHERE

The type of SELECT statement we've worked with so far retrieves all the rows from a given table and uses them in the statement's result set. This is great if you really do need to see all the information the table contains. But what if you want to find only the rows that apply to a specific person, a specific place, a particular numeric value, or a range of dates? These are not unusual requests. In fact, they are the impetus behind many of the questions you commonly pose to the database. You might, for example, have a need to ask the following types of questions:

> *"Who are our customers in Seattle?"*
>
> *"Show me a current list of our Bellevue employees and their phone numbers."*
>
> *"What kind of music classes do we currently offer?"*
>
> *"Give me a list of classes that earn three credits."*
>
> *"Which entertainers maintain a Web site?"*
>
> *"Give me a list of engagements for the Caroline Coie Trio."*
>
> *"Give me a list of customers who placed orders in May."*
>
> *"Give me the names of our staff members who were hired on May 16, 1985."*
>
> *"What is the current tournament schedule for Red Rooster Lanes?"*
>
> *"Which bowlers are on team 5?"*

To answer these questions, you'll have to expand your SQL vocabulary once again by adding another clause to your SELECT statement: the WHERE clause.

The WHERE Clause

You use a WHERE clause in a SELECT statement to filter the data the statement draws from a table. The WHERE clause contains a *search condition* that it uses as the filter. This search condition provides the mechanism needed to select only the rows you need or exclude the ones you don't want. Your database system applies the search condition to each row in the logical table defined by the FROM clause. Figure 6-1 shows the syntax of the SELECT statement with the WHERE clause.

A search condition contains one or more *predicates*, each of which is an expression that tests one or more value expressions and returns a true, false, or unknown answer. As you'll learn later, you can combine multiple predicates into a search condition using AND or OR Boolean operators. When the entire search condition evaluates to true for a particular row, you will see that row in the final result set. Note that when a search condition contains only one predicate, the terms *search condition* and *predicate* are synonymous.

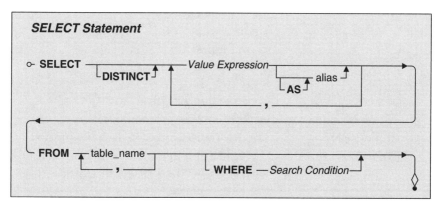

Figure 6-1 *The syntax diagram for a SELECT statement with a WHERE clause*

Remember from Chapter 5, "Getting More Than Simple Columns," that a value expression can contain column names, literal values, functions, or other value expressions. When you construct a predicate, you will typically include at least one value expression that refers to a column from the tables you specify in the FROM clause.

The simplest and perhaps most commonly used predicate compares one value expression (a column) to another (a literal). For example, if you want only the rows from the Customers table in which the value of the customer last name column is Smith, you write a predicate that compares the last name column to the literal value "Smith."

SQL	SELECT CustLastName
	FROM Customers
	WHERE CustLastName = 'Smith'

The predicate in the WHERE clause is equivalent to asking this question for each row in the Customers table: "Does the customer last name equal

'Smith'?" When the answer to this question is yes (true) for any given row in the Customers table, that row appears in the result set.

The SQL Standard defines 18 predicates, but I'll cover the five basic ones in this chapter: Comparison, BETWEEN, IN, LIKE, and IS NULL.

COMPARISON	Use one of the six comparison operators to compare one value expression to another value expression. The six operators and their meanings are = equal to <> not equal to < less than > greater than <= less than or equal to >= greater than or equal to
BETWEEN (RANGE)	The BETWEEN predicate lets you test whether the value of a given value expression falls within a specified range of values. You specify the range using two value expressions separated by the AND keyword.
IN (MEMBERSHIP)	You can test whether the value of a given value expression matches an item in a given list of values using the IN predicate.
LIKE (PATTERN MATCH)	The LIKE predicate allows you to test whether a character string value expression matches a specified character string pattern.
IS NULL	Use the IS NULL predicate to determine whether a value expression evaluates to Null.

> ❖ **Note** Don't worry too much about the other 13 predicates defined in the current SQL Standard (Similar, Regex, Quantified, Exists, Unique, Normalized, Match, Overlaps, Distinct, Member, Submultiset, Set, and Type). Of these, I could not find any commercial implementation of 10 of them. MySQL and PostgreSQL support Regex. I'll cover the other two—Quantified and Exists—in Chapter 11, "Subqueries."

Using a WHERE Clause

Before I explore each of the basic predicates in the SQL Standard, let's first take a look at another example of how to construct a simple WHERE clause. This time, I'll give you a detailed walkthrough of the steps to build your request.

> ❖ **Note** Throughout this chapter, I use the "Request/Translation/Clean Up/SQL" technique introduced in Chapter 4, "Creating a Simple Query."

Suppose you're making the following request to the database:

> *"What are the names of our customers who live in the state of Washington?"*

When composing a translation statement for this type of request, you must try to indicate the information you want to see in the result set as explicitly and clearly as possible. You'll expend more effort to rephrase a request than you've been accustomed to so far, but the results will be well worth the extra work. Here's how you translate this particular request:

Translation	Select first name and last name from the customers table for those customers who live in Washington State

You'll clean up this statement in the usual fashion, but you'll also perform two extra tasks. First, look for any words or phrases that indicate or imply some type of restriction. Dead giveaways are the words "where," "who," and "for." Here are some examples of the types of phrases you're trying to identify:

> *". . . who live in Bellevue."*
>
> *". . . for everyone whose ZIP Code is 98125."*
>
> *". . . who placed orders in May."*
>
> *". . . for suppliers in California."*
>
> *". . . who were hired on May 16, 1985."*
>
> *". . . where the area code is 425."*
>
> *". . . for Mike Hernandez."*

When you find such a restriction, you're ready for the second task. Study the phrase, and try to determine which column is going to be tested, what value that column is going to be tested against, and how the column is going to be tested. The answers to these questions will help you formulate the search condition for your WHERE clause. Let's apply these questions to your translation statement.

Which column is going to be tested? **State**

What value is it going to be tested against? **'WA'**

How is the column going to be tested? **Using the "equal to" operator**

You need to be familiar with the structure of the table you're using to answer the request. If necessary, have a copy of the table structure handy before you begin to answer these questions.

> ❖ **Note** Sometimes the answers to these questions are evident, and other times the answers are implied. I'll show you how to make the distinction and decipher the correct answers as I work through other examples in this chapter.

After answering the questions, take them and create the appropriate condition. Next, cross out the original restriction, and replace it with the word WHERE and the search condition you just created. Here's how your Clean Up statement will look after you have completed this task:

Clean Up	Select first name and last name from ~~the~~ customers ~~table~~ ~~for those customers who live in~~ where state ~~is equal to~~ = 'WA' ~~Washington State~~

Now you can turn this into a proper SELECT statement:

SQL	SELECT CustFirstName, CustLastName
	FROM Customers
	WHERE CustState = 'WA'

The result set of your completed SELECT statement will display only those customers who live in the state of Washington.

That's all there is to defining a WHERE clause. As I indicated at the beginning of this section, it's simply a matter of creating the appropriate search condition and placing it in the WHERE clause. The real work, however, is in defining the search conditions.

Defining Search Conditions

Now that you have an idea of how to create a simple WHERE clause, let's take a closer look at the five basic types of predicates you can define.

Comparison

The most common type of condition is one that uses a comparison predicate to compare two value expressions to each other. As you can see in Figure 6-2, you can define six different types of comparisons using the following comparison predicate operators:

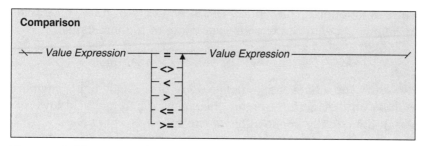

Figure 6-2 *The syntax diagram for the comparison condition*

= Equal To	< Less Than	<= Less Than or Equal To
<> Not Equal To	> Greater Than	>= Greater Than or Equal To

Comparing String Values: A Caution

You can easily compare numeric or datetime data, but you must pay close attention when you compare character strings. For example, you might not get the results you expect when you compare two seemingly similar strings such as "Mike" and "MIKE." The determining factor for all character string comparisons is the collating sequence used by your database system. The collating sequence also determines how character strings are sorted and impacts how you use other comparison conditions as well.

Because many different vendors have implemented SQL on machines with different architectures and for many languages other than English, the SQL Standard does not define any default collating sequence for character string sorting or comparison. How characters are sorted from "lowest" to "highest" depends on the database software you are using and, in many cases, how the software was installed.

Many database systems use the ASCII collating sequence, which places numbers before letters and all uppercase letters before all lowercase letters. If your database supports the ASCII collating sequence, the characters are in the following sequence from lowest value to highest value:

>   ... 0123456789 ... ABC ... XYZ ... abc ... xyz ...

Some systems, however, offer a case-insensitive option. In these, for example, lowercase *a* is considered equal to uppercase *A*. When your database supports this option using ASCII as a base, characters are in the following sequence from lowest value to highest value:

>   ... 0123456789 ... {Aa}{Bb}{Cc} ... {Xx}{Yy}{Zz} ...

Note that the characters enclosed in braces ({}) are considered equal because no distinction is made between uppercase and lowercase. They sort alphabetically irrespective of the case.

Database systems running on IBM mainframe systems use the IBM-proprietary EBCDIC sequence. In a database system that uses EBCDIC, all lowercase letters come first, then all uppercase letters, and finally numbers. If your database supports EBCDIC, characters are in the following sequence from lowest value to highest value:

>   ... abc ... xyz ... ABC ... XYZ ... 0123456789 ...

To drive this point home, let's look at a set of sample column values to see how different collating sequences affect how your database system defines higher, lower, or equal values.

Here is a table of column values sorted using the ASCII character set, case sensitive (numbers first, then uppercase, and then lowercase).

Company Name
3rd Street Warehouse
5th Avenue Market
Al's Auto Shop
Ashby's Cleaners
Zebra Printing
Zercon Productions
allegheny & associates
anderson tree farm
zorn credit services
ztech consulting

Now, let's turn off case sensitivity so that lowercase letters and their uppercase equivalents are considered equal. The next table shows what happens.

Company Name
3rd Street Warehouse
5th Avenue Market
Al's Auto Shop
allegheny & associates
anderson tree farm
Ashby's Cleaners
Zebra Printing
Zercon Productions
zorn credit services
ztech consulting

Finally, let's see how these values are sorted on an IBM system using the EBCDIC collating sequence (lowercase letters, uppercase letters, and then numbers).

Company Name
allegheny & associates
anderson tree farm
zorn credit services
ztech consulting
Al's Auto Shop
Ashby's Cleaners
Zebra Printing
Zercon Productions
3rd Street Warehouse
5th Avenue Market

You can also encounter unexpected results when trying to compare two character strings of unequal length, such as "John" and "John" or "Mitch" and "Mitchell." Fortunately, the SQL Standard clearly specifies how the database system must handle this. Before your database compares two character strings of unequal length, it must add the special *default pad character* to the right of the smaller string until it is the same length as the larger string. (The default pad character is a space in most database systems.) Your database then uses its collating sequence to determine whether the two strings are now equal to each other. As a result, "John" and "John" are equal (after the padding takes place) and "Mitch" and "Mitchell" are unequal.

❖ **Note**   Some database systems differ from the SQL Standard in that they ignore trailing blanks rather than pad the shorter string with a default space. Therefore, "John" and "John " are considered equal in some systems, but for a different reason—because the trailing blanks in the second item are disregarded. Be sure to test your database system to determine how it handles this type of comparison and whether it returns the type of results you expect.

In summary, check your database system's documentation to determine how it collates uppercase letters, lowercase letters, and numbers.

Equality and Inequality

Although you've already seen a couple of examples, let's take another look at an equality comparison condition using the "equal to" operator.

Assume you're making this request to the database:

"Show me the first and last names of all the agents who were hired on March 14, 1977."

Because you are going to search for a specific hire date, you can use an equality comparison condition with an "equal to" operator to retrieve the appropriate information. Now I'll run this through the translation process to define the appropriate SELECT statement:

Translation	Select first name and last name from the agents table for all agents hired on March 14, 1977
Clean Up	Select first name ~~and~~ last name from ~~the~~ agents ~~table for all agents hired on~~ where date hired = ~~March 14, 1977~~ '1977-03-14'
SQL	SELECT AgtFirstName, AgtLastName FROM Agents WHERE DateHired = '1977-03-14'

In this example, I tested the values of a specific column to determine whether any values matched a given date value. In essence, I executed an *inclusive* process—a given row in the Agents table will be included in the result set *only* if the current value of the DateHired column for that row matches the specified date. But what if you wanted to do the exact opposite and *exclude* certain rows from the result set? In that case, you would use a comparison condition with a "not equal to" operator.

Suppose you submit the following request:

"Give me a list of vendor names and phone numbers for all our vendors, with the exception of those here in Bellevue."

You've probably already determined that you need to exclude those vendors based in Bellevue and that you'll use a "not equal to" condition for the task. The phrase "with the exception of" provides a clear indication that the "not equal to" condition is appropriate. Keep this in mind as you look at the translation process.

Translation	Select vendor name and phone number from the vendors table for all vendors except those based in 'Bellevue'
Clean Up	Select vendor name ~~and~~ phone number from ~~the~~ vendors ~~table for all vendors except those based in~~ where city <> 'Bellevue'
SQL	SELECT VendName, VendPhone FROM Vendors WHERE VendCity <> 'Bellevue'

> ❖ **Note** The SQL Standard uses the <> symbol for the "not equal to" operator. Several RDBMS programs provide alternate notations, such as != (supported by Microsoft SQL Server and Sybase) and ¬= (supported by IBM's DB2). Be sure to check your database system's documentation for the appropriate notation of this operator.

You've effectively excluded all vendors from Bellevue with this simple condition. Later in this chapter, I'll show you a different method for excluding rows from a result set.

Less Than and Greater Than

Often you want rows returned where a particular value in a column is smaller or larger than the comparison value. This type of comparison employs the "less than" (<), "less than or equal to" (<=), "greater than" (>), or "greater than or equal to" (>=) comparison operators. The type of data you compare determines the relationship between those values.

CHARACTER STRINGS	This comparison determines whether the value of the first value expression precedes (<) or follows (>) the value of the second value expression in your database system's collating sequence. For example, you can interpret $a < c$ as "Does a precede c?" For details about collating sequences, see the previous section, "Comparing String Values: A Caution."
NUMBERS	This comparison determines whether the value of the first value expression is smaller (<) or larger (>) than the value of the second value expression. For example, you can interpret $10 > 5$ as "Is 10 larger than 5?"

DATES/TIMES   This comparison determines whether the value of the first value expression is earlier (<) or later (>) than the value of the second value expression. For example, you can interpret *'2007-05-16' < '2007-12-15'* as "Is May 16, 2007, earlier than December 15, 2007?" Dates and times are evaluated in chronological order.

Let's take a look at how you might use these comparison predicates to answer a request.

"Are there any orders where the ship date was accidentally posted earlier than the order date?"

You'll use a "less than" comparison operator in this instance because you want to determine whether any ship date was posted earlier than its respective order date. Here's how you translate this:

Translation	Select order number from the orders table where the ship date is earlier than the order date
Clean Up	Select order number from ~~the~~ orders ~~table~~ where ~~the~~ ship date ~~is earlier than the~~ < order date
SQL	SELECT OrderNumber FROM Orders WHERE ShipDate < OrderDate

The SELECT statement's result set will include only those rows from the Orders table where the search condition is true.

The next example requires a "greater than" comparison operator to retrieve the appropriate information.

"Are there any classes that earn more than four credits?"

Translation	Select class ID from the classes table for all classes that earn more than four credits
Clean Up	Select class ID from ~~the~~ classes ~~table for all classes that earn more than four~~ where credits > 4
SQL	SELECT ClassID FROM Classes WHERE Credits > 4

The result set generated by this SELECT statement includes only classes that earn five credits or more, such as Intermediate Algebra and Engineering Physics.

Now, let's take a look at some examples where you're interested not only in the values that might be greater than or less than but also equal to the comparison value.

"I need the names of everyone we've hired since January 1, 1989."

You use a "greater than or equal to" comparison for this because you want to retrieve all hire dates from January 1, 1989, to the present, *including* employees hired on that date. As you run through the translation process, be sure to identify all the columns you need for the SELECT clause.

Translation	Select first name and last name as EmployeeName from the employees table for all employees hired since January 1, 1989
Clean Up	Select first name ~~and~~ || '' || last name as EmployeeName from ~~the~~ employees ~~table for all employees hired since~~ where date hired >= ~~January 1, 1989~~ '1989-01-01'
SQL	SELECT FirstName || ' ' || LastName AS EmployeeName FROM Employees WHERE DateHired >= '1989-01-01'

Here's another request you might make to the database:

"Show me a list of products with a retail price of fifty dollars or less."

As you've probably deduced, you'll use a "less than or equal to" comparison for this request. This ensures that the SELECT statement's result set contains only those products that cost anywhere from one cent to exactly fifty dollars. Here's how you translate this request:

Translation	Select product name from the products table for all products with a retail price of fifty dollars or less
Clean Up	Select product name from ~~the~~ products ~~table for all products with a~~ where retail price ~~of~~ <= 50 ~~fifty dollars or less~~
SQL	SELECT ProductName FROM Products WHERE RetailPrice <= 50

The examples you've seen so far use only a single type of comparison. Later in this chapter, I'll show you how to combine comparisons using AND and OR.

Range

You can test the value of a value expression against a specific range of values with a range condition. Figure 6-3 shows the syntax for this condition.

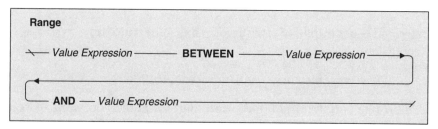

Figure 6-3 *The syntax diagram for the range condition*

The range condition tests the value of a given value expression against a range of values defined by two other value expressions. The BETWEEN . . . AND predicate defines the range by using the value of the second value expression as the start point and the value of the third value expression as the end point. Both the start point and end point are part of the range. A row is included in the result set only if the value of the first value expression falls within the specified range.

There's one "gotcha" about using BETWEEN . . . AND. The SQL Standard actually defines two types of BETWEEN comparisons: ASYMMETRIC and SYMMETRIC. The default, ASYMMETRIC, dictates that Value1 BETWEEN Value2 AND Value3 is the same as Value1 >= Value2 AND Value1 <= Value3. This means that Value2 must be less than or equal to Value3 for the predicate to work properly. For example, the SQL Standard states that

```
MyColumn BETWEEN 5 AND 10
```

should be processed as

```
MyColumn >= 5 AND MyColumn <= 10
```

So, putting the larger value first, as in

```
MyColumn BETWEEN 10 AND 5
```

is interpreted according to the SQL Standard as

```
MyColumn >=10 AND MyColumn <= 5
```

which can never be true! (The column value can't both be greater than or equal to 10 and at the same time less than or equal to 5.) However, some database systems allow Value2 to be greater than or equal to Value3—the equivalent of using the SYMMETRIC keyword in the SQL Standard. (I'm not aware of any major implementation that yet supports the ASYMMETRIC and SYMMETRIC keywords.) Check your database system documentation for details.

Here are a couple of examples that illustrate how you use a range condition:

"Which staff members were hired in July 1986?"

The range condition is appropriate here because you want to retrieve the names of everyone who was hired within a specific set of dates, in this case, between July 1, 1986, and July 31, 1986. Let's now run this through the translation process and build the appropriate SELECT statement.

Translation	Select first name and last name from the staff table where the date hired is between July 1, 1986, and July 31, 1986
Clean Up	Select first name and last name from ~~the~~ staff ~~table~~ where ~~the~~ date hired is between ~~July 1, 1986~~ '1986-07-01' and ~~July 31, 1986~~ '1986-07-31'
SQL	SELECT FirstName, LastName FROM Staff WHERE DateHired BETWEEN '1986-07-01' AND '1986-07-31'

Notice that I stated the range of dates more explicitly in the translation statement than in the request. Use this technique to translate the request as clearly as possible and thus define the appropriate SELECT statement.

You can also use a range condition on character string data quite effectively, as shown in this example:

"Give me a list of students—along with their phone numbers—whose last names begin with the letter B."

Translation	Select last name, first name, and phone number from the students table for all students whose last name begins with the letter 'B'
Clean Up	Select last name, first name, ~~and~~ phone number from ~~the~~ students ~~table for all students whose name begins with the letter 'B'~~ where last name between 'B' and 'Bz'
SQL	SELECT StudLastName, StudFirstName, StudPhoneNumber FROM Students WHERE StudLastName BETWEEN 'B' AND 'Bz'

When creating a range for character string data, think carefully about the values you want to include. For example, here are three possible ways you might have indicated the start and end points for the required range in this request. The results are quite different!

BETWEEN 'A' AND 'B'	I know that many of you would not have indicated 'A' as the start point because you know the range would then include everyone whose name begins with that letter. However, this is a fairly typical mistake.
BETWEEN 'B' AND 'C'	Indicating the start and end points in this manner probably returns the desired results for my example. However, you might get unexpected results based on the character data you're trying to compare. Remember that the BETWEEN operator *includes* the start and end points in the range. Consequently, a student whose last name is only the letter 'C' will be included in the result set.
BETWEEN 'B' AND 'BZ'	This is the clearest and most explicit method of indicating the start and end points—in most cases, it will return the desired results. In the end, you must understand your data in order to define the correct range.

One more thing before I leave BETWEEN. Notice that the diagram in Figure 6-3 says that you can use a *value expression* not only for the two values in the BETWEEN clause but also for the first value. As I've explained, a value expression can be as simple as a column name or a simple literal or as complex as a character, mathematical, or datetime expression. When you have a table that has two columns that define a range of values (for example, StartDate and EndDate in the Engagements table in the Entertainment Agency sample database), you can also use BETWEEN to search for rows that contain a value BETWEEN the values in the two columns. Here's an example.

"Show me all engagements that are scheduled to occur on October 10, 2017."

Translation	Select engagement number, start date, and end date from the engagements table for engagements where October 10, 2017, is between the start date and the end date
Clean Up	Select engagement number, start date, ~~and~~ end date from ~~the~~ engagements ~~table for engagements~~ where ~~October 10, 2017 is~~ '2017-10-10' between ~~the~~ start date and ~~the~~ end date
SQL	SELECT EngagementNumber, StartDate, EndDate FROM Engagements WHERE '2017-10-10' BETWEEN StartDate AND EndDate

So far, I've shown you how to narrow the scope of your request using a broad range of values and a more specific range of values. Now, let's take a look at how you can refine your requests even further by using an explicit list of values.

Set Membership

You'll use the membership condition to test the value of a value expression against a list of explicitly defined values. As you can see in Figure 6-4, the membership condition uses the IN predicate to determine whether the value of the first value expression matches any value within a parenthetical list of values defined by one or more value expressions.

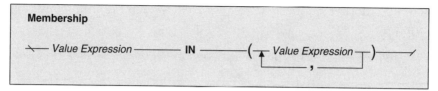

Figure 6-4 *The syntax diagram for the membership condition*

Although theoretically, you can include an almost limitless number of value expressions in the list, it makes more sense to use only a few. You already have two conditions at your disposal that you can use to indicate broader ranges of values. You can use the membership condition most effectively when you define a finite list of values, as you'll see in the following examples.

Here's a request you might make to the database:

> *"I need to know which bowling lanes sponsored tournaments for the following 2017 dates: September 18, October 9, and November 6."*

This type of request lends itself to a membership condition because it focuses on searching for a specific set of values. If the request were not so explicit, you would most likely use a range condition instead. Here's how to translate this request:

Translation	Select tourney location from the tournaments table where the tourney date is in this list of dates: September 18, 2017; October 9, 2017; November 6, 2017
Clean Up	Select tourney location from ~~the~~ tournaments ~~table~~ where ~~the~~ tourney date is in ~~this list of dates~~: (~~September 18, 2017~~; '2017-09-18',~~October 9 2017~~; '2017-10-09', ~~November 6, 2017~~ '2017-11-06')

SQL	SELECT TourneyLocation
	FROM Tournaments
	WHERE TourneyDate
	    IN ('2017-09-18', '2017-10-09',
	    '2017-11-06')

Here's another request that requires a membership condition for its answer:

"Which entertainers do we represent in Seattle, Redmond, and Bothell?"

Translation	Select stage name from the entertainers table for all entertainers based in Seattle, Redmond, or Bothell
Clean Up	Select stage name from the entertainers ~~table for all entertainers based~~ where city in ('Seattle', 'Redmond', ~~or~~ 'Bothell')
SQL	SELECT EntStageName FROM Entertainers WHERE EntCity IN ('Seattle', 'Redmond', 'Bothell')

You might have noticed that I used the word "or" in the translation statement's list of cities instead of "and" as it appears in the original request. The reason and logic for this is simple: There is only one entry in the EntCity column for a given entertainer. A given row can't contain Seattle *and* Redmond *and* Bothell all at the same time, but a single row could contain Seattle *or* Redmond *or* Bothell. This might seem a trivial point, but using the proper words and phrases helps to clarify your Translation and Clean Up statements and ensures that you define the most appropriate SELECT statement for your request. You'll see that this small point becomes even more important later in the chapter when you begin using multiple conditions.

All the conditions you've learned so far use complete values as their criteria. Now I'll take a look at a condition that allows you to use partial values as a criterion.

Pattern Match

The pattern match condition is useful when you need to find values that are similar to a given pattern string or when you have only a partial piece of information to use as a search criterion. Figure 6-5 shows the syntax for this type of condition.

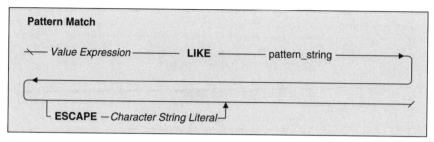

Figure 6-5 *The syntax diagram for the pattern match condition*

This condition takes the value of a value expression and uses the LIKE predicate to test whether the value matches a defined pattern string. A pattern string can consist of any logical combination of regular string characters and two special wildcard characters: the percent sign (%) and the underscore (_). The percent sign represents zero or more arbitrary regular characters, and the underscore represents a single arbitrary regular character. The manner in which you define the pattern string determines which values are retrieved from the value expression. Table 6-1 shows samples of the different types of pattern strings you can define.

❖ **Note** One of the most popular database systems, Microsoft Office Access, uses an asterisk (*) instead of the percent sign (%) and a question mark (?) instead of an underscore (_). Access also supports using a hashtag (#) to search for numeric characters in specific positions. If you're using Microsoft Access, substitute these characters in your pattern strings for the LIKE predicate.

Table 6-1 *Samples of Defined Pattern Strings*

Pattern String	Criterion Processed	Sample Return Values
'Sha%'	Character string can be any length but must begin with "Sha"	**Sha**nnon, **Sha**ron, **Sha**wn
'%son'	Character string can be any length but must end with "son"	Ben**son**, John**son**, Morri**son**
'%han%'	Character string can be any length but must contain "han"	Buc**han**an, **han**del, Jo**han**sen, Nat**han**son

Pattern String	Criterion Processed	Sample Return Values
`'Ro_'`	Character string can be only three characters in length and must have "Ro" as the first and second letters	**Ro**b, **Ro**n, **Ro**y
`'_im'`	Character string can be only three characters in length and must have "im" as the second and third letters	J**im**, K**im**, T**im**
`'_ar_'`	Character string can be only four characters in length and must have "ar" as the second and third letters	B**ar**t, G**ar**y, M**ar**k
`'_at%''`	Character string can be any length but must have "at" as the second and third letters	G**at**es, M**at**thews, P**at**terson
`'%ac_'`	Character string can be any length but must have "ac" as the second and third letters from the end of the string	Apod**ac**a, Tr**ac**y, Wall**ac**e

Let's take a look at how you can use a pattern match condition by considering the following request:

"Give me a list of customers whose last names begin with 'Mar'."

Requests such as this one typically use phrases that indicate the need for a pattern match condition. Here are a few examples of the types of phrases you're likely to encounter:

". . . begin with 'Her'."

". . . start with 'Ba'."

". . . include the word 'Park'."

". . . contain the letters 'han'."

". . . have 'ave' in the middle of it."

". . . with 'son' at the end."

". . . ending in 'ez'."

❖ **Caution** In many database systems, string comparison is case sensitive. Several major database systems allow system administrators to specify an option to use either case-sensitive or case-insensitive comparison when they install database servers. If your database system is case sensitive, LIKE '%chi%' will find "roast chicken," but it won't find "Chicken a la King" because the lowercase 'c' in the pattern string is not equal to the uppercase 'C' in the column. Check your database documentation to find out whether you need to deal with the difference between upper- and lowercase letters.

As you can see, it can be relatively easy to determine the type of pattern string you need for a request. After you know the type of pattern you need to create, you can continue with the translation process.

Translation	Select last name and first name from the customers table where the last name begins with 'Mar'
Clean Up	Select last name ~~and~~ first name from ~~the~~ customers ~~table~~ where ~~the~~ last name ~~begins with~~ like 'Mar%'
SQL	SELECT CustLastName, CustFirstName FROM Customers WHERE CustLastName LIKE 'Mar%'

The result set for this SELECT statement includes names such as Marks, Marshall, Martinez, and Marx because I was only concerned with matching the first three letters of the last name.

Here's how you might answer another request using a pattern match condition:

"Show me a list of vendor names where the word 'Forest' appears in the street address."

Translation	Select vendor name from the vendors table where the street address contains the word 'Forest'
Clean Up	Select vendor name from ~~the~~ vendors ~~table~~ where ~~the~~ street address ~~contains the word~~ like '%Forest%'
SQL	SELECT VendName FROM Vendors WHERE VendStreetAddress LIKE '%Forest%'

In this case, a row from the Vendors table is included in the result set only if the street address contains a street name such as Forest Park Place, Forest Ridge Avenue, Evergreen Forest Drive, or Black Forest Road.

Although you can search for any pattern string using the appropriate wild-card characters, you'll run into a problem if the values you want to retrieve include a percent sign or an underscore character. For example, you will have a problem trying to retrieve the value MX_445 because it contains an underscore character. You can circumvent this potential dilemma by using the ESCAPE option of the LIKE predicate, as shown in Figure 6-5.

The ESCAPE option allows you to designate a *single* character string literal—known as an *escape character*—to indicate how the database system should interpret a percent sign or underscore character within a pattern string. Place the escape character after the ESCAPE keyword and enclose it within single quotes, as you would any character string literal. When the escape character precedes a wildcard character in a pattern string, the database system interprets that wildcard character *literally* within the pattern string.

Here's an example of how you might use the ESCAPE option:

"Show me a list of products that have product codes beginning with 'G_00' and ending in a single number or letter."

Translation	Select product name and product code from the products table where the product code begins with 'G_00' and ends in a single number or letter
Clean Up	Select product name ~~and~~ product code from ~~the~~ products ~~table~~ where ~~the~~ product code ~~begins with~~ like 'G_00_' ~~and ends in a single number or letter~~
SQL	SELECT ProductName, ProductCode FROM Products WHERE ProductCode LIKE 'G_00_' ESCAPE '\'

It's evident that you need to use the ESCAPE option to help answer this request—otherwise, the database system interprets the underscore character in the pattern string as a wildcard character. Note that I included the escape character in the Clean Up statement. You should do so in your Clean Up statements as well because it ensures that you remember to use the ESCAPE option when you define your SELECT statement.

This SELECT statement will retrieve product codes such as G_002 and G_00X. Because I want to search for one of the two characters that are defined in the standard as a wildcard, I *must* include the ESCAPE clause. If I ask for LIKE 'G_00_', the database system will return rows where the product code has a 'G' for the first letter, *any* character in the second position (because of the wildcard character), zeros in the third and fourth positions, and any character in the fifth position. When I define "\" as the escape character, the database system ignores the escape character but interprets the first underscore character literally, not as a wildcard. Because I did not use the escape character just before the second underscore, the database system interprets the second underscore as a true wildcard character.

Keep in mind that the character you use as an escape character should not be part of the values you're trying to retrieve. It doesn't make sense to use "&" as an escape character if you're searching for values such as Martin & Lewis, Smith & Kearns, or Hernandez & Viescas. Also, remember that the escape character affects only the wildcard character that immediately follows it. However, you can use as many escape characters in your pattern string as are appropriate.

Null

Now that you've learned how to search for complete values and partial values, let's discuss searching for *unknown* values. You learned in Chapter 5 that a Null *does not* represent a zero, a character string of one or more blank spaces, or a zero-length character string (a character string that has no characters in it) because each of these items can be meaningful in a variety of circumstances. You also learned that a Null *does* represent a missing or unknown value. To retrieve Null values from a value expression, you use the *Null condition* shown in Figure 6-6.

Figure 6-6 *The syntax diagram for the Null condition*

This condition takes the value of the value expression and determines whether it is Null using the IS NULL predicate. It's quite a straightforward operation. Let's take a look at how you might use this condition in the following examples:

"Give me a list of customers who didn't specify what county they live in."

Translation	Select first name and last name as Customer from the customers table where the county name is unspecified
Clean Up	Select first name || ' ' || ~~and~~ last name as Customer from ~~the~~ customers ~~table~~ where ~~the~~ county name is null ~~unspecified~~
SQL	SELECT CustFirstName || ' ' || CustLastName AS Customer FROM Customers WHERE CustCounty IS NULL

The only customers who appear in the result set for this SELECT statement are those who didn't know or couldn't remember what county they live in, or those folks who live in Washington, D.C. (Washington, by the way, is the only city in the entire United States that isn't situated within a county.)

Here's another request you might make to the database:

"Which engagements do not yet have a contract price?"

Translation	Select engagement number and contract price from the engagements table for any engagement that does not have a contract price
Clean Up	Select engagement number ~~and~~ contract price from ~~the~~ engagements ~~table for any engagement that does not have a~~ where contract price is null
SQL	SELECT EngagementNumber, ContractPrice FROM Engagements WHERE ContractPrice IS NULL

On the surface, this seems like a straightforward request—you'll just search for any engagement that has 0 as the contract price. But looks can be deceiving, and they can lull you into making incorrect assumptions. If the entertainment agency in this example uses 0 as the contract price for any promotional engagement, then zero is a valid, meaningful value. Therefore, any contract price that is yet to be determined or negotiated is indeed (or should be) Null.

This example illustrates the fact that you do need to understand your data in order to make meaningful, accurate requests to the database. If you execute a SELECT statement and then think that the information you see in a result set is erroneous, don't panic. Your first impulse will probably be to rewrite the entire SELECT statement because you believe you've made some disastrous mistake in the syntax. Before you do anything drastic, review the data you're working with, and make certain you have a clear idea of how it's being used. After you have a better understanding of the data, you'll often find that you need to make only minor changes to your SELECT statement in order for it to retrieve the proper information.

❖ **Note** You must use the Null condition to search for Null values within a value expression. A condition such as `<ValueExpression>` = `Null` is invalid because the value of the value expression cannot be compared to something that is, by definition, unknown. In fact, using Null in any comparison predicate yields "unknown," and because unknown is not "true," the comparison will fail.

Excluding Rows with NOT

Up to this point, I've shown you how to *include* specific rows in a result set. Let's now take a look at how you *exclude* rows from a result set by using the NOT operator. I've already shown you one simple way to exclude rows from a result set by using an equality comparison condition with a "not equal to" operator. You can also exclude rows with other types of conditions by using the NOT operator. As you can see in Figure 6-7, this operator is an optional component of the BETWEEN, IN, LIKE, and IS NULL predicates. A SELECT statement will disregard any rows that meet the condition expressed by any of these predicates when you include the NOT operator. The rows that will be in the result set instead are those that *did not meet* the condition.

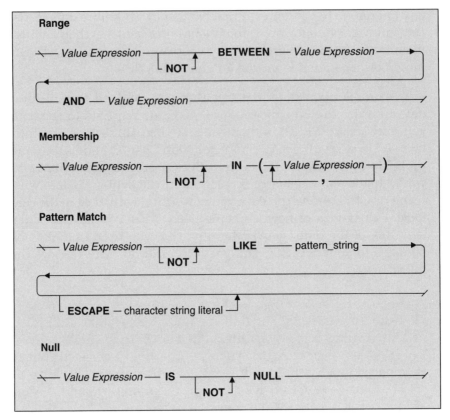

Figure 6-7 *The syntax diagram for the NOT operator*

The following examples illustrate how you can use NOT as part of a search condition:

> *"Show me a list of all the orders we've taken, except for those posted in July."*

A request such as this requires you to define a SELECT statement that excludes rows meeting a specific criterion and commonly contains phrases that indicate the need for a NOT operator as part of the search condition. The types of phrases you'll encounter are similar to those listed here.

> *". . . that don't begin with 'Her'."*

> *". . . that aren't in the Administrative or Personnel departments."*

> *". . . who have a fax number."*

> *". . . who were hired before June 1 or after August 31."*

You have to perform a bit of deductive work sometimes in order to translate a phrase properly. Some phrases, such as the third phrase listed above, do not explicitly indicate the need for a NOT operator. In this case, the requirement is implied because you want to *exclude* everyone who *does not* have a fax number. As you begin to work with requests that contain these types of phrases, you'll often find that you need to analyze them carefully and possibly rewrite them in order to determine whether you need to exclude certain rows from the result set. There's no easy rule of thumb I can give you here, but with a little patience and practice it will become easier for you to determine whether you need a NOT operator for a specific request.

After you've determined whether you need to exclude any information from the result set, you can continue with the translation process.

"Show me a list of all the orders we've taken, except for those posted in October."

Translation	Select order ID and order date from the orders table where the order date does not fall between October 1, 2017, and October 31, 2017
Clean Up	Select order ID ~~and~~ order date from ~~the~~ orders ~~table~~ where ~~the~~ order date ~~does~~ not ~~fall~~ between ~~October 1, 2017,~~ '2017-10-01' and ~~October 31, 2017~~ '2017-10-31'
SQL	SELECT OrderID, OrderDate FROM Orders WHERE OrderDate NOT BETWEEN '2017-10-01' AND '2017-10-31'

This SELECT statement produces a result set that will *not* contain any orders posted between October 1, 2017, and October 31, 2017. It will, however, contain every other order in the Orders table. You can further restrict the rows sent to the result set to only those orders taken in 2017 by using multiple conditions, which is an issue I'll cover in the next section.

Now let's assume you're working with the following request:

"I need the identification numbers of all faculty members who are not professors or associate professors."

Translation	Select staff ID and title from the faculty table where the title is not 'professor' or 'associate professor'
Clean Up	Select staff ID ~~and~~ title from ~~the~~ faculty ~~table~~ where ~~the~~ title ~~is~~ not in ('professor', ~~or~~ 'associate professor')
SQL	SELECT StaffID, Title FROM Faculty WHERE Title NOT IN ('Professor', 'Associate Professor')

In this case, you need to exclude any staff member whose title is one of those specified within the request, so you use a membership condition with a NOT operator to send the correct rows to the result set.

Excluding rows from a result set becomes a relatively straightforward process after you get accustomed to analyzing and rephrasing your requests as the situation dictates. The real key, as you've seen so far, is being able to determine the type of condition you need to answer a given request.

Using Multiple Conditions

The requests I've worked with up to this point have been simple and have required only a single condition to supply the answer. Now I'll look at how you can answer complex requests using multiple conditions. Let's begin by considering the following request:

> *"Give me the first and last names of customers who live in Seattle and whose last names start with the letter 'H'."*

Based on the knowledge you've gained thus far, you can ascertain that this request requires an equality comparison condition and a pattern match condition to supply an answer. You've identified the conditions you need, but how do you combine them into one search condition? The answer lies in the way the SQL Standard defines the syntax for a search condition, as shown in Figure 6-8.

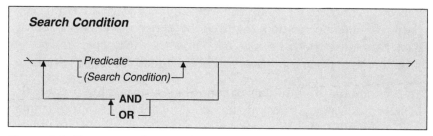

Figure 6-8 *The syntax diagram for the search condition*

Introducing AND and OR

You can combine two or more conditions by using the AND and OR operators, and the complete set of conditions you've combined to answer a given request constitutes a single search condition. As Figure 6-8 shows, you can also combine a complete search condition with other conditions by enclosing the search condition in parentheses. All this allows you to create very complex WHERE clauses that precisely control which rows are selected to be included in a result set.

Using AND

The first way you can combine two or more conditions is by using the AND operator. You use this operator when *all* the conditions you combine must be met in order for a row to be included in a result set. Let's use the sample request I made at the beginning of this section as an example and apply this operator during the translation process.

> *"Give me the first and last names of customers who live in Seattle and whose last names start with the letter 'H'."*

Translation	Select first name and last name from the customers table where the city is 'Seattle' and the last name begins with 'H'
Clean Up	Select first name ~~and~~ last name from ~~the~~ customers ~~table~~ where ~~the~~ city ~~is~~ = 'Seattle' and ~~the~~ last name ~~begins with~~ like 'H%'
SQL	SELECT CustFirstName, CustLastName FROM Customers WHERE CustCity = 'Seattle' AND CustLastName LIKE 'H%'

You've accounted for both the equality comparison condition and the pattern match condition required by the request, and you've ensured that they must both be met by using the AND operator. Any row that fails to meet either condition will be excluded from the result set.

You can chain any number of conditions you need to answer the request at hand. Just keep in mind that *all* the conditions you've combined with ANDs *must* be met in order for a row to be included in the result set. Remember that the entire search condition must evaluate to true for a row to appear in the result set. Figure 6-9 shows the result when you combine two predicate expressions using the AND operator. If *either* of the expressions evaluates to false, then the row is not selected.

Second Expression

AND	True	False
True	True (Rows are selected)	False (Rows are rejected)
False	False (Rows are rejected)	False (Rows are rejected)

First Expression

Figure 6-9 *The result of combining two predicate expressions with the AND operator*

Using OR

The second way to combine two or more conditions is by using the OR operator. You use this operator when *either* of the conditions you combine can be met for a row to be included in a result set. Here's an example of how you might use an OR operator in a search condition:

> *"I need the name, city, and state of every staff member who lives in Seattle or is from the state of Oregon."*

Translation	Select first name, last name, city, and state from the staff table where the city is 'Seattle' or the state is 'OR'
Clean Up	Select first name, last name, city, ~~and~~ state from ~~the~~ staff ~~table~~ where ~~the~~ city ~~is~~ = 'Seattle' or ~~the~~ state ~~is~~ = 'OR'
SQL	SELECT StfFirstName, StfLastName, StfCity, StfState FROM Staff WHERE StfCity = 'Seattle' OR StfState = 'OR'

In this case, you've accounted for both of the equality comparison conditions you need to answer this request, and you've ensured that *only one* of the conditions has to be met by using the OR operator. As long as a row fulfills either condition, it will be included in the result set. To help clarify the matter, Figure 6-10 shows the result of combining two predicate expressions with an OR operator.

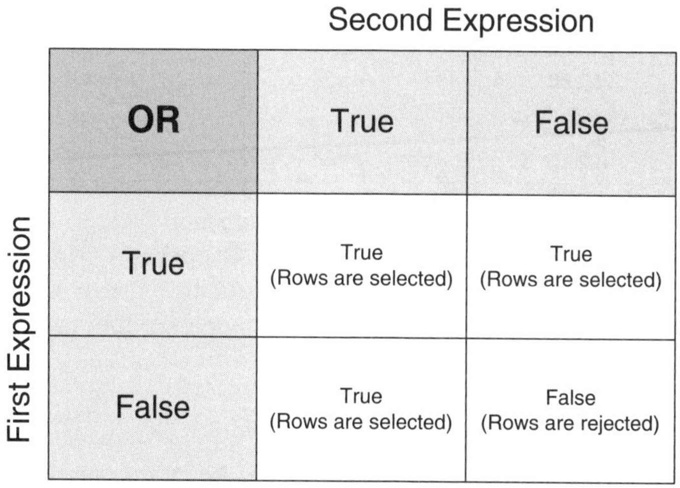

Figure 6-10 *The result of combining two predicate expressions with the OR operator*

Determining whether to use an AND operator to combine conditions is relatively easy and straightforward. However, determining whether to use an OR operator can be tricky sometimes. For example, consider the following request:

> "*Show me a list of vendor names and phone numbers for all vendors based in Washington and California.*"

Your first impulse might be to use an AND operator because the condition seems obvious—you want vendors in Washington *and* California. Unfortunately, you would be wrong. If you think about it, a vendor will be based in *either* Washington *or* California because *you can enter only one state value in the state column for that vendor.* The actual condition is much clearer now, isn't it? As I mentioned earlier in the chapter, you must get into the habit of studying and analyzing your requests as they become more complex. Try to look for implied conditions as best as you can.

Let's continue and run this request through the translation process.

> *"Show me a list of vendor names and phone numbers for all vendors based in Washington and California."*

Translation	Select name, phone number, and state from the vendors table where the state is 'WA' or 'CA'
Clean Up	Select name, phone number, ~~and~~ state from ~~the~~ vendors ~~table~~ where ~~the~~ state ~~is~~ = 'WA' or state = 'CA'
SQL	SELECT VendName, VendPhoneNumber, VendState FROM Vendors WHERE VendState = 'WA' OR VendState = 'CA'

You've accounted for both equality comparison conditions and ensured that either one must be met by using the OR operator. Note, however, that "state" appears in the search condition of the Clean Up and SQL statements twice. This is necessary because each comparison condition follows the same -syntax:

```
Value Expression <comparison operator> Value Expression
```

Remember that you cannot omit any clause, keyword, or defined term from the syntax unless it is explicitly defined as an optional item. Thus, a condition such as WHERE VendState = 'WA' OR 'CA' is completely invalid. You might ask why this is so. I'll explain more about the sequence in which expression operators get evaluated—the order of precedence—later.

In this case, your database system evaluates the expression in strict left-to-right sequence. So, VendState = 'WA' will be evaluated first. For any given row, the result will be true if the state is Washington, and false if it is not. Next, this true or false result gets "ORed" with the literal value 'CA'—which is not a true or false value! Your database system might return an error at this point ('CA'—a character string literal—is an invalid data type for the OR operator), or it might return only the rows where the state is Washington, or it might even first evaluate 'CA' OR 'WA' as a Boolean expression and then compare VendState to True or False!

Always make certain that your conditions are completely and correctly defined. Otherwise, the search condition for your SELECT statement will fail.

> ❖ **Note** I used this example to illustrate a common trap you'll encounter when you use the OR operator. However, if you thought you could use a membership condition such as WHERE VendState IN ('WA', 'CA') to answer this request, you are absolutely correct. In some instances, you'll find that there's more than one way to express a condition.

Using AND and OR Together

You can use both AND and OR to answer particularly tricky requests. For example, you can answer the following type of request by using both operators:

> *"I need to see the names of staff members who have a 425 area code and a phone number that begins with 555, along with anyone who was hired between October 1 and December 31 of 2007."*

It should be easy for you to decide what types of conditions you need for this request by now. You've probably already determined that you need three conditions to answer this request: an equality comparison condition to find the area code, a pattern match condition to find the phone numbers, and a range condition to find those staff members hired between October 1 and December 31. All you have to do now is determine how you're going to combine the conditions.

You need to combine the comparison and pattern match conditions with an AND operator because they identify the phone numbers you're searching for and because both conditions must be met in order for a row to be included in the result set. You then treat this combination of conditions as a single unit and combine it with the range condition using an OR operator. Now a row will be included in the result set as long as it meets *either* the combined condition or the range condition.

Here's the request again and the translation:

"I need to see the names of staff members who have a 425 area code and a phone number that begins with 555, along with anyone who was hired between October 1 and December 31 of 2017."

Translation	Select first name, last name, area code, phone number, and date hired from the staff table where the area code is 425 and the phone number begins with 555 or the date hired falls between October 1, 2017, and December 31, 2017
Clean Up	Select first name, last name, area code, phone number, ~~and~~ date hired from ~~the~~ staff ~~table~~ where ~~the~~ area code ~~is~~ = '425' and ~~the~~ phone number ~~begins with~~ like '555%' or ~~the~~ date hired ~~falls~~ between ~~October 1, 2017,~~ '2017-10-01' and ~~December 31, 2017~~ '2017-12-31'
| SQL | ```
SELECT StfFirstName, StfLastName, StfAreaCode,
    StfPhoneNumber, DateHired
FROM Staff
WHERE (StfAreaCode = '425'
    AND StfPhoneNumber LIKE '555%')
OR DateHired
    BETWEEN '2017-10-01' AND '2017-12-31'
``` |

The previous example clearly demonstrates a situation where you can use a search condition within a search condition. Before you translated the request, I said that you needed to combine the comparison and pattern match conditions with an AND operator and then treat them as a single unit. When you treat a combined set of conditions as a single unit, by definition, it becomes a search condition, and you should enclose it in parentheses, exactly as I did in the example. It's worth noting, however, that the SQL Standard and most database systems give AND precedence over OR as well as processing left to right, so I probably could have gotten away with not placing parentheses around the two comparisons linked with AND. Always use parentheses to make it crystal clear
```

how you want the comparisons to be processed. See the topic "Order of Precedence," later in this chapter.

Here's another example using AND and OR:

"I need the name and title of every professor or associate professor who was hired on May 16, 1989."

Translation	Select first name, last name, title, and date hired from the staff table where the title is 'professor' or 'associate professor' and the date hired is May 16, 1989
Clean Up	Select first name, last name, title, ~~and~~ date hired from ~~the~~ staff ~~table~~ where the title ~~is~~ = 'professor' or title = 'associate professor' and ~~the~~ date hired ~~is~~ = ~~May 16, 1989~~ '1989-05-16'

SQL	SELECT StfFirstName, StfLastName, Title, DateHired
	FROM Staff
	WHERE (Title = 'Professor'
	   OR Title = 'Associate Professor')
	   AND DateHired = '1989-05-16'

You've probably guessed that the two conditions combined with the OR operator are being treated as a single search condition. This example merely reinforces the fact that you can define a search condition with either the AND or the OR operators. But once again, the key is making certain that you enclose the search condition within parentheses to make it perfectly clear how the comparisons should be processed.

Excluding Rows: Take Two

If you're feeling a bit of déjà vu, don't worry—I did discuss this already. Well, at least to some extent. You learned earlier in this chapter that the NOT operator is an option of the BETWEEN, IN, LIKE, and IS NULL predicates. But as Figure 6-11 illustrates, NOT is also an option as the first keyword of a search condition, and it allows you to exclude rows from a result set just as you can by using NOT within a predicate. You use this particular NOT operator *before* a single condition (predicate) or an embedded search condition. Once again, you can express the same condition in various ways.

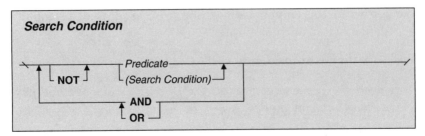

Figure 6-11 *Including the NOT operator in a search condition*

Let's assume you're posing the following request to the database:

> *"Show me the location and date of any tournament not being held at Bolero Lanes, Imperial Lanes, or Thunderbird Lanes."*

You've probably already determined that you'll use a membership condition to answer this request. Now you just need to determine how you'll define it. One approach you can take is using the NOT operator within the predicate.

```
WHERE TourneyLocation NOT IN ('Bolero Lanes',
    'Imperial Lanes', 'Thunderbird Lanes')
```

Another approach you might consider is using the NOT operator as the first keyword before the search condition.

```
WHERE NOT TourneyLocation IN ('Bolero Lanes',
    'Imperial Lanes', 'Thunderbird Lanes')
```

Either condition will exclude tournaments held at Bolero Lanes, Imperial Lanes, and Thunderbird Lanes from the result set. However, one advantage of using NOT before a search condition is that you can apply it to a comparison condition. (Remember that the syntax for a comparison condition does not include NOT as an optional operator.) But now you can use a comparison condition to exclude rows from a result set. The following example shows how you might use this type of condition:

> *"Show me the bowlers who live outside of Bellevue."*

Translation	Select first name, last name, and city from the bowlers table where the city is not 'Bellevue'
Clean Up	Select first name, last name, ~~and~~ city from ~~the~~ bowlers ~~table~~ where ~~the~~ city ~~is~~ not = 'Bellevue'

SQL	SELECT BowlerFirstName, BowlerLastName, BowlerCity
	FROM Bowlers
	WHERE NOT BowlerCity = 'Bellevue'

Yes, I know that you could have expressed this condition as WHERE BowlerCity <> 'Bellevue'. This example simply emphasizes that you can express a condition in various ways.

Now that you've learned how to use a NOT operator within a single condition and a complete search condition, be aware of a problem that can occur when you define a search condition with two NOT operators that will *include* rows instead of *excluding* them. Here's an example:

"Which staff members are not teachers or teacher's aides?"

Translation	Select first name, last name, and title from the staff table where the title is not 'teacher' or 'teacher's aide'
Clean Up	Select first name, last name, ~~and~~ title from ~~the~~ staff ~~table~~ where ~~the~~ title ~~is~~ not in ('teacher', ~~or~~ 'teacher''s aide')
SQL	SELECT StfFirstName, StfLastName, Title
	FROM Staff
	WHERE NOT Title
	NOT IN ('Teacher', 'Teacher''s Aide')

❖ **Note** I bet you're wondering about the two single quotes in the 'Teacher''s Aide' character string literal. The SQL Standard dictates that you use a single quote to delimit a character string or date-time literal. When you need to embed a single quote within a character string literal, you must "clue in" your database system by entering the single quote twice. If you don't do that, the single quote acts as the end delimiter of the character string. The "s Aide'" that would occur after the second single quote would generate a syntax error!

I assume, of course, that one of the two NOT operators appears by mistake. You can still execute this SELECT statement, but it will send the wrong rows to the result set. In this case, the two NOT operators cancel each other—exactly like a double negative in arithmetic or in language—and the IN predicate now determines which rows are sent to the result set. So instead of seeing anyone *other than* a teacher or teacher's aide in the result set, you'll see *only* teachers and teacher's aides. Although you would not consciously define a search condition in this manner, you could very well do it accidentally. Remember that it's often the simple mistakes that cause the most problems.

Order of Precedence

The SQL Standard specifies how a database system should evaluate single conditions within a search condition and the order in which those evaluations take place. You've already learned in this chapter *how* a database evaluates each type of condition. Now I'll show you how the database determines *when* to evaluate each single condition.

By default, the database evaluates conditions from left to right. This is particularly true in the case of simple conditions. In the following example, the SELECT statement first searches for rows where the ship date is equal to the order date and then determines which of those rows contain customer number 1001. The rows that meet both conditions are then sent to the result set.

SQL	SELECT CustomerID, OrderDate, ShipDate
	FROM Orders
	WHERE ShipDate = OrderDate
	AND CustomerID = 1001

To have the SELECT statement search for a specific customer number before evaluating the ship date, just switch the position of the conditions. I'll discuss why you might want to do this later in this section.

When a search condition contains various types of single conditions, the database evaluates them in a specific order based on the operator used in each condition. The SQL Standard defines the following order of precedence for operator evaluation.

Evaluation Order	Type of Operator
1	Positive sign (+), negative sign (−)
2	Multiplication (*), division (/)

Evaluation Order	Type of Operator
3	Addition (+), subtraction (−)
4	=, <>, <, >, <=, >=, BETWEEN, IN, LIKE, IS NULL
5	NOT
6	AND
7	OR

The following SELECT statement contains an example of the type of search condition that causes the database system to follow the order of precedence. In this case, the database performs the addition operation, executes the comparisons, and determines whether either condition has been met. Any row that meets either condition is then sent to the result set.

```
SQL              SELECT CustomerID, OrderDate, ShipDate
                 FROM Orders
                 WHERE CustomerID = 1001
                    OR ShipDate = OrderDate + 4
```

Prioritizing Conditions

You can greatly increase the accuracy of your search conditions by understanding the order of precedence. This knowledge will help you formulate exactly the right condition for the request at hand. But you must be careful to avoid defining ambiguous conditions because they can produce unexpected results.

Let's use the following example to take a look at this potential problem:

```
SQL              SELECT CustFirstName, CustLastName, CustState,
                    CustZipCode
                 FROM Orders
                 WHERE CustLastName = 'Patterson'
                    AND CustState = 'CA'
                    OR CustZipCode LIKE '%9'
```

In this instance, it's difficult to determine the true intent of the search condition because there are two ways you can interpret it.

> You're looking for everyone named Patterson in the state of California *or* anyone with a ZIP Code that ends with a 9.

> You're specifically looking for everyone named Patterson *and* anyone who lives in California or has a ZIP Code that ends with a 9.

If you have memorized the evaluation order table, you know that the first way is correct because your system should evaluate AND before OR. But are you always going to remember the evaluation sequence? You can avoid this ambiguity and make the search condition clearer by using parentheses to combine and prioritize certain conditions. For example, to follow the first interpretation of the search condition, you define the WHERE clause in this manner.

```
WHERE (CustLastName = 'Patterson' AND CustState = 'CA') OR
CustZipCode LIKE '%9'
```

The parentheses ensure that the database analyzes and evaluates the two comparison conditions *before* it performs the same processes on the pattern match condition.

You could instead follow the second interpretation and define the WHERE clause in this manner:

```
WHERE CustLastName = 'Patterson' AND (CustState = 'CA' OR
CustZipCode LIKE '%9')
```

In this case, the database analyzes and evaluates the first comparison condition *after* it performs those processes on the second comparison condition and the pattern match condition.

The idea of enclosing conditions in parentheses should be familiar to you by now. You learned how to do this when I discussed combining conditions earlier in this chapter. Now I'm trying to emphasize that the placement of the parentheses can have a serious impact on the outcome of the search condition.

You can define any number of parenthetical conditions and even embed them as necessary. Similar to processing expressions, search conditions are processed left to right and then innermost to outermost *except* that when two or more conditions are at an equal level, the database system processes AND first and then OR. Here's how the database handles parenthetical search conditions:

- Parenthetical search conditions are processed before nonparenthetical search conditions.

- Two or more parenthetical search conditions are processed from left to right.

- Embedded parenthetical search conditions within a search condition are processed from innermost to outermost.

After the database begins to analyze a given parenthetical condition, it evaluates all expressions within the condition using the normal order of precedence. If you carefully translate your request and make effective use of parentheses within the search condition, you'll have better results.

Less Is Better Than More

I said at the beginning of this section that the database initially evaluates conditions from left to right and that it invokes the order of precedence when you define and use complex conditions. I also said that the manner in which you use parentheses in a search condition has a direct impact on its outcome. Now I'll pass along a simple, generic tip for speeding up the search condition process: Ask for less. That is, select only those columns you need to fulfill the request, and make the search condition as specific as you can so that your database processes the fewest rows possible. When you need to use multiple conditions, make certain that the condition that excludes the most rows from the result set is processed first so that your database can potentially find the answer faster. (Here's where your understanding of the order of precedence is really beneficial.)

I'll demonstrate this tip with an example I used earlier in this section.

SQL

```
SELECT CustomerID, OrderDate, ShipDate
FROM Orders
WHERE ShipDate = OrderDate
    AND CustomerID = 1001
```

In this instance, a row must fulfill both conditions for it to be included in the result set. Placing the predicates in this order tells your database to search for each ship date that is equal to its respective order date first. Depending on the number of rows in the table, it could take the database quite some time to evaluate this condition. Then the database will search the rows that met the first condition to identify which ones contain customer ID 1001.

Here's perhaps a better way to define the condition:

SQL

```
SELECT CustomerID, OrderDate, ShipDate
FROM Orders
WHERE CustomerID = 1001
  AND ShipDate = OrderDate
```

Now the database is more likely to search for the customer ID first. This condition is more likely to produce a small number of rows, which means that the database will need less time to search for the rows that match the ship date predicate.

You should make this technique a common practice and apply it when you define your search conditions. This will go a long way in helping to ensure that your SELECT statements execute quickly and efficiently. Be sure to study your database system's documentation to learn what other techniques you can apply to optimize the SELECT statement even further.

> ❖ **Note** Virtually all commercial database systems include a query optimizer that looks at your entire request and tries to figure out the fastest way to return the answer. The indexes that your database administrator has defined on columns in your tables have the biggest influence on what most optimizers choose to do. But it doesn't hurt to make it a practice to include the most exclusive search condition first to further influence your database system's optimizer.

Now that you understand combining search conditions, let's take a short side trip to something more complex. What do you do when you want to find rows that contain a range of values compared to another range of values? Read on!

Checking for Overlapping Ranges

BETWEEN works really well when you're looking for a value in a single column that is within a range of values. You also learned that you can test a single value to see whether it is within the range defined by a pair of start/end or low/high columns in your table. But what should you do if you want to find out whether one range overlaps with another? For example, you might want to know all the engagements (each has a start date and an end date) that occur any time during the week of November 12, 2017, through November 18, 2017. You might be tempted to solve the problem using BETWEEN like this:

"Show me the engagements that occur during the week of November 12, 2017, through November 18, 2017."

Translation	Select engagement number, start date, and end date from the engagements table where start date is between November 12, 2017, and November 18, 2017 and end date is between November 12, 2017, and November 18, 2017
Clean Up	Select engagement number, start date, ~~and~~ end date from ~~the~~ engagements ~~table~~ where start date ~~is~~ between ~~November 12, 2017~~ '2017-11-12' and ~~November 18, 2017~~ '2017-11-18' and end date is between ~~November 12, 2017~~ '2017-11-17' and ~~November 18, 2017~~ '2017-11-18'

SQL	`SELECT EngagementNumber, StartDate, EndDate`
	`FROM Engagements`
	`WHERE StartDate`
	`    BETWEEN '2017-11-12' AND '2017-11-18'`
	`AND EndDate BETWEEN '2017-11-12' AND '2017-11-18'`

Close, but no cigar. You really want any engagement that has any date that falls between the two dates in November. To understand why a simple combination of BETWEEN clauses doesn't work, consider Figure 6-12.

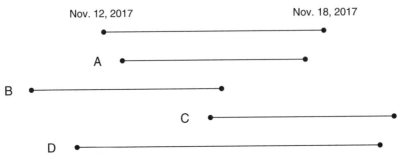

Figure 6-12 *Engagements that occur within the desired date span*

As you can see in the figure, there are four possible engagement date spans that can occur either entirely or partially within the week you want.

- Some engagements occur entirely within the date span, as represented by line A.

- Some start before the date span but end within the date span, as represented by line B.

- Others might start within the date span but end after the date span, as represented by line C.

- And finally, some engagements might start before the date span and not end until after the date span, as shown in line D.

If you think about the request as originally stated, the only engagements you'll find are those that are like line A. B gets excluded because the start date is not between November 12 and November 18 even though part of the engagement occurs within the desired date span. C gets excluded because the end date is not between the two dates of interest. And D gets excluded because both the start and end dates are outside the range even though some dates of the engagement *do* occur entirely within the date span of interest.

So, how do you solve this problem? You explicitly create a search condition for each of the four possible scenarios, like this:

```
WHERE (StartDate BETWEEN '2017-11-12' AND '2017-11-18'
AND EndDate BETWEEN '2017-11-12' AND '2017-11-18')
OR (StartDate <= '2017-11-12')
```

```
AND EndDate BETWEEN '2017-11-12' AND '2017-11-18')
OR (StartDate BETWEEN '2017-11-12' AND '2017-11-18'
AND EndDate >= '2017-11-18')
OR (StartDate <= '2017-11-12'
AND EndDate >= '2017-11-18')
```

Not pretty, is it? But take a look at the figure again. What one thing do all the start dates have in common? They're all less than or equal to the end date of the span! Likewise, the end dates are all greater than or equal to the start date of the span. So the simple answer is as follows:

SQL	
	`SELECT EngagementNumber, StartDate, EndDate`
	`FROM Engagements`
	`WHERE StartDate <= '2017-11-18'`
	`AND EndDate >= '2017-11-12'`

Isn't that a lot simpler? Keep this solution in mind—you'll need it to solve one of the sample problems at the end of the chapter. Now back to my regular programming—let's revisit Nulls.

Nulls Revisited: A Cautionary Note

Now is as good a time as any to remind you about Nulls. You learned in Chapter 5 that a Null represents the absence of a value and that an expression processing a Null value will return a Null value. The same holds true for search conditions as well. A predicate that evaluates a Null value *can never be true*. This might seem confusing, but the predicate can never be false either! The SQL Standard defines the result of any predicate that evaluates a Null as *unknown*. Remember that a predicate must be true for a row to be selected, so a false or unknown result will reject the row.

To help clarify the matter, let's reexamine in Figures 6-13 and 6-14 the truth tables I first showed you in Figures 6-9 and 6-10. But this time, let's include the unknown result you will get if a Null is involved.

Second Expression

AND	True	False	Unknown
True	True (Rows are selected)	False (Rows are rejected)	Unknown (Rows are rejected)
False	False (Rows are rejected)	False (Rows are rejected)	False (Rows are rejected)
Unknown	Unknown (Rows are rejected)	False (Rows are rejected)	Unknown (Rows are rejected)

(First Expression labels the rows on the left)

Figure 6-13 *The result of combining two predicate expressions with the AND operator when either expression is Null (unknown)*

Second Expression

OR	True	False	Unknown
True	True (Rows are selected)	True (Rows are selected)	True (Rows are selected)
False	True (Rows are selected)	False (Rows are rejected)	Unknown (Rows are rejected)
Unknown	True (Rows are selected)	Unknown (Rows are rejected)	Unknown (Rows are rejected)

(First Expression labels the rows on the left)

Figure 6-14 *The result of combining two predicate expressions with the OR operator when either expression is Null (unknown)*

You can see that an unknown result from evaluating a predicate on a Null column really throws a monkey wrench into the picture! For example, let's assume you have a simple comparison predicate: A = B. If either A or B for a given row is the Null value, then the result of the comparison is unknown. Because the result is not true, the row won't be selected. If A = B is not true, you might expect that NOT (A = B) would be true. No! This is unknown also. Figure 6-15 helps you understand how this is so.

(Expression)	NOT (Expression)
True	False
False	True
Unknown	Unknown

Figure 6-15 *The result of applying NOT to a true/false/unknown value*

Suppose you're making the following request to the database:

"Let me see the names and phone numbers of King County residents whose last names are Hernandez."

Translation	Select first name, last name, and phone number from the customers table where the county name is 'King' and the last name is 'Hernandez'
Clean Up	Select first name, last name, ~~and~~ phone number from ~~the~~ customers ~~table~~ where ~~the~~ county ~~name is~~ = 'King' and ~~the~~ last name ~~is~~ = 'Hernandez'
SQL	SELECT CustFirstName, CustLastName, CustPhoneNumber FROM Customers WHERE CustCounty = 'King' AND CustLastName = 'Hernandez'

As you know, a row must meet *both* conditions to be included in the result set. If either the county name or the last name is Null, the database disregards the row completely.

Let's now consider this request:

"Show me the names of all staff members who are graduate counselors or were hired on September 1, 2007."

Translation	Select last name and first name from the staff table where the title is 'graduate counselor' or date hired is September 1, 2007
Clean Up	Select last name ~~and~~ first name from ~~the~~ staff ~~table~~ where ~~the~~ title ~~is~~ = 'graduate counselor' or date hired ~~is~~ = ~~September 1,2007~~ '2007-09-01'
SQL	SELECT StfLastName, StfFirstName FROM Staff WHERE Title = 'Graduate Counselor' OR DateHired = '2007-09-01'

Although you might expect Nulls to have the same effect on conditions combined with OR as they do on conditions combined with AND, that is not necessarily the case. A row still has a chance of being included in the result set as long as it meets *either* of these conditions. Take a look at Figure 6-14 again. Based on the values of Title and DateHired, Table 6-2 shows how the database determines whether to send a row to the result set when you combine the predicates with OR.

Table 6-2 *Determining the Result Set with OR*

Value of Title	Value of DateHired	Result
Graduate Counselor	2007-09-01	The row is included in the result set because it meets both conditions.
Graduate Counselor	2007-11-15	The row is included in the result set because it meets the first condition.
Registrar	2007-09-01	The row is included in the result set because it meets the second condition.
Graduate Counselor	Null	The row is included in the result set because it meets the first condition.
Null	2007-09-01	The row is included in the result set because it meets the second condition.
Null	Null	The row is excluded from the result set because it does not meet either condition.

When you suspect that a result set is displaying incorrect information, test any columns you're using as criteria with the Null condition. This will give you the opportunity to deal with any Null values as appropriate, and you can then execute your original SELECT statement once again. For example, if you think there might be a few graduate counselors missing from the result set, you could execute the following SELECT statement to determine whether this is true:

SQL	`SELECT StfLastName, StfFirstName, Title`
	`FROM Staff`
	`WHERE Title IS NULL`

If there are Null values in the Title column, this SELECT statement will produce a result set that contains the names of all staff members who do not have a title specified in the database. Now you can deal with this data as appropriate and then return to your original SELECT statement.

I'm not done dealing with Nulls just yet. I'll revisit Nulls once more in Chapter 12, "Simple Totals," when I discuss SELECT statements that summarize data.

Expressing Conditions in Different Ways

One side benefit to everything you've learned in this chapter is that you now can express a given condition in various ways. Let's take a look at this by considering the following request:

"Give me the name of every employee who was hired in October 2007."

You need to search for hire dates that fall between October 1, 2007, and October 31, 2007, to answer this request. Based on what you've already learned, you can define the condition in two ways:

```
DateHired BETWEEN '2007-10-01' AND '2007-10-31'
DateHired >= '2007-10-01' AND DateHired <= '2007-10-31'
```

Both of these conditions will send the same rows to the result set—the condition you choose to use is only a matter of preference. Some people find the first expression easier to understand, although others prefer the second expression.

Here are some other examples of equivalent conditions:

"Show me the vendors who are based in California, Oregon, or Washington."

```
VendState IN ('CA', 'OR', 'WA')
VendState = 'CA' OR VendState = 'OR' OR VendState = 'WA'
```

"Give me a list of customers whose last name begins with 'H'."

```
CustLastName >= 'H' AND CustLastName <= 'HZ'
CustLastName BETWEEN 'H' AND 'HZ'
CustLastName LIKE 'H%'
```

"Show me all the students who do not live in Seattle or Redmond."

```
StudCity <> 'Seattle' AND StudCity <> 'Redmond'
StudCity NOT IN ('Seattle', 'Redmond')
NOT (StudCity = 'Seattle' OR StudCity = 'Redmond')
```

There's no wrong way for you to define a condition, but you can define a condition incorrectly by blatantly disregarding its syntax. (As you know, this will cause the condition to fail.) However, some database systems optimize certain types of conditions for speedy processing, making them preferable to other equivalent conditions. Check your database system's documentation to determine whether your system has any preferred methods for defining conditions.

Sample Statements

You've now learned all the techniques you need to build solid search conditions. Let's take a look at some examples of various types of search conditions using the tables from each of the sample databases. These examples illustrate the use of search conditions to filter your data.

I've also included sample result sets that would be returned by these operations and placed them immediately after the SQL syntax line. The name that appears immediately above a result set is the name I gave each query in the sample data on the companion website for the book, www.informit.com/title/9780134858333. I stored each query in the appropriate sample database (as indicated within the example) and pre-fixed the names of the queries relevant to this chapter with "CH06."

You can follow the instructions in the Introduction of this book to load the samples onto your computer and try them.

> ❖ **Note** I've combined the Translation and Clean Up steps for all the examples once again so that you can continue to learn how to consolidate the process.

Sales Orders Database

"Show me all the orders for customer number 1001."

Translation/ Clean Up	Select ~~the~~ order number ~~and~~ customer ID from ~~the~~ orders ~~table~~ where ~~the~~ customer ID ~~is equal to~~ = 1001
SQL	SELECT OrderNumber, CustomerID FROM Orders WHERE CustomerID = 1001

CH06_Orders_for_Customer_1001 (44 Rows)

OrderNumber	CustomerID
2	1001
7	1001
16	1001
52	1001
55	1001
107	1001
137	1001
138	1001
151	1001
154	1001
<< more rows here >>	

"Show me an alphabetized list of products with names that begin with 'Dog'."

Translation/ Clean Up	Select ~~the~~ product name from ~~the~~ products ~~table~~ where ~~the~~ product name like 'Dog%' ~~and~~ order by product name
SQL	SELECT ProductName FROM Products WHERE ProductName LIKE 'Dog%' ORDER BY ProductName

CH06_Products_That_Begin_With_DOG (4 Rows)

ProductName
Dog Ear Aero-Flow Floor Pump
Dog Ear Cyclecomputer
Dog Ear Helmet Mount Mirrors
Dog Ear Monster Grip Gloves

❖ **Note** I just wanted to remind you that you place the ORDER BY clause at *the end* of a SELECT statement. If necessary, review the Sorting Information section in Chapter 4. Also, remember that if you execute a SELECT against the saved view in Microsoft SQL Server, it ignores the ORDER BY specification saved in the view. You have to open the view in the designer and execute it from there to see the sequence displayed above.

Entertainment Agency Database

"Show me an alphabetical list of entertainers based in Bellevue, Redmond, or Woodinville."

Translation/ Clean Up	Select stage name, phone number, ~~and~~ city from ~~the~~ entertainers ~~table~~ where ~~the~~ city ~~is~~ in ('Bellevue', 'Redmond', ~~or~~ 'Woodinville') ~~and~~ order by stage name
SQL	SELECT EntStageName, EntPhoneNumber, EntCity FROM Entertainers WHERE EntCity IN ('Bellevue', 'Redmond', 'Woodinville') ORDER BY EntStageName

CH06_Eastside_Entertainers (7 Rows)

EntStageName	EntPhoneNumber	EntCity
Carol Peacock Trio	555-2691	Redmond
Jazz Persuasion	555-2541	Bellevue
Jim Glynn	555-2531	Bellevue
JV & the Deep Six	555-2511	Redmond
Katherine Ehrlich	555-0399	Woodinville
Modern Dance	555-2631	Woodinville
Susan McLain	555-2301	Bellevue

"Show me all the engagements that run for four days."

Translation/ Clean Up	Select engagement number, start date, ~~and~~ end date from ~~the~~ engagements ~~table~~ where ~~the~~ CAST(end date ~~minus~~ - start date AS INTEGER) ~~is equal to~~ = 3
SQL	SELECT EngagementNumber, StartDate, EndDate FROM Engagements WHERE CAST(EndDate - StartDate AS INTEGER) = 3

CH06_FourDay Engagements (15 Rows)

EngagementNumber	StartDate	EndDate
5	2017-09-12	2017-09-15
13	2017-09-18	2017-09-22
17	2017-09-30	2017-10-03
21	2017-10-01	2017-10-04
56	2017-11-26	2017-11-29
58	2017-12-02	2017-12-05
59	2017-12-02	2017-12-05
63	2017-12-19	2017-12-22
70	2017-12-24	2017-12-27
95	2018-01-16	2018-01-19

<< more rows here >>

> ❖ **Note** An engagement runs from the start date *through* the end date. When subtracting StartDate from EndDate, you get one less day than the total number of days for the engagement. For this reason, I compared the result of the calculation to 3, not 4.

School Scheduling Database

"Show me an alphabetical list of all the staff members and their salaries if they make between $40,000 and $50,000 a year."

Translation/ Clean Up	Select first name, last name, ~~and~~ salary from ~~the~~ staff ~~table~~ where ~~the~~ salary ~~is~~ between 40000 and 50000, ~~then~~ order by last name, ~~and~~ first name
SQL	SELECT StfFirstName, StfLastName, Salary FROM Staff WHERE Salary BETWEEN 40000 AND 50000 ORDER BY StfLastname, StfFirstName

CH06_Staff_Salaries_40K_TO_50K (14 Rows)

StfFirstName	StfLastName	Salary
Robert	Brown	$49,000.00
Kirk	DeGrasse	$45,000.00
Katherine	Ehrlich	$45,000.00
Jim	Glynn	$45,000.00
Liz	Keyser	$48,000.00
Ann	Patterson	$45,000.00
Maria	Patterson	$48,000.00
Mariya	Sergienko	$45,000.00
Tim	Smith	$40,000.00
Caleb	Viescas	$45,000.00

<< more rows here >>

"Show me a list of students whose last name is 'Kennedy' or who live in Seattle."

Translation/ Clean Up	Select first name, last name, ~~and~~ city from ~~the~~ students ~~table~~ where ~~the~~ last name ~~is~~ = 'Kennedy' or ~~the~~ city ~~is~~ = 'Seattle'
SQL	SELECT StudFirstName, StudLastName, StudCity FROM Students WHERE StudLastName = 'Kennedy' 　　OR StudCity = 'Seattle'

CH06_Seattle_Students_And_Students_Named_Kennedy (4 Rows)

StudFirstName	StudLastName	StudCity
Doris	Hartwig	Seattle
John	Kennedy	Portland
Kendra	Bonnicksen	Seattle
Richard	Lum	Seattle

Bowling League Database

"List the ID numbers of the teams that won one or more of the first ten matches in Game 3."

Translation/ Clean Up	Select the team ID, match ID, ~~and~~ game number from ~~the~~ match_games ~~table~~ where ~~the~~ game number ~~is~~ = 3 and ~~the~~ match ID ~~is~~ between 1 and 10
SQL	SELECT WinningTeamID, MatchID, GameNumber FROM Match_Games WHERE GameNumber = 3 AND MatchID BETWEEN 1 AND 10

CH06_Game3_Top_Ten_Matches (10 Rows)

WinningTeamID	MatchID	GameNumber
1	1	3
3	2	3

WinningTeamID	MatchID	GameNumber
5	3	3
7	4	3
3	5	3
4	6	3
5	7	3
8	8	3
2	9	3
1	10	3

"List the bowlers in teams 3, 4, and 5 whose last names begin with the letter 'H'."

Translation/ Clean Up	Select first name, last name, ~~and~~ team ID from ~~the~~ bowlers ~~table~~ where ~~the~~ team ID ~~is either~~ in (3, 4, ~~or~~ 5) and ~~the~~ last name ~~begins with the letter~~ like 'H%'
SQL	SELECT BowlerFirstName, BowlerLastName, TeamID FROM Bowlers WHERE (TeamID IN (3,4,5)) AND (BowlerLastName LIKE 'H%')

CH06_H_Bowlers_Teams_3_Through_5 (4 Rows)

BowlerFirstName	BowlerLastName	TeamID
Elizabeth	Hallmark	4
Gary	Hallmark	4
Kendra	Hernandez	5
Michael	Hernandez	5

Recipes Database

"List the recipes that have no notes."

Translation/ Clean Up	Select ~~the~~ recipe title from ~~the~~ recipes ~~table~~ where notes is ~~empty~~ Null
SQL	SELECT RecipeTitle FROM Recipes WHERE Notes IS NULL

CH06_Recipes_With_No_Notes (6 rows)

RecipeTitle
Irish Stew
Salsa Buena
Fettuccini Alfredo
Mike's Summer Salad
Roast Beef
Yorkshire Pudding

"Show the ingredients that are meats (ingredient class is 2) but that aren't chicken."

Translation/ Clean Up	Select ingredient name from ~~the~~ ingredients ~~table~~ where ingredient class ID ~~is equal to~~ = 2 and ingredient name ~~does~~ not ~~contain~~ like '%chicken%'
SQL	SELECT IngredientName FROM Ingredients WHERE (IngredientClassID = 2) AND (IngredientName NOT LIKE '%chicken%')

CH06_Meats_That_Are_Not_Chicken (5 rows)

IngredientName
Beef
Bacon
T-bone Steak
New York Steak
Ground Pork

❖ **Note** PostgreSQL is case-sensitive, so the above query won't work as written because all the ingredient names contain 'Chicken', not 'chicken'. Be sure to use `IngredientName NOT LIKE '%Chicken%'` in PostgreSQL. Of course, there could be an ingredient named "Ground chicken," so changing to an upper case "C" won't catch that. To be sure, you would have to include a second predicate to test for both upper and lower case. You will need to do the same thing for SQL Server or MySQL if your database was installed with the case-sensitive option. (The default for both is not case-sensitive.)

Summary

In this chapter, I introduced you to the idea of filtering the information you see in a result set by using a search condition in a WHERE clause. You learned that a search condition uses combinations of predicates to filter the data sent to the result set and that predicates are specific tests you can apply to a value expression. I then introduced you to the five basic types of predicates.

My discussion continued with an in-depth look at each of the five basic types of predicates you can define within a search condition of a WHERE clause. You learned how to compare values and how to test whether a value falls within a specified range of values. You also learned how to test whether a value matches one of a defined list of values or is part of a specific pattern string. Additionally, you learned that you could use the NOT operator to exclude rows from a result set.

I then discussed how to use multiple conditions by combining them with AND and OR operators. You learned that a row must meet all conditions combined with AND before it can be included in the result set, whereas it must meet *only one* of those conditions if the conditions are combined with OR. You also learned how to use AND and OR together to answer complex requests. I then took a second look at using NOT to exclude rows from a result set, and you learned that NOT can be used at two different levels in a search condition.

The order of precedence was the next topic of discussion, and you learned how the database analyzes and evaluates conditions. You now know that the database evaluates conditions in a specific order based on the operator used in each condition. You also learned how to use parentheses to alter the order in which the database evaluates certain conditions and to ensure that you avoid defining ambiguous conditions.

I took a brief detour to show you how to search for a range across another range. The answer is surprisingly simple, and it doesn't involve using BETWEEN.

I next took another look at Nulls. Here you learned that Nulls affect conditions in much the way that they affect expressions. You also know that you should test for Null values if you suspect that a result set is displaying incorrect information.

Finally, I discussed the fact that the same condition can be expressed in various ways. You now know, for example, that you can use three different types of conditions to search for people whose last names begin with the letter "H."

In the next part of the book, I'll introduce you to the idea of *sets* and the types of operations you can perform on them. After you learn about sets, you'll be well on your way to learning how to define SELECT statements using multiple tables.

The following section presents several requests that you can work out on your own.

Problems for You to Solve

Below, I show you the request statement and the name of the solution query in the sample databases. If you want some practice, you can work out the SQL you need for each request and then check your answer with the query I saved in the samples. Don't worry if your syntax doesn't exactly match the syntax of the queries I saved—as long as your result set is the same.

Sales Orders Database

1. *"Give me the names of all vendors based in Ballard, Bellevue, and Redmond."*

   You can find the solution in CH06_Ballard_Bellevue_Redmond_ Vendors (3 rows).

2. *"Show me an alphabetized list of products with a retail price of $125.00 or more."*

   (Hint: You'll alphabetize the list using a clause I discussed in a previous chapter.)

   You can find the solution in CH06_Products_Priced_Over_125 (13 rows).

3. *"Which vendors do we work with that don't have a Web site?"*

   You can find the solution in CH06_Vendors_With_No_Website (4 rows).

Entertainment Agency Database

1. *"Let me see a list of all engagements that occurred during October 2017."*

   (Hint: You need to solve this problem by testing for values in a range in the table that contain any values in another range—the first and last dates in October.)

   You can find the solution in CH06_October_2017_Engagements (24 rows).

2. *"Show me any engagements in October 2017 that start between noon and 5 p.m."*

   You can find the solution in CH06_October_Dates_Between_ Noon_and_Five (17 rows).

3. *"List all the engagements that start and end on the same day."*

   You can find the solution in CH06_Single_Day_Engagements (5 rows).

School Scheduling Database

1. *"Show me which staff members use a post office box as their address."*

   You can find the solution in CH06_Staff_Using_POBoxes (3 rows).

2. *"Can you show me which students live outside of the Pacific Northwest?"*

   You can find the solution in CH06_Students_Residing_Outside_ PNW (5 rows).

3. *"List all the subjects that have a subject code starting 'MUS'."*

   You can find the solution in CH06_Subjects_With_MUS_In_ SubjectCode (4 rows).

4. *"Produce a list of the ID numbers all the Associate Professors who are employed full time."*

   You can find the solution in CH06_Full_Time_Associate_ Professors (4 rows).

Bowling League Database

1. *"Give me a list of the tournaments held during September 2017."*

   You can find the solution in CH06_September_2017_Tournament_ Schedule (4 rows).

2. *"What are the tournament schedules for Bolero, Red Rooster, and Thunderbird Lanes?"*

   You can find the solution in CH06_Eastside_Tournaments (9 rows).

3. *"List the bowlers who live on the Eastside (you know—Bellevue, Bothell, Duvall, Redmond, and Woodinville) and who are on teams 5, 6, 7, or 8."*

   (Hint: Use IN for the city list and BETWEEN for the team numbers.)

   You can find the solution in CH06_Eastside_Bowlers_On_ Teams_5_Through_8 (9 rows).

Recipes Database

1. *"List all recipes that are main courses (recipe class is 1) and that have notes."*

   You can find the solution in CH06_Main_Courses_With_Notes (4 rows).

2. *"Display the first five recipes."*

   (Hint: Use BETWEEN on the primary key of the table.)

   You can find the solution in CH06_First_5_Recipes (5 rows).

Part III
Working with Multiple Tables

Thinking in Sets

"Small cheer and a great welcome makes a merry feast."
—William Shakespeare Comedy of Errors, Act 3, scene 1

Topics Covered in This Chapter

What Is a Set, Anyway?

Operations on Sets

Intersection

Difference

Union

SQL Set Operations

Summary

By now, you know how to create a set of information by asking for specific columns or expressions on columns (SELECT), how to sort the rows (ORDER BY), and how to restrict the rows returned (WHERE). Up to this point, I've been focusing on basic exercises involving a single table. But what if you want to know something about information contained in multiple tables? What if you want to compare or contrast sets of information from the same or different tables?

Creating a meal by peeling, slicing, and dicing a single pile of potatoes or a single bunch of carrots is easy. From here on out, most of the problems I'm going to show you how to solve will involve getting data from *multiple* tables. I'm not only going to show you how to put together a good stew—I'm going to teach you how to be a chef!

Before digging into this chapter, you need to know that it's all about the *concepts* you must understand in order to successfully link two or more sets of information. I'm also going to give you a brief overview of some specific syntax defined in the SQL Standard that directly supports the pure definition of these concepts. Be forewarned, however, that many current commercial implementations of SQL do not yet support this "pure" syntax. In later chapters, I'll show you how to implement the concepts you'll learn here using SQL syntax that is commonly supported by most major database systems. What I'm after here is not the letter of the law but rather the spirit of the law.

What Is a Set, Anyway?

If you were a teenager any time from the mid-1960s onward, you might have studied set theory in a mathematics course. (Remember New Math? Maybe you're not old enough!) If you were introduced to set algebra, you probably wondered why any of it would ever be useful.

Now you're trying to learn about relational databases and this quirky language called SQL to build applications, solve problems, or just get answers to your questions. Were you paying attention in algebra class? If so, solving problems—particularly complex ones—in SQL will be much easier.

Actually, you've been working with sets from the beginning of this book. In Chapter 1, "What Is Relational?," you learned about the basic structure of a relational database—tables containing rows that are made up of one or more columns. Each table in your database is a *set* of information about one subject. In Chapter 2, "Ensuring Your Database Structure Is Sound," you learned how to verify that the structure of your database is sound. Each table should contain the *set* of information related to one and only one subject or action.

In Chapter 4, "Creating a Simple Query," you learned how to build a basic SELECT statement in SQL to retrieve a result *set* of information that contains specific columns from a single table and how to sort those result sets. In Chapter 5, "Getting More Than Simple Columns," you learned how to glean a new *set* of information from a table by writing expressions that operate on one or more columns. In Chapter 6, "Filtering Your Data," you learned how to restrict further the *set* of information you retrieve from your tables by adding a filter (WHERE clause) to your query.

As you can see, a set can be as little as the data from one column from one row in one table. Actually, you can construct a request in SQL that returns no rows—an empty set. Sometimes it's useful to discover that something does *not* exist. A set can also be multiple columns (including columns you create with expressions) from multiple rows fetched from multiple tables. Each row in a result set is a *member* of the set. The values in the columns are specific *attributes* of each member—data items that describe the member of the set. In the next several chapters, I'll show how to ask for information from multiple sets of data and link these sets together to get answers to more complex questions. First, however, you need to understand more about sets and the logical ways to combine them.

Operations on Sets

In Chapter 1, I discussed how Dr. E. F. Codd invented the relational model on which most modern databases and SQL are based. Two branches of mathematics—set theory and first-order predicate logic—formed the foundation of his new model.

To graduate beyond getting answers from only a single table, you need to learn how to use result sets of information to solve more complex problems. These complex problems usually require using one of the common set operations to link data from two or more tables. Sometimes, you'll need to get two different result sets from the same table and then combine them to get your answer.

The three most common set operations are as follows:

- **Intersection**—You use this to find the common elements in two or more different sets: "List all students and the classes for which they are currently enrolled." "Show me the recipes that contain *both lamb and rice*." "*Show me the customers who ordered both bicycles and helmets.*"

- **Difference**—You use this to find items that are in one set but not another: "Show me the recipes that contain lamb *but do not contain rice*." "Show me the customers who ordered a bicycle *but not a helmet*."

- **Union**—You use this to combine two or more similar sets: "Show me all the recipes that contain *either lamb or rice*." "Show me the customers who ordered *either a bicycle or a helmet*." "List the names and addresses *for both staff and students*."

In the following three sections, I'll explain these basic set operations—the ones you should have learned in high school algebra. The "SQL Set Operations" section later in this chapter gives an overview of how these operations are implemented in "pure" SQL.

Intersection

No, it's not your local street corner. An *intersection* of two sets contains the common elements of two sets. Let's first take a look at an intersection from the pure perspective of set theory and then see how you can use an intersection to solve business problems.

Intersection in Set Theory

An intersection is a very powerful mathematical tool often used by scientists and engineers. As a scientist, you might be interested in finding common points between two sets of chemical or physical sample data. For example, a pharmaceutical research chemist might have two compounds that seem to provide a certain beneficial effect. Finding the commonality (the intersection) between the two compounds might help discover what it is that makes the two compounds effective. Or, an engineer might be interested in finding the intersection between one alloy that is hard but brittle and another alloy that is soft but resilient.

Let's take a look at intersection in action by examining two sets of numbers. In this example, each single number is a member of the set. The first set of numbers is as follows:

1, 5, 8, 9, 32, 55, 78

The second set of numbers is as follows:

3, 7, 8, 22, 55, 71, 99

The intersection of these two sets of numbers is the numbers common to both sets:

8, 55

The individual entries—the members—of each set don't have to be just single values. In fact, when solving problems with SQL, you'll probably deal with sets of rows.

According to set theory, when a member of a set is something more than a single number or value, each member (or object) of the set has multiple attributes or bits of data that describe the properties of each member. For example, your favorite stew recipe is a complex member of the set of all recipes that contains many different ingredients. Each ingredient is an attribute of your complex stew member.

To find the intersection between two sets of complex set members, you have to find the members that match on all the attributes. Also, all the members in each set you're trying to compare must have the same number and type of attributes. For example, suppose you have a complex set like the one below, in which each row represents a member of the set (a stew recipe), and each column denotes a particular attribute (an ingredient).

Potatoes	Water	Lamb	Peas
Rice	Chicken Stock	Chicken	Carrots
Pasta	Water	Tofu	Snap Peas
Potatoes	Beef Stock	Beef	Cabbage
Pasta	Water	Pork	Onions

A second set might look like the following:

Potatoes	Water	Lamb	Onions
Rice	Chicken Stock	Turkey	Carrots
Pasta	Vegetable Stock	Tofu	Snap Peas
Potatoes	Beef Stock	Beef	Cabbage
Beans	Water	Pork	Onions

The intersection of these two sets is the one member whose attributes all match in both sets:

Potatoes	Beef Stock	Beef	Cabbage

Intersection between Result Sets

If the previous examples look like rows in a table or a result set to you, you're on the right track! When you're dealing with rows in a set of data that you fetch with SQL, the attributes are the individual columns. For example, suppose you have a set of rows returned by a query like the following one. (These are recipes from my cookbook.)

Recipe	Starch	Stock	Meat	Vegetable
Lamb Stew	Potatoes	Water	Lamb	Peas
Chicken Stew	Rice	Chicken Stock	Chicken	Carrots
Veggie Stew	Pasta	Water	Tofu	Snap Peas
Irish Stew	Potatoes	Beef Stock	Beef	Cabbage
Pork Stew	Pasta	Water	Pork	Onions

A second query result set might look like the following. (These are recipes from my friend Mike's cookbook.)

Recipe	Starch	Stock	Meat	Vegetable
Lamb Stew	Potatoes	Water	Lamb	Peas
Turkey Stew	Rice	Chicken Stock	Turkey	Carrots
Veggie Stew	Pasta	Vegetable Stock	Tofu	Snap Peas
Irish Stew	Potatoes	Beef Stock	Beef	Cabbage
Pork Stew	Beans	Water	Pork	Onions

The intersection of these two sets is the two members whose attributes all match in both sets—that is, the two recipes that Mike and John have in common.

Recipe	Starch	Stock	Meat	Vegetable
Lamb Stew	Potatoes	Water	Lamb	Peas
Irish Stew	Potatoes	Beef Stock	Beef	Cabbage

Sometimes it's easier to see how intersection works using a set diagram. A *set diagram* is an elegant yet simple way to diagram sets of information and graphically represent how the sets intersect or overlap. You might also have heard this sort of diagram called a Euler or Venn diagram. (By the way, Leonard Euler was an eighteenth-century Swiss mathematician, and John Venn used this particular type of logic diagram in 1880 in a paper he wrote while a Fellow at Cambridge University. So you can see that "thinking in sets" is not a particularly modern concept!)

Let's assume you have a nice database containing all your favorite recipes. You really like the way onions enhance the flavor of beef, so you're interested in finding all recipes that contain both beef and onions. Figure 7-1 shows the set diagram that helps you visualize how to solve this problem.

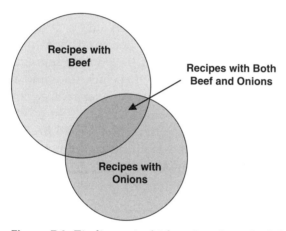

Figure 7-1 *Finding out which recipes have both beef and onions*

The upper circle represents the set of recipes that contain beef. The lower circle represents the set of recipes that contain onions. Where the two circles overlap is where you'll find the recipes that contain both—the intersection of the two sets. As you can imagine, you first ask SQL to fetch all the recipes that have beef. In the second query, you ask SQL to fetch all the recipes that have onions. As you'll see later, you can use a special SQL keyword—INTERSECT—to link the two queries to get the final answer.

Yes, I know what you're thinking. If your recipe table looks like the samples above, you could simply say the following:

"Show me the recipes that have beef as the meat ingredient and onions as the vegetable ingredient."

Translation	Select the recipe name from the recipes table where meat ingredient is beef and vegetable ingredient is onions
Clean Up	Select ~~the~~ recipe name from ~~the~~ recipes ~~table~~ where meat ingredient ~~is~~ = 'beef' and vegetable ingredient ~~is~~ = 'onions'
SQL	SELECT RecipeName FROM Recipes WHERE MeatIngredient = 'Beef' AND VegetableIngredient = 'Onions'

Hold on now! If you remember the lessons you learned in Chapter 2, you know that a single Recipes table probably won't cut it. (Pun intended!) What about recipes that have ingredients other than meat and vegetables? What about the fact that some recipes have many ingredients and others have only a few? A correctly designed recipes database will have a separate Recipe_Ingredients table with one row per recipe per ingredient. Each ingredient row will have only one ingredient, so no single row can be both beef and onions at the same time. You'll need first to find all the beef rows, then find all the onions rows, and then intersect them on RecipeID. (If you're confused about why I'm criticizing the previous table design, be sure to go back and read Chapter 2!)

How about a more complex problem? Let's say you want to add carrots to the mix. A set diagram to visualize the solution might look like Figure 7-2.

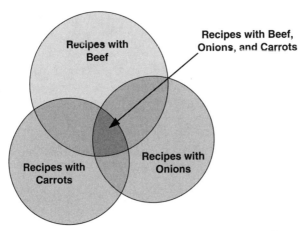

Figure 7-2 *Determining which recipes have beef, onions, and carrots*

Got the hang of it? The bottom line is that when you're faced with solving a problem involving complex criteria, a set diagram can be an invaluable way to see the solution expressed as the intersection of SQL result sets.

Problems You Can Solve with an Intersection

As you might guess, you can use an intersection to find the matches between two or more sets of information. Here's just a small sample of the problems you can solve using an intersection technique with data from the sample databases:

> *"Show me customers and employees who have the same name."*
>
> *"Find all the customers who ordered a bicycle and also ordered a helmet."*
>
> *"List the entertainers who played engagements for customers Bonnicksen and Rosales."*
>
> *"Show me the students who have an average score of 85 or better in Art and who also have an average score of 85 or better in Computer Science."*
>
> *"Find the bowlers who had a raw score of 155 or better at both Thunderbird Lanes and Bolero Lanes."*
>
> *"Show me the recipes that have beef and garlic."*

One of the limitations of using a pure intersection is that the values must match in all the columns in each result set. This works well if you're intersecting two or more sets from the same table—for example, customers who ordered bicycles and customers who ordered helmets. It also works well when you're intersecting sets from tables that have similar columns—for example, customer names and employee names. In many cases, however, you'll want to find solutions that require a match on only a few column values from each set. For this type of problem, SQL provides an operation called a JOIN—an intersection on key values. Here's a sample of problems you can solve with a JOIN:

> *"Show me customers and employees who live in the same city."* (JOIN on the city name.)
>
> *"List customers and the entertainers they booked."* (JOIN on the engagement number.)

"Find the agents and entertainers who live in the same ZIP Code."
(JOIN on the ZIP Code.)

"Show me the students and their teachers who have the same first name." (JOIN on the first name.)

"Find the bowlers who are on the same team." (JOIN on the team ID.)

"Display all the ingredients for recipes that contain carrots." (JOIN on the ingredient ID.)

Never fear. In the next chapter I'll show you all about solving these problems (and more) by using JOINs. And because so few commercial implementations of SQL support INTERSECT, I'll show how to use a JOIN to solve many problems that might otherwise require an INTERSECT.

Difference

What's the difference between 21 and 10? If you answered 11, you're on the right track! A *difference* operation (sometimes also called subtract, minus, or except) takes one set of values and removes the set of values from a second set. What remains is the set of values in the first set that are *not* in the second set. (As you'll see later, EXCEPT is the keyword used in the SQL Standard.)

Difference in Set Theory

Difference is another very powerful mathematical tool. As a scientist, you might be interested in finding what's different about two sets of chemical or physical sample data. For example, a pharmaceutical research chemist might have two compounds that seem to be very similar, but one provides a certain beneficial effect and the other does not. Finding what's different about the two compounds might help uncover why one works and the other does not. As an engineer, you might have two similar designs, but one works better than the other. Finding the difference between the two designs could be crucial to eliminating structural flaws in future buildings.

Let's take a look at difference in action by examining two sets of numbers. The first set of numbers is as follows:

1, 5, 8, 9, 32, 55, 78

The second set of numbers is as follows:

3, 7, 8, 22, 55, 71, 99

The difference of the first set of numbers minus the second set of numbers is the numbers that exist in the first set but not the second:

1, 5, 9, 32, 78

Note that you can turn the previous difference operation around. Thus, the difference of the second set minus the first set is

3, 7, 22, 71, 99

The members of each set don't have to be single values. In fact, you'll most likely be dealing with sets of rows when trying to solve problems with SQL.

Earlier in this chapter I said that when a member of a set is something more than a single number or value, each member of the set has multiple attributes (bits of information that describe the properties of each member). For example, your favorite stew recipe is a complex member of the set of all recipes that contains many different ingredients. You can think of each ingredient as an attribute of your complex stew member.

To find the difference between two sets of complex set members, you have to find the members that match on all the attributes in the second set with members in the first set. Don't forget that all of the members in each set you're trying to compare must have the same number and type of attributes. Remove from the first set all the matching members you find in the second set, and the result is the difference. For example, suppose you have a complex set like the one below. Each row represents a member of the set (a stew recipe), and each column denotes a particular attribute (an ingredient).

Potatoes	Water	Lamb	Peas
Rice	Chicken Stock	Chicken	Carrots
Pasta	Water	Tofu	Snap Peas
Potatoes	Beef Stock	Beef	Cabbage
Pasta	Water	Pork	Onions

A second set might look like this:

Potatoes	Water	Lamb	Onions
Rice	Chicken Stock	Turkey	Carrots
Pasta	Vegetable Stock	Tofu	Snap Peas
Potatoes	Beef Stock	Beef	Cabbage
Beans	Water	Pork	Onions

The difference of the first set minus the second set is the objects in the first set that don't exist in the second set:

Potatoes	Water	Lamb	Peas
Rice	Chicken Stock	Chicken	Carrots
Pasta	Water	Tofu	Snap Peas
Pasta	Water	Pork	Onions

Difference between Result Sets

When you're dealing with rows in a set of data fetched with SQL, the attributes are the individual columns. For example, suppose you have a set of rows returned by a query like the following one. (These are recipes from John's cookbook.)

Recipe	Starch	Stock	Meat	Vegetable
Lamb Stew	Potatoes	Water	Lamb	Peas
Chicken Stew	Rice	Chicken Stock	Chicken	Carrots
Veggie Stew	Pasta	Water	Tofu	Snap Peas
Irish Stew	Potatoes	Beef Stock	Beef	Cabbage
Pork Stew	Pasta	Water	Pork	Onions

A second query result set might look like the following. (These are recipes from Mike's cookbook.)

Recipe	Starch	Stock	Meat	Vegetable
Lamb Stew	Potatoes	Water	Lamb	Peas
Turkey Stew	Rice	Chicken Stock	Turkey	Carrots
Veggie Stew	Pasta	Vegetable Stock	Tofu	Snap Peas
Irish Stew	Potatoes	Beef Stock	Beef	Cabbage
Pork Stew	Beans	Water	Pork	Onions

The difference between John's recipes and Mike's recipes (John's minus Mike's) is all the recipes in John's cookbook that *do not* appear in Mike's cookbook.

Recipe	Starch	Stock	Meat	Vegetable
Chicken Stew	Rice	Chicken Stock	Chicken	Carrots
Veggie Stew	Pasta	Water	Tofu	Snap Peas
Pork Stew	Pasta	Water	Pork	Onions

You can also turn this problem around. Suppose you want to find the recipes in Mike's cookbook that *are not* in John's cookbook. Here's the answer:

Recipe	Starch	Stock	Meat	Vegetable
Turkey Stew	Rice	Chicken Stock	Turkey	Carrots
Veggie Stew	Pasta	Vegetable Stock	Tofu	Snap Peas
Pork Stew	Beans	Water	Pork	Onions

Again, I can use a set diagram to help visualize how a difference operation works. Let's assume you have a nice database containing all your favorite recipes. You really do not like the way onions taste with beef, so you're interested in finding all recipes that contain beef but not onions. Figure 7-3 shows you the set diagram that helps you visualize how to solve this problem.

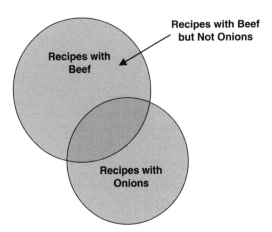

Figure 7-3 *Finding out which recipes have beef but not onions*

The upper full circle represents the set of recipes that contain beef. The lower full circle represents the set of recipes that contain onions. As you remember from the discussion about INTERSECT, where the two circles overlap is where you'll find the recipes that contain both. The dark-shaded part of the upper circle that's not part of the overlapping area represents the set of recipes that contain beef but do not contain onions. Likewise, the part of the lower circle that's not part of the overlapping area represents the set of recipes that contain onions but do not contain beef.

You probably know that you first ask SQL to fetch all the recipes that have beef. Next, you ask SQL to fetch all the recipes that have onions. (As you'll see later in this chapter, the special SQL keyword EXCEPT links the two queries to get the final answer.)

Are you falling into the trap again? (You *did* read Chapter 2, didn't you?) If your recipe table looks like the samples earlier, you might think that you could simply say the following:

"Show me the recipes that have beef as the meat ingredient and that do not have onions as the vegetable ingredient."

Translation	Select the recipe name from the recipes table where meat ingredient is beef and vegetable ingredient is not onions
Clean Up	Select ~~the~~ recipe name from ~~the~~ recipes ~~table~~ where meat ingredient ~~is~~ = 'beef' and vegetable ingredient ~~is not~~ <> 'onions'
SQL	SELECT RecipeName FROM Recipes WHERE MeatIngredient = 'Beef' AND VegetableIngredient <> 'Onions'

Again, as you learned in Chapter 2, a single Recipes table isn't such a hot idea. (Pun intended!) What about recipes that have ingredients other than meat and vegetables? What about the fact that some recipes have many ingredients and others have only a few? A correctly designed Recipes database will have a separate Recipe_Ingredients table with one row per recipe per ingredient. Each ingredient row will have only one ingredient, so no one row can be both beef and onions at the same time. You'll need first to find all the beef rows, then find all the onions rows, then difference them on RecipeID.

How about a more complex problem? Let's say you hate carrots, too. A set diagram to visualize the solution might look like Figure 7-4.

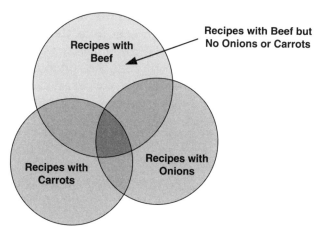

Figure 7-4 *Finding out which recipes have beef but no onions or carrots*

First you need to find the set of recipes that have beef, and then get the difference with either the set of recipes containing onions or the set containing carrots. Take that result and get the difference again with the remaining set (onions or carrots) to leave only the recipes that have beef but no carrots or onions (the light-shaded area in the upper circle).

Problems You Can Solve with Difference

Unlike intersection (which looks for common members of two sets), difference looks for members that are in one set but *not* in another set. Here's just a small sample of the problems you can solve using a difference technique with data from the sample databases:

> *"Show me customers whose names are not the same as any employee."*
>
> *"Find all the customers who ordered a bicycle but did not order a helmet."*
>
> *"List the entertainers who played engagements for customer Bonnicksen but did not play any engagement for customer Rosales."*
>
> *"Show me the students who have an average score of 85 or better in Art but do not have an average score of 85 or better in Computer Science."*
>
> *"Find the bowlers who had a raw score of 155 or better at Thunderbird Lanes but not at Bolero Lanes."*
>
> *"Show me the recipes that have beef but not garlic."*

One of the limitations of using a pure difference is that the values must match in all the columns in each result set. This works well if you're finding the difference between two or more sets from the same table—for example, customers who ordered bicycles and customers who ordered helmets. It also works well when you're finding the difference between sets from tables that have similar columns—for example, customer names and employee names.

In many cases, however, you'll want to find solutions that require a match on only a few column values from each set. For this type of problem, SQL provides an OUTER JOIN operation, which is an intersection on key values that includes the unmatched values from one or both of the two sets. Here's a sample of problems you can solve with an OUTER JOIN:

> *"Show me customers who do not live in the same city as any employees."* (OUTER JOIN on the city name.)
>
> *"List customers and the entertainers they did not book."* (OUTER JOIN on the engagement number.)

"Find the agents who are not in the same ZIP Code as any enter-tainer." (OUTER JOIN on the ZIP Code.)

"Show me the students who do not have the same first name as any teachers." (OUTER JOIN on the first name.)

"Find the bowlers who have an average of 150 or higher who have never bowled a game below 125." (OUTER JOIN on the bowler ID from two different tables.)

"Display all the ingredients for recipes that do not have carrots." (OUTER JOIN on the recipe ID.)

Don't worry! I'll show you all about solving these problems (and more) using OUTER JOINs in Chapter 9, "OUTER JOINs." Also, because only a few commercial implementations of SQL support EXCEPT (the keyword for difference), I'll show how to use an OUTER JOIN to solve many problems that might otherwise require an EXCEPT. In Chapter 18, "'NOT' and 'AND' Problems," I'll show you additional ways to solve EXCEPT problems.

Union

So far I've discussed finding the items that are common in two sets (intersection) and the items that are different (difference). The third type of set operation involves adding two sets (union).

Union in Set Theory

Union lets you combine two sets of similar information into one set. As a scientist, you might be interested in combining two sets of chemical or physical sample data. For example, a pharmaceutical research chemist might have two different sets of compounds that seem to provide a certain beneficial effect. The chemist can union the two sets to obtain a single list of all effective compounds.

Let's take a look at union in action by examining two sets of numbers. The first set of numbers is as follows:

1, 5, 8, 9, 32, 55, 78

The second set of numbers is as follows:

3, 7, 8, 22, 55, 71, 99

The union of these two sets of numbers is the numbers in both sets combined into one new set:

1, 5, 8, 9, 32, 55, 78, 3, 7, 22, 71, 99

Note that the values common to both sets, 8 and 55, appear only once in the answer. Also, the sequence of the numbers in the result set is not necessarily in any specific order. When you ask a database system to perform a UNION, the values returned won't necessarily be in sequence unless you explicitly include an ORDER BY clause. In SQL, you can also ask for a UNION ALL if you want to see the duplicate members.

The members of each set don't have to be just single values. In fact, you'll probably deal with sets of rows when working with SQL.

To find the union of two or more sets of complex members, all the members in each set you're trying to union must have the same number and type of attributes. For example, suppose you have a complex set like the one below. Each row represents a member of the set (a stew recipe), and each column denotes a particular attribute (an ingredient).

Potatoes	Water	Lamb	Peas
Rice	Chicken Stock	Chicken	Carrots
Pasta	Water	Tofu	Snap Peas
Potatoes	Beef Stock	Beef	Cabbage
Pasta	Water	Pork	Onions

A second set might look like the following:

Potatoes	Water	Lamb	Onions
Rice	Chicken Stock	Turkey	Carrots
Pasta	Vegetable Stock	Tofu	Snap Peas
Potatoes	Beef Stock	Beef	Cabbage
Beans	Water	Pork	Onions

The union of these two sets is the set of objects from both sets. Duplicates are eliminated.

Potatoes	Water	Lamb	Peas
Rice	Chicken Stock	Chicken	Carrots
Pasta	Water	Tofu	Snap Peas
Potatoes	Beef Stock	Beef	Cabbage
Pasta	Water	Pork	Onions
Potatoes	Water	Lamb	Onions
Rice	Chicken Stock	Turkey	Carrots
Pasta	Vegetable Stock	Tofu	Snap Peas
Beans	Water	Pork	Onions

Combining Result Sets Using a Union

It's a small leap from sets of complex objects to rows in SQL result sets. When you're dealing with rows in a set of data that you fetch with SQL, the attributes are the individual columns. For example, suppose you have a set of rows returned by a query like the following one. (These are recipes from John's cookbook.)

Recipe	Starch	Stock	Meat	Vegetable
Lamb Stew	Potatoes	Water	Lamb	Peas
Chicken Stew	Rice	Chicken Stock	Chicken	Carrots
Veggie Stew	Pasta	Water	Tofu	Snap Peas
Irish Stew	Potatoes	Beef Stock	Beef	Cabbage
Pork Stew	Pasta	Water	Pork	Onions

A second query result set might look like this one. (These are recipes from Mike's cookbook).

Recipe	Starch	Stock	Meat	Vegetable
Lamb Stew	Potatoes	Water	Lamb	Peas
Turkey Stew	Rice	Chicken Stock	Turkey	Carrots
Veggie Stew	Pasta	Vegetable Stock	Tofu	Snap Peas
Irish Stew	Potatoes	Beef Stock	Beef	Cabbage
Pork Stew	Beans	Water	Pork	Onions

The union of these two sets is all the rows in both sets. Maybe John and Mike decided to write a cookbook together, too!

Recipe	Starch	Stock	Meat	Vegetable
Lamb Stew	Potatoes	Water	Lamb	Peas
Chicken Stew	Rice	Chicken Stock	Chicken	Carrots
Veggie Stew	Pasta	Water	Tofu	Snap Peas
Irish Stew	Potatoes	Beef Stock	Beef	Cabbage
Pork Stew	Pasta	Water	Pork	Onions
Turkey Stew	Rice	Chicken Stock	Turkey	Carrots
Veggie Stew	Pasta	Vegetable Stock	Tofu	Snap Peas
Pork Stew	Beans	Water	Pork	Onions

Let's assume you have a nice database containing all your favorite recipes. You really like recipes with either beef or onions, so you want a list of recipes that contain either ingredient. Figure 7-5 shows you the set diagram that helps you visualize how to solve this problem.

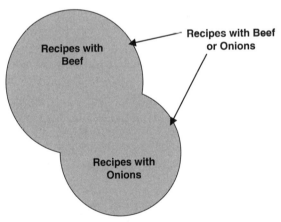

Figure 7-5 *Finding out which recipes have either beef or onions*

The upper circle represents the set of recipes that contain beef. The lower circle represents the set of recipes that contain onions. The union of the two circles gives you all the recipes that contain either ingredient, with duplicates eliminated where the two sets overlap. As you probably know, you first ask SQL to fetch all the recipes that have beef. In the second query, you ask SQL to fetch all the recipes that have onions. As you'll see later, the SQL keyword UNION links the two queries to get the final answer.

By now you know that it's not a good idea to design a recipes database with a single table. Instead, a correctly designed recipes database will have a separate Recipe_Ingredients table with one row per recipe per ingredient. Each ingredient row will have only one ingredient, so no one row can be both beef or onions at the same time. You'll need to first find all the recipes that have a beef row, then find all the recipes that have an onions row, and then union them.

Problems You Can Solve with Union

A union lets you "mush together" rows from two similar sets—with the added advantage of no duplicate rows. Here's a sample of the problems you can solve using a union technique with data from the sample databases:

> *"Show me all the customer and employee names and addresses."*
>
> *"List all the customers who ordered a bicycle combined with all the customers who ordered a helmet."*
>
> *"List the entertainers who played engagements for customer Bonnicksen combined with all the entertainers who played engagements for customer Rosales."*
>
> *"Show me the students who have an average score of 85 or better in Art together with the students who have an average score of 85 or better in Computer Science."*
>
> *"Find the bowlers who had a raw score of 155 or better at Thunderbird Lanes combined with bowlers who had a raw score of 140 or better at Bolero Lanes."*
>
> *"Show me the recipes that have beef together with the recipes that have garlic."*

As with other "pure" set operations, one of the limitations is that the values must match in all the columns in each result set. This works well if you're unioning two or more sets from the same table—for example, customers who ordered bicycles and customers who ordered helmets. It also works well when you're performing a union on sets from tables that have like columns—for example, customer names and addresses and employee names and addresses. I'll explore the uses of the SQL UNION operator in detail in Chapter 10, "UNIONs."

In many cases where you would otherwise union rows from the same table, you'll find that using DISTINCT (to eliminate the duplicate rows) with complex criteria on joined tables will serve as well. I'll show you all about solving problems this way using JOINs in Chapter 8, "INNER JOINs."

SQL Set Operations

Now that you have a basic understanding of set operations, let's look briefly at how they're implemented in SQL.

Classic Set Operations versus SQL

As noted earlier, not many commercial database systems yet support set intersection (INTERSECT) or set difference (EXCEPT) directly. The current SQL Standard, however, clearly defines how these operations should be implemented. I think that these set operations are important enough to at least warrant an overview of the syntax.

As promised, I'll show you alternative ways to solve an intersection or difference problem in later chapters using JOINs. Because most database systems do support UNION, Chapter 10 is devoted to its use. The remainder of this chapter gives you an overview of all three operations.

Finding Common Values: INTERSECT

Let's say you're trying to solve the following seemingly simple problem:

"Show me the orders that contain both a bike and a helmet."

Translation	Select the distinct order numbers from the order details table where the product number is in the list of bike and helmet product numbers
Clean Up	Select ~~the~~ distinct order numbers from ~~the~~ order details ~~table~~ where ~~the~~ product number ~~is~~ in ~~the list of~~ bike and helmet product numbers
SQL	SELECT DISTINCT OrderNumber FROM Order_Details WHERE ProductNumber IN (1, 2, 6, 10, 11, 25, 26)

❖ **Note** Readers familiar with SQL might ask why I didn't JOIN Order_Details to Products and look for bike or helmet product names. The simple answer is that I haven't introduced the concept of a JOIN yet, so I built this example on a single table using IN and a list of known bike and helmet product numbers.

That seems to do the trick at first, but the answer includes orders that contain either a bike *or* a helmet, and you really want to find ones that contain *both* a bike *and* a helmet! If you visualize orders with bicycles and orders with helmets as two distinct sets, it's easier to understand the problem. Figure 7-6 shows one possible relationship between the two sets of orders using a set diagram.

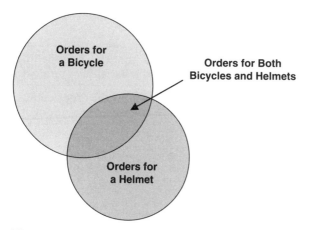

Figure 7-6 *One possible relationship between two sets of orders*

Actually, there's no way to predict in advance what the relationship between two sets of data might be. In Figure 7-6, some orders have a bicycle in the list of products ordered, but no helmet. Some have a helmet, but no bicycle. The overlapping area, or intersection, of the two sets is where you'll find orders that have both a bicycle and a helmet. Figure 7-7 shows another case where *all* orders that contain a helmet also contain a bicycle, but some orders that contain a bicycle do not contain a helmet.

Seeing "both" in your request suggests you're probably going to have to break the solution into separate sets of data and then link the two sets in some way. (Your request also needs to be broken into two parts.)

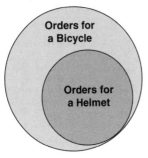

Figure 7-7 *All orders for a helmet also contain an order for a bicycle*

"Show me the orders that contain a bike."

Translation	Select the distinct order numbers from the order details table where the product number is in the list of bike product numbers
Clean Up	Select ~~the~~ distinct order numbers from ~~the~~ order details ~~table~~ where ~~the~~ product number ~~is~~ in ~~the list of~~ bike product numbers
SQL	SELECT DISTINCT OrderNumber FROM Order_Details WHERE ProductNumber IN (1, 2, 6, 11)

"Show me the orders that contain a helmet."

Translation	Select the distinct order numbers from the order details table where the product number is in the list of helmet product numbers
Clean Up	Select ~~the~~ distinct order numbers from ~~the~~ order details ~~table~~ where ~~the~~ product number ~~is~~ in ~~the list of~~ helmet product numbers
SQL	SELECT DISTINCT OrderNumber FROM Order_Details WHERE ProductNumber IN (10, 25, 26)

Now you're ready to get the final solution by using—you guessed it—an *intersection* of the two sets. Figure 7-8 shows the SQL syntax diagram that handles this problem. (Note that you can use INTERSECT more than once to combine multiple SELECT statements.)

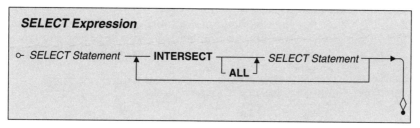

Figure 7-8 *Linking two SELECT statements with INTERSECT*

You can now take the two parts of your request and link them with an INTERSECT operator to get the correct answer:

SQL	
| | ```
SELECT DISTINCT OrderNumber
FROM Order_Details
WHERE ProductNumber IN (1, 2, 6, 11)
INTERSECT
SELECT DISTINCT OrderNumber
FROM Order_Details
WHERE ProductNumber IN (10, 25, 26)
``` |

The sad news is that not many commercial implementations of SQL yet support the INTERSECT operator. But all is not lost! Remember that the primary key of a table uniquely identifies each row. (You don't have to match on all the fields in a row—just the primary key—to find unique rows that intersect.) I'll show you an alternative method (JOIN) in Chapter 8 that can solve this type of problem in another way. The good news is that virtually all commercial implementations of SQL *do* support JOIN.

Finding Missing Values: EXCEPT (DIFFERENCE)

Okay, let's go back to the bicycles and helmets problem again. Let's say you're trying to solve this seemingly simple request as follows:

"Show me the orders that contain a bike but not a helmet."
```

Translation	Select the distinct order numbers from the order details table where the product number is in the list of bike product numbers and product number is not in the list of helmet product numbers
Clean Up	Select ~~the~~ distinct order numbers from ~~the~~ order details ~~table~~ where ~~the~~ product number ~~is~~ in ~~the list of~~ bike product numbers and product number ~~is~~ not in ~~the list of~~ helmet product numbers
| SQL | ```
SELECT DISTINCT OrderNumber
FROM Order_Details
WHERE ProductNumber IN (1, 2, 6, 11)
    AND ProductNumber NOT IN (10, 25, 26)
``` |

Unfortunately, the answer shows you orders that contain only a bike! The problem is that the first IN clause finds detail rows containing a bicycle, but the second IN clause simply eliminates helmet rows. If you visualize orders with bicycles and orders with helmets as two distinct sets, you'll find this easier to understand. Figure 7-9 shows one possible relationship between the two sets of orders.

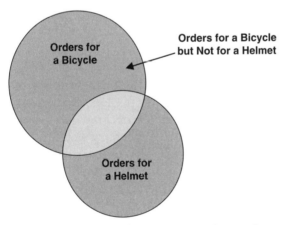

Figure 7-9 *Orders for a bicycle that do not also contain a helmet*

Seeing "except" or "but not" in your request suggests you're probably going to have to break the solution into separate sets of data and then link the two sets in some way. (Your request also needs to be broken into two parts.)
```

"Show me the orders that contain a bike."

Translation	Select the distinct order numbers from the order details table where the product number is in the list of bike product numbers
Clean Up	Select ~~the~~ distinct order numbers from ~~the~~ order details ~~table~~ where ~~the~~ product number ~~is~~ in ~~the list of~~ bike product numbers
SQL	SELECT DISTINCT OrderNumber FROM Order_Details WHERE ProductNumber IN (1, 2, 6, 11)

"Show me the orders that contain a helmet."

Translation	Select the distinct order numbers from the order details table where the product number is in the list of helmet product numbers
Clean Up	Select ~~the~~ distinct order numbers from ~~the~~ order details ~~table~~ where ~~the~~ product number ~~is~~ in ~~the list of~~ helmet product numbers
SQL	SELECT DISTINCT OrderNumber FROM Order_Details WHERE ProductNumber IN (10, 25, 26)

Now you're ready to get the final solution by using—you guessed it—a *difference* of the two sets. SQL uses the EXCEPT keyword to denote a difference operation. Figure 7-10 shows you the SQL syntax diagram that handles this problem.

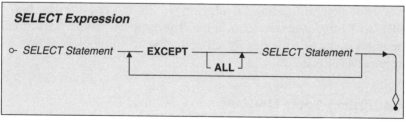

Figure 7-10 *Linking two SELECT statements with EXCEPT*

You can now take the two parts of your request and link them with an EXCEPT operator to get the correct answer:

```
SQL        SELECT DISTINCT OrderNumber
           FROM Order_Details
           WHERE ProductNumber IN (1, 2, 6, 11)
           EXCEPT
           SELECT DISTINCT OrderNumber
           FROM Order_Details
           WHERE ProductNumber IN (10, 25, 26)
```

Remember from my earlier discussion about the difference operation that the sequence of the sets matters. In this case, you're asking for bikes "except" helmets. If you want to find out the opposite case—orders for helmets that do not include bikes—you can turn it around as follows:

```
SQL        SELECT DISTINCT OrderNumber
           FROM Order_Details
           WHERE ProductNumber IN (10, 25, 26)
           EXCEPT
           SELECT DISTINCT OrderNumber
           FROM Order_Details
           WHERE ProductNumber IN (1, 2, 6, 11)
```

The sad news is that not many commercial implementations of SQL yet support the EXCEPT operator. Hang on to your helmet! Remember that the primary key of a table uniquely identifies each row. (You don't have to match on all the fields in a row—just the primary key—to find unique rows that are different.) I'll show you an alternative method (OUTER JOIN) in Chapter 9 that can solve this type of problem in another way. The good news is that nearly all commercial implementations of SQL *do* support OUTER JOIN.

Combining Sets: UNION

One more problem about bicycles and helmets, then I'll pedal on to the next chapter. Let's say you're trying to solve this request, which looks simple enough on the surface:

"Show me the orders that contain either a bike or a helmet."

Translation	Select the distinct order numbers from the order details table where the product number is in the list of bike and helmet product numbers
Clean Up	Select ~~the~~ distinct order numbers from ~~the~~ order details ~~table~~ where ~~the~~ product number ~~is~~ in ~~the list of~~ bike and helmet product numbers
SQL	SELECT DISTINCT OrderNumber FROM Order_Details WHERE ProductNumber IN (1, 2, 6, 10, 11, 25, 26)

Actually, that works just fine! So why use a UNION to solve this problem? The truth is, you probably would not. However, if I make the problem more complicated, a UNION would be useful:

"List the customers who ordered a bicycle together with the vendors who provide bicycles."

Unfortunately, answering this request involves creating a couple of queries using JOIN operations, then using UNION to get the final result. Because I haven't shown you how to do a JOIN yet, I'll save solving this problem for Chapter 10. Gives you something to look forward to, doesn't it?

Let's get back to the "bicycles or helmets" problem and solve it with a UNION. If you visualize orders with bicycles and orders with helmets as two distinct sets, then you'll find it easier to understand the problem. Figure 7-11 shows you one possible relationship between the two sets of orders.

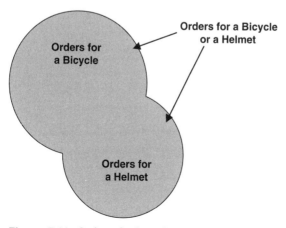

Figure 7-11 *Orders for bicycles or helmets*

Seeing "either," "or," or "together" in your request suggests that you'll need to break the solution into separate sets of data and then link the two sets with a UNION. This particular request can be broken into two parts:

"Show me the orders that contain a bike."

Translation	Select the distinct order numbers from the order details table where the product number is in the list of bike product numbers
Clean Up	Select ~~the~~ distinct order numbers from ~~the~~ order details ~~table~~ where ~~the~~ product number ~~is~~ in ~~the list of~~ bike product numbers
SQL	SELECT DISTINCT OrderNumber FROM Order_Details WHERE ProductNumber IN (1, 2, 6, 11)

"Show me the orders that contain a helmet."

Translation	Select the distinct order numbers from the order details table where the product number is in the list of helmet product numbers
Clean Up	Select ~~the~~ distinct order numbers from ~~the~~ order details ~~table~~ where ~~the~~ product number ~~is~~ in ~~the list of~~ helmet product numbers
SQL	SELECT DISTINCT OrderNumber FROM Order_Details WHERE ProductNumber IN (10, 25, 26)

Now you're ready to get the final solution by using—you guessed it—a *union* of the two sets. Figure 7-12 shows the SQL syntax diagram that handles this problem.

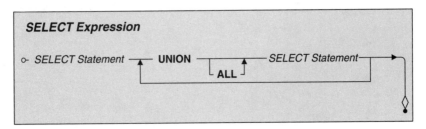

Figure 7-12 *Linking two SELECT statements with UNION*

You can now take the two parts of your request and link them with a UNION operator to get the correct answer:

```
SQL        SELECT DISTINCT OrderNumber
           FROM Order_Details
           WHERE ProductNumber IN (1, 2, 6, 11)
           UNION
           SELECT DISTINCT OrderNumber
           FROM Order_Details
           WHERE ProductNumber IN (10, 25, 26)
```

The good news is that nearly all commercial implementations of SQL support the UNION operator. As is perhaps obvious from the examples, a UNION might be doing it the hard way when you want to get an "either-or" result from a single table. UNION is most useful for compiling a list from several similarly structured but different tables. I'll explore UNION in much more detail in Chapter 10.

Summary

I began this chapter by discussing the concept of a set. Next, I discussed each of the major set operations implemented in SQL in detail—intersection, difference, and union. I showed how to use set diagrams to visualize the problem you're trying to solve. Finally, I introduced you to the basic SQL syntax and keywords (INTERSECT, EXCEPT, and UNION) for all three operations just to whet your appetite.

At this point you're probably saying, "Wait a minute, why did you show me three kinds of set operations—two of which I probably can't use?" Remember the title of the chapter: "Thinking in Sets." If you're going to be at all successful solving complex problems, you'll need to break your problem into result sets of information that you then link back together.

So, if your problem involves "it must be this, *and* it must be that," you might need to solve the "this" and then the "that" and then link them to get your final solution. The SQL Standard defines a handy INTERSECT operation—but an INNER JOIN might work just as well. Read on in Chapter 8.

Likewise, if your problem involves "it must be this, *but it must not be that*," you might need to solve the "this" and then the "that" and then subtract the "that" from the "this" to get your answer. I showed you the SQL Standard EXCEPT operation, but an OUTER JOIN might also do the trick. Get the details in Chapters 9 and 18.

Finally, I showed you how to add sets of information using a UNION. As promised, I'll really get into UNION in Chapter 10.

8

INNER JOINs

"Do not quench your inspiration and your imagination;
do not become the slave of your model."

—Vincent van Gogh

Topics Covered in This Chapter

What Is a JOIN?

The INNER JOIN

Uses for INNER JOINs

Sample Statements

Summary

Problems for You to Solve

Up to this point, I have primarily focused on solving problems using single tables. You now know how to get simple answers from one table. You also know how to get slightly more complex answers by using expressions or by sorting the result set. In other words, you now can draw the perfect eyes, chin, mouth, or nose. In this chapter, I'll show you how to link or join multiple parts to form a portrait.

What Is a JOIN?

In Chapter 2, "Ensuring Your Database Structure Is Sound," I emphasized the importance of separating the data in your tables into individual subjects. Most problems you need to solve in real life, however, require that you link data from multiple tables—customers and their orders, customers and the entertainers they booked, bowlers and their scores, students and the classes they took, or recipes and the ingredients you need. To solve these more complex problems, you must link, or join, multiple tables to find your answer. You use the *JOIN* keyword to do so.

The previous chapter showed how useful it is to intersect two sets of data to solve problems. As you recall, however, an INTERSECT involves matching all the columns in both result sets to get the answer. A JOIN is also an intersection, but it's different because you ask your database system to perform a JOIN only on the columns you specify. Thus, a JOIN lets you intersect two very dissimilar tables on matching column values. For example, you can use a JOIN to link customers to their orders by matching the CustomerID in the Customers table to the CustomerID in the Orders table.

As you'll see later, you specify a JOIN as part of the FROM clause in an SQL statement. A JOIN defines a "logical table" that is the result of linking two tables or result sets. By placing the JOIN in a FROM clause, you define a linking of tables *from* which the query extracts the final result set. In other words, the JOIN replaces the single table name you learned to use in the FROM clause in earlier chapters. As you'll learn later in this chapter, you can also specify multiple JOIN operations to create a complex result set on more than two tables.

The INNER JOIN

The SQL Standard defines several ways to perform a JOIN, the most common of which is the *INNER JOIN*. Imagine for a moment that you're linking students and the classes for which they registered. You might have some students who have been accepted to attend the school but have not yet registered for any classes, and you might also have some classes that are on the schedule but do not yet have any students registered.

An INNER JOIN between the Students table and the Classes table returns rows in the Students table linked with the related rows in the Classes table (via the Student_Schedules table)—but it returns neither students who have not yet registered for any classes nor any classes for which no student is registered. An INNER JOIN returns only those rows where the linking values match in both of the tables or in result sets.

What's "Legal" to JOIN?

Most of the time, you specify the primary key from one table and the related foreign key from the second table as the link that JOIN uses. If you remember from Chapter 2, a foreign key must be the same data type as its related primary key. However, it's also "legal" to JOIN two tables or result sets on any columns that have what the SQL Standard calls "JOIN eligible" data types.

In general, you can join a character column to another character column or expression, any type of number column (for example, an integer) to any other type of number column (perhaps a floating-point value), and any date column to another date column. This allows you, for example, to JOIN rows from the Customers table to rows from the Employees table on the city or ZIP Code columns (perhaps to find out which Customers and Employees live in the same city or postal region).

❖ **Note** Just because you *can* define a JOIN on any JOIN eligible columns in two tables doesn't mean you *should*. The linking columns must have the same data meaning for the JOIN to make sense. For example, it doesn't make sense to JOIN customer name with employee address even though both columns are character data type. You won't get any rows in the result set unless someone has put a name in the employee address column by mistake. Likewise, it doesn't make sense to JOIN StudentID with ClassID even though both are numbers. You might get some rows in the result set, but they won't make any sense.

Even when it makes sense to JOIN linking columns, you might end up constructing a request that takes a long time to solve. For example, if you ask for a JOIN on columns for which your database administrator has not defined an index, your database system might have to do a lot of extra work. Also, if you ask for a JOIN on expressions—for example, a concatenation of first name and last name from two tables—your database system must not only form the result column from your expression for all rows but also might have to perform multiple scans of all the data in both tables to return the correct result.

Column References

Before I jump into the syntax for a JOIN, there's a key bit of information that I haven't covered yet. Because you've been creating queries on a single table, you haven't had to worry about qualifying column names. But when you start to build queries that include multiple tables (as you will when you use a JOIN), you'll often include two or more tables that each have columns with the same name. If you remember from Chapter 2, I recommended that you create a foreign key in a related table by copying the primary key—including its name—from one table into another.

So, how do you make it crystal clear to your database system which copy of a field you are talking about in your query syntax? The simple answer is that you provide a *column reference* that includes the table name. Figure 8-1 shows the diagram for a column reference.

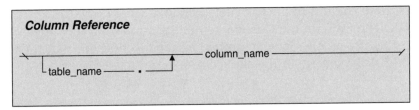

Figure 8-1 *The syntax diagram of a column reference*

Although you can use only the column name by itself in any clause in a statement that you write in SQL, you can also explicitly qualify a column name with the name of its parent table. If the column name isn't unique in all the tables you include in your FROM clause, then you *must* qualify the column name with the name of its parent table. Here's how you would write a simple SELECT statement on the Employees table to incorporate qualified column names:

SQL

```
SELECT Employees.FirstName, Employees.LastName,
    Employees.PhoneNumber
FROM Employees
```

Now that I've covered that little tidbit, you can move on to studying the syntax of a JOIN operation.

Syntax

You can think of what you've studied so far as taking a nice ride down a country lane or a quick jaunt across town to pick up some groceries. Now let's strap on our seat belts and venture out onto the highway—let's examine the INNER JOIN syntax.

Using Tables

I'll start with something simple—an INNER JOIN on two tables. Figure 8-2 shows the syntax for creating the query.

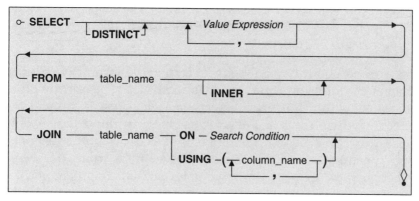

Figure 8-2 *The syntax diagram of a query using an INNER JOIN on two tables*

As you can see, the FROM clause is now just a little more complicated. (I left out the WHERE and ORDER BY clauses for now to simplify things.) Instead of a single table name, you specify two table names and link them with the JOIN keyword. Note that the INNER keyword, which is optional, specifies the type of JOIN. As you'll learn in the next chapter, you can also specify an OUTER JOIN. If you don't explicitly state the type of JOIN you want, the default is INNER. I recommend that you always explicitly state the type of JOIN you want so that the nature of your request is clear.

❖ **Note** Those who are following along with the complete syntax diagrams in Appendix A, "SQL Standard Diagrams," will find `Table Reference JOIN Table Reference` described as part of the *Joined Table* defined term. *Table Reference* can be either a `table_name` or a `Joined Table`, and the FROM clause of a SELECT statement uses `Table Reference`. I "rolled up" these complex definitions into a single diagram to make it easy to study a simple two-table JOIN. I'll be using this same simplification technique in diagrams throughout the remainder of this chapter.

The critical part of an INNER JOIN is the ON or USING clause that follows the second table and tells your database system how to perform the

JOIN. To solve the JOIN, your database system logically combines every row in the first table with every row in the second table. (This combination of all rows from one table with all rows from a second table is called a *Cartesian product*. I show you how to use a Cartesian product to solve problems in Chapter 20, "Using Unlinked Data and 'Driver' Tables.") It then applies the criteria in the ON or USING clauses to filter out the actual rows to be returned.

You learned about using a *search condition* to form a WHERE clause in Chapter 6, "Filtering Your Data." You can use a search condition in the ON clause within a JOIN to specify a logical test that must be true in order to return any two linked rows. Keep in mind that it only makes sense to write a search condition that compares at least one column from the first table with at least one column from the second table. Although you can write a very complex search condition, you'll typically specify a simple equals comparison test on the primary key columns from one table with the foreign key columns from the other table.

Let's look at a simple example. In a well-designed database, you should break out complex classification names into a second table and then link the names back to the primary subject table via a simple key value. You do this to help prevent data entry errors. Anyone using your database chooses from a list of classification names rather than typing the name (and perhaps misspelling it) in each row. For example, in the Recipes sample database, recipe classes appear in a table separate from recipes. Figure 8-3 shows the relationship between the Recipe_Classes and Recipes tables.

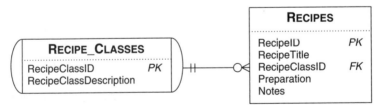

Figure 8-3 *Recipe class descriptions are in a table separate from the Recipes table*

When you want to retrieve information about recipes and the related RecipeClassDescription from the database, you don't want to see the RecipeClassID code numbers from the Recipes table. Let's see how to approach this problem with a JOIN.

❖ **Note** Throughout this chapter, I use the "Request/Translation/ Clean Up/SQL" technique introduced in Chapter 4, "Creating a Simple Query."

"Show me the recipe title, preparation, and recipe class description of all recipes in my database."

Translation	Select recipe title, preparation, and recipe class description from the recipe classes table joined with the recipes table on recipe class ID in the recipe classes table matching recipe class ID in the recipes table
Clean Up	Select recipe title, preparation, ~~and~~ recipe class description from ~~the~~ recipe classes ~~table~~ inner join~~ed with the~~ recipes ~~table~~ on recipe_classes.recipe class ID ~~in the recipe classes table matching~~ = recipes.recipe class ID ~~in the recipes table~~

SQL	SELECT RecipeTitle, Preparation,
	          RecipeClassDescription
	FROM Recipe_Classes INNER JOIN Recipes
	    ON Recipe_Classes.RecipeClassID =
	          Recipes.RecipeClassID

❖ **Note** You might have noticed that I've started to format the Clean Up step into phrases that more closely mirror the final set of clauses I need in SQL. As you begin to build more complex queries, I recommend this technique to help you move from the Clean Up step to the final SQL.

When beginning to use multiple tables in your FROM clause, you should always fully qualify each column name with the table name, wherever you use it, to make absolutely clear what column from what table you want. (Now you know why I took a minute to explain a column reference!) Note that I *had to* qualify the name of RecipeClassID in the ON clause because there are two columns named RecipeClassID—one in the Recipes table and one in the Recipe_Classes table. I didn't have to qualify RecipeTitle, Preparation, or RecipeClassDescription in the SELECT clause because each of these column names appears only once in all the tables. If I want to include RecipeClassID in the output, I must tell the database system *which* RecipeClassID I want—the one from Recipe_ Classes or the one from Recipes. To write the query with all the names fully qualified, I should say this:

SQL
```
SELECT Recipes.RecipeTitle,
       Recipes.Preparation,
       Recipe_Classes.RecipeClassDescription
FROM Recipe_Classes INNER JOIN Recipes
   ON Recipe_Classes.RecipeClassID =
       Recipes.RecipeClassID
```

❖ **Note** Although most commercial implementations of SQL support the JOIN keyword, some do not. If your database does not support JOIN, you can still solve the previous problem by listing all the tables you need in the FROM clause and then moving your search condition from the ON clause to the WHERE clause. In databases that do not support JOIN, you solve the example problem like this:

```
SELECT Recipes.RecipeTitle, Recipes.Preparation,
    Recipe_Classes.RecipeClassDescription
FROM Recipe_Classes, Recipes
WHERE Recipe_Classes.RecipeClassID =
    Recipes.RecipeClassID
```

For a beginner, this syntax is probably much more intuitive for simple queries. However, the SQL Standard syntax allows you to fully define the source for the final result set entirely within the FROM clause. Think of the FROM clause as fully defining a linked result set from which the database system obtains your answer. In the SQL Standard, you use the WHERE clause only to filter rows out of the result set defined by the FROM clause.

Not too difficult, is it? But what happened to the USING clause that I showed you in Figure 8-2? If the matching columns in the two tables have the same name and all you want to do is join on equal values, use the USING clause and list the column names. Let's do the previous problem again with USING.

"Show me the recipe title, preparation, and recipe class description of all recipes in my database."

Translation	Select recipe title, preparation, and recipe class description from the recipe classes table joined with the recipes table using recipe class ID
Clean Up	Select recipe title, preparation, ~~and~~ recipe class description from ~~the~~ recipe classes ~~table~~ inner join~~ed with the~~ recipes ~~table~~ using recipe class ID

SQL	SELECT Recipes.RecipeTitle,
	   Recipes.Preparation,
	   Recipe_Classes.RecipeClassDescription
	FROM Recipe_Classes
	INNER JOIN Recipes
	USING (RecipeClassID)

Some database systems do not yet support USING. If you find that you can't use USING with your database, you can always get the same result with an ON clause and an equals comparison.

> ❖ **Note** The SQL Standard also defines a NATURAL JOIN, which links the two specified tables by matching all the columns with the same name. If the only common columns are the linking columns and your database supports NATURAL JOIN, you can solve the example problem like this:
>
> ```
> SELECT Recipes.RecipeTitle, Recipes.Preparation,
>     Recipe_Classes.RecipeClassDescription
> FROM Recipe_Classes
> NATURAL INNER JOIN Recipes
> ```
>
> Do not specify an ON or USING clause when using the NATURAL keyword. Keep in mind that the INNER keyword is optional. If you specify NATURAL JOIN, an INNER JOIN is assumed.

As mentioned earlier in this section, your database system logically creates the combination of every row in the first table with every row in the second table and then applies the criteria you specify in ON or USING. This sounds like a lot of extra work for your database to first build all the combinations and then filter out the potentially few matching rows.

Rest assured that all modern relational database systems evaluate the entire JOIN clause before starting to fetch rows. In the example I have been using so far, many database systems begin to solve this request by first fetching a row from Recipe_Classes. The database then uses an internal link—an index (if one has been defined by the designer of the tables)—to quickly find any matching rows in the Recipes table for the first row in the Recipe_Classes table before moving on to the next row in Recipe_Classes. In other words, your database uses a smart or optimized plan to fetch only the rows that match. This won't seem important when your database tables contain only a few hundred rows, but it makes a big difference when your database has to deal with hundreds of thousands of rows!

Assigning Correlation (Alias) Names to Tables

The SQL Standard defines a way to assign an alias name—known as a *correlation name* in the Standard—to any table you list in your FROM clause. This feature can be very handy for building complex queries using tables that have long, descriptive names. You can assign a short correlation name to a table to make it easier to explicitly reference columns in a table with a long name.

Figure 8-4 shows how to assign a correlation name to a table in a FROM clause.

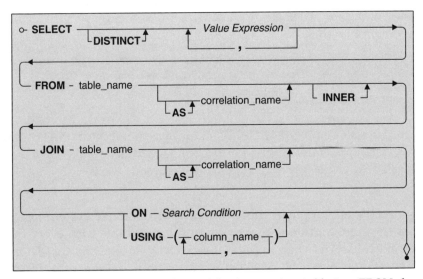

Figure 8-4 *Assigning a correlation (alias) name to a table in a FROM clause*

To assign a correlation name to a table, follow the table name with the optional keyword AS and then the correlation name you want to assign.

(As with all optional keywords, I recommend including AS in order to make the query easier to read and understand.) After you have assigned a correlation name to a table, you use that name in place of the original table name in all other clauses, including the SELECT clause, the search conditions in the ON and WHERE clauses, and the ORDER BY clause. This can be confusing because you tend to write the SELECT clause before you write the FROM clause. If you plan to give a table an alias in the FROM clause, you must use that alias when you qualify column names in the SELECT clause.

Let's reformulate the sample query I've been using with correlation names just to see how it looks. The query using R as the correlation name for the Recipes table and RC as the correlation name for the Recipe_Classes table is shown here:

```
SQL                SELECT R.RecipeTitle, R.Preparation,
                      RC.RecipeClassDescription
                   FROM Recipe_Classes AS RC
                     INNER JOIN Recipes AS R
                       ON RC.RecipeClassID = R.RecipeClassID
```

Suppose you want to add a filter to see only recipes of class Main course or Dessert. (See Chapter 6 for details about defining filters.) After you assign a correlation name, you must continue to use the new name in all references to the table. Here's the SQL:

```
SQL                SELECT R.RecipeTitle, R.Preparation,
                      RC.RecipeClassDescription
                   FROM Recipe_Classes AS RC
                     INNER JOIN Recipes AS R
                       ON RC.RecipeClassID = R.RecipeClassID
                   WHERE RC.RecipeClassDescription = 'Main course'
                   OR RC.RecipeClassDescription = 'Dessert'
```

You don't have to assign a correlation name to all tables. In the previous example, I could have assigned a correlation name only to Recipes or only to Recipe_Classes.

In some cases, you *must* assign a correlation name to a table in a complex JOIN. Let's hop over to the Bowling League database to examine a case where this is true. Figure 8-5 shows you the relationship between the Teams and Bowlers tables.

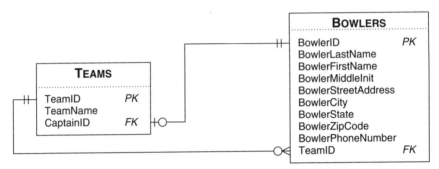

Figure 8-5 *The relationships between Teams and Bowlers*

As you can see, TeamID is a foreign key in the Bowlers table that lets you find the information for all bowlers on a team. One of the bowlers on a team is the team captain, so there's also a link from BowlerID in the Bowlers table to CaptainID in the Teams table.

If you want to list the team name, the name of the team captain, and the names of all the bowlers in one request, you must include *two* copies of the Bowlers table in your query—one to link to CaptainID to retrieve the name of the team captain and another to link to TeamID to get a list of all the team members. In this case, you *must* assign an alias name to one or both copies of the Bowlers table so that your database system can differentiate between the copy that links in the captain's name and the copy that provides the list of all team members. Later in this chapter, I'll show an example that requires including multiple copies of one table and assigning alias names. You can find this example using the Bowling League database in the "More Than Two Tables" subsection of "Sample Statements."

Embedding a SELECT Statement

Let's make it more interesting. In most implementations of SQL, you can substitute an entire SELECT statement for any table name in your FROM clause. In the SQL Standard, an embedded SELECT statement like this is called a *derived table*. If you think about it, using a SELECT statement is simply a way to derive a subset of data from one or more tables. Of course, you must assign a correlation name so that the result of evaluating your embedded query has a name. Figure 8-6 shows how to assemble a JOIN clause using embedded SELECT statements.

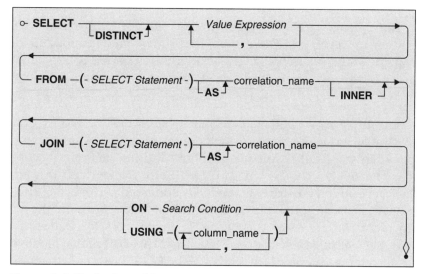

Figure 8-6 *Replacing table names with SELECT statements in a JOIN*

Notice in the figure that a SELECT statement can include all query clauses except an ORDER BY clause. Also, you can mix and match SELECT statements with table names on either side of the INNER JOIN keywords.

Let's look at the Recipes and Recipe_Classes tables again. I'll assume that your request still needs only main courses and desserts. Here's the query again with the Recipe_Classes table filtered in a SELECT statement that's part of the INNER JOIN:

```
SQL          SELECT R.RecipeTitle, R.Preparation,
                 RCFiltered.ClassName
             FROM
               (SELECT RecipeClassID,
                  RecipeClassDescription AS ClassName
               FROM Recipe_Classes AS RC
               WHERE RC.ClassName = 'Main course' OR
                 RC.ClassName = 'Dessert') AS RCFiltered
             INNER JOIN Recipes AS R
               ON RCFiltered.RecipeClassID = R.RecipeClassID
```

❖ **Note** Some database systems do not support embedding a SELECT statement inside a FROM clause. If your system does not support this feature, you can often save the inner SELECT statement as a view, and use the view name in place of the select statement.

Watch out! First, when you decide to substitute a SELECT statement for a table name, be sure to include not only the columns you want to appear in the final result but also any linking columns needed to perform the JOIN. That's why you see both RecipeClassID and Recipe-ClassDescription in the embedded statement. Just for fun, I gave RecipeClassDescription an alias name of ClassName in the embedded statement. As a result, the SELECT clause asks for ClassName rather than RecipeClassDescription. Note that the ON clause now references the correlation name of the embedded SELECT statement—RCFiltered—rather than the original name of the table or the correlation name I assigned the table inside the embedded SELECT statement.

If your database system has a very smart optimizer, defining your request this way should be just as fast as the previous example where the filter on RecipeClassDescription was applied via a WHERE clause *after* the JOIN. You would like to think that your database system, in order to answer your request most efficiently, would first filter the rows from Recipe_Classes before attempting to find any matching rows in Recipes. It could be much slower to first join all rows from Recipe_Classes with matching rows from Recipes and *then* apply the filter. If you find it's taking longer to solve this request than it should, moving the WHERE clause into a SELECT statement within the JOIN might force your database system to do the filtering on Recipe_Classes first.

Embedding JOINs within JOINs

Although you can solve many problems by linking only two tables, you'll often need to link three, four, or more tables to get all the data you require. For example, you might want to fetch all the relevant information about recipes—the type of recipe, the recipe name, and all the ingredients for the recipe—in one query. Figure 8-7 shows the tables required to answer this request.

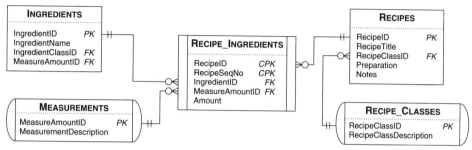

Figure 8-7 *The tables needed from the Recipes sample database to fetch all the information about recipes*

Looks like you need to get data from *five* different tables! (The Measurements and Recipe_Classes tables are "lookup" tables, hence the difference in the diagram.) Never fear—you can do this by constructing a more complex FROM clause, embedding JOIN clauses within JOIN clauses. Here's the trick: Everywhere you can specify a table name, you can also specify an entire JOIN clause surrounded with parentheses. Figure 8-8 is a simplified version of Figure 8-4. (I've left off correlation name clauses and chosen the ON clause to form a simple JOIN of two tables.)

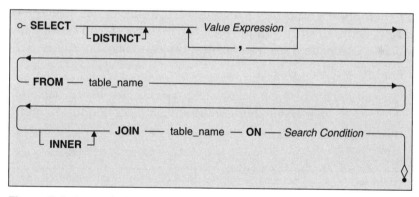

Figure 8-8 *A simple INNER JOIN of two tables*

To add a third table to the mix, just place an open parenthesis before the first table name, add a close parenthesis after the search condition, and insert INNER JOIN, a table name, the ON keyword, and another search condition. Figure 8-9 shows how to do this.

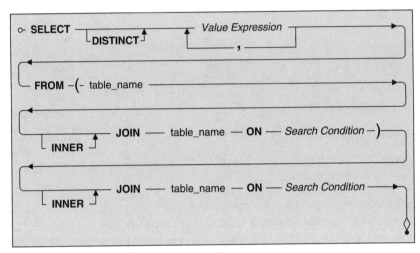

Figure 8-9 *A simple INNER JOIN of three tables*

If you think about it, the INNER JOIN of two tables inside the parentheses forms a logical table, or inner result set. This result set now takes the place of the first simple table name in Figure 8-8. You can continue this process of enclosing an entire JOIN clause in parentheses and then adding another JOIN keyword, table name, ON keyword, and search condition until you have all the result sets you need. Let's make a request that needs data from all the tables shown in Figure 8-7 and see how it turns out:

"I need the recipe type, recipe name, preparation instructions, ingredient names, ingredient step numbers, ingredient quantities, and ingredient measurements from my recipes database, sorted in step number sequence."

Translation	Select the recipe class description, recipe title, preparation instructions, ingredient name, recipe sequence number, amount, and measurement description from the recipe classes table joined with the recipes table on recipe class ID in the recipe classes table matching recipe class ID in the recipes table, then joined with the recipe ingredients table on recipe ID in the recipes table matching recipe ID in the recipe ingredients table, then joined with the ingredients table on ingredient ID in the ingredients table matching ingredient ID in the recipe ingredients table, and then finally joined with the measurements table on measurement amount ID in the measurements table matching measurement amount ID in the recipe ingredients table, order by recipe title and recipe sequence number

Clean Up	Select ~~the~~ recipe class description, recipe title, preparation ~~instructions~~, ingredient name, recipe sequence number, amount, ~~and~~ measurement description from ~~the~~ recipe classes ~~table~~ inner joined ~~with the~~ recipes ~~table~~ on recipe_classes.recipe class ID ~~in the recipe classes table matching~~ = recipes.recipe class ID ~~in the recipes table, then~~ inner joined ~~with the~~ recipe ingredients ~~table~~ on recipes.recipe ID ~~in the recipes table matching~~ = recipe_ingredients.recipe ID ~~in the recipe ingredients table, then~~ inner joined ~~with the~~ ingredients ~~table~~ on ingredients. ingredient ID ~~in the ingredients table matching~~ = ingredients.ingredient ID ~~in the recipe ingredients table, and then finally~~ inner joined ~~with the~~ measurements ~~table~~ on measurements.measurement amount ID ~~in the measurements table matching~~ = recipe ingredients. measurement amount ID ~~in the recipe ingredients table,~~ order by recipe title and recipe sequence number
| SQL | ```
SELECT Recipe_Classes.RecipeClassDescription,
      Recipes.RecipeTitle, Recipes.Preparation,
      Ingredients.IngredientName,
      Recipe_Ingredients.RecipeSeqNo,
      Recipe_Ingredients.Amount,
      Measurements.MeasurementDescription
FROM (((Recipe_Classes
  INNER JOIN Recipes
  ON Recipe_Classes.RecipeClassID =
      Recipes.RecipeClassID)
  INNER JOIN Recipe_Ingredients
  ON Recipes.RecipeID =
      Recipe_Ingredients.RecipeID)
  INNER JOIN Ingredients
  ON Ingredients.IngredientID =
      Recipe_Ingredients.IngredientID)
  INNER JOIN Measurements
  ON Measurements.MeasureAmountID =
      Recipe_Ingredients.MeasureAmountID
ORDER BY RecipeTitle, RecipeSeqNo
``` |
```

Wow! Anyone care to jump in and add a filter for recipe class Main courses? If you said you need to add the WHERE clause just before the ORDER BY clause, you guessed the correct way to do it.

In truth, you can substitute an entire JOIN of two tables anywhere you could otherwise place only a table name. In Figure 8-9, I implied that you must first join the first table with the second table and then join that result with the third table. You could also join the second and third tables first (as long as the third table is, in fact, related to the second table and not the first one) and then perform the final join with the first table. Figure 8-10 shows this alternate method.

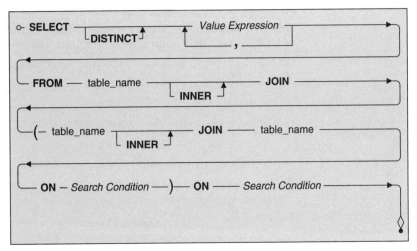

Figure 8-10 *Joining more than two tables in an alternate sequence*

Let's look at the problem from a painting perspective. If you're trying to get pastel green, the mixing sequence doesn't matter that much. You can mix white with blue to get pastel blue and then mix in some yellow, or you can mix blue with yellow to get green and then add some white to get the final color.

To solve the request I just showed you using five tables, I could also have stated the SQL as follows:

SQL
```
SELECT Recipe_Classes.RecipeClassDescription,
    Recipes.RecipeTitle, Recipes.Preparation,
    Ingredients.IngredientName,
    Recipe_Ingredients.RecipeSeqNo,
    Recipe_Ingredients.Amount,
    Measurements.MeasurementDescription
FROM Recipe_Classes
  INNER JOIN (((Recipes
  INNER JOIN Recipe_Ingredients
    ON Recipes.RecipeID =
        Recipe_Ingredients.RecipeID)
  INNER JOIN Ingredients
  ON Ingredients.IngredientID =
      Recipe_Ingredients.IngredientID)
  INNER JOIN Measurements
  ON Measurements.MeasureAmountID =
      Recipe_Ingredients.MeasureAmountID)
  ON Recipe_Classes.RecipeClassID =
      Recipes.RecipeClassID
ORDER BY RecipeTitle, RecipeSeqNo
```

You need to be aware of this feature because you might run into this sort of construction either in queries others have written or in the SQL built for you by Query By Example software. Also, the optimizers in some database systems are sensitive to the sequence of the JOIN definitions. If you find your query using many JOINs is taking a long time to execute on a large database, you might be able to get it to run faster by changing the sequence of JOINs in your SQL statement. For simplicity, I'll build most of the examples later in this chapter using a direct construction of JOINs by following a simple path from left to right and top to bottom, using the diagrams that you can find in Appendix B, "Schema for the Sample Databases."

Check Those Relationships!

It should be obvious at this point that knowing the relationships between your tables is of utmost importance. When you find that the columns of data you need reside in different tables, you might need to construct a FROM clause as complicated as the one I just showed you to be able to gather all the pieces in a way that logically makes sense. If you don't know the relationships between your tables and the linking columns that form the relationships, you'll paint yourself into a corner!

In many cases, you might have to follow a path through several relationships to get the data you want. For example, let's simplify the previous request and just ask for recipe name and ingredient names:

"Show me the names of all my recipes and the names of all the ingredients for each of those recipes."

Translation	Select the recipe title and the ingredient name from the recipes table joined with the recipe ingredients table on recipe ID in the recipes table matching recipe ID in the recipe ingredients table, and then joined with the ingredients table on ingredient ID in the ingredients table matching ingredient ID in the recipe ingredients table
Clean Up	Select ~~the~~ recipe title ~~and the~~ ingredient name from ~~the~~ recipes ~~table~~ inner joined ~~with the~~ recipe ingredients ~~table~~ on recipes.recipe ID ~~in the recipes table matching~~ = recipe_ingredients.recipe ID ~~in the recipe ingredients table, and then~~ inner joined ~~with the~~ ingredients ~~table~~ on ingredients.ingredient ID ~~in the ingredients table matching~~ = recipe_ingredients.ingredient ID ~~in the recipe ingredients table~~

SQL	SELECT Recipes.RecipeTitle,
	    Ingredients.IngredientName
	FROM (Recipes
	INNER JOIN Recipe_Ingredients
	  ON Recipes.RecipeID =
	  Recipe_Ingredients.RecipeID)
	INNER JOIN Ingredients
	  ON Ingredients.IngredientID =
	  Recipe_Ingredients.IngredientID

Did you notice that even though you don't need *any* columns from the Recipe_Ingredients table, you still must include it in the query? You must do so because the only way that Recipes and Ingredients are related is *through* the Recipe_Ingredients table.

Uses for INNER JOINs

Now that you have a basic understanding of the mechanics for constructing an INNER JOIN, let's look at some of the types of problems you can solve with it.

Find Related Rows

As you know, the most common use for an INNER JOIN is to link tables so that you can fetch columns from different tables that are related. Following is a sample list of the kinds of requests you can solve from the sample databases using an INNER JOIN:

> "Show me the vendors and the products they supply to us."
>
> "List employees and the customers for whom they booked an order."
>
> "Display agents and the engagement dates they booked."
>
> "List customers and the entertainers they booked."
>
> "Find the entertainers who played engagements for customers Berg or Hallmark."
>
> "Display buildings and all the classrooms in each building."
>
> "List the faculty staff and the subject each teaches."
>
> "Display bowling teams and the name of each team captain."
>
> "List the bowling teams and all the team members."
>
> "Show me the recipes that have beef or garlic."
>
> "Display all the ingredients for recipes that contain carrots."

I'll show how to construct queries to answer requests like these (and more) in the Sample Statements section of this chapter.

Find Matching Values

A more esoteric use of an INNER JOIN is finding rows in two or more tables or result sets that match on one or more values that are *not* the related key values. Remember that in Chapter 7, 'Thinking in Sets,' I promised to show you how to perform the equivalent of an INTERSECT using an INNER JOIN. Following is a small sample of just some of the requests you can solve using this technique:

> *"Show me customers and employees who have the same name."*
>
> *"Show me customers and employees who live in the same city."*
>
> *"Find all the customers who ordered a bicycle and also ordered a helmet."*
>
> *"Find the agents and entertainers who live in the same postal code."*
>
> *"List the entertainers who played engagements for customers Bonnick-sen and Rosales."*
>
> *"Show me the students and their teachers who have the same first name."*
>
> *"Show me the students who have an average score of 85 or better in Art and who also have an average score of 85 or better in Computer Science."*
>
> *"Find the bowlers who live in the same ZIP Code."*
>
> *"Find the bowlers who had a raw score of 155 or better at both Thunder-bird Lanes and Bolero Lanes."*
>
> *"Find the ingredients that use the same default measurement amount."*
>
> *"Show me the recipes that have beef and garlic."*

The next section shows how to solve several problems like these.

Sample Statements

You now know the mechanics of constructing queries using INNER JOIN and have seen some of the types of requests you can answer with an INNER JOIN. Let's take a look at a fairly robust set of samples, all of which use INNER JOIN. These examples come from each of the sample databases, and they illustrate how you can use an INNER JOIN to fetch data from two tables, fetch data from more than two tables, and solve a problem using matching values.

I've also included sample result sets that would be returned by these operations and placed them immediately after the SQL syntax line. The name that appears immediately above a result set is the name I gave each query in the sample data on the companion website for the book, www.informit.com/title/978013485833.

I stored each query in the appropriate sample database (as indicated within the example) and prefixed the names of the queries relevant to this chapter with "CH08." You can follow the instructions in the Introduction of this book to load the samples onto your computer and try them.

> ❖ **Note** Because many of these examples use complex JOINs, your database system might choose a different way to solve these queries. For this reason, the first few rows I show you might not exactly match the result you obtain, but the total number of rows should be the same. To simplify the process, I have combined the Translation and Clean Up steps for all the following examples.

Two Tables

I'll start out with simple primary colors and show you sample requests that require an INNER JOIN on only two tables.

Sales Orders Database

"Display all products and their categories."

Translation/ Clean Up	Select category description ~~and~~ product name from ~~the~~ categories ~~table~~ inner joined ~~with the~~ products ~~table~~ on categories.category ID ~~in the categories table matching~~ = products.category ID ~~in the products table~~

SQL	SELECT Categories.CategoryDescription,
	    Products.ProductName
	FROM Categories
	  INNER JOIN Products
	    ON Categories.CategoryID =
	      Products.CategoryID

CH08_Products_And_Categories (40 rows)

CategoryDescription	ProductName
Accessories	Dog Ear Cyclecomputer
Accessories	Dog Ear Helmet Mount Mirrors
Accessories	Viscount C-500 Wireless Bike Computer
Accessories	Kryptonite Advanced 2000 U-Lock
Accessories	Nikoma Lok-Tight U-Lock
Accessories	Viscount Microshell Helmet
Accessories	Viscount CardioSport Sport Watch
Accessories	Viscount Tru-Beat Heart Transmitter
Accessories	Dog Ear Monster Grip Gloves
<< more rows here >>	

❖ **Note** Remember that in the absence of an ORDER BY clause, each database system might return rows in a different sequence. The sequence you see above matches that from Microsoft Access and MySQL because both systems appear to fetch rows from Categories first and then find the matching rows in Products, so the rows appear in order by accessory name. In Microsoft SQL Server and PostgreSQL, the systems fetch Products first and then look up the matching row in Categories, so the sequence is different. Expect to see a difference between systems whenever the query does not use ORDER BY.

Entertainment Agency Database

"Show me entertainers, the start and end dates of their contracts, and the contract price."

Translation/ Clean Up	Select entertainer stage name, start date, end date, ~~and~~ contract price from ~~the~~ entertainers ~~table~~ inner joined ~~with the~~ engagements ~~table~~ on entertainers.entertainer ID ~~in the entertainers table matching~~ = engagements. entertainer ID ~~in the engagements table~~

SQL	SELECT Entertainers.EntStageName,
	
	    Engagements.StartDate, Engagements.EndDate,
	
	    Engagements.ContractPrice
	
	FROM Entertainers
	
	  INNER JOIN Engagements
	
	    ON Entertainers.EntertainerID =
	
	      Engagements.EntertainerID

CH08_Entertainers_And_Contracts (111 rows)

EntStageName	StartDate	EndDate	ContractPrice
Carol Peacock Trio	2017-09-18	2017-09-26	$1,670.00
Carol Peacock Trio	2017-10-01	2017-10-07	$1,940.00
Carol Peacock Trio	2017-10-14	2017-10-15	$410.00
Carol Peacock Trio	2017-10-21	2017-10-21	$140.00
Carol Peacock Trio	2017-11-13	2017-11-19	$680.00
Carol Peacock Trio	2017-12-23	2017-12-26	$410.00
Carol Peacock Trio	2017-12-29	2018-01-07	$1,400.00
Carol Peacock Trio	2018-01-08	2018-01-08	$320.00
Carol Peacock Trio	2018-01-22	2018-01-30	$1,670.00
Carol Peacock Trio	2018-02-11	2018-02-19	$1,670.00
Carol Peacock Trio	2018-02-25	2018-02-28	$770.00
Topazz	2017-09-11	2017-09-18	$770.00
<< more rows here >>			

School Scheduling Database

"List the subjects taught on Wednesday."

Translation/ Clean Up	Select subject name from ~~the~~ subjects table inner ~~joined with the~~ classes ~~table~~ on subjects.subject ID ~~in the subjects table matching~~ = classes.subject ID ~~in the classes table~~ where Wednesday schedule ~~is~~ = true

| SQL | ```
SELECT DISTINCT Subjects.SubjectName
FROM Subjects
INNER JOIN Classes
   ON Subjects.SubjectID
    = Classes.SubjectID
WHERE Classes.WednesdaySchedule = -1
``` |

❖ **Note** Because several sections of the same class might be scheduled on the same day of the week, I included the DISTINCT keyword to eliminate the duplicates. Some databases do support a TRUE keyword, but I chose to use a more universal "integer with all bits on" value: –1. If your database system stores a true/false value as a single bit, you can also test for a true value of 1. A false value is always the number zero (0).

CH08_Subjects_On_Wednesday (34 rows)

SubjectName

Advanced English Grammar

Art History

Biological Principles

Chemistry

Composition—Fundamentals

Composition—Intermediate

Design

Drawing

Elementary Algebra

<< more rows here >>

Bowling League Database

"Display bowling teams and the name of each team captain."

| Translation/ Clean Up | Select team name ~~and~~ captain full name from ~~the~~ teams ~~table~~ inner join~~ed with the~~ bowlers ~~table~~ on team captain ID ~~equals~~ = bowler ID |
```

| SQL | `SELECT Teams.TeamName, (Bowlers.BowlerLastName`
`   || ', ' || Bowlers.BowlerFirstName)`
`      AS CaptainName`
`FROM Teams`
`INNER JOIN Bowlers`
`   ON Teams.CaptainID = Bowlers.BowlerID` |

CH08_Teams_And_Captains (10 rows)

TeamName	CaptainName
Marlins	Fournier, David
Sharks	Patterson, Ann
Terrapins	Viescas, Carol
Barracudas	Sheskey, Richard
Dolphins	Viescas, Suzanne
Orcas	Thompson, Sarah
Manatees	Viescas, Michael
Swordfish	Rosales, Joe
Huckleberrys	Viescas, David
MintJuleps	Hallmark, Alaina

Recipes Database

"Show me the recipes that have beef or garlic."

Translation/ Clean Up	Select ~~unique~~ distinct recipe title from ~~the~~ recipes ~~table~~ joined ~~with the~~ recipe ingredients ~~table~~ on recipes.recipe ID ~~in the recipes table matching~~ = recipe_ingredients. recipe ID ~~in the recipe ingredients table~~ where ingredient ID ~~is in the list of beef and garlic IDs~~ (1, 9)

SQL	`SELECT DISTINCT Recipes.RecipeTitle`
	`FROM Recipes`
	`INNER JOIN Recipe_Ingredients`
	`   ON Recipes.RecipeID =`
	`      Recipe_Ingredients.RecipeID`
	`WHERE Recipe_Ingredients.IngredientID IN (1, 9)`

> ❖ **Note** Because some recipes might have both beef and garlic, I added the DISTINCT keyword to eliminate potential duplicate rows.

CH08_Beef_Or_Garlic_Recipes (5 rows)
RecipeTitle
Asparagus
Garlic Green Beans
Irish Stew
Pollo Picoso
Roast Beef

More Than Two Tables

Next, let's add some spice by making requests that require a JOIN of more than two tables.

Sales Orders Database

"Find all the customers who have ever ordered a bicycle helmet."

Translation/ Clean Up	Select customer first name, customer last name from ~~the~~ customers ~~table~~ inner join~~ed with the~~ orders ~~table~~ on customers.customer ID ~~in the customers table matching~~ = orders.customer ID ~~in the orders table, then~~ inner join~~ed with the~~ order details ~~table~~ on orders.order number ~~in the orders table matching~~ = order_details.order number ~~in the order details table, then~~ inner join~~ed with the~~ products ~~table~~ on products.product number ~~in the products table matching~~ = order_details.product number ~~in the order details table~~ where product name ~~contains~~ LIKE '%Helmet%'

SQL	`SELECT DISTINCT Customers.CustFirstName,`
	`    Customers.CustLastName`
	`FROM ((Customers INNER JOIN Orders`
	`    ON Customers.CustomerID = Orders.CustomerID)`
	`INNER JOIN Order_Details`
	`    ON Orders.OrderNumber =`
	`        Order_Details.OrderNumber)`

```
INNER JOIN Products
   ON Products.ProductNumber =
      Order_Details.ProductNumber
WHERE Products.ProductName LIKE '%Helmet%'
```

❖ **Caution** If your database system is case sensitive when performing searches in character fields, you must be careful to enter the search criteria using the correct case for the letters. For example, in many database systems, 'helmet' is not the same as 'Helmet'.

❖ **Note** Because a customer might have ordered a helmet more than once, I included the DISTINCT keyword to eliminate duplicate rows.

CH08_Customers_Who_Ordered_Helmets (25 rows)

CustFirstName	CustLastName
Andrew	Cencini
Angel	Kennedy
Caleb	Viescas
Darren	Gehring
David	Smith
Dean	McCrae
Estella	Pundt
Gary	Hallmark
Jim	Wilson
John	Viescas

<< more rows here >>

Entertainment Agency Database

"Find the entertainers who played engagements for customers Berg or Hallmark."

Translation/ Clean Up	Select ~~unique~~ distinct entertainer stage name from ~~the~~ entertainers ~~table~~ inner join~~ed with the~~ engagements ~~table~~ on entertainers.entertainer ID ~~in the entertainers table matching~~ = engagements.entertainer ID ~~in the engagements table, then~~ inner join~~ed with the~~ customers ~~table~~ on customers.customer ID ~~in the customers table matching~~ = engagements.customer ID ~~in the engagements table~~ where ~~the~~ customer last name ~~is~~ = 'Berg' or ~~the~~ customer last name ~~is~~ = 'Hallmark'

SQL	SELECT DISTINCT Entertainers.EntStageName
	
	FROM (Entertainers
	
	INNER JOIN Engagements
	
	    ON Entertainers.EntertainerID =
	
	        Engagements.EntertainerID)
	
	INNER JOIN Customers
	
	    ON Customers.CustomerID =
	
	        Engagements.CustomerID
	
	WHERE Customers.CustLastName = 'Berg'
	
	    OR Customers.CustLastName = 'Hallmark'

CH08_Entertainers_For_Berg_ OR_Hallmark (8 rows)

EntStageName
Carol Peacock Trio
Coldwater Cattle Company
Country Feeling
Jim Glynn
JV & the Deep Six
Modern Dance
Susan McLain
Topazz

Bowling League Database

"List all the tournaments, the tournament matches, and the game results."

Translation/ Clean Up	Select tourney ID, tourney location, match ID, lanes, odd lane team, even lane team, game number, game winner from ~~the~~ tournaments ~~table~~ inner joined ~~with the~~ tourney matches ~~table~~ on tournaments.tourney ID ~~in the tournaments table matching~~ = tourney_matches.tourney ID ~~in the tourney matches table, then~~ inner joined ~~with the~~ teams ~~table aliased~~ as odd team on oddteam.team ID ~~in the odd team table matches~~ = tourney_matches.odd lane team ID ~~in the tourney matches table, then~~ inner joined ~~with the~~ teams ~~table aliased~~ as even team on eventeam.team ID ~~in the even team table matches~~ = tourney_matches.even lane team ID ~~in the tourney matches table, then~~ inner joined ~~with the~~ match games ~~table~~ on match_games.match ID ~~in the match games table matches~~ = tourney_matches.match ID ~~in the tourney matches table, then~~ inner joined ~~with the~~ teams ~~table aliased~~ as winner on winner.team ID ~~in the winner table matches~~ = match_games.winning team ID ~~in the match games table~~

SQL	```SELECT Tournaments.TourneyID AS Tourney,```
	`        Tournaments.TourneyLocation AS Location,`
	`        Tourney_Matches.MatchID,`
	`        Tourney_Matches.Lanes,`
	`        OddTeam.TeamName AS OddLaneTeam,`
	`        EvenTeam.TeamName AS EvenLaneTeam,`
	`        Match_Games.GameNumber AS GameNo,`
	`        Winner.TeamName   AS Winner`
	`FROM ((((Tournaments`
	`    INNER JOIN Tourney_Matches`
	`      ON Tournaments.TourneyID`
	`      = Tourney_Matches.TourneyID)`
	`    INNER JOIN Teams AS OddTeam`
	`      ON OddTeam.TeamID`
	`      = Tourney_Matches.OddLaneTeamID)`
	`    INNER JOIN Teams AS EvenTeam`
	`      ON EvenTeam.TeamID`
	`      = Tourney_Matches.EvenLaneTeamID)`
	`    INNER JOIN Match_Games`
	`      ON Match_Games.MatchID`
	`      = Tourney_Matches.MatchID)`
	`    INNER JOIN Teams AS Winner`
	`      ON Winner.TeamID`
	`      = Match_Games.WinningTeamID`

> ❖ **Note** This is a really fun query because it requires *three* copies of one table (Teams) to get the job done. I had to assign correlation names to at least two of the tables to keep everything legal, but I went ahead and gave them all alias names to reflect their specific roles in the query.

CH08_Tournament_Match_Game_Results (168 rows)

Tourney	Location	MatchID	Lanes	OddLane Team	EvenLane Team	GameNo	Winner
1	Red Rooster Lanes	1	01-02	Marlins	Sharks	1	Marlins
1	Red Rooster Lanes	1	01-02	Marlins	Sharks	2	Sharks
1	Red Rooster Lanes	1	01-02	Marlins	Sharks	3	Marlins
1	Red Rooster Lanes	2	03-04	Terrapins	Barracudas	1	Terrapins
1	Red Rooster Lanes	2	03-04	Terrapins	Barracudas	2	Barracudas
1	Red Rooster Lanes	2	03-04	Terrapins	Barracudas	3	Terrapins
1	Red Rooster Lanes	3	05-06	Dolphins	Orcas	1	Dolphins
1	Red Rooster Lanes	3	05-06	Dolphins	Orcas	2	Orcas
1	Red Rooster Lanes	3	05-06	Dolphins	Orcas	3	Dolphins

<< more rows here >>

> ❖ **Note** Although the records appear to be sorted by tournament and match, this is simply the sequence in which the database system I used (in this case, Microsoft Access) chose to return the records. If you want to ensure that the records are sorted in a specific sequence, you must supply an ORDER BY clause.

Recipes Database

"Show me the main course recipes and list all the ingredients."

Translation/ Clean Up	Select recipe title, ingredient name, measurement description, ~~and~~ amount from ~~the~~ recipe classes ~~table~~ inner joined ~~with the~~ recipes ~~table~~ on recipes.recipe class ID ~~in the recipes table matches~~ = recipe_classes.recipe class ID ~~in the recipe classes table~~, then inner join~~ed with the~~ recipe ingredients ~~table~~ on recipes.recipe ID ~~in the recipes table matches~~ = recipe_ingredients.recipe ID ~~in the recipe ingredients table, then~~ inner joined ~~with the~~ ingredients ~~table~~ on ingredients.ingredient ID ~~in the ingredients table matches~~ = recipe_ingredients.ingredient ID ~~in the recipe ingredients table, and finally~~ inner join~~ed with the~~ measurements ~~table~~ on measurements.measure amount ID ~~in the measurements table matches~~ = recipe_ingredients.measure amount ID ~~in the recipe ingredients table~~, where recipe class description is = 'Main course'
| SQL | ```
SELECT Recipes.RecipeTitle,
    Ingredients.IngredientName,
    Measurements.MeasurementDescription,
    Recipe_Ingredients.Amount
FROM (((Recipe_Classes
INNER JOIN Recipes
  ON Recipes.RecipeClassID =
    Recipe_Classes.RecipeClassID)
INNER JOIN Recipe_Ingredients
  ON Recipes.RecipeID =
    Recipe_Ingredients.RecipeID)
INNER JOIN Ingredients
  ON Ingredients.IngredientID =
    Recipe_Ingredients.IngredientID)
INNER JOIN Measurements
  ON Measurements.MeasureAmountID =
    Recipe_Ingredients.MeasureAmountID
WHERE Recipe_Classes.RecipeClassDescription
    = 'Main course'
``` |
```

❖ **Caution** You can find a MeasureAmountID in both the Ingredients and the Recipe_Ingredients tables. If you define the final JOIN on MeasureAmountID using the Ingredients table instead of the Recipe_Ingredients table, you'll get the default measurement for the ingredient rather than the one specified for the ingredient in the recipe.

CH08_Main_Course_Ingredients (53 rows)

RecipeTitle	IngredientName	Measurement Description	Amount
Irish Stew	Beef	Pound	1
Irish Stew	Onion	Whole	2
Irish Stew	Potato	Whole	4
Irish Stew	Carrot	Whole	6
Irish Stew	Water	Quarts	4
Irish Stew	Guinness Beer	Ounce	12
Fettuccini Alfredo	Fettuccini Pasta	Ounce	16
Fettuccini Alfredo	Vegetable Oil	Tablespoon	1
Fettuccini Alfredo	Salt	Teaspoon	3

<< more rows here >>

Looking for Matching Values

Finally, let's add a third dimension to the picture. This last set of examples shows requests that use a JOIN on common values from two or more result sets or tables. (If your database supports the INTERSECT keyword, you can also solve many of these problems by intersecting the result sets.)

Sales Orders Database

"Find all the customers who ordered a bicycle and also ordered a helmet."

This request seems simple enough—perhaps too simple. Let's ask it a different way so that it's clearer what I need the database to do.

"Find all the customers who ordered a bicycle, then find all the cus-tomers who ordered a helmet, and finally list the common customers so that we know who ordered both a bicycle and a helmet."

Translation 1	Select customer first name and customer last name from those common to the set of customers who ordered bicycles and the set of customers who ordered helmets
Translation 2/ Clean Up	Select customer first name ~~and~~ customer last name from (Select ~~unique~~ distinct customer name, customer first name, customer last name from ~~the~~ customers ~~table~~ inner joined ~~with the~~ orders ~~table~~ on customers.customer ID ~~in the customers table matches~~ = orders.customer ID ~~in the orders table, then~~ inner joined ~~with the~~ order details ~~table~~ on orders.order number ~~in the orders table matches~~ = order_details.order number ~~in the order details table, then~~ inner joined ~~with the~~ products table on products.product number ~~in the products table matches~~ = order_details.product number ~~in the order details table~~ where product name ~~contains~~ LIKE '%Bike') as cust bikes inner joined ~~with~~ (Select ~~unique~~ distinct customer ID from ~~the~~ customers ~~table~~ inner joined ~~with the~~ orders ~~table~~ on customers.customer ID ~~in the customers table matches~~ = orders.customer ID in ~~the~~ orders ~~table, then~~ inner joined ~~with the~~ order details ~~table~~ on orders.order number ~~in the orders table matches~~ = order_details.order number ~~in the order details table, then~~ joined ~~with the~~ products table on products.product number ~~in the products table matches~~ = order_details.product number ~~in the order details table~~ where product name ~~contains~~ LIKE '%Helmet') as cust helmets on cust bikes.customer ID ~~in the cust bikes table matches~~ = cust helmets.customer ID ~~in the cust helmets table~~
| SQL | ```
SELECT CustBikes.CustFirstName,
    CustBikes.CustLastName
FROM
    (SELECT DISTINCT Customers.CustomerID,
        Customers.CustFirstName,
        Customers.CustLastName
    FROM ((Customers
    INNER JOIN Orders
        ON Customers.CustomerID
        = Orders.CustomerID)
    INNER JOIN Order_Details
        ON Orders.OrderNumber =
        Order_Details.OrderNumber)
``` |
```

```
        INNER JOIN Products
          ON Products.ProductNumber =
          Order_Details.ProductNumber
        WHERE Products.ProductName LIKE '%Bike')
      AS CustBikes
    INNER JOIN
      (SELECT DISTINCT Customers.CustomerID
        FROM ((Customers
        INNER JOIN Orders
          ON Customers.CustomerID =
            Orders.CustomerID)
        INNER JOIN Order_Details
          ON Orders.OrderNumber =
            Order_Details.OrderNumber)
        INNER JOIN Products
          ON Products.ProductNumber =
            Order_Details.ProductNumber
        WHERE Products.ProductName LIKE '%Helmet')
          AS CustHelmets
  ON CustBikes.CustomerID =
    CustHelmets.CustomerID
```

❖ **Note** I simplified the second embedded SELECT statement to fetch only the CustomerID because that's the only column I need for the INNER JOIN of the two sets to work. I could have actually eliminated the JOIN to the Customers table and fetched the CustomerID from the Orders table. Remember that you can think of a SELECT statement embedded in a FROM clause as a "logical table," and I assigned a unique name to each statement so that I could write the final ON clause.

You could also solve this problem as the INTERSECT of the two sets, but you would need to include all the output columns in both of the result sets that you intersect. Quite frankly, this might not be the best way to solve this problem. I'll show you how to solve this problem more efficiently in Chapter 11, "Subqueries," when I teach you how to use subqueries.

CH08_Customers_Both_Bikes_And_Helmets (21 rows)

CustFirstName	CustLastName
William	Thompson
Robert	Brown
Dean	McCrae
John	Viescas
Mariya	Sergienko
Neil	Patterson
Andrew	Cencini
Angel	Kennedy
Liz	Keyser
Rachel	Patterson
<< more rows here >>	

Entertainment Agency Database

> "List the entertainers who played engagements for both customers Berg and Hallmark."

As you saw earlier, solving for Berg *or* Hallmark is easy. Let's phrase the request a different way so that it's clearer what we need the database to do for us.

> "Find all the entertainers who played an engagement for Berg, then find all the entertainers who played an engagement for Hallmark, and finally list the common entertainers so that we know who played an engagement for both."

Translation 1	Select entertainer stage name from those common to the set of entertainers who played for Berg and the set of entertainers who played for Hallmark
Translation 2/ Clean Up	Select entertainer stage name from (Select ~~unique~~ distinct entertainer stage name from ~~the~~ entertainers ~~table~~ inner join~~ed with the~~ engagements ~~table~~ on entertainers.entertainer ID ~~in the entertainers table matches~~ = engagements.entertainer ID ~~in the engagements table,~~ ~~then~~ inner join~~ed with the~~ customers ~~table~~ on customers.customer ID ~~in the customers table matches~~ = engagements.customer ID ~~in the engagements table~~

where customer last name ~~is~~ = 'Berg') as entberg inner joi~~ned with~~ (Select ~~unique~~ distinct entertainer stage names from ~~the~~ entertainers ~~table~~ inner join~~ed with the~~ engagements ~~table~~ on entertainers.entertainer ID ~~in the entertainers table matches~~ = engagements. entertainer ID ~~in the engagements table, then~~ join~~ed with the~~ customers ~~table~~ on customers.customer ID in the customers ~~table matches~~ = engagements.customer ID ~~in the engagements table~~ where customer last name ~~is~~ = 'Hallmark') as enthallmark　on entberg.entertainer ID ~~in the entberg table matches~~ = enthallmark.entertainer ID ~~in the enthallmark table~~

SQL	

```
SELECT EntBerg.EntStageName
FROM
    (SELECT DISTINCT Entertainers.EntertainerID,
        Entertainers.EntStageName
    FROM (Entertainers
    INNER JOIN Engagements
      ON Entertainers.EntertainerID =
        Engagements.EntertainerID)
    INNER JOIN Customers
      ON Customers.CustomerID =
        Engagements.CustomerID
    WHERE Customers.CustLastName = 'Berg')
  AS EntBerg INNER JOIN
    (SELECT DISTINCT Entertainers.EntertainerID,
        Entertainers.EntStageName
    FROM (Entertainers
    INNER JOIN Engagements
      ON Entertainers.EntertainerID =
        Engagements.EntertainerID)
    INNER JOIN Customers
      ON Customers.CustomerID =
        Engagements.CustomerID
    WHERE Customers.CustLastName = 'Hallmark')
  AS EntHallmark
ON EntBerg.EntertainerID =
    EntHallmark.EntertainerID
```

CH08_Entertainers_Berg_AND_Hallmark (4 rows)

EntStageName
Carol Peacock Trio
JV & the Deep Six
Modern Dance
Country Feeling

❖ **Note** This is another example of a request that can also be solved with INTERSECT. It can also be solved more efficiently with subqueries, which you'll learn about in Chapter 11.

School Scheduling Database

"Show me the students and teachers who have the same first name."

Translation/ Clean Up	Select student full name ~~and~~ staff full name from ~~the~~ students ~~table~~ inner joined ~~with the~~ staff ~~table~~ on students.first name ~~in the students table matches~~ = staff.first name ~~in the staff table~~
SQL	SELECT (Students.StudFirstName || ' ' ||
	Students.StudLastName) AS StudFullName,
	(Staff.StfFirstName || ' ' ||
	Staff.StfLastName) AS StfFullName
	FROM Students
	INNER JOIN Staff
	ON Students.StudFirstName = Staff.StfFirstName

CH08_Students_Staff_Same_FirstName (2 rows)

StudFullName	StfFullName
Michael Viescas	Michael Hernandez
David Hamilton	David Smith

Bowling League Database

"Find the bowlers who had a raw score of 170 or better at both Thunderbird Lanes and Bolero Lanes."

Yes, this is another "solve an intersection with a JOIN" problem. Let's ask it a different way so that it's clearer what I need the database to do for us:

"Find all the bowlers who had a raw score of 170 or better at Thunderbird Lanes, then find all the bowlers who had a raw score of 170 or better at Bolero Lanes, and finally list the common bowlers so that we know who had good scores at both bowling alleys."

Translation 1	Select bowler full name from those common to the set of bowlers who have a score of 170 or better at Thunderbird Lanes and the set of bowlers who have a score of 170 or better at Bolero Lanes
Translation 2/ Clean Up	Select bowler full name from (Select ~~unique~~ distinct bowler ID ~~and~~ bowler full name from ~~the~~ bowlers ~~table~~ inner join~~ed with the~~ bowler scores ~~table~~ on bowlers. bowler ID ~~in the bowlers table matches~~ = bowler_scores. bowler ID ~~in the bowler scores table, then~~ inner join~~ed with the~~ tourney matches ~~table~~ on tourney_matches. match ID ~~in the tourney matches table matches~~ = bowler_ scores.match ID ~~in the bowler scores table, and finally~~ inner join~~ed with the~~ tournaments ~~table~~ on tournaments. tourney ID ~~in the tournaments table matches~~ = tourney_ matches.tourney ID ~~in the tourney matches table~~ where tourney location ~~is~~ = 'Thunderbird Lanes' and raw score ~~is greater than or equal to~~ >= 170) as bowlertbird inner join~~ed with~~ (Select ~~unique~~ distinct bowler ID ~~and~~ bowler full name from ~~the~~ bowlers ~~table~~ inner join~~ed with the~~ bowler scores ~~table~~ on bowlers.bowler ID ~~in the bowlers table matches~~ = bowler_scores.bowler ID ~~in the bowler scores table, then~~ inner join~~ed with the~~ tourney matches ~~table~~ on tourney_matches.match ID ~~in the tourney matches table matches~~ = bowler_scores.match ID ~~in the bowler scores table, and finally~~ inner join~~ed with the~~ tournaments ~~table~~ on tournaments.tourney ID ~~in the tournaments table matches~~ = tourney_matches.tourney ID ~~in the tourney matches table~~ where tourney location ~~is~~ = 'Bolero Lanes' and raw score ~~is greater than or equal to~~ >= 170) as bowlerbolero on bowlertbird.bowler ID ~~in the bowlertbird table matches~~ = bowlerbolero.bowler ID ~~in the bowlerbolero table~~

SQL	``SELECT BowlerTbird.BowlerFullName``
	``FROM``
	``    (SELECT DISTINCT Bowlers.BowlerID,``
	``        (Bowlers.BowlerLastName || ', ' ||``
	``        Bowlers.BowlerFirstName) AS BowlerFullName``
	``    FROM ((Bowlers``
	``    INNER JOIN Bowler_Scores``

```
        ON Bowlers.BowlerID = Bowler_Scores.
BowlerID)
    INNER JOIN Tourney_Matches
    ON Tourney_Matches.MatchID =
        Bowler_Scores.MatchID)
    INNER JOIN Tournaments
    ON Tournaments.TourneyID =
        Tourney_Matches.TourneyID
    WHERE Tournaments.TourneyLocation =
        'Thunderbird Lanes'
    AND Bowler_Scores.RawScore >= 170)
  AS BowlerTbird INNER JOIN
    (SELECT DISTINCT Bowlers.BowlerID,
        (Bowlers.BowlerLastName || ', ' ||
        Bowlers.BowlerFirstName) AS
BowlerFullName
    FROM ((Bowlers
    INNER JOIN Bowler_Scores
    ON Bowlers.BowlerID = Bowler_Scores.
BowlerID)
    INNER JOIN Tourney_Matches
    ON Tourney_Matches.MatchID =
        Bowler_Scores MatchID)
    INNER JOIN Tournaments
    ON Tournaments.TourneyID =
        Tourney_Matches.TourneyID
    WHERE Tournaments.TourneyLocation =
        'Bolero Lanes'
    AND Bowler_Scores.RawScore >= 170)
  AS BowlerBolero
ON BowlerTbird.BowlerID = BowlerBolero.BowlerID
```

❖ **Note** Because a bowler might have had a high score at either bowling alley more than once, I added the DISTINCT keyword to eliminate the duplicates. Again, this is a problem that might be better solved with subqueries, which you'll learn about in Chapter 11.

CH08_Good_Bowlers_TBird_And_Bolero (11 rows)

BowlerFullName
Kennedy, John
Patterson, Neil
Kennedy, Angel
Patterson, Kathryn
Viescas, John
Viescas, Caleb
Thompson, Sarah
Thompson, Mary
Thompson, William
Patterson, Rachel
Clothier, Ben

Recipes Database

"Display all the ingredients for recipes that contain carrots."

Translation/ Clean Up	Select recipe ID, recipe title, ~~and~~ ingredient name from ~~the~~ recipes ~~table~~ inner joined ~~with the~~ recipe ingredients ~~table~~ on recipes.recipe ID ~~in the recipes table matches~~ = recipe_ingredients.recipe ID ~~in the recipe ingredients table~~, inner joined ~~with the ingredients table~~ on ingredients.ingredient ID ~~in the ingredients table matches~~ = recipe_ingredients.ingredient ID ~~in the recipe ingredients table, then finally~~ inner joined ~~with~~ (Select recipe ID from ~~the~~ ingredients ~~table~~ inner joined ~~with the recipe ingredients table~~ on ingredients.ingredient ID ~~in the ingredients table matches~~ = recipe_ingredients.ingredient ID ~~in the recipe ingredients table~~ where ingredient name ~~is~~ = 'Carrot') as carrots on recipes.recipe ID ~~in the recipes table matches~~ = carrots.recipe ID ~~in the carrots table~~

SQL	`SELECT Recipes.RecipeID, Recipes.RecipeTitle,`
	`    Ingredients.IngredientName`
	`FROM ((Recipes`
	`INNER JOIN Recipe_Ingredients`
	`  ON Recipes.RecipeID =`
	`    Recipe_Ingredients.RecipeID)`

```
INNER JOIN Ingredients
   ON Ingredients.IngredientID =
      Recipe_Ingredients.IngredientID)
INNER JOIN
   (SELECT Recipe_Ingredients.RecipeID
    FROM Ingredients
    INNER JOIN Recipe_Ingredients
      ON Ingredients.IngredientID =
         Recipe_Ingredients.IngredientID
      WHERE Ingredients.IngredientName = 'Carrot')
   AS Carrots
ON Recipes.RecipeID = Carrots.RecipeID
```

❖ **Note** This request can be solved more simply with a subquery. I'll show you how to do that in Chapter 11.

CH08_Recipes_Containing_Carrots (16 rows)

RecipeID	RecipeTitle	IngredientName
1	Irish Stew	Beef
1	Irish Stew	Onion
1	Irish Stew	Potato
1	Irish Stew	Carrot
1	Irish Stew	Water
1	Irish Stew	Guinness Beer
14	Salmon Filets in Parchment Paper	Salmon
14	Salmon Filets in Parchment Paper	Carrot
14	Salmon Filets in Parchment Paper	Leek
14	Salmon Filets in Parchment Paper	Red Bell Pepper
14	Salmon Filets in Parchment Paper	Butter

<< more rows here >>

Summary

In this chapter, I thoroughly discussed how to link two or more tables or result sets on matching values. I began by defining the concept of a JOIN, and then I went into the details about forming an INNER JOIN. I discussed what is "legal" to use as the criteria for a JOIN but cautioned you about making nonsensical JOINs.

I started out simply with examples joining two tables. I next showed how to assign correlation (alias) names to tables within your FROM clause. You might want to do this for convenience—or you might be required to assign correlation names when you include the same table more than once or use an embedded SELECT statement.

I showed how to replace a reference to a table with a SELECT statement within your FROM clause. I next showed how to extend your horizons by joining more than two tables or result sets. I wrapped up the discussion of the syntax of an INNER JOIN by reemphasizing the importance of having a good database design and understanding how your tables are related.

I discussed some reasons why INNER JOINs are useful and gave you specific examples. The rest of the chapter provided more than a dozen examples of using INNER JOIN. I broke these examples into JOINs on two tables, JOINs on more than two tables, and JOINs on matching values. In the next chapter, I'll explore another variant of JOIN—an OUTER JOIN.

The following section presents some requests to work out on your own.

Problems for You to Solve

Below, I show you the request statement and the name of the solution query in the sample databases. If you want some practice, you can work out the SQL you need for each request and then check your answer with the query I saved in the samples. Don't worry if your syntax doesn't exactly match the syntax of the queries I saved—as long as your result set is the same.

Sales Orders Database

1. *"List customers and the dates they placed an order, sorted in order date sequence."*

   (Hint: The solution requires a JOIN of two tables.)

   You can find the solution in CH08_Customers_And_OrderDates (944 rows).

2. *"List employees and the customers for whom they booked an order."*

   (Hint: The solution requires a JOIN of more than two tables.)

   You can find the solution in CH08_Employees_And_Customers (211 rows).

3. *"Display all orders, the products in each order, and the amount owed for each product, in order number sequence."*

   (Hint: The solution requires a JOIN of more than two tables.)

   You can find the solution in CH08_Orders_With_Products (3,973 rows).

4. *"Show me the vendors and the products they supply to us for products that cost less than $100."*

   (Hint: The solution requires a JOIN of more than two tables.)

   You can find the solution in CH08_Vendors_And_Products_Less_Than_100 (66 rows).

5. *"Show me customers and employees who have the same last name."*

   (Hint: The solution requires a JOIN on matching values.)

   You can find the solution in CH08_Customers_Employees_Same_LastName (16 rows).

6. *"Show me customers and employees who live in the same city."*

   (Hint: The solution requires a JOIN on matching values.)

   You can find the solution in CH08_Customers_Employees_Same_City (10 rows).

Entertainment Agency Database

1. *"Display agents and the engagement dates they booked, sorted by booking start date."*

   (Hint: The solution requires a JOIN of two tables.)

   You can find the solution in CH08_Agents_Booked_Dates (111 rows).

2. *"List customers and the entertainers they booked."*

   (Hint: The solution requires a JOIN of more than two tables.)

   You can find the solution in CH08_Customers_Booked_
   Entertainers (75 rows).

3. *"Find the agents and entertainers who live in the same postal code."*

   (Hint: The solution requires a JOIN on matching values.)

   You can find the solution in CH08_Agents_Entertainers_Same_
   Postal (10 rows).

School Scheduling Database

1. *"Display buildings and all the classrooms in each building."*

   (Hint: The solution requires a JOIN of two tables.)

   You can find the solution in CH08_Buildings_Classrooms
   (47 rows).

2. *"List students and all the classes in which they are currently enrolled."*

   (Hint: The solution requires a JOIN of more than two tables.)

   You can find the solution in CH08_Student_Enrollments
   (50 rows).

3. *"List the faculty staff and the subject each teaches."*

   (Hint: The solution requires a JOIN of more than two tables.)

   You can find the solution in CH08_Staff_Subjects (110 rows).

4. *"Show me the students who have a grade of 85 or better in art and who also have a grade of 85 or better in any computer course."*

   (Hint: The solution requires a JOIN on matching values.)

   You can find the solution in CH08_Good_Art_CS_Students
   (1 row).

Bowling League Database

1. *"List the bowling teams and all the team members."*

   (Hint: The solution requires a JOIN of two tables.)

   You can find the solution in CH08_Teams_And_Bowlers (32 rows).

2. *"Display the bowlers, the matches they played in, and the bowler game scores."*

   (Hint: The solution requires a JOIN of more than two tables.)

   You can find the solution in CH08_Bowler_Game_Scores (1,344 rows).

3. *"Find the bowlers who live in the same ZIP Code."*

   (Hint: The solution requires a JOIN on matching values, and be sure to not match bowlers with themselves.)

   You can find the solution in CH08_Bowlers_Same_ZipCode (92 rows).

Recipes Database

1. *"List all the recipes for salads."*

   (Hint: The solution requires a JOIN of two tables.)

   You can find the solution in CH08_Salads (1 row).

2. *"List all recipes that contain a dairy ingredient."*

   (Hint: The solution requires a JOIN of more than two tables.)

   You can find the solution in CH08_Recipes_Containing_Dairy (2 rows).

3. *"Find the ingredients that use the same default measurement amount."*

   (Hint: The solution requires a JOIN on matching values.)

   You can find the solution in CH08_Ingredients_Same_Measure (628 rows).

4. *"Show me the recipes that have beef and garlic."*

   (Hint: The solution requires a JOIN on matching values.)

   You can find the solution in CH08_Beef_And_Garlic_Recipes (1 row).

9

OUTER JOINs

*"The only difference between a problem and
a solution is people understand the solution."*
—Charles Franklin Kettering Inventor, 1876–1958

Topics Covered in This Chapter

What Is an OUTER JOIN?

The LEFT/RIGHT OUTER JOIN

The FULL OUTER JOIN

Uses for OUTER JOINs

Sample Statements

Summary

Problems for You to Solve

In the previous chapter, I covered all the "ins" of JOINs—linking two or more tables or result sets using INNER JOIN to find all the rows that match. Now it's time to talk about the "outs"—linking tables and finding out not only the rows that match but also the rows that don't match.

What Is an OUTER JOIN?

As I explained in the previous chapter, the SQL Standard defines several types of JOIN operations to link two or more tables or result sets. An OUTER JOIN asks your database system to return not only the rows that match on the criteria you specify but also the unmatched rows from either one or both of the two sets you want to link.

Let's suppose, for example, that you want to fetch information from the School Scheduling database about students and the classes for which they're registered. As you learned in the previous chapter, an INNER JOIN returns only students who have registered for a class and classes for which a student has registered. It won't return any students who have been accepted at the school but haven't signed up for any classes yet, nor will it return any classes that are on the schedule but for which no student has yet shown an interest.

What if you want to list *all* students and the classes for which they are registered, if any? Conversely, suppose you want a list of *all* the classes and the students who have registered for those classes, if any. To solve this sort of problem, you need to ask for an OUTER JOIN.

Figure 9-1 uses a set diagram to show one possible relationship between students and classes. As you can see, a few students haven't registered for a class yet, and a few classes do not yet have any students signed up to take the class.

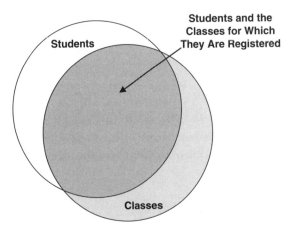

Figure 9-1 *A possible relationship between students and classes*

If you ask for *all* students and the classes for which they are registered, you'll get a result set resembling Figure 9-2.

You might ask, "What will I see for the students who haven't registered for any classes?" If you remember the concept of a Null or "nothing" value discussed in Chapter 5, "Getting More Than Simple Columns," you know what you'll see: When you ask for all students joined with any classes, your database system will return a Null value in all columns from the Classes table when it finds a student who is not yet registered for any classes. If you think about the concept of a difference between two sets (discussed in Chapter 7, "Thinking in Sets"), the rows with a Null value in the columns from the Classes table represent the difference between the set of all students and the set of students who have registered for a class.

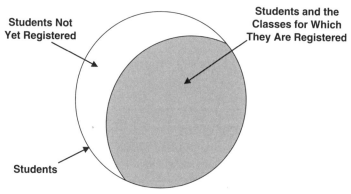

Figure 9-2 *All students and the classes for which they are registered*

Likewise, if you ask for all classes and any students who registered for classes, the rows with Null values in the columns from the Students table represent the difference between the set of all classes and the set of classes for which students have registered. As I promised, using an OUTER JOIN with a test for Null values is an alternate way to discover the difference between two sets. Unlike a true EXCEPT operation that matches on entire rows from the two sets, you can specify the match in a JOIN operation on just a few specific columns (usually the primary key and the foreign key).

The LEFT/RIGHT OUTER JOIN

You'll generally use the OUTER JOIN form that asks for all the rows from one table or result set and any matching rows from a second table or result set. To do this, you specify either a LEFT OUTER JOIN or a RIGHT OUTER JOIN.

What's the difference between LEFT and RIGHT? Remember from the previous chapter that to specify an INNER JOIN on two tables, you name the first table, include the JOIN keyword, and then name the second table. When you begin building queries using OUTER JOIN, the SQL Standard considers the first table you name as the one on the "left," and the second table as the one on the "right." So, if you want all the rows from the first table and any matching rows from the second table, you'll use a LEFT OUTER JOIN. Conversely, if you want all the rows from the second table and any matching rows from the first table, you'll specify a RIGHT OUTER JOIN.

Syntax

Let's examine the syntax needed to build either a LEFT or RIGHT OUTER JOIN.

Using Tables

I'll start simply with defining an OUTER JOIN using tables. Figure 9-3 shows the syntax diagram for creating a query with an OUTER JOIN on two tables.

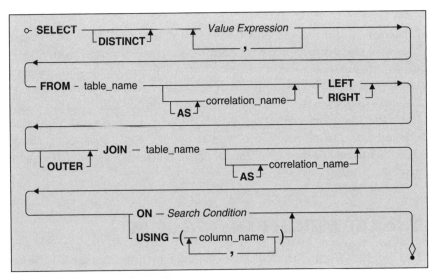

Figure 9-3 *Defining an OUTER JOIN on two tables*

Just like INNER JOIN (covered in Chapter 8, "INNER JOINs"), all the action happens in the FROM clause. (I left out the WHERE and ORDER

BY clauses for now to simplify things.) Instead of specifying a single table name, you specify two table names and link them with the JOIN keyword. If you do not specify the type of JOIN you want, your database system assumes you want an INNER JOIN. In this case, because you want an OUTER JOIN, you must explicitly state that you want either a LEFT JOIN or a RIGHT JOIN. The OUTER keyword is optional.

> ❖ **Note** For those of you following along with the complete syntax diagrams in Appendix A, "SQL Standard Diagrams," note that I've pulled together the applicable parts (from *Select Statement, Table Reference,* and *Joined Table*) into simpler diagrams that explain the specific syntax I'm discussing.

The critical part of any JOIN is the ON or USING clause that follows the second table and tells your database system how to perform the JOIN. Your database system logically combines every row in the first table with every row in the second table to solve the JOIN. (This combination of all rows from one table with all rows from a second table is called a *Cartesian product.*) It then applies the criteria in the ON or USING clause to find the matching rows to be returned. Because you asked for an OUTER JOIN, your database system also returns the unmatched rows from either the "left" or "right" table.

You learned about using a search condition to form a WHERE clause in Chapter 6, "Filtering Your Data." You can use a search condition in the ON clause within a JOIN to specify a logical test that must be true to return any two linked rows. It only makes sense to write a search condition that compares at least one column from the first table with at least one column from the second table. Although you can write a very complex search condition, you can usually specify a simple equals comparison test on the primary key columns from one table with the foreign key columns from the other table.

To keep things simple, let's start with the same recipe classes and recipes example I used in the last chapter. Remember that in a well-designed database, you should break out complex classification names into a second table and then link the names back to the primary subject table via a simple key value. In the Recipes sample database, recipe classes appear in a table separate from recipes. Figure 9-4 shows the relationship between the Recipe_Classes and Recipes tables.

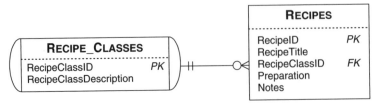

Figure 9-4 *Recipe classes are in a separate table from recipes*

When you originally set up the kinds of recipes to save in your database, you might have started by entering all the recipe classes that came to mind. Now that you've entered a number of recipes, you might be interested in finding out which classes don't have any recipes entered yet. You might also be interested in listing *all* the recipe classes along with the names of recipes entered so far for each class. You can solve either problem with an OUTER JOIN.

> ❖ **Note** Throughout this chapter, I use the "Request/Translation/ Clean Up/SQL" technique introduced in Chapter 4, "Creating a Simple Query."

"Show me all the recipe types and any matching recipes in my database."

Translation	Select recipe class description and recipe title from the recipe classes table left outer joined with the recipes table on recipe class ID in the recipe classes table matching recipe class ID in the recipes table
Clean Up	Select recipe class description ~~and~~ recipe title from ~~the~~ recipe classes ~~table~~ left outer join~~ed with the~~ recipes ~~table~~ on recipe_classes.recipe class ID ~~in the recipe classes table matching~~ = recipes.recipe class ID ~~in the recipes table~~

SQL	SELECT Recipe_Classes.RecipeClassDescription,
	        Recipes.RecipeTitle
	FROM Recipe_Classes
	LEFT OUTER JOIN Recipes
	    ON Recipe_Classes.RecipeClassID =
	        Recipes.RecipeClassID

When using multiple tables in your FROM clause, remember to qualify fully each column name with the table name wherever you use it so that it's absolutely clear which column from which table you want. Note that I *had to* qualify the name of RecipeClassID in the ON clause because there are two columns named RecipeClassID—one in the Recipes table and one in the Recipe_Classes table.

> ❖ **Note** Although most commercial implementations of SQL support OUTER JOIN, some do not. If your database does not support OUTER JOIN, you can still solve the problem by listing all the tables you need in the FROM clause, then moving your search condition from the ON clause to the WHERE clause. You must consult your database documentation to learn the specific nonstandard syntax that your database requires to define the OUTER JOIN. For example, earlier versions of Microsoft SQL Server support this syntax. (Notice the asterisk in the WHERE clause.)
>
> ```
> SELECT Recipe_Classes.RecipeClassDescription,
>     Recipes.RecipeTitle
> FROM Recipe_Classes, Recipes
> WHERE Recipe_Classes.RecipeClassID *=
>     Recipes.RecipeClassID
> ```
>
> If you're using Oracle, the optional syntax is as follows. (Notice the plus sign in the WHERE clause.)
>
> ```
> SELECT Recipe_Classes.RecipeClassDescription,
>     Recipes.RecipeTitle
> FROM Recipe_Classes, Recipes
> WHERE Recipe_Classes.RecipeClassID =
>     Recipes.RecipeClassID(+)
> ```
>
> Quite frankly, these strange syntaxes were invented by database vendors that wanted to provide this feature long before a clearer syntax was defined in the SQL Standard. Thankfully, the SQL Standard syntax allows you to fully define the source for the final result set entirely within the FROM clause. Think of the FROM clause as fully defining a linked result set from which the database system obtains your answer. In the SQL Standard, you use the WHERE clause only to filter rows out of the result set defined by the FROM clause. Also, because the specific syntax for defining an OUTER JOIN via the WHERE clause varies by product, you might have to learn several different syntaxes if you work with multiple nonstandard products.

If you execute the example query in the Recipes sample database, you should see 16 rows returned. Because I didn't enter any soup recipes in the database, you'll get a Null value for RecipeTitle in the row where RecipeClassDescription is 'Soup'. To find only this one row, use this approach.

"List the recipe classes that do not yet have any recipes."

Translation	Select recipe class description from the recipe classes table left outer joined with the recipes table on recipe class ID where recipe ID is empty
Clean Up	Select recipe class description from ~~the~~ recipe classes ~~table~~ left outer join~~ed with the~~ recipes ~~table~~ on recipe_classes.recipe class ID ~~in the recipes table matches~~ = recipes.recipe class ID ~~in the recipes table~~ where recipe ID is ~~empty~~ NULL

SQL	SELECT Recipe_Classes.RecipeClassDescription
	FROM Recipe_Classes
	LEFT OUTER JOIN Recipes
	  ON Recipe_Classes.RecipeClassID =
	      Recipes.RecipeClassID
	WHERE Recipes.RecipeID IS NULL

If you think about it, I've just done a difference or EXCEPT operation (see Chapter 7) using a JOIN. It's somewhat like saying, *"Show me all the recipe classes except the ones that already appear in the recipes table."* The set diagram in Figure 9-5 should help you visualize what's going on.

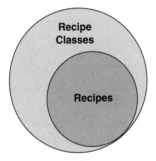

Figure 9-5 *A possible relationship between recipe classes and recipes*

In Figure 9-5, all recipes have a recipe class, but some recipe classes exist for which no recipe has yet been defined. When I add the IS NULL test, I'm asking for all the rows in the lighter outer circle that don't have any matches in the set of recipes represented by the darker inner circle.

Notice that the diagram for an OUTER JOIN on tables in Figure 9-3 also has the optional USING clause. If the matching columns in the two tables have the same name and you want to join only on equal values, you can use the USING clause and list the column names. Let's do the previous problem again with USING.

"Display the recipe classes that do not yet have any recipes."

Translation	Select recipe class description from the recipe classes table left outer joined with the recipes table using recipe class ID where recipe ID is empty
Clean Up	Select recipe class description from ~~the~~ recipe classes ~~table~~ left outer join~~ed with the~~ recipes ~~table~~ using recipe class ID where recipe ID is ~~empty~~ NULL
SQL	SELECT Recipe_Classes.RecipeClassDescription FROM Recipe_Classes LEFT OUTER JOIN Recipes USING (RecipeClassID) WHERE Recipes.RecipeID IS NULL

The USING syntax is a lot simpler, isn't it? There's one small catch: Any column in the USING clause loses its table identity because the SQL Standard dictates that the database system must "coalesce" the two columns into a single column. In this example, there's only one RecipeClassID column as a result, so you can't reference Recipes.RecipeClassID or Recipe_Classes.RecipeClassID in the SELECT clause or any other clause.

Be aware that some database systems do not yet support USING. If you find that you can't use USING with your database, you can always get the same result with an ON clause and an equals comparison.

❖ **Note** The SQL Standard also defines a type of JOIN operation called a NATURAL JOIN. A NATURAL JOIN links the two specified tables by matching all the columns with the same name. If the only

common columns are the linking columns and your database supports NATURAL JOIN, you can solve the example problem like this:

```
SELECT Recipe_Classes.RecipeClassDescription
FROM Recipe_Classes
NATURAL LEFT OUTER JOIN Recipes
WHERE Recipes.RecipeID IS NULL
```

Do not specify an ON or USING clause if you use the NATURAL
keyword.

Embedding a SELECT Statement

As you recall from Chapter 8, most SQL implementations let you substitute an entire SELECT statement for any table name in your FROM
clause. Of course, you must then assign a correlation name (see the section "Assigning Correlation (Alias) Names to Tables" in Chapter 8) so that
the result of evaluating your embedded query has a name. Figure 9-6
shows how to assemble an OUTER JOIN clause using embedded
SELECT statements.

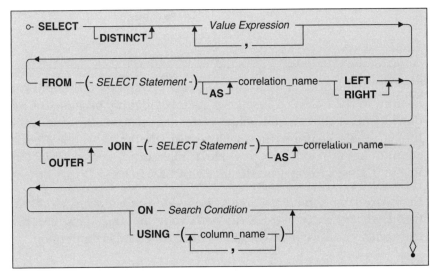

Figure 9-6 *An OUTER JOIN using SELECT statements*

Note that a SELECT statement can include all query clauses *except* an ORDER BY clause. Also, you can mix and match SELECT statements with table names on either side of the OUTER JOIN keywords.

Let's look at the Recipes and Recipe_Classes tables again. For this example, let's also assume that you are interested only in classes Salads, Soups, and Main courses. Here's the query with the Recipe_Classes table filtered in a SELECT statement that participates in a LEFT OUTER JOIN with the Recipes table:

```
SQL          SELECT RCFiltered.ClassName, R.RecipeTitle
             FROM
                  (SELECT RecipeClassID,
                       RecipeClassDescription AS ClassName
                   FROM Recipe_Classes AS RC
                   WHERE RC.ClassName = 'Salads'
                       OR RC.ClassName = 'Soup'
                       OR RC.ClassName = 'Main Course')
                  AS RCFiltered
             LEFT OUTER JOIN Recipes AS R
                  ON RCFiltered.RecipeClassID = R.RecipeClassID
```

You must be careful when using a SELECT statement in a FROM clause. First, when you decide to substitute a SELECT statement for a table name, you must be sure to include not only the columns you want to appear in the final result but also any linking columns you need to perform the JOIN. That's why you see both RecipeClassID and RecipeClassDescription in the embedded statement. Just for fun, I gave RecipeClassDescription an alias name of ClassName in the embedded statement. As a result, the SELECT clause asks for ClassName rather than RecipeClassDescription. Note that the ON clause now references the correlation name (RCFiltered) of the embedded SELECT statement rather than the original name of the table or the correlation name I assigned the table inside the embedded SELECT statement.

As the query is stated for the actual Recipes sample database, you see one row with RecipeClassDescription of Soup with a Null value returned for RecipeTitle because there are no soup recipes in the sample database. I could just as easily have built a SELECT statement on the Recipes table on the right side of the OUTER JOIN. For example, I could have asked for recipes that contain the word "beef" in their titles, as in the following statement:

```
SQL      SELECT RCFiltered.ClassName, R.RecipeTitle
         FROM
             (SELECT RecipeClassID,
                 RecipeClassDescription AS ClassName
             FROM Recipe_Classes AS RC
             WHERE RC.ClassName = 'Salads'
                 OR RC.ClassName = 'Soup'
                 OR RC.ClassName = 'Main Course')   AS RCFiltered
         LEFT OUTER JOIN
             (SELECT Recipes.RecipeClassID, Recipes.Recipe
                 Title
             FROM Recipes
             WHERE Recipes.RecipeTitle LIKE '%beef%')
             AS R
             ON RCFiltered.RecipeClassID = R.RecipeClassID
```

Keep in mind that the LEFT OUTER JOIN asks for *all* rows from the result set or table on the left side of the JOIN, regardless of whether any matching rows exist on the right side. The previous query not only returns a Soup row with a Null RecipeTitle (because there are no soups in the database at all) but also a Salad row with a Null. You might conclude that there are no salad recipes in the database. Actually, there *are* salads in the database but no salads with "beef" in the title of the recipe!

❖ **Note** You might have noticed that you can enter a full search condition as part of the ON clause in a JOIN. This is absolutely true, so it is perfectly legal in the SQL Standard to solve the example problem as follows:

```
SELECT Recipe_Classes.RecipeClassDescription,
    Recipes.RecipeTitle
FROM Recipe_Classes
LEFT OUTER JOIN Recipes
```

```
ON Recipe_Classes.RecipeClassID =
   Recipes.RecipeClassID
AND
   (Recipe_Classes.RecipeClassDescription = 'Salads'
OR Recipe_Classes.RecipeClassDescription = 'Soup'
OR Recipe_Classes.RecipeClassDescription =
   'Main Course')
AND Recipes.RecipeTitle LIKE '%beef%'
```

Unfortunately, I have discovered that some major implementations of SQL solve this problem incorrectly or do not accept this syntax at all! Therefore, I recommend that you always enter in the search condition in the ON clause only criteria that compare columns from the two tables or result sets. If you want to filter the rows from the underlying tables, do so with a separate search condition in a WHERE clause in an embedded SELECT statement.

Embedding JOINs within JOINs

Although you can solve many problems by linking just two tables, many times you'll need to link three, four, or more tables to get all the data to solve your request. For example, you might want to fetch all the relevant information about recipes—the type of recipe, the recipe name, and all the ingredients for the recipe—in one query. Now that you understand what you can do with an OUTER JOIN, you might also want to list *all* recipe classes—even those that have no recipes defined yet—and all the details about recipes and their ingredients. Figure 9-7 shows all the tables needed to answer this request.

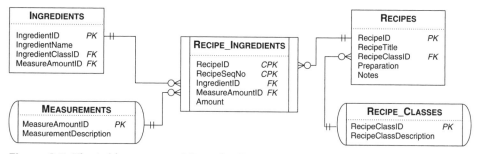

Figure 9-7 *The tables you need from the Recipes sample database to fetch all the information about recipes*

Looks like you need data from *five* different tables! Just as in Chapter 8, you can do this by constructing a more complex FROM clause, embedding JOIN clauses within JOIN clauses. Here's the trick: Everywhere you can specify a table name, you can also specify an entire JOIN clause surrounded with parentheses. Figure 9-8 shows a simplified version of joining two tables. (I've left off the correlation name clauses and chosen the ON clause to form a simple INNER or OUTER JOIN of two tables.)

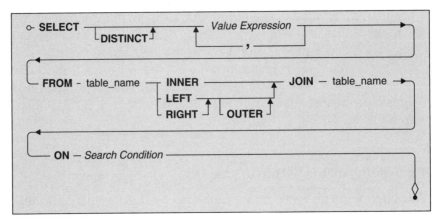

Figure 9-8 *A simple JOIN of two tables*

To add a third table to the mix, just place an open parenthesis before the first table name, add a close parenthesis after the search condition, and then insert another JOIN, a table name, the ON keyword, and another search condition. Figure 9-9 shows how to do this.

If you think about it, the JOIN of two tables inside the parentheses forms a logical table, or inner result set. This result set now takes the place of the first simple table name in Figure 9-8. You can continue this process of enclosing an entire JOIN clause in parentheses and then adding another JOIN keyword, table name, ON keyword, and search condition until you have all the result sets you need. Let's make a request that needs data from all the tables shown in Figure 9-7 and see how it turns out. (You might use this type of request for a report that lists all recipe types with details about the recipes in each type.)

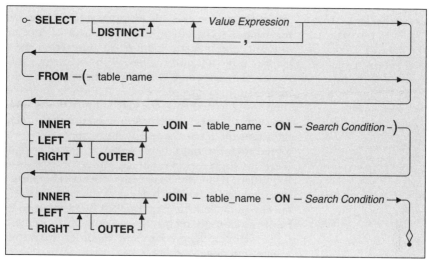

Figure 9-9 *A simple JOIN of three tables*

"I need all the recipe types, and then the matching recipe names, preparation instructions, ingredient names, ingredient step numbers, ingredient quantities, and ingredient measurements from my recipes database, sorted in recipe title and step number sequence."

Translation	Select the recipe class description, recipe title, preparation instructions, ingredient name, recipe sequence number, amount, and measurement description from the recipe classes table left outer joined with the recipes table on recipe class ID in the recipe classes table matching recipe ID in the recipes table, then joined with the recipe ingredients table on recipe ID in the recipes table matching recipe ID in the recipe ingredients table, then joined with the ingredients table on ingredient ID in the ingredients table matching ingredient ID in the recipe ingredients table, and then finally joined with the measurements table on measurement amount ID in the measurements table matching measurement amount ID in the recipe ingredients table, order by recipe title and recipe sequence number

Clean Up	Select ~~the~~ recipe class description, recipe title, preparation ~~instructions~~, ingredient name, recipe sequence number, amount, ~~and~~ measurement description from ~~the~~ recipe classes ~~table~~ left outer joined ~~with the~~ recipes ~~table~~ on recipe_classes.recipe class ID ~~in the recipe classes table matching~~ = recipes.recipe class ID ~~in the recipes table,~~ ~~then~~ inner joined ~~with the~~ recipe ingredients ~~table~~ on recipes.recipe ID ~~in the recipes table matching~~ = recipe_ingredients.recipe ID ~~in the recipe ingredients table, then~~ inner joined ~~with the~~ ingredients ~~table~~ on ingredients.ingredient ID ~~in the ingredients table matching~~ = recipe_ingredients.ingredient ID ~~in the recipe ingredients table, and then~~ ~~finally~~ inner joined ~~with the~~ measurements ~~table~~ on measurements.measurement amount ID ~~in the measurements table matching~~ = recipe_ingredients.measurement amount ID ~~in the recipe ingredients table,~~ order by recipe title, ~~and~~ recipe sequence number

SQL	`SELECT Recipe_Classes.RecipeClassDescription,`
	`    Recipes.RecipeTitle, Recipes.Preparation,`
	`    Ingredients.IngredientName,`
	`    Recipe_Ingredients.RecipeSeqNo,`
	`    Recipe_Ingredients.Amount,`
	`    Measurements.MeasurementDescription`
	`FROM (((Recipe_Classes`
	`LEFT OUTER JOIN Recipes`
	`  ON Recipe_Classes.RecipeClassID =`
	`    Recipes.RecipeClassID)`
	`INNER JOIN Recipe_Ingredients`
	`  ON Recipes.RecipeID =`
	`    Recipe_Ingredients.RecipeID)`
	`INNER JOIN Ingredients`
	`  ON Ingredients.IngredientID =`
	`    Recipe_Ingredients.IngredientID)`
	`INNER JOIN Measurements`
	`  ON Measurements.MeasureAmountID =`
	`    Recipe_Ingredients.MeasureAmountID`
	`ORDER BY RecipeTitle, RecipeSeqNo`

In truth, you can substitute an entire JOIN of two tables anywhere you might otherwise place only a table name. In Figure 9-9, I implied that you must first join the first table with the second table and then join that result with the third table. You could also join the second and third tables first (as long as the third table is, in fact, related to the second table and not the first one) and then perform the final JOIN with the first table. Figure 9-10 shows you this alternate method.

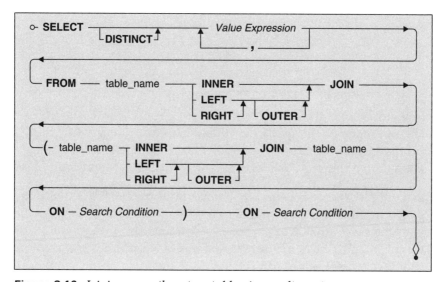

Figure 9-10 *Joining more than two tables in an alternate sequence*

To solve the request I just showed you using five tables, I could have also stated the SQL as follows:

SQL

```
SELECT Recipe_Classes.RecipeClassDescription,
       Recipes.RecipeTitle, Recipes.Preparation,
       Ingredients.IngredientName,
       Recipe_Ingredients.RecipeSeqNo,
       Recipe_Ingredients.Amount,
       Measurements.MeasurementDescription
FROM Recipe_Classes LEFT OUTER JOIN
     (((Recipes
     INNER JOIN Recipe_Ingredients
```

```
ON Recipes.RecipeID =
    Recipe_Ingredients.RecipeID)
INNER JOIN Ingredients
ON Ingredients.IngredientID =
    Recipe_Ingredients.IngredientID)
INNER JOIN Measurements
ON Measurements.MeasureAmountID =
    Recipe_Ingredients.MeasureAmountID)
ON Recipe_Classes.RecipeClassID =
    Recipes.RecipeClassID
ORDER BY RecipeTitle, RecipeSeqNo
```

Remember that the optimizers in some database systems are sensitive to the sequence of the JOIN definitions. If your query with many JOINs is taking a long time to execute on a large database, it might run faster if you change the sequence of JOINs in your SQL statement.

You might have noticed that I used only one OUTER JOIN in the previous multiple-JOIN examples. You're probably wondering whether it's possible or even makes sense to use more than one OUTER JOIN in a complex JOIN. Let's assume that there are not only some recipe classes that don't have matching recipe rows but also some recipes that don't have any ingredients defined yet. In the previous example, you won't see any rows from the Recipes table that do not have any matching rows in the Recipe_Ingredients table because the INNER JOIN eliminates them. Let's ask for all recipes as well.

> *"I need all the recipe types, and then all the recipe names and preparation instructions, and then any matching ingredient names, ingredient step numbers, ingredient quantities, and ingredient measurements from my recipes database, sorted in recipe title and step number sequence."*

| Translation | Select the recipe class description, recipe title, preparation instructions, ingredient name, recipe sequence number, amount, and measurement description from the recipe classes table left outer joined with the recipes table on |

recipe class ID in the recipe classes table matching recipe class ID in the recipes table, then left outer joined with the recipe ingredients table on recipe ID in the recipes table matching recipe ID in the recipe ingredients table, then joined with the ingredients table on ingredient ID in the ingredients table matching ingredient ID in the recipe ingredients table, and then finally joined with the measurements table on measurement amount ID in the measurements table matching measurement amount ID in the recipe ingredients table, order by recipe title and recipe sequence number

Clean Up	Select ~~the~~ recipe class description, recipe title, preparation ~~instructions~~, ingredient name, recipe sequence number, amount, ~~and~~ measurement description from ~~the~~ recipe classes ~~table~~ left outer ~~joined with the~~ recipes ~~table~~ on recipe_classes.recipe class ID ~~in the recipe classes table matching~~ = recipes.recipe class ID ~~in the recipes table,~~ ~~then~~ left outer ~~joined with the~~ recipe ingredients ~~table~~ on recipes.recipe ID ~~in the recipes table matching~~ = recipe_ingredients.recipe ID ~~in the recipe ingredients table, then~~ inner ~~joined with the~~ ingredients ~~table~~ on ingredients.ingredient ID ~~in the ingredients table matching~~ = recipe_ingredients.ingredient ID ~~in the recipe ingredients table,~~ ~~and then finally~~ inner ~~joined with the~~ measurements ~~table~~ on measurements.measurement amount ID ~~in the mea-surements table matching~~ = recipe_ingredients.measurement amount ID ~~in the recipe ingredients table,~~ order by recipe title ~~and~~ recipe sequence number
SQL	```SELECT Recipe_Classes.RecipeClassDescription,``` ```Recipes.RecipeTitle, Recipes.Preparation,``` ```Ingredients.IngredientName,``` ```Recipe_Ingredients.RecipeSeqNo,``` ```Recipe_Ingredients.Amount,``` ```Measurements.MeasurementDescription``` ```FROM (((Recipe_Classes``` ```LEFT OUTER JOIN Recipes``` ```ON Recipe_Classes.RecipeClassID =``` ```Recipes.RecipeClassID)```

```
LEFT OUTER JOIN Recipe_Ingredients
    ON Recipes.RecipeID =
        Recipe_Ingredients.RecipeID)
INNER JOIN Ingredients
    ON Ingredients.IngredientID =
        Recipe_Ingredients.IngredientID)
INNER JOIN Measurements
    ON Measurements.MeasureAmountID =
        Recipe_Ingredients.MeasureAmountID
ORDER BY RecipeTitle, RecipeSeqNo
```

Be careful! This sort of multiple OUTER JOIN works as expected only if you're following a path of one-to-many relationships. Let's look at the relationships between Recipe_Classes, Recipes, and Recipe_Ingredients again, as shown in Figure 9-11.

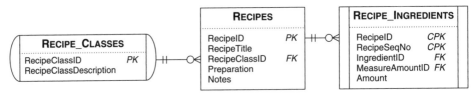

Figure 9-11 *The relationships between the Recipe_Classes, Recipes, and Recipe_Ingredients tables*

You might see a one-to-many relationship sometimes called a *parent-child relationship*. Each parent row (on the "one" side of the relationship) might have zero or more children rows (on the "many" side of the relationship). Unless you have orphaned rows on the "many" side (for example, a row in Recipes that has a Null in its RecipeClassID column), *every* row in the child table should have a matching row in the parent table. So it makes sense to say `Recipe_Classes LEFT JOIN Recipes` to pick up any parent rows in Recipe_Classes that don't have any children yet in Recipes. `Recipe_Classes RIGHT JOIN Recipes` should (barring any orphaned rows) give you the same result as an INNER JOIN.

Likewise, it makes sense to ask for `Recipes LEFT JOIN Recipe_Ingredients` because you might have some recipes for which no ingredients have yet been entered. `Recipes RIGHT JOIN Recipe_Ingredients` doesn't work because the linking column (RecipeID) in Recipe_Ingredients is also part of that table's compound primary key. Therefore, you are guaranteed to have no orphaned rows in Recipe_Ingredients because no column in a primary key can contain a Null value.

Now, let's take it one step further and ask for all ingredients, including those not yet included in any recipes. First, take a close look at the relationships between the tables, including the Ingredients table, as shown in Figure 9-12.

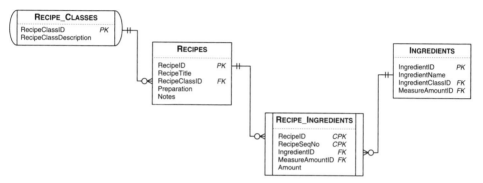

Figure 9-12 *The relationships between the Recipe_Classes, Recipes, Recipe_Ingredients, and Ingredients tables*

Let's try this request. (Caution: There's a trap here!)

"I need all the recipe types, and then all the recipe names and preparation instructions, and then any matching ingredient step numbers, ingredient quantities, and ingredient measurements, and finally all ingredient names from my recipes database, sorted in recipe title and step number sequence."

Translation	Select the recipe class description, recipe title, preparation instructions, ingredient name, recipe sequence number, amount, and measurement description from the recipe classes table left outer joined with the recipes table on recipe class ID in the recipe classes table matches class ID in the recipes table, then left outer joined with the recipe ingredients table on recipe ID in the recipes table matches recipe ID in the recipe ingredients table, then joined with the measurements table on measurement amount ID in the measurements table matches measurement amount ID in the measurements table, and then finally right outer joined with the ingredients table on ingredient ID in the ingredients table matches ingredient ID in the recipe ingredients table, order by recipe title and recipe sequence number

Clean Up	Select ~~the~~ recipe class description, recipe title, preparation ~~instructions~~, ingredient name, recipe sequence number, amount, ~~and~~ measurement description from ~~the~~ recipe classes ~~table~~ left outer joined ~~with the~~ recipes ~~table~~ on recipe_classes.recipe class ID ~~in the recipe classes table matches~~ = recipes.class ID ~~in the recipes table,~~ then left outer joined ~~with the~~ recipe ingredients ~~table~~ on recipes.recipe ID ~~in the recipes table matches~~ = recipe_ingredients.recipe ID ~~in the recipe ingredients table,~~ then inner joined ~~with the~~ measurements ~~table~~ on measurements.measurement amount ID ~~in the measurements table matches~~ = measurements.measurement amount ID ~~in the measurements table, and then finally~~ right outer joined ~~with the~~ ingredients ~~table~~ on ingredients.ingredient ID ~~in the ingredients table matches~~ = recipe_ingredients.ingredient ID ~~in the recipe ingredients table,~~ order by recipe title, ~~and~~ recipe sequence number

| SQL | ```
SELECT Recipe_Classes.RecipeClassDescription,
       Recipes.RecipeTitle, Recipes.Preparation,
       Ingredients.IngredientName,
       Recipe_Ingredients.RecipeSeqNo,
       Recipe_Ingredients.Amount,
       Measurements.MeasurementDescription
FROM (((Recipe_Classes
LEFT OUTER JOIN Recipes
  ON Recipe_Classes.RecipeClassID =
     Recipes.RecipeClassID)
LEFT OUTER JOIN Recipe_Ingredients
  ON Recipes.RecipeID =
     Recipe_Ingredients.RecipeID)
INNER JOIN Measurements
  ON Measurements.MeasureAmountID =
     Recipe_Ingredients.MeasureAmountID)
RIGHT OUTER JOIN Ingredients
  ON Ingredients.IngredientID =
     Recipe_Ingredients.IngredientID
ORDER BY RecipeTitle, RecipeSeqNo
``` |
```

Do you think this will work? Actually, the answer is a resounding NO! Most database systems analyze the entire FROM clause and then try to determine the most efficient way to assemble the table links. Let's assume, however, that the database decides to fully honor how I've grouped the JOINs within parentheses. This means that the database system will work from the innermost JOIN first (Recipe_Classes joined with Recipes) and then work outward.

Because some rows in Recipe_Classes might not have any matching rows in Recipes, this first JOIN returns rows that have a Null value in Recipes.RecipeClassID. Looking back at Figure 9-12, you can see that there's a one-to-many relationship between Recipe_Classes and Recipes. Unless some recipes exist that haven't been assigned a recipe class, I should get *all* the rows from the Recipes table anyway! The next JOIN with the Recipe_Ingredients table also asks for a LEFT OUTER JOIN. I want all the rows, regardless of any Null values, from the previous JOIN (of Recipe_Classes with Recipes) and any matching rows in Recipe_Ingredients. Again, because some rows in Recipe_Classes might not have matching rows in Recipes or some rows in Recipes might not have matching rows in Recipe_Ingredients, several of the rows might have a Null in the IngredientID column from the Recipe_Ingredients table. What I'm doing with both JOINs is "walking down" the one-to-many relationships from Recipe_Classes to Recipes and then from Recipes to Recipe_Ingredients. So far, so good. (By the way, the final INNER JOIN with Measurements is inconsequential—I know that all Ingredients have a valid MeasureAmountID.)

Now the trouble starts. The final RIGHT OUTER JOIN asks for all the rows from Ingredients and *any matching* rows from the result of the previous JOINs. Remember from Chapter 5 that a Null is a very special value—it cannot be equal to any other value, not even another Null. When I ask for *all* the rows in Ingredients, the IngredientID in all these rows has a non-Null value. None of the rows from the previous JOIN that have a Null in IngredientID will match at all, so the final JOIN throws them away! You will see any ingredient that isn't used yet in any recipe, but you won't see recipe classes that have no recipes or recipes that have no ingredients.

If your database system decides to solve the query by performing the JOINs in a different order, you might see recipe classes that have no recipes and recipes that have no ingredients, but you won't see ingredients not yet used in any recipe because of the Null matching problem. Some database systems might recognize this logic problem and refuse to solve your query at all—you'll see something like an "ambiguous OUTER JOINs" error message. The problem I'm now experiencing results from trying to "walk back up" a many-to-one relationship with an OUTER JOIN going in the other direction. Walking down the hill is easy, but walking back up the other side requires special tools. What's the solution to this problem? Read on to the next section to find out!

The FULL OUTER JOIN

A FULL OUTER JOIN is neither "left" nor "right"—it's both! It includes *all* the rows from both of the tables or result sets participating in the JOIN. When no matching rows exist for rows on the "left" side of the JOIN, you see Null values from the result set on the "right." Conversely, when no matching rows exist for rows on the "right" side of the JOIN, you see Null values from the result set on the "left."

Syntax

Now that you've been working with JOINs for a while, the syntax for a FULL OUTER JOIN should be pretty obvious. You can study the syntax diagram for a FULL OUTER JOIN in Figure 9-13.

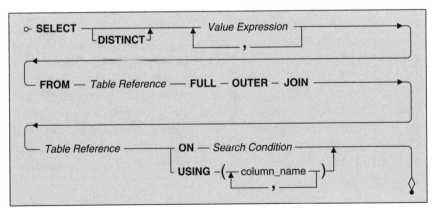

Figure 9-13 *The syntax diagram for a FULL OUTER JOIN*

To simplify things, I'm now using the term *table reference* in place of a table name, a SELECT statement, or the result of another JOIN. Let's take another look at the problem I introduced at the end of the previous section. I can now solve it properly using a FULL OUTER JOIN.

> *"I need all the recipe types, and then all the recipe names and preparation instructions, and then any matching ingredient step numbers, ingredient quantities, and ingredient measurements, and finally all ingredient names from my recipes database, sorted in recipe title and step number sequence."*

Translation	Select the recipe class description, recipe title, preparation instructions, ingredient name, recipe sequence number, amount, and measurement description from the recipe classes table full outer joined with the recipes table on recipe class ID in the recipe classes table matches recipe class ID in the recipes table, then left outer joined with the recipe ingredients table on recipe ID in the recipes table matches recipe ID in the recipe ingredients table, then joined with the measurements table on measurement amount ID in the measurements table matches measurement amount ID in the recipe ingredients table, and then finally full outer joined with the ingredients table on ingredient ID in the ingredients table matches ingredient ID in the recipe ingredients table, order by recipe title and recipe sequence number
Clean Up	Select ~~the~~ recipe class description, recipe title, preparation ~~instructions~~, ingredient name, recipe sequence number, amount, ~~and~~ measurement description from ~~the~~ recipe classes ~~table~~ full outer join~~ed with the~~ recipes ~~table~~ on recipe_classes.recipe class ID ~~in the recipe classes table matches~~ = recipes.recipe class ID ~~in the recipes table, then~~ left outer join~~ed with the~~ recipe ingredients ~~table~~ on recipes.recipe ID ~~in the recipes table matches~~ = recipe_ingredients.recipe ID ~~in the recipe ingredients table, then~~ inner join~~ed with the~~ measurements ~~table~~ on measurements.measurement amount ID ~~in the measurements table matches~~ = recipe_ingredients.measurement amount ID ~~in the recipe ingredients table, and then finally~~ full outer join~~ed with the~~ ingredients ~~table~~ on ingredients.ingredient ID ~~in the ingredients table matches~~ = recipe_ingredients.ingredient ID ~~in the recipe ingredients table,~~ order by recipe title ~~and~~ recipe sequence number

| SQL | ```
SELECT Recipe_Classes.RecipeClassDescription,
       Recipes.RecipeTitle, Recipes.Preparation,
       Ingredients.IngredientName,
       Recipe_Ingredients.RecipeSeqNo,
       Recipe_Ingredients.Amount,
       Measurements.MeasurementDescription
FROM (((Recipe_Classes
FULL OUTER JOIN Recipes
    ON Recipe_Classes.RecipeClassID =
        Recipes.RecipeClassID)
    LEFT OUTER JOIN Recipe_Ingredients
    ON Recipes.RecipeID =
        Recipe_Ingredients.RecipeID)
    INNER JOIN Measurements
    ON Measurements.MeasureAmountID =
        Recipe_Ingredients.MeasureAmountID)
    FULL OUTER JOIN Ingredients
    ON Ingredients.IngredientID =
        Recipe_Ingredients.IngredientID
ORDER BY RecipeTitle, RecipeSeqNo
``` |
| --- | --- |

The first and last JOINs now ask for *all* rows from both sides of the JOIN, so the problem with Nulls not matching is solved. You should now see not only recipe classes for which there are no recipes and recipes for which there are no ingredients but also ingredients that haven't been used in a recipe yet. You might get away with using a LEFT OUTER JOIN for the first JOIN, but because you can't predict in advance how your database system decides to nest the JOINs, you should ask for a FULL OUTER JOIN on both ends to ensure the right answer.

❖ **Note** As you might expect, database systems that do not support the SQL Standard syntax for LEFT OUTER JOIN or RIGHT OUTER JOIN also have a special syntax for FULL OUTER JOIN. You must consult your database documentation to learn the specific nonstandard syntax that your database requires to define the OUTER JOIN. For
```

example, earlier versions of Microsoft SQL Server support the following syntax. (Notice the asterisks in the WHERE clause.)

```
SELECT Recipe_Classes.RecipeClassDescription,
    Recipes.RecipeTitle
FROM Recipe_Classes, Recipes
WHERE Recipe_Classes.RecipeClassID *=*
    Recipes.RecipeClassID
```

Products that do not support any FULL OUTER JOIN syntax but do support LEFT or RIGHT OUTER JOINs yield an equivalent result by performing a UNION on a LEFT and RIGHT OUTER JOIN. I'll discuss UNION in more detail in the next chapter. Because the specific syntax for defining a FULL OUTER JOIN using the WHERE clause varies by product, you might have to learn several different syntaxes if you work with multiple nonstandard products.

FULL OUTER JOIN on Non-Key Values

Thus far, I have been discussing using OUTER JOINs to link tables or result sets on related key values. You can, however, solve some interesting problems by using an OUTER JOIN on non-key values. For example, the previous chapter showed how to find students and staff who have the same first name in the School Scheduling database. Suppose you're interested in listing *all* staff members and *all* students and showing the ones who have the same first name as well the staff who do not match any student on first name and the students who do not match any staff on first name. You can do that with a FULL OUTER JOIN.

> *"Show me all the students and all the teachers and list together those who have the same first name."*

Translation	Select student full name and staff full name from the students table full outer joined with the staff table on first name in the students table matches first name in the staff table

Clean Up	Select student full name ~~and~~ staff full name from ~~the~~ students ~~table~~ full outer joined ~~with the~~ staff ~~table~~ on students.first name ~~in the students table matches~~ = staff.first name ~~in the staff table~~
| SQL | ```
SELECT (Students.StudFirstName || ' ' ||
      Students.StudLastName) AS StudFullName,
      (Staff.StfFirstName || ' ' ||
      Staff.StfLastName) AS StfFullName
FROM Students
FULL OUTER JOIN Staff
ON Students.StudFirstName =
      Staff.StfFirstName
``` |

UNION JOIN

No discussion of OUTER JOINs would be complete without at least an honorable mention to UNION JOIN. In the SQL Standard, a UNION JOIN is a FULL OUTER JOIN with the matching rows removed. Figure 9-14 shows the syntax.

As you might expect, not many commercial implementations support a UNION JOIN. Quite frankly, I'm hard pressed to think of a good reason why you would want to do a UNION JOIN.

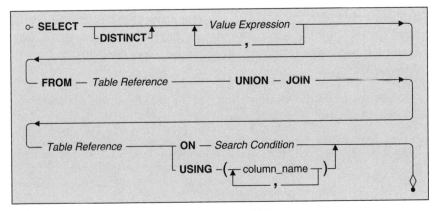

Figure 9-14 *The SQL syntax for a UNION JOIN*
```

Uses for OUTER JOINs

Because an OUTER JOIN lets you see not only the matched rows but also the unmatched ones, it's great for finding out which, if any, rows in one table do not have a matching related row in another table. It also helps you find rows that have matches on a few rows but not on all. In addition, it's useful for creating input to a report where you want to show all categories (regardless of whether matching rows exist in other tables) or all customers (regardless of whether a customer has placed an order). Following is a small sample of the kinds of requests you can solve with an OUTER JOIN.

Find Missing Values

Sometimes you just want to find what's missing. You do so by using an OUTER JOIN with a test for Null. Here are some "missing value" problems you can solve:

"What products have never been ordered?"

"Show me customers who have never ordered a helmet."

"List entertainers who have never been booked."

"Display agents who haven't booked an entertainer."

"Show me tournaments that haven't been played yet."

"List the faculty members not teaching a class."

"Display students who have never withdrawn from a class."

"Show me classes that have no students enrolled."

"List ingredients not used in any recipe yet."

"Display missing types of recipes."

Find Partially Matched Information

Particularly for reports, it's useful to be able to list all the rows from one or more tables along with any matching rows from related tables. Here's a sample of "partially matched" problems you can solve with an OUTER JOIN:

"List all products and the dates for any orders."

"Display all customers and any orders for bicycles."

"Show me all entertainment styles and the customers who prefer those styles."

"List all entertainers and any engagements they have booked."

"List all bowlers and any games they bowled over 160."

"Display all tournaments and any matches that have been played."

"Show me all subject categories and any classes for all subjects."

"List all students and the classes for which they are currently enrolled."

"Display all faculty and the classes they are scheduled to teach."

"List all recipe types, all recipes, and any ingredients involved."

"Show me all ingredients and any recipes they're used in."

Sample Statements

You now know the mechanics of constructing queries using OUTER JOIN and have seen some of the types of requests you can answer with an OUTER JOIN. Let's look at a fairly robust set of samples, all of which use OUTER JOIN. These examples come from each of the sample databases, and they illustrate the use of the OUTER JOIN to find either missing values or partially matched values.

I've also included sample result sets that would be returned by these operations and placed them immediately after the SQL syntax line. The name that appears immediately above a result set is the name I gave each query in the sample data on the companion website for the book, www.informit.com/title/9780134858333. I stored each query in the appropriate sample database (as indicated within the example) and prefixed the names of the queries relevant to this chapter with "CH09." You can follow the instructions in the Introduction of this book to load the samples onto your computer and try them.

> ❖ **Note** Because many of these examples use complex JOINs, the optimizer for your database system might choose a different way to solve these queries. For this reason, the first few rows might not exactly match the result you obtain, but the total number of rows should be the same. To simplify the process, I have combined the Translation and Clean Up steps for all the following examples.

Sales Orders Database

"What products have never been ordered?"

Translation/ Clean Up	Select product number ~~and~~ product name from ~~the~~ products ~~table~~ left outer join~~ed with the~~ order details ~~table~~ on products.product number ~~in the products table matches~~ = order_details.product number ~~in the order details table~~ where ~~the~~ order detail order number is null

SQL	SELECT Products.ProductNumber,
	        Products.ProductName
	FROM Products
	LEFT OUTER JOIN Order_Details
	  ON Products.ProductNumber =
	        Order_Details.ProductNumber
	WHERE Order_Details.OrderNumber IS NULL

CH09_Products_Never_Ordered (2 rows)

ProductNumber	ProductName
4	Victoria Pro All Weather Tires
23	Ultra-Pro Rain Jacket

"Display all customers and any orders for bicycles."

Translation 1	Select customer full name, order date, product name, quantity ordered, and quoted price from the customers table left outer joined with the orders table on customer ID, then joined with the order details table on order number, then joined with the products table on product number, then finally joined with the categories table on category ID where category description is "Bikes"
Translation 2/ Clean Up	Select customer full name, order date, product name, quantity ordered, ~~and~~ quoted price from ~~the~~ customers ~~table~~ left outer join~~ed with~~ (Select customer ID, order date, product name, quantity ordered, ~~and~~ quoted price from ~~the~~ orders ~~table~~ inner join~~ed with the~~ order details ~~table~~ on orders.order number ~~in the orders table matches~~ = order_details.order number ~~in the order details table, then~~

joined with the products table on order_details.product number in the order details table matches = products. product number in the products table, then finally joined with the categories table on categories.category ID in the categories table matches = products.category ID in the products table where category description is = 'Bikes') as rd on customers.customer ID in the customers table matches = rd.customerID in the embedded SELECT statement

❖ **Note** Because I'm looking for specific orders (bicycles), I split the translation process into two steps to show that the orders need to be filtered before applying an OUTER JOIN.

```
SQL        SELECT Customers.CustFirstName || ' ' ||
               Customers.CustLastName AS CustFullName,
               RD.OrderDate, RD.ProductName,
               RD.QuantityOrdered, RD.QuotedPrice
           FROM Customers
           LEFT OUTER JOIN
               (SELECT Orders.CustomerID, Orders.OrderDate,
                   Products.ProductName,
                   Order_Details.QuantityOrdered,
                   Order_Details.QuotedPrice      FROM ((Orders
                 INNER JOIN Order_Details
                   ON Orders.OrderNumber =
                       Order_Details.OrderNumber)
                 INNER JOIN Products
                   ON Order_Details.ProductNumber =
                       Products.ProductNumber)
                 INNER JOIN Categories
                   ON Categories.CategoryID =
                       Products.CategoryID
               WHERE Categories.CategoryDescription =
                       'Bikes')
               AS RD
           ON Customers.CustomerID = RD.CustomerID
```

> ❖ **Note** This request is really tricky because you want to list *all* customers OUTER JOINed with only the orders for bikes. If you turn Translation 1 directly into SQL, you won't find any of the customers who have not ordered a bike! An OUTER JOIN from Customers to Orders *will* return all customers and any orders. When you add the filter to select only bike orders, that's all you will get—customers who ordered bikes.
>
> Translation 2 shows you how to do it correctly—create an inner result set that returns only orders for bikes, and then OUTER JOIN that with Customers to get the final answer.

CH09_All_Customers_And_Any_Bike_Orders (914 rows)

CustFullName	OrderDate	ProductName	Quantity Ordered	QuotedPrice
Suzanne Viescas				
William Thompson	2017-12-24	Trek 9000 Mountain Bike	5	$1,164.00
William Thompson	2018-01-16	Trek 9000 Mountain Bike	6	$1,164.00
William Thompson	2017-10-12	Viscount Mountain Bike	2	$635.00
William Thompson	2017-10-06	Viscount Mountain Bike	5	$615.95
William Thompson	2018-01-16	Trek 9000 Mountain Bike	4	$1,200.00
William Thompson	2017-10-12	Trek 9000 Mountain Bike	3	$1,200.00
William Thompson	2018-01-08	Trek 9000 Mountain Bike	2	$1,200.00
		<< more rows here >>		

(Looks like William Thompson is a really good customer!)

Entertainment Agency Database

"List entertainers who have never been booked."

Translation/ Clean Up	Select entertainer ID ~~and~~ entertainer stage name from ~~the~~ entertainers ~~table~~ left outer join~~ed with the~~ engagements ~~table~~ on entertainers.entertainer ID ~~in the entertainers table matches~~ = engagements.entertainer ID ~~in the engagements table~~ where engagement number is null

SQL	SELECT Entertainers.EntertainerID,
	      Entertainers.EntStageName
	FROM Entertainers
	LEFT OUTER JOIN Engagements
	  ON Entertainers.EntertainerID =
	      Engagements.EntertainerID
	WHERE Engagements.EngagementNumber IS NULL

CH09_Entertainers_Never_Booked (1 row)

EntertainerID	EntStageName
1009	Katherine Ehrlich

"Show me all musical styles and the customers who prefer those styles."

Translation/ Clean Up	Select style ID, style name, customer ID, customer first name, ~~and~~ customer last name from ~~the~~ musical styles ~~table~~ left outer join~~ed with~~ (the musical preferences ~~table~~ inner join~~ed with the~~ customers ~~table~~ on musical_preferences.customer ID ~~in the musical preferences table matches~~ = customers.customer ID ~~in the customers table~~) on musical_styles.style ID ~~in the musical styles table matches~~ = musical_preferences.style ID ~~in the musical preferences table~~

SQL	SELECT Musical_Styles.StyleID,
	      Musical_Styles.StyleName,
	      Customers.CustomerID,
	      Customers.CustFirstName,
	      Customers.CustLastName

```
FROM Musical_Styles
LEFT OUTER JOIN (Musical_Preferences
    INNER JOIN Customers
    ON Musical_Preferences.CustomerID =
        Customers.CustomerID)
    ON Musical_Styles.StyleID =
        Musical_Preferences.StyleID
```

CH09_All_Styles_And_Any_Customers (41 rows)

StyleID	StyleName	CustomerID	CustFirstName	CustLastName
1	40s Ballroom Music	10015	Carol	Viescas
1	40s Ballroom Music	10011	Joyce	Bonnicksen
2	50s Music			
3	60s Music	10002	Deb	Waldal
4	70s Music	10007	Liz	Keyser
5	80s Music	10014	Mark	Rosales
6	Country	10009	Sarah	Thompson
7	Classical	10005	Elizabeth	Hallmark
	<< more rows here >>			

(Looks like nobody likes 50s music!)

> ❖ **Note** I very carefully phrased the FROM clause to influence the database system to first perform the INNER JOIN between Musical_Preferences and Customers, and then OUTER JOINed that with Musical_Styles. If your database tends to process JOINs from left to right, you might have to state the FROM clause with the INNER JOIN first followed by a RIGHT OUTER JOIN to Musical_Styles. In Microsoft Office Access, I had to state the INNER JOIN as an embedded SELECT statement to get it to return the correct answer.

School Scheduling Database

"List the faculty members not teaching a class."

Translation/ Clean Up	Select staff first name ~~and~~ staff last name from ~~the~~ staff ~~table~~ left outer join~~ed with the~~ faculty classes ~~table~~ on staff.staff ID ~~in the staff table matches~~ = faculty_classes.staff ID ~~in the faculty classes table~~ where class ID is null
SQL	SELECT Staff.StfFirstName, Staff.StfLastName, FROM Staff LEFT OUTER JOIN Faculty_Classes ON Staff.StaffID = Faculty_Classes.StaffID WHERE Faculty_Classes.ClassID IS NULL

CH09_Staff_Not_Teaching (5 rows)

StfFirstName	StfLastName
Jeffrey	Smith
Tim	Smith
Kathryn	Patterson
Joe	Rosales III
Carolyn	Coie

"Display students who have never withdrawn from a class."

Translation/ Clean Up	Select student full name from ~~the~~ students ~~table~~ left outer join~~ed with~~ (Select student ID from ~~the~~ student schedules ~~table~~ inner join~~ed with the~~ student class status ~~table~~ on student_class_status.class status ~~in the student class status table~~ matches = student_schedules.class status ~~in the student schedules table~~ where class status description ~~is~~ = 'withdrew') as withdrew on students.student ID ~~in the students table matches~~ = withdrew.student ID ~~in the embeddedd SELECT statement~~ where ~~the~~ student_schedules.student ID ~~in the student schedules table~~ is null

SQL	`SELECT Students.StudLastName || ', ' ||`
	`    Students.StudFirstName AS StudFullName`
	`FROM Students`
	`LEFT OUTER JOIN`
	`    (SELECT Student_Schedules.StudentID`
	`     FROM Student_Class_Status`
	`     INNER JOIN Student_Schedules`
	`       ON Student_Class_Status.ClassStatus =`
	`          Student_Schedules.ClassStatus`
	`     WHERE Student_Class_Status.ClassStatus`
	`       Description = 'withdrew')`
	`    AS Withdrew`
	`ON Students.StudentID = Withdrew.StudentID`
	`WHERE Withdrew.StudentID IS NULL`

❖ **Note** This is another example where you must apply the filter on "withdrew" in an embedded SELECT statement. If you use that filter in the WHERE clause of the main query, you will get no results. Remember that when you need to apply a filter to the "right" side of a "left" join (or vice-versa), you must do it in an embedded SELECT statement.

CH09_Students_Never_Withdrawn (16 rows)

StudFullName
Patterson, Kerry
Stadick, Betsy
Galvin, Janice
Hartwig, Doris
Bishop, Scott
Hallmark, Elizabeth
Sheskey, Sara
Smith, Karen

<< more rows here >>

"Show me all subject categories and any classes for all subjects."

Translation/ Clean Up	Select category description, subject name, classroom ID, start date, start time, ~~and~~ duration from ~~the~~ categories ~~table~~ left outer joined ~~with the~~ subjects ~~table~~ on categories.category ID ~~in the categories table matches~~ = subjects.category ID ~~in the subjects table,~~ then left outer joined ~~with the~~ classes ~~table~~ on subjects.subject ID ~~in the subjects table matches~~ = classes.subject ID ~~in the classes table~~
SQL	```SELECT Categories.CategoryDescription,``` ``` Subjects.SubjectName, Classes.ClassroomID,``` ``` Classes.StartDate, Classes.StartTime,``` ``` Classes.Duration``` ```FROM (Categories``` ```LEFT OUTER JOIN Subjects``` ``` ON Categories.CategoryID = Subjects.CategoryID)``` ```LEFT OUTER JOIN Classes``` ``` ON Subjects.SubjectID = Classes.SubjectID```

❖ **Note** I was very careful again to construct the sequence and nesting of JOINs to be sure I got the answer I expected.

CH09_All_Categories_All_Subjects_Any_Classes (145 rows)

Category Description	SubjectName	ClassroomID	StartDate	StartTime	Duration
Accounting	Financial Accounting Fundamentals I	3305	2017-09-11	16:00	50
Accounting	Financial Accounting Fundamentals I	3305	2018-01-15	16:00	50
Accounting	Financial Accounting Fundamentals II	3307	2017-09-12	13:00	80

Category Description	SubjectName	ClassroomID	StartDate	StartTime	Duration
Accounting	Fundamentals of Managerial Accounting	3307	2018-01-16	13:00	80
Accounting	Intermediate Accounting				
Accounting	Business Tax Accounting				
Art	Introduction to Art	1231	2017-09-12	10:00	50
Art	Introduction to Art	1231	2018-01-16	10:00	50

<< *more rows here* >>

Further down in the result set, you'll find no classes scheduled for Introduction to Business, Developing a Feasibility Plan, Introduction to Entrepreneurship, and Information Technology I and II. You'll also find no subjects scheduled for categories Psychology, French, or German.

Bowling League Database

"Show me tournaments that haven't been played yet."

Translation/ Clean Up	Select tourney ID, tourney date, ~~and~~ tourney location from ~~the~~ tournaments ~~table~~ left outer joined ~~with the~~ tourney matches ~~table~~ on tournaments.tourney ID ~~in the tournaments table matches~~ = tourney_matches.tourney ID ~~in the tourney matches table~~ where match ID is null
SQL	SELECT Tournaments.TourneyID, Tournaments.TourneyDate, Tournaments.TourneyLocation FROM Tournaments LEFT OUTER JOIN Tourney_Matches ON Tournaments.TourneyID = Tourney_Matches.TourneyID WHERE Tourney_Matches.MatchID IS NULL

```
SELECT Tournaments.TourneyID,
       Tournaments.TourneyDate,
       Tournaments.TourneyLocation
FROM Tournaments
LEFT OUTER JOIN Tourney_Matches
  ON Tournaments.TourneyID =
     Tourney_Matches.TourneyID
WHERE Tourney_Matches.MatchID IS NULL
```

CH09_Tourney_Not_Yet_Played (6 rows)

TourneyID	TourneyDate	TourneyLocation
15	2018-07-12	Red Rooster Lanes
16	2018-07-19	Thunderbird Lanes
17	2018-07-26	Bolero Lanes
18	2018-08-02	Sports World Lanes
19	2018-08-09	Imperial Lanes
20	2018-08-16	Totem Lanes

List all bowlers and any games they bowled over 180."

Translation 1	Select bowler name, tourney date, tourney location, match ID, and raw score from the bowlers table left outer joined with the bowler scores table on bowler ID, then inner joined with the tourney matches table on match ID, then finally inner joined with the tournaments table on tournament ID where raw score in the bowler scores table is greater than 180

Can you see why the above translation won't work? You need a filter on one of the tables that is on the right side of the left join, so you need to put the filter in an embedded SELECT statement. Let's restate the Translation step, clean it up, and solve the problem.

Translation 2/ Clean Up	Select bowler name, tourney date, tourney location, match ID, ~~and~~ raw score from ~~the~~ bowlers ~~table~~ left outer join~~ed with~~ (Select tourney date, tourney location, match ID, bowler ID, ~~and~~ raw score from ~~the~~ bowler scores ~~table~~ inner join~~ed with the~~ tourney matches ~~table~~ on bowler_scores.match ID ~~in the bowler scores table matches~~ = tourney_matches.match ID ~~in the tourney matches table, then~~ inner join~~ed with the~~ tournaments ~~table~~ on tournaments.tournament ID ~~in the tournaments table matches~~ = tourney_matches.tournament ID ~~in the tourney matches table~~ where raw score ~~is greater than~~ > 180) as ti on bowlers.bowler ID ~~in the bowlers table matches~~ = ti.bowler ID ~~in the embedded SELECT statement~~

SQL	`SELECT Bowlers.BowlerLastName || ', ' ||`
	`Bowlers.BowlerFirstName AS BowlerName,`
	`TI.TourneyDate, TI.TourneyLocation,`
	`TI.MatchID, TI.RawScore FROM Bowlers`
	`LEFT OUTER JOIN`
	`(SELECT Tournaments.TourneyDate,`

```
                  Tournaments.TourneyLocation,
                  Bowler_Scores.MatchID,
                  Bowler_Scores.BowlerID,
                  Bowler_Scores.RawScore
             FROM (Bowler_Scores
              INNER JOIN Tourney_Matches
                ON Bowler_Scores.MatchID =
                   Tourney_Matches.MatchID)
              INNER JOIN Tournaments
                ON Tournaments.TourneyID =
                   Tourney_Matches.TourneyID
              WHERE Bowler_Scores.RawScore > 180)
             AS TI
          ON Bowlers.BowlerID = TI.BowlerID
```

CH09_All_Bowlers_And_Scores_Over_180 (106 rows)

BowlerName	TourneyDate	TourneyLocation	MatchID	RawScore
Black, Alastair				
Cunningham, David				
Ehrlich, Zachary				
Fournier, Barbara				
Fournier, David				
Hallmark, Alaina				
Hallmark, Bailey				
Hallmark, Elizabeth				
Hallmark, Gary				
Hernandez, Kendra				
Hernandez, Michael				
Kennedy, Angel	2017-11-20	Sports World Lanes	46	185
Kennedy, Angel	2017-10-09	Totem Lanes	22	182

<< more rows here >>

> ❖ **Note** You guessed it! This is another example where you must build the filtered INNER JOIN result set first and then OUTER JOIN that with the table from which you want "all" rows.

Recipes Database

"List ingredients not used in any recipe yet."

Translation/ Clean Up	Select ingredient name from ~~the~~ ingredients ~~table~~ left outer join~~ed with the~~ recipe ingredients ~~table~~ on ingredients.ingredient ID ~~in the ingredients table matches~~ = recipe_ingredients.ingredient ID ~~in the recipe ingredients table~~ where recipe ID is null

SQL	SELECT Ingredients.IngredientName
	
	FROM Ingredients
	
	LEFT OUTER JOIN Recipe_Ingredients
	
	  ON Ingredients.IngredientID =
	
	    Recipe_Ingredients.IngredientID
	
	WHERE Recipe_Ingredients.RecipeID IS NULL

CH09_Ingredients_Not_Used (20 rows)

IngredientName
Halibut
Chicken, Fryer
Bacon
Iceberg Lettuce
Butterhead Lettuce
Scallop
Vinegar
Red Wine

<< more rows here >>

"I need all the recipe types, and then all the recipe names, and then any matching ingredient step numbers, ingredient quantities, and ingredient measurements, and finally all ingredient names from my recipes database, sorted by recipe class description in descending order, then by recipe title and recipe sequence number."

Translation/ Clean Up	Select ~~the~~ recipe class description, recipe title, ingredient name, recipe sequence number, amount, ~~and~~ measurement description from ~~the~~ recipes ~~table~~ left outer joined ~~with the~~ recipe ingredients ~~table~~ on recipes.recipe ID ~~in the recipes table matches~~ = recipe_ingredients.recipe ID ~~in the recipe ingredients table, then~~ inner joined ~~with the~~ measurements ~~table~~ on measurements.measurement amount ID ~~in the measurements table matches~~ = recipe_ingredients.measurement amount ID ~~in the recipe ingredients table, and then~~ full outer joined ~~with the~~ ingredients ~~table~~ on ingredients.ingredient ID ~~in the ingredients table matches~~ = recipe_ingredients.ingredient ID ~~in the recipe ingredients table, then finally~~ full outer joined ~~with the~~ recipe classes ~~table~~ on recipe_classes.recipe class ID ~~in the recipe classes table matches~~ = recipes.recipe class ID, ~~sorted~~ order by RecipeClassDescription descending, RecipeTitle, ~~and~~ RecipeSeqNo.

SQL	`SELECT Recipe_Classes.RecipeClassDescription,`
	`        Recipes.RecipeTitle,`
	`        Ingredients.IngredientName,`
	`        Recipe_Ingredients.RecipeSeqNo,`
	`        Recipe_Ingredients.Amount,`
	`        Measurements.MeasurementDescription`
	`FROM (((Recipe_Classes`
	`FULL OUTER JOIN Recipes`
	`   ON Recipe_Classes.RecipeClassID =`
	`      Recipes.RecipeClassID)`
	`   LEFT OUTER JOIN Recipe_Ingredients`
	`   ON Recipes.RecipeID =`
	`      Recipe_Ingredients.RecipeID)`
	`   INNER JOIN Measurements`
	`   ON Measurements.MeasureAmountID =`
	`      Recipe_Ingredients.MeasureAmountID)`

```
FULL OUTER JOIN Ingredients
  ON Ingredients.IngredientID =
       Recipe_Ingredients.IngredientID
  ON Recipe_Classes.RecipeClassID =
       Recipes.RecipeClassID
  ORDER BY RecipeClassDescription Desc,
    RecipeTitle, RecipeSeqNo
```

> ❖ **Note** This sample is a request you saw me solve in the section on FULL OUTER JOIN. I decided to include it here so that you can see the actual result. You won't find this query saved using this syntax in the Microsoft Access or MySQL version of the sample database because neither product supports a FULL OUTER JOIN. Instead, you can find this problem solved with a UNION of two OUTER JOIN queries that achieves the same result. You'll learn about using UNION in the next chapter. The result shown here is what you'll see when you run the query in Microsoft SQL Server or PostgreSQL.

CH09_All_Recipe_Classes_All_Recipes (109 rows)

RecipeClass Description	RecipeTitle	Ingredient Name	Recipe SeqNo	Amount	Measurement Description
Main course	Irish Stew	Beef	1	1	Pound
Main course	Irish Stew	Onion	2	2	Whole
Main course	Irish Stew	Potato	3	4	Whole
Main course	Irish Stew	Carrot	4	6	Whole
Main course	Irish Stew	Water	5	4	Quarts
Main course	Irish Stew	Guinness Beer	6	12	Ounce
Hors d'oeuvres	Salsa Buena	Jalapeno	1	6	Whole
Hors d'oeuvres	Salsa Buena	Tomato	2	2	Whole

<< more rows here >>

❖ **Note** At the 33rd row in PostgreSQL, you'll find the Recipe Class "Soup" with no recipes or ingredients. At the end of the output in SQL Server, you'll find a number of ingredients beginning with Blue Cheese and Halibut that have no Recipe Class or Recipe, with the Soup row at the end.

Summary

In this chapter, I led you through the world of OUTER JOINs. I began by defining an OUTER JOIN and comparing it to the INNER JOIN you learned about in Chapter 8.

I next explained how to construct a LEFT or RIGHT OUTER JOIN, beginning with simple examples using two tables, and then progressing to embedding SELECT statements and constructing statements using multiple JOINs. I showed how an OUTER JOIN combined with a Null test is equivalent to the difference (EXCEPT) operation I covered in Chapter 7. I also discussed some of the difficulties you might encounter when constructing statements using multiple OUTER JOINs. I closed the discussion of the LEFT and RIGHT OUTER JOIN with a problem requiring multiple OUTER JOINs that can't be solved with only LEFT or RIGHT.

In my discussion of FULL OUTER JOIN, I showed how you might need to use this type of JOIN in combination with other INNER and OUTER JOINs to get the correct answer. I also briefly explained a variant of the FULL OUTER JOIN—the UNION JOIN.

I explained how OUTER JOINs are useful and listed a variety of requests that you can solve using OUTER JOINs. The rest of the chapter showed nearly a dozen examples of how to use OUTER JOIN. I provided several examples for each of the sample databases and showed you the logic behind constructing the solution statement for each request.

The following section presents a number of requests that you can work out on your own.

Problems for You to Solve

Below, I show you the request statement and the name of the solution query in the sample databases. If you want some practice, you can work out the SQL you need for each request and then check your answer with the query I saved in the samples. Don't worry if your syntax doesn't exactly match the syntax of the queries I saved—as long as your result set is the same.

Sales Orders Database

1. *"Show me customers who have never ordered a helmet."*

   (Hint: This is another request where you must first build an INNER JOIN to find all orders containing helmets and then do an OUTER JOIN with Customers.)

   You can find the solution in CH09_Customers_No_Helmets (3 rows).

2. *"Display customers who have no sales rep (employees) in the same ZIP Code."*

   You can find the solution in CH09_Customers_No_Rep_Same_Zip (18 rows).

3. *"List all products and the dates for any orders."*

   You can find the solution in CH09_All_Products_Any_Order_Dates (2,681 rows).

Entertainment Agency Database

1. *"Display agents who haven't booked an entertainer."*

   You can find the solution in CH09_Agents_No_Contracts (1 row).

2. *"List customers with no bookings."*

   You can find the solution in CH09_Customers_No_Bookings (2 rows).

3. *"List all entertainers and any engagements they have booked."*

   You can find the solution in CH09_All_Entertainers_And_Any_Engagements (112 rows).

School Scheduling Database

1. *"Show me classes that have no students enrolled."*

   (Hint: You need only "enrolled" rows from Student_Classes, not "completed" or "withdrew.")

   You can find the solution in CH09_Classes_No_Students_Enrolled (118 rows).

2. *"Display subjects with no faculty assigned."*

   You can find the solution in CH09_Subjects_No_Faculty (1 row).

3. *"List students not currently enrolled in any classes."*

   (Hint: You need to find which students have an "enrolled" class status in student schedules and then find the students who are not in this set.)

   You can find the solution in CH09_Students_Not_Currently_Enrolled (2 rows).

4. *"Display all faculty and the classes they are scheduled to teach."*

   You can find the solution in CH09_All_Faculty_And_Any_Classes (135 rows).

Bowling League Database

1. *"Display matches with no game data."*

   You can find the solution in CH09_Matches_Not_Played_Yet (1 row).

2. *"Display all tournaments and any matches that have been played."*

   You can find the solution in CH09_All_Tourneys_Match_Results (174 rows).

Recipes Database

1. *"Display missing types of recipes."*

   You can find the solution in CH09_Recipe_Classes_No_Recipes (1 row).

2. *"Show me all ingredients and any recipes they're used in."*

   You can find the solution in CH09_All_Ingredients_Any_Recipes (108 rows).

3. *"List the salad, soup, and main course categories and any recipes."*

   You can find the solution in CH09_Salad_Soup_Main_Courses (9 rows).

4. *"Display all recipe classes and any recipes."*

   You can find the solution in CH09_All_RecipeClasses_And_Matching_Recipes (16 rows).

UNIONs

*"I beseech those whose piety will permit them reverently
to petition, that they will pray for this union."*
—SAM HOUSTON, TEXAS HERO

Topics Covered in This Chapter

What Is a UNION?

Writing Requests with UNION

Uses for UNION

Sample Statements

Summary

Problems for You to Solve

In Chapter 7, "Thinking in Sets," I introduced three fundamental set operations—intersection, difference, and union. Chapter 8, "INNER JOINs," showed how to perform the equivalent of an intersection operation by linking result sets on key values using INNER JOIN. Chapter 9, "OUTER JOINs," discussed how to ask for a set difference by using an OUTER JOIN and testing for the Null value. This chapter explains how to do the third operation, a UNION.

What Is a UNION?

A UNION lets you select the rows from two or more similar result sets and combine them into a single result set. Notice that I said "rows," not "columns." In Chapters 8 and 9, you learned how to bring together columns from two or more result sets using a JOIN. When you ask for a JOIN, the columns from the result sets appear side by side. For example, if you ask for the RecipeClassDescription from the Recipe_Classes table and the RecipeTitle from the Recipes table with a JOIN, you get a result set that looks like Figure 10-1.

RecipeClassDescription	RecipeTitle
Main course	Irish Stew
Main course	Fettuccini Alfredo
Main course	Pollo Picoso
Main course	Roast Beef
Main course	Huachinango Veracruzana (Red Snapper, Veracruz style)
Main course	Tourtière (French-Canadian Pork Pie)
Main course	Salmon Filets in Parchment Paper
Vegetable	Garlic Green Beans
<< more rows here >>	

Figure 10-1 *Fetching data from two tables using a JOIN*

Let's first take a quick look at the syntax for a basic UNION, as shown in Figure 10-2.

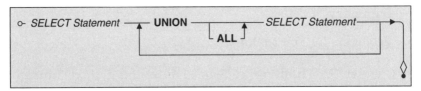

Figure 10-2 *The syntax diagram for a basic UNION statement*

A UNION interleaves the rows from one result set with the rows from another result set. You define each result set by writing a SELECT statement that can include not only a complex JOIN in the FROM clause but also WHERE, HAVING, and GROUP BY clauses. You then link them with the UNION keyword. (You'll learn about the GROUP BY clause in Chapter 13, "Grouping Data," and the HAVING clause in Chapter 14, "Filtering Grouped Data.") If you ask for RecipeClassDescription from the Recipe_Classes table UNION RecipeTitle from the Recipes table, you get an answer that looks like Figure 10-3.

Notice that I get only one column in the result set. The name of the column is inherited from the column in the first table we chose to include in the SELECT expression, but it includes information on both RecipeTitle (Asparagus) and RecipeClassDescription (Dessert). Instead of appearing side by side, the data from the two columns is interleaved vertically.

RecipeClassDescription
Asparagus
Coupe Colonel
Dessert
Fettuccini Alfredo
Garlic Green Beans
Hors d'oeuvres
Huachinango Veracruzana (Red Snapper, Veracruz style)
Irish Stew
<< more rows here >>

Figure 10-3 *Fetching data from two tables using a UNION*

If you studied the diagram in Figure 10-2, you're probably wondering what the optional keyword ALL is about. When you leave out that keyword, your database system eliminates any rows that have duplicate values. For example, if there's a RecipeClassDescription of Dessert and a RecipeTitle of Dessert, you get only one Dessert row in the final result set. Conversely, when you include the ALL keyword, no duplicate rows are removed. Note that UNION ALL is likely to be much more efficient because your database system doesn't have to do extra work to look for and eliminate any duplicate rows. If you're certain that the queries you are combining with UNION don't contain any duplicate rows (or you don't care about duplicates), then always use the ALL keyword.

To perform a UNION, the two result sets must meet certain requirements. First, each of the two SELECT statements that you're linking with a UNION must have the same number of output columns specified after the SELECT keyword so that the result set will have the same number of columns. Secondly, each corresponding column must be what the SQL Standard calls "comparable."

❖ **Note** The full SQL:2016 Standard allows you to UNION dissimilar sets. However, most commercial implementations support the basic or entry-level standard I'm describing here. You might find that your database system allows you to use UNION in more creative ways.

As discussed in Chapter 6, "Filtering Your Data," you should compare only character values with character values, number values with number values, or datetime values with datetime values. Although some database systems allow mixing data types in a comparison, it really doesn't make sense to compare a character value such as "John" to a numeric value such as 55. If it makes sense to compare two columns in a WHERE clause, then the columns are comparable. This is what the SQL Standard means when it requires that a column from one result set that you want to UNION with a column from another result set must be of a comparable data type.

Writing Requests with UNION

In the previous chapters on INNER JOIN and OUTER JOIN, you studied how to construct a SELECT statement using the SELECT, FROM, and WHERE clauses. The focus of those two chapters was on constructing complex JOINs within the FROM clause. To construct a UNION, you now have to graduate to a *SELECT expression* that links two or more SELECT statements with the UNION operator. Each SELECT statement can have as simple or complex a FROM clause as you need to get the job done.

Using Simple SELECT Statements

Let's start simply by creating a UNION of two simple SELECT statements that use a single table in the FROM clause. Figure 10-4 shows the syntax diagram for a UNION of two simple SELECT statements.

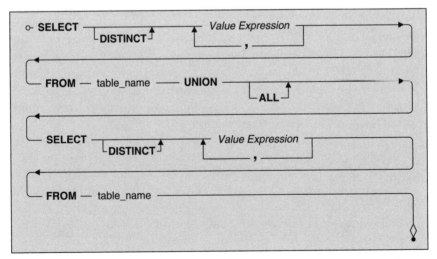

Figure 10-4 *Using a UNION to combine two simple SELECT statements*

Unlike when you ask for a JOIN, all the action happens in the UNION operator that you specify to combine the two SELECT statements. As mentioned earlier, if you leave out the optional ALL keyword, your database system eliminates any duplicate rows it finds. This means that the result set from your request might have fewer rows than the sum of the number of rows returned from each result set participating in the UNION. On the other hand, if you include the ALL keyword, the number of rows in the result set will be equal to the sum of the number of rows in the two participating result sets.

❖ **Note** The SQL Standard also defines a CORRESPONDING clause that you can place after the UNION keyword to indicate that you want the UNION performed by comparing columns that have the same name in each result set. You can also further restrict the comparison set by including a specific list of column names after the CORRE-SPONDING keyword. I could not find a major commercial implementation of this feature, but you might find it supported in future releases of the product you use.

Let's create a simple UNION—a mailing list for customers and vendors from the Sales Orders sample database. Figure 10-5 shows the two tables needed.

CUSTOMERS		VENDORS	
CustomerID	*PK*	VendorID	*PK*
CustFirstName		VendName	
CustLastName		VendStreetAddress	
CustStreetAddress		VendCity	
CustCity		VendState	
CustState		VendZipCode	
CustZipCode		VendPhoneNumber	
CustAreaCode		VendFaxNumber	
CustPhoneNumber		VendWebPage	
		VendEmailAddress	

Figure 10-5 *The Customers and Vendors tables from the Sales Orders sample database*

Notice that there's no "natural" relationship between these two tables, but they do both contain columns that have similar meanings and data types. In a mailing list, you need a name, street address, city, state, and ZIP Code. Because all these fields in both tables are comparable character data, I don't need to worry about data types. (Some database designers might make ZIP Code a number, but that's OK too, as long as the ZIP Code column from one table is a data type that's comparable with the data type of the ZIP Code column from the second table.)

One problem is that the name in the Vendors table is a single column, but there are two name fields in Customers: CustFirstName and CustLastName. To come up with the same number of columns from both tables, I need to build an expression on the two columns from Customers to create a single column expression to UNION with the single name column from Vendors. Let's build the query.

> ❖ **Note** Throughout this chapter, I use the "Request/Translation/Clean Up/SQL" technique introduced in Chapter 4, "Creating a Simple Query."

"Build a single mailing list that consists of the name, address, city, state, and ZIP Code for customers and the name, address, city, state, and ZIP Code for vendors."

Translation	Select customer full name, customer address, customer city, customer state, and customer ZIP Code from the customers table combined with vendor name, vendor address, vendor city, vendor state, and vendor ZIP Code from the vendors table
Clean Up	Select customer full name, customer address, customer city, customer state, ~~and~~ customer ZIP Code from ~~the~~ customers ~~table combined with~~ union Select vendor name, vendor address, vendor city, vendor state, ~~and~~ vendor ZIP Code from ~~the~~ vendors ~~table~~

SQL	SELECT Customers.CustLastName || ', ' ||
	    Customers.CustFirstName AS MailingName,
	Customers.CustStreetAddress, Customers.CustCity,
	    Customers.CustState, Customers.CustZipCode
	FROM Customers
	UNION
	SELECT Vendors.VendName,
	    Vendors.VendStreetAddress, Vendors.VendCity,
	    Vendors.VendState, Vendors.VendZipCode
	FROM Vendors

Notice that each SELECT statement generates five columns, but I had to use an expression to combine the two name columns in the Customers table into a single column. All the columns from both SELECT statements are character data, so I have no problem with them being comparable.

You might be wondering: "What are the names of the columns that are output from this query?" Good question! The SQL Standard specifies that when the names of respective columns are the same (for example, the name of the fourth column of the first SELECT statement is the same as the name of the fourth column of the second SELECT statement), that's the name of the output column. If the column names are different (as in the example I just constructed), the SQL Standard states: "If a <query expression body> immediately contains UNION or INTERSECT, and the <column name>s of a pair of corresponding columns of the operand tables are not equivalent, then the result column has an implementation-dependent <column name>."

In plain English, this means that your database system decides what names to assign to the output columns. Your system is compliant with the SQL Standard as long as the name doesn't appear in some other column position in one of the result sets participating in the UNION. Most commercial database systems default to the names of the columns in the first SELECT statement. For the previous example, this means that you'll see column names of MailingName, CustStreetAddress, CustCity, CustState, and CustZipCode.

Notice that I did not include the ALL keyword in the UNION. Although it is unlikely that a customer last name and first name will match a vendor name (never mind the address, city, state, and ZIP Code), I wanted to avoid duplicate mailing addresses. If you're certain that you won't have any duplicates in two or more UNION sets, you can include the ALL keyword. Using ALL most likely will cause the request to run faster because your database system won't have to do extra work attempting to remove duplicates.

Combining Complex SELECT Statements

As you might imagine, the SELECT statements you combine with a UNION operator can be as complex as you need to get the job done. The only restriction is that both SELECT statements must ultimately provide the same number of columns, and the columns in each relative position must be comparable data types.

Suppose you want a list of all the customers and the bikes they ordered combined with all the vendors and the bikes they supply. First, let's identify all the tables I need. Figure 10-6 shows the tables needed to link customers to products.

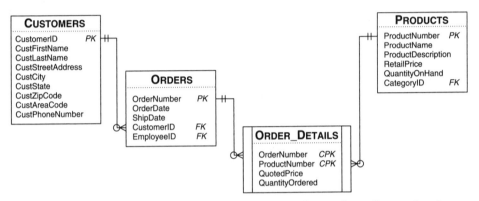

Figure 10-6 *Table relationships to link customers to the products they ordered*

Looks like I need to JOIN four tables. If I want to find vendors and the products they sell, I need the tables shown in Figure 10-7.

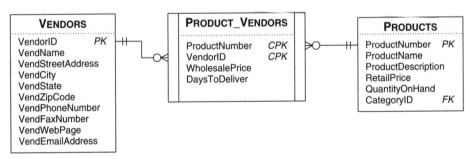

Figure 10-7 *Table relationships to link vendors to the products they sell*

As discussed in Chapter 8, you can nest multiple JOIN clauses to link several tables to gather the information you need to solve a complex problem. For review, Figure 10-8 shows the syntax for nesting three tables.

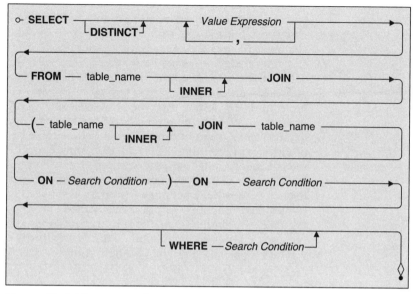

Figure 10-8 *The syntax for JOINing three tables*

I now have all the pieces needed to solve the puzzle. I can build a compound INNER JOIN to fetch the customer information, insert a UNION keyword, and then build the compound INNER JOIN for the vendor information.

"List customers and the bikes they ordered combined with vendors and the bikes they sell."

Translation	Select customer full name and product name from the customers table joined with the orders table on customer ID in the customers table matches customer ID in the orders table, then joined with the order details table on order number in the orders table matches order number in the order details table, and then joined with the products table on product number in the products table matches product number in the order details table where product name contains 'bike', combined with select vendor name and product name from the vendors table joined with the product vendors table on vendor ID in the vendors table matches vendor ID in the product vendors table, and then joined with the products table on product number in the products table matches product number in the product vendors table where product name contains 'bike'

Clean Up	Select customer full name ~~and~~ product name from ~~the~~ customers ~~table~~ ~~joined with the~~ orders ~~table~~ on customers.customer ID ~~in the customers table matches~~ = orders.customer ID ~~in the orders table, then~~ joined ~~with the~~ order details ~~table~~ on orders.order number ~~in the orders table matches~~ = order_details.order number ~~in the order details table, and then~~ joined ~~with the~~ products ~~table~~ on products.product number ~~in the products table matches~~ = order_details.product number ~~in the order details table~~ where product name ~~contains~~ like '%bike%', ~~combined with~~ union select vendor name ~~and~~ product name from ~~the~~ vendors ~~table~~ joined ~~with the~~ product vendors ~~table~~ on vendors.vendor ID ~~in the vendors table matches~~ = product_vendors.vendor ID ~~in the product vendors table, and then~~ joined ~~with the~~ products ~~table~~ on products.product number ~~in the products table matches~~ = product_vendors.product number ~~in the product vendors table~~ where product name ~~contains~~ like '%bike%'
SQL	

```
SELECT Customers.CustLastName || ', ' ||
    Customers.CustFirstName AS FullName,
    Products.ProductName, 'Customer' AS RowID
FROM ((Customers INNER JOIN Orders
  ON Customers.CustomerID = Orders.CustomerID)
INNER JOIN Order_Details
  ON Orders.OrderNumber =
    Order_Details.OrderNumber)
INNER JOIN Products
  ON Products.ProductNumber =
    Order_Details.ProductNumber
WHERE Products.ProductName LIKE '%bike%'
UNION
SELECT Vendors.VendName, Products.ProductName,
    'Vendor' AS RowID
FROM (Vendors
INNER JOIN Product_Vendors
  ON Vendors.VendorID = Product_Vendors.VendorID)
INNER JOIN Products
  ON Products.ProductNumber =
    Product_Vendors.ProductNumber
WHERE Products.ProductName LIKE '%bike%'
```

Well, that's about the size of the King Ranch, but it gets the job done! Notice that I also threw in a character string literal that I named RowID in both SELECT statements so that it will be easy to see which rows originate from Customers and which ones come from Vendors. You might be tempted to insert a DISTINCT keyword in the first SELECT statement because a really good customer might have ordered a particular bike model more than once. Because I didn't use the ALL keyword on the UNION, the request will eliminate any duplicates anyway. If you add DISTINCT, you might be asking your database system to perform extra work to eliminate duplicates twice!

When you need to build a UNION query, I recommend that you build the separate SELECT statements first. It's easy then to copy and paste the syntax for each SELECT statement into a new query, separating each statement with the UNION keyword.

Using UNION More Than Once

So far, I have shown you only how to use a UNION to combine two result sets. In truth, you can follow the second SELECT statement specification with another UNION keyword and another SELECT statement. Although some implementations limit the number of result sets you can combine with UNION, in theory, you can keep adding UNION SELECT to your heart's content.

Suppose you need to build a single mailing list from three different tables—Customers, Employees, and Vendors—perhaps to create a combined list for holiday greeting labels. Figure 10-9 shows a diagram of the syntax to build this list.

You can see that you need to create one SELECT statement to fetch all the names and addresses from the Customers table, UNION that first statement with a SELECT statement for the same information from the Employees table, and finally, UNION that with a SELECT statement for names and addresses from the Vendors table. (To simplify the process, I have combined the Translation and Clean Up steps in this example.)

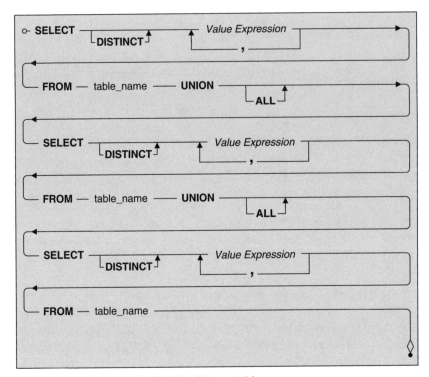

Figure 10-9 *Creating a UNION of three tables*

"Create a single mailing list for customers, employees, and vendors."

Translation/ Clean Up	Select customer full name, customer street address, customer city, customer state, ~~and~~ customer ZIP Code from ~~the~~ customers ~~table combined with~~ union Select employee full name, employee street address, employee city, employee state, ~~and~~ employee ZIP Code from ~~the~~ employees ~~table combined with~~ union Select vendor name, vendor street address, vendor city, vendor state, ~~and~~ vendor ZIP Code from ~~the~~ vendors ~~table~~

SQL	SELECT Customers.CustFirstName || ' ' ||
	        Customers.CustLastName AS CustFullName,
	        Customers.CustStreetAddress,
	        Customers.CustCity,
	        Customers.CustState, Customers.CustZipCode

```
FROM Customers
UNION
SELECT Employees.EmpFirstName || ' ' ||
       Employees.EmpLastName AS EmpFullName,
       Employees.EmpStreetAddress, Employees.EmpCity,
       Employees.EmpState,
       Employees.EmpZipCode
FROM Employees
UNION
SELECT Vendors.VendName, Vendors.VendStreetAddress,
       Vendors.VendCity, Vendors.VendState,
       Vendors.VendZipCode
FROM Vendors
```

Of course, if you want to filter the mailing list for a particular city, state, or range of ZIP Codes, you can add a WHERE clause to any or all of the SELECT statements. If, for example, you want to create a list of the customers, employees, and vendors only in a particular state, you must add a WHERE clause to *each* of the embedded SELECT statements. You could also apply a filter to just one of the SELECT statements, for example, to create a list of vendors in the state of Texas combined with all customers and all employees.

Sorting a UNION

What about sorting the result of a UNION? You'll find on many database systems that the result set appears as though it is sorted by the output columns from left to right. For example, in the UNION of three tables I just built in the previous section, the rows will appear in sequence first by name, then by street address, and so on.

To keep the postal service happy (and perhaps get a discount for a large mailing), sort your rows by ZIP Code. You can add an ORDER BY clause to do this, but the trick is that this clause must appear at the very end after the last SELECT statement. The ORDER BY applies to the result of the UNION, not the last SELECT statement. Figure 10-10 shows how to do this.

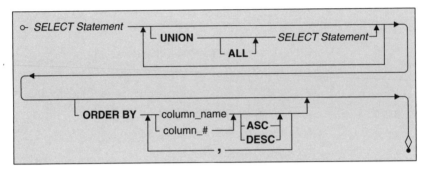

Figure 10-10 *Adding a sorting specification to a UNION query*

As the diagram shows, you can loop through a UNION SELECT statement as many times as you like to pick up all the result sets you need to combine, but the ORDER BY clause must appear at the end. You might ask, "What do I use for column_name or column_# in the ORDER BY clause?" Remember that you're sorting the output of all the previous parts of the SELECT expression. As discussed earlier, the output names of the columns are "implementation-dependent," but most database systems use the column names generated by the first SELECT statement.

You can also specify the relative column number, starting with 1, as the first output column. In a query that outputs name, street address, city, state, and ZIP Code, you need to specify a column_# of 5 (ZIP Code is the fifth column) to sort by ZIP.

Let's sort the mailing list query using both techniques. Here's the correct syntax for sorting by column name:

```
SQL    SELECT Customers.CustFirstName || ' ' ||
          Customers.CustLastName AS CustFullName,
          Customers.CustStreetAddress, Customers.CustCity,
          Customers.CustState, Customers.CustZipCode
       FROM Customers
       UNION
       SELECT Employees.EmpFirstName || ' ' ||
          Employees.EmpLastName AS EmpFullName,
          Employees.EmpStreetAddress, Employees.EmpCity,
          Employees.EmpState, Employees.EmpZipCode
```

```
FROM Employees
UNION
SELECT Vendors.VendName, Vendors.VendStreetAddress,
    Vendors.VendCity, Vendors.VendState,
    Vendors.VendZipCode
FROM Vendors
ORDER BY CustZipCode
```

Of course, I'm assuming that the name of the output column I want to sort is the name of the column from the first SELECT statement. Using a relative column number to specify the sort looks like this:

SQL

```
SELECT Customers.CustFirstName || ' ' ||
    Customers.CustLastName AS CustFullName,
    Customers.CustStreetAddress,
    Customers.CustCity,
    Customers.CustState, Customers.CustZipCode
FROM Customers
UNION
SELECT Employees.EmpFirstName || ' ' ||
    Employees.EmpLastName AS EmpFullName,
    Employees.EmpStreetAddress, Employees.EmpCity,
    Employees.EmpState, Employees.EmpZipCode
FROM Employees
UNION
SELECT Vendors.VendName, Vendors.VendStreetAddress,
    Vendors.VendCity, Vendors.VendState,
    Vendors.VendZipCode
FROM Vendors
ORDER BY 5
```

Uses for UNION

You probably won't use UNION as much as INNER JOIN and OUTER JOIN. You most likely will use UNION to combine two or more similar result sets from different tables. Although you *can* use UNION to combine two result sets from the same table or set of tables, you usually can solve those sorts of problems with a simple SELECT statement containing a more complex WHERE clause. I include a couple of examples in the "Sample Statements" section and show you the more efficient way to solve the same problem with a WHERE clause instead of a UNION.

Here's just a small sample of the types of problems you can solve with UNION using the sample databases:

> *"Show me all the customer and employee names and addresses."*
>
> *"List all the customers who ordered a bicycle combined with all the customers who ordered a helmet." (This is one of those problems that can also be solved with a single SELECT statement and a complex WHERE clause.)*
>
> *"Produce a mailing list for customers and vendors."*
>
> *"List the customers who ordered a bicycle together with the vendors who provide bicycles."*
>
> *"Create a list that combines agents and entertainers."*
>
> *"Display a combined list of customers and entertainers."*
>
> *"Produce a list of customers who like contemporary music together with a list of entertainers who play contemporary music."*
>
> *"Create a mailing list for students and staff."*
>
> *"Show me the students who have an average score of 85 or better in Art together with the faculty members who teach Art and have a proficiency rating of 9 or better."*
>
> *"Find the bowlers who had a raw score of 155 or better at Thunderbird Lanes combined with bowlers who had a raw score of 140 or better at Bolero Lanes." (This is another problem that can also be solved with a single SELECT statement and a complex WHERE clause.)*
>
> *"List the tourney matches, team names, and team captains for the teams starting on the odd lane together with the tourney matches, team names, and team captains for the teams starting on the even lane."*
>
> *"Create an index list of all the recipe titles and ingredients."*
>
> *"Display a list of all ingredients and their default measurement amounts together with ingredients used in recipes and the measurement amount for each recipe."*

Sample Statements

You now know the mechanics of constructing queries using UNION and have seen some of the types of requests you can answer with a UNION. Let's take a look at a fairly robust set of samples using UNION from each of the sample databases. These examples illustrate the use of the UNION operation to combine sets of rows.

I've also included sample result sets that would be returned by these operations and placed them immediately after the SQL syntax line. The name that appears immediately above a result set is the name I gave each query in the sample data on the companion website for this book, www.informit.com/title/9780134858333. I stored each query in the appropriate sample database (as indicated within the example), and I prefixed the names of the queries relevant to this chapter with "CH10." You can follow the instructions in the Introduction of this book to load the samples onto your computer and try them.

> ❖ **Note** Because many of these examples use complex JOINs, the optimizer for your database system might choose a different way to solve these queries. For this reason, the first few rows might not exactly match the result you obtain, but the total number of rows should be the same. To simplify the process, I have combined the Translation and Clean Up steps for all the following examples.

Sales Orders Database

> *"Show me all the customer and employee names and addresses, including any duplicates, sorted by ZIP Code."*

Translation/ Clean Up	Select ~~customer~~ first name, ~~customer~~ last name, ~~customer~~ street address, ~~customer~~ city, ~~customer~~ state, ~~and~~ ~~customer~~ ZIP Code from ~~the~~ customers ~~table~~ ~~combined with~~ union all Select ~~employee~~ first name, ~~employee~~ last name, ~~employee~~ street address, ~~employee~~ city, ~~employee~~ state, ~~and~~ ~~employee~~ ZIP Code from ~~the~~ employees ~~table~~, order by ZIP Code

```
SQL        SELECT Customers.CustFirstName,
                  Customers.CustLastName,
                  Customers.CustStreetAddress,
                  Customers.CustCity,
                  Customers.CustState, Customers.CustZipCode
           FROM Customers
           UNION ALL
           SELECT Employees.EmpFirstName,
                  Employees.EmpLastName,
                  Employees.EmpStreetAddress, Employees.EmpCity,
                  Employees.EmpState, Employees.EmpZipCode
           FROM Employees
           ORDER BY CustZipCode
```

CH10_Customers_UNION_ALL_Employees (36 rows)

CustFirst Name	CustLast Name	CustStreet Address	CustCity	CustState	CustZip Code
Estella	Pundt	2500 Rosales Lane	Dallas	TX	75260
Robert	Brown	672 Lamont Ave	Houston	TX	77201
Kirk	DeGrasse	455 West Palm Ave	San Antonio	TX	78284
Kirk	DeGrasse	455 West Palm Ave	San Antonio	TX	78284
Angel	Kennedy	667 Red River Road	Austin	TX	78710
Maria	Patterson	3445 Cheyenne Road	El Paso	TX	79915
Mark	Rosales	323 Advocate Lane	El Paso	TX	79915
Caleb	Viescas	4501 Wetland Road	Long Beach	CA	90809

<< more rows here >>

(Notice that Kirk DeGrasse must be both a customer and an employee.)

"List all the customers who ordered a bicycle combined with all the customers who ordered a helmet."

Translation/ Clean Up	Select customer first name, customer last name, ~~and the constant~~ 'Bike' from ~~the~~ customers ~~table~~ joined ~~with the~~ orders ~~table~~ on customers. customer ID ~~in the customers table matches~~ = orders.customer ID ~~in the orders table, then~~ joined ~~with the~~ order details ~~table~~ on orders.order number ~~in the orders table matches~~ = order_details.order number ~~in the order details table, and then~~ joined ~~with the~~ products ~~table~~ on product number ~~in the products table matches~~ = order_details.product number ~~in the order details table~~ where product name ~~contains~~ like '%bike%,' ~~combined with~~ union Select customer first name, customer last name, ~~and the constant~~ 'Helmet' from ~~the~~ customers ~~table~~ joined ~~with the~~ orders ~~table~~ on customers.customer ID ~~in the customers table matches~~ = orders.customer ID ~~in the orders table,~~ ~~then~~ joined ~~with the~~ order details ~~table~~ on orders. order number ~~in the orders table matches~~ = order_details.order number ~~in the order details table, and then~~ joined ~~with the~~ products ~~table~~ on product number ~~in the products table matches~~ = order_details.product number ~~in the order details table~~ where product name ~~contains~~ like '%helmet%'

| SQL | ```sql
SELECT Customers.CustFirstName,
    Customers.CustLastName, 'Bike' AS ProdType
FROM ((Customers INNER JOIN Orders
  ON Customers.CustomerID = Orders.CustomerID)
INNER JOIN Order_Details
  ON Orders.OrderNumber =
    Order_Details.OrderNumber)
INNER JOIN Products
  ON Products.ProductNumber =
    Order_Details.ProductNumber
WHERE Products.ProductName LIKE '%bike%'
UNION
SELECT Customers.CustFirstName,
    Customers.CustLastName, 'Helmet' AS ProdType
FROM ((Customers INNER JOIN Orders
  ON Customers.CustomerID = Orders.CustomerID)
INNER JOIN Order_Details
  ON Orders.OrderNumber = Order_Details.OrderNumber)
INNER JOIN Products
  ON Products.ProductNumber =
    Order_Details.ProductNumber
WHERE Products.ProductName LIKE '%helmet%'
``` |
```

CH10_Customer_Order_Bikes_UNION_Customer_Order_Helmets (52 rows)

CustFirstName	CustLastName	ProdType
Alaina	Hallmark	Bike
Andrew	Cencini	Bike
Andrew	Cencini	Helmet
Angel	Kennedy	Bike
Angel	Kennedy	Helmet
Caleb	Viescas	Bike
Caleb	Viescas	Helmet
Darren	Gehring	Bike

<< more rows here >>

Notice that this is one of those problems that can also be solved with a single SELECT statement and a slightly more complex WHERE clause. The one advantage of using a UNION is that it's easy to add an artificial "set identifier" column (in this case, the ProdType column) to each result set so that you can see which customers came from which result set. However, most database systems solve a WHERE clause—even one with complex criteria—much faster than they solve a UNION. Following is the SQL to solve the same problem with a WHERE clause, but note that this eliminates rows in which a customer ordered both a bike and a helmet because I didn't include the ProdType column. Doing so would have required a CASE statement in the SELECT clause, which you won't learn about until Chapter 19, "Condition Testing."

```
SQL       SELECT DISTINCT Customers.CustFirstName,
               Customers.CustLastName
          FROM ((Customers INNER JOIN Orders
            ON Customers.CustomerID = Orders.CustomerID)
          INNER JOIN Order_Details
            ON Orders.OrderNumber = Order_Details.OrderNumber)
          INNER JOIN Products
            ON Products.ProductNumber =
               Order_Details.ProductNumber
          WHERE Products.ProductName LIKE '%bike%'
            OR Products.ProductName LIKE '%helmet%'
```

CH10_Customers_Bikes_Or_Helmets (27 rows)

CustFirstName	CustLastName
Alaina	Hallmark
Andrew	Cencini
Angel	Kennedy
Caleb	Viescas
Darren	Gehring
David	Smith
Dean	McCrae
Estella	Pundt
<< more rows here >>	

❖ **Note** You can see that you need a DISTINCT keyword to eliminate duplicates when you don't use UNION. Remember that UNION automatically eliminates duplicates unless you specify UNION ALL. You can specify DISTINCT in the UNION examples, but you're asking your database system to do more work than necessary.

Entertainment Agency Database

"Create a list that combines agents and entertainers."

Translation/ Clean Up	Select agent full name, ~~and the constant~~ 'Agent' from ~~the~~ agents ~~table combined with~~ union Select ~~entertainer~~ stage name, ~~and the constant~~ 'Entertainer' from ~~the~~ entertainers ~~table~~
| SQL | ```
SELECT Agents.AgtLastName || ', ' ||
       Agents.AgtFirstName AS Name, 'Agent' AS Type
FROM Agents
UNION
SELECT Entertainers.EntStageName,
       'Entertainer' AS Type
FROM Entertainers
``` |
```

CH10_Agents_UNION_Entertainers (22 rows)

Name	Type
Bishop, Scott	Agent
Carol Peacock Trio	Entertainer
Caroline Coie Cuartet	Entertainer
Coldwater Cattle Company	Entertainer
Country Feeling	Entertainer
Dumbwit, Daffy	Agent
Jazz Persuasion	Entertainer
Jim Glynn	Entertainer

<< more rows here >>

School Scheduling Database

"Show me the students who have a grade of 85 or better in Art together with the faculty members who teach Art and have a proficiency rating of 9 or better."

Translation/ Clean Up	Select student first name ~~aliased~~ as FirstName, student last name ~~aliased~~ as LastName, ~~and~~ grade ~~aliased~~ as Score from the students table joined ~~with the~~ student schedules ~~table~~ on students.student ID ~~in the students table matches~~ = student_schedules.student ID ~~in the student schedules table, then~~ joined ~~with the~~ student class status ~~table~~ on student_class_status.class status ~~in the student class status table matches~~ = student_schedules.class status ~~in the student schedules table,~~ ~~then~~ joined ~~with the~~ classes ~~table~~ on classes.class ID ~~in the classes table matches~~ = student_schedules.class ID ~~in the student schedules table, and then~~ joined ~~with the~~ subjects ~~table~~ on subjects.subject ID ~~in the subjects table matches~~ = classes.subject ID ~~in the classes table~~ where class status description ~~is~~ = 'completed' and grade ~~is greater than or equal to~~ >= 85 and category ID ~~is~~ = 'ART' ~~combined with~~ union Select staff first name, staff last name, ~~and~~ proficiency rating ~~aliased~~ as Score from ~~the~~ staff ~~table~~ joined ~~with the~~ faculty subjects ~~table~~ on staff.staff ID ~~in the staff table matches~~ = faculty_subjects.staff ID ~~in the faculty subjects table, and then~~ joined ~~with the~~ subjects ~~table~~ on subjects.subject ID ~~in the subjects table matches~~ = faculty_subjects.subject ID ~~in the faculty subjects table~~ where proficiency rating ~~is greater than~~ > 8 and category ID ~~is~~ = 'ART'

SQL

```
SELECT Students.StudFirstName AS FirstName,
    Students.StudLastName AS LastName,
    Student_Schedules.Grade AS Score,
    'Student' AS Type
FROM (((Students INNER JOIN Student_Schedules
  ON Students.StudentID =
    Student_Schedules.StudentID)
INNER JOIN Student_Class_Status
  ON Student_Class_Status.ClassStatus =
    Student_Schedules.ClassStatus)
INNER JOIN Classes
  ON Classes.ClassID = Student_Schedules.ClassID)
INNER JOIN Subjects
  ON Subjects.SubjectID = Classes.SubjectID
WHERE Student_Class_Status.ClassStatusDescription =
    'Completed'
  AND Student_Schedules.Grade >= 85
  AND Subjects.CategoryID = 'ART'
UNION
SELECT Staff.StfFirstName, Staff.StfLastName,
    Faculty_Subjects.ProficiencyRating AS Score,
    'Faculty' AS Type
FROM (Staff INNER JOIN Faculty_Subjects
  ON Staff.StaffID = Faculty_Subjects.StaffID)
INNER JOIN Subjects
  ON Subjects.SubjectID = Faculty_Subjects.SubjectID
WHERE Faculty_Subjects.ProficiencyRating > 8
  AND Subjects.CategoryID = 'ART'
```

CH10_Good_Art_Students_And_Faculty (12 rows)

FirstName	LastName	Score	Type
Alaina	Hallmark	10	Faculty
George	Chavez	97.81	Student
John	Kennedy	87.65	Student
Kerry	Patterson	99.83	Student
Liz	Keyser	10	Faculty
Mariya	Sergienko	9	Faculty
Michael	Hernandez	10	Faculty
<< more rows here >>			

Bowling League Database

"List the tourney matches, team names, and team captains for the teams starting on the odd lane together with the tourney matches, team names, and team captains for the teams starting on the even lane, and sort by tournament date and match number."

Translation/ Clean Up	Select tourney location, tourney date, match ID, team name, captain name ~~and the constant~~ 'Odd Lane' from ~~the~~ tournaments ~~table~~ joined ~~with the~~ tourney matches ~~table~~ on tournaments.tourney ID ~~in the tournaments table equals~~ = tourney_matches.tourney ID ~~in the tourney matches table, then~~ joined ~~with the~~ teams ~~table~~ on tourney_matches.odd lane team ID ~~in the tourney matches table equals~~ = teams.team ID ~~in the teams table, and then~~ joined ~~with the~~ bowlers ~~table~~ on teams.captain ID ~~in the teams table equals~~ = bowlers.bowler ID ~~in the bowlers table, combined with~~ union all Select tourney location, tourney date, match ID, team name, captain name ~~and the constant~~ 'Even Lane' from ~~the~~ tournaments ~~table~~ joined ~~with the~~ tourney matches ~~table~~ on tournaments.tourney ID ~~in the tournaments tab-le equals~~ = tourney_matches.tourney ID ~~in the tourney matches table, then~~ joined ~~with the~~ teams ~~table~~ on tourney_matches.even lane team ID ~~in the tourney matches table equals~~ = teams.team ID ~~in the teams table, and then~~ joined ~~with the~~ bowlers ~~table~~ on teams.captain ID ~~in the teams table equals~~ = bowlers.bowler ID ~~in the bowlers table~~, order by ~~tourney date~~ 2, ~~and match ID~~ 3

SQL

```
SELECT Tournaments.TourneyLocation,
       Tournaments.TourneyDate,
       Tourney_Matches.MatchID, Teams.TeamName,
       Bowlers.BowlerLastName || ', ' ||
       Bowlers.BowlerFirstName AS Captain,
       'Odd Lane' AS Lane
FROM ((Tournaments INNER JOIN Tourney_Matches
  ON Tournaments.TourneyID =
     Tourney_Matches.TourneyID)
INNER JOIN Teams
  ON Teams.TeamID =
     Tourney_Matches.OddLaneTeamID)
INNER JOIN Bowlers
  ON Bowlers.BowlerID = Teams.CaptainID
UNION ALL
SELECT Tournaments.TourneyLocation,
       Tournaments.TourneyDate,
       Tourney_Matches.MatchID, Teams.TeamName,
       Bowlers.BowlerLastName || ', ' ||
       Bowlers.BowlerFirstName AS Captain,
       'Even Lane' AS Lane
FROM ((Tournaments INNER JOIN Tourney_Matches
  ON Tournaments.TourneyID =
     Tourney_Matches.TourneyID)
INNER JOIN Teams  ON Teams.TeamID =
     Tourney_Matches.EvenLaneTeamID)
INNER JOIN Bowlers
  ON Bowlers.BowlerID = Teams.CaptainID
ORDER BY 2, 3
```

Notice that the two SELECT statements are almost identical! The only difference is the first SELECT statement links Tourney_Matches with Teams on OddLaneTeamID, and the second uses EvenLaneTeamID. Also, note that I decided in the final solution to sort by relative column number (the second and third columns) rather than column name

(TourneyDate and MatchID). Finally, you can use UNION ALL because a team is never going to compete against itself.

CH10_Bowling_Schedule (114 rows)

Tourney Location	Tourney Date	MatchID	TeamName	Captain	Lane
Red Rooster Lanes	2017-09-04	1	Marlins	Fournier, David	Odd Lane
Red Rooster Lanes	2017-09-04	1	Sharks	Patterson, Ann	Even Lane
Red Rooster Lanes	2017-09-04	2	Barracudas	Sheskey, Richard	Even Lane
Red Rooster Lanes	2017-09-04	2	Terrapins	Viescas, Carol	Odd Lane
Red Rooster Lanes	2017-09-04	3	Dolphins	Viescas, Suzanne	Odd Lane
Red Rooster Lanes	2017-09-04	3	Orcas	Thompson, Sarah	Even Lane
Red Rooster Lanes	2017-09-04	4	Manatees	Viescas, Michael	Odd Lane
Red Rooster Lanes	2017-09-04	4	Swordfish	Rosales, Joe	Even Lane
Thunderbird Lanes	2017-09-11	5	Marlins	Fournier, David	Even Lane
Thunderbird Lanes	2017-09-11	5	Terrapins	Viescas, Carol	Odd Lane

<< more rows here >>

Recipes Database

"Create an index list of all the recipe classes, recipe titles, and ingredients."

Translation/ Clean Up	Select recipe class description, ~~and the constant~~ 'Recipe Class' from ~~the~~ recipe classes ~~table combined with~~ union Select recipe title, ~~and the constant~~ 'Recipe' from ~~the~~ recipes ~~table combined with~~ union Select ingredient name, ~~and the constant~~ 'Ingredient' from ~~the~~ ingredients ~~table~~

```
SQL        SELECT Recipe_Classes.RecipeClassDescription
               AS IndexName, 'Recipe Class' AS Type
           FROM Recipe_Classes
           UNION
           SELECT Recipes.RecipeTitle, 'Recipe' AS Type FROM
              Recipes
           UNION
           SELECT Ingredients.IngredientName,
               'Ingredient' AS Type
           FROM Ingredients
```

CH10_Classes_Recipes_Ingredients (101 rows)

IndexName	Type
Asparagus	Ingredient
Asparagus	Recipe
Bacon	Ingredient
Balsamic vinaigrette dressing	Ingredient
Beef	Ingredient
Beef drippings	Ingredient
Bird's custard powder	Ingredient
Black olives	Ingredient

<< more rows here >>

Summary

I began the chapter by defining UNION and showing you the difference between linking two tables with a JOIN and combining two tables with a UNION.

I next explained how to construct a simple UNION using two SELECT statements, each of which asked for columns from a single table. I explained the significance of the ALL keyword and recommended that you use it either when you know the queries produce no duplicates or when you don't care. I then progressed to combining two complex

SELECT statements that each used a JOIN on multiple tables. Next, I showed how to use UNION to combine more than two result sets. I wrapped up my discussion of UNION syntax by showing how to sort the result.

I explained how UNION is useful and listed a variety of requests that you can solve using UNION. The "Sample Statements" section showed you one or two examples of how to use UNION in each of the sample databases, including the logic behind constructing these requests.

The following section presents some requests that you can work out on your own.

Problems for You to Solve

Below, I show you the request statement and the name of the solution query in the sample databases. If you want some practice, you can work out the SQL you need for each request and then check your answer with the query I saved in the samples. Don't worry if your syntax doesn't exactly match the syntax of the queries I saved—as long as your result set is the same.

Sales Orders Database

1. *"List the customers who ordered a helmet together with the vendors who provide helmets."*

   (Hint: This involves creating a UNION of two complex JOINs.)

   You can find the solution in CH10_Customer_Helmets_Vendor_Helmets (91 rows).

Entertainment Agency Database

1. *"Display a combined list of customers and entertainers."*

   (IIint: Be careful to create an expression for one of the names so that you have the same number of columns in both SELECT statements.)

   You can find the solution in CH10_Customers_UNION_Entertainers (28 rows).

2. *"Produce a list of customers who like contemporary music together with a list of entertainers who play contemporary music."*

(Hint: You need to UNION two complex JOINs to solve this one.)

You can find the solution in CH10_Customers_Entertainers_Contemporary (5 rows).

School Scheduling Database

1. *"Create a mailing list for students and staff, sorted by ZIP Code."*

(Hint: Try using a relative column number for the sort.)

You can find the solution in CH10_Student_Staff_Mailing_List (45 rows).

Bowling League Database

1. *"Find the bowlers who had a raw score of 165 or better at Thunderbird Lanes combined with bowlers who had a raw score of 150 or better at Bolero Lanes."*

(Hint: This is another of those problems that can also be solved with a single SELECT statement and a complex WHERE clause.)

You can find the solution using UNION in CH10_Good_Bowlers_TBird_Bolero_UNION (129 rows). You can find the solution using WHERE in CH10_Good_Bowlers_TBird_Bolero_WHERE (135 rows).

2. *"Can you explain why the row counts are different in the previous solution queries?"*

(Hint: Try using UNION ALL in the first query.)

Recipes Database

1. *"Display a list of all ingredients and their default measurement amounts together with ingredients used in recipes and the measurement amount for each recipe."*

(Hint: You need one simple JOIN and one complex JOIN to solve this.)

You can find the solution in CH10_Ingredient_Recipe_Measurements (144 rows).

Subqueries

"We can't solve problems by using the same kind of thinking we used when we created them."

—ALBERT EINSTEIN

Topics Covered in This Chapter

What Is a Subquery?

Subqueries as Column Expressions

Subqueries as Filters

Uses for Subqueries

Sample Statements

Summary

Problems for You to Solve

In the previous three chapters, I showed you many ways to work with data from more than one table. All the techniques I've covered to this point have been focused on linking subsets of information—one or more columns and one or more rows from an entire table or a query embedded in the FROM clause. I've also explored combining sets of information using the UNION operator. In this chapter, I'll show you effective ways to fetch a single column from a table or query and use it as a value expression in either a SELECT clause or a WHERE clause.

There are two significant points you should learn in this chapter:

1. There's always more than one way to solve a particular problem in SQL. In fact, this chapter will show you new ways to solve problems already covered in previous chapters.

2. You can build complex filters that do not rely on the tables in your FROM clause. This is an important concept because using a subquery in a WHERE clause is the only way to get the correct number of rows in your answer when you want rows from one table based on the filtered contents from other related tables. I'll explain this in more detail later in the chapter.

> ❖ **Note** This chapter covers advanced concepts and assumes that you've read and thoroughly understood Chapter 7, "Thinking in Sets"; Chapter 8, "INNER JOINs"; and Chapter 9, "OUTER JOINs."

What Is a Subquery?

Simply put, a *subquery* is a SELECT expression that you embed inside one of the clauses of a SELECT statement to form your final query statement. In this chapter, I'll define more formally a subquery and show how to use it other than in the FROM clause.

The SQL Standard defines three types of subqueries:

1. **Row subquery**—an embedded SELECT expression that returns more than one column and no more than one row

2. **Table subquery**—an embedded SELECT expression that returns one or more columns and zero to many rows

3. **Scalar subquery**—an embedded SELECT expression that returns only one column and no more than one row

Row Subqueries

You've already created queries that embed a SELECT statement in a FROM clause to let you filter rows before joining that result with other tables or queries. (That's called a table subquery, as you'll learn below.)

A *row subquery* is a special form of a SELECT statement that returns more than one column but only one row.

In the SQL Standard, you can use a row subquery to build something the standard calls a *row value constructor*. When you create a WHERE clause, you build a search condition that is typically some sort of comparison of one column from one of your tables either with another column or with a literal. The SQL Standard, however, allows you to build a search condition that compares multiple values as a logical row with another set of values as a logical row (two row value constructors). You can enter the list of comparison values either by making a list in parentheses or by using a row subquery to fetch a single row from one of your tables. The bad news is that not many commercial database systems support this syntax.

Why might this be useful? Consider a Products table that has a compound part identifier in two separate fields. The first part of the identifier might be characters that indicate the subclass of parts (SKUClass), such as CPU or DSK for a computer parts manufacturer. The second part of the identifier could be a number that identifies the part within the subclass (SKUNumber). Let's say you want all parts that have a combined identifier of DSK09775 or higher. Here's an example of a WHERE clause that uses a row value constructor to solve the problem:

```
SQL        SELECT SKUClass, SKUNumber, ProductName
           FROM Products
           WHERE
              (SKUClass, SKUNumber)
              >= ('DSK', 9775)
```

The preceding WHERE clause asks for rows where the combination of SKUClass and SKUNumber is greater than the combination of DSK and 9775. It's the same as requesting the following:

```
SQL        SELECT SKUClass, SKUNumber, ProductName
           FROM Products
           WHERE (SKUClass > 'DSK')
           OR ((SKUClass = 'DSK')
           AND (SKUNumber >= 9775))
```

Here's where you could substitute a SELECT statement that returns a single row of two columns—a row subquery—for the second part of the comparison (probably using a WHERE clause to limit the result to one row). Most commercial databases support neither a row value constructor nor row subqueries. That's all I'm going to say about them in this chapter.

Table Subqueries

Wait a minute! Didn't I already show you how to embed a SELECT expression returning multiple rows and columns inside a FROM clause in the previous three chapters? The answer is yes—I snuck it in on you! I've already liberally used table subqueries in the previous chapters to specify a complex result that I then embedded in the FROM clause of another query. In this chapter, I'll show you how to use a table subquery as the source for the list of comparison values for an IN predicate— something about which you learned the basics in Chapter 6, "Filtering Your Data." I'll also teach you a few new comparison predicate keywords that are used only with table subqueries.

Scalar Subqueries

In this chapter, I'll also show how to use a scalar subquery anywhere you might otherwise use a value expression. A scalar subquery lets you fetch a single column or calculated expression from another table that does not have to be in the FROM clause of the main query. You can use the single value fetched by a scalar subquery in the list of columns you request in a SELECT clause or as a comparison value in a WHERE clause.

Subqueries as Column Expressions

In Chapter 5, "Getting More Than Simple Columns," you learned a lot about using expressions to generate calculated columns to be output by your query. I didn't tell you then that you can also use a special type of SELECT statement—a subquery—to fetch data from another table, even if the table isn't in your FROM clause.

Syntax

Let's go back to the basics and take a look at a simple form of a SELECT statement in Figure 11-1.

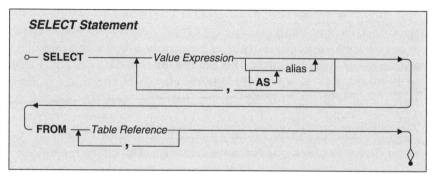

Figure 11-1 *The syntax diagram for a simple SELECT statement*

This looks simple, but it really isn't! In fact, the value expression part can be quite complex. Figure 11-2 shows all the options that can constitute a value expression.

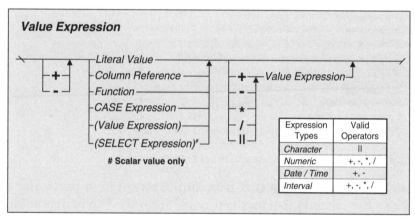

Figure 11-2 *The syntax diagram for a value expression*

In Chapter 5, I showed you how to create basic value expressions using literal values, column references, and functions. I'll explore *CASE Expression* in Chapter 19, "Condition Testing." Notice that *SELECT Expression* now appears on the list. This means that you can embed a scalar subquery in the list of expressions immediately following the SELECT keyword. As noted earlier, a scalar subquery is a SELECT expression that returns exactly one column and no more than one row. This makes sense because you're substituting the subquery where you would normally enter a single column name or expression that results in a single column.

You might be wondering at this point, "Why is this useful?" A subquery used in this way lets you pluck a single value from some other table or query to include in the output of your query. You don't need to reference the table or query that is the source of the data in the FROM clause of the subquery at all in the FROM clause of the outer query. In most cases, you will need to add criteria in the WHERE clause of the subquery to make certain it returns no more than one row. You can even have the criteria in the subquery reference a value being returned by the outer query to pluck out the data related to the current row.

Let's look at some simple examples using only the Customers and Orders tables from the Sales Orders example database. Figure 11-3 shows the relationship between these two tables.

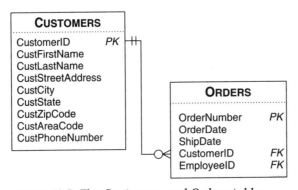

Figure 11-3 *The Customers and Orders tables*

Now, let's build a query that lists all the orders for a particular date and plucks the related customer last name from the Customers table using a subquery.

> ❖ **Note** Throughout this chapter, I use the "Request/Translation/ Clean Up/SQL" technique introduced in Chapter 4, "Creating a Simple Query." Also, I include parentheses around the parts that are subqueries in the Clean Up step and indent the subqueries where possible to help you see how I am using them.

"Show me all the orders shipped on October 3, 2017, and each order's related customer last name."

Translation	Select order number, order date, ship date, and also select the related customer last name out of the customers table from the orders table where ship date is October 3, 2017
Clean Up	Select order number, order date, ship date, ~~and also~~ (select ~~the related~~ customer last name ~~out of the~~ from customers ~~table~~) from ~~the~~ orders ~~table~~ where ship date ~~is~~ = ~~October 3, 2017~~ '2017-10-03'
SQL	SELECT Orders.OrderNumber, Orders.OrderDate, 　　Orders.ShipDate, 　　(SELECT Customers.CustLastName 　　FROM Customers 　　WHERE Customers.CustomerID = 　　　Orders.CustomerID) FROM Orders WHERE Orders.ShipDate = '2017-10-03'

Notice that I had to restrict the value of the CustomerID in the subquery to the value of the CustomerID in each row I'm fetching from the Orders table. Otherwise, I'll get *all* the rows in Customers in the subquery. Remember that this must be a scalar subquery—a query that returns only one value from one row—so I must do something to restrict what gets returned to no more than one row. Because CustomerID is the primary key of the Customers table, I can be confident that the match on the CustomerID column from the Orders table will return exactly one row.

Those of you who caught on to the concept of INNER JOIN in Chapter 8 are probably wondering why you would want to solve this problem as just described rather than to JOIN Orders to Customers in the FROM clause of the outer query. Right now I'm focusing on the *concept* of using a subquery to create an output column with a very simple example. In truth, you probably should solve this particular problem with the following query using an INNER JOIN:

SQL	SELECT Orders.OrderNumber, Orders.OrderDate, 　　Orders.ShipDate, Customers.CustLastName FROM Customers INNER JOIN Orders ON Customers.CustomerID = Orders.OrderID WHERE Orders.ShipDate = '2017-10-03'

An Introduction to Aggregate Functions: COUNT and MAX

Now that you understand the basic concept of using a subquery to generate an output column, let's expand your horizons and see how this feature can be really useful. First, I need to give you an overview of a couple of aggregate functions. (I'll cover all the aggregate functions in detail in the next chapter.)

The SQL Standard defines many functions that calculate values in a query. One subclass of functions—aggregate functions—lets you calculate a single value for a group of rows in a result set. For example, you can use an aggregate function to count the rows, find the largest or smallest value within the set of rows, or calculate the average or total of some value or expression across the result set.

Let's take a look at a couple of these functions and then see how they can be most useful in a subquery. Figure 11-4 shows the diagram for the COUNT and MAX functions, which can generate an output column in a SELECT clause.

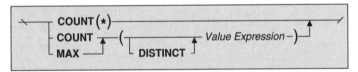

Figure 11-4 *Using the COUNT and MAX aggregate functions*

You can use COUNT to determine the number of rows or the number of non-Null values in a result set. Use COUNT(*) to find out how many rows arc in the entire set. If you specify a particular column in the result set using COUNT(*column_name*), the database system counts the number of rows with non-Null values in that column. You can also ask to count only the unique values by adding the DISTINCT keyword.

Likewise, you can find the largest value in a column by using MAX. If the value expression is numeric, you get the largest number value from the column or expression you specify. If the value expression returns a character data type, the largest value will depend on the collating sequence of your database system. If the value expression is a date or time, you get the latest date or time value from the column or expression.

Let's use these functions in a subquery to solve a couple of interesting problems:

"List all the customer names and a count of the orders they placed."

Translation	Select customer first name, customer last name, and also select the count of orders from the orders table for this customer from the customers table
Clean Up	Select cust~~omer~~ first name, cust~~omer~~ last name, ~~and also~~ (select ~~the~~ count ~~of orders~~ (*) from ~~the~~ orders ~~table for this customer~~ where orders.customer ID = customers.customer ID) from ~~the~~ customers ~~table~~

SQL	SELECT Customers.CustFirstName,
	    Customers.CustLastName,
	    (SELECT COUNT(*)
	    FROM Orders
	    WHERE Orders.CustomerID =
	        Customers.CustomerID)
	AS CountOfOrders
	FROM Customers

Subqueries as output columns are starting to look interesting now! In Part IV, "Summarizing and Grouping Data," you'll learn more about creative ways to use aggregate functions. But if all you want is a count of related rows, a subquery is a good way to do it. In fact, if you don't want anything other than the customer name and the count of orders, this is just about the only way to solve the problem. If you add the Orders table to the FROM clause of the main query (FROM Customers INNER JOIN Orders ON Customers.CustomerID = Orders.CustomerID), you'll get multiple rows for each customer who placed more than one order. In Chapter 13, "Grouping Data," you'll learn about another way that involves grouping the rows on customer name.

Let's look at an interesting problem that takes advantage of another aggregate function—MAX:

"Show me a list of customers and the last date on which they placed an order."

Translation	Select customer first name, customer last name, and also select the highest order date from the orders table for this customer from the customers table
Clean Up	Select cust~~omer~~ first name, cust~~omer~~ last name, ~~and also~~ (select ~~the highest~~ max(order date) from ~~the~~ orders ~~table for this customer~~ where orders.customer ID = customers.customer ID) from ~~the~~ customers ~~table~~

SQL	SELECT Customers.CustFirstName,
	Customers.CustLastName,
	(SELECT MAX(OrderDate)
	FROM Orders
	WHERE Orders.CustomerID =
	Customers.CustomerID) AS LastOrderDate
	FROM Customers

As you can imagine, using MAX in this way works well for finding the highest or most recent value from any related table. I'll show you several other ways to use these functions in the "Sample Statements" section later in this chapter.

Subqueries as Filters

In Chapter 6, you learned how to filter the information retrieved by adding a WHERE clause. You also learned how to use both simple and complex comparisons to get only the rows you want in your result set. Now I'll build on your skills and show you how to use a subquery as one of the comparison arguments to do more sophisticated filtering.

Syntax

Let's revisit the SELECT statement from Figure 11-1 and look at the syntax for building a query with a simple comparison predicate in a WHERE clause. Figure 11-5 shows the simplified diagram.

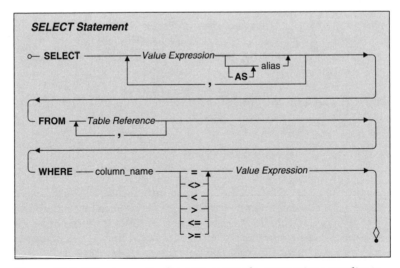

Figure 11-5 *Filtering a result using a simple comparison predicate*

As you remember from Figure 11-2, a value expression can be a subquery. In the simple example in Figure 11-5, you're comparing the value expression to a single column. Thus, the value expression must be a single value—that is, a scalar subquery that returns exactly one column and no more than one row. Let's solve a simple problem requiring a comparison to a value returned from a subquery. In this example, I am going to ask for all the details about customer orders, but I want only the *last* order for each customer. Figure 11-6 shows the tables needed.

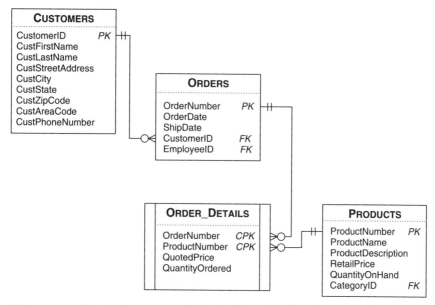

Figure 11-6 *The tables required to list all the details about an order*

"List customers and all the details from their last order."

Translation	Select customer first name, customer last name, order number, order date, product number, product name, and quantity ordered from the customers table joined with the orders table on customer ID in the customers table equals customer ID in the orders table, then joined with the order details table on order number in the orders table equals order number in the order details table, and then joined with the products table on product number in the products table equals product number in the order details table where the order date equals the maximum order date from the orders table for this customer

Clean Up	Select ~~customer~~ first name, ~~customer~~ last name, order number, order date, product number, product name, ~~and~~ quantity ordered from ~~the~~ customers ~~table~~ inner joine~~d with the~~ orders ~~table~~ on customers.customer ID ~~in the customers table equals~~ = orders. customer ID ~~in the orders table, then~~ inner joine~~d with the~~ order details ~~table~~ on orders.order number ~~in the orders table equals~~ = order_details.order number ~~in the order details table, and then~~ inner joine~~d with the~~ products ~~table~~ on products.product number ~~in the products table equals~~ = order_details.product number ~~in the order details table~~ where ~~the~~ order date ~~equals~~ = (select ~~the maximum~~ (order date) from ~~the~~ orders ~~table for this customer~~ where orders.customer ID = customers.customer ID)

SQL	SELECT Customers.CustFirstName,
	
	    Customers.CustLastName, Orders.OrderNumber,
	
	    Orders.OrderDate,
	
	    Order_Details.ProductNumber,
	
	    Products.ProductName,
	
	    Order_Details.QuantityOrdered
	
	FROM ((Customers
	
	INNER JOIN Orders
	
	  ON Customers.CustomerID = Orders.CustomerID)
	
	INNER JOIN Order_Details
	
	  ON Orders OrderNumber =
	
	      Order_Details.OrderNumber)
	
	INNER JOIN Products
	
	  ON Products.ProductNumber =
	
	  Order_Details.ProductNumber
	
	WHERE Orders.OrderDate =
	
	  (SELECT MAX(OrderDate)
	
	  FROM Orders AS O2
	
	  WHERE O2.CustomerID = Customers.CustomerID)

Did you notice that I gave an alias name to the second reference to the Orders table (that is, the Orders table in the subquery)? Even if you leave out the alias name, many database systems will recognize that you mean the copy of the Orders table within the subquery. In fact, the SQL Standard dictates that any unqualified reference should be resolved from the innermost query first. Still, I added the alias reference to make it crystal clear that the copy of the Orders table I'm referencing in the WHERE clause of the subquery is the one in the FROM clause of the subquery. If you follow this practice, your request will be much easier to understand—either by you when you come back to it some months later or by someone else who has to figure out what your request meant.

Special Predicate Keywords for Subqueries

The SQL Standard defines a number of special predicate keywords for use in a WHERE clause with a subquery.

Set Membership: IN

You learned in Chapter 6 how to use the IN keyword in a WHERE clause to compare a column or expression to a list of values. You now know that each value expression in the IN list *could* be a scalar subquery. How about using a subquery to generate the entire list? As Figure 11-7 shows, you can certainly do that!

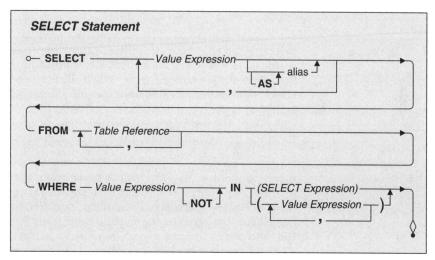

Figure 11-7 *Using a subquery with an IN predicate*

In this case, you can use a table subquery that returns one column and as many rows as necessary to build the list. Let's use the Recipes sample database for an example. Figure 11-8 shows the tables of interest.

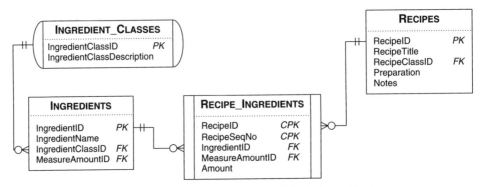

Figure 11-8 *The tables needed to list recipes and their ingredients*

Let's suppose you're having someone over for dinner who just adores seafood. Although you know you have some recipes containing seafood ingredients, you're not sure of all the ingredient names in your database. You do know that you have an IngredientClassDescription of Seafood, so you can join all the tables and filter on IngredientClassDescription—or you can get creative and use subqueries and the IN predicate instead.

"List all my recipes that have a seafood ingredient."

Translation	Select recipe title from the recipes table where the recipe ID is in the selection of recipe IDs from the recipe ingredients table where the ingredient ID is in the selection of ingredient IDs from the ingredients table joined with the ingredient classes table on ingredient class ID in the ingredients table matches ingredient class ID in the ingredient classes table where ingredient class description is 'seafood'
Clean Up	Select recipe title from ~~the~~ recipes ~~table~~ where ~~the~~ recipe ID ~~is~~ in ~~the~~ (selection of recipe IDs from ~~the~~ recipe ingredients ~~table~~ where ~~the~~ ingredient ID ~~is~~ in ~~the~~ (selection of ingredient IDs from ~~the~~ ingredients ~~table~~ inner join~~ed with the~~ ingredient classes ~~table~~ on ingredients.ingredient class ID ~~in the ingredients table matches~~ = ingredient_classes. ingredient class ID ~~in the ingredient classes table~~ where ingredient class description ~~is~~ = 'seafood'))

```
SQL          SELECT RecipeTitle
             FROM Recipes
             WHERE Recipes.RecipeID IN
               (SELECT RecipeID
               FROM Recipe_Ingredients
               WHERE Recipe_Ingredients.IngredientID IN
               (SELECT IngredientID
               FROM Ingredients
               INNER JOIN Ingredient_Classes
                 ON Ingredients.IngredientClassID =
                     Ingredient_Classes.IngredientClassID
               WHERE
               Ingredient_Classes.IngredientClassDescription
                 = 'Seafood'))
```

Did it occur to you that you could put a subquery within a subquery? I actually could have gone one level deeper by eliminating the INNER JOIN from the second subquery. I could have stated the second subquery using the following syntax:

```
SQL          (SELECT IngredientID
             FROM Ingredients
             WHERE Ingredients.IngredientClassID IN
               (SELECT IngredientClassID
               FROM Ingredient_Classes
               WHERE
               Ingredient_Classes.IngredientClassDescription
                 = 'Seafood'))
```

That would be overkill, however, because embedding IN clauses within IN clauses only makes the query harder to read. I did so in the previous example to show you that you *can* do it. It's worth restating, though, that just because you *can* do something doesn't mean you *should!* I think you'll agree that it's easier to see what's going on by using a single IN predicate and a more complex JOIN in the subquery. Here's another solution using this technique:

SQL	
	SELECT RecipeTitle
	FROM Recipes
	WHERE Recipes.RecipeID IN
	(SELECT RecipeID
	FROM (Recipe_Ingredients
	INNER JOIN Ingredients
	ON Recipe_Ingredients.IngredientID =
	Ingredients.IngredientID)
	INNER JOIN Ingredient_Classes
	ON Ingredients.IngredientClassID =
	Ingredient_Classes.IngredientClassID
	WHERE
	Ingredient_Classes.IngredientClassDescription
	= 'Seafood'

You might be asking at this point, "Why go to all this trouble? Why not just do the complex JOIN in the outer query and be done with it?" The reason is that you'll get the wrong answer! Actually, the rows returned will all be rows from the Recipes table for seafood recipes, but you might get some rows more than once. Let's try to solve this without the subquery to see why you get duplicate rows.

SQL	
	SELECT RecipeTitle
	FROM ((Recipes
	INNER JOIN Recipe_Ingredients
	ON Recipes.RecipeID =
	Recipe_Ingredients.RecipeID)
	INNER JOIN Ingredients
	ON Recipe_Ingredients.IngredientID =
	Ingredients.IngredientID)
	INNER JOIN Ingredient_Classes
	ON Ingredients.IngredientClassID =
	Ingredient_Classes.IngredientClassID
	WHERE
	Ingredient_Classes.IngredientClassDescription
	= 'Seafood'

If you look back at Figure 11-8, you can see that the Recipe_Ingredients table might have many rows for each row in the Recipes table. The result set defined by the FROM clause will contain at least as many rows as there are in Recipe_Ingredients, with the RecipeTitle column value repeated many times. Even when I add the filter to restrict the result to ingredients in class Seafood, I will still get more than one row per recipe in any recipe that has more than one seafood ingredient.

Yes, you could include the DISTINCT keyword, but the odds are your database system will have to do more work to eliminate the duplicates. Although this statement saved as a view probably won't be updatable in most database systems because the single output column might have duplicate values in many rows, keep in mind that a view using DISTINCT will never be updatable because DISTINCT masks the unique identity of each underlying row, so your database system won't know which row to update.

Using this subquery technique also becomes really important when you want to list more than just the recipe title. For example, suppose you also want to list *all* the ingredients from *any* recipe that has a seafood ingredient. If you use a complex JOIN in the outer query and filter for an ingredient class of Seafood as I just did, all you will get is seafood ingredients—you won't get all the other ingredients for the recipes. Let's ask one additional and slightly more complex request:

> *"List recipes and all ingredients for each recipe for recipes that have a seafood ingredient."*

Translation	Select recipe title and ingredient name from the recipes table joined with the recipe ingredients table on recipe ID in the recipes table equals recipe ID in the recipe ingredients table, and then joined with the ingredients table on ingredient ID in the ingredients table equals ingredient ID in the recipe ingredients table where the recipe ID is in the selection of recipe IDs from the recipe ingredients table joined with the ingredients table on ingredient ID in the recipe ingredients table equals ingredient ID in the ingredients table, and then joined with the ingredient classes table on ingredient class ID in the ingredients table equals ingredient class ID in the ingredient classes table where ingredient class description is 'seafood'

Clean Up	Select recipe title, ~~and~~ ingredient name from ~~the~~ recipes ~~table~~ inner joined ~~with the~~ recipe ingredients ~~table~~ on recipes.recipe ID ~~in the recipes table equals~~ = recipe_ingredients.recipe ID ~~in the recipe ingredients table, and then~~ inner joined ~~with the~~ ingredients ~~table~~ on ingredients.ingredient ID ~~in the ingredients table equals~~ = recipe_ingredients.ingredient ID ~~in the recipe ingredients table~~ where ~~the~~ recipe ID ~~is~~ in ~~the~~ (selection ~~of~~ recipe IDs from ~~the~~ recipe ingredients ~~table~~ inner joined ~~with the~~ ingredients ~~table~~ on recipe_ingredients.ingredient ID ~~in the recipe ingredients table equals~~ = ingredients.ingredient ID ~~in the ingredients table, and then~~ inner joined ~~with the~~ ingredient classes ~~table~~ on ingredients.ingredient class ID ~~in the ingredients table equals~~ = ingredient_classes.ingredient class ID ~~in the ingredient classes table~~ where ingredient class description ~~is~~ = 'seafood')
SQL	```SELECT Recipes.RecipeTitle,
Ingredients.IngredientName
FROM (Recipes
INNER JOIN Recipe_Ingredients
ON Recipes.RecipeID =
Recipe_Ingredients.RecipeID)
INNER JOIN Ingredients
ON Ingredients.IngredientID =
Recipe_Ingredients.IngredientID
WHERE Recipes.RecipeID IN
(SELECT RecipeID
FROM (Recipe_Ingredients
INNER JOIN Ingredients
ON Recipe_Ingredients.IngredientID =
Ingredients.IngredientID)
INNER JOIN Ingredient_Classes
ON Ingredients.IngredientClassID =
Ingredient_Classes.IngredientClassID
WHERE
Ingredient_Classes.IngredientClassDescription
= 'Seafood')```

The key here is that the complex INNER JOIN in the main part of the query retrieves *all* the ingredients for the recipes selected, and the complex subquery returns a list of recipe IDs for just the seafood recipes. It seems like I'm doing a complex JOIN twice, but there's method in the madness!

Quantified: ALL, SOME, and ANY

As you have just seen, the IN predicate lets you compare a column or expression to a list to see whether that column or expression is *in* the list. In other words, the column or expression *equals* one of the members of the list. If you want to find out whether the column or expression is greater than or less than any, all, or some of the items in the list, you can use a *quantified predicate*. Figure 11-9 shows the syntax.

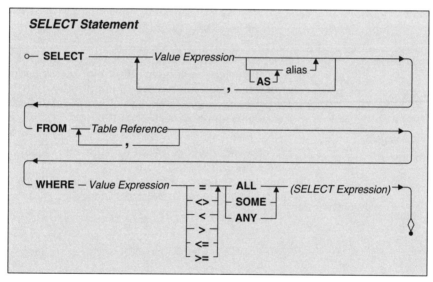

Figure 11-9 *Using a quantified predicate in a SELECT statement*

In this case, the SELECT expression must be a table subquery that returns exactly one column and zero or more rows. When the subquery returns more than one row, the values in the rows make up a list. As you can see, this predicate combines a comparison operator with a keyword that tells your database system how to apply the operator to the members of the list. When you use the keyword ALL, the comparison must be true for all the values returned by the subquery. When you use either of the keywords SOME or ANY, the comparison need be true for only one value in the list.

If you think about it, when the subquery returns multiple rows, asking for = ALL will always be false unless all the values returned by the subquery are the same and the value expression on the left of the comparison equals all of them. By the same logic, you might think that <> ANY will always be false if the value expression on the left *does* equal any of the values in the list. In truth, the SQL Standard treats SOME and ANY the same. So if you say <> SOME or <> ANY, then the predicate is true if the value expression on the left does not equal at least one of the values in the list. Another confusing point is that if the subquery returns no rows, then any comparison predicate with the ALL keyword is true, and any comparison predicate with the SOME or ANY keyword is false.

Let's work through a couple of requests to see quantified predicates in action. First, let's do a problem in the Recipes database. Refer to Figure 11-8 to see the tables I'll use.

"Show me the recipes that have beef or garlic."

Translation	Select recipe title from the recipes table where recipe ID is in the selection of recipe IDs from the recipe ingredients table where ingredient ID equals any of the selection of ingredient IDs from the ingredients table where ingredient name is 'beef' or 'garlic'
Clean Up	Select recipe title from ~~the~~ recipes ~~table~~ where recipe ID ~~is in the~~ (~~selection of~~ recipe IDs from ~~the~~ recipe ingredients ~~table~~ where ingredient ID ~~equals~~ = any ~~of the~~ (~~selection of~~ ingredient IDs from ~~the~~ ingredients ~~table~~ where ingredient name ~~is~~ in 'beef' ~~or~~ 'garlic'))

SQL	SELECT Recipes.RecipeTitle
	FROM Recipes
	WHERE Recipes.RecipeID IN
	    (SELECT Recipe_Ingredients.RecipeID
	    FROM Recipe_Ingredients
	    WHERE Recipe_Ingredients.IngredientID = ANY
	    (SELECT Ingredients.IngredientID
	    FROM Ingredients
	    WHERE Ingredients.IngredientName
	    IN ('Beef', 'Garlic')))

Do you get the feeling I could have also used IN instead of = ANY? If so, you're right! I could have also created a JOIN between Recipe_Ingredients and Ingredients in the first subquery to return the requisite list of RecipeIDs. As I stated at the beginning of the chapter, there's almost always more than one way to solve a particular problem in SQL. Sometimes, using a quantified predicate might make your request clearer.

Let's now solve a more complex problem to show you the real power of quantified predicates. This example uses the Sales Orders sample database, and Figure 11-10 shows the tables involved.

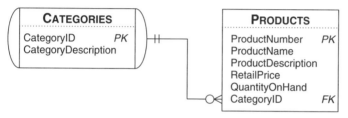

Figure 11-10 *The relationship of the Categories and Products tables*

"Find all accessories that are priced greater than any clothing item."

Translation	Select product name and retail price from the products table joined with the categories table on category ID in the products table matches category ID in the categories table where category description is 'accessories' and retail price is greater than all the selection of retail price from the products table joined with the categories table on category ID in the products table matches category ID in the categories table where category name is 'clothing'
Clean Up	Select product name ~~and~~ retail price from ~~the~~ products ~~table~~ inner join~~ed with the~~ categories ~~table~~ on products. category ID ~~in the products table~~ ~~matches~~ = catego- ries.category ID ~~in the categories table~~ where category description ~~is~~ = 'accessories' and retail price ~~is greater than~~ > all ~~the~~ (select~~ion of~~ retail price from ~~the~~ products ~~table~~ inner join~~ed with the~~ categories ~~table~~ on products. category ID ~~in the products table~~ ~~matches~~ = categories. category ID ~~in the categories table~~ where category name ~~is~~ = 'clothing')

```
SQL          SELECT Products.ProductName,
                Products.RetailPrice
             FROM Products
             INNER JOIN Categories
               ON Products.CategoryID
                  = Categories.CategoryID
             WHERE Categories.CategoryDescription =
                'Accessories'
             AND Products.RetailPrice > ALL
                (SELECT Products.RetailPrice
                FROM Products
                INNER JOIN Categories
                  ON Products.CategoryID =
                     Categories.CategoryID
                WHERE Categories.CategoryDescription =
                   'Clothing')
```

What's happening here? The subquery fetches all the prices for clothing items. The outer query then lists all accessories whose prices are greater than *all* the prices in the clothing items subquery. Note that you could also solve this query by finding the RetailPrice that is greater than the MAX price fetched in a subquery, but the point here is to demonstrate a use of ALL.

Existence: EXISTS

Both set membership (IN) and quantified (SOME, ANY, ALL) predicates perform a comparison with a value expression—usually a column from the source you specify in the FROM clause of your outer query. Sometimes it's useful to know simply that a related row EXISTS in the result set returned by a subquery. In Chapter 8, I showed a technique for solving AND problems using complex INNER JOINs. You can also use EXISTS to solve those same sorts of problems. Let's take another look at a problem I solved in Chapter 8.

"Find all the customers who ordered a bicycle."

Translation	Select customer ID, customer first name, and customer last name from the customers table where there exists some row from the orders table joined with the order details table on order ID in the orders table equals order ID in the order details table, and then joined with the products table on product ID in the products table equals product ID in the order details table where category ID equals 2 (Bikes) and the orders table customer ID equals the customers table customer ID
Clean Up	Select customer ID, cust~~omer~~ first name, ~~and~~ cust~~omer~~ last name from ~~the~~ customers ~~table~~ where ~~there~~ exists ~~some row~~ (select * from ~~the~~ orders ~~table~~ inner join~~ed with the~~ order details ~~table~~ on orders.order ID ~~in the orders table equals~~ = order_details.order ID ~~in the order details table, and then~~ inner join~~ed with the~~ products ~~table~~ on products.product ID ~~in the products table equals~~ = order_details.product ID ~~in the order details table~~ where product name category ID ~~equals~~ = 2 ~~(Bikes)~~ and ~~the~~ orders ~~table~~ customer ID ~~equals~~ = ~~the~~ customers ~~table~~ customer ID)

SQL	`SELECT Customers.CustomerID,`
	`        Customers.CustFirstName,`
	`        Customers.CustLastName`
	`FROM Customers`
	`WHERE EXISTS`
	`    (SELECT *`
	`    FROM (Orders`
	`    INNER JOIN Order_Details`
	`      ON Orders.OrderNumber =`
	`        Order_Details.OrderNumber)`
	`    INNER JOIN Products`
	`      ON Products.ProductNumber =`
	`        Order_Details.ProductNumber`
	`    WHERE Products.CategoryID = 2`
	`      AND Orders.CustomerID =`
	`        Customers.CustomerID)`

Notice that you can use any column name from any of the tables in the FROM clause as the column to be fetched in the SELECT clause of the subquery. I chose to use the shorthand "*" for all columns. (Remember from the discussion earlier in "An Introduction to Aggregate Functions: COUNT and MAX," that using * or a column name in the COUNT function does make a difference. It does not matter in this case.) Stated another way, this query is asking, "Give me the customers for whom there exists some row in order details for a bike." Because I didn't match on the OrderID column, I don't care which column gets returned by the subquery. Also, I took a shortcut by using `CategoryID = 2` because I know that this category covers all bike products. That's more efficient than doing an additional JOIN to the Products table and using a test on the ProductName column for `LIKE '%Bike%'`.

> ❖ **Note** Because this is such an interesting query, I saved this solution as CH11_Customer_Ordered_Bikes_EXISTS in the sample database. You can find the INNER JOIN solution in CH11_Customers_Ordered_Bikes_JOIN. Because the INNER JOIN depends on using DISTINCT to avoid returning duplicate rows, the JOIN solution won't be updatable. You can also solve this using IN, but I'll leave that as a challenge for you to solve! (Hint: I saved a sample query using IN in the sample database so that you can check your work.)

Uses for Subqueries

At this point, you should have a pretty good understanding of the concept of using a subquery either to generate an output column or to perform a complex comparison in a WHERE clause. The best way to give you an idea of the wide range of uses for subqueries is to list some problems you can solve with subqueries and then present a robust set of examples in the "Sample Statements" section.

Build Subqueries as Column Expressions

As mentioned earlier in this chapter, using a subquery to fetch a single value from a related table is probably more effectively done with a JOIN. When you consider aggregate functions, however, subqueries to fetch the result of a function calculation make the idea much more interesting. I'll explore this use of aggregate functions further in the next chapter. In the meantime, here are some problems you can solve using a subquery to generate an output column:

"List vendors and a count of the products they sell to us."

"Display products and the latest date the product was ordered."

"Show me entertainers and the count of each entertainer's engagements."

"Display all customers and the date of the last booking each made."

"List all staff members and the count of classes each teaches."

"Display all subjects and the count of classes for each subject on Monday."

"Show me all the bowlers and a count of games each bowled."

"Display the bowlers and the highest game each bowled."

"List all the meats and the count of recipes each appears in."

"Show me the types of recipes and the count of recipes in each type."

Use Subqueries as Filters

Now that you know about subqueries, you can really expand your kit of tools for solving complex queries. In this chapter, I explored many interesting ways to use subqueries as filters in a WHERE clause. In Chapter 14, "Filtering Grouped Data," I'll show you how to use subqueries as filters for groups of information in a HAVING clause.

Here's a sample of problems you can solve using subqueries as a filter for rows in a WHERE clause. Note that I solved many of these same problems in earlier chapters. Now, you get to think about solving them an alternate way by using a subquery!

> ❖ **Note** As a hint, I've included the keyword(s) you can use to solve the problem in parentheses after the problem statement.

"List customers who ordered bikes." (IN)

"Display customers who ordered clothing or accessories." (= SOME)

"Find all the customers who ordered a bicycle helmet." (IN)

"What products have never been ordered?" (NOT IN)

"List customers who have booked entertainers who play country or country rock." (IN)

"Find the entertainers who played engagements for customers Bonnicksen or Rosales." (= SOME)

"Display agents who haven't booked an entertainer." (NOT IN)

"List the entertainers who played engagements for customer Bonnicksen." (EXISTS)

"Display students enrolled in a class on Tuesday." (IN)

"Display students who have never withdrawn from a class." (NOT IN)

"List the subjects taught on Wednesday." (IN)

"Display team captains with a current average higher than all other members on their team." (> ALL)

"List all the bowlers who have a current average that's less than all the other bowlers on the same team." (< ALL)

"Display all the ingredients for recipes that contain carrots." (IN)

"List the ingredients that are used in some recipe where the measurement amount in the recipe is not the default measurement amount." (<> SOME)

Sample Statements

You now know the mechanics of constructing queries using subqueries and have seen some of the types of requests you can answer with a subquery. Let's take a look at a fairly robust set of samples, all of which use one or more subqueries. These examples come from each of the sample databases, and they illustrate the use of the subqueries to either generate an output column or act as a filter.

I've also included sample result sets that would be returned by these operations and placed them immediately after the SQL syntax line. The name that appears immediately above a result set is the name I gave each query in the sample data on the companion website for this book, www.informit.com/title/9780134858333. I stored each query in the appropriate sample database (as indicated within the example), and I prefixed the names of the queries relevant to this chapter with "CH11."

You can follow the instructions in the Introduction of this book to load the samples onto your computer and try them.

> ❖ **Note** Remember that all the column names and table names used in these examples are drawn from the sample database structures shown in Appendix B, "Schema for the Sample Databases." Because many of these examples use complex JOINs, your database system might choose a different way to solve these queries. For this reason, the first few rows might not exactly match the result you obtain, but the total number of rows should be the same. To simplify the process, I have combined the Translation and Clean Up steps for all the following examples.

Subqueries in Expressions

Sales Orders Database

"List vendors and a count of the products they sell to us."

Translation/ Clean Up	Select vendor name ~~and also~~ (select ~~the~~ count(*) ~~of prod-~~ ~~ucts~~ from ~~the~~ product vendors ~~table~~ where ~~the~~ product vendor ~~table~~ vendor ID ~~equals~~ = ~~the~~ vendors ~~table~~ vendor ID) from ~~the~~ vendors ~~table~~

SQL	`SELECT VendName,`
	`    (SELECT COUNT(*)`
	`    FROM Product_Vendors`
	`    WHERE Product_Vendors.VendorID =`
	`        Vendors.VendorID)`
	`    AS VendProductCount`
	`FROM Vendors`

> ❖ **Note** I assigned an alias name to the subquery in the SELECT clause so that the output displays a meaningful name. If you don't do that, your database system will generate something like Expr1.

CH11_Vendors_Product_Count (10 rows)

VendName	VendProductCount
Shinoman, Incorporated	3
Viscount	6
Nikoma of America	5
ProFormance	3
Kona, Incorporated	1
Big Sky Mountain Bikes	22
Dog Ear	9
Sun Sports Suppliers	5
Lone Star Bike Supply	30
Armadillo Brand	6

Entertainment Agency Database

"Display all customers and the date of the last booking each made."

Translation/ Clean Up	Select ~~customer~~ first name, ~~customer~~ last name, ~~and also~~ (select ~~the highest~~ MAX(start date) from ~~the~~ engagements ~~table~~ where ~~the~~ engagements ~~table~~ customer ID ~~equals~~ = ~~the~~ customers ~~table~~ customer ID) from ~~the~~ customers ~~table~~
| SQL | ```
SELECT Customers.CustFirstName,
       Customers.CustLastName,
       (SELECT MAX(StartDate)
        FROM Engagements
        WHERE Engagements.CustomerID =
           Customers.CustomerID)
       AS LastBooking
FROM Customers
``` |

CH11_Customers_Last_Booking (15 rows)

CustFirstName	CustLastName	LastBooking
Doris	Hartwig	2018-02-24
Deb	Waldal	2018-02-18
```

CustFirstName	CustLastName	LastBooking
Peter	Brehm	2018-02-27
Dean	McCrae	2018-02-25
Elizabeth	Hallmark	2018-02-20
Matt	Berg	2018-02-24
Liz	Keyser	2018-02-20
Darren	Gehring	
Sarah	Thompson	2018-02-25
<< more rows here >>		

❖ **Note** The LastBooking column for some customers is blank (Null) because those customers have no bookings.

School Scheduling Database

"Display all subjects and the count of classes for each subject on Monday."

Translation/ Clean Up	Select subject name ~~and also~~ (select ~~the~~ count(*) ~~of classes~~ from ~~the~~ classes ~~table~~ where Monday schedule ~~is~~ = true and ~~the~~ classes ~~table~~ subject ID ~~equals~~ = ~~the~~ subjects ~~table~~ subject ID) from ~~the~~ subjects ~~table~~

SQL	SELECT Subjects.SubjectName,
	
	    (SELECT COUNT(*)
	
	    FROM Classes
	
	    WHERE MondaySchedule = 1
	
	    AND Classes.SubjectID = Subjects.SubjectID)
	
	    AS MondayCount
	
	FROM Subjects

❖ **Note** Be sure to use the test for true that your database system supports. Remember that some database systems require you to compare to a keyword TRUE or to the integer value 1 or –1.

CH11_Subjects_Monday_Count (56 rows)

SubjectName	MondayCount
Financial Accounting Fundamentals I	2
Financial Accounting Fundamentals II	0
Fundamentals of Managerial Accounting	0
Intermediate Accounting	0
Business Tax Accounting	0
Introduction to Business	0
Developing A Feasibility Plan	0
Introduction to Entrepreneurship	0

<< more rows here >>

> ❖ **Note** Rather than return a Null value when there are no rows, the COUNT aggregate function returns a zero.

Bowling League Database

"Display the bowlers and the highest game each bowled."

Translation/ Clean Up	Select bowler first name, bowler last name, ~~and also~~ (select ~~the highest~~ MAX(raw score) from ~~the~~ bowler scores ~~table~~ where ~~the~~ bowler scores ~~table~~ bowler ID ~~equals~~ = ~~the~~ bowlers ~~table~~ bowler ID) from ~~the~~ bowlers ~~table~~

SQL	```SELECT Bowlers.BowlerFirstName,```
	``` Bowlers.BowlerLastName,```
	``` (SELECT MAX(RawScore)```
	``` FROM Bowler_Scores```
	``` WHERE Bowler_Scores.BowlerID =```
	``` Bowlers.BowlerID)```
	``` AS HighScore```
	```FROM Bowlers```

CH11_Bowler_High_Score (32 rows)

BowlerFirstName	BowlerLastName	HighScore
Barbara	Fournier	164
David	Fournier	178
John	Kennedy	191
Sara	Sheskey	149
Ann	Patterson	165
Neil	Patterson	179
David	Viescas	195
Stephanie	Viescas	150

<< more rows here >>

Recipes Database

"List all the meats and the count of recipes each appears in."

Translation/ Clean Up	Select ingredient class description, ingredient name, ~~and also~~ (select ~~the~~ count(*) ~~of rows~~ from ~~the~~ recipe ingredients ~~table~~ where ~~the~~ recipe ingredients ~~table~~ ingredient ID ~~equals~~ = ~~the~~ ingredients ~~table~~ ingredient ID) from ~~the~~ ingredient classes ~~table~~ inner joined ~~with the~~ ingredients ~~table~~ on ingredient_classes.ingredient class ID ~~in the ingredients classes table matches~~ = ingredients.ingredient class ID ~~in the ingredients table~~ where ingredient class description ~~is~~ = 'meat'
| SQL | ```
SELECT Ingredient_Classes.IngredientClassDescription,
    Ingredients.IngredientName,
    (SELECT COUNT(*)
    FROM Recipe_Ingredients
    WHERE Recipe_Ingredients.IngredientID =
        Ingredients.IngredientID)
AS RecipeCount
FROM Ingredient_Classes
INNER JOIN Ingredients
  ON Ingredient_Classes.IngredientClassID =
      Ingredients.IngredientClassID
WHERE
    Ingredient_Classes.IngredientClassDescription
    = 'Meat'
``` |
```

CH11_Meat_Ingredient_Recipe_Count (11 rows)

IngredientClassDescription	IngredientName	RecipeCount
Meat	Beef	2
Meat	Chicken, Fryer	0
Meat	Bacon	0
Meat	Chicken, Pre-cut	0
Meat	T-bone Steak	0
Meat	Chicken Breast	0
Meat	Chicken Leg	1
Meat	Chicken Wing	0
Meat	Chicken Thigh	1
Meat	New York Steak	0
Meat	Ground Pork	1

Subqueries in Filters

Sales Orders Database

"Display customers who ordered clothing or accessories."

Translation/ Clean Up	Select customer ID, ~~customer~~ first name, ~~customer~~ last name from ~~the~~ customers ~~table~~ where customer ID ~~is equal to~~ = any ~~of the~~ (~~selection of~~ customer ID from ~~the~~ orders ~~table~~ inner ~~joined with the~~ order details ~~table~~ on orders. order number ~~in the orders table matches~~ = order_details. order number ~~in the order details table, then~~ inner joined ~~with the~~ products ~~table~~ on products.product number ~~in the products table matches~~ = order_details.product number ~~in the order details table, and then~~ inner joined ~~with the~~ categories ~~table~~ on categories.category ID ~~in the categories table matches~~ = products.category ID ~~in the products table~~ where ~~-~~category description ~~is~~ = 'clothing' or category description ~~is~~ = 'accessories')

SQL	SELECT Customers.CustomerID,
	Customers.CustFirstName,
	Customers.CustLastName
	FROM Customers
	WHERE Customers.CustomerID = ANY
	(SELECT Orders.CustomerID
	FROM ((Orders
	INNER JOIN Order_Details
	ON Orders.OrderNumber =
	Order_Details.OrderNumber)
	INNER JOIN Products
	ON Products.ProductNumber =
	Order_Details.ProductNumber)
	INNER JOIN Categories
	ON Categories.CategoryID =
	Products.CategoryID
	WHERE Categories.CategoryDescription
	= 'Clothing'
	OR Categories.CategoryDescription
	= 'Accessories')

CH11_Customers_Clothing_OR_Accessories (27 rows)

CustomerID	CustFirstName	CustLastName
1001	Suzanne	Viescas
1002	William	Thompson
1003	Gary	Hallmark
1004	Robert	Brown
1005	Dean	McCrae
1006	John	Viescas
1007	Mariya	Sergienko
1008	Neil	Patterson
	<< more rows here >>	

> ❖ **Note** Just for fun, I solved this query by using = ANY. Can you think of a solution using IN or EXISTS? You can find these solutions in the sample database saved as CH11_Customers_Clothing_OR_Accessories_IN and CH11_Customers_Clothing_OR_Accessories_EXISTS. If you look at the scripts I supplied for MySQL, you'll find that I used ANY in the script, but if you look in the sample database, you'll find that MySQL and PostgreSQL converted the actual stored view to use IN. Go figure.

Entertainment Agency Database

"List the entertainers who played engagements for customer Berg."

Translation/ Clean Up	Select entertainer ID, ~~and entertainer~~ stage name from ~~the~~ entertainers ~~table~~ where ~~there~~ exists (select * ~~some row~~ from ~~the~~ customers ~~table~~ inner join~~ed with the~~ engagements ~~table~~ on customers.customer ID ~~in the customers table matches~~ = engagements.customer ID ~~in the engagements table~~ where customer last name ~~is~~ = 'Berg' and ~~the~~ engagements ~~table~~ entertainer ID ~~equals~~ = ~~the~~ entertainers ~~table~~ entertainer ID)

SQL	SELECT Entertainers.EntertainerID,
	
	    Entertainers.EntStageName FROM Entertainers WHERE EXISTS
	
	(SELECT *
	
	FROM Customers
	
	INNER JOIN Engagements
	
	  ON Customers.CustomerID =
	
	    Engagements.CustomerID
	
	WHERE Customers.CustLastName - 'Berg'
	
	AND Engagements.EntertainerID =
	
	    Entertainers.EntertainerID)

CH11_Entertainers_Berg_EXISTS (6 rows)

EntertainerID	EntStageName
1001	Carol Peacock Trio
1003	JV & the Deep Six
1004	Jim Glynn

EntertainerID	EntStageName
1006	Modern Dance
1007	Coldwater Cattle Company
1008	Country Feeling

> ❖ **Note** Just for a bit of challenge, I decided to solve this problem using EXISTS. Can you solve it using IN? You can find the second solution in CH11_Entertainers_Berg_IN.

School Scheduling Database

"Display students who have never withdrawn from a class."

Translation/ Clean Up	Select student ID, stud~~ent~~ first name, ~~and~~ stud~~ent~~ last name from ~~the~~ students ~~table~~ where ~~the~~ student ID ~~is~~ not in ~~the~~ (select~~ion of~~ student ID from ~~the~~ student schedules ~~table~~ inner join~~ed with the~~ student class status ~~table~~ on student_schedules.class status ~~in the student schedules table matches~~ = student_class_status.class status ~~in the student class status table~~ where class status description ~~is~~ = 'withdrew')

SQL	`SELECT Students.StudentID,`
	`        Students.StudFirstName,`
	`        Students.StudLastName`
	`FROM Students`
	`WHERE Students.StudentID NOT IN`
	`    (SELECT Student_Schedules.StudentID`
	`    FROM Student_Schedules`
	`    INNER JOIN Student_Class_Status`
	`      ON Student_Schedules.ClassStatus =`
	`          Student_Class_Status.ClassStatus`
	`    WHERE`
	`      Student_Class_Status.ClassStatusDescription`
	`      = 'Withdrew')`

> ❖ **Note** This is a pretty simple query that finds all the students who ever withdrew from a class in the subquery and then asks for all the students NOT IN this list. Can you think how you would solve this with an OUTER JOIN?

CH11_Students_Never_Withdrawn (16 rows)

StudentID	StudFirstName	StudLastName
1001	Kerry	Patterson
1003	Betsey	Stadick
1004	Janice	Galvin
1005	Doris	Hartwig
1006	Scott	Bishop
1007	Elizabeth	Hallmark
1008	Sara	Sheskey
1009	Karen	Smith

<< more rows here >>

Bowling League Database

"Display team captains with a handicap score higher than all other members on their teams."

Translation/ Clean Up	Select team name, bowler ID, bowler first name, bowler last name, ~~and~~ handicap score from ~~the~~ bowlers ~~table~~ inner joined ~~with the~~ teams ~~table~~ on bowlers.bowler ID ~~in the bowlers table matches~~ = teams.captain ID ~~in the teams table~~ inner joined ~~with the~~ bowler scores ~~table~~ on bowlers.bowler ID ~~in the bowlers table matches~~ = bowler_scores.bowler ID ~~in the bowler scores table~~ where ~~the~~ handicap score ~~is greater than~~ > all ~~the~~ (selection ~~of~~ handicap score from bowlers as B2 inner joined ~~with the~~ bowler scores ~~table~~ as BS2 on B2.bowler ID ~~in the B2 table matches~~ = BS2.bowler ID ~~in the BS2 table~~ where ~~the~~ B2 ~~table~~ bowler ID ~~is not equal~~ <> ~~the~~ bowlers ~~table~~ bowler ID and ~~the~~ B2 ~~table~~ team ID ~~is equal~~ = ~~to the~~ bowlers ~~table~~ team ID)

SQL	SELECT Teams.TeamName, Bowlers.BowlerID,
	   Bowlers.BowlerFirstName,
	   Bowlers.BowlerLastName,
	   Bowler_Scores.HandiCapScore
	FROM (Bowlers
	INNER JOIN Teams
	  ON Bowlers.BowlerID = Teams.CaptainID)
	INNER JOIN Bowler_Scores
	  ON Bowlers.BowlerID = Bowler_Scores.BowlerID
	WHERE Bowler_Scores.HandiCapScore > All
	  (SELECT BS2.HandiCapScore
	  FROM Bowlers AS B2
	  INNER JOIN Bowler_Scores AS BS2
	    ON B2.BowlerID = BS2.BowlerID
	  WHERE B2.BowlerID <> Bowlers.BowlerID
	    AND B2.TeamID = Bowlers.TeamID)

❖ **Note** I explicitly gave aliases to the second copy of the Bowlers table and the second copy of the Bowler_Scores table in the subquery to make it crystal clear what's going on. I specifically do not want to compare against the score of the current bowler—that would cause the > ALL predicate to fail. I also want to compare only with the other bowlers on the same team.

CH11_Team_Captains_High_Score (1 row)

TeamName	BowlerID	BowlerFirstName	BowlerLastName	HandiCapScore
Huckleberrys	7	David	Viescas	224

Recipes Database

"Display all the ingredients for recipes that contain carrots."

❖ **Note** I promised in Chapter 8 that I would show you how to solve this problem with a subquery. I keep my promises!

Translation/ Clean Up	Select recipe title ~~and~~ ingredient name from ~~the~~ recipes ~~table~~ inner join~~ed with the~~ recipe ingredients ~~table~~ on recipes.recipe ID ~~in the recipes table matches~~ = recipe_ingredients.recipe ID ~~in the recipe ingredients table; and then~~ inner join~~ed with the~~ ingredients ~~table~~ on ingredients.ingredient ID ~~in the ingredients table matches~~ = recipe_ingredients.ingredient ID ~~in the recipe ingredients table~~ where recipe ID ~~is~~ in ~~the~~ (select~~ion of~~ recipe ID from ~~the~~ ingredients ~~table~~ inner join~~ed with the~~ recipe ingredients ~~table~~ on ingredients.ingredient ID ~~in the ingredients table matches~~ = recipe_ingredients.ingredient ID ~~in the recipe ingredients table~~ where ingredient name ~~is~~ = 'carrot')

SQL	`SELECT Recipes.RecipeTitle,`
	`    Ingredients.IngredientName`
	`FROM (Recipes`
	`INNER JOIN Recipe_Ingredients`
	`  ON Recipes.RecipeID =`
	`    Recipe_Ingredients.RecipeID)`
	`INNER JOIN Ingredients`
	`  ON Ingredients.IngredientID =`
	`    Recipe_Ingredients.IngredientID`
	`WHERE Recipes.RecipeID`
	`IN`
	`    (SELECT Recipe_Ingredients.RecipeID`
	`    FROM Ingredients`
	`    INNER JOIN Recipe_Ingredients`
	`      ON Ingredients.IngredientID =`
	`        Recipe_Ingredients.IngredientID`
	`    WHERE Ingredients.IngredientName = 'carrot')`

❖ **Note** If you place the filter for 'carrot' in the outer query, you will see only carrot ingredients in the output. In this problem, you want to see *all* the ingredients from any recipe that uses carrots, so the subquery is a good way to solve it. This query result appears to be sorted by recipe title even though there is no ORDER BY clause. If you want to ensure this sequence in any database system, be sure to include an ORDER BY clause.

CH11_Recipes_Ingredients_With_Carrots (16 rows)

RecipeTitle	IngredientName
Irish Stew	Beef
Irish Stew	Onion
Irish Stew	Potato
Irish Stew	Carrot
Irish Stew	Water
Irish Stew	Guinness Beer
Salmon Filets in Parchment Paper	Salmon
Salmon Filets in Parchment Paper	Carrot
Salmon Filets in Parchment Paper	Leek

<< more rows here >>

Summary

I began the chapter with a definition of the three types of subqueries defined by the SQL Standard—row, table, and scalar—and recalled that I had already covered how to use table subqueries in a FROM clause. I also briefly described the use of a row subquery and explained that not many commercial implementations support this yet.

Next, I showed how to use a subquery to generate a column expression in a SELECT clause. I discussed a simple example and then introduced two aggregate functions that are useful for fetching related summary information from another table. (I'll cover all the aggregate functions in detail in the next chapter.)

I then discussed using subqueries to create complex filters in the WHERE clause. I first covered simple comparisons and then introduced special comparison keywords—IN, SOME, ANY, ALL, and EXISTS—that are useful for building predicates with subqueries.

I summarized why subqueries are useful and provided a sample list of problems to solve using subqueries. The rest of the chapter showed examples of how to use subqueries. I broke these examples into two groups: using subqueries in column expressions and using subqueries in filters.

The following section presents several requests that you can work out on your own.

Problems for You to Solve

Below, I show you the request statement and the name of the solution query in the sample databases. If you want some practice, you can work out the SQL you need for each request and then check your answer with the query I saved in the samples. Don't worry if your syntax doesn't exactly match the syntax of the queries I saved—as long as your result set is the same.

Sales Orders Database

1. *"Display products and the latest date each product was ordered."*

   (Hint: Use the MAX aggregate function.)

   You can find the solution in CH11_Products_Last_Date (40 rows). Do you see any blank dates in the result? Can you explain why?

2. *"List customers who ordered bikes."*

   (Hint: Build a filter using IN.)

   You can find the solution in CH11_Customers_Ordered_Bikes_IN (23 rows).

3. *"What products have never been ordered?"*

   (Hint: Build a filter using NOT IN.)

   You can find the solution in CH11_Products_Not_Ordered (2 rows).

Entertainment Agency Database

1. *"Show me all entertainers and the count of each entertainer's engagements."*

   (Hint: Use the COUNT aggregate function.)

   You can find the solution in CH11_Entertainer_Engagement_Count (13 rows).

2. *"List customers who have booked entertainers who play country or country rock."*

   (Hint: Build a filter using IN.)

   You can find the solution in CH11_Customers_Who_Like_Country (13 rows).

3. *"Find the entertainers who played engagements for customers Berg or Hallmark."*

   (Hint: Build a filter using = SOME.)

   You can find the solution in CH11_Entertainers_Berg_OR_Hallmark_SOME (8 rows).

4. *"Display agents who haven't booked an entertainer."*

   (Hint: Build a filter using NOT IN.)

   You can find the solution in CH11_Bad_Agents (1 row).

School Scheduling Database

1. *"List all staff members and the count of classes each teaches."*

   (Hint: Use the COUNT aggregate function.)

   You can find the solution in CH11_Staff_Class_Count (27 rows).

2. *"Display students enrolled in a class on Tuesday."*

   (Hint: Build a filter using IN.)

   You can find the solution in CH11_Students_In_Class_Tuesdays (18 rows).

3. *"List the subjects taught on Wednesday."*

   (Hint: Build a filter using IN.)

   You can find the solution in CH11_Subjects_On_Wednesday (34 rows).

Bowling League Database

1. *"Show me all the bowlers and a count of games each bowled."*

   (Hint: Use the COUNT aggregate function.)

   You can find the solution in CH11_Bowlers_And_Count_Games (32 rows).

2. *"List all the bowlers who have a raw score that's less than all of the other bowlers on the same team."*

   (Hint: Build a filter using < ALL. Also use DISTINCT in case a bowler has multiple games with the same low score.)

   You can find the solution in CH11_Bowlers_Low_Score (3 rows).

Recipes Database

1. *"Show me the types of recipes and the count of recipes in each type."*

   (Hint: Use the COUNT aggregate function.)

   You can find the solution in CH11_Count_Of_Recipe_Types (7 rows).

2. *"List the ingredients that are used in some recipe where the measurement amount in the recipe is not the default measurement amount."*

   (Hint: Build a filter using <> SOME.)

   You can find the solution in CH11_Ingredients_Using_NonStandard_Measure (21 rows).

■■■■■■■■■■ Part IV
Summarizing and Grouping Data

Simple Totals

"There are two kinds of statistics: the kind
you look up and the kind you make up."
—REX STOUT *DEATH OF A DOXY: A NERO WOLFE NOVEL*

Topics Covered in This Chapter

Aggregate Functions

Using Aggregate Functions in Filters

Sample Statements

Summary

Problems for You to Solve

You now know how to select the columns you need for a given request, define expressions that add extra levels of detail, join the appropriate tables that supply the columns you require, and define conditions to filter the data sent to the result set. I've shown you all these techniques so that you can learn how to retrieve detailed information from one or more tables in the database. In this and the next two chapters, I'll show you how to take a step back and look at the data from a much broader perspective, otherwise known as "seeing the big picture."

In this chapter, you'll learn how to use aggregate functions to produce basic summary information. In Chapter 13, "Grouping Data," I'll show you how to organize data into groups with the GROUP BY clause of the SELECT statement, and in Chapter 14, "Filtering Grouped Data," I'll show you various filtering techniques you can apply to the data after it is grouped. And finally in Chapter 21, "Complex Calculations on Groups," you'll learn how to become a "grouping master."

Aggregate Functions

The requests you've been working with so far have required answers involving individual column values from the rows returned by the FROM and WHERE clauses. However, you'll often encounter requests, such as the following, that require only calculated values across multiple rows for an answer:

> *"How many of our customers live in Seattle?"*
>
> *"What is the lowest price and highest price we've assigned to any item in our inventory?"*
>
> *"How many classes is Mike Hernandez teaching?"*
>
> *"What time does our earliest class begin?"*
>
> *"What is the average length of a class?"*
>
> *"What is the total amount for order number 12?"*

The SQL Standard provides a set of *aggregate functions* that allow you to calculate a single value from the rows in a result set or from the values returned by a value expression. You can apply a given function to all the rows or values, or you can use a WHERE clause to apply the function to a specific set of rows or values. For example, you can use an aggregate function to determine the largest or smallest value of a value expression, count the number of rows in a result set, or calculate a total using only distinct values from a value expression. Figure 12-1 shows the syntax for the basic aggregate functions supported by all database systems.

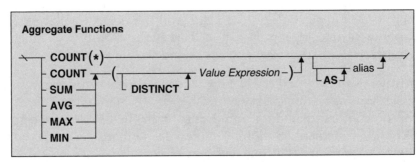

Figure 12-1 *The syntax diagram for aggregate functions*

As you can see, aggregate functions have a very simple and straight-forward syntax. In the previous chapter, I discussed using two of the aggregate functions in a subquery either to return a single calculated value in a SELECT clause or to fetch a calculated value that you can use in a predicate in a WHERE clause. I'll show you a few more examples of this usage in this chapter.

> ❖ **Note** The 2016 SQL Standard defines a dozen or more additional aggregate operations, but many are not yet implemented in any major commercial database system. In this chapter, I focus on the basic aggregate functions supported by all major systems. After you learn how to work with these, consult your database documentation to learn whether more functions are available to use in your SQL statements.

Each aggregate function returns a single value, regardless of whether it is processing the rows in a result set or the values returned by a value expression. Except COUNT(*), all aggregate functions automatically disregard Null values. You can use several aggregate functions at the same time in the list of value expressions immediately following the SELECT keyword, and you can even mix value expressions containing aggregate functions with value expressions containing literal values. But you need to be careful once you've started including aggregate expressions.

When you include an aggregate expression, you're asking your database system to calculate one value across a group of rows. You'll learn in the next chapter that you can define the groups you want by using the GROUP BY clause. However, in this chapter, I'm looking at simple queries that do not explicitly specify groups. In the absence of a group specification, the group of records that your database uses to calculate any aggregate expression is all the rows returned by your FROM and WHERE clauses.

If you think about it, it doesn't make sense to also include a value expression using a column from one of your tables that isn't inside an aggregate function. Remember that I introduced you to the COUNT and MAX aggregate functions in Chapter 11, "Subqueries." Consider the following SQL:

SQL	SELECT LastName, COUNT(*) As CountOfStudents
	FROM Students

Including the COUNT function without specifying any groups asks your database system to count all the rows in the result set returned from the

FROM clause. COUNT(*) returns a single value—the count of all the rows in the Students table—so the query should return one row. Which Last-Name should your database system display? The answer is it can't figure out which one to choose, so the above statement is illegal.

It is valid, however, to include a literal expression to enhance your output further. You can do this because a literal expression is simply a constant—it has the same value for all rows. So, it's perfectly legal to use the following SQL:

SQL	SELECT 'The number of students is: ', COUNT(*)
	As CountOfStudents
	FROM Students

This returns one row:

The number of students is:	18

Now that I've gotten that little warning out of the way, let's look at each of these aggregate functions and how you might use them to answer a request.

Counting Rows and Values with COUNT

The SQL Standard defines two versions of the COUNT function. COUNT(*) processes rows in a result set and COUNT (*value expression*) processes values returned by a value expression.

Counting All the Rows

You use COUNT(*) to determine how many rows exist in a result set. The COUNT(*) function counts *all* the rows in a result set, including redundant rows and rows containing Null values. Here's a simple example of the type of question you can answer with this function.

> ❖ **Note** Throughout this chapter, I use the "Request/Translation/Clean Up/SQL" technique introduced in Chapter 4, "Creating a Simple Query." All examples assume you have thoroughly studied and understood the concepts covered in previous chapters, especially the chapters on JOINs and subqueries.

"Show me the total number of employees we have in our company."

Translation	Select the count of employees from the employees table
Clean Up	Select ~~the~~ count ~~of employees~~ (*)
	from ~~the~~ employees ~~table~~
SQL	SELECT COUNT(*)
	FROM Employees

Note that I use "(*)" in the Clean Up statement to indicate that I want to count *all* the rows in the Employees table. You should add the asterisk in your Clean Up step when you work with this type of request because it helps ensure that you use the correct COUNT function. The SELECT statement in this example generates a result set consisting of a single-column row containing a numeric value that represents the total number of rows in the Employees table.

There is virtually no restriction on the number of rows the COUNT(*) function processes. I say "virtually" because most database systems return the count as an integer, which limits the value to 2,147,483,647 rows. You can indicate which rows COUNT(*) should include by using a WHERE clause. For example, here's how you define a SELECT statement that counts all the rows in the Employees table for those employees who live in Washington state:

SQL	SELECT COUNT(*)
	FROM Employees
	WHERE EmpState = 'WA'

As I work through this chapter, you'll see that you can use a WHERE clause to filter the rows or values processed by any aggregate function.

When you use an aggregate function in a SELECT statement, you might or might not see a column name in the result set for the return value of the function. Some database systems provide a default column name, and others do not. But you can use the AS option of the function's syntax to provide a meaningful column name for the result set. Here's how you might apply this option to the previous example:

SQL	SELECT COUNT(*) AS TotalWashingtonEmployees
	FROM Employees
	WHERE EmpState = 'WA'

Now the result set consists of a column called TotalWashingtonEmployees that contains the return value of the COUNT(*) function. As the syntax diagram in Figure 12-1 indicates, you can apply this technique to any aggregate function.

Counting Values in a Column or Expression

You use the COUNT(*value expression*) function to count the total number of *non-Null* values returned by a value expression. (This expression is more commonly known as COUNT, which is the name I'll use for the remainder of the book.) It counts all values returned by a value expression, regardless of whether they are unique or duplicate, but automatically excludes any Null values from the final count. You can use COUNT to answer this type of request:

"How many customers were able to indicate which county they live in?"

Here you need to determine how many actual values exist in the county column. Remember that COUNT(*) *includes* Null values as well, so it won't provide you with the correct answer. Instead, you use the COUNT function and translate the request in this manner:

Translation	Select the count of non-Null county values as NumberOfKnownCounties from the customers table
Clean Up	Select ~~the~~ count ~~of non-Null~~ (county) ~~values~~ as NumberOfKnownCounties from ~~the~~ customers ~~table~~
SQL	SELECT COUNT(CustCounty) AS NumberOfKnownCounties FROM Customers

Note that the Translation and Clean Up statements explicitly ask for non-Null values. Although you already know that this function processes only non-Null values, it's a good idea to add this to both statements so that you'll be sure to use the correct COUNT function. The SELECT statement defined here will generate a single row that contains a numeric value representing the count of rows containing non-Null county names found in the CustCounty column. Basically, you get the same answer using COUNT(*) if you include WHERE CustCounty IS NOT NULL.

Remember that the COUNT function treats duplicate county names as though they were unique and includes every one of them in the final count. You can, however, use the function's DISTINCT option to exclude duplicate values from the count. The next example shows how you might apply it to a given request.

"How many unique county names are there in the customers table?"

Translation	Select the count of unique non-Null county names as NumberOfUniqueCounties from the customers table
Clean Up	Select ~~the~~ count ~~of unique non-Null~~ (distinct county) ~~names~~ as NumberOfUniqueCounties from ~~the~~ customers ~~table~~
SQL	SELECT COUNT(DISTINCT CustCounty) AS NumberOfUniqueCounties FROM Customers

When you use the DISTINCT option, the database retrieves all the non-Null values from the county column, eliminates the duplicates, and *then* counts the values that remain. The database goes through much of this same process whenever you use DISTINCT with the SUM, AVG, MIN, or MAX functions.

In this next example, I use a slightly altered version of the previous request to show that you can apply a filter to the COUNT function.

"How many unique county names are there in the customers table for the state of Oregon?"

Translation	Select the count of unique non-Null county names as NumberOfUniqueOregonCounties from the customers table where the state is 'OR'
Clean Up	Select ~~the~~ count ~~of unique non-Null~~ (distinct county) ~~names~~ as NumberOfUniqueOregonCounties from ~~the~~ customers ~~table~~ where ~~the~~ state ~~is~~ = 'OR'
SQL	SELECT COUNT(DISTINCT CustCounty) AS NumberOfUniqueOregonCounties FROM Customers WHERE CustState = 'OR'

It's important to note that you *cannot* use DISTINCT with COUNT(*). This is a reasonable restriction because COUNT(*) counts *all* rows in a table, regardless of whether any are redundant or contain Null values.

Computing a Total with SUM

You can calculate a total for a *numeric* value expression with the SUM function. It processes all the non-Null values of the value expression and returns a final total to the result set. Note that if the value expression in all the rows is Null or if the result of evaluating the FROM and WHERE clauses is an empty set, then SUM returns a Null. Here's a sample request you can answer with SUM:

"What is the total amount we pay in salaries to our employees in Washington?"

Translation	Select the sum of salary as TotalSalaryAmount from the employees table where the state is 'WA'
Clean Up	Select ~~the~~ sum ~~of~~ (salary) as TotalSalaryAmount from ~~the~~ employees ~~table~~ where ~~the~~ state ~~is~~ = 'WA'
SQL	SELECT SUM(Salary) AS TotalSalaryAmount FROM Employees WHERE EmpState = 'WA'

The value expression I used here was a simple column reference. However, you can also use SUM on a value expression consisting of a numeric expression, as I demonstrate in the next example:

"How much is our current inventory worth?"

Translation	Select the sum of wholesale price times quantity on hand as TotalInventoryValue from the products table
Clean Up	Select ~~the~~ sum of (wholesale price ~~times~~ * quantity on hand) as TotalInventoryValue from ~~the~~ products ~~table~~
SQL	SELECT SUM(WholesalePrice * QuantityOnHand) AS TotalInventoryValue FROM Products

As you know, a row must contain actual values in the WholesalePrice and QuantityOnHand columns in order for it to be processed by the SUM function. In this instance, the database processes the expression for all qualifying rows in the Products table, totals the results with the SUM function, and then sends the grand total to the result set.

Here's an example of how to use SUM to calculate a total for a unique set of numeric values:

"Calculate a total of all unique wholesale costs for the products we sell."

Translation	Select the sum of unique wholesale costs as SumOfUniqueWholesaleCosts from the products table
Clean Up	Select ~~the~~ sum ~~of unique~~ (distinct wholesale costs) as SumOfUniqueWholesaleCosts from ~~the~~ products ~~table~~
SQL	SELECT SUM(DISTINCT WholesaleCost) AS SumOfUniqueWholesaleCosts FROM Products

Calculating a Mean Value with AVG

Another function you can use on *numeric* values is AVG, which calculates the arithmetic mean of all non-Null values returned by a value expression. You can use AVG to answer a request such as this:

"What is the average contract amount for vendor number 10014?"

Translation	Select the average of contract price as AverageContractPrice from the vendor contracts table where the vendor ID is 10014
Clean Up	Select ~~the average of~~ avg (contract price) as AverageContractPrice from ~~the~~ vendor contracts ~~table~~ where the vendor ID ~~is~~ = 10014
SQL	SELECT AVG(ContractPrice) AS AverageContractPrice FROM Vendor_Contracts WHERE VendorID = 10014

As you work with your Clean Up statement, be sure to cross out the word "average" and replace it with "avg" to help keep you from accidentally using "Average" in the SELECT clause. "Average" is not a valid SQL keyword, so the SELECT statement will fail if you try to use it.

You can also use AVG to process a numeric expression, just as you did with the SUM function. Remember that you cannot use AVG with a value expression that is not numeric. Most database systems will give you an error if you try to use these functions with character string or datetime data.

"What is the average item total for order 64?"

Translation	Select the average of price times quantity ordered as AverageItemTotal from the order details table where order ID is 64
Clean Up	Select ~~the average of~~ avg (price ~~times~~ * quantity ordered) as AverageItemTotal from ~~the~~ order details ~~table~~ where order ID ~~is~~ = 64
SQL	SELECT AVG(Price * QuantityOrdered) AS AverageItemTotal FROM Order_Details WHERE OrderID = 64

Keep in mind that a row must contain actual values in the columns Price and QuantityOrdered for that row to be processed by the AVG function. Otherwise, the numeric expression evaluates to Null, and the AVG function disregards the row entirely. As with SUM, if the value expression in all rows is Null or the result of evaluating the FROM and WHERE clauses is an empty set, AVG returns a Null value.

In this next example, I use the DISTINCT option to average a unique set of numeric values:

"Calculate an average of all unique product prices."

Translation	Select the average of unique prices as UniqueProductPrices from the products table
Clean Up	Select ~~the average of unique~~ avg (distinct prices) as UniqueProductPrices from ~~the~~ products ~~table~~
SQL	SELECT AVG(DISTINCT Price) AS UniqueProductPrices FROM Products

Finding the Largest Value with MAX

You can determine the *largest* value returned by a value expression with the MAX function. The MAX function can process any type of data, and the value it returns depends on the data it processes.

CHARACTER STRINGS	The value that MAX returns is based on the collating sequence used by your database system or computer. For example, if your database uses the ASCII character set and is case-insensitive, it sorts company names in this manner: ". . . 4th Dimension Productions . . . Al's Auto Shop . . . allegheny & associates . . . Zercon Productions . . . zorn credit services." In this instance, MAX will return "zorn credit services" as the MAX value.
NUMBERS	MAX returns the largest number.
DATETIME	MAX evaluates dates and times in chronological order and returns the *most recent* (or latest) date or time.

Here are a couple of examples of how you might use MAX to answer a request:

"What is the largest amount paid on a contract?"

Translation	Select the maximum contract price as LargestContractPrice from the engagements table
Clean Up	Select ~~the~~ maximum (contract price) as LargestContractPrice from ~~the~~ engagements ~~table~~
SQL	SELECT MAX(ContractPrice) AS LargestContractPrice FROM Engagements

"What was the largest line item total for order 3314?"

Translation	Select the maximum price times quantity ordered as LargestItemTotal from the order details table where the order ID is 3314
Clean Up	Select ~~the~~ maximum (price ~~times~~ * quantity ordered) as LargestItemTotal from ~~the~~ order details ~~table~~ where ~~the~~ order ID ~~is~~ = 3314
SQL	SELECT MAX(Price * QuantityOrdered) AS LargestItemTotal FROM Order_Details WHERE OrderID = 3314

You might be tempted to use the DISTINCT option to return a unique instance of the highest or most recent value. Although the SQL Standard specifies DISTINCT as an option for the MAX function, DISTINCT *does not affect* the MAX function whatsoever. There can be only one maximum value, regardless of whether or not it is distinct. For example, if you're looking for the most recent hire date in the Agents table, both of the following expressions return the same value:

```
SELECT MAX(DateHired) FROM Agents
SELECT MAX(DISTINCT DateHired) FROM Agents
```

I present both versions of the function because they are part of the current SQL Standard, but I recommend that you use the MAX function without the DISTINCT option. When you include DISTINCT, you're asking your database system to do extra and unnecessary work first to find the unique values and then figure out which one is the largest or latest.

Finding the Smallest Value with MIN

The MIN function allows you to determine the *smallest* value returned by a value expression. It works like the MAX function but returns the opposite value: the first character string (based on the collating sequence), the smallest number, and the earliest date or time.

You can answer requests such as these with the MIN function:

"What is the lowest price we charge for a product?"

Translation	Select the minimum price as LowestProductPrice from the products table
Clean Up	Select ~~the minimum~~ (price) as LowestProductPrice from ~~the~~ products ~~table~~
SQL	SELECT MIN(Price) AS LowestProductPrice FROM Products

"What was the lowest line item total for order 3314?"

Translation	Select the minimum price times quantity ordered as LowestItemTotal from the order details table where the order ID is 3314

Clean Up	Select ~~the~~ minimum (price ~~times~~ * quantity ordered) as LowestItemTotal from ~~the~~ order details ~~table~~ where ~~the~~ order ID ~~is~~ = 3314

SQL	`SELECT MIN(Price * QuantityOrdered)`
	`    AS LowestItemTotal`
	`FROM Order_Details`
	`WHERE OrderID = 3314`

It's important to note that the DISTINCT option *has no affect* whatsoever on the MIN function. (As you know, this was the case with the MAX function as well.) There can be only one minimum value, regardless of whether or not it is distinct. For example, both of the following expressions return the same value:

```
SELECT MIN(DateHired) FROM Agents
SELECT MIN(DISTINCT DateHired) FROM Agents
```

I present both versions of the function because they are part of the current SQL Standard, but, just as I mentioned for MAX, I recommend that you use the MIN function without the DISTINCT option. When you include DISTINCT, you're asking your database system to do extra and unnecessary work first to find the unique values and then figure out which one is the lowest or earliest.

Using More Than One Function

As I mentioned at the beginning of this section, you can use several aggregate functions at the same time. This gives you the ability to show contrasting information using a single SELECT statement. For example, you can use the MIN and MAX functions to show the earliest and most recent order dates for a specific customer, or the MAX, MIN, and AVG functions to show the highest, lowest, and average grades for a given student. Here are other examples of how you might use two or more aggregate functions:

> *"Show me the earliest and most recent review dates for the employees in the advertising department."*

Translation	Select the minimum review date as EarliestReviewDate and the maximum review date as RecentReviewDate from the employees table where the department is 'Advertising'

Clean Up	Select ~~the minimum~~ review date as EarliestReviewDate, ~~and the~~ maximum review date as RecentReviewDate from ~~the~~ employees ~~table~~ where ~~the~~ department ~~is~~ = 'Advertising'
SQL	SELECT MIN(ReviewDate) AS EarliestReviewDate, MAX(ReviewDate) AS RecentReviewDate FROM Employees WHERE Department = 'Advertising'

"How many different products were ordered on order number 553, and what was the total cost of that order?"

Translation	Select the unique count of product ID as TotalProductsPurchased and the sum of price times quantity ordered as OrderAmount from the order details table where the order number is 553
Clean Up	Select ~~the unique~~ count ~~of~~ (DISINCT product ID) as TotalProductsPurchased, ~~and the~~ sum ~~of~~ (price ~~times~~ * quantity ordered) as OrderAmount from ~~the~~ order details ~~table~~ where ~~the~~ order number ~~is~~ = 553
SQL	SELECT COUNT(DISTINCT ProductID) AS TotalProductsPurchased, SUM(Price * QuantityOrdered) AS OrderAmount FROM Order_Details WHERE OrderNumber = 553

You must keep in mind a couple of restrictions when you work with two or more aggregate functions. The first is that you cannot embed one aggregate function within another. (The one exception is you can embed an aggregate function inside another if you're using it in a Window function. See Chapter 22.) This restriction makes the following expression illegal:

```
SUM(AVG(LineItemTotal))
```

The second is that you cannot use a subquery as the value expression of an aggregate function. For example, the following expression is illegal under this restriction:

```
AVG((SELECT Price FROM Products WHERE Category = 'Bikes'))
```

Despite these restrictions, you've learned how easily you can use aggregate functions in a SELECT clause to retrieve relatively complex statistical information. Let's now look at how you might use aggregate functions to filter the information in a result set.

Using Aggregate Functions in Filters

Because an aggregate function returns a single value, you can use it as part of a comparison predicate in a search condition. You have to place the aggregate function within a subquery, however, and then use the subquery as part of the comparison predicate. If you're thinking that this sounds familiar, you're right. In Chapter 11, you learned how to use a subquery as part of a search condition in a WHERE clause and an aggregate function within a subquery. So you already know, in a general sense, how to use an aggregate function to filter the data sent to a result set. Now let's expand on that knowledge.

Using an aggregate function as part of a comparison predicate allows you to test the value of a value expression against a single statistical value. Although you could use a literal value for the task, a subquery gives you more flexibility and provides a more dynamic aspect to the condition. For example, suppose you're making the following request to the database:

> *"List the products that have a retail price less than or equal to the overall average retail price."*

One method you can use to answer this request is to calculate the overall average retail price manually and then plug that specific value into a comparison predicate.

Translation	Select the product name from the products table where the retail price is less than or equal to $196.03
Clean Up	Select ~~the~~ product name from ~~the~~ products ~~table~~ where ~~the~~ retail price ~~is less than or equal to~~ <= $196.03
SQL	SELECT ProductName FROM Products WHERE RetailPrice <= 196.03

Hey, why do more work than necessary? You can use an aggregate function in a subquery and let the database system do the work for you.

Translation	Select the product name from the products table where the retail price is less than or equal to the overall average retail price in the products table
Clean Up	Select ~~the~~ product name from ~~the~~ products ~~table~~ where ~~the~~ retail price ~~is less than or equal to the~~ <= ~~overall~~ (select ~~average~~ avg retail price ~~in the~~ from products ~~table~~)

SQL	SELECT ProductName
	
	FROM Products
	
	WHERE RetailPrice <=
	
	    (SELECT AVG(RetailPrice)
	
	    FROM Products)

I saved this query as CH12_Products_LTE_Avg_Price in the Sales Orders sample database.

It should be obvious that using a subquery with an aggregate function is your best course of action. If you use a literal value, you must be certain that you always recalculate the average contract price before executing the SELECT statement, just in case you've modified any existing retail prices. You then have to make sure that you enter the value correctly in the comparison predicate. But you won't have to worry about any of this if you use a subquery instead. The AVG function is always evaluated whenever you execute the SELECT statement, and it always returns the correct value regardless of whether you've modified any of the contract prices. (This is true for any aggregate function you use in a subquery.)

You can limit the rows that an aggregate function evaluates by using a WHERE clause in the subquery. This allows you to narrow the scope of the statistical value returned by the aggregate function. You already learned how to apply a WHERE clause to a subquery back in Chapter 11, so let's look at an example of how you might apply this technique:

"List the engagement number and contract price of all engagements that have a contract price larger than the total amount of all contract prices for the entire month of September 2017."

Translation	Select engagement number and contract price from the engagements table where the contract price is greater than the sum of all contract prices of engagements dated between September 1, 2017, and September 30, 2017

Clean Up	Select engagement number, ~~and~~ contract price from ~~the~~ engagements ~~table~~ where ~~the~~ contract price ~~is greater than~~ > ~~the~~ (select sum ~~of all~~ (contract prices) from engagements where ~~dated~~ start date between ~~September 1, 2017~~, '2017-09-01' and ~~September 30, 2017~~ '2017-09-30')

SQL	SELECT EngagementNumber, ContractPrice
	
	FROM Engagements
	
	WHERE ContractPrice >
	
	   (SELECT SUM(ContractPrice) FROM Engagements
	
	     WHERE StartDate BETWEEN '2017-09-01'
	
	     AND '2017-09-30')

I saved this query as CH12_Engagements_GT_SUM_September in the Entertainment Agency sample database.

You might find that you rarely have a need to use aggregate functions in filters, but they certainly come in handy when you have to answer those occasional off-the-wall requests.

Sample Statements

In this chapter, you've learned how to use aggregate functions in a SELECT clause and within a subquery being used as part of a comparison predicate. Now let's look at some examples of working with aggregate functions using the tables from each of the sample databases. These examples illustrate the use of the aggregate functions as output columns and in subqueries.

I've also included sample result sets that would be returned by these operations and placed them immediately after the SQL syntax line. The name that appears immediately above a result set is the name I gave each query in the sample data on the companion website for this book, www.informit.com/title/9780134858333. I stored each query in the appropriate sample database (as indicated within the example), and I prefixed the names of the queries relevant to this chapter with "CH12." You can follow the instructions in the Introduction of this book to load the samples onto your computer and try them.

❖ **Note** Remember that all the column names and table names used in these examples are drawn from the sample database structures shown in Appendix B, "Schema for the Sample Databases." Because many of these examples use complex JOINs, your database system might choose a different way to solve these queries. For this reason, the first few rows might not exactly match the result you obtain, but the total number of rows should be the same. To simplify the process, I have combined the Translation and Clean Up steps for all the following examples.

Sales Orders Database

"How many customers do we have in the state of California?"

Translation/ Clean Up	Select ~~the~~ count(*) as NumberOfCACustomers ~~of all customers~~ from ~~the~~ customers ~~table~~ where ~~the~~ state ~~is~~ = 'CA'
SQL	SELECT COUNT(*) AS NumberOfCACustomers
	FROM Customers
	WHERE CustState = 'CA'

CH12_Number_Of_California_Customers (1 Row)

NumberOfCACustomers
7

"List the product names and numbers that have a quoted price greater than or equal to the overall average retail price in the products table."

Translation/ Clean Up	Select ~~the~~ product name, ~~and the~~ product number from ~~the~~ products ~~table~~ inner ~~joined with the~~ order details ~~table~~ on products.product number ~~in the products table matches~~ = order_details.product number ~~in the order details table~~ where ~~the~~ quoted price ~~is greater than or equal to~~ >= (select ~~the average~~ avg(retail price) ~~in the~~ from products ~~table~~)

SQL	`SELECT DISTINCT Products.ProductName,`
	`    Products.ProductNumber`
	`FROM Products`
	`INNER JOIN Order_Details`
	`ON Products.ProductNumber =`
	`    Order_Details.ProductNumber`
	`WHERE Order_Details.QuotedPrice >=`
	`    (SELECT AVG(RetailPrice)`
	`    FROM Products)`

❖ **Note** I chose to ask for DISTINCT products because (I hope) a particular product might have been ordered more than once. I need to see each product name and number only once.

CH12_Quoted_Price_vs_Average_Retail_Price (4 Rows)

ProductName	ProductNumber
Eagle FS-3 Mountain Bike	2
GT RTS-2 Mountain Bike	11
Trek 9000 Mountain Bike	1
Viscount Mountain Bike	6

Entertainment Agency Database

"List the engagement number and contract price of contracts that occur on the earliest date."

Translation/ Clean Up	Select engagement number, ~~and~~ contract price from ~~the~~ engagements ~~table~~ where ~~the~~ start date ~~is equal to the~~ = ~~earliest~~ (select min(start date) ~~in the~~ from engagements ~~table~~)
SQL	`SELECT EngagementNumber, ContractPrice`
	`FROM Engagements`
	`WHERE StartDate =`
	`    (SELECT MIN(StartDate) FROM Engagements)`

CH12_Earliest_Contracts (1 Row)

EngagementNumber	ContractPrice
2	$200.00

"What was the total value of all engagements booked in October 2017?"

Translation/ Clean Up	Select ~~the~~ sum ~~of~~ (contract price) as TotalBookedValue from ~~the~~ engagements ~~table~~ where ~~the~~ start date ~~is~~ between ~~October 1, 2017~~ '2017-10-01' and ~~October 31, 2017~~ '2017-10-31'
SQL	SELECT SUM(ContractPrice) AS TotalBookedValue FROM Engagements WHERE StartDate BETWEEN '2017-10-01' AND '2017-10-31'

CH12_Total_Booked_Value_For_October_2017 (1 Row)

TotalBookedValue
$30,125.00

School Scheduling Database

"What is the largest salary we pay to any staff member?"

Translation/ Clean Up	Select ~~the~~ maximum (salary) as LargestStaffSalary from ~~the~~ staff ~~table~~
SQL	SELECT Max(Salary) AS LargestStaffSalary FROM Staff

CH12_Largest_Staff_Salary (1 Row)

LargestStaffSalary
$60,000.00

"What is the total salary amount paid to our staff in California?"

Translation/ Clean Up	Select ~~the~~ sum ~~of~~ (salary) as TotalAmountPaid from ~~the~~ staff ~~table for all our California staff~~ where state = 'CA'
SQL	SELECT SUM(Salary) AS TotalAmountPaid FROM Staff WHERE StfState = 'CA'

CH12_Total_Salary_Paid_To_California_Staff (1 Row)

TotalAmountPaid
$209,000.00

Bowling League Database

"How many tournaments have been played at Red Rooster Lanes?"

Translation/ Clean Up	Select ~~the~~ count ~~of~~ (tourney location)~~s~~ as NumberOfTournaments from ~~the~~ tournaments ~~table~~ where ~~the~~ tourney location ~~is~~ = 'Red Rooster Lanes'
SQL	SELECT COUNT(TourneyLocation) AS NumberOfTournaments FROM Tournaments WHERE TourneyLocation = 'Red Rooster Lanes'

❖ **Note** Because the query filters on TourneyLocation, I could have also used COUNT(*).

CH12_Number_Of_Tournaments_At_Red_Rooster_Lanes (1 Row)

NumberOfTournaments
3

"List the last name and first name, in alphabetical order, of every bowler whose personal average score is greater than or equal to the overall average score."

Translation/ Clean Up	Select ~~the~~ last name, ~~and~~ first name from ~~the~~ bowlers ~~table~~ where ~~the~~ (select ~~average~~ avg(raw score) from ~~the~~ bowlers scores ~~table~~ as BS ~~for the current bowler~~ where BS.bowler ID = bowlers.bowler ID) ~~is greater than or equal to the~~ >= ~~overall~~ (select avg(raw score) ~~score in the~~ from bowler scores ~~table~~) ~~sorted~~ order by last name, ~~and~~ first name

SQL	SELECT Bowlers.BowlerLastName,
	        Bowlers.BowlerFirstName
	FROM Bowlers
	WHERE (SELECT AVG(RawScore)
	FROM Bowler_Scores AS BS
	WHERE BS.BowlerID = Bowlers.BowlerID)
	>=(SELECT AVG(RawScore) FROM Bowler_Scores)
	ORDER BY Bowlers.BowlerLastName,
	        Bowlers.BowlerFirstName

CH12_Better_Than_Overall_Average (17 Rows)

BowlerLastName	BowlerFirstName
Cunningham	David
Fournier	David
Hallmark	Alaina
Hallmark	Gary
Hernandez	Michael
Kennedy	Angel
Kennedy	John
Patterson	Kathryn
Patterson	Neil
Patterson	Rachel
Clothier	Ben

BowlerLastName	BowlerFirstName
Thompson	Mary
Thompson	Sarah
Thompson	William
Viescas	Caleb
Viescas	David
Viescas	John

❖ **Note** You can see that this is a creative use of two subqueries in the WHERE clause to solve the problem.

Recipes Database

"How many recipes contain a beef ingredient?"

Translation/ Clean Up	Select ~~the~~ count (*) ~~of recipes~~ as NumberOfRecipes from ~~the~~ recipes ~~table~~ where ~~the~~ recipe ID ~~is~~ in ~~the~~ (selection of recipe ~~IDs in the~~ from recipe ingredients ~~table~~ inner joined ~~with the~~ ingredients ~~table~~ on recipe_ingredients.ingredient ID ~~in the recipe ingredients table matches~~ = ingredients. ingredient ID ~~in the ingredients table~~ where ~~the~~ ingredient name ~~is~~ like '%Beef%')
| SQL | ```
SELECT COUNT(*) AS NumberOfRecipes
FROM Recipes
WHERE Recipes.RecipeID IN
    (SELECT RecipeID
    FROM Recipe_Ingredients
    INNER JOIN Ingredients ON
        Recipe_Ingredients.IngredientID =
        Ingredients.IngredientID
    WHERE Ingredients.IngredientName
        LIKE '%Beef%')
``` |
```

CH12_Recipes_With_Beef_Ingredient (1 Row)

NumberOfRecipes
3

"How many ingredients are measured by the cup?"

Translation/ Clean Up	Select ~~the~~ count (*) ~~of ingredients~~ as NumberOfIngredients from ~~the~~ ingredients ~~table~~ inner join~~ed with the~~ measurements ~~table~~ on ingredients.measure amount ID ~~in the ingredients table matches~~ = measurements.measure amount ID ~~in the measurements table~~ where ~~the~~ measurement description ~~is~~ = 'Cup'

SQL	`SELECT COUNT(*) AS NumberOfIngredients`
	`FROM Ingredients`
	`INNER JOIN Measurements`
	`ON Ingredients.MeasureAmountID =`
	`    Measurements.MeasureAmountID`
	`WHERE MeasurementDescription = 'Cup'`

CH12_Number_of_Ingredients_Measured_by_the_Cup (1 Row)

NumberOfIngredients
12

Summary

I began this chapter by introducing you to aggregate functions. You learned about five different functions and that you can use them in the SELECT and WHERE clauses of a SELECT statement. You also learned that each aggregate function—except COUNT(*)—disregards all Null values as it performs its operation.

Next, I showed how to use each aggregate function. You learned how to count rows or values with the COUNT functions, how to find the largest and smallest values with the MAX and MIN functions, how to calculate a mean average with the AVG function, and how to total a set of values with the SUM function. I also showed how to use the DISTINCT option with each function and explained that DISTINCT does not affect the MAX and MIN functions.

I closed the chapter by showing you how to use aggregate functions in filters. You now know that you can use an aggregate function within a subquery and then use the subquery as part of the filter. You also learned that you can apply a filter to the subquery as well so that the aggregate function bases its value on a specific set of data.

I've only just begun to show you what you can do with aggregate functions. In the next two chapters, I'll show you how to provide more sophisticated statistical information by using aggregate functions on *grouped* data and how to apply a filter to aggregate calculations.

The following section presents some requests that you can work out on your own.

Problems for You to Solve

Below, I show you the request statement and the name of the solution query in the sample databases. If you want some practice, you can work out the SQL you need for each request and then check your answer with the query I saved in the samples. Don't worry if your syntax doesn't exactly match the syntax of the queries I saved—as long as your result set is the same.

Sales Orders Database

1. *"What is the average retail price of a mountain bike?"*

    You can find the solution in CH12_Average_Price_Of_A_ Mountain_Bike (1 row – value: $1321.25).

2. *"What was the date of our most recent order?"*

    You can find the solution in CH12_Most_Recent_Order_Date (1 row – value: 2018-03-01).

3. *"What was the total amount for order number 8?"*

    You can find the solution in CH12_Total_Amount_For_Order_ Number_8 (1 row – value: $1492.60).

Entertainment Agency Database

1. *"What is the average salary of a booking agent?"*

   You can find the solution in CH12_Average_Agent_Salary (1 row – value: $24850.00).

2. *"Show me the engagement numbers for all engagements that have a contract price greater than or equal to the overall average contract price."*

   (Hint: You'll have to use a subquery to answer this request.)

   You can find the solution in CH12_Contract_Price_GE_Average_Contract_Price (43 rows).

3. *"How many of our entertainers are based in Bellevue?"*

   You can find the solution in CH12_Number_Of_Bellevue_Entertainers (1 row – value: 3).

4. *"Which engagements occur earliest in October 2017?"*

   You can find the solution in CH12_Earliest_October_Engagements (3 rows).

School Scheduling Database

1. *"What is the current average class duration?"*

   You can find the solution in CH12_Average_Class_Duration (1 row – value: 78.939 – but SQL Server truncates to 78).

2. *"List the last name and first name of each staff member who has been with us since the earliest hire date."*

   (Hint: You'll have to use a subquery containing an aggregate function that evaluates the DateHired column.)

   You can find the solution in CH12_Most_Senior_Staff_Members (1 row – value: "Alborous, Sam").

3. *"How many classes are held in room 3346?"*

   You can find the solution in CH12_Number_Of_Classes_Held_In_Room_3346 (1 row – value: 10).

Bowling League Database

1. *"What is the largest handicap held by any bowler at the current time?"*

   You can find the solution in CH12_Current_Highest_Handicap (1 row – value: 52).

2. *"Which locations hosted tournaments on the earliest tournament date?"*

   You can find the solution in CH12_Tourney_Locations_For_ Earliest_Date (1 row – value: "Red Rooster Lanes").

3. *"What is the last tournament date we have on our schedule?"*

   You can find the solution in CH12_Last_Tourney_Date (1 row – value: 2018-08-16).

Recipes Database

1. *"Which recipe requires the most cloves of garlic?"*

   (Hint: You'll need to use INNER JOINs and a subquery to answer this request. Note that the measurement is "cloves" for all recipes, so you don't have to filter for that.)

   You can find the solution in CH12_Recipe_With_Most_Cloves_of_ Garlic (1 row – value: "Roast Beef").

2. *"Count the number of main course recipes."*

   (Hint: To search on "Main course" recipes requires a JOIN between Recipe_Classes and Recipes, but you can also cheat and just look for RecipeClassID = 1.)

   You can find the solution in CH12_Number_Of_Main_Course_ Recipes (1 row – value: 7).

3. *"Calculate the total number of teaspoons of salt in all recipes."*

   (Hint: Salt happens to be measured in teaspoons in all recipes, so you don't have to filter for that.)

   You can find the solution in CH12_Total_Salt_Used (1 row – value: 8.75).

13

Grouping Data

"Don't drown yourself with details. Look at the whole."
—Marshal Ferdinand Foch Commander-in-Chief, Allied Armies in France

Topics Covered in This Chapter

Why Group Data?

The GROUP BY Clause

"Some Restrictions Apply"

Uses for GROUP BY

Sample Statements

Summary

Problems for You to Solve

Chapter 12, "Simple Totals," explained how to use the aggregate functions (COUNT, MIN, MAX, AVG, and SUM) to ask SQL to calculate a value across all the rows in the table defined in your FROM and WHERE clauses. I pointed out, however, that after you include any value expression that contains an aggregate function in your SELECT clause, *all* your value expressions must either be a literal constant or contain an aggregate function. This characteristic is useful if you want to see only one row of totals across a result set, but what if you want to see some subtotals? In this chapter, I'll show you how to ask for subtotals by grouping your data. I'll show you how to do more complex subtotals in Chapter 21, "Performing Complex Calculations on Groups."

Why Group Data?

When you're working in the Sales Orders database, finding out the number of orders (COUNT), the total sales (SUM), the average of sales (AVG), the smallest order (MIN), or the largest order (MAX) is useful, indeed. And if you want to calculate any of these values by customer, order date, or product, you can add a filter (WHERE) to fetch the rows for one particular customer or product. But what if you want to see subtotals for *all* customers, displaying the customer name along with the subtotals? To do that, you need to ask your database system to *group* the rows.

Likewise, in the Entertainment Agency database, it's easy to find out the number of contracts, the total contract price, the smallest contract price, or the largest contract price for all contracts. You can even filter the rows so that you see these calculations for one particular entertainer, one particular customer, or across a specific range of dates. Again, if you want to see one total row for each customer or entertainer, you must group the rows.

Are you starting to get the idea? When you ask your database system to group rows on column values or expressions, it forms subsets of rows based on matching values. You can then ask your database to calculate aggregate values *on each group*. Let's look at a simple example from the Entertainment Agency database. First, I need to build a query that fetches the columns of interest—entertainer name and contract price. Here's the SQL:

SQL	SELECT Entertainers.EntStageName,
	    Engagements.ContractPrice
	FROM Entertainers
	INNER JOIN Engagements
	ON Entertainers.EntertainerID =
	    Engagements.EntertainerID
	ORDER BY EntStageName

The result looks like the following table. (In the sample database, I saved this request as CH13_Entertainers_And_ContractPrices.)

EntStageName	ContractPrice
Carol Peacock Trio	$140.00
Carol Peacock Trio	$1,670.00
Carol Peacock Trio	$770.00
Carol Peacock Trio	$1,670.00
Carol Peacock Trio	$1,670.00
Carol Peacock Trio	$320.00
Carol Peacock Trio	$1,400.00
Carol Peacock Trio	$680.00
Carol Peacock Trio	$410.00
Carol Peacock Trio	$1,940.00
Carol Peacock Trio	$410.00
Caroline Coie Cuartet	$1,250.00
Caroline Coie Cuartet	$2,450.00
Caroline Coie Cuartet	$1,490.00
Caroline Coie Cuartet	$1,370.00
<< more rows here >>	

You already know that you can count all the rows, or find the smallest, largest, sum, or average of the ContractPrice column—as long as you eliminate the EntStageName column. However, you can keep this column if you ask your database to group on it. If you ask to group on entertainer stage name, your database will form one group containing the first eleven rows ("Carol Peacock Trio"), a second group containing the next eleven rows ("Caroline Coie Cuartet"), and so on through the entire table. You can now ask for the COUNT of the rows or the SUM, MIN, MAX, or AVG of the ContractPrice column, and you will get one aggregate row per entertainment group. The result looks like the following table.

EntStageName	NumContracts	TotPrice	MinPrice	MaxPrice	AvgPrice
Carol Peacock Trio	11	$11,080.00	$140.00	$1,940.00	$1,007.27
Caroline Coie Cuartet	11	$15,070.00	$290.00	$2,450.00	$1,370.00
Coldwater Cattle Company	8	$14,875.00	$350.00	$3,800.00	$1,859.38
Country Feeling	15	$34,080.00	$275.00	$14,105.00	$2,272.00
Jazz Persuasion	7	$5,480.00	$500.00	$1,670.00	$782.86
Jim Glynn	9	$3,030.00	$110.00	$770.00	$336.67
Julia Schnebly	8	$4,345.00	$275.00	$875.00	$543.13
JV & the Deep Six	10	$17,150.00	$950.00	$3,650.00	$1,715.00
Modern Dance	10	$14,600.00	$650.00	$2,930.00	$1,460.00
Saturday Revue	9	$11,550.00	$290.00	$2,930.00	$1,283.33
Susan McLain	6	$2,670.00	$230.00	$800.00	$445.00
Topazz	7	$6,620.00	$590.00	$1,550.00	$945.71
<< more rows here >>					

Looks interesting, doesn't it? I bet you'd like to know how I did that! I'll show you all the details in the following sections.

❖ **Note** Remember in the Introduction that I warned you that results from each database system won't necessarily match the sort order you see in examples in this book unless you include an ORDER BY clause. Even when you include that specification, the system might return results in columns not included in the ORDER BY clause in a different sequence because of different optimization techniques.

If you're running the examples in Microsoft SQL Server, simply selecting the rows from the view does not honor any ORDER BY clause specified in the view. You must open the design of the view and execute it from there for the ORDER BY clause to be honored.

The GROUP BY Clause

As you discovered in Chapter 12, you can find out all sorts of interesting information by using aggregate functions. However, you might have noticed that all the examples I gave you applied the aggregate functions across *all* the rows returned by the FROM and WHERE clauses. You could filter the result set down to one group using the WHERE clause, but there was really no way to look at the results from multiple groups in one request. To accomplish this summarizing by group in a single request, I need to add one more major clause to your SQL vocabulary—GROUP BY.

Syntax

Let's take a close look at the GROUP BY clause. Figure 13-1 shows the basic diagram for a SELECT statement with GROUP BY added.

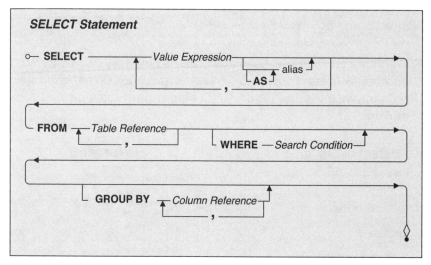

Figure 13-1 *The syntax diagram of a SELECT statement with a GROUP BY clause*

As you recall from earlier chapters, you define the tables that are the source of your data in the FROM clause. Your FROM clause can be as simple as a single table name or as complex as a JOIN of multiple tables. As discussed in Chapter 8, "INNER JOINs," you can even embed an entire table subquery (a SELECT statement) as a table reference. Next, you can optionally provide a WHERE clause to include or exclude certain rows supplied by the FROM clause. I covered the WHERE clause in detail in Chapter 6, "Filtering Your Data."

When you add a GROUP BY clause, you specify the columns in the logical table formed by the FROM and WHERE clauses that you want your database system to use as the definition for groups of rows. Rows that have the same values in the list of columns you specify will be gathered into a group. You can use the columns that you list in the GROUP BY clause in value expressions in your SELECT clause, and you can use any of the aggregate functions I discussed in the previous chapter to perform calculations across each group.

> ❖ **Note** When you use GROUP BY, you'll often see the results returned by your database system as though they are sorted by the columns you specified. This happens because some optimizers first sort the data internally to make it faster to process your GROUP BY. Keep in mind that if you want a specific sort order, you must also include an ORDER BY clause.

Let's apply the GROUP BY clause to see how you can calculate information about contract prices by entertainment group—the sample I tantalized you with earlier. Figure 13-2 shows the tables needed to solve this problem.

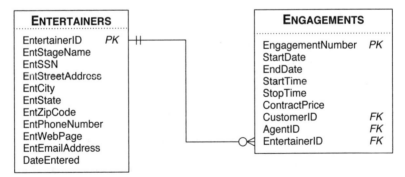

Figure 13-2 *The relationship between the Entertainers and Engagements tables*

> ❖ **Note** Throughout this chapter, I use the "Request/Translation/Clean Up/SQL" technique introduced in Chapter 4, "Creating a Simple Query."

"Show me for each entertainment group the group name, the count of contracts for the group, the total price of all the contracts, the lowest contract price, the highest contract price, and the average price of all the contracts."

(Hint: When you see a request that wants the count, total, smallest, largest, or average of values at a detail level [contracts] *for each* value at a higher level [entertainers], you are going to need to use aggregate functions and grouping in your request. Remember that for each entertainer there are most likely many contracts.)

Translation	Select entertainer name, the count of contracts, the sum of the contract price, the lowest contract price, the highest contract price, and the average contract price from the entertainers table joined with the engagements table on entertainer ID, grouped by entertainer name
Clean Up	Select entertainer name, ~~the~~ count ~~of~~ (*) ~~contracts~~, ~~the~~ sum ~~of the~~ (contract price), ~~the lowest~~ min(contract price), ~~the highest~~ max(contract price), ~~and the average~~ avg(contract price) from ~~the~~ entertainers ~~table~~ inner join~~ed with the~~ engagements ~~table~~ on entertainers.entertainer ID ~~in the entertainers table matches~~ = engagements.entertainer ID ~~in the engagements table~~, group~~ed~~ by entertainer name

SQL	SELECT Entertainers.EntStageName,
	    COUNT(*) AS NumContracts,
	    SUM(Engagements.ContractPrice) AS TotPrice,
	    MIN(Engagements.ContractPrice) AS MinPrice,
	    MAX(Engagements.ContractPrice) AS MaxPrice,
	    AVG(Engagements.ContractPrice) AS AvgPrice
	FROM Entertainers
	INNER JOIN Engagements
	ON Entertainers.EntertainerID =
	    Engagements.EntertainerID
	GROUP BY Entertainers.EntStageName

Note that I substituted MIN for "lowest," MAX for "highest," and AVG for "average," as I showed you in the previous chapter. I also asked for

COUNT(*) because I want to count all the engagement (contract) rows regardless of any Null values. Adding the GROUP BY clause is what gets me the aggregate calculations *per entertainment group*. It also allows me to include the entertainer name in the SELECT clause. (I saved this request as CH13_Aggregate_Contract_Info_By_Entertainer in the sample database.)

Do you suppose the above query returns a row for each entertainer? What about entertainers who have never been booked? If you remember what you learned in Chapter 9 about OUTER JOIN, you might be tempted to solve the problem like this:

```
SQL          SELECT Entertainers.EntStageName,
                 COUNT(*) AS NumContracts,
                 SUM(Engagements.ContractPrice) AS TotPrice,
                 MIN(Engagements.ContractPrice) AS MinPrice,
                 MAX(Engagements.ContractPrice) AS MaxPrice,
                 AVG(Engagements.ContractPrice) AS AvgPrice
             FROM Entertainers
             LEFT OUTER JOIN Engagements
             ON Entertainers.EntertainerID =
                 Engagements.EntertainerID
             GROUP BY Entertainers.EntStageName
```

One interesting point about all the aggregate functions is that they ignore rows that have a Null value. The above query will return a blank or Null value for TotPrice, MinPrice, MaxPrice, and AvgPrice for the one entertainer who has no engagements, but you'll find that NumContracts is 1! How can that be? Well, this SQL asks for COUNT(*)—count any row returned. The OUTER JOIN returns exactly one row for the entertainer with no booking, so the count of 1 is correct. (I saved this request as CH13_Aggregate_Contract_Info_All_Entertainers_WRONG in the sample database.) However, if you remember from the previous chapter, you can also COUNT(*value expression*), and that tells your database system to add to the count only if it finds a non-Null value in the value expression or column name you specify. Let's tweak the query one more time.

SQL

```
SELECT Entertainers.EntStageName,
    COUNT(Engagements.EntertainerID) AS NumContracts,
    SUM(Engagements.ContractPrice) AS TotPrice,
    MIN(Engagements.ContractPrice) AS MinPrice,
    MAX(Engagements.ContractPrice) AS MaxPrice,
    AVG(Engagements.ContractPrice) AS AvgPrice
FROM Entertainers
LEFT OUTER JOIN Engagements
ON Entertainers.EntertainerID =
    Engagements.EntertainerID
GROUP BY Entertainers.EntStageName
```

Because the EntertainerID column from the Engagements table for the one entertainer who has no bookings is Null, nothing gets counted. If you run this query, you should see the correct value 0 in NumContracts for the one entertainer who has no engagements. (I saved this request as CH13_Aggregate_Contract_Info_All_Entertainers in the sample database.)

What if you want (or need) to group on more than one value? Let's look at this same problem, but from the perspective of customers rather than entertainers, and let's assume you want to display in your result set both the customer's last name and first name. Figure 13-3 shows the necessary tables.

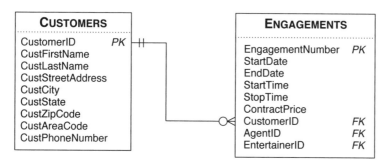

Figure 13-3 *The relationship between the Customers and Engagements tables*

> *"Show me for each customer the customer first and last names, the count of contracts for the customer, the total price of all the contracts, the lowest contract price, the highest contract price, and the average price of all the contracts."*

Translation	Select customer last name, customer first name, the count of contracts, the sum of the contract price, the lowest contract price, the highest contract price, and the average contract price from the customers table joined with the engagements table on customer ID, grouped by customer last name and customer first name
Clean Up	Select ~~customer~~ last name, ~~customer~~ first name, ~~the~~ count ~~of~~ (*) ~~contracts,~~ ~~the~~ sum ~~of the~~ (contract price), ~~the lowest~~ min(contract price), ~~the highest~~ max(contract price), ~~and the average~~ avg(contract price) from ~~the~~ customers ~~table~~ inner joine~~d with the~~ engagements ~~table~~ on customers.customer ID ~~in the customers table matches~~ = engagements.customer ID ~~in the engagements table,~~ grouped by customer last name, ~~and~~ customer first name

SQL	SELECT Customers.CustLastName,
	    Customers.CustFirstName,
	    COUNT(*) AS NumContracts,
	    SUM(Engagements.ContractPrice) AS TotPrice,
	    MIN(Engagements.ContractPrice) AS MinPrice,
	    MAX(Engagements.ContractPrice) AS MaxPrice,
	    AVG(Engagements.ContractPrice) AS AvgPrice
	FROM Customers
	INNER JOIN Engagements
	ON Customers.CustomerID =
	    Engagements.CustomerID
	GROUP BY Customers.CustLastName,
	    Customers.CustFirstName

The result looks like the following table. (In the Entertainment Agency sample database, I saved this request as CH13_Aggregate_Contract_Info_By_Customer.)

CustLast Name	CustFirst Name	Num Contracts	TotPrice	MinPrice	MaxPrice	AvgPrice
Berg	Matt	9	$13,170.00	$200.00	$2,675.00	$1,463.33
Brehm	Peter	7	$7,250.00	$290.00	$3,800.00	$1,035.71
Ehrlich	Zachary	13	$12,455.00	$230.00	$1,550.00	$958.08

CustLast Name	CustFirst Name	Num Contracts	TotPrice	MinPrice	MaxPrice	AvgPrice
Hallmark	Elizabeth	8	$25,585.00	$410.00	$14,105.00	$3,198.13
Hartwig	Doris	8	$10,795.00	$140.00	$2,750.00	$1,349.38
Keyser	Liz	7	$4,685.00	$200.00	$1,490.00	$669.29
McCrae	Dean	11	$11,800.00	$290.00	$2,570.00	$1,072.73
Patterson	Kerry	7	$6,815.00	$110.00	$2,930.00	$973.57
		<< more rows here >>				

Because it takes two columns to display the customer name, I had to include them *both* in the GROUP BY clause. Remember that if you want to include a column in the output that is not the result of an aggregate calculation, you must also include it in the GROUP BY clause. I did not include ContractPrice in the GROUP BY clause because that's the column I'm using in many of the aggregate function expressions. If I had included ContractPrice, I would have gotten unique groups of customers and prices. MIN, MAX, and AVG will all return that grouped price. COUNT will be greater than one only if more than one contract with the same price exists for a given customer. If you think about it, though, grouping by customer and price and asking for a COUNT would be a good way to find customers who have multiple contracts at the same price.

Do you suppose this query includes customers who have no bookings? If you answered "No," you're correct! To fetch data for all customers regardless of whether they've booked an engagement, you must use an OUTER JOIN and be careful to COUNT one of the columns from the Engagements table. The solution is similar to the problem discussed earlier for entertainers and engagements.

Mixing Columns and Expressions

Suppose you want to list the customer name as one output column, the full customer address as another output column, the last engagement date, and the sum of engagement contract prices. The customer name is in two columns: CustFirstName and CustLastName. The columns you need for a full address are CustStreetAddress, CustCity, CustState, and CustZipCode. Let's see how you should construct the SQL for this request. (I saved this request as CH13_Customers_Last_Booking in the Entertainment Agency sample database.)

"Show me for each customer the customer full name, the customer full address, the latest contract date for the customer, and the total price of all the contracts."

Translation	Select customer last name and customer first name as CustomerFullName; street address, city, state, and ZIP Code as CustomerFullAddress; the latest contract start date; and the sum of the contract price from the customers table joined with the engagements table on customer ID, grouped by customer last name, customer first name, customer street address, customer city, customer state, and customer ZIP Code
Clean Up	Select ~~customer~~ last name ~~and~~ || ', ' || ~~customer~~ first name as CustomerFullName, street address~~,~~ || ', ' || city~~,~~ || ', ' || state~~, and~~ || ' ' || ZIP Code as CustomerFullAddress, ~~the latest~~ max(contract start date) as latest date, ~~and the~~ sum ~~of the~~ (contract price) as total contract price from ~~the~~ customers ~~table~~ inner ~~joined with the~~ engagements ~~table~~ on customers. customer ID ~~in the customers table matches~~ = engagements. customer ID ~~in the engagements table~~ grouped by ~~customer~~ last name, ~~customer~~ first name, ~~customer~~ street address, ~~customer~~ city, ~~customer~~ state, ~~and customer~~ ZIP Code
SQL	``` SELECT Customers.CustLastName || ', ' || ```

```
SELECT Customers.CustLastName || ', ' ||
    Customers.CustFirstName AS CustomerFullName,
    Customers.CustStreetAddress || ', ' ||
    Customers.CustCity || ', ' ||
    Customers.CustState || ' ' ||
    Customers.CustZipCode AS CustomerFullAddress,
    MAX(Engagements.StartDate) AS LatestDate,
    SUM(Engagements.ContractPrice),
    AS TotalContractPrice
FROM Customers
INNER JOIN Engagements
ON Customers.CustomerID =
    Engagements.CustomerID
GROUP BY Customers.CustLastName,
    Customers.CustFirstName,
    Customers.CustStreetAddress,
    Customers.CustCity, Customers.CustState,
    Customers.CustZipCode
```

Notice that I had to list every one of the columns that I used in an output expression that did not include an aggregate function. I used Start-Date and ContractPrice in aggregate expressions, so I don't need to list them in the GROUP BY clause. In fact, it doesn't make sense to group on either StartDate or ContractPrice because I want to use these in an aggregate calculation across multiple customers. If, for example, I grouped on StartDate, MAX(StartDate) would return the grouping value, and the expression SUM(ContractPrice) would return only the sum of contract prices for a customer on any given date. You wouldn't get the sum of more than one contract unless a customer had more than one contract for a given date—not likely.

Using GROUP BY in a Subquery in a WHERE Clause

In Chapter 11, "Subqueries," I introduced the COUNT and MAX aggregate functions to show how to filter rows using an aggregate value fetched with a subquery. In Chapter 12 I showed how to use MIN, AVG, and SUM in a subquery filter as well. Let's look at a request that requires both a subquery with an aggregate function and a GROUP BY clause in the subquery:

"Display the engagement contract whose price is greater than the sum of all contracts for any other customer."

Translation	Select customer first name, customer last name, engagement start date, and engagement contract price from the customers table joined with the engagements table on customer ID where the contract price is greater than the sum of all contract prices from the engagements table for customers other than the current customer, grouped by customer ID
Clean Up	Select customer ~~first~~ name, customer ~~last~~ name, engagement start date, ~~and~~ engagement contract price from ~~the~~ customers ~~table~~ inner join~~ed with the~~ engagements ~~table~~ on customers. customer ID ~~in the customers table matches~~ = engagements. customer ID ~~in the engagements table~~ where ~~the~~ contract price ~~is greater than~~ > ALL (select ~~the~~ sum ~~of all~~ (contract price~~s~~) from ~~the~~ engagements ~~table~~ as E2 ~~for~~ where E2.customer~~s~~ ID <> ~~other than the current~~ customers.customer ID~~,~~ grouped by E2.customer ID)

SQL

```
SELECT Customers.CustFirstName,
    Customers.CustLastName,
    Engagements.StartDate,
    Engagements.ContractPrice
FROM Customers
INNER JOIN Engagements
ON Customers.CustomerID =
    Engagements.CustomerID
WHERE Engagements.ContractPrice > ALL
    (Select SUM(ContractPrice)
    FROM Engagements AS E2
    WHERE E2.CustomerID <> Customers.CustomerID
    GROUP BY E2.CustomerID)
```

Let's analyze what the subquery is doing. For each engagement that the query looks at in the JOIN of the Customers and Engagements tables, the subquery calculates the SUM of all contract prices for all *other* customers and groups them by customer ID. Because there are multiple customers in the database, the subquery will return multiple SUM values—one for each of the other customers. For this reason, I cannot ask for a simple greater than (>) comparison. I can, however, use the quantified greater than all (> ALL) comparison to check a set of values as you learned in Chapter 11. If you run this query in the sample Entertainment Agency database for this chapter (I saved it as CH13_Biggest_Big_Contract), you'll find that one contract fits the bill, as shown here:

CustFirstName	CustLastName	StartDate	ContractPrice
Elizabeth	Hallmark	2018-01-22	$14,105.00

Simulating a SELECT DISTINCT Statement

Did it occur to you that you can use a GROUP BY clause and not include any aggregate functions in your SELECT clause? Sure you can! When you do this, you get the same effect as using the DISTINCT keyword covered in Chapter 4. (See the "Eliminating Duplicate Rows" section in that chapter.)

Let's look at a simple request that requires unique values and solve it using both techniques:

"Show me the unique city names from the customers table."

Translation 1	Select the unique city names from the customers table
Clean Up	Select ~~the unique~~ distinct city ~~names~~ from ~~the~~ customers ~~table~~
SQL	`SELECT DISTINCT Customers.CustCity` `FROM Customers`
Translation 2	Select city name from the customers table, grouped by city name
Clean Up	Select city ~~name~~ from ~~the~~ customers ~~table,~~ grouped by city name

SQL	`SELECT Customers.CustCity`
	`FROM Customers`
	`GROUP BY Customers.CustCityName`

Remember that GROUP BY groups all the rows on the grouping column(s) you specify and returns one row per group. This is a slightly different way to get to the same result that you obtain with the DISTINCT keyword. Which one is better? I think that DISTINCT might be a clearer statement of what you want if all you want is unique rows, but you might find that your database system solves the problem faster when you use GROUP BY. In addition, GROUP BY lets you obtain more information about your data. Consider the following query:

SQL	`SELECT Customers.CustCity, Count(*) as`
	`    CustPerCity`
	`FROM Customers`
	`GROUP BY Customers.CustCityName`

With this query, you not only fetch the unique city names but also find out how many customers are in each city. Is that cool or what?

"Some Restrictions Apply"

I already mentioned that adding a GROUP BY clause places certain restrictions on constructing your request. Let's review those restrictions to make sure you don't fall into common traps.

Column Restrictions

When you add a GROUP BY clause, you're asking your database system to form unique groups of rows from those returned by the tables defined in your FROM clause and filtered by your WHERE clause. You can use as many aggregate expressions as you like in your SELECT clause, and these expressions can use any of the columns in the table defined by the FROM and WHERE clauses. As I pointed out in an earlier example, it probably does not make sense to reference a column in an aggregate expression and also include that column in your grouping specification.

If you choose to also include expressions that reference columns but do not include an aggregate function, you must list *all* columns you use this way in the GROUP BY clause. One of the most common mistakes is to assume that you can reference columns in nonaggregate expressions as long as the columns come from unique rows. For example, let's look at an incorrect request that includes a primary key value—something that I know by definition is unique:

"Display the customer ID, customer full name, and the total of all engagement contract prices."

Translation	Select customer ID, customer first name, and customer last name as CustFullName, and the sum of contract prices as TotalPrice from the customers table joined with the engagements table on customer ID, grouped by customer ID
Clean Up	Select customer ID, ~~customer~~ first name ~~and~~ || ' ' || ~~customer~~ last name as CustFullName, ~~and the~~ sum ~~of~~ (contract price)s as TotalPrice from ~~the~~ customers ~~table~~ inner join~~ed with the~~ engagements ~~table~~ on customers.customer ID ~~in the customers table matches~~ = engagements.customer ID ~~in the engagements table,~~ grouped by customer ID

SQL	`SELECT Customers.CustomerID,`
	`    Customers.CustFirstName || ' ' ||`
	`    Customers.CustLastName AS CustFullName,`
	`    SUM(Engagements.ContractPrice) AS TotalPrice`
	`FROM Customers`
	`INNER JOIN Engagements`
	`ON Customers.CustomerID =`
	`    Engagements.CustomerID`
	`GROUP BY Customers.CustomerID`

I *know* that CustomerID is unique per customer. Grouping on CustomerID alone should be sufficient to fetch unique customer first and last name information within the groups formed by CustomerID. However, SQL is a language based on syntax, not semantics. In other words, SQL does not take into account any knowledge that could be implied by the design of your database tables—including whether columns are primary keys. SQL demands that your request be syntactically "pure" and translatable without any knowledge of the underlying table design. So, the above SQL statement will fail on a database system that is fully compliant with the SQL Standard because I've included columns in the SELECT clause that are not in an aggregate function and are also not in the GROUP BY clause (CustFirstName and CustLastName). (Surprisingly, a query constructed like the above does work in MySQL and PostgreSQL.) The correct SQL request is as follows:

```
SQL         SELECT Customers.CustomerID,
                Customers.CustFirstName || ' ' ||
                Customers.CustLastName AS CustFullName,
                SUM(Engagements.ContractPrice) AS TotalPrice
            FROM Customers
            INNER JOIN Engagements
            ON Customers.CustomerID =
                Engagements.CustomerID
            GROUP BY Customers.CustomerID,
                Customers.CustFirstName,
                Customers.CustLastName
```

This might seem like overkill, but it's the correct way to do it!

❖ **Note** In some database systems, you must exactly duplicate the *expressions* you use in the SELECT clause in the GROUP BY clause. Oracle and Microsoft Office Access are examples of systems that either support or require this. (Microsoft Office Access lets you do it either way.) In my example, instead of listing the separate columns, you would have to end the SQL with this:

```
GROUP BY Customers.CustomerID,
    Customers.CustFirstName || ' ||
    Customers.CustLastName
```

> This isn't compliant with the SQL Standard, but you might find that
> this is the only way you can get your request to work on your system.

Grouping on Expressions

I showed you earlier some correct examples of creating expressions that
do not include aggregate functions. One of the most common mistakes is
to attempt to group on the expression you create in the SELECT clause
rather than on the individual columns. Remember that the GROUP BY
clause must refer to columns created by the FROM and WHERE clauses.
It cannot use an expression you create in your SELECT clause.

Let's take another look at an example I solved earlier to show you what
I mean, but this time, let's make the mistake. (I'm skipping the Translation and Clean Up steps here because I covered them earlier.)

*"Show me for each customer in the state of Washington the customer
full name, the customer full address, the latest contract date for the
customer, and the total price of all the contracts."*

```
SQL          SELECT Customers.CustLastName || ', ' ||
                 Customers.CustFirstName AS CustomerFullName,
                 Customers.CustStreetAddress || ', ' ||
                 Customers.CustCity || ', ' ||
                 Customers.CustState || ' ' ||
                 Customers.CustZipCode AS CustomerFullAddress,
                 MAX(Engagements.StartDate) AS LatestDate,
                 SUM(Engagements.ContractPrice)
                 AS TotalContractPrice
             FROM Customers
             INNER JOIN Engagements
             ON Customers.CustomerID =
                 Engagements.CustomerID
             WHERE Customers.CustState = 'WA'
             GROUP BY CustomerFullName,
                 CustomerFullAddress
```

Some database systems will let you get away with this, but it's not correct. The CustomerFullName and CustomerFullAddress columns don't exist until *after* your database system has evaluated the FROM, WHERE, and GROUP BY clauses. The GROUP BY clause won't find these columns in the result created in the FROM and WHERE clauses, so on a database system that strictly adheres to the SQL Standard you'll get a syntax error.

I showed you earlier one correct way to solve this: You must list all the columns you use in both the CustomerFullName and CustomerFullAddress expressions. Another way is to make the FROM clause generate the calculated columns by embedding a table subquery. Here's what it looks like:

| SQL | ```
SELECT CE.CustomerFullName,
    CE.CustomerFullAddress,
    MAX(CE.StartDate) AS LatestDate,
    SUM(CE.ContractPrice) AS TotalContractPrice
FROM
    (SELECT Customers.CustLastName || ', ' ||
    Customers.CustFirstName AS CustomerFullName,
      Customers.CustStreetAddress || ', ' ||
      Customers.CustCity || ', ' ||
      Customers.CustState || ' ' ||
      Customers.CustZipCode AS CustomerFullAddress,
      Engagements.StartDate,
      Engagements.ContractPrice
    FROM Customers
    INNER JOIN Engagements
    ON Customers.CustomerID =
        Engagements.CustomerID
    WHERE Customers.CustState = 'WA')
  AS CE
GROUP BY CE.CustomerFullName,
    CE.CustomerFullAddress
``` |
```

This works now because I've generated the CustomerFullName and CustomerFullAddress columns as output in the FROM clause. You have to admit, though, that this makes the query very complex. In truth, it's better to just list all the individual columns you plan to use in nonaggregate expressions rather than try to generate the expressions as columns inside the FROM clause. I saved this last request as CH13_Customers_ Total_Contract in the Entertainment Agency sample database.

Uses for GROUP BY

At this point, you should have a fairly good understanding of how to ask for subtotals across groups using aggregate functions and the GROUP BY clause. The best way to give you an idea of the wide range of uses for GROUP BY is to list some problems you can solve with this new clause and then present a robust set of examples in the "Sample Statements" section:

"Show me each vendor and the average by vendor of the number of days to deliver products."

"Display for each product the product name and the total sales."

"List for each customer and order date the customer full name and the total cost of items ordered on each date."

"Display each entertainment group ID, entertainment group member, and the amount of pay for each member based on the total contract price divided by the number of members in the group."

"Show each agent name, the sum of the contract price for the engagements booked, and the agent's total commission."

"For completed classes, list by category and student the category name, the student name, and the student's average grade in all classes taken in that category."

"Display by category the category name and the count of classes offered."

"List each staff member and the count of classes each is scheduled to teach."

"Show me for each tournament and match the tournament ID, the tournament location, the match number, the name of each team, and the total of the handicap score for each team."

"Display for each bowler the bowler name and the average of the bowler's raw game scores."

"Show me how many recipes exist for each class of ingredient."

"If I want to cook all the recipes in my cookbook, how much of each ingredient must I have on hand?"

Sample Statements

You now know the mechanics of constructing queries using a GROUP BY clause and have seen some of the types of requests you can answer. Let's take a look at a set of samples, all of which request that the information be grouped. These examples come from each of the sample databases.

I've also included sample result sets that would be returned by these operations and placed them immediately after the SQL syntax line. The name that appears immediately above a result set is the name I gave each query in the sample data on the companion website for this book, www.informit.com/title/9780134858333. I stored each query in the appropriate sample database (as indicated within the example), and I prefixed the names of the queries relevant to this chapter with "CH13." You can follow the instructions in the Introduction of this book to load the samples onto your computer and try them.

❖ **Note** Remember that all the column names and table names used in these examples are drawn from the sample database structures shown in Appendix B, "Schema for the Sample Databases." To simplify the process, I have combined the Translation and Clean Up steps for all the examples.

These samples assume you have thoroughly studied and understood the concepts covered in previous chapters, especially the chapters on JOINs and subqueries.

Sales Orders Database

"List for each customer and order date the customer full name and the total cost of items ordered on each date."

Translation/ Clean Up	Select customer first name ~~and~~ || ' ' || customer last name as CustFullName, order date, ~~and the~~ sum ~~of~~ (quoted price ~~times~~ * quantity ordered) as TotalCost from ~~the~~ customers ~~table~~ inner joined ~~with the~~ orders ~~table~~ on customers.customer ID ~~in the customers table matches~~ = orders.customer ID ~~in the orders table, and then inner~~ joined ~~with the~~ order details ~~table~~ on orders.order number ~~in the orders table matches~~ = order_details.order number ~~in the order details table,~~ grouped by customer first name, customer last name, ~~and~~ order date

SQL	`SELECT Customers.CustFirstName || ' ' ||`
	    `Customers.CustLastName AS CustFullName,`
	    `Orders.OrderDate,`
	    `SUM(Order_Details.QuotedPrice *`
	    `Order_Details.QuantityOrdered) AS TotalCost`
	`FROM (Customers`
	`INNER JOIN Orders`
	`ON Customers.CustomerID = Orders.CustomerID)`
	`INNER JOIN Order_Details`
	`ON Orders.OrderNumber =`
	    `Order_Details.OrderNumber`
	`GROUP BY Customers.CustFirstName,`
	    `Customers.CustLastName, Orders.OrderDate`

CH13_Order_Totals_By_Customer_And_Date (847 rows)

CustFullName	OrderDate	TotalCost
Alaina Hallmark	2017-09-03	$4,699.98
Alaina Hallmark	2017-09-15	$4,433.95
Alaina Hallmark	2017-09-22	$353.25
Alaina Hallmark	2017-09-23	$3,951.90
Alaina Hallmark	2017-10-01	$10,388.68
Alaina Hallmark	2017-10-13	$3,088.00
Alaina Hallmark	2017-10-23	$6,775.06
Alaina Hallmark	2017-10-31	$15,781.10

<< more rows here >>

Entertainment Agency Database

"Display each entertainment group ID, entertainment group member, and the amount of pay for each member based on the total contract price divided by the number of members in the group."

❖ **Note** This one is really tricky because each member might belong to more than one entertainer group. You must sum the contract prices for each entertainer and then divide by the count of members in that group (assuming each member gets equal pay). Fetching the count requires a subquery filtered on the current entertainer ID (the ID of the group, not the ID of the member), which means you also must group by entertainer ID. Oh yes, and don't forget to exclude members who are not active (Status = 3).

Translation/ Clean Up	Select entertainer ID, ~~mem~~ber first name, ~~mem~~ber last name, ~~and the~~ sum ~~of~~ (contract price)~~s divided by~~ / ~~the~~ (select count(*) ~~of active members~~ from entertainer members as EM2 ~~in the current entertainer group~~ where status ~~is not equal to~~ <> ~~not active~~ 3 and ~~the~~ EM2 ~~table~~ entertainer ID ~~equals~~ = ~~the~~ entertainer members ~~table~~ entertainer ID) from ~~the~~ members ~~table~~ inner join~~ed with the~~ entertainer members ~~table~~ on members.member ID ~~in the members table matches~~ = entertainer_members. member ID ~~in the entertainer members table, then~~ inner join~~ed with the~~ entertainers ~~table~~ on entertainers. entertainer ID ~~in the entertainers table matches~~ = enter- tainer_members.entertainer ID ~~in the entertainer members table, and finally~~ inner join~~ed with the~~ engage- ments ~~table~~ on entertainers.entertainer ID ~~in the entertainers table matches~~ = engagements.entertainer ID ~~in the engagements table,~~ where member status ~~is not equal to~~ <> ~~not active~~ 3~~,~~ group~~ed~~ by entertainer ID, member first name, ~~and~~ member last name, ~~sorted~~ order by member last name
| SQL | ```
SELECT Entertainers.EntertainerID,
    Members.MbrFirstName, Members.MbrLastName,
    SUM(Engagements.ContractPrice)/
        (SELECT COUNT(*)
        FROM Entertainer_Members AS EM2
``` |
```

```
              WHERE EM2.Status <> 3
              AND EM2.EntertainerID =
              Entertainers.EntertainerID)
           AS MemberPay
      FROM ((Members
      INNER JOIN Entertainer_Members
      ON Members.MemberID =
         Entertainer_Members.MemberID)
      INNER JOIN Entertainers
      ON Entertainers.EntertainerID =
         Entertainer_Members.EntertainerID)
      INNER JOIN Engagements
      ON Entertainers.EntertainerID =
         Engagements.EntertainerID
      WHERE Entertainer_Members.Status <> 3
      GROUP BY Entertainers.EntertainerID,
         Members.MbrFirstName, Members.MbrLastName
      ORDER BY Members.MbrLastName
```

CH13_Member_Pay (39 rows)

EntertainerID	MbrFirstName	MbrLastName	MemberPay
1010	Kendra	Bonnicksen	$2,887.50
1013	Kendra	Bonnicksen	$3,767.50
1007	Robert	Brown	$2,975.00
1008	Robert	Brown	$6,816.00
1008	George	Chavez	$6,816.00
1013	George	Chavez	$3,767.50
1010	Caroline	Coie	$2,887.50
1013	Caroline	Coie	$3,767.50
	<< more rows here >>		

School Scheduling Database

"For completed classes, list by category and student the category name, the student name, and the student's average grade of all classes taken in that category."

Translation/ Clean Up	Select category description, ~~student~~ first name, ~~student~~ last name, ~~and the average~~ AVG(~~of~~ grade) as AvgOfGrade from ~~the~~ categories ~~table~~ inner joined ~~with the~~ subjects ~~table~~ on categories.category ID ~~in the categories table matches~~ = subjects. category ID ~~in the subjects table, then~~ inner joined ~~with the~~ classes ~~table~~ on subjects.subject ID ~~in the subjects table matches~~ = classes.subject ID ~~in the classes table, then~~ inner joined ~~with the~~ student schedules ~~table~~ on classes.class ID ~~in the classes table matches~~ = student_schedules.class ID ~~in the student schedules table, then~~ inner joined ~~with the~~ student class status ~~table~~ on student_class_status.class status ~~in the student class status table matches~~ = student_schedules.class status ~~in the student schedules table,~~ ~~and finally~~ inner joined ~~with the~~ students ~~table~~ on students.student ID ~~in the students table matches~~ = student_schedules.student ID ~~in the student schedules table~~ where class status description ~~is~~ = 'Completed~~;~~' grouped by category description, student first name, ~~and~~ student last name

SQL	`SELECT Categories.CategoryDescription,`
	`    Students.StudFirstName,`
	`    Students.StudLastName,`
	`    AVG(Student_Schedules.Grade) AS AvgOfGrade`
	`FROM ((((Categories`
	`INNER JOIN Subjects`
	`ON Categories.CategoryID = Subjects.CategoryID)`
	`INNER JOIN Classes`
	`ON Subjects.SubjectID = Classes.SubjectID)`
	`INNER JOIN Student_Schedules`
	`ON Classes.ClassID = Student_Schedules.ClassID)`
	`INNER JOIN Student_Class_Status`
	`ON Student_Class_Status.ClassStatus =`
	`    Student_Schedules.ClassStatus)`

```
INNER JOIN Students

ON Students.StudentID =

    Student_Schedules.StudentID

WHERE Student_Class_Status.ClassStatusDescription =

    'Completed'

GROUP BY Categories.CategoryDescription,

    Students.StudFirstName,

    Students.StudLastName
```

CH13_Student_GradeAverage_By_Category (63 rows)

Category Description	StudFirst Name	StudLast Name	AvgOfGrade
Accounting	Doris	Hartwig	80.51
Accounting	Elizabeth	Hallmark	91.12
Accounting	Kendra	Bonnicksen	88.50
Accounting	Richard	Lum	79.61
Accounting	Sarah	Thompson	77.34
Art	Doris	Hartwig	82.19
Art	George	Chavez	83.63
Art	John	Kennedy	87.65
Art	Kerry	Patterson	99.83
Art	Michael	Viescas	73.37

<< more rows here >>

Bowling League Database

"Show me for each tournament and match the tournament ID, the tournament location, the match number, the name of each team, and the total of the handicap score for each team."

Translation/ Clean Up	Select tourney ID, tourney location, match ID, team name, ~~and the~~ sum ~~of~~ (handicap score) as TotHandiCapScore from ~~the~~ tournaments ~~table~~ inner joined ~~with the~~ tourney matches ~~table~~ on tournaments.tourney ID ~~in the tournaments table matches~~ = tourney_matches.tourney ID ~~in the tourney matches table, then~~ inner joined ~~with the~~ match games ~~table~~ on tourney_matches.match ID ~~in the tourney matches table matches~~ = match_games.match ID ~~in the match games table, then~~ inner joined ~~with the~~ bowler scores ~~table~~ on match_games.match ID ~~in the match games table matches~~ = bowler_scores.match ID ~~in the bowler scores table~~ and match_games.game number ~~in the match games table matches~~ = bowler_scores.game number ~~in the bowler scores table, then~~ inner joined ~~with the~~ bowlers ~~table~~ on bowlers.bowler ID ~~in the bowlers table matches~~ = bowler_scores.bowler ID ~~in the bowler scores table, and finally~~ inner joined ~~with the~~ teams ~~table~~ on teams.team ID ~~in the teams table matches~~ = bowlers.team ID ~~in the bowlers table,~~ grouped by tourney ID, tourney location, match ID, ~~and~~ team name

SQL	```sql
	SELECT Tournaments.TourneyID,
	    Tournaments.TourneyLocation,
	    Tourney_Matches.MatchID, Teams.TeamName,
	    SUM(Bowler_Scores.HandicapScore)
	    AS TotHandiCapScore
	FROM ((((Tournaments
	INNER JOIN Tourney_Matches
	ON Tournaments.TourneyID =
	    Tourney_Matches.TourneyID)
	INNER JOIN Match_Games
	ON Tourney_Matches.MatchID =
	    Match_Games.MatchID)
	INNER JOIN Bowler_Scores
	ON (Match_Games.MatchID =
	    Bowler_Scores.MatchID) AND
	    (Match_Games.GameNumber =
	    Bowler_Scores.GameNumber))
	INNER JOIN Bowlers
	ON Bowlers.BowlerID = Bowler_Scores.BowlerID)
	``

```
INNER JOIN Teams
ON Teams.TeamID = Bowlers.TeamID
GROUP BY Tournaments.TourneyID,
    Tournaments.TourneyLocation,
    Tourney_Matches.MatchID, Teams.TeamName
```

As you can see, the difficult part of this request is assembling the complex JOIN clauses to link all the tables in the correct manner.

CH13_Tournament_Match_Team_Results (112 rows)

Tourney ID	Tourney Location	MatchID	TeamName	TotHandi CapScore
1	Red Rooster Lanes	1	Marlins	2351
1	Red Rooster Lanes	1	Sharks	2348
1	Red Rooster Lanes	2	Barracudas	2289
1	Red Rooster Lanes	2	Terrapins	2391
1	Red Rooster Lanes	3	Dolphins	2389
1	Red Rooster Lanes	3	Orcas	2395
1	Red Rooster Lanes	4	Manatees	2292
1	Red Rooster Lanes	4	Swordfish	2353
2	Thunderbird Lanes	5	Marlins	2297
2	Thunderbird Lanes	5	Terrapins	2279

<< more rows here >>

"Display the highest raw score for each bowler."

Translation/ Clean Up	Select bowler first name, bowler last name, ~~and the~~ maximum (raw score) as HighScore from ~~the~~ bowlers ~~table~~ inner join~~ed with the~~ bowler scores ~~table~~ on bowlers.bowler ID ~~in the bowlers table matches~~ = bowler_scores.bowler ID ~~in the bowler scores table,~~ group~~ed~~ by bowler first name, ~~and~~ bowler last name

SQL	SELECT Bowlers.BowlerFirstName,
	    Bowlers.BowlerLastName,
	    MAX(Bowler_Scores.RawScore) AS HighScore
	FROM Bowlers
	INNER JOIN Bowler_Scores
	ON Bowlers.BowlerID = Bowler_Scores.BowlerID
	GROUP BY Bowlers.BowlerFirstName,
	    Bowlers.BowlerLastName

CH13_Bowler_High_Score_Group (32 rows)

BowlerFirstName	BowlerLastName	HighScore
Alaina	Hallmark	180
Alastair	Black	164
Angel	Kennedy	194
Ann	Patterson	165
Bailey	Hallmark	164
Barbara	Fournier	164
Caleb	Viescas	193
Carol	Viescas	150
David	Cunningham	180
David	Fournier	178
	<< more rows here >>	

Recipes Database

"Show me how many recipes exist for each class of ingredient."

❖ **Note** The challenge here is that you don't want to count a particular recipe class more than once per recipe. For example, if a recipe contains multiple herbs or dairy ingredients, that recipe should be counted only once per class. Sounds like it's time to use COUNT(DISTINCT *value expression*), doesn't it?

Translation/ Clean Up	Select ingredient class description, ~~and the unique~~ count ~~of~~ (distinct recipe ID) as CountOfRecipeID from ~~the~~ ingredient classes ~~table~~ inner join~~ed with the~~ ingredients ~~table~~ on ingredient_classes.ingredient class ID ~~in the ingredient classes table matches~~ = ingredients.ingredient class ID ~~in the ingredients table, and then~~ inner join~~ed with the~~ recipe ingredients ~~table~~ on ingredients.ingredient ID ~~in the ingredients table matches~~ = recipe_ingredients.ingredient ID ~~in the recipe ingredients table,~~ grouped by ingredient class description

| SQL | ```
SELECT
    Ingredient_Classes.IngredientClassDescription,
    Count(DISTINCT RecipeID) AS CountOfRecipeID
FROM (Ingredient_Classes
INNER JOIN Ingredients
ON Ingredient_Classes.IngredientClassID =
    Ingredients.IngredientClassID)
INNER JOIN Recipe_Ingredients
ON Ingredients.IngredientID =
    Recipe_Ingredients.IngredientID
GROUP BY
    Ingredient_Classes.IngredientClassDescription
``` |

CH13_IngredientClass_Distinct_Recipe_Count (19 rows)

IngredientClassDescription	CountOfRecipeID
Bottle	1
Butter	3
Cheese	2
Chips	1
Condiment	2
Dairy	2
Fruit	1
Grain	2
Herb	1

<< more rows here >>
```

> ❖ **Note** Because Microsoft Access does not support COUNT DISTINCT, you'll find that the query in the Access sample database first selects the DISTINCT values of RecipeID using a table subquery in the FROM clause and then counts the resulting rows.

Summary

I began the chapter by explaining to you why you might want to group data to get multiple subtotals from a result set. After tantalizing you with an example, I proceeded to show how to use the GROUP BY clause to solve the example problem and several others. I also showed how to mix column expressions with aggregate functions.

I next explored an interesting example of using GROUP BY in a subquery that acts as a filter in a WHERE clause. I subsequently pointed out that constructing a query using GROUP BY and no aggregate functions is the same as using DISTINCT in your SELECT clause. Then I warned you to carefully construct your GROUP BY clause to include the columns and not the expressions.

I wrapped up my discussion of the GROUP BY clause by explaining some common pitfalls. I showed that SQL does not consider any knowledge of primary keys. I also explained common mistakes you might make when using column expressions in your SELECT clause.

I summarized why the GROUP BY clause is useful and gave you a sample list of problems you can solve using GROUP BY. The rest of the chapter provided examples of how to build requests that require the GROUP BY clause.

The following section presents several requests that you can work out on your own.

Problems for You to Solve

Below, I show you the request statement and the name of the solution query in the sample databases. If you want some practice, you can work out the SQL you need for each request and then check your answer with the query I saved in the samples. Don't worry if your syntax doesn't exactly match the syntax of the queries I saved—as long as your result set is the same.

Sales Orders Database

1. *"Show me each vendor and the average by vendor of the number of days to deliver products."*

   (Hint: Use the AVG aggregate function and group on vendor.)

   You can find the solution in CH13_Vendor_Avg_Delivery (10 rows).

2. *"Display for each product the product name and the total sales."*

   (Hint: Use SUM with a calculation of quantity times price and group on product name.)

   You can find the solution in CH13_Sales_By_Product (38 rows).

3. *"List all vendors and the count of products sold by each."*

   You can find the solution in CH13_Vendor_Product_Count_Group (10 rows).

4. Challenge: Now solve problem 3 by using a subquery.

   You can find the solution in CH13_Vendor_Product_Count_Subquery (10 rows).

Entertainment Agency Database

1. *"Show each agent's name, the sum of the contract price for the engagements booked, and the agent's total commission."*

   (Hint: You must multiply the sum of the contract prices by the agent's commission. Be sure to group on the commission rate as well!)

   You can find the solution in CH13_Agent_Sales_And_Commissions (8 rows).

School Scheduling Database

1. *"Display by category the category name and the count of classes offered."*

   (Hint: Use COUNT and group on category name.)

   You can find the solution in CH13_Category_Class_Count (15 rows).

2. *"List each staff member and the count of classes each is scheduled to teach."*

   (Hint: Use COUNT and group on staff name.)

   You can find the solution in CH13_Staff_Class_Count (22 rows).

3. Challenge: Now solve problem 2 by using a subquery.

   You can find the solution in CH13_Staff_Class_Count_Subquery (27 rows).

4. Can you explain why the subquery solution returns five more rows? Is it possible to modify the query in question 2 to return 27 rows? If so, how would you do it?

   (Hint: Think about using an OUTER JOIN.)

Bowling League Database

1. *"Display for each bowler the bowler name and the average of the bowler's raw game scores."*

   (Hint: Use the AVG aggregate function and group on bowler name.)

   You can find the solution in CH13_Bowler_Averages (32 rows).

2. *"Calculate the current average and handicap for each bowler."*

   (Hint: This is a "friendly" league, so the handicap is 90 percent of 200 minus the raw average. Be sure to round the raw average and convert it to an integer before subtracting it from 200, and then round and truncate the final result. Although the SQL Standard doesn't define a ROUND function, most commercial database systems provide one. Check your product documentation for details.)

   You can find the solution in CH13_Bowler_Average_Handicap (32 rows).

3. Challenge: *"Display the highest raw score for each bowler,"* but solve it by using a subquery.

   You can find the solution in CH13_Bowler_High_Score_Subquery (32 rows).

Recipes Database

1. *"If I want to cook all the recipes in my cookbook, how much of each ingredient must I have on hand?"*

   (Hint: Use SUM and group on ingredient name and measurement description.)

   You can find the solution in CH13_Total_Ingredients_Needed (65 rows).

2. *"List all meat ingredients and the count of recipes that include each one."*

   You can find the solution in CH13_Meat_Ingredient_Recipe_Count_Group (4 rows).

3. Challenge: Now solve problem 2 by using a subquery.

   You can find the solution in CH13_Meat_Ingredient_Recipe_Count_Subquery (11 rows).

4. Can you explain why the subquery solution returns seven more rows? Is it possible to modify the query in question 2 to return 11 rows? If so, how would you do it?

   (Hint: Think about using an OUTER JOIN.)

Filtering Grouped Data

"Let schoolmasters puzzle their brain,
With grammar, and nonsense, and learning; Good liquor,
I stoutly maintain, Gives genius a better discerning."
—OLIVER GOLDSMITH

Topics Covered in This Chapter

A New Meaning of "Focus Groups"

Where You Filter Makes a Difference

Uses for HAVING

Sample Statements

Summary

Problems for You to Solve

In Chapter 12, "Simple Totals," I gave you the details about all the aggregate functions defined in the SQL Standard. I followed that up in Chapter 13, "Grouping Data," with a discussion of how to ask your database system to group sets of rows and then calculate aggregate values in each group. One of the advantages to grouping is that you can also display value expressions based on the grouping columns to identify each group.

In this chapter, I'll put the final piece of the summarizing and grouping puzzle into place. After you group rows and calculate aggregate values, it's often useful to filter further the final result using a predicate on an aggregate calculation. As you will soon see, you need the last piece of this puzzle—the HAVING clause—to do that.

A New Meaning for "Focus Groups"

You now know that once you've gathered your information into groups of rows, you can request the MIN, MAX, AVG, SUM, or COUNT of all the values in each group. Suppose you want to refine further the final result set—to focus the groups—by testing one of the aggregate values. Let's take a look at a simple request:

> *"Show me the entertainer groups that play in a jazz style and have more than three members."*

Doesn't sound too difficult, does it? Figure 14-1 shows the tables needed to solve this request.

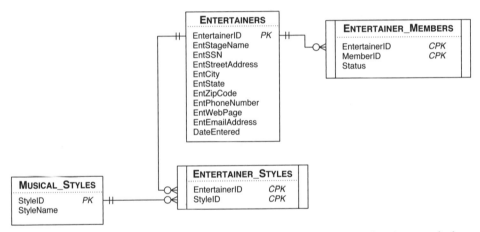

Figure 14-1 *The tables needed to figure out which entertainers play jazz and also have more than three members*

> ❖ **Note** I again use the "Request/Translation/Clean Up/SQL" technique introduced in Chapter 4, "Creating a Simple Query." I also use some JOIN and subquery techniques you learned in Chapter 8, "INNER JOINs"; Chapter 9, "OUTER JOINs"; and Chapter 11, "Subqueries."

Without knowing about the HAVING clause, you'd probably be tempted to solve it in the following incorrect manner:

Translation	Select the entertainer stage name and the count of members from the entertainers table joined with the entertainer members table on entertainer ID in the entertainers table matches entertainer ID in the entertainer members table where the entertainer ID is in the selection of entertainer IDs from the entertainer styles table joined with the musical styles table on style ID in the entertainer styles table matches style ID in the musical styles table where the stylename is 'Jazz' and where the count of the members is greater than 3, grouped by entertainer stage name
Clean Up	Select ~~the entertainer~~ stage name ~~and the~~ count(*) ~~of members~~ as CountOfMembers from ~~the~~ entertainers ~~table~~ inner join~~ed with the~~ entertainer members ~~table~~ on entertainers.entertainer ID ~~in the entertainers table matches~~ = entertainer_members.entertainer ID ~~in the entertainer members table~~ where ~~the~~ entertainer ID ~~is~~ in ~~the~~ (select~~ion of~~ entertainer IDs from ~~the~~ entertainer styles ~~table~~ inner join~~ed with the~~ musical styles ~~table~~ on entertainer_styles.style ID ~~in the entertainer styles table matches~~ = musical_styles.style ID ~~in the musical styles table~~ where ~~the~~ style name ~~is~~ = 'Jazz') and ~~where the~~ count(*) ~~of the members is greater than~~ > 3~~,~~ group~~ed~~ by entertainer stage name
| SQL | ```
SELECT Entertainers.EntStageName,
    COUNT(*) AS CountOfMembers
FROM Entertainers
INNER JOIN Entertainer_Members
ON Entertainers.EntertainerID =
    Entertainer_Members.EntertainerID
WHERE Entertainers.EntertainerID
IN
  (SELECT Entertainer_Styles.EntertainerID
   FROM Entertainer_Styles
   INNER JOIN Musical_Styles
   ON Entertainer_Styles.StyleID =
      Musical_Styles.StyleID
   WHERE Musical_Styles.StyleName = 'Jazz')
AND COUNT(*) > 3
GROUP BY Entertainers.EntStageName
``` |
```

What's wrong with this picture? The key is that any column you reference in a WHERE clause (remember Chapter 6, "Filtering Your Data"?) *must* be a column in one of the tables defined in the FROM clause. Is COUNT(*) a column generated from the FROM clause? I don't think so! In fact, you can calculate COUNT for each group only after the rows are grouped.

Looks like I need a new clause after GROUP BY. Figure 14-2 shows the entire syntax for a SELECT statement, including the new HAVING clause.

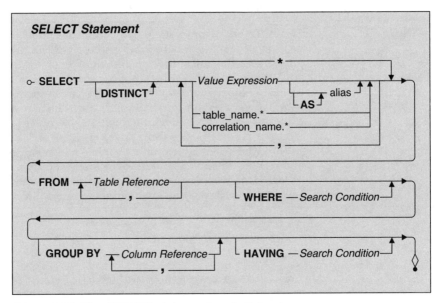

Figure 14-2 *The SELECT statement and all its clauses*

Because the HAVING clause acts on rows *after* they have been grouped, the SQL Standard defines some restrictions on the columns you reference in any predicate in the search condition. Note that when you do not have a GROUP BY clause, the HAVING clause operates on all rows returned by the FROM and WHERE clauses as though they are a single group. Frankly, I can't think of a good reason why you would want to construct a request with a HAVING clause and no GROUP BY clause.

The restrictions are the same as those for columns referenced in the SELECT clause of a grouped query. Any reference to a column in a predicate within the search condition of a HAVING clause either must name a column listed in the GROUP BY clause or must be enclosed within an aggregate function. This makes sense because any column comparisons must use something generated from the grouped rows—either a grouping value or an aggregate calculation across rows in each group.

Now that you know a bit about HAVING, let's solve the earlier problem in the correct way:

"Show me the entertainer groups that play in a jazz style and have more than three members."

Translation	Select the entertainer stage name and the count of members from the entertainers table joined with the entertainer members table on entertainer ID in the entertainers table matches entertainer ID in the entertainer members table then inner joined with the entertainer styles table on style ID in the entertainers table matches style ID in the entertainer styles table, then inner joined with the musical styles table on style ID in the entertainer styles table matches style ID in the musical styles table where the style name is 'Jazz,' grouped by entertainer stage name, and having the count of the members greater than 3
Clean Up	Select ~~the entertainer~~ stage name ~~and the~~ count(*) ~~of members~~ as CountOfMembers from ~~the~~ entertainers ~~table~~ inner join~~ed with the~~ entertainer members ~~table~~ on entertainers. entertainer ID ~~in the entertainers table matches~~ = entertainer_members.entertainer ID ~~in the entertainer members table then~~ inner join~~ed with the~~ entertainer styles ~~table~~ on entertainers.style ID ~~in the entertainers table matches~~ = entertainer_styles.style ID ~~in the entertainer styles table,~~ ~~then~~ inner join~~ed with the~~ musical styles ~~table~~ on entertainer_styles.style ID ~~in the entertainer styles table matches~~ = musical_styles.style ID ~~in the musical styles table~~ where ~~the~~ style name ~~is~~ = 'Jazz'~~,~~ grouped by entertainer stage name~~, and~~ having ~~the~~ count(*) ~~of the members greater than~~ > 3

SQL	`SELECT Entertainers.EntertainerID,`
	`    Entertainers.EntStageName,`
	`    Count(Entertainer_Members.EntertainerID)`
	`    AS CountOfMembers`
	`FROM ((Entertainers INNER JOIN Entertainer_Members`
	`ON Entertainers.EntertainerID =`
	`    Entertainer_Members.EntertainerID)`
	`INNER JOIN Entertainer_Styles`
	`ON Entertainers.EntertainerID =`
	`    Entertainer_Styles.EntertainerID)`
	`INNER JOIN Musical_Styles`
	`ON Musical_Styles.StyleID =`
	`    Entertainer_Styles.StyleID`

```
WHERE Musical_Styles.StyleName = 'Jazz'
GROUP BY Entertainers.EntertainerID,
    Entertainers.EntStageName
HAVING
Count(Entertainer_Members.EntertainerID) > 3
```

Although I also included the COUNT in the final output of the request, I didn't need to do that to ask for COUNT(*) in the HAVING clause. As long as any calculated value or column reference I use in HAVING can be derived from the grouped rows, I'm OK. I saved this query in the Entertainment Agency sample database as CH14_Jazz_Entertainers_More_Than_3.

Where You Filter Makes a Difference

You now know two ways to filter your final result set: WHERE and HAVING. You also know that there are certain limitations on the predicates you can use within a search condition in a HAVING clause. In some cases, however, you have the choice of placing a predicate in either clause. Let's take a look at the reasons for putting your filter in the WHERE clause instead of the HAVING clause.

Should You Filter in WHERE or in HAVING?

You learned in Chapter 6 about five major types of predicates you can build to filter the rows returned by the FROM clause of your request. These are comparison (=, <>, <, >, >=, <=), range (BETWEEN), set membership (IN), pattern match (LIKE), and Null (IS NULL). In Chapter 11, I expanded your horizons by showing you how to use a subquery as one of the arguments in comparison and set membership predicates. Also, I introduced you to two additional classes of predicates—quantified (ANY, SOME, ALL) and existence (EXISTS)—that require a subquery as one of the arguments.

Keep in mind that the search condition in a WHERE clause filters rows *before* your database system groups them. In general, when you want to ultimately group only a subset of rows, it's better to eliminate unwanted rows first in the WHERE clause. For example, let's assume you want to solve the following problem:

"Show me the states on the west coast of the United States where the total of the orders is greater than $1 million."

Figure 14-3 shows the tables needed to solve this problem.

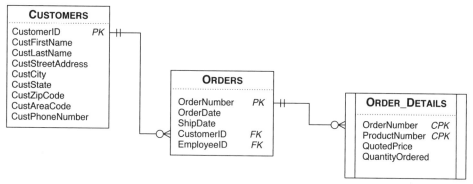

Figure 14-3 *The tables needed to sum all orders by state*

You could legitimately state the request in the following manner, placing the predicate on customer state into the HAVING clause:

SQL

```
SELECT Customers.CustState,
    SUM(Order_Details.QuantityOrdered *
    Order_Details.QuotedPrice) AS SumOfOrders
FROM (Customers
    INNER JOIN Orders
    ON Customers.CustomerID = Orders.CustomerID)
INNER JOIN Order_Details
ON Orders.OrderNumber =
    Order_Details.OrderNumber
GROUP BY Customers.CustState
HAVING SUM(Order_Details.QuantityOrdered *
    Order_Details.QuotedPrice) > 1000000
AND CustState IN ('WA', 'OR', 'CA')
```

Because you are grouping on the state column, you *can* construct a predicate on that column in the HAVING clause, but you might be asking your database system to do more work than necessary. As it turns out, the total of all orders for customers in the state of Texas also exceeds $1 million. If you place the filter on customer state in the HAVING clause as shown here, your database will calculate the total for all the rows in Texas as well, evaluate the first predicate in the HAVING clause and keep the result, and then finally throw it out when the Texas group isn't one you want. In my sample database, I have customers only in the states of CA, TX, OR, and WA. You can imagine how this performance problem would be compounded if you had customers in all 50 states. Your database would do the calculation for all states and then throw out all but three of them!

If you want to calculate a result based on grouping by customer state but want only customers in Washington, Oregon, and California, it makes more sense to filter down to the rows in those three states using a WHERE clause before you ask to GROUP BY state. If you don't do so, the FROM clause returns rows for all customers in all states and must do extra work to group rows you're not even going to need. Here's the better way to solve the problem:

Translation	Select customer state and the sum of quantity ordered times quoted price as SumOfOrders from the customers table joined with the orders table on customer ID in the customers table matches customer ID in the orders table, and then joined with the order details table on order number in the orders table matches order number in the order details table where customer state is in the list 'WA', 'OR', 'CA', grouped by customer state, and having the sum of the orders greater than $1 million
Clean Up	Select cus~~tomer~~ state, ~~and the~~ sum ~~of~~ (quantity ordered ~~times~~ * quoted price) as SumOfOrders from ~~the~~ customers ~~table~~ inner join~~ed with the~~ orders ~~table~~ on customers. customer ID ~~in the customers table matches~~ = orders. customer ID ~~in the orders table, and then~~ join~~ed with the~~ order details ~~table~~ on orders.order number ~~in the orders table matches~~ = order_details.order number ~~in the order details table~~ where customer state ~~is~~ in ~~the list~~ ('WA', 'OR', 'CA')~~,~~ grouped by customer state~~, and~~ having ~~the~~ sum ~~of the orders~~ (quantity ordered * quoted price) ~~greater than~~ > ~~$1 million~~ 1000000

SQL	SELECT Customers.CustState,
	    SUM(Order_Details.QuantityOrdered *
	    Order_Details.QuotedPrice) AS SumOfOrders
	FROM (Customers
	    INNER JOIN Orders
	ON Customers.CustomerID = Orders.CustomerID)
	INNER JOIN Order_Details

```
ON Orders.OrderNumber =
    Order_Details.OrderNumber
WHERE Customers.CustState IN ('WA', 'OR', 'CA')
GROUP BY Customers.CustState
HAVING SUM(Order_Details.QuantityOrdered *
    Order_Details.QuotedPrice) > 1000000
```

Notice that you must repeat the expression in the HAVING clause; you cannot use the alias name assigned in the SELECT clause. I saved this query in the sample database as CH14_West_Coast_Big_Order_States.

Avoiding the HAVING COUNT Trap

Often, you might want to know which categories of items have fewer than a certain number of members. For example, you might want to know which entertainment groups have two or fewer members, which recipes have two or fewer dairy ingredients, or which subjects have three or fewer full-time professors teaching. The trick here is you *also* want to know which categories have *zero* members.

Let's look at a request that illustrates the trap you can fall into:

"Show me the subject categories that have fewer than three full professors teaching that subject."

Figure 14-4 shows the tables needed to solve this problem.

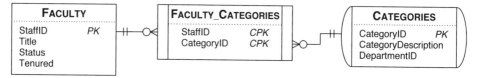

Figure 14-4 *The tables needed to find out which categories have fewer than three faculty teaching in that category*

Translation	Select category description and the count of staff ID as ProfCount from the categories table joined with the faculty categories table on category ID in the categories table matches category ID in the faculty categories table, and then joined with the faculty table on staff ID in the faculty table matches staff ID in the faculty categories table where title is 'Professor,' grouped by category description, and having the count of staff ID less than 3

Clean Up	Select category description ~~and the~~ count ~~of~~ (staff ID) as ProfCount from ~~the~~ categories ~~table~~ inner joined ~~with the~~ faculty categories ~~table~~ on categories.category ID ~~in the categories table matches~~ = faculty_categories. category ID ~~in the faculty categories table, and then~~ inner joined ~~with the~~ faculty ~~table~~ on faculty.staff ID ~~in the faculty table matches~~ = faculty_categories.staff ID ~~in the faculty categories table~~ where title ~~is~~ = 'Professor;' grouped by category description~~, and~~ having ~~the~~ count ~~of~~ (staff ID) ~~less than~~ < 3

SQL	SELECT Categories.CategoryDescription,
	    COUNT(Faculty_Categories.StaffID) AS
	    ProfCount
	FROM (Categories
	INNER JOIN Faculty_Categories
	ON Categories.CategoryID =
	    Faculty_Categories.CategoryID)
	INNER JOIN Faculty
	ON Faculty.StaffID = Faculty_Categories.StaffID
	WHERE Faculty.Title = 'Professor'
	GROUP BY Categories.CategoryDescription
	HAVING COUNT(Faculty_Categories.StaffID) < 3

Looks good, doesn't it? Below is the result set returned from this query.

CH14_Subjects_Fewer_3_Professors_WRONG

CategoryDescription	ProfCount
Accounting	1
Business	2
Computer Information Systems	1
Economics	1
Geography	1
History	1
Journalism	1
Math	1
Political Science	1

Do you notice that the result set lists *no* subject categories with zero professors? This happened because the COUNT function is counting only the rows that are left in the Faculty_Categories table after filtering for full professors. I threw away any potential zero rows with the WHERE clause!

Just to confirm my suspicions that some categories exist with no full professors, let's construct a query that will test my theory. Remember that the COUNT aggregate function will return a zero if I ask it to count an empty set, and I can get an empty set if I force the request to consider how many rows exist for a specific subject category. I do this by forcing the query to look at the subject categories one at a time. I'll be counting category rows, not faculty subject rows. Consider the following SELECT statement:

SQL

```
SELECT COUNT(Faculty.StaffID)
AS BiologyProfessors
FROM (Faculty
INNER JOIN Faculty_Categories
ON Faculty.StaffID =
    Faculty_Categories.StaffID)
INNER JOIN Categories
ON Categories.CategoryID =
    Faculty_Categories.CategoryID
WHERE Categories.CategoryDescription =
    'Biology'
AND Faculty.Title = 'Professor'
```

BiologyProfessors
0

I saved this query as CH14_Count_Of_Biology_Professors in the sample database. As you can see, there really are no full professors in the School Scheduling sample database who teach biology. I asked the query to consider just one subject category. Because there are no rows that are both Professor and Biology, I get a legitimate empty set. The COUNT function, therefore, returns a zero.

Now that I know this, I can embed this request as a subquery in a WHERE clause that extracts a match on category ID from the outer query. This forces the request to consider the categories one at a time as it fetches the category descriptions one row at a time from the Categories table in the outer request. The SQL is as follows:

SQL

```
SELECT Categories.CategoryDescription,
   (SELECT COUNT(Faculty.StaffID)
   FROM (Faculty
   INNER JOIN Faculty_Categories
   ON Faculty.StaffID =
      Faculty_Categories.StaffID)
   INNER JOIN Categories AS C2
   ON C2.CategoryID =
      Faculty_Categories.CategoryID
   WHERE C2.CategoryID = Categories.CategoryID
     AND Faculty.Title = 'Professor')
   AS ProfCount
FROM Categories
WHERE
   (SELECT COUNT(Faculty.StaffID)
   FROM (Faculty
   INNER JOIN Faculty_Categories
   ON Faculty.StaffID =
      Faculty_Categories.StaffID)
   INNER JOIN Categories AS C3
   ON C3.CategoryID =
      Faculty_Categories.CategoryID
   WHERE C3.CategoryID = Categories.CategoryID
   AND Faculty.Title = 'Professor') < 3
```

I saved this query as CH14_Subjects_Fewer_3_Professors_RIGHT in the sample database. Notice that I also included a copy of the subquery in the SELECT clause so that I can see the actual counts per category. This now works correctly because the subquery in the WHERE clause legitimately returns zero for a category that has no full professors. The correct result is below.

CH14_Subjects_Fewer_3_Professors_RIGHT

CategoryDescription	ProfCount
Accounting	1
Biology	0
Business	2
Chemistry	0
Computer Information Systems	1
Computer Science	0
Economics	1
Geography	1
History	1
Journalism	1
Math	1
Physics	0
Political Science	1
Psychology	0
French	0
German	0

As you can see, many subject categories actually have *no* full professors assigned to teach the subject. Although this final solution does not use HAVING at all, I include it to make you aware that HAVING isn't always the clear solution for this type of problem. Keep in mind that you can still use HAVING for many ". . . having fewer than . . ." problems. For example, if you want to see all customers who spent less than $500 last month, but you don't care about customers who bought nothing at all, then the HAVING solution works just fine (and will most likely execute faster). However, if you also need to see customers who bought nothing, you will have to use the non-HAVING technique I just showed you.

But "having" said all that (pun intended), there actually *is* a way to solve this problem using GROUP BY and HAVING. Recall from Chapter 13 that I showed you how to get a zero count in a query that joined entertainers and engagements using an OUTER JOIN. The trick to solve the subject categories and professors problem is to use a subquery in the FROM clause that filters for professors. You must do this so that the result set you use in the JOIN is already filtered *before* you do the JOIN. I have left the final solution up to you in the "Problems for You to Solve" section at the end of this chapter. Never fear—the solution is in the sample database!

Uses for HAVING

At this point, you should have a good understanding of how to ask for subtotals across groups using aggregate functions and the GROUP BY clause and how to filter the grouped data using HAVING. The best way to give you an idea of the wide range of uses for HAVING is to list some problems you can solve with this new clause and then present a set of examples in the "Sample Statements" section.

> *"Show me each vendor and for each vendor, the average of the number of days to deliver products, but display only the vendors whose average number of days to deliver is greater than the average number of delivery days for all vendors."*

> *"Display for each product the product name and the total sales that are greater than the average of sales for all products in that category."*

> *"List for each customer and order date the customer full name and the total cost of items ordered that is greater than $1,000."*

> *"How many orders are for only one product?"*

> *"Which agents booked more than $3,000 worth of business in December 2017?"*

> *"Show me the entertainers who have more than two overlapped bookings."*

> *"Show each agent name, the sum of the contract price for the engagements booked, and the agent's total commission for agents whose total commission is more than $1,000."*

> *"Do any team captains have a raw score that is higher than any other member of the team?"*

> *"Display for each bowler the bowler name and the average of the bowler's raw game scores for bowlers whose average is greater than 155."*

> *"List the bowlers whose highest raw scores are at least 20 higher than their current averages."*

"For completed classes, list by category and student the category name, the student name, and the student's average grade of all classes taken in that category for those students who have an average of 90 or better."

"Display by category the category name and the count of classes offered for those categories that have three or more classes."

"List each staff member and the count of classes each is scheduled to teach for those staff members who teach at least one but fewer than three classes."

"List the recipes that contain both beef and garlic."

"Sum the amount of salt by recipe class, and display those recipe classes that require more than three teaspoons."

"For what type of recipe do I have two or more recipes?"

Sample Statements

You now know the mechanics of constructing queries using a HAVING clause and have seen some of the types of requests you can answer. Let's take a look at a set of samples, all of which request that the information be grouped and then filtered on an aggregate value from the group. These examples come from each of the sample databases.

> ❖ **Note** Remember in the Introduction that I warned you that results from each database system won't necessarily match the sort order you see in examples in this book unless you include an ORDER BY clause. Even when you include that specification, the system might return results in columns not included in the ORDER BY clause in a different sequence because of different optimization techniques.
>
> If you're running the examples in Microsoft SQL Server, simply selecting the rows from the view does not honor any ORDER BY clause specified in the view. For the ORDER BY clause to be honored, you must open the design of the view and execute it from there.
>
> Also, when you use GROUP BY, you'll often see the results returned by your database system as though they are sorted by the columns you specified. This happens because some optimizers first sort the data internally to make it faster to process your GROUP BY. Keep in mind that if you want a specific sort order, you must also include an ORDER BY clause.

I've also included sample result sets that would be returned by these operations and placed them immediately after the SQL syntax line. The name that appears immediately above a result set is the name I gave each query in the sample data on the companion website for this book, www.informit.com/title/9780134858333. I stored each query in the appropriate sample database (as indicated within the example), and I prefixed the names of the queries relevant to this chapter with "CH14." You can follow the instructions in the Introduction of this book to load the samples onto your computer and try them.

> ❖ **Note** Remember that all the column names and table names used in these examples are drawn from the sample database structures shown in Appendix B, "Schema for the Sample Databases." To simplify the process, I have combined the Translation and Clean Up steps for all the examples. These samples assume you have thoroughly studied and understood the concepts covered in previous chapters, especially the chapters on JOINs and subqueries.

Sales Orders Database

"List for each customer and order date the customer's full name and the total cost of items ordered that is greater than $1,000."

Translation/ Clean Up	Select customer first name ~~and~~ || ' ' || customer last name as CustFullName, order date, ~~and the~~ sum ~~of~~ (quoted price ~~times~~ * quantity ordered) as TotalCost from ~~the~~ customers ~~table~~ inner join~~ed with the~~ orders ~~table~~ on customers. customer ID ~~in the customers table matches~~ = orders. customer ID ~~in the orders table, and then~~ inner joined ~~with the~~ order details ~~table~~ on orders.order number ~~in the orders table matches~~ = order_details.order number ~~in the order details table,~~ grouped by customer first name, customer last name, ~~and~~ order date, having ~~the~~ sum ~~of~~ (quoted price ~~times~~ * quantity ordered) ~~greater than~~ > 1000

SQL	`SELECT Customers.CustFirstName || ' ' ||`
	`    Customers.CustLastName AS CustFullName,`
	`    Orders.OrderDate,`
	`    SUM(Order_Details.QuotedPrice *`
	`    Order_Details.QuantityOrdered)`
	`    AS TotalCost`
	`FROM (Customers`

```
INNER JOIN Orders
ON Customers.CustomerID = Orders.CustomerID)
INNER JOIN Order_Details
ON Orders.OrderNumber =
    Order_Details.OrderNumber
GROUP BY Customers.CustFirstName,
    Customers.CustLastName, Orders.OrderDate
HAVING SUM(Order_Details.QuotedPrice *
    Order_Details.QuantityOrdered) > 1000
```

CH14_Order_Totals_By_Customer_And_Date_GT1000 (649 rows)

CustFullName	OrderDate	TotalCost
Alaina Hallmark	2017-09-03	$4,699.98
Alaina Hallmark	2017-09-15	$4,433.95
Alaina Hallmark	2017-09-22	$3,951.90
Alaina Hallmark	2017-09-23	$10,388.68
Alaina Hallmark	2017-10-01	$3,088.00
Alaina Hallmark	2017-10-13	$6,775.06
Alaina Hallmark	2017-10-23	$15,781.10
Alaina Hallmark	2017-10-31	$15,969.50

<< more rows here >>

Entertainment Agency Database

"Which agents booked more than $3,000 worth of business in December 2017?"

Translation/ Clean Up	Select ~~the~~ agent first name, agent last name, ~~and the~~ sum ~~of~~ (contract price) as TotalBooked from ~~the~~ agents ~~table~~ inner join~~ed with the~~ engagements ~~table~~ on agents.agent ID ~~in the agents table matches~~ = engagements.agent ID ~~in the engagements table~~ where ~~the~~ engagement start date ~~is~~ between ~~December 1, 2017,~~ '2017-12-01' and ~~December 31, 2017,~~ '2017-12-31'; grouped by agent first name, ~~and~~ agent last name~~, and~~ having ~~the~~ sum ~~of~~ (contract price) ~~greater than~~ > 3000

SQL	SELECT Agents.AgtFirstName, Agents.AgtLastName,
	SUM(Engagements.ContractPrice)
	AS TotalBooked
	FROM Agents
	INNER JOIN Engagements
	ON Agents.AgentID = Engagements.AgentID
	WHERE Engagements.StartDate
	BETWEEN '2017-12-01' AND '2017-12-31'
	GROUP BY Agents.AgtFirstName, Agents.AgtLastName
	HAVING SUM(Engagements.ContractPrice) > 3000

CH14_Agents_Book_Over_3000_12_2017 (2 rows)

AgtFirstName	AgtLastName	TotalBooked
Marianne	Weir	$6,000.00
William	Thompson	$3,340.00

❖ **Caution** If your database uses a data type that stores both dates and times, the BETWEEN search condition might not work as expected because the user could have entered both a date and a time value in what you expect to contain only a date. (I entered only dates in the Microsoft Office Access samples where I was forced to use the Date/Time data type.) When a date and time column contains both a date and a time, the value is greater than just the date portion. For example, 2017-12-31 12:00:00 is greater than 2017-12-31, so the BETWEEN search condition will fail to fetch that row. If you suspect this might be the case, you should write the above search condition as

```
StartDate >= '2017-12-01' AND StartDate < '2018-01-01'
```

The second search condition ensures that you fetch all the rows for December 31, 2017, even if some of the rows have a time value in them.

School Scheduling Database

"For completed classes, list by category and student the category name, the student name, and the student's average grade of all classes taken in that category for those students who have an average higher than 90."

Translation/ Clean Up	Select category description, student first name, student last name, ~~and the average~~ avg(~~of~~ grade) as AvgOfGrade from ~~the~~ categories ~~table~~ inner joined ~~with the~~ subjects ~~table~~ on categories. category ID ~~in the categories table matches~~ = subjects.category ID ~~in the subjects table, then~~ inner joined ~~with the~~ classes ~~table~~ on subjects.subject ID ~~in the subjects table matches~~ = classes. subject ID ~~in the classes table, then~~ inner joined ~~with the~~ student schedules ~~table~~ on classes.class ID ~~in the classes table matches~~ = student_schedules.class ID ~~in the student schedules table, then~~ inner joined ~~with the~~ student class status ~~table~~ on student_class_status.class status ~~in the student class status table matches~~ = student_schedules.class status ~~in the student schedules table, and finally~~ inner joined ~~with the~~ students ~~table~~ on students.student ID ~~in the students table matches~~ = student_ schedules.student ID ~~in the student schedules table~~ where class status description ~~is~~ = 'Completed~~;~~' grouped by category description, student first name, ~~and~~ student last name~~, and~~ having ~~the average~~ avg(~~of~~ grade) ~~greater than~~ > 90
| SQL | ```
SELECT Categories.CategoryDescription,
       Students.StudFirstName,
       Students.StudLastName,
       AVG(Student_Schedules.Grade) AS AvgOfGrade
FROM ((((Categories
INNER JOIN Subjects
ON Categories.CategoryID = Subjects.CategoryID)
INNER JOIN Classes
ON Subjects.SubjectID = Classes.SubjectID)
INNER JOIN Student_Schedules
ON Classes.ClassID = Student_Schedules.ClassID)
INNER JOIN Student_Class_Status
ON Student_Class_Status.ClassStatus =
   Student_Schedules.ClassStatus)
INNER JOIN Students
ON Students.StudentID =
   Student_Schedules.StudentID
WHERE Student_Class_Status.ClassStatusDescription =
   'Completed'
GROUP BY Categories.CategoryDescription,
``` |
```

```
                    Students.StudFirstName,
                    Students.StudLastName
            HAVING AVG(Student_Schedules.Grade) > 90
```

CH14_A_Students (17 rows)

CategoryDescription	StudFirstName	StudLastName	AvgOfGrade
Accounting	Elizabeth	Hallmark	91.12
Art	Kerry	Patterson	99.83
Biology	Brannon	Jones	94.54
Biology	Karen	Smith	93.05
Chemistry	Richard	Lum	98.31
Computer Information Systems	Janice	Galvin	90.56
Computer Information Systems	John	Kennedy	92.36
Computer Information Systems	Steve	Pundt	98.01
English	Brannon	Jones	91.66
English	Janice	Galvin	91.44

<< more rows here >>

"List each staff member and the count of classes each is scheduled to teach for those staff members who teach at least one but fewer than three classes."

❖ **Note** I avoided the HAVING COUNT zero problem by specifically stating that I want staff members who teach at least one class.

Translation/ Clean Up	Select staff first name, staff last name, ~~and the~~ count ~~of classes~~ (*) as ClassCount from ~~the~~ staff ~~table~~ inner joined ~~with the~~ faculty classes ~~table~~ on staff.staff ID ~~in the staff table matches~~ = faculty_classes.staff ID ~~in the faculty classes table,~~ grouped by staff first name, ~~and~~ staff last name~~, and~~ having ~~the~~ count ~~of classes~~ (*) ~~less than~~ < 3

SQL	`SELECT Staff.StfFirstName, Staff.StfLastName,`
	    `COUNT(*) AS ClassCount`
	`FROM Staff`
	`INNER JOIN Faculty_Classes`
	`ON Staff.StaffID = Faculty_Classes.StaffID`
	`GROUP BY Staff.StfFirstName, Staff.StfLastName`
	`HAVING COUNT(*) < 3`

CH14_Staff_Class_Count_1_To_3 (2 rows)

StfFirstName	StfLastName	ClassCount
Luke	Patterson	2
Michael	Hernandez	2

Bowling League Database

"List the bowlers whose highest raw scores are more than 20 pins higher than their current averages."

Translation/ Clean Up	Select bowler first name, bowler last name, ~~the average~~ avg(raw score) as CurrentAverage, ~~and the~~ maximum (raw score) as HighGame from ~~the~~ bowlers ~~table~~ inner joined ~~with the~~ bowler scores ~~table~~ on bowlers.bowler ID ~~in the bowlers table matches~~ = bowler_scores.bowler ID ~~in the bowler scores table,~~ grouped by bowler first name, ~~and~~ bowler last name~~, and~~ having ~~the~~ maximum (raw score) ~~greater than~~ > ~~the average~~ avg(raw score) ~~plus~~ + 20

SQL	`SELECT Bowlers.BowlerFirstName,`
	        `Bowlers.BowlerLastName,`
	     `AVG(Bowler_Scores.RawScore) AS CurrentAverage,`
	     `MAX(Bowler_Scores.RawScore) AS HighGame`
	`FROM Bowlers INNER JOIN Bowler_Scores`
	`ON Bowlers.BowlerID = Bowler_Scores.BowlerID`
	`GROUP BY Bowlers.BowlerFirstName,`
	        `Bowlers.BowlerLastName`
	`HAVING MAX(Bowler_Scores.RawScore) >`
	     `(AVG(Bowler_Scores.RawScore) + 20)`

CH14_Bowlers_Big_High_Score (15 rows)

BowlerFirstName	BowlerLastName	CurrentAverage	HighGame
Alaina	Hallmark	158	180
Angel	Kennedy	163	194
Ben	Clothier	163	192
Caleb	Viescas	164	193
David	Fournier	157	178
David	Viescas	168	195
Gary	Hallmark	157	179
John	Kennedy	166	191
John	Viescas	168	193
	<< more rows here >>		

Recipes Database

"List the recipes that contain both beef and garlic."

Translation/ Clean Up	Select recipe title from ~~the~~ recipes ~~table~~ where ~~the~~ recipe ID ~~is~~ in ~~the~~ (selection of recipe ID from ~~the~~ ingredients ~~table~~ inner joined ~~with the~~ recipe ingredients ~~table~~ on recipe_ingredients.ingredient ID ~~in the recipe ingredients table matches~~ = ingredients.ingredient ID ~~in the ingredients table~~ where ~~the~~ ingredient name ~~is~~ = 'Beef' or ~~the~~ ingredient name ~~is~~ = 'Garlic;' grouped by recipe ID ~~and~~ having ~~the~~ count ~~of the values in~~ (recipe ID) ~~equal to~~ = 2)

SQL	SELECT Recipes.RecipeTitle
	
	FROM Recipes
	
	WHERE Recipes.RecipeID
	
	IN (SELECT Recipe_Ingredients.RecipeID
	
	  FROM Ingredients
	
	  INNER JOIN Recipe_Ingredients
	
	  ON Ingredients.IngredientID =
	
	    Recipe_Ingredients.IngredientID
	
	  WHERE Ingredients.IngredientName = 'Beef'
	
	  OR Ingredients.IngredientName = 'Garlic'
	
	  GROUP BY Recipe_Ingredients.RecipeID
	
	  HAVING COUNT(Recipe_Ingredients.RecipeID) = 2)

CH14_Recipes_Beef_And_Garlic (1 row)

RecipeTitle
Roast Beef

> ❖ **Note** This illustrates a creative use of GROUP BY and HAVING in a subquery to find recipes that have *both* ingredients. When a recipe has neither of the ingredients, the recipe won't appear in the sub-query. When a recipe has only one of the ingredients, the count will be 1, so the row will be eliminated. Only when a recipe has both will the COUNT be 2. Be careful, though. If a particular recipe calls for both minced and whole garlic but no beef, this technique won't work! You will get a COUNT of 2 for the two garlic entries, so the recipe will be selected even though it has no beef.
>
> If you wonder why I used an OR operator when I want both beef and garlic, be sure to review the Using OR topic in the Using Multiple Conditions section in Chapter 6. I showed you an alternative way to solve this problem in Chapter 8. In Chapter 18, "'Not' and 'And' Problems," I'll show you another creative way to solve this problem.

Summary

I started the chapter with a discussion about focusing the groups you form by using the HAVING clause to filter out groups based on aggregate calculations. I introduced the syntax of this final clause for a SELECT statement and explained a simple example.

Next, I showed an example of when to use the WHERE clause rather than the HAVING clause to filter rows. I explained that when you have a choice, you're better off placing your filter in the WHERE clause. Before you got too comfortable with HAVING, I showed you a common trap to avoid when counting groups that might contain a zero result. I also showed you an alternative way to solve this type of problem.

Finally, I summarized why the HAVING clause is useful and gave you a sample list of problems you can solve using HAVING. The rest of the chapter provided examples of how to build requests that require the HAVING clause.

The following section presents several requests that you can work out on your own.

Problems for You to Solve

Below, I show you the request statement and the name of the solution query in the sample databases. If you want some practice, you can work out the SQL you need for each request and then check your answer with the query I saved in the samples. Don't worry if your syntax doesn't exactly match the syntax of the queries I saved—as long as your result set is the same.

Sales Orders Database

1. *"Show me each vendor and the average by vendor of the number of days to deliver products that are greater than the average delivery days for all vendors."*

   (Hint: You need a subquery to fetch the average delivery time for all vendors.)

   You can find the solution in CH14_Vendor_Avg_Delivery_GT_Overall_Avg (5 rows).

2. *"Display for each product the product name and the total sales that is greater than the average of sales for all products in that category."*

   (Hint: To calculate the comparison value, you must first SUM the sales for each product within a category and then AVG those sums by category.)

   You can find the solution in CH14_Sales_By_Product_GT_Category_Avg (13 rows).

3. *"How many orders are for only one product?"*

   (Hint: You need to use an inner query in the FROM clause that lists the order numbers for orders having only one row and then COUNT those rows in the outer SELECT clause.)

   You can find the solution in CH14_Single_Item_Order_Count (1 row).

Entertainment Agency Database

1. *"Show me the entertainers who have more than two overlapped bookings."*

   (Hint: Use a subquery to find those entertainers with overlapped bookings HAVING a COUNT greater than 2. Remember that in Chapter 6, I showed you how to compare for overlapping ranges efficiently.)

   You can find the solution in CH14_Entertainers_MoreThan_2_Overlap (1 row).

2. *"Show each agent's name, the sum of the contract price for the engagements booked, and the agent's total commission for agents whose total commission is more than $1,000."*

   (Hint: Use the similar problem from Chapter 13 and add a HAVING clause.)

   You can find the solution in CH14_Agent_Sales_Big_Commissions (4 rows).

School Scheduling Database

1. *"Display by category the category name and the count of classes offered for those categories that have three or more classes."*

   (Hint: JOIN categories to subjects and then to classes. COUNT the rows and add a HAVING clause to get the final result.)

   You can find the solution in CH14_Category_Class_Count_3_Or_More (14 rows).

2. *"List each staff member and the count of classes each is scheduled to teach for those staff members who teach fewer than three classes."*

   (Hint: This is a HAVING COUNT zero trap! Use subqueries instead.)

   You can find the solution in CH14_Staff_Teaching_LessThan_3 (7 rows).

3. *"Show me the subject categories that have fewer than three full professors teaching that subject."*

   I did show you one way to correctly solve this problem in the section "Avoiding the HAVING COUNT Trap" using subqueries. Now try to solve it correctly using JOINs and GROUP BY.

(Hint: Consider using OUTER JOIN and a subquery in the FROM clause.)

You can find the solution in CH14_Subjects_Fewer_3_Professors_Join_RIGHT (16 rows).

4. *"Count the classes taught by every staff member."*

(Hint: This really isn't a HAVING problem, but you might be tempted to solve it incorrectly using a GROUP BY using COUNT(*).)

You can find the correct solution in CH14_Staff_Class_Count_Subquery (27 rows) and CH14_Staff_Class_Count_GROUPED_RIGHT (27 rows). The incorrect solution is in CH14_Staff_Class_Count_GROUPED_WRONG (22 rows).

Bowling League Database

1. *"Do any team captains have a raw score that is higher than any other member of the team?"*

(Hint: You find out the top raw score for captains by JOINing teams to bowlers on captain ID and then to bowler scores. Use a HAVING clause to compare the MAX value for all other members from a subquery.)

You can find the solution in CH14_Captains_Who_Are_Hotshots (0 rows). (There are no captains who bowl better than their teammates!)

2. *"Display for each bowler the bowler name and the average of the bowler's raw game scores for bowlers whose average is greater than 155."*

(Hint: You need a simple HAVING clause comparing the AVG to a numeric literal.)

You can find the solution in CH14_Good_Bowlers (17 rows).

3. *"List the last name and first name of every bowler whose average raw score is greater than or equal to the overall average score."*

(Hint: I showed you how to solve this in Chapter 12 in the "Sample Statements" section with a subquery in a WHERE clause. Now solve it using HAVING!) (use closing parenthesis, not backslash)

You can find the solution in CH14_Better_Than_Overall_Average_HAVING (17 rows).

Recipes Database

1. *"Sum the amount of salt by recipe class, and display those recipe classes that require more than three teaspoons."*

   (Hint: This requires a complex JOIN of five tables to filter out salt and teaspoon, SUM the result, and then eliminate recipe classes that use more than three teaspoons.)

   You can find the solution in CH14_Recipe_Classes_Lots_Of_Salt (1 row).

2. *"For what class of recipe do I have two or more recipes?"*

   (Hint: JOIN recipe classes with recipes, count the result, and keep the ones with two or more with a HAVING clause.)

   You can find the solution in CH14_Recipe_Classes_Two_Or_More (4 rows).

Part V

Modifying Sets of Data

15

Updating Sets of Data

"It is change, continuing change, inevitable change, that is the dominant factor in society today."

—Isaac Asimov

Topics Covered in This Chapter

What Is an UPDATE?

The UPDATE Statement

Uses for UPDATE

Sample Statements

Summary

Problems for You to Solve

As you learned in Part II, "SQL Basics"; Part III, "Working with Multiple Tables"; and Part IV, "Summarizing and Grouping Data"; using the SELECT statement to fetch data from your tables can be both fun and challenging. (Okay, so maybe some of it is a lot more challenging than fun!) If all you need to do is answer questions, then you don't need this part of my book. However, most real-world applications not only answer complex questions but also allow the user to change, add, or delete data. In addition to defining the SELECT statement that you've been learning about to retrieve data, the SQL Standard also defines three statements that allow you to modify your data. In this chapter, you'll learn about the first of those statements—UPDATE.

What Is an UPDATE?

The SELECT statement lets you retrieve sets of data from your tables. The UPDATE statement also works with sets of data, but you can use it to *change* the values in one or more columns and in one or more rows. By now, you should also be very familiar with expressions. To change a value in a column, you simply assign an expression to the column.

But you must be careful because UPDATE is very powerful. Most of the time you'll want to update only one or a few rows. If you're not careful, you can end up changing thousands of rows. To avoid this problem, I'll show you a technique for testing your statement first.

> ❖ **Note** You can find all the sample statements and solutions in the "modify" version of the respective sample databases—SalesOrdersModify, EntertainmentAgencyModify, SchoolScheduling-Modify, and BowlingLeagueModify.

The UPDATE Statement

The UPDATE statement is actually much simpler than the SELECT statement that you have been learning about in the previous chapters. The UPDATE statement has only three clauses: UPDATE, SET, and an optional WHERE clause, as shown in Figure 15-1.

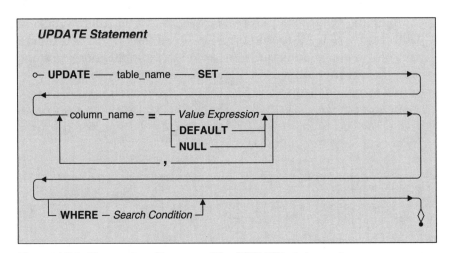

Figure 15-1 *The syntax diagram of the UPDATE statement*

After the UPDATE keyword, you specify the name of the table that you want to update. The SET keyword begins one or more clauses that assign a new value to a column in the table. You must include at least one assignment clause, and you can include as many assignment clauses as you need to change the value of multiple columns in each row. Use the optional WHERE clause to restrict the rows that are to be updated in the target table.

Using a Simple UPDATE Expression

Let's look at an example using a simple assignment of an expression to the column you want to update.

> ❖ **Note** Throughout this chapter, I use the "Request/Translation/ Clean Up/SQL" technique introduced in Chapter 4, "Creating a Simple Query."

"Increase the retail price of all products by 10 percent."

Ah, this is somewhat tricky. You'll find it tough to directly translate your original request into SQL-like English because you don't usually state the clauses in the same order required by the UPDATE statement. Take a close look at your request and figure out (a) the name of the target table and (b) the names of the columns you need to update. Restate your request in that order, and then proceed with the translation, like this:

"Change products by increasing the retail price by 10 percent."

Translation	Update the products table by setting the retail price equal to the retail price plus 10 percent of the price
Clean Up	Update ~~the~~ products ~~table by~~ setting ~~the~~ retail price ~~equal to~~ = ~~the~~ retail price ~~plus~~ + (.~~10 percent of the~~ * retail price)
SQL	`UPDATE Products` `SET Price = Price + (0.1 * Price)`

Notice that you cannot say `SET Price + 10 percent`. You must state the column to be updated to the left of the equals sign and then create an expression to calculate the new value you want. If the new value involves using the old or current value of the column, then you must reference the column name as needed to the right of the equals sign. One rule that's very clear in the SQL Standard is that your database system must evaluate all the assignment expressions *before* it updates any rows. So your database will resolve the two references to the Price column to the right of the equals sign by fetching the value of the Price column before it makes any changes.

You'll find this sort of assignment statement common in any programming language. Although it might appear to you that you're assigning the value of a column to itself, you're really grabbing the value before it changes, adding 10 percent of the value, and then assigning the result to the column to update it to a new value.

Updating Selected Rows

Are you always going to want to update all rows in a table? Probably not. To limit the rows changed by your UPDATE statement, you need to add a WHERE clause. Let's consider another problem:

> *"My clothing supplier just announced a price increase of 4 percent. Update the price of the clothing products and add 4 percent."*

Let's restate that:

> *"Modify products by increasing the retail price by 4 percent for products that are clothing (category 3)."*

Translation	Update the products table by setting the retail price equal to retail price times 1.04 for all products in category 3
Clean Up	Update ~~the~~ products ~~table by~~ ~~setting the~~ retail price ~~equal to~~ = retail price ~~times~~ * 1.04 ~~for all~~ where ~~products in~~ category ID = 3
SQL	UPDATE Products SET RetailPrice = RetailPrice * 1.04 WHERE CategoryID = 3

❖ **Note** I simplified the calculation in the query by multiplying the original value by 1.04 rather than adding the original value to 0.04 times the original value. The result is mathematically the same and might actually execute faster because one mathematical operation (price times 1.04) is more efficient than two (price plus price times .04).

After tackling subqueries in Chapter 11, this was easy, right? Just wait—you'll use subqueries extensively in your WHERE clauses, and I'll cover that later in this chapter.

Safety First: Ensure You're Updating the Correct Rows

Even for simple UPDATE queries, I strongly recommend that you verify that you're going to be updating the correct rows. How do you do that? As I mentioned, most of the time you'll add a WHERE clause to select a subset of rows to update. Why not build a SELECT query first to return the rows that you intend to update? Continuing with my example, let's ask the database to return a column that lets me ensure that I have the correct rows, the value I want to update, and the expression I intend to assign to the column I'm changing.

> *"List the product name, retail price, and retail price plus 4 percent from the products table for the products in category 3."*

Translation	Select product name, retail price, and retail price times 1.04 from the products table for products in category ID 3
Clean Up	Select product name, retail price, ~~and~~ retail price ~~times~~ * 1.04 from ~~the~~ products ~~table for~~ where ~~products in~~ category ID = 3
SQL	SELECT ProductName, RetailPrice, RetailPrice * 1.04 As NewPrice FROM Products WHERE CategoryID = 3

Figure 15-2 shows the result.

ProductName	RetailPrice	NewPrice
Ultra-Pro Rain Jacket	$85.00	$88.40
StaDry Cycling Pants	$69.00	$71.76
Kool-Breeze Rocket Top Jersey	$32.00	$33.28
Wonder Wool Cycle Socks	$19.00	$19.76

Figure 15-2 *Verifying the rows you want to update*

Note that I included the product name so I can see exactly what I want to update. If this is the result I want, I can transform the SELECT statement into the correct UPDATE statement by removing elements I don't need and swapping the FROM and SELECT clauses. Figure 15-3 shows how to transform this SELECT statement into the correct UPDATE syntax.

Simply cross out the words you don't need, move the table name to the UPDATE clause, move the target field and expression to the SET clause separated by an equals sign, copy your WHERE clause, and you're done.

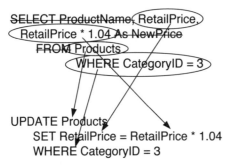

Figure 15-3 *Converting a SELECT query into an UPDATE statement*

A Brief Aside: Transactions

Before I get too much further into changing data, you need to know about an important feature available in SQL. The SQL Standard defines something called a *transaction* that you can use to protect a series of changes you're making to the data in your tables. You can think of a transaction in SQL just like a transaction you might make online or at a store to buy something. You initiate the transaction when you send in your order. Paying for the item you ordered is part of the transaction. The transaction is completed when you receive and accept the merchandise. But if the merchandise doesn't arrive, you might apply for a refund. Or if the merchandise is unsatisfactory, you return it and ask for your money back.

The SQL Standard provides three statements that mimic this scenario. You can use START TRANSACTION before you begin your changes to indicate that you want to protect and verify the changes you're about to make. Think of this as sending in your order. You make the changes to your database—register the payment and register the receipt. If everything completes satisfactorily, you can use COMMIT to make the changes permanent. If something went wrong (the payment or receipt update failed), you can use ROLLBACK to restore the data as it was before you started the transaction.

This buying and selling example might seem silly, but transactions are a very powerful feature of SQL, especially when you need to make changes to multiple rows or to rows in several tables. Using a transaction ensures that either all changes are successful or none are. You don't want to register the payment without receipt of the goods, and you don't want to mark the goods received without receiving the payment. Note that this applies to changing your data not only with the UPDATE statement described in this chapter but also with INSERT and DELETE, which are described in the next two chapters.

Not all database systems implement transactions, and the syntax to use transaction processing varies slightly depending on the particular database system. Some database systems allow you to nest transactions inside each other so that you can establish multiple commit points. Some end-user database systems, such as Microsoft Office Access, start a transaction for you behind the scenes every time you run a query that changes your data. If you've used Microsoft Access, you know that it prompts you with a message indicating how many rows will be changed and whether any will fail—and you can either accept the changes or cancel them (ROLLBACK). As always, consult your database documentation for details.

Updating Multiple Columns

As implied by the diagram of the UPDATE statement in Figure 15-1, you can specify more than one column to change by including additional assignment statements separated by columns. Keep in mind that your database applies all the changes you specify to every row returned as a result of evaluating your WHERE clause. Let's take a look at an update you might want to perform in the School Scheduling database:

> *"Modify classes by changing the classroom to 1635 and the schedule dates from Monday-Wednesday-Friday to Tuesday-Thursday-Saturday for all drawing classes (subject ID 13)."*

Translation	Update classes and set classroom ID to 1635, Monday schedule to false, Wednesday schedule to false, Friday schedule to false, Tuesday schedule to true, Thursday schedule to true, and Saturday schedule to true for all classes that are subject ID 13

Clean Up	Update classes ~~and~~ set classroom ID ~~to~~ = 1635, Monday schedule ~~to~~ = 0 ~~false~~, Wednesday schedule ~~to~~ = 0 ~~false~~, Friday schedule ~~to~~ = 0 ~~false~~, Tuesday schedule ~~to~~ = 1 ~~true~~, Thursday schedule ~~to~~ = 1 ~~true~~, ~~and~~ Saturday schedule ~~to~~ = 1 ~~true for all classes that are~~ where subject ID = 13

SQL	UPDATE Classes SET ClassRoomID = 1635,
	
	    MondaySchedule = 0,
	
	    WednesdaySchedule = 0,
	
	    FridaySchedule = 0,
	
	    TuesdaySchedule = 1,
	
	    ThursdaySchedule = 1,
	
	    SaturdaySchedule = 1
	
	WHERE SubjectID = 13

> ❖ **Note** Remember that most database systems use the value 0 for
> false and the value 1 or –1 for true. Check your database documenta-
> tion for details.

Perhaps you want to make doubly sure that you're changing only the
classes scheduled on Monday-Wednesday-Friday. To do that, add criteria
to your WHERE clause like this:

SQL	UPDATE Classes SET ClassRoomID = 1635,
	
	    MondaySchedule = 0,
	
	    WednesdaySchedule = 0, FridaySchedule = 0,
	
	    TuesdaySchedule = 1, ThursdaySchedule = 1,
	
	    SaturdaySchedule = 1
	
	WHERE SubjectID = 13
	
	    AND MondaySchedule = 1
	
	    AND WednesdaySchedule = 1
	
	    AND FridaySchedule = 1

Notice that you're filtering for the value you expect to find in the field
before your UPDATE statement changes the value. With this modified
query, you're finding all rows for SubjectID 13 that have a true (1) value

in the Monday, Wednesday, and Friday schedule fields. For each row that matches these criteria, your UPDATE statement will change the Class-RoomID and the schedule fields. If you try to run this query a second time, you should find that your database updates no rows because you eliminated all rows that qualify by changing the field values the first time you ran the query.

Using a Subquery to Filter Rows

In the examples in previous sections, I've updated the products in category 3 and the classes in subject 13. In the real world, code values like this don't have much meaning. You'd probably much rather say "clothing products" or "drawing classes." In a SELECT query, you can add the related tables to your FROM clause with JOIN specifications and then display the more meaningful value from the related table. As always, you must be familiar with your table relationships to make this connection. Figure 15-4 shows the tables I need for my example.

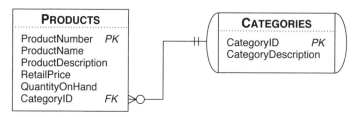

Figure 15-4 *The tables needed to relate category descriptions to products*

Let's look again at the verification query I built to check my update of products, but this time, let's add the Categories table:

SQL

```
SELECT ProductName, RetailPrice,
    RetailPrice * 1.04 As NewPrice
FROM Products INNER JOIN Categories
    ON Products.CategoryID = Categories.CategoryID
WHERE Categories.CategoryDescription = 'Clothing'
```

Filtering on the value Clothing makes a lot more sense than selecting the category ID value 3. However, notice that the diagram of the UPDATE statement in Figure 15-1 shows that I can supply only a table name following the UPDATE keyword. I cannot specify the INNER JOIN needed to include the Categories table so that I can filter on the more meaningful value. So what's the solution?

Remember from Chapter 11, "Subqueries," that I can create a filter in a WHERE clause to test a value fetched from a related table. Let's solve the price update problem again using a subquery so that I can apply a more meaningful filter value.

"Modify products by increasing the retail price by 4 percent for products that are clothing."

Translation	Update the products table by setting the retail price equal to retail price times 1.04 for the products whose category ID is equal to the selection of the category ID from the categories table where the category description is clothing
Clean Up	Update ~~the~~ products ~~table by~~ setting ~~the~~ retail price ~~equal to~~ = retail price ~~times~~ * 1.04 ~~for the products whose~~ where category ID ~~is equal to~~ = ~~the~~ (selection ~~of the~~ category ID from ~~the~~ categories ~~table~~ where ~~the~~ category description ~~is~~ = 'Clothing')

SQL	UPDATE Products
	SET RetailPrice = RetailPrice * 1.04
	WHERE CategoryID =
	   (SELECT CategoryID
	   FROM Categories
	   WHERE CategoryDescription = 'Clothing')

That's not as straightforward as a simple WHERE clause on a column from a joined table, but it gets the job done.

❖ **Caution** Notice that I used an equals comparison for the CategoryID column in the Products table and the value returned by the subquery. As I noted in Chapter 11, if you want to use an equals comparison in a predicate with a subquery, the subquery must return only one value. If more than one row in the Categories table had the value Clothing in the category description field, this query would fail. However, in my example, I'm reasonably certain that filtering for

Clothing will return only one value for CategoryID. Whenever you're not sure that a subquery will return only one value, you should use the IN predicate rather than the "equal to" operator.

Let's solve the problem of updating classes by using the same technique. I want to use the subject code or subject name from the Subjects table rather than the numeric and meaningless subject ID. Figure 15-5 shows the tables involved.

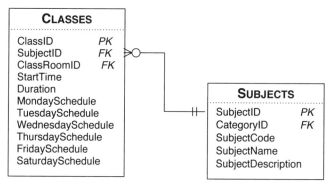

Figure 15-5 *The tables needed to relate subject names to classes*

Let's solve the update problem again by using a subquery filter.

> *"Modify classes by changing the classroom to 1635 and the schedule dates from Monday-Wednesday-Friday to Tuesday-Thursday-Saturday for all drawing classes."*

Translation	Update classes and set classroom ID to 1635, Monday schedule to false, Wednesday schedule to false, Friday schedule to false, Tuesday schedule to true, Thursday schedule to true, and Saturday schedule to true for all classes whose subject ID is in the selection of subject IDs from the subjects table where subject name is 'Drawing'
Clean Up	Update classes ~~and~~ set classroom ID ~~to~~ = 1635, Monday schedule ~~to~~ = 0 ~~false~~, Wednesday schedule ~~to~~ = 0 ~~false~~, Friday schedule ~~to~~ = 0 ~~false~~, Tuesday schedule ~~to~~ = 1 ~~true~~, Thursday schedule ~~to~~ = 1 ~~true~~, ~~and~~ Saturday schedule ~~to~~ = 1 ~~true for all classes whose~~ where subject ID ~~is in the~~ (~~selection of~~ subject IDs from ~~the~~ subjects ~~table~~ where subject name ~~is~~ = 'Drawing')

```
SQL              UPDATE Classes SET ClassRoomID = 1635,
                     MondaySchedule = 0,
                     WednesdaySchedule = 0, FridaySchedule = 0,
                     TuesdaySchedule = 1, ThursdaySchedule = 1,
                     SaturdaySchedule = 1
                 WHERE SubjectID IN
                     (SELECT SubjectID
                     FROM Subjects
                     WHERE SubjectName = 'Drawing')
```

Notice that even though I'm fairly certain that only one subject ID has a subject name equal to Drawing, I decided to play it safe and use the IN predicate.

Some Database Systems Allow a JOIN in the UPDATE Clause

Several database systems, most notably the ones from Microsoft (Microsoft Access and Microsoft SQL Server), allow you to specify a joined table in the FROM clause of an UPDATE query. The restriction is that the JOIN must be from the primary key in one table to the foreign key in another table so that the database system can figure out which specific row or rows you intend to update. This allows you to avoid a subquery in the WHERE clause when you want to filter rows based on a value in a related table.

If your database system allows this, you can solve the problem of modifying the information on drawing classes as follows:

```
SQL              UPDATE Classes INNER JOIN Subject
                     ON Classes.SubjectID = Subjects.SubjectID
                 SET ClassRoomID = 1635, MondaySchedule = 0,
                     WednesdaySchedule = 0, FridaySchedule = 0,
                     TuesdaySchedule = 1, ThursdaySchedule = 1,
                     SaturdaySchedule = 1
                 WHERE Subjects.SubjectName = 'Drawing'
```

As you can see, this avoids having to use a subquery to filter the rows. In some ways, this syntax is also easier to understand. You can also use this syntax to join a related table that supplies one of the values in your update calculation rather than use a subquery in the SET clause. Be sure to check the documentation for your database system to see if this feature is supported. You'll note that I've used this technique to solve some of the sample queries in the Microsoft Access versions of the sample databases.

By the way, the SQL Standard allows the target table to be a view, which could imply a joined table. However, the standard specifies that the rules for updating a view are defined by the implementation, which allows database system vendors to either always require a simple table name or otherwise restrict what you can do using a view or joined table. As always, check your database documentation for details.

As you might imagine, you can make the subquery as complex as necessary to allow you to filter the target table properly. For example, if you want to change the start time for all classes taught by one professor, you need to JOIN the Faculty_Classes and Staff tables in the FROM clause of the subquery. Figure 15-6 shows the tables involved.

Let's say you want to change the start time of all classes taught by Kathryn Patterson to 2:00 PM. (You probably wouldn't want to do this because you might end up with multiple classes starting at the same time, but this makes an interesting example.) Your solution might look as follows.

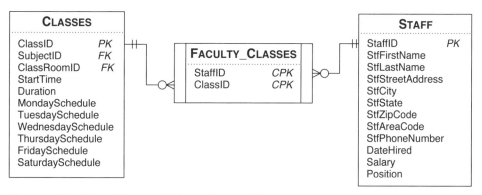

Figure 15-6 *The tables needed to relate staff names to classes*

"Change the classes table by setting the start time to 2:00 PM for all classes taught by Kathryn Patterson."

Translation	Update the classes table by setting the start time to 2:00 PM for all classes whose class ID is in the selection of class IDs of faculty classes joined with staff on staff ID in the faculty classes table matches staff ID in the staff table where the staff first name is 'Kathryn' and the staff last name is 'Patterson'
Clean Up	Update ~~the~~ classes ~~table by~~ ~~setting the~~ start time ~~to~~ = ~~2:00 PM.~~ '14:00:00' ~~for all classes whose~~ where class ID ~~is~~ in ~~the~~ (~~selection of~~ class IDs ~~of~~ from faculty classes inner join~~ed with~~ staff on faculty_classes.staff ID ~~in the~~ ~~faculty classes table matches~~ = staff.staff ID ~~in the staff~~ ~~table~~ where ~~the~~ staff first name ~~is~~ = 'Kathryn' and ~~the~~ staff last name ~~is~~ = 'Patterson')

SQL	UPDATE Classes SET StartTime = '14:00:00'
	 WHERE ClassID IN
	    (SELECT ClassID
	    FROM Faculty_Classes INNER JOIN Staff
	      ON Faculty_Classes.StaffID = Staff.StaffID
	    WHERE StfFirstName = 'Kathryn'
	    AND StfLastName = 'Patterson')

So the trick is to identify the relationships between the target table and any related table(s) you need to specify the criteria in the WHERE clause. You did this in Chapter 8, "INNER JOINs," and Chapter 9, "OUTER JOINs," as you assembled the FROM clause of queries on multiple tables. When building an UPDATE statement, you can put only the target table after the UPDATE keyword, so you must take the other tables and put them in a subquery that returns the column that you can link back to the target table.

Using a Subquery UPDATE Expression

If you thought I was done using subqueries, you were wrong. Notice in Figure 15-1 that the value that you can assign to a column in a SET clause can be a value expression. Just for review, Figure 15-7 shows how to construct a value expression.

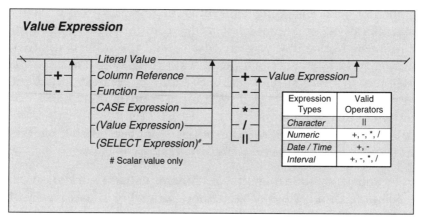

Figure 15-7 *The syntax diagram for a value expression*

In Chapter 2, "Ensuring Your Database Structure Is Sound," I advised you to not include calculated fields in your tables. As with most rules, there are exceptions. Consider the Orders table in the Sales Orders sample database. If your business handles extremely large orders (thousands of order detail rows), you might want to consider including an order total field in the Orders table. Including this calculated field lets you run queries to examine the total of all items ordered without having to fetch and total thousands of detail rows. If you choose to do this, you must include code in your application that keeps the calculated total up to date every time a change is made to any related order detail row.

❖ **Note** Many database systems provide a feature—often called a *trigger*—that enables you to run code within the database system whenever data is added, updated, or deleted. (The act of adding, updating, or deleting data "triggers" your code.) The trigger code can then perform additional complex validations or even run additional update, insert, or delete queries to modify data in related tables. You can imagine how code you write in a trigger could potentially update calculated values in related tables.

Some database systems (notably Microsoft SQL Server) also enable you to define calculated columns as part of your table design. Clearly, such features cause your database system to do additional work whenever you work with the data in your tables, so you should carefully consider using such features and do so sparingly. Consult your database documentation for details.

So far, I've been assigning a literal value or a value expression containing a literal value, an operator, and a column name to columns in the SET clause. Notice that you can also assign the value of another column in the target table, but you'll rarely want to do that. The most interesting possibility is that you can use a SELECT expression (a subquery) that returns a single value (such as a sum) from another table and assign that value to your column. You can include criteria in the subquery (a WHERE clause) that filters the values from the other table based on a value in the table you're updating.

So, to update a total in one table (Orders) using a sum of an expression on columns in a related table (Order_Details), you can run an UPDATE query using a subquery. In the subquery, you'll sum the value of quantity ordered times quoted price and place it in the calculated field, and you'll add a WHERE clause to make sure you're summing values from related rows in the Order_Details table for each row in the Orders table. Your request might look like this:

"Change the orders table by setting the order total to the sum of quantity ordered times quoted price for all related order detail rows."

Translation	Update the orders table by setting the order total to the sum of quantity ordered times quoted price from the order details table where the order number matches the order number in the orders table
Clean Up	Update ~~the~~ orders ~~table by~~ setting ~~the~~ order total ~~to~~ = ~~the~~ (select sum ~~of~~ (quantity ordered ~~times~~ * quoted price) from ~~the~~ order details ~~table~~ where ~~the~~ order_details.order number ~~matches the~~ = orders.order number ~~in the orders table~~)

SQL	UPDATE Orders
	SET OrderTotal =
	    (SELECT SUM(QuantityOrdered * QuotedPrice)
	    FROM Order_Details
	    WHERE Order_Details.OrderNumber =
	    Orders.OrderNumber)

❖ **Note** I saved this query as CH15_Update_Order_Totals_Subquery in the Sales Orders Modify sample database.

Notice that I didn't include a WHERE clause to filter the orders that the database will update. If you execute this query in application code, you'll probably want to filter the order number so that the database updates only the order that you know was changed. Some database systems actually let you define a calculated field like this and specify how the field should be updated by your database system. As noted earlier, most database systems also support something called a *trigger* that the database system runs on your behalf each time a row in a specified table is changed, added, or deleted. For systems that include these features, you can use this UPDATE query syntax in either the definition of the table or in the trigger you define to run when a value changes. As usual, consult your database documentation for details.

Uses for UPDATE

At this point, you should have a good understanding of how to update one or more columns in a table using either a simple literal or a complex subquery expression. You also know how to filter the rows that will be changed by your UPDATE statement. The best way to give you an idea of the wide range of uses for the UPDATE statement is to list some problems you can solve with this statement and then present a set of examples in the "Sample Statements" section.

> *"Reduce the quoted price by 2 percent for orders shipped more than 30 days after the order date."*
>
> *"Add 6 percent to all agent salaries."*
>
> *"Change the tournament location to 'Oasis Lanes' for all tournaments originally scheduled at 'Sports World Lanes.'"*
>
> *"Recalculate the grade point average for all students based on classes completed."*
>
> *"Apply a 5 percent discount to all orders for customers who purchased more than $50,000 in the month of October 2017."*
>
> *"Correct the engagement contract price by multiplying the entertainer daily rate times number of days and adding a 15 percent commission."*
>
> *"Update the city and state for all bowlers by looking up the names by ZIP Code."*

"For all students and staff in ZIP codes 98270 and 98271, change the area code to 360."

"Make sure the retail price for all bikes is at least a 45 percent markup over the wholesale price of the vendor with the lowest cost."

"Apply a 2 percent discount to all engagements for customers who booked more than $3,000 worth of business in the month of October 2017."

"Change the name of the 'Huckleberrys' bowling team to 'Manta Rays.'"

"Increase the salary of full-time tenured staff by 5 percent."

"Set the retail price of accessories to the wholesale price of the highest priced vendor plus 35 percent."

"Add 0.5 percent to the commission rate of agents who have sold more than $20,000 in engagements."

"Calculate and update the total pins, games bowled, current average, and current handicap for all bowlers."

Sample Statements

You now know the mechanics of constructing UPDATE queries. Let's look at a set of samples, all of which request that one or more columns in a table be changed in some way. These examples come from four of the sample databases.

❖ **Caution** Because the sample queries you'll find in the modified versions of the sample databases change your data, be aware that some of the queries will work as expected only once. For example, after you run an UPDATE query to change the name of a customer or bowling team using a WHERE clause to find the row you want to change, subsequent attempts to find the row to change will fail because of the change you made the first time you ran the query. Consider restoring the databases from the sample scripts or a backup copy if you want to work through the problems again.

Also, if you're using MySQL, the default in the Query Editor in MySQL Workbench is to allow only "safe" updates that include specification of the Primary Key in the WHERE clause. Many of the queries shown here won't run with that enabled. Go to Edit / Preferences / SQL Editor and clear the Safe Updates checkbox near the bottom.

I've also included a view of each target table before and after executing the update and a count of the number of rows that should be changed by each sample UPDATE statement. The name that appears immediately before the count of rows changed is the name I gave each query in the sample data on the companion website for the book. Also, I created a companion SELECT query (stored as a View in MySQL, PostgreSQL, and Microsoft SQL Server) for each UPDATE query that you can use to see exactly what will be changed. The name of the companion query is the name of the original query with _Query appended to the name. I stored each query in the appropriate sample database (as indicated within the example) and prefixed the names of the queries relevant to this chapter with "CH15." You can find the sample data on the companion website for this book, www.informit.com/title/9780134858333. You can follow the instructions in the Introduction of this book to load the samples onto your computer and try them.

❖ **Note** Remember that all the column names and table names used in these examples are drawn from the sample database structures shown in Appendix B, "Schema for the Sample Databases." To simplify the process, I have combined the Translation and Clean Up steps for all the examples. These samples assume you have thoroughly studied and understood the concepts covered in previous chapters, especially the chapter on subqueries.

All of the sample statements have a companion SELECT statement that shows the rows affected and any new values before you run the actual UPDATE statement. These additional queries (views) have the name of the actual UPDATE statement appended with _Query. For example, the UPDATE statement named CH15_Update_Order_Totals_Subquery has a companion CH15_Update_Order_Totals_Subquery_Query that simply shows you the rows affected without changing any data.

Sales Orders Database

"Reduce the quoted price by 2 percent for orders shipped more than 30 days after the order date."

Let's restate the problem so that it more closely follows the SQL syntax.

"Change order details by setting the quoted price to quoted price times 0.98 for all orders where the shipped date is more than 30 days later than the order date."

Translation/ Clean Up	Update ~~the~~ order details ~~table by~~ setting ~~the~~ quoted price ~~equal to~~ = ~~the~~ quoted price ~~times~~ * 0.98 where ~~the~~ order ID ~~is~~ in ~~the~~ (~~selection of~~ order IDs from ~~the~~ orders ~~table~~ where ship date ~~minus~~ – order date ~~is greater than~~ > 30

SQL	UPDATE Order_Details
	
	SET QuotedPrice = QuotedPrice * 0.98
	
	WHERE OrderID IN
	
	    (SELECT OrderID
	
	    FROM Orders
	
	    WHERE (ShipDate - OrderDate) > 30)

❖ **Note** This query solution assumes your database system allows you to subtract one date from another to obtain the number of days between the two dates. Consult your database documentation for details.

Order_Details Table Before Executing the UPDATE Query – CH15_Adjust_Late_Order_Prices_Query

OrderNumber	ProductNumber	QuotedPrice	UpdatedPrice
291	1	$1,200.00	1176
291	14	$139.95	137.15
291	30	$43.65	42.78
371	9	$32.01	31.37
371	22	$79.54	77.95

OrderNumber	ProductNumber	QuotedPrice	UpdatedPrice
371	35	$37.83	37.07
387	1	$1,200.00	1176
387	6	$635.00	622.3

<< more rows here >>

Order_Details Table After Executing CH15_Adjust_Late_Order_Prices (29 rows changed)

OrderNumber	ProductNumber	QuotedPrice	QuantityOrdered
291	1	$1,176.00	4
291	14	$137.15	2
291	30	$42.78	6
371	9	$31.37	6
371	22	$77.95	5
371	35	$37.07	6
387	1	$1,176.00	4
387	6	$622.30	4

<< more rows here >>

"Make sure the retail price for all bikes is at least a 45 percent markup over the wholesale price of the vendor with the lowest cost."

Restated, the request is as follows:

"Change the products table by setting the retail price equal to 1.45 times the wholesale price of the vendor that has the lowest cost for the product where the retail price is not already equal to 1.45 times the wholesale price and the category ID is 2."

Translation/ Clean Up	Update ~~the~~ products ~~table by~~ setting~~the~~ retail price ~~equal to~~ = 1.45 ~~times~~ * ~~the~~ (~~selection of the unique~~ distinct wholesale price from ~~the~~ product vendors ~~table~~ where ~~the~~ product vendors ~~table's~~ product number ~~is equal to~~ = ~~the~~ products ~~table's~~ product number and ~~the~~

wholesale price ~~is equal to~~ = the (selection of the minimum (wholesale price) from ~~the~~ product vendors table where ~~the~~ product vendors ~~table's~~ product number ~~is equal to~~ = the products ~~table's~~ product number)) where ~~the~~ retail price ~~is less than~~ < 1.45 times ~~the~~ (selection of the unique distinct wholesale price from ~~the~~ product vendors ~~table~~ where ~~the~~ product vendors ~~table's~~ product number ~~is equal to~~ = the products ~~table's~~ product number and ~~the~~ wholesale price ~~is equal to~~ = the (selection of the minimum (wholesale price) from ~~the~~ product vendors ~~table~~ where ~~the~~ product vendors ~~table's~~ product number ~~is equal to~~ = the products ~~table's~~ product number)) and ~~the~~ category ID ~~is equal to~~ = 2

SQL	

```
UPDATE Products
SET RetailPrice = ROUND(1.45 *
   (SELECT DISTINCT WholeSalePrice
    FROM Product_Vendors
    WHERE Product_Vendors.ProductNumber
     = Products.ProductNumber
    AND WholeSalePrice =
       (SELECT MIN(WholeSalePrice)
        FROM Product_Vendors
        WHERE Product_Vendors.ProductNumber
         = Products.ProductNumber)), 0)
WHERE RetailPrice < 1.45 *
    (SELECT DISTINCT WholeSalePrice
     FROM Product_Vendors
     WHERE Product_Vendors.ProductNumber
      = Products.ProductNumber
     AND WholeSalePrice =
        (SELECT MIN(WholeSalePrice)
         FROM Product_Vendors
         WHERE Product_Vendors.ProductNumber
            = Products.ProductNumber))
   AND CategoryID = 2
```

❖ **Note** You'll find this query solved with a JOIN in the UPDATE clause in the Microsoft Access sample database because Access does not support a subquery that uses DISTINCT in the SET clause. (It declares the query not updatable because of the DISTINCT.)

Notice also that the solution rounds the resulting price to the nearest dollar (zero decimal places). You'll find that most commercial implementations support a ROUND function even though this function is not explicitly defined in the SQL Standard.

I could have also included a subquery to find the category ID that is equal to (or IN) the category IDs from the Categories table where category description is equal to Bikes, but I thought the query was complex enough without adding another subquery. Finally, I selected the DISTINCT wholesale price because more than one vendor might have the same low price. I want only one value from the subquery for the comparison.

Products Table Before Executing the UPDATE Query – CH15_Adjust_Bike_ Retail_Price_Query (1 row)

ProductNumber	ProductName	RetailPrice	UpdatedPrice
2	Eagle FS-3 Mountain Bike	$1,800.00	1840

Products Table After Executing CH15_Adjust_Bike_Retail_Price (1 row changed)

ProductNumber	ProductName	RetailPrice
2	Eagle FS-3 Mountain Bike	$1,840.00

❖ **Note** If you scan the Product_Vendors table for all the bikes (product IDs 1, 2, 6, and 11), you'll find that only product 2 has a current retail price that is less than 1.45 times the lowest wholesale price for that product from any vendor. The wholesale price for bike 2 from vendor ID 6 is $1,269, and 1.45 times this amount is $1,840.05, which the query rounded to the nearest dollar.

Entertainment Agency Database

"Add 6 percent to all agent salaries."

Restated, the request is as follows:

"Change the agents table by adding 6 percent to all salaries."

Translation/ Clean Up	Update ~~the~~ agents ~~table by~~ setting salary ~~equal to~~ = salary ~~times~~ * 1.06
SQL	UPDATE Agents SET Salary = ROUND(Salary * 1.06, 0)

❖ **Note** I've again used the common ROUND function found in most commercial implementations and have specified rounding to zero decimal places. Check your database system documentation for specific details about rounding in your implementation.

Agents Table Before Executing the UPDATE Query – CH15_Give_Agents_6Percent_Raise_Query (9 rows)

AgentID	AgtFirstName	AgtLastName	Salary	NewSalary
1	William	Thompson	$35,000.00	37100
2	Scott	Bishop	$27,000.00	28620
3	Carol	Viescas	$30,000.00	31800
4	Karen	Smith	$22,000.00	23320
5	Marianne	Wier	$24,500.00	25970
6	John	Kennedy	$33,000.00	34980
7	Caleb	Viescas	$22,100.00	23426
8	Maria	Patterson	$30,000.00	31800
9	Daffy	Dumbwit	$50.00	53

Agents Table After Executing CH15_Give_Agents_6Percent_Raise (9 rows changed)

AgentID	AgtFirstName	AgtLastName	Salary
1	William	Thompson	$37,100.00
2	Scott	Bishop	$28,620.00
3	Carol	Viescas	$31,800.00
4	Karen	Smith	$23,320.00
5	Marianne	Wier	$25,970.00
6	John	Kennedy	$34,980.00
7	Caleb	Viescas	$23,426.00
8	Maria	Patterson	$31,800.00
9	Daffy	Dumbwit	$53.00

"Correct the engagement contract price by multiplying the entertainer daily rate by the number of days and adding a 15 percent commission."

Let's restate that:

"Modify the engagements table by setting the contract price to 1.15 times the number of days for the contract times the entertainer daily rate."

Translation/ Clean Up	Update ~~the~~ engagements ~~table by~~ ~~setting the~~ contract price ~~equal to~~ = 1.15 ~~times~~ * ~~the~~ (end date ~~minus~~ – ~~the~~ start date ~~plus~~ + 1) ~~and then times the~~ * (~~selection of the~~ entertainer price per day from ~~the~~ entertainers ~~table~~ where ~~the~~ entertainers ~~table~~ entertainer ID ~~is equal to~~ = ~~the~~ engagements ~~table~~ entertainer ID

SQL	UPDATE Engagements
	
	SET Engagements.ContractPrice =
	
	    ROUND(1.15 * (EndDate - StartDate + 1) *
	
	    (SELECT EntPricePerDay
	
	     FROM Entertainers
	
	      WHERE Entertainers.EntertainerID =
	
	        Engagements.EntertainerID), 0)

❖ **Note** This query solution assumes your database system allows you to subtract one date from another to obtain the number of days between the two dates. Consult your database documentation for details.

I add 1 to the difference to obtain the actual number of days because the entertainment occurs on both the first and the last days of the engagement. It's clear you need to do this for an engagement that is booked for only one day. The start and end days are the same, so the difference is zero, but the engagement played for exactly one day.

Microsoft Access uses "banker's rounding" on fractions equal to exactly 0.5, so the result is rounded to the nearest even number. For example, 3.5 rounds to 4, and 2.5 rounds to 2. This can make some results different by one dollar.

Entertainer Prices per Day

EntertainerID	EntStageName	EntPricePerDay
1001	Carol Peacock Trio	$175.00
1002	Topazz	$120.00
1003	JV & the Deep Six	$275.00
1004	Jim Glynn	$60.00
1005	Jazz Persuasion	$125.00
1006	Modern Dance	$250.00
1007	Coldwater Cattle Company	$275.00
1008	Country Feeling	$280.00
1009	Katherine Ehrlich	$145.00
1010	Saturday Revue	$250.00
1011	Julia Schnebly	$90.00
1012	Susan McLain	$75.00
1013	Caroline Coie Cuartet	$250.00

Engagements Table Before Executing the UPDATE Query – CH15_Calculate_ Entertainment_ContractPrice_Query (111 rows)

Engagement Number	ContractPrice	NewContractPrice	EntertainerID
2	$200.00	345	1004
3	$590.00	863	1005
4	$470.00	483	1004
5	$1,130.00	1265	1003
6	$2,300.00	1610	1008
7	$770.00	1104	1002
8	$1,850.00	2530	1007
9	$1,370.00	3163	1010
10	$3,650.00	3163	1003

<< more rows here >>

Engagements Table After Executing CH15_Calculate_Entertainment_ContractPrice (111 rows changed)

EngagementNumber	Contract Price	EntertainerID
2	$345.00	1004
3	$862.00	1005
4	$483.00	1004
5	$1,265.00	1003
6	$1,610.00	1008
7	$1,104.00	1002
8	$2,530.00	1007
9	$3,162.00	1010
10	$3,162.00	1003

<< more rows here >>

> ❖ **Note** The original contract price values in the Engagements table are simply random values within a reasonable range that I chose when I created the original sample data. This update query clearly corrects each value to a more reasonable charge based on each entertainer's daily rate.

School Scheduling Database

"For all students in ZIP Codes 98270 and 98271, change the area code to 360."

Restated, the problem is as follows:

"Change the students table by setting the area code to 360 for all students who live in ZIP Codes 98270 and 98271."

Translation/ Clean Up	Update ~~the~~ students ~~table by~~ setting ~~the~~ area code ~~equal to~~ = '360' where ~~the~~ student zip code ~~is in the list~~ ('98270', ~~and~~ '98271')
SQL	UPDATE Students SET Students.StudAreaCode = '360' WHERE Students.StudZipCode IN ('98270', '98271')

Students Table Before Executing the UPDATE Query CH15_Fix_Student_AreaCode_Query (2 rows)

Student ID	Stud FirstName	Stud LastName	Stud ZipCode	Stud AreaCode	NewStud AreaCode
1007	Elizabeth	Hallmark	98271	253	360
1017	George	Chavez	98270	206	360

Students Table After Executing CH15_Fix_Student_AreaCode (2 rows changed)

StudentID	StudFirstName	StudLastName	StudZipCode	StudAreaCode
1001	Kerry	Patterson	78284	210
1007	Elizabeth	Hallmark	98271	360
1008	Sara	Sheskey	97208	503
		<< more rows here >>		

StudentID	StudFirstName	StudLastName	StudZipCode	StudAreaCode
1016	Steve	Pundt	75204	972
1017	George	Chavez	98270	360
1018	Richard	Lum	98115	206
1019	Daffy	Dumbwit	98002	425

"Recalculate the grade point average for all students based on classes completed."

Restated, the request looks like this:

"Modify the students table by setting the grade point average to the sum of the credits times the grade divided by the sum of the credits."

Translation/ Clean Up	Update ~~the~~ students ~~table by~~ ~~setting the~~ student GPA ~~equal to~~ = the (~~selection of the~~ sum of (credits ~~times~~ * grade) ~~divided by~~ / the sum ~~of~~ (credits) from ~~the~~ classes ~~table~~ inner joined ~~with the~~ student schedules ~~table~~ on classes.class ID ~~in the classes table matches~~ = student_ schedules.class ID ~~in the student schedules table~~ where ~~the~~ class status ~~is~~ = ~~complete~~ 2 and ~~the~~ student schedules ~~table~~ student ID ~~is equal to~~ = ~~the~~ students ~~table~~ student ID)

SQL	`UPDATE Students SET Students.StudGPA =`
	`    (SELECT ROUND (SUM(Classes.Credits *`
	`        Student_Schedules.Grade) /`
	`        SUM(Classes.Credits), 3)`
	`    FROM Classes`
	`    INNER JOIN Student_Schedules`
	`    ON Classes.ClassID = Student_`
	`        Schedules.ClassID`
	`    WHERE (Student_Schedules.ClassStatus = 2)`
	`    AND (Student_Schedules.StudentID =`
	`        Students.StudentID))`

Students Table Before Executing the UPDATE Query – CH15_Update_Student_ GPA_Query (19 rows)

StudentID	StudFirstName	StudLastName	StudGPA	NewStudGPA
1001	Kerry	Patterson	74.465	81.075
1002	David	Hamilton	78.755	80.09
1003	Betsy	Stadick	85.235	80.31
1004	Janice	Galvin	81	85.042
1005	Doris	Hartwig	72.225	85.135
1006	Scott	Bishop	88.5	77.512
1007	Elizabeth	Hallmark	87.65	72.098
1008	Sara	Sheskey	84.625	85.695

<< more rows here >>

Students Table After Executing the CH15_Update_Student_GPA Query (19 rows changed)

StudentID	StudFirstName	StudLastName	StudGPA
1001	Kerry	Patterson	81.075
1002	David	Hamilton	80.09
1003	Betsy	Stadick	80.31
1004	Janice	Galvin	85.042
1005	Doris	Hartwig	85.135
1006	Scott	Bishop	77.512
1007	Elizabeth	Hallmark	72.098
1008	Sara	Sheskey	85.695

<< more rows here >>

❖ **Note** Because Microsoft Access does not support using subqueries with aggregate functions, you'll find this query solved as a series of calls to built-in functions using a predefined view on the Student_ Schedules and Classes tables. Also, if you use the SQL shown above, you will get a Null result for the last student who hasn't registered for any classes. In all four sample databases, I avoid the Null and substitute a 0 value using functions available in each database system. In Chapter 19, "Condition Testing," I'll show you how to avoid this problem using CASE.

Bowling League Database

"Calculate and update the total pins, games bowled, current average, and current handicap for all bowlers."

❖ **Note** You calculated the handicap using a SELECT query in the "Problems for You to Solve" section of Chapter 13, "Grouping Data." For a hint, see the CH13_Bowler_Average_Handicap query in the Bowling League sample database. Remember that the handicap is 90 percent of 200 minus the bowler's average.

Let's restate the problem like this:

"Modify the bowlers table by calculating the total pins, games bowled, current average, and current handicap from the bowler scores table."

Translation/ Clean Up	Update ~~the~~ bowlers ~~table by~~ setting ~~the~~ total pins ~~equal to~~ = ~~the~~ (select~~ion of the~~ sum ~~of the~~ (raw score) from ~~the~~ bowler scores ~~table~~ where ~~the~~ bowler scores ~~table~~ bowler ID ~~is equal to~~ = ~~the~~ bowlers ~~table~~ bowler ID), ~~and the~~ games bowled ~~equal to~~ = ~~the~~ (select~~ion of the~~ count ~~of the~~ (raw score) from ~~the~~ bowler scores ~~table~~ where ~~the~~ bowler scores ~~table~~ bowler ID ~~is equal to~~ = ~~the~~ bowlers ~~table~~ bowler ID), ~~and the~~ current average ~~equal to~~ = ~~the~~ (select~~ion of the average~~ avg ~~of the~~ (raw score) from ~~the~~ bowler scores ~~table~~ where ~~the~~ bowler scores ~~table~~ bowler ID ~~is equal to~~ = ~~the~~ bowlers ~~table~~ bowler ID), ~~and the~~ current handicap ~~equal to~~ = ~~the~~ (select~~ion of~~ 0.9 ~~times~~ * (200 ~~minus~~ – ~~the average~~ avg ~~of the~~ (raw score)) from ~~the~~ bowler scores ~~table~~ where ~~the~~ bowler scores ~~table~~ bowler ID ~~is equal to~~ = ~~the~~ bowlers ~~table~~ bowler ID)

SQL

```
UPDATE Bowlers SET Bowlers.BowlerTotalPins =
    (SELECT SUM(RawScore)
    FROM Bowler_Scores
    WHERE Bowler_Scores.BowlerID =
        Bowlers.BowlerID),
     Bowlers.BowlerGamesBowled =
    (SELECT COUNT(Bowler_Scores.RawScore)
    FROM Bowler_Scores
    WHERE Bowler_Scores.BowlerID =
        Bowlers.BowlerID),
     Bowlers.BowlerCurrentAverage =
    (SELECT ROUND(AVG(Bowler_Scores.RawScore), 0)
    FROM Bowler_Scores
    WHERE Bowler_Scores.BowlerID =
        Bowlers.BowlerID),
     Bowlers.BowlerCurrentHcp =
    (SELECT ROUND(0.9 *
        (200 - ROUND(AVG(Bowler_Scores.RawScore),
        0)), 0)
    FROM Bowler_Scores
    WHERE Bowler_Scores.BowlerID =
        Bowlers.BowlerID)
```

Bowlers Table Before Executing the UPDATE Query – CH15_Calc_Bowler_Pins_Avg_Hcp_Query (34 rows)

Bowler ID	Bowler Total Pins	New Bowler Total Pins	Bowler Games Bowled	New Bowler Games Bowled	Bowler Current Average	New Bowler Current Average	Bowler Current Hcp	New Bowler Current Hcp
1	5790	6242	39	42	148	149	47	46
2	6152	6581	39	42	158	157	38	39
3	6435	6956	39	42	165	166	32	31
4	5534	5963	39	42	142	142	52	52
5	5819	6269	39	42	149	149	46	46
6	6150	6654	39	42	158	158	38	38

Bowler ID	Bowler Total Pins	New Bowler Total Pins	Bowler Games Bowled	New Bowler Games Bowled	Bowler Current Average	New Bowler Current Average	Bowler Current Hcp	New Bowler Current Hcp
7	6607	7042	39	42	169	168	28	29
8	5558	5983	39	42	143	142	51	52
9	5874	6319	39	42	151	150	44	45
10	6184	6702	39	42	159	160	37	36

<< more rows here >>

Bowlers Table After Executing CH15_Calc_Bowler_Pins_Avg_Hcp (34 rows changed)

BowlerID	<<other columns>>	Bowler TotalPins	Bowler GamesBowled	Bowler CurrentAverage	Bowler CurrentHcp
1	…	6242	42	149	46
2	…	6581	42	157	39
3	…	6956	42	166	31
4	…	5963	42	142	52
5	…	6269	42	149	46
6	…	6654	42	158	38
7	…	7042	42	168	29
8	…	5983	42	142	52
9	…	6319	42	150	45
10	…	6702	42	160	36

<< more rows here >>

❖ **Note** Because Microsoft Access does not support using subqueries with aggregate functions, you'll find this query solved as a series of calls to built-in functions. Also, if you use the SQL shown above, you will get a Null result for the last two bowlers who haven't bowled any games. In all four sample databases, I avoid the Null and substitute a 0 value using functions available in each database system. In Chapter 19, I'll show you how to avoid this problem using CASE.

"Change the tournament location to 'Oasis Lanes' for all tournaments originally scheduled at 'Sports World Lanes.'"

Restated, the problem is as follows:

"Modify the tournaments table by changing the tournament location to 'Oasis Lanes' for all tournaments originally scheduled at 'Sports World Lanes.'"

Translation/ Clean Up	Update ~~the~~ tournaments ~~table by~~ ~~setting the~~ tourney location ~~equal to~~ = 'Oasis Lanes' where ~~the original~~ tourney location ~~is equal to~~ = 'Sports World Lanes'
SQL	UPDATE Tournaments SET TourneyLocation = 'Oasis Lanes' WHERE TourneyLocation = 'Sports World Lanes'

Tournaments Table Before Executing the UPDATE Query – CH15_Change_Tourney_Location_Query (3 rows)

TourneyID	TourneyLocation	NewTourneyLocation
5	Sports World Lanes	Oasis Lanes
12	Sports World Lanes	Oasis Lanes
18	Sports World Lanes	Oasis Lanes

Tournaments Table After Executing CH15_Change_Tourney_Location (3 rows changed)

TourneyID	TourneyDate	TourneyLocation
	<< more rows here >>	
5	2017-10-02	Oasis Lanes
	<< more rows here >>	
12	2017-11-20	Oasis Lanes
	<< more rows here >>	
18	2018-08-02	Oasis Lanes
19	2018-08-09	Imperial Lanes
20	2018-08-16	Totem Lanes

Summary

I started the chapter with a brief discussion about the UPDATE statement used to change data in tables rather than to fetch data. I introduced the syntax of the UPDATE statement and explained a simple example to update one column in all the rows in a table using an expression.

Next, I showed an example of how to use the WHERE clause to filter the rows you are updating. I also showed you how to construct a SELECT query first to verify that you'll be updating the correct rows, and I showed you how to map the clauses in your SELECT query into the UPDATE statement you need. Next, I explained the importance of transactions and how you can use them to protect against errors or to ensure that either all changes or no changes are made to your tables. I continued my discussion by showing you how to update multiple columns in a table with a single UPDATE query.

Then I entered the realm of using subqueries in your UPDATE queries. I explained how to use a subquery to create a more complex filter in your WHERE clause. Finally, I showed you how to use a subquery to generate a new value to assign to a column in your SET clause. The rest of the chapter provided examples of how to build UPDATE queries.

The following section presents several problems that you can work out on your own.

Problems for You to Solve

Below, I show you the request statement and the name of the solution query in the sample databases. If you want some practice, you can work out the SQL you need for each request and then check your answer with the query I saved in the samples. Don't worry if your syntax doesn't exactly match the syntax of the queries I saved—as long as your result is the same.

Sales Orders Database

1. *"Apply a 5 percent discount to all orders for customers who purchased more than $50,000 in the month of October 2017."*

   (Hint: You need a subquery within a subquery to fetch the order numbers for all orders where the customer ID of the order is in the set of customers who ordered more than $50,000 in the month of October.)

   You can find the solution in CH15_Give_Discount_To_Good_October_Customers (639 rows changed). Be sure to run CH15_Update_Order_Totals_Subquery to correct the totals in the Orders table after executing this query.

2. *"Set the retail price of accessories (category = 1) to the wholesale price of the highest-priced vendor plus 35 percent."*

   (Hint: See CH15_Adjust_Bike_Retail_Price in the Sample Statements for the technique.)

   You can find the solution in CH15_Adjust_Accessory_Retail_Price (11 rows changed).

Entertainment Agency Database

1. *"Apply a 2 percent discount to all engagements for customers who booked more than $3,000 worth of business in the month of October 2017."*

   (Hint: Use an aggregate subquery to find those customers with engagements in October HAVING total bookings greater than $3,000.)

   You can find the solution in CH15_Discount_Good_Customers_October (34 rows changed).

2. *"Add 0.5 percent to the commission rate of agents who have sold more than $20,000 in engagements."*

   (Hint: Use an aggregate subquery to find those agents HAVING total bookings greater than $20,000.)

   You can find the solution in CH15_Reward_Good_Agents (3 rows changed).

School Scheduling Database

1. *"Increase the salary of full-time tenured staff by 5 percent."*

   (Hint: Use a subquery in the WHERE clause to find matching staff IDs in the faculty table that have a status of full-time and a tenured field value of true, that is, 1 or –1, depending on your database system.)

   You can find the solution in CH15_Give_FullTime_Tenured_Raise (21 rows changed).

2. *"For all staff in zip codes 98270 and 98271, change the area code to 360."*

   You can find the solution in CH15_Fix_Staff_AreaCode (2 rows changed).

Bowling League Database

1. *"Change the name of the 'Huckleberrys' bowling team to 'Manta Rays.'"*

   You can find the solution in CH15_Change_Huckleberry_Name (1 row changed).

2. *"Update the city and state for all bowlers by looking up the names by ZIP Code."*

   (Hint: Use a subquery to fetch the matching city name and another subquery to fetch the matching state from the WAZips table.)

   You can find the solution in CH15_Update_Bowler_City_State (6 rows changed).

16

Inserting Sets of Data

*"I was brought up to believe that the only thing worth
doing was to add to the sum of accurate information in the world."*

—MARGARET MEADE

Topics Covered in This Chapter

What Is an INSERT?

The INSERT Statement

Uses for INSERT

Sample Statements

Summary

Problems for You to Solve

To this point, you have learned how to fetch information from your tables in creative ways. In the previous chapter, you learned how to modify existing data by using the UPDATE statement. But how do you put data into your tables to begin with? The data certainly doesn't appear magically on its own! You'll learn the answer in this chapter—how to use the INSERT statement to add rows into your tables.

What Is an INSERT?

Most commercial database systems come with one or more graphical interface programs that let you work with data displayed on your screen. For example, you can open any table in Microsoft Office Access by simply finding the table object and opening it. Access displays the data in something it calls a datasheet that looks like a grid with columns and rows. You scroll to the end of the display to find a blank row, type data into the columns on that row, and then move to another row to insert a new row in your table. You can also use Access to work with tables in Microsoft SQL Server in the same manner. You can do something similar using the MySQL query browser, and Microsoft's SQL Server, IBM's DB2, and Oracle Corporation's Oracle database provide equivalent tools. Also, you can purchase graphical design tools for PostgreSQL from third-party providers such as SQL Maestro.

But what's really happening when you type in new data and tell the system to save it? The graphical interface tools actually execute a command using SQL to add the data you just entered to your table. The SQL statement that these programs use is INSERT. If you browse through the sample files, you can find scripts that I generated to load the data into the sample databases. For example, the first few lines of the 01 EntertainmentAgencyData.SQL file look like this:

```
USE EntertainmentAgencyExample;
INSERT INTO Customers
    (CustomerID, CustFirstName, CustLastName, CustStreetAddress,
    CustCity, CustState, CustZipCode, CustPhoneNumber)
    VALUES (10001, 'Doris', 'Hartwig', '4726 - 11th Ave. N.E. ',
    'Seattle' 'WA', '98105', '555-2671');
INSERT INTO Customers
    (CustomerID, CustFirstName, CustLastName, CustStreetAddress,
    CustCity, CustState, CustZipCode, CustPhoneNumber)
    VALUES (10002, 'Deb', 'Waldal', '908 W. Capital Way',
    'Tacoma', 'WA', '98413', '555-2496');
```

The first command (USE) tells the database system which database to use for the following commands. Each INSERT statement tells the database system to add exactly one row to a specific table. This might seem like a tedious process to load thousands of records into a sample database, but you'll find that each script to load data actually runs in just a few seconds. For some of the simpler tables, I used the graphical user interface to directly type in the data. To generate data for other sample tables, I wrote some application code to create and execute the INSERT statements. If you're familiar with Microsoft Office Access and Visual Basic, you can find code to generate sample data in the zfrmSellProducts form in the Sales Orders sample database.

If you write any applications—whether for desktop systems or for the Web—you'll create code to generate and execute the appropriate INSERT statement when your user enters new data. Most of the time, you'll use the INSERT . . . VALUES version to add the data. In this chapter, you'll also learn about a second form of the INSERT statement that makes it easy to copy data from one table to another.

> ❖ **Note** You can find all the sample statements and solutions in the "modify" version of the respective sample databases—SalesOrdersModify, EntertainmentAgencyModify, SchoolScheduling-Modify, and BowlingLeagueModify.

The INSERT Statement

SQL has two main versions of the INSERT statement. In the first version, you include the VALUES keyword and list the values that you want your database system to add as a single new row in a specified target table. The second version lets you use a SELECT clause to fetch data from a table to insert into your target table. Let's take a look at the VALUES version first.

Inserting Values

Although SQL is primarily designed to work with sets of data, much of the time you'll use INSERT to add a single row of data to one of your tables. The simplest way to add one row to a table is to use the INSERT statement with the VALUES clause. Figure 16-1 shows the diagram for this statement.

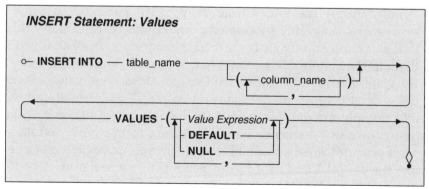

Figure 16-1 *The syntax diagram of the INSERT statement using the VALUES clause*

As you can see, you begin the statement with the INSERT INTO keywords. Next, specify the name of the table where you want to add the row. If you're going to supply values for all the columns in the sequence in which those columns are defined in the table, you can omit the column name list. (For example, I could have omitted specifying the column name list in the INSERT statements I use to load the sample data because I'm supplying a value for every column.) However, even when you plan to supply values for all columns, I recommend that you include the list of columns for which you intend to specify a data value. If you don't do that, your query will break if someone later adds a column to the table definition or changes the sequence of columns in the table. You specify the column name list by entering a left parenthesis, the column names separated by commas if you specify more than one, and a closing right parenthesis.

> ❖ **Note** The SQL Standard indicates that table_name can also be a view name, but the view must be "updatable and insertable." Many database systems support inserting rows into views, and each database system has its own rules about what constitutes an updatable or insertable view.
>
> In most cases, a view isn't insertable if you use the DISTINCT keyword or if one of the output columns is the result of an expression or an aggregate function. Some database systems also support defining the view using JOIN and ON keywords in place of table_name. Consult your database system documentation for details. In this chapter, I'll exclusively use a single table as the target for each INSERT statement.

Finally, specify the VALUES keyword, a left parenthesis, a list of value expressions separated by commas, and a closing right parenthesis. Note that you must specify each value in the same sequence that you specified them in the column name list. That is, the first value expression supplies the value for the first column in the list, the second value expression for the second column in the list, and so on. If you're including values for all columns and did not include the column name list, your values must be in the same sequence as the columns in the table definition. If you want your database system to use the default value defined for a column, use the DEFAULT keyword. (But you'll get an error if no default value is defined.) To supply the Null value, use the NULL keyword. (But you'll get an error if the column is defined to not allow Null values.)

Remember from earlier chapters that a value expression can be quite complex and can even include a subquery to fetch a single value from the target table or another table. For review, Figure 16-2 shows the diagram of a value expression.

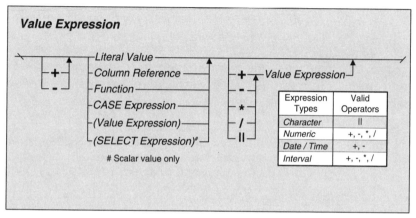

Figure 16-2 *Use a value expression, whose syntax is shown here, in a VALUES clause to specify the value of each column in your target table*

> ❖ **Note** Not all database systems allow you to use a SELECT expression or a CASE expression in the VALUES clause of an INSERT statement. Check your database documentation for details.

Let's look at how to add one row to the Employees table in the Sales Orders sample database. As with all queries, you should know the structure of the table. Figure 16-3 shows the design of the Employees table.

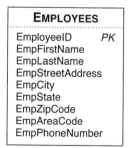

Figure 16-3 *The Employees table in the Sales Orders sample database*

Now let's formulate a request.

> ❖ **Note** Throughout this chapter, I use the "Request/Translation/ Clean Up/SQL" technique introduced in Chapter 4, "Creating a Simple Query."

"Add new employee Susan Metters at 16547 NE 132nd St, Woodinville, WA 98072, with area code 425 and phone number 555-7825."

You typically won't list the columns you need in your original request, but keep them in mind as you go to the Translation step. Here's how you might translate the request to add a new employee row:

Translation	Insert into the employees table in the columns first name, last name, street address, city, state, ZIP Code, area code, and phone number the values Susan, Metters, 16547 NE 132nd St, Woodinville, WA, 98072, 425, and 555-7825
Clean Up	Insert into ~~the~~ employees ~~table in the columns~~ (first name, last name, street address, city, state, ZIP Code, area code, ~~and~~ phone number) ~~the~~ values ('Susan', 'Metters', '16547 NE 132nd St', 'Woodinville', 'WA', '98072', 425, ~~and~~ '555-7825')

SQL	INSERT INTO Employees
	    (EmpFirstName, EmpLastName,
	    EmpStreetAddress, EmpCity, EmpState,
	    EmpZipCode, EmpAreaCode, EmpPhoneNumber)
	VALUES ('Susan', 'Metters',
	    '16547 NE 132nd St', 'Woodinville', 'WA',
	    '98072', 425, '555-7825')

You can find this query saved as CH16_Add_Employee in the modify version of the Sales Orders sample database.

Are you wondering why I didn't include the primary key (EmployeeID) of the Employees table? If so, read on!

Generating the Next Primary Key Value

In the example query in the previous section, I didn't include the primary key—EmployeeID. In all database systems, the primary key must have a value. Won't this query fail?

The answer is no, but only because I took advantage of a special feature that you'll find in nearly all commercial database implementations. When you're not concerned about the value of the primary key in a table—except that the value must be unique—you can usually define the primary key using a special data type that the database system will increment for you every time you insert a new row. In Microsoft Access, use the data type called AutoNumber. (The data type is actually an integer with special attributes.) In Microsoft SQL Server and IBM DB2, use the Identity data type (also an integer), and in PostgreSQL, use the serial data type (also an integer). For MySQL, use an integer with the special AUTO_INCREMENT attribute. The SQL syntax used in my example works in all three types of sample databases because I used this special feature for the primary key fields in nearly all the sample tables in the modify versions.

The Oracle database system is a bit different. Rather than provide a special data type, Oracle lets you define a Sequence pseudo-column, and you reference the NEXTVAL property of the pseudo-column every time you need a unique value for a new row. In Oracle, let's assume you previously defined a pseudo-column called EmpID. You can write your SQL like this:

```
SQL            INSERT INTO Employees (EmployeeID, EmpFirstName,
                  EmpLastName, EmpStreetAddress, EmpCity,
                  EmpState, EmpZipCode, EmpAreaCode,
                  EmpPhoneNumber)
               VALUES (EmpID.NEXTVAL, 'Susan', 'Metters',
                  '16547 NE 132nd St', 'Woodinville', 'WA',
                  '98072', 425, '555-7825')
```

Note that I'm now providing a value for each column in the table in the sequence that the columns are defined in the table definition. I could eliminate the optional column name list and write the SQL like this:

```
SQL            INSERT INTO Employees
               VALUES (EmpID.NEXTVAL, 'Susan', 'Metters',
                  '16547 NE 132nd St', 'Woodinville', 'WA',
                  '98072', 425, '555-7825')
```

As noted earlier, I don't recommend that you omit the column name list because your query will fail if your database administrator adds a column or changes the sequence of the column definitions. I present this option only for completeness.

If you really have your thinking cap on, you might wonder whether you could just as easily generate the next value by using a subquery expression. The SQL standard certainly supports this, and your SQL might look like this:

SQL
```
INSERT INTO Employees (EmployeeID, EmpFirstName,
    EmpLastName, EmpStreetAddress, EmpCity,
    EmpState, EmpZipCode, EmpAreaCode,
    EmpPhoneNumber)
VALUES ((SELECT MAX(EmployeeID)
        FROM Employees) + 1, 'Susan', 'Metters',
    '16547 NE 132nd St', 'Woodinville', 'WA',
    '98072', 425, '555-7825')
```

Unfortunately, several of the major database systems do not yet support a subquery in a VALUES clause. Check your database documentation for details.

> ❖ **Note** If you want to insert a value into an IDENTITY column in Microsoft SQL Server, you must first execute this command:
>
> ```
> SET IDENTITY_INSERT <table_name> ON;
> ```
>
> Be sure to set the option to OFF after you have finished the INSERT.
>
> When you insert your own values into an auto-increment column in Microsoft Access, Microsoft SQL Server, or MySQL, those database systems automatically update the "next" value when appropriate; however, PostgreSQL does not. After you insert rows providing your own number for a SERIAL column in PostgreSQL, you must reset the last value like this:
>
> ```
> SELECT setval('tablename_serialcolname_seq', <number>)
> ```
>
> In this command, tablename is the name of your table, serialcolname is the name of the SERIAL column in that table, and <number> is the last value you supplied.

Inserting Data by Using SELECT

Because I've focused so far on inserting only a single row at a time, you're probably wondering why I named this chapter "Inserting Sets of Data." In one sense, values for multiple columns in one row is a set of data, but you probably think of a set as consisting of multiple rows. Never fear—you can also insert a set of rows by using a SELECT expression in place of the VALUES clause. Because a SELECT expression fetches rows from one or more tables, you can think of an INSERT statement with SELECT as a powerful way to copy data. Figure 16-4 shows the syntax diagram for an INSERT statement using a SELECT expression.

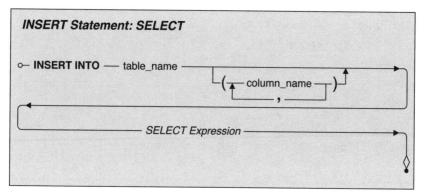

Figure 16-4 *The syntax diagram of the INSERT statement using a SELECT expression*

Notice that this variant of the INSERT statement begins in the same way. Following the INSERT INTO keywords, specify the name of the table that is the target of this insert. If your SELECT expression returns the same number of columns and in the same order as in your target table, you can omit the optional column name list. But as I recommended earlier, even when you plan to supply values for all columns, I recommend that you include the list of columns for which you intend to specify a data value. If you don't do that, your query will break if someone later adds a column to the table definition or changes the sequence of columns in the table.

If you examine the SQL diagrams in Appendix A, "SQL Standard Diagrams," you'll find that a SELECT expression is simply a SELECT statement that is optionally combined with additional SELECT statements using the UNION, INTERSECT, or EXCEPT operations. (See Chapter 7,

"Thinking in Sets," for an explanation of these three operations and Chapter 10, "UNIONs," for a detailed description of UNION.) Figure 16-5 shows the syntax diagram for a SELECT statement.

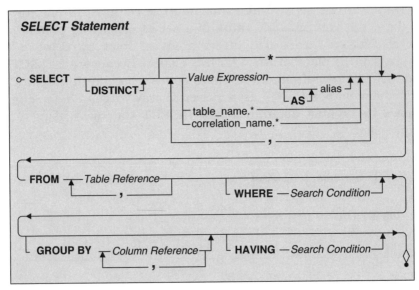

Figure 16-5 *The syntax diagram of a SELECT statement*

You might recall from earlier chapters that a table reference can be a single table name, a list of tables separated by commas, or a complex JOIN of two or more tables. A search condition can be a simple comparison of a column to a value; a more complex test using BETWEEN, IN, LIKE, or NULL; or a very complex predicate using subqueries. In short, you have all the power of SELECT queries that you've learned about in earlier chapters at your disposal to specify the set of rows that you want to copy to a table.

Let's dig in and work through some examples that you can solve using INSERT with a SELECT expression. Here's a simple request that requires copying the data from a row in one table into another table:

> *"We just hired customer David Smith. Copy to the Employees table all the details for David Smith from the Customers table."*

As when building any query, you need to be familiar with the structure of the tables involved. Figure 16-6 shows the design of the two tables.

CUSTOMERS	
CustomerID	*PK*
CustFirstName	
CustLastName	
CustStreetAddress	
CustCity	
CustState	
CustZipCode	
CustAreaCode	
CustPhoneNumber	

EMPLOYEES	
EmployeeID	*PK*
EmpFirstName	
EmpLastName	
EmpStreetAddress	
EmpCity	
EmpState	
EmpZipCode	
EmpAreaCode	
EmpPhoneNumber	

Figure 16-6 *The Customers and Employees tables in the Sales Orders sample database*

Let's restate the request so that it's easier to translate into an INSERT query:

"Copy to the Employees table the relevant columns in the Customers table for customer David Smith."

Translation	Insert into the employees table in the columns first name, last name, street address, city, state, ZIP code, area code, and phone number the selection of the first name, last name, street address, city, state, ZIP code, area code, and phone number columns from the customers table where the customer first name is 'David' and the customer last name is 'Smith'
Clean Up	Insert into ~~the~~ employees ~~table in the columns~~ (first name, last name, street address, city, state, ZIP code, area code, ~~and~~ phone number) ~~the~~ (~~selection of the~~ first name, last name, street address, city, state, ZIP code, area code, ~~and~~ phone number ~~columns~~ from ~~the~~ customers ~~table~~ where ~~the~~ customer first name ~~is~~ = 'David' and ~~the~~ customer last name ~~is~~ = 'Smith')

SQL	INSERT INTO Employees
	    (EmpFirstName, EmpLastName, EmpStreetAddress,
	        EmpCity, EmpState, EmpZipCode,
	        EmpAreaCode, EmpPhoneNumber)
	    SELECT Customers.CustFirstName,
	        Customers.CustLastName,
	        Customers.CustStreetAddress,
	        Customers.CustCity,
	        Customers.CustState, Customers.CustZipCode,
	        Customers.CustAreaCode,
	        Customers.CustPhoneNumber

```
                    FROM Customers
                    WHERE (Customers.CustFirstName = 'David')
                    AND (Customers.CustLastName = 'Smith')
```

Notice that I did not include the EmployeeID column because I'm depending on the database system to generate the next unique value for the new row(s) being inserted. You can find this query saved as CH16_Copy_Customer_To_Employee in the modified version of the Sales Orders sample database.

Because there's only one customer named David Smith, this query copies exactly one row to the Employees table. This still isn't a set of rows, but you can see how easy it is to use a SELECT expression to fetch the values you need to insert when they're available in another table.

Let's move on to a problem that could potentially insert hundreds of rows. In every active database application that collects new information over time, you might want to design a feature that allows the user to archive or copy to a backup table all transactions that occurred at some point in the past. The idea is that you don't want old historical data slowing down the processing of new data by making your application wade through thousands of rows that represent transactions that occurred long ago.

So, you might want to write an INSERT statement that copies transactions that happened earlier than a specific date into a table reserved for historical data. (In the next chapter, I'll show you how to delete the copied or archived transactions from the active table.) A typical request might look like this:

"Archive all engagements earlier than January 1, 2018."

In this particular case, both the Engagements table and the Engagements_Archive table have the same design, as shown in Figure 16-7.

ENGAGEMENTS		**ENGAGEMENTS_ARCHIVE**	
EngagementNumber	*PK*	EngagementNumber	*PK*
StartDate		StartDate	
EndDate		EndDate	
StartTime		StartTime	
StopTime		StopTime	
ContractPrice		ContractPrice	
CustomerID	*FK*	CustomerID	
AgentID	*FK*	AgentID	
EntertainerID	*FK*	EntertainerID	

Figure 16-7 *The Engagements and Engagements_Archive tables in the Entertainment Agency sample database*

This is one case where you can safely leave out the column name list. The translation is very easy, and it looks like this:

Translation	Insert into the engagements archive table the selection of all columns from the engagements table where the engagement end date is earlier than January 1, 2018
Clean Up	Insert into ~~the~~ engagements archive ~~table~~ ~~the~~ selection ~~of all columns~~ * from ~~the~~ engagements ~~table~~ where ~~the~~ engagement end date ~~is earlier than~~ < ~~January 1, 2018~~ '2018-01-01'

SQL	INSERT INTO Engagements_Archive
	
	   SELECT Engagements.*
	
	   FROM Engagements
	
	   WHERE Engagements.EndDate
	
	     < '2018-01-01'

That's almost too easy, right? But remember that I recommended that you always explicitly list the column names. If you do that, your query will still run even if someone adds a new column to either table or changes the sequence of the columns. It's a bit more effort, but I recommend writing your SQL for this problem to look like this:

SQL	INSERT INTO Engagements_Archive
	
	  (EngagementNumber, StartDate, EndDate,
	
	   StartTime, StopTime, ContractPrice,
	
	   CustomerID, AgentID, EntertainerID)
	
	  SELECT Engagements.EngagementNumber,
	
	    Engagements.StartDate, Engagements.EndDate,
	
	    Engagements.StartTime, Engagements.StopTime,
	
	    Engagements.ContractPrice,
	
	    Engagements.CustomerID,
	
	    Engagements.AgentID,
	
	  Engagements.EntertainerID FROM Engagements
	
	   WHERE Engagements.EndDate < '2018-01-01'

You'll find this query saved as CH16_Archive_Engagements in the modify version of the Entertainment Agency sample database.

Now let's look at a creative way to use a SELECT expression. Consider the following request:

> *"Add a new product named 'Hot Dog Spinner' with a retail price of $895 in the Bikes category."*

You can see the tables you need in Figure 16-8.

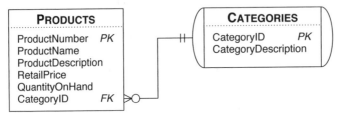

Figure 16-8 *The Products table and the related Categories table in the Sales Orders database*

Your target table is clearly the Products table, but that table requires a numeric value in the CategoryID field. The request says "in the Bikes category," so how do you suppose you can find the related CategoryID that you need for the Products table? Use a SELECT expression! You want to supply values also for the ProductName and RetailPrice columns, but remember that a SELECT statement can include literal values for some or all output columns. So you can fetch the related category ID from the Categories table and supply the other values you intend to insert as literal values. Let's restate the request and then solve it. (You can find this query saved as CH16_Add_Product in the sample Sales Orders Modify database.)

> *"Add a row to the products table using the values 'Hot Dog Spinner' for the product name, $895 for the retail price, and the category ID from the categories table for the category 'Bikes.'"*

Translation	Insert into the products table in the columns product name, retail price, and category ID the selection of 'Hot Dog Spinner' as the product name, 895 as the retail price, and category ID from the categories table where the category description is equal to 'Bikes'
Clean Up	Insert into ~~the~~ products ~~table in the columns~~ (product name, retail price, ~~and~~ category ID) ~~the selection of~~ 'Hot Dog Spinner' as ~~the~~ product name, 895 as ~~the~~ retail price, ~~and~~ category ID from ~~the~~ categories ~~table~~ where ~~the~~ category description ~~is equal to~~ = 'Bikes'

SQL	INSERT INTO Products
	(ProductName, RetailPrice, CategoryID)
	SELECT 'Hot Dog Spinner' AS ProductName,
	895 AS RetailPrice, CategoryID
	FROM Categories
	WHERE CategoryDescription = 'Bikes'

You might think using a SELECT expression is useful only for copying entire rows, but as you have just seen, it's also useful to fetch one or more discrete values from a table that can supply the values you need. You'll find some interesting applications of this technique in the "Sample Statements" section later in this chapter.

Uses for INSERT

At this point, you should have a good understanding of how to insert one or more rows in a table using either a simple VALUES clause or a SELECT expression. The best way to give you an idea of the wide range of uses for the INSERT statement is to list some problems you can solve with this statement and then present a set of examples in the "Sample Statements" section. Here's just a small list of the types of problems you can solve with INSERT:

> "*Create a new bowler record for Matthew Patterson by copying the record for Neil Patterson.*"

> "*In the Entertainment database, create a new customer record for Kendra Hernandez at 457 211th St NE, Bothell, WA 98200, with a phone number of 555-3945.*"

> "*In the Sales Order database, create a new customer record for Mary Baker at 7834 W 32nd Ct, Bothell, WA 98011, with area code 425 and phone number 555-9876.*"

> "*Create a new subject category called 'Italian' with a subject code of 'ITA' in the Humanities department.*"

> "*Add a new team called the 'Aardvarks' with no captain assigned.*"

> "*Add a new engagement for customer Matt Berg booking entertainer Jazz Persuasion from 7 PM to 11 PM on August 15 and 16, 2018, that was booked by agent Karen Smith.*"

"Add a new vendor named Hot Dog Bikes at 1234 Main Street, Chicago, IL 60620, with phone number (773) 555-6543, fax number (773) 555-6542, website address http://www.hotdogbikes.com/, and e-mail address Sales@hotdogbikes.com."

"Add a new class for subject ID 4 (Intermediate Accounting) to be taught in classroom 3315 for five credits starting on January 16, 2018, at 3:00 PM for 80 minutes on Tuesdays and Thursdays."

"Archive the tournament, tourney match, match game, and bowler scores for all matches played in 2017."

"Add 'New Age' to the list of musical styles."

"Archive all orders and order details for orders placed before January 1, 2018."

"Angel Kennedy wants to register as a student. Her husband is already enrolled. Create a new student record for Angel using the information from John's record."

"Duplicate all the tournaments and tourney matches played in 2017 for the same week in 2019."

"Agent Marianne Wier would like to book some entertainers, so create a new customer record by copying relevant fields from the agents table."

"Customer Liz Keyser wants to order again the products ordered on December 11, 2017. Use June 12, 2018, as the order date and June 15, 2018, as the shipped date."

"Staff member Tim Smith wants to enroll as a student. Create a new student record from Tim's staff record."

"Customer Doris Hartwig would like to rebook the entertainers she hired to play on December 1, 2017, for August 1, 2018."

"Customer Angel Kennedy wants to order again all the products ordered during the month of November 2017. Use June 15, 2018, as the order date and June 18, 2018, as the shipped date."

Sample Statements

You now know the mechanics of constructing INSERT queries. Let's look at a set of samples, all of which request that one or more rows be added to a table. These examples come from four of the sample databases.

❖ **Caution** Because the sample queries you'll find in the modified versions of the sample databases change your data, be aware that some of the queries will work as expected only once. For example, after you run an INSERT query to archive orders using a WHERE clause to find the rows you want to copy, subsequent attempts to archive the data again will fail because you will be inserting duplicate Primary Key values in the archive tables. Consider restoring the databases from the sample scripts or a backup copy if you want to work through the problems again.

I've also included a view of the data that the sample INSERT statement should add to the target table and a count of the number of rows that should be added. The name that appears immediately before the count of rows inserted is the name I gave each query in the sample data on the companion website for the book. Also, I created a companion SELECT query (stored as a View in MySQL and Microsoft SQL Server) for each INSERT query that you can use to see exactly what will be added. The name of the companion query is the name of the original query with _Query appended to the name. I stored each query in the appropriate sample database (as indicated within the example) and prefixed the names of the queries relevant to this chapter with "CH16." You can find the sample data on the companion website for this book, www.informit.com/title/9780134858333. You can follow the instructions in the Introduction of this book to load the samples onto your computer and try them.

❖ **Note** Remember that all the column names and table names used in these examples are drawn from the sample database structures shown in Appendix B, "Schema for the Sample Databases." To simplify the process, I have combined the Translation and Clean Up steps for all the examples. These samples assume you have thoroughly studied and understood the concepts covered in previous chapters.

Sales Orders Database

"Add a new vendor named Hot Dog Bikes at 1234 Main Street, Chicago, IL 60620, with phone number (773) 555-6543, fax number (773) 555-6542, Web site address http://www.hotdogbikes.com/, and e-mail address Sales@hotdogbikes.com."

Translation/ Clean Up	Insert into ~~the~~ vendors ~~table in the columns~~ (VendName, VendStreetAddress, VendCity, VendState, VendZipCode, VendPhoneNumber, VendFaxNumber, VendWebPage, ~~and~~ VendEMailAddress) ~~the~~ values ('Hot Dog Bikes', '1234 Main Street', 'Chicago', 'IL', '60620', '(773) 555-6543', '(773) 555-6542', 'http://www.hotdogbikes.com/', ~~and~~ 'Sales@ hotdogbikes.com')
SQL	```INSERT INTO Vendors
(VendName, VendStreetAddress, VendCity,
VendState, VendZipCode, VendPhoneNumber,
VendFaxNumber, VendWebPage,
VendEMailAddress)
VALUES ('Hot Dog Bikes', '1234 Main Street',
'Chicago', 'IL', '60620', '(773) 555-6543',
'(773) 555-6542', 'http://www.hotdogbikes.com/',
'Sales@hotdogbikes.com')```

Row Inserted into the Vendors Table by CH16_Add_Vendor (1 row added)

Vend Name	Vend Street Address	Vend City	Vend State	Vend ZipCode	Vend Phone Number	Vend Fax Number	Vend Web Page	Vend EMail Address
Hot Dog Bikes	1234 Main Street	Chicago	IL	60620	(773) 555-6543	(773) 555-6542	http://www .hotdogbikes .com/	Sales@ hotdog-bikes.com

"Archive all orders and order details for orders placed before January 1, 2018."

❖ **Note** To archive all the information about an order, you need to copy data from both the Orders and the Order_Details tables, so you need two queries. Be sure to run the INSERT query for the orders first because rows in the Orders_Details_Archive table have foreign keys in the OrderID column that point to the same column in the Orders_ Archive table.

If your system supports transactions (see the discussion in Chapter 15, "Updating Sets of Data"), you can start a transaction, run the query to copy orders followed by the query to copy order details, and then commit both INSERT actions if both ran with no errors. If the second query causes an error, you can roll back the transaction, which will ensure that none of the orders rows are copied. There's no point in copying only half the information about orders.

Because you're archiving rows by date, the query to archive order details must use a subquery filter for all order ID values that appear in the Orders table before the specified date.

Translation 1/ Clean Up	Insert into ~~the~~ orders archive ~~table the~~ selection ~~of~~ order number, order date, ship date, customer ID, employee ID, ~~and~~ order total from ~~the~~ orders ~~table~~ where ~~the~~ order date ~~is earlier than~~ < '2018-01-01'

SQL	INSERT INTO Orders_Archive
	    SELECT OrderNumber, OrderDate, ShipDate,
	        CustomerID, EmployeeID, OrderTotal
	    FROM Orders
	    WHERE OrderDate < '2018-01-01'

Rows Inserted into the Orders_Archive Table by CH16_Archive_2017_Orders (594 rows added)

Order Number	OrderDate	ShipDate	CustomerID	EmployeeID	OrderTotal
1	2017-09-02	2017-09-05	1018	707	$12,751.85
2	2017-09-02	2017-09-04	1001	703	$816.00
3	2017-09-02	2017-09-05	1002	707	$11,912.45
4	2017-09-02	2017-09-04	1009	703	$6,601.73
5	2017-09-02	2017-09-02	1024	708	$5,544.75
6	2017-09-02	2017-09-06	1014	702	$9,820.29
7	2017-09-02	2017-09-05	1001	708	$467.85
8	2017-09-02	2017-09-02	1003	703	$1,492.60
9	2017-09-02	2017-09-05	1007	708	$69.00
10	2017-09-02	2017-09-05	1012	701	$2,607.00

<< more rows here >>

Translation 2/ Clean Up	Insert into ~~the~~ order details archive ~~table the~~ selection of order number, product number, quoted price, ~~and~~ quantity ordered from ~~the~~ order details ~~table~~ where ~~the~~ order number ~~is~~ in ~~the~~ (selection ~~of the~~ order number from ~~the~~ orders ~~table~~ where ~~the~~ order date ~~is earlier than~~ < '2018-01-01')

SQL	INSERT INTO Order_Details_Archive
	    SELECT OrderNumber, ProductNumber,
	        QuotedPrice, QuantityOrdered
	  FROM Order_Details
	  WHERE Order_Details.OrderNumber IN
	    (SELECT OrderNumber
	    FROM Orders
	    WHERE Orders.OrderDate < '2018-01-01')

Rows Inserted into the Order_Details_Archive Table by CH16_Archive_2017_Order_Details (2499 rows added)

OrderNumber	ProductNumber	QuotedPrice	QuantityOrdered
1	1	$1,200.00	2
1	6	$635.00	3
1	11	$1,650.00	4
1	16	$28.00	1
1	21	$55.00	3
1	26	$121.25	5
1	40	$174.60	6
2	27	$24.00	4
2	40	$180.00	4
3	1	$1,164.00	5

<< more rows here >>

❖ **Note** Neither query follows my recommendation to always include the column name list, but I wrote these two queries this way to show you examples where the column name list is not absolutely required.

Entertainment Agency Database

"Create a new customer record for Kendra Hernandez at 457 211th St NE, Bothell, WA 98200, with a phone number of 555-3945."

Translation/ Clean Up	Insert into ~~the~~ customers ~~table in the columns~~ (customer first name, customer last name, customer street address, customer city, customer state, customer ZIP Code, ~~and~~ customer phone number) ~~the~~ values ('Kendra', 'Hernandez', '457 211th St NE', 'Bothell', 'WA', '98200', ~~and~~ '555-3945')
SQL	``` INSERT INTO Customers (CustFirstName, CustLastName, CustStreetAddress, CustCity, CustState, CustZipCode, CustPhoneNumber) VALUES ('Kendra', 'Hernandez', '457 211th St NE', 'Bothell', 'WA', '98200', '555-3945') ```

Row Inserted into the Customers Table by CH16_Add_Customer (1 row added)

CustFirst Name	CustLast Name	CustStreet Address	Cust City	Cust State	Cust ZipCode	CustPhone Number
Kendra	Hernandez	457 211th St NE	Bothell	WA	98200	555-3945

"Add a new engagement for customer Matt Berg booking entertainer Jazz Persuasion from 7 PM to 11 PM on August 15 and 16, 2018, which was booked by agent Karen Smith."

❖ **Note** If you look at the Engagements table, you'll find that you need the customer ID for Matt Berg from the Customers table, the entertainer ID for Jazz Persuasion from the Entertainers table, and the agent ID for Karen Smith from the Agents table. You can fetch these values by using a SELECT expression.

Be careful that you include the three tables you need in the FROM clause with no JOIN criteria. Also, don't forget to calculate the contract price by using the price per day from the Entertainers table with a 15 percent markup. This technique works because there is only one customer named Matt Berg, only one agent named Karen Smith, and only one entertainment group called Jazz Persuasion. If there happens to be more than one agent or customer with these names, you'll get more than one row inserted into the Engagements table.

Translation/ Clean Up	Insert into ~~the~~ engagements ~~table into the~~ (customer ID, entertainer ID, agent ID, start date, end date, start time, end time, ~~and~~ contract price) ~~columns the~~ selection of customer ID, entertainer ID, agent ID, ~~and the values August 15, 2018~~ '2018-08-15', ~~August 16, 2018~~ '2018-08-16', ~~'07:00:00 p.m.'~~ '19:00:00', ~~'11:00:00 p.m.'~~ '23:00:00', ~~and the~~ (~~entertainer~~ price per day ~~times~~ * 2 ~~times~~ * 1.15) from ~~the~~ customers, entertainers, ~~and~~ agents ~~tables~~ where ~~the~~ customer first name ~~is~~ = 'Matt' and ~~the~~ customer last name ~~is~~ = 'Berg' and ~~the~~ entertainer stage name ~~is~~ = 'Jazz Persuasion' and ~~the~~ agent first name ~~is~~ = 'Karen' and ~~the~~ agent last name ~~is~~ = 'Smith'

SQL	`INSERT INTO Engagements`
	`    (CustomerID, EntertainerID, AgentID,`
	`    StartDate, EndDate,`
	`    StartTime, StopTime,`
	`    ContractPrice)`
	`SELECT Customers.CustomerID,`
	`    Entertainers.EntertainerID, Agents.AgentID,`
	`    '2018-08-15', '2018-08-16',`
	`    '19:00:00', '23:00:00',`
	`    ROUND(EntPricePerDay * 2 * 1.15, 0)`
	`FROM Customers, Entertainers, Agents`
	`WHERE (Customers.CustFirstName = 'Matt')`
	`    AND (Customers.CustLastName = 'Berg')`
	`    AND (Entertainers.EntStageName =`
	`            'Jazz Persuasion')`
	`    AND (Agents.AgtFirstName = 'Karen')`
	`    AND (Agents.AgtLastName = 'Smith')`

❖ **Note** You might have noticed that I used three tables with no JOIN in the FROM clause. When you do this, you get all rows from the first table combined with all rows from the second table and all rows from the third table—something called a *Cartesian* product. It works in this case because I am filtering out the specific customer, entertainer, and agent combination that I want, getting one row from each table, which results in one row returned by the SELECT. I'll go into more detail about using tables in this way in Chapter 20, "Using Unlinked Data and 'Driver' Tables."

Row Inserted into the Engagements Table by CH16_Add_Engagement (1 row added)

Customer ID	Entertainer ID	Agent ID	Start Date	End Date	Start Time	Stop Time	Contract Price
10006	1005	4	2018-08-15	2018-08-16	19:00:00	23:00:00	$288.00

School Scheduling Database

"Create a new subject category called 'Italian' with a subject code of 'ITA' in the Humanities department."

> ❖ **Note** You need the department ID for the Humanities department, so the solution requires a SELECT expression using the Departments table.

Translation/ Clean Up	Insert into ~~the~~ categories ~~table the~~ selection ~~of~~ 'ITA' as ~~the~~ category ID, 'Italian' as ~~the~~ category description, ~~and~~ department ID from ~~the~~ departments ~~table~~ where department name ~~is~~ = 'Humanities'
SQL	``` INSERT INTO Categories SELECT 'ITA' AS CategoryID, 'Italian' AS CategoryDescription, Departments.DepartmentID FROM Departments WHERE Departments.DeptName = 'Humanities' ```

Row Inserted into the Categories Table by CH16_Add_Category (1 row added)

CategoryID	CategoryDescription	DepartmentID
ITA	Italian	3

"Add a new class for subject ID 4 (Intermediate Accounting) to be taught in classroom 3315 for five credits starting on January 16, 2018, at 3:00 PM for 80 minutes on Tuesdays and Thursdays."

> ❖ **Note** You can assume that the default value for all schedule days is zero or false, so you need to include a true or 1 value only for Tuesday and Thursday.

Translation/ Clean Up	Insert into ~~the~~ classes ~~table into the columns~~ (subject ID, classroom ID, credits, start date, start time, duration, Tuesday schedule, ~~and~~ Thursday schedule) ~~the~~ values (4, 3315, 5, ~~January 16, 2018~~ '2018-01-16', ~~3 PM~~ '15:00:00', 80, 1, ~~and~~ 1)

SQL	INSERT INTO Classes
	
	        (SubjectID, ClassRoomID, Credits,
	
	        StartDate, StartTime, Duration,
	
	        TuesdaySchedule, ThursdaySchedule)
	
	    VALUES (4, 3315, 5, '2018-01-16', '15:00:00',
	
	        80, 1, 1)

Row Inserted into the Classes Table by CH16_Add_New_Accounting_Class (1 row added)

Subject ID	ClassRoom ID	Credits	Start Date	Start Time	Duration	Tuesday Schedule	Thursday Schedule
4	3315	5	2018-01-16	15:00:00	80	1	1

Bowling League Database

"Create a new bowler record for Matthew Patterson by copying the record for Neil Patterson."

❖ **Note** Be sure to set the total pins, games bowled, current average, and current handicap columns to zero.

Translation/ Clean Up	Insert into ~~the~~ bowlers ~~table into the columns~~ (bowler last name, bowler first name, bowler address, bowler city, bowler state, bowler zip, bowler phone number, team ID, bowler total pins, bowler games bowled, bowler current average, ~~and~~ bowler current handicap) ~~the~~ selection ~~of~~ bowler last name, ~~the value~~ 'Matthew', bowler address, bowler city, bowler state, bowler zip, bowler phone number, team ID, ~~and the values~~ 0, 0, 0, ~~and~~ 0 from ~~the~~ bowlers ~~table~~ where ~~the~~ bowler last name ~~is~~ = 'Patterson' and ~~the~~ bowler first name ~~is~~ = 'Neil'

SQL	INSERT INTO Bowlers
	
	        (BowlerLastName, BowlerFirstName,
	
	        BowlerAddress, BowlerCity,

```
            BowlerState, BowlerZip,
            BowlerPhoneNumber, TeamID,
            BowlerTotalPins, BowlerGamesBowled,
            BowlerCurrentAverage, BowlerCurrentHcp)
        SELECT Bowlers.BowlerLastName, 'Matthew',
            Bowlers.BowlerAddress, Bowlers.BowlerCity,
            Bowlers.BowlerState, Bowlers.BowlerZip,
            Bowlers.BowlerPhoneNumber, Bowlers.TeamID,
            0, 0,
            0, 0
        FROM Bowlers
        WHERE (Bowlers.BowlerLastName = 'Patterson')
            AND (Bowlers.BowlerFirstName = 'Neil')
```

Row Inserted into the Bowlers Table by CH16_Add_Bowler (1 row added)

Bowler LastName	Bowler FirstName	Bowler Address	Bowler City	Bowler State	Bowler Zip
Patterson	Matthew	16 Maple	Auburn	WA	98002

Bowler PhoneNumber	TeamID	Bowler TotalPins	Bowler GamesBowled	BowlerCurrent Average	Bowler CurrentHcp
(206) 555-3487	2	0	0	0	0

"Add a new team called the 'Aardvarks' with no captain assigned."

Translation/ Clean Up	Insert into ~~the~~ teams ~~table into the columns~~ (team name, ~~and~~ captain ID) ~~the~~ values ('Aardvarks', ~~and~~ Null)
SQL	INSERT INTO Teams (TeamName, CaptainID) VALUES ('Aardvarks', NULL)

Row Inserted into the Teams Table by CH16_Add_Team (1 row added)

TeamName	CaptainID
Aardvarks	NULL

Summary

I started the chapter with a brief discussion about the INSERT statement used to add data in tables. I introduced the syntax of the INSERT statement and explained a simple example of adding one row using a values list.

Next, I discussed the features in most database systems that allow you to generate the next unique value in a table to use as the primary key value for new rows. I explained that Microsoft SQL Server provides an Identity data type, Microsoft Access provides an AutoNumber data type, and MySQL has an AUTO_INCREMENT attribute for this purpose. I briefly explained the use of the Sequence pseudo-column in the Oracle database system. And finally, I explained how to use a subquery in a VALUES clause to obtain the previous maximum value and add 1.

I explored using a SELECT expression in your INSERT statements to copy one or more rows. First, I reviewed the syntax of the SELECT expression. Next, I showed you how to copy one row from one table to another. I explored copying multiple rows using an example to copy old records to history archive tables. Finally, I showed you how a SELECT expression is often useful for fetching one or more values from a related table to create values to add to your table. The rest of the chapter provided examples of how to build UPDATE queries.

The following section presents several problems that you can work out on your own.

Problems for You to Solve

Below, I show you the request statement and the name of the solution query in the sample databases. If you want some practice, you can work out the SQL you need for each request and then check your answer with the query I saved in the samples. Don't worry if your syntax doesn't exactly match the syntax of the queries I saved—as long as your result is the same.

Sales Orders Database

1. *"Customer Liz Keyser wants to order again the products ordered on December 12, 2017. Use June 12, 2018, as the order date and June 15, 2018, as the shipped date."*

   (Hint: You need to copy rows in both the Orders and Order_ Details tables, in that order. Assume that you can add 1000 to the OrderID column value that you find for the December 12 order for Liz Keyser to generate the new order number. If you're working in Microsoft SQL Server, be sure to SET IDENTITY_ INSERT Orders ON for the insertion into the Orders table. And if you're working in PostgreSQL, be sure to use SetVal to set the value of Orders_OrderNumber_seq after the INSERT.)

   You can find the solution in CH16_Copy_Dec12_Order_For_Keyser (1 row added) and CH16_Copy_Dec12_OrderDetails_For_Keyser (4 rows added).

   ❖ **Note** Adding a fixed value to generate a new primary key value isn't recommended because you would have to determine in advance how many numbers you could safely skip to get your query to work. In truth, there are ways to avoid using system functions within each database type that will return the "next" valid value for you to use. However, that sort of programming is beyond the scope of a *"Mere Mortals"* book. I tell you to add a safe fixed number to make it easy to answer the problem question, but understand that this isn't the best way to do it.

2. *"Create a new customer record for Mary Baker at 7834 W 32nd Ct., Bothell, WA, 98011, with area code 425 and phone number 555-9876."*

   You can find the solution in CH16_Add_Sales_Customer (1 row added).

3. *"Customer Angel Kennedy wants to order again all the products ordered during the month of November 2017. Use June 15, 2018, as the order date and June 18, 2018, as the shipped date."*

   (Hint: You need to copy rows in both the Orders and Order_ Details tables. Assume that you can add 1000 to the OrderID column value that you find for the November orders for Angel

Kennedy to generate the new order number. See the reminders for problem #1 above if you're working in Microsoft SQL Server or PostgreSQL.)

You can find the solution in CH16_Copy_November_Orders_For_AKennedy (6 rows added) and CH16_Copy_November_OrderDetails_For_AKennedy (34 rows added).

Entertainment Agency Database

1. *"Agent Marianne Wier would like to book some entertainers, so create a new customer record by copying relevant fields from the Agents table."*

   (Hint: Simply copy the relevant columns from the Agents table to the Customers table.)

   You can find the solution in CH16_Copy_Agent_To_Customer (1 row added).

2. *"Add 'New Age' to the list of musical styles."*

   You can find the solution in CH16_Add_Style (1 row added).

3. *"Customer Doris Hartwig would like to rebook the entertainers she hired to play on December 2, 2017, for August 1, 2018."*

   (Hint: Use a SELECT expression that joins the Customers and Engagements tables, and provide the new engagement dates as literal values.)

   You can find the solution in CH16_Duplicate_Engagement (1 row added).

School Scheduling Database

1. *"Angel Kennedy wants to register as a student. Her husband, John, is already enrolled. Create a new student record for Angel using the information from John's record."*

   You can find the solution in CH16_Add_Student (1 row added).

2. *"Staff member Tim Smith wants to enroll as a student. Create a new student record from Tim's staff record."*

   You can find the solution in CH16_Enroll_Staff (1 row added).

Bowling League Database

1. *"Archive the tournament, tourney match, match game, and bowler scores for all matches played in 2017."*

   (Hint: You need to write four queries to archive rows in the Tournaments, Tourney_Matches, Match_Games, and Bowler_Scores tables. You must copy Tournaments first, Tourney_Matches second, Match_Games third, and finally Bowler_Scores in order to honor referential integrity rules.)

   You can find the solution in CH16_Archive_2017_Tournaments_1 (14 rows added), CH16_Archive_2017_Tournaments_2 (57 rows added), CH16_Archive_2017_Tournaments_3 (168 rows added), and CH16_Archive_2017_Tournaments_4 (1,344 rows added).

2. *"Duplicate all the tournaments and tourney matches played in 2017 for the same week in 2019."*

   (Hint: Assume that you can add 25 to the TourneyID column value for the 2017 tournaments to generate the new tournament ID. You'll need to copy rows in both the Tournaments and the Tourney_Matches tables. If you're working in Microsoft SQL Server, be sure to SET IDENTITY_INSERT Orders ON for the insertion into the Tournaments table. And if you're working in PostgreSQL, be sure to use SetVal to set the value of Tournaments_TournamentID_seq after the INSERT.)

   Note also that you cannot simply add two years or 730 days to the dates because the objective is to play the tournaments on the same day of the week—52 weeks times 7 is 364, not 365. Also, be sure you filter for the correct dates in both statements—you'll need a subquery in the second one. You can find the solution in CH16_Copy_2017_Tournaments_1 (14 rows added) and CH16_Copy_2017_Tournaments_2 (57 rows added).

17

Deleting Sets of Data

"I came to love my rows, my beans,
though so many more than I wanted."
—Henry David Thoreau

Topics Covered in This Chapter

What Is a DELETE?

The DELETE Statement

Uses for DELETE

Sample Statements

Summary

Problems for You to Solve

Now you know how to change data by using an UPDATE statement. You also have learned how to add data by using an INSERT statement. But what about getting rid of unwanted data? For that, you need to use what is arguably the simplest but also the most dangerous statement in SQL—DELETE.

What Is a DELETE?

You learned in the previous chapter that adding data to your tables is fairly straightforward. You can add one row at a time by using a VALUES clause, or you can copy multiple rows by using a SELECT expression. But what do you do if you added a row in error? How do you remove rows you've copied to archive tables? How do you delete a customer who isn't sending you any orders? How do you remove a student who applied for admission but then didn't sign up for any classes? If you want to start over with empty tables, how do you remove all the rows? The answer to all these questions is this: Use a DELETE statement. Just like all the other statements in SQL, a DELETE statement works with sets of rows. As you'll learn in this chapter, the simplest DELETE statement removes all the rows from the table you specify. But most of the time you'll want to specify the subset of rows to delete. If you guessed that you add a WHERE clause to do that, you're absolutely correct.

> ❖ **Note** You can find all the sample statements and solutions in the "modify" version of the respective sample databases— SalesOrdersModify, EntertainmentAgencyModify, SchoolSchedulingModify, and BowlingLeagueModify.

The DELETE Statement

The DELETE statement has only three keywords: DELETE, FROM, and WHERE. You can see the diagram of the DELETE statement in Figure 17-1.

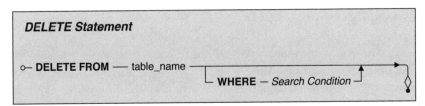

Figure 17-1 *The syntax diagram of the DELETE statement*

I said that the DELETE statement is perhaps the simplest statement in SQL, and I wasn't kidding! But it's also the most dangerous statement that you can execute. If you do not include a WHERE clause, the statement removes all the rows in the table you specify. This can be useful when you're testing a new application, for example, so you can empty all the rows from existing tables but keep the table structure. You might also design an application that has working or temporary tables that you load with data to perform a specific task. For example, it's common to use an INSERT statement to copy rows from a very complex SELECT expression into a table that you subsequently use for several static reports. A DELETE statement with no WHERE clause is handy in this case to clean out the old rows before running a new set of reports.

> ❖ **Note** The SQL Standard indicates that table_name can also be a query (or view) name, but the table implied by the query name must be "updatable." Many database systems support deleting rows from views, and each database system has its own rules about what constitutes an updatable view. In most cases, a view isn't updatable if you use the DISTINCT keyword or if one of the output columns is the result of an expression or an aggregate function.
>
> Some database systems also support defining the view (a derived table in SQL Standard terminology) using JOIN and ON keywords in place of table_name. In systems that support using a derived table, you must also specify which table in the JOIN is the target of the delete immediately after the FROM keyword in the form table_name.*. Consult your database system documentation for details. In this chapter, I'll exclusively use a single table as the target for each DELETE statement.

Deleting All Rows

Deleting all rows is almost too easy. Let's construct a DELETE statement using the Bowlers table in the Bowling League sample database.

> ❖ **Note** Throughout this chapter, I use the "Request/Translation/Clean Up/SQL" technique introduced in Chapter 4, "Creating a Simple Query."

"Delete all bowlers."

Translation	Delete all rows from the bowlers table
Clean Up	Delete ~~all rows~~ from ~~the~~ bowlers ~~table~~
SQL	DELETE FROM Bowlers

If you execute this statement in the sample database, will it actually delete all rows? The answer is no, because I defined a constraint (a referential integrity rule as discussed in Chapter 2, "Ensuring Your Database Structure Is Sound") between the Bowlers table and the Bowler_Scores table. If any rows exist for a particular bowler in the Bowler_Scores table, your database system should not allow you to delete the row in the Bowlers table for that bowler.

Two bowlers in the modified version of the Bowling League sample database do not have any scores, so you should be able to delete those records with this simple DELETE statement. Even if you really didn't mean to delete any rows at all, those two rows will be gone forever. Well, maybe. First, many database systems maintain a log of changes you make to tables. It is sometimes possible to recover lost data from the system logs. Remember also my brief discussion about transactions in Chapter 15, "Updating Sets of Data." If you start a transaction (or the system starts one for you), you can roll back any pending changes if you encounter any errors.

You might also remember that I told you that Microsoft Office Access is one database system that automatically starts a transaction for you whenever you execute a query from the user program interface. If you try to run this query in Microsoft Access, it will first prompt you with a warning about how many rows are about to be deleted. You can cancel the delete at that point when you realize that the database is about to attempt to delete all the rows in the table. If you let the system continue beyond the first warning, you'll receive the error dialog box shown in Figure 17-2.

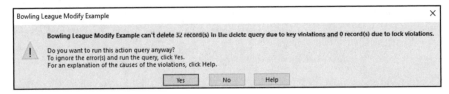

Figure 17-2 *Some database systems warn you if executing a DELETE statement will cause errors*

You can see that 32 of the 34 records in the table won't be deleted because of "key violations." This is an obtuse way to tell you: "Hey, dummy, you've still got rows in the Bowler_Scores table for some of these bowlers you're trying to delete." Click No at this point, and the database system will execute a ROLLBACK on your behalf—none of the rows will be deleted. Click Yes, and the database system executes a COMMIT to permanently delete the two rows for bowlers who have no scores.

In the "Sample Statements" section later in this chapter, I'll show you two ways to safely delete bowlers who haven't bowled any games if that's what you really want to do.

Deleting Some Rows

Most of the time, you'll want to limit the rows that you delete. You can do that by adding a WHERE clause to specifically filter the rows to be deleted. Your WHERE clause can be as simple or as complex as any you've learned about for SELECT or UPDATE statements.

Using a Simple WHERE Clause

Let's start with something simple. Suppose you want to delete in the Sales Orders database any orders that have a zero order total. Your request might look like this:

"Delete orders that have a zero order total."

Translation	Delete from the orders table where the order total is zero
Clean Up	Delete from ~~the~~ orders ~~table~~ where ~~the~~ order total ~~is = zero~~ 0
SQL	DELETE FROM Orders WHERE OrderTotal = 0

The WHERE clause uses a simple comparison predicate to find only the rows that have an order total equal to zero. If you execute this query in the sample database, you'll find that it deletes 11 rows. You can find this query saved as CH17_Delete_Zero_OrdersA.

Safety First: Ensuring That You're Deleting the Correct Rows

Even for simple DELETE queries, I strongly recommend that you verify that you'll be deleting the correct rows. How do you do that? As I mentioned, most of the time you'll add a WHERE clause to select a subset of rows to delete. Why not build a SELECT query first to return the rows that you intend to remove?

"List all the columns from the Orders table for the orders that have a zero order total."

Translation	Select all columns from the orders table where the order total is zero
Clean Up	Select ~~all columns~~ * from ~~the~~ orders ~~table~~ where ~~the~~ order total ~~is = zero~~ 0
SQL	SELECT * FROM Orders WHERE OrderTotal = 0

If you run this query on the Sales Orders sample database, your result should look like Figure 17-3.

OrderNumb ▾	OrderDate ▾	ShipDate ▾	CustomerID ▾	EmployeeID ▾	OrderTotal ▾
198	2017-10-08	2017-10-10	1002	703	$0.00
216	2017-10-12	2017-10-12	1016	707	$0.00
305	2017-11-01	2017-11-05	1013	708	$0.00
361	2017-11-12	2017-11-13	1016	706	$0.00
484	2017-12-09	2017-12-10	1021	707	$0.00
523	2017-12-15	2017-12-17	1003	704	$0.00
629	2018-01-08	2018-01-12	1014	704	$0.00
632	2018-01-08	2018-01-12	1001	706	$0.00
689	2018-01-15	2018-01-16	1015	705	$0.00
753	2018-01-28	2018-01-30	1013	701	$0.00
816	2018-02-09	2018-02-12	1011	701	$0.00

Figure 17-3 *Verifying the rows you want to delete*

Note that I used the shortcut * character to indicate I wanted to see all columns. If the result set shows all the rows you want to delete, you can transform your SELECT statement into the correct DELETE statement by simply replacing SELECT * with DELETE. Figure 17-4 shows how to transform this SELECT statement into the correct DELETE syntax.

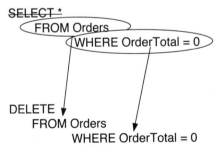

Figure 17-4 *Converting a verifying SELECT query into a DELETE statement*

This conversion is so simple that it would be silly not to create the SELECT statement first to make sure you're deleting the rows you want. Remember, unless you've protected your DELETE inside a transaction, after you execute a DELETE statement, the rows are gone for good.

Using a Subquery

The query explained in the previous section to delete all orders that have a zero order total seems simple enough. But keep in mind that the Order Total column is a calculated value. (I showed you how to calculate and set the total using an UPDATE query in Chapter 15.) What if the user or the application failed to run the update after adding, changing, or deleting one or more order detail rows? Your simple query might attempt to delete an order that still has rows in the Order_Details table, and it might miss some orders that had all the order details removed but didn't have the total updated.

A safer way to ensure that you're deleting orders that have no order details is to use a subquery to check for matching rows in the Order_ Details table. Your request might look like this:

"Delete all orders that have no items ordered."

Translation	Delete the rows from the orders table where the order number is not in the selection of the order number from the order details table
Clean Up	Delete ~~the rows~~ from ~~the~~ orders ~~table~~ where ~~the~~ order number ~~is~~ not in ~~the~~ (selection ~~of the~~ order number from ~~the~~ order details) ~~table~~
SQL	DELETE FROM Orders WHERE OrderNumber NOT IN 　(SELECT OrderNumber 　FROM Order_Details)

That's a bit more complex than the simple comparison for an order total equal to zero, but it ensures that you delete only orders that have no matching rows in the Order_Details table. You can find this query saved as CH17_Delete_Zero_OrdersB in the sample database. This more complex query might actually find and delete some rows that have a nonzero order total that wasn't correctly updated when the last order item was deleted.

To construct the WHERE clause for DELETE queries, you'll probably use IN, NOT IN, EXISTS, or NOT EXISTS quite frequently. (Reread Chapter 11, "Subqueries," if you need a refresher.) Let's look at one more example that requires a complex WHERE clause to filter the rows to be deleted.

> *"Delete all orders and order details for orders placed before January 1, 2018, which have been copied to the archive tables."*

Remember that in Chapter 16, "Inserting Sets of Data," I showed you how to use INSERT to copy a set of old rows to one or more archive tables. After you copy the rows, you can often make the processing in the main part of your application more efficient by deleting the rows that you have archived. As implied by the request, you need to delete rows from two tables, so let's break it down into two requests. You need to delete from the Order_Details table first because a defined referential integrity rule won't let you delete rows in the Orders table if matching rows exist in the Order_Details table.

> *"Delete all order details for orders placed before January 1, 2018, which have been copied to the archive table."*

Do you see a potential danger here? One way to solve the problem would be to simply delete rows from orders that were placed before January 1, 2018.

Translation	Delete rows from the order details table where the order number is in the selection of the order number from the orders table where the order date is earlier than January 1, 2018
Clean Up	Delete ~~rows~~ from ~~the~~ order details ~~table~~ where ~~the~~ order number ~~is~~ in ~~the~~ (~~selection of the~~ order number from ~~the~~ orders ~~table~~ where ~~the~~ order date ~~is earlier than~~ < ~~January 1, 2018~~ '2018-01-01')

SQL	DELETE FROM Order_Details
	
	WHERE OrderNumber IN
	
	  (SELECT OrderNumber
	
	  FROM Orders
	
	  WHERE OrderDate < '2018-01-01')

You can find this query saved as CH17_Delete_Archived_Order_Details_ Unsafe. What if someone else promised to run the INSERT query to archive the rows but really didn't? If you run this query, you'll delete all the order details for orders placed before January 1, 2018, regardless of whether the rows actually exist in the archive table. A safer way is to delete only the rows that you first verify are in the archive table. Let's try again.

Translation	Delete rows from the order details table where the order number is in the selection of order number from the order details archive table
Clean Up	Delete ~~rows~~ from ~~the~~ order details ~~table~~ where ~~the~~ order number ~~is~~ in ~~the~~ (~~selection of~~ order number from ~~the~~ order details archive) ~~table~~

SQL	DELETE FROM Order_Details
	WHERE OrderNumber IN
	   (SELECT OrderNumber
	    FROM Order_Details_Archive)

You can find this query saved as CH17_Delete_Archived_Order_Details_OK. Notice that the query doesn't care at all about the order date. However, it is much safer because it is deleting only the rows in the main table that have a matching order number in the archive table. If you want to be sure you're deleting rows from orders that are before January 1, 2018, and that are already in the archive table, you can use both IN predicates in your query combined with the AND Boolean operator.

Uses for DELETE

At this point, you should have a good understanding of how to delete one or more rows in a table—either all the rows or a selection of rows determined by using a WHERE clause. The best way to give you an idea of the wide range of uses for the DELETE statement is to list some problems you can solve with this statement and then present a set of examples in the "Sample Statements" section. Here's just a small list of the types of problems that you can solve with DELETE:

"Delete products that have never been ordered."

"Delete all entertainers who have never been hired."

"Delete bowlers who have not bowled any games."

"Delete all students who are not registered for any class."

"Delete any categories that have no products."

"Delete customers who have never booked an entertainer."

"Delete teams that have no bowlers assigned."

"Delete all classes that have never had a student registered."

"Delete customers who haven't placed an order."

"Delete musical styles that aren't played by any entertainer."

"Delete all bowling matches that have not been played."

"Delete subjects that have no classes."

"Delete all engagements that have been copied to the archive table."

"Delete all the tournament data that has been copied to the archive tables."

"Delete vendors who do not provide any products."

"Delete members who are not part of an entertainment group."

"Delete employees who haven't sold anything."

Sample Statements

You now know the mechanics of constructing DELETE queries. Let's take a look at a set of samples, all of which request that one or more rows be deleted from a table. These examples come from four of the sample databases.

> ❖ **Caution** Because the sample queries you'll find in the modified versions of the sample databases change your data, be aware that some of the queries will work as expected only once. For example, after you run a DELETE query to remove orders using a WHERE clause to find the rows you want to copy, subsequent attempts to delete the data again will fail because those rows were deleted the first time you ran the query. Consider restoring the databases from the sample scripts or a backup copy if you want to work through the problems again.

I've also included a view of the data that the sample DELETE statement should remove from the target table and a count of the number of rows that should be deleted. The name that appears immediately before the count of rows deleted is the name I gave each query in the sample data on the companion website for the book, www.informit.com/

title/9780134858333. Also, I created a companion SELECT query (stored as a View in MySQL and Microsoft SQL Server) for each DELETE query that you can use to see exactly what will be deleted. The name of the companion query is the name of the original query with _Query appended to the name. I stored each query in the appropriate sample database (as indicated within the example) and prefixed the names of the queries relevant to this chapter with "CH17." You can find the sample data on the companion website for this book, www.informit.com/title/9780134858333. You can follow the instructions in the Introduction of this book to load the samples onto your computer and try them.

> ❖ **Note** Remember that all the column names and table names used in these examples are drawn from the sample database structures shown in Appendix B, "Schema for the Sample Databases." To simplify the process, I have combined the Translation and Clean Up steps for all the examples. These samples assume you have thoroughly studied and understood the concepts covered in previous chapters.

Sales Orders Database

"Delete customers who haven't placed an order."

Translation/ Clean Up	Delete ~~rows~~ from ~~the~~ customers ~~table~~ where ~~the~~ customer ID ~~is~~ not in ~~the~~ (~~selection of the~~ customer ID from ~~the~~ orders) ~~table~~

SQL	DELETE
	FROM Customers
	WHERE CustomerID NOT IN
	    (SELECT CustomerID
	    FROM Orders)

Row Deleted from the Customers Table by CH17_Delete_Customers_Never_Ordered (1 row deleted)

Customer ID	Cust First Name	Cust Last Name	Cust Street Address	Cust City	Cust State	Cust Zip Code	Cust Area Code	Cust Phone Number
1028	Jeffrey	Tirekicker	15622 NE 42nd Ct	Redmond	WA	98052	425	555-9999

❖ **Note** If you ran the CH16_Add_Customer query from the previous chapter, you will see two rows deleted. The second row will be for Kendra Hernandez.

"Delete vendors who do not provide any products."

Translation/ Clean Up	Delete ~~rows~~ from ~~the~~ vendors ~~table~~ where ~~the~~ vendor ID ~~is~~ not in ~~the~~ (~~selection of~~ vendor ID from ~~the~~ product vendors) ~~table~~

SQL	DELETE
	FROM Vendors
	WHERE VendorID NOT IN
	    (SELECT VendorID
	      FROM Product_Vendors)

Row Deleted from the Vendors Table by CH17_Delete_Vendors_No_Products (1 row deleted)

Vendor ID	VendName	VendStreet Address	Vend City	Vend State	Vend ZipCode	<<other columns>>
11	Astro Paper-Products	5639N. Riverside	Chicago	IL	60637	...

❖ **Note** If you executed the CH16_Add_Vendor query from the previous chapter, you will see two rows deleted. The second row will be for Hot Dog Bikes.

Entertainment Agency Database

"Delete all entertainers who have never been hired."

❖ **Note** Before you can delete any Entertainer row, you must first delete any related rows from both Entertainer_Members and Entertainer_Styles.

Translation 1/ Clean Up	Delete ~~rows~~ from ~~the~~ entertainer members ~~table~~ where ~~the~~ entertainer ID ~~is~~ not in ~~the~~ (selection of entertainer ID from ~~the~~ engagements) ~~table~~

SQL	DELETE
	
	FROM Entertainer_Members
	
	WHERE EntertainerID NOT IN
	
	   (SELECT EntertainerID
	
	   FROM Engagements)

Row Deleted from the Entertainer_Members Table by CH17_Delete_Entertainers_Not_Booked1 (1 row deleted)

EntertainerID	MemberID	Status
1009	121	2

Translation 2/ Clean Up	Delete ~~rows~~ from ~~the~~ entertainer styles ~~table~~ where ~~the~~ entertainer ID ~~is~~ not in ~~the~~ (selection of entertainer ID from ~~the~~ engagements) ~~table~~

SQL	DELETE
	
	FROM Entertainer_Styles
	
	WHERE EntertainerID NOT IN
	
	   (SELECT EntertainerID
	
	   FROM Engagements)

Rows Deleted from the Entertainer_Styles Table by CH17_Delete_Entertainers_Not_Booked2 (3 rows deleted)

EntertainerID	StyleID
1009	7
1009	14
1009	21

Translation 3/ Clean Up	Delete ~~rows~~ from ~~the~~ entertainers ~~table~~ where ~~the~~ entertainer ID ~~is~~ not in ~~the~~ (selection of entertainer ID from ~~the~~ engagements) ~~table~~

SQL	DELETE
	FROM Entertainers
	WHERE EntertainerID NOT IN
	(SELECT EntertainerID
	FROM Engagements)

Row Deleted from the Entertainers Table by CH17_Delete_Entertainers_Not_Booked3 (1 row deleted)

Entertainer ID	EntStage Name	Ent SSN	EntStreet Address	Ent City	Ent State	Ent ZipCode	<<other columns>>
1009	Katherine Ehrlich	888-61-1103	777 Fenexet Blvd	Woodin-ville	WA	98072	...

"Delete all engagements that have been copied to the archive table."

Translation/ Clean Up	Delete ~~rows~~ from ~~the~~ engagements ~~table~~ where ~~the~~ engagement ID ~~is~~ in ~~the~~ (selection of engagement ID from ~~the~~ engagements archive) ~~table~~
SQL	DELETE
	FROM Engagements
	WHERE EngagementID IN
	(SELECT EngagementID
	FROM Engagements_Archive)

❖ **Note** To find rows to delete, you must first run the CH16_Archive_Engagements query to copy data to the archive table. The archive table in the original sample database is empty.

Rows Deleted from the Engagements Table by CH17_Remove_Archived_Engagements (56 rows deleted if you first run CH16_Archive_Engagements)

Engage-ment Number	Start Date	End Date	Start Time	Stop Time	Contract Price	Customer ID	Agent ID	Enter-tainer ID
2	2017-09-02	2017-09-06	13:00	15:00	$200.00	10006	4	1004
3	2017-09-11	2017-09-16	13:00	15:00	$590.00	10001	3	1005

Engage-ment Number	Start Date	End Date	Start Time	Stop Time	Contract Price	Customer ID	Agent ID	Enter-tainer ID
4	2017-09-12	2017-09-18	20:00	0:00	$470.00	10007	3	1004
5	2017-09-12	2017-09-15	16:00	19:00	$1,130.00	10006	5	1003
6	2017-09-11	2017-09-15	15:00	21:00	$2,300.00	10014	7	1008

<< more rows here >>

School Scheduling Database

"Delete all classes that have never had a student registered."

❖ **Note** You need to delete the rows from the Faculty_Classes table first and then delete from the Classes table because the database has an integrity rule that won't let you delete rows in the Classes table when matching rows exist in the Faculty_Classes table.

Translation 1/ Clean Up	Delete from ~~the~~ faculty classes ~~table~~ where ~~the~~ class ID ~~is~~ not in ~~the~~ (~~selection of~~ class ID from ~~the~~ student schedules) ~~table~~

SQL	DELETE
	FROM Faculty_Classes
	WHERE ClassID NOT IN
	    (SELECT ClassID
	      FROM Student_Classes)

Rows Deleted from the Faculty_Classes Table by CH17_Delete_Classes_No_Students_1 (113 rows deleted)

ClassID	StaffID
1002	98036
1002	98036
1004	98019
1006	98045
1012	98030

ClassID	StaffID
1031	98005
1183	98005
1184	98011
1196	98028
1560	98028

<< more rows here >>

Translation 2/ Clean Up	Delete from ~~the~~ classes ~~table~~ where ~~the~~ class ID ~~is~~ not in ~~the~~ (selection ~~of~~ class ID from ~~the~~ student schedules) ~~table~~
SQL	DELETE FROM Classes WHERE ClassID NOT IN (SELECT ClassID FROM Student_Schedules)

Rows Deleted from the Classes Table by CH17_Delete_Classes_No_Students_2 (115 rows deleted)

Class ID	Subject ID	Classroom ID	Credits	Start Date	Start Time	Duration	Monday Schedule	<<other columns>>
1002	12	1619	4	2017-09-11	15:30	110	Yes	...
1004	13	1627	4	2017-09-11	8:00	50	Yes	...
1006	13	1627	4	2017-09-11	9:00	110	Yes	...
1012	14	1627	4	2017-10-11	13:00	110	No	...
1031	16	1231	5	2017-09-11	14:00	50	Yes	...
1183	38	3415	5	2017-09-11	13:00	50	Yes	...
1184	38	3415	5	2017-09-11	14:00	50	Yes	...
1196	39	3415	5	2017-09-11	15:00	50	Yes	...

<< more rows here >>

Bowling League Database

"Delete bowlers who have not bowled any games."

❖ **Note** You can solve this request by deleting bowlers whose number of games bowled is zero or by deleting bowlers who have no rows in the Bowler_Scores table. The second method is safer because it doesn't depend on the calculated value of the games bowled, but let's solve it both ways.

Translation 1/ Clean Up	Delete ~~rows~~ from ~~the~~ bowlers ~~table~~ where ~~the~~ bowler games bowled ~~is = zero~~ 0
SQL	DELETE FROM Bowlers WHERE BowlerGamesBowled = 0

Rows Deleted from the Bowlers Table by CH17_Delete_Bowlers_No_Games (2 rows deleted)

Bowler ID	Bowler LastName	Bowler FirstName	<<other columns>>	Bowler Games Bowled	Bowler Current Average	Bowler Current Hcp
33	Patterson	Kerry	...	0	0	0
34	Patterson	Maria	...	0	0	0

Translation 2/ Clean Up	Delete ~~rows~~ from ~~the~~ bowlers ~~table~~ where ~~the~~ bowler ID ~~is~~ not in ~~the~~ (~~selection of~~ bowler ID from ~~the~~ bowler scores) ~~table~~

SQL	DELETE
	FROM Bowlers
	WHERE BowlerID NOT IN
	  (SELECT BowlerID
	   FROM Bowler_Scores)

Rows Deleted from the Bowlers Table by CH17_Delete_Bowlers_No_Games_Safe (2 rows deleted)

Bowler ID	Bowler LastName	Bowler FirstName	<<other columns>>	Bowler Games Bowled	Bowler Current Average	Bowler Current Hcp
33	Patterson	Kerry	...	0	0	0
34	Patterson	Maria	...	0	0	0

❖ **Note** If you ran the CH16_Add_Bowler query in the previous chapter, you should see three rows deleted in both queries. (Matthew Patterson will be the third row.)

"Delete teams that have no bowlers assigned."

Translation/ Clean Up	Delete from ~~the~~ teams ~~table~~ where ~~the~~ team ID ~~is~~ not in ~~the~~ (~~selection of~~ team ID from ~~the~~ bowlers) ~~table~~

SQL	DELETE
	
	FROM Teams
	
	WHERE TeamID NOT IN
	
	    (SELECT TeamID
	
	      FROM Bowlers)

Rows Deleted from the Bowlers Table by CH17_Delete_Teams_No_Bowlers (2 rows deleted)

TeamID	TeamName	CaptainID
9	Huckleberrys	7
10	Never Show Ups	22

❖ **Note** If you ran the CH16_Add_Team query in the previous chapter, you should see three rows deleted in both queries. (Aardvarks will be the third row.)

Summary

I started the chapter with a brief discussion about the DELETE statement used to delete rows from tables. I introduced the syntax of the DELETE statement and explained a simple example of deleting all the rows in a table. I briefly reviewed transactions and showed you how the Microsoft Access database system uses transactions to help protect you from mistakes.

Next, I discussed using a WHERE clause to limit the rows you are deleting. I explained how to use a SELECT statement to verify the rows you plan to delete and how to convert the SELECT statement into a DELETE statement. Finally, I extensively explored using subqueries to test for rows to delete based on the existence or nonexistence of related rows in other tables. The rest of the chapter provided examples of how to build DELETE queries.

The following section presents several problems that you can work out on your own.

Problems for You to Solve

Below, I show you the request statement and the name of the solution query in the sample databases. If you want some practice, you can work out the SQL you need for each request and then check your answer with the query I saved in the samples. Don't worry if your syntax doesn't exactly match the syntax of the queries I saved—as long as your result is the same.

Sales Orders Database

1. *"Delete products that have never been ordered."*

   (Hint: You need to delete from the Product_Vendors table first and then from the Products table.)

   You can find the solution in CH17_Delete_Products_Never_Ordered_1 (4 rows deleted) and CH17_Delete_Products_Never_Ordered_2 (2 rows deleted). Note that you will see three rows deleted in the second query if you ran the CH16_Add_Product query in the previous chapter.

2. *"Delete employees who haven't sold anything."*

   You can find the solution in CH17_Delete_Employees_No_Orders (1 row deleted). Note that you will see two rows deleted if you executed the CH16_Add_Employee query from the previous chapter.

3. *"Delete any categories that have no products."*

   You can find the solution in CH17_Delete_Categories_No_Products (1 row deleted).

Entertainment Agency Database

1. *"Delete customers who have never booked an entertainer."*

   Caution: Before you can delete a customer, you must ensure no rows exist in both the Engagements and the Musical_Preferences table.

   You can find the solutions in CH17_Delete_Customers_Never_Booked1 (5 rows deleted) and CH17_Delete_Customers_Never_Booked2 (2 rows deleted). Note that you will see three rows deleted in the second query if you ran the CH16_Add_Customer query in the previous chapter.

2. *"Delete musical styles that aren't played by any entertainer."*

   Caution: If you look for StyleID values that do not exist only in the Entertainer_Styles table, the query will fail because some of the selected styles also exist in the Musical_Preferences table.

   You can find the solution in CH17_Delete_Styles_No_Entertainer (5 rows deleted). You will see eight rows deleted if you executed the CH16_Add_Style query in the previous chapter.

3. *"Delete members who are not part of an entertainment group."*

   You can find the solution in CH17_Delete_Members_Not_In_Group (0 rows deleted).

School Scheduling Database

1. *"Delete all students who are not registered for any class."*

   You can find the solution in CH17_Delete_Students_No_Classes (1 row deleted). You will see two rows deleted if you ran the CH16_Add_Student query from the previous chapter.

2. *"Delete subjects that have no classes."*

   (Hint: You need to delete rows from both the Faculty_Subjects and the Subjects tables. In the second query, be sure that you don't delete subjects that are a prerequisite for another subject that has classes scheduled.)

   You can find the solution in CH17_Delete_Subjects_No_Classes_1 (64 rows deleted if you ran CH17_Delete_Classes_No_Studentss_2 first; 8 rows deleted otherwise) and

CH17_Delete_Subjects_No_Classes_2 (33 rows deleted if you ran CH17_Delete_Classes_No_Students_2 first; 4 rows deleted otherwise).

Bowling League Database

1. *"Delete all the tournament data that has been copied to the archive tables."*

   (Hint: You need to delete rows from the Bowler_Scores, Match_Games, Tourney_Matches, and Tournaments tables. You should find no rows to delete unless you have executed the four archive queries from Chapter 16.)

   You can find the solution in CH17_Delete_Archived_2017_Tournaments_1 (1,344 rows deleted), CH17_Delete_Archived_2017_Tournaments_2 (168 rows deleted), CH17_Delete_Archived_2017_Tournaments_3 (57 rows deleted), and CH17_Delete_Archived_2017_Tournaments_4 (14 rows deleted). You are incorrect if your solution looks like CH17_Delete_Archived_Tournaments_1_WRONG.

2. *"Delete all bowling matches that have not been played."*

   Caution: Make sure there are no matching rows in both the Bowler_Scores table and the Match_Games table.

   You can find the solution in CH17_Delete_Matches_Not_Played (58 rows deleted if you ran the CH16_Copy_2017_Tournaments queries; 1 row deleted otherwise).

■ Part VI

Introduction to Solving Tough Problems

18

"NOT" and "AND" Problems

"For every complex problem, there's an answer
that is clear, simple, and wrong."

—H. L. MENCKEN

Topics Covered in This Chapter

A Short Review of Sets

Finding Out the "NOT" Case

Finding Multiple Match in the Same Tables

Sample Statements

Summary

Problems for You to Solve

At this point (especially if you've been a good student and have worked through all the sample statements and problems), you should be very comfortable with the basics of the SQL database language. Now, in the words of a famous Louisiana chef, it's time to "kick it up a notch." In this chapter, I'm going to walk you through more complex problems to find out when something "is not" and when something "is" under multiple conditions. In Chapter 19, "Condition Testing," I'll introduce you to logic testing in a Value Expression using CASE. In Chapter 20, "Using Unlinked Data and 'Driver' Tables," I'll prompt you to "think outside the box" using disconnected tables to solve problems. In Chapter 21, "Performing Complex Calculations on Groups," I'll show you how to get subtotals when you group data, and in Chapter 22, "Partitioning Data into 'Windows,'" I'll lead you through looking at "windows" of related data. Let's get started!

A Short Review of Sets

Remember in Chapter 7, "Thinking in Sets," I used Venn diagrams to help you visualize how you need the overlapping part of two sets to solve "and" problems and the excluded part of two sets to solve "not" problems. Solving a problem requiring something to be "not" one criterion is easy (recipes that do not have beef), but it starts to get tough when your result must satisfy two or more "not" criteria (recipes that do not have beef OR carrots OR onions). The same is surely true when you're looking for something that "is" with one criterion (recipes that have cheese). It gets a bit tougher when a set of things must satisfy two (recipes that have beef AND onions), and it becomes a head-scratcher when a set must satisfy three or more criteria (recipes that have beef AND onions AND carrots). And it can be mind-boggling to visualize a set of things that IS one or more criteria but is also NOT several other criteria.

Sets with Multiple AND Criteria

Let's take a look at the multiple "AND" ("IS") case first because that's easier to visualize. Figure 18-1 shows you a possible solution for recipes that have beef AND onions AND carrots.

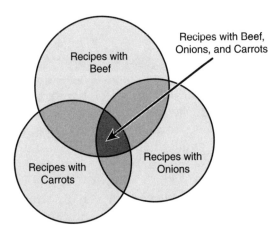

Figure 18-1 *Recipes that have beef and onions and carrots*

Looks pretty simple, doesn't it? But keep in mind that recipes with their ingredients are themselves sets of data with two or more rows. (You can't think of a recipe that has only one ingredient, can you?) If you try to solve the problem with a search condition like this:

```
WHERE Ingredient IN ('Beef', 'Onions', 'Carrots')
```

you'll get the wrong answer! Why? Well, remember that your database system tests each row against the search condition. If a recipe has beef OR onions OR carrots, the preceding search condition will be true. You want recipes that have all three, not just one. You need something more complex to find the recipes that have all three items, not just one, so you should state the problem like this:

"Find the recipes whose list of ingredients includes beef AND whose list of ingredients includes onions AND whose list of ingredients includes carrots."

In Chapter 8, "INNER JOINs," I showed you one way to search for recipes with two ingredients using individual SELECT statements inside the FROM clause (CH08_Beef_And_Garlic_Recipes). In Chapter 14, "Filtering Grouped Data," I showed another way to do this for two ingredients with a creative use of GROUP BY and HAVING (CH14_Beef_And_Garlic_Recipes). In this chapter, I'll show you some additional ways to tackle a problem like this.

Sets with Multiple NOT Criteria

Excluding multiple criteria involves finding all the items that DO include one of the criteria and then subtracting (removing) them all from the set of all items. If I want to find all recipes that do not have beef or onions or carrots, the Venn diagram looks like Figure 18-2.

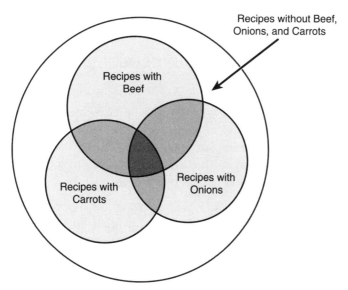

Figure 18-2 *Recipes that do not have beef, onions, or carrots*

Think of it as finding all the recipes that have beef and removing them from the set of all recipes, then finding the recipes that have onions and removing all of those, and finally finding the set of recipes that includes carrots and removing those as well. What you have left is the answer. Again, you might be tempted to solve it with a search condition like this:

```
WHERE Ingredient NOT IN ('Beef', 'Onions', 'Carrots')
```

From the previous discussion, you should be able to see why this won't work. A search condition like the preceding one will return any recipe that has some ingredient other than beef, onions, or carrots. It *will* find and eliminate a recipe that has ONLY those three ingredients, but that would be a strange recipe, indeed! Because ingredients for any recipe form a set, you need to think of the problem like this:

> *"Find the recipes whose list of ingredients does not include beef, and whose list of ingredients does not include onions, and whose list of ingredients does not include carrots."*

Stated another way, you could also do:

> *"Find the recipes that are NOT in the list of recipes whose list of ingredients includes beef or onions or carrots."*

I haven't solved this particular problem in previous chapters, but rest assured I will show you some ways to do it in this one.

Sets Including Some Criteria but Excluding Others

Just for completeness, let's take a quick look at the case where you want to include items that meet one or more criteria but exclude items that also meet one or more criteria. Suppose you want all recipes that have beef but do not want any recipes that have onions or carrots. Figure 18-3 shows you a possible situation for this problem.

I bet you can figure this one out on your own, but to make sure you really "get it," you should not try to solve the problem like this:

```
WHERE Ingredient = 'Beef' AND Ingredient NOT IN ('Onions',
'Carrot')
```

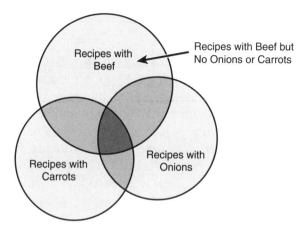

Figure 18-3 *Recipes that have beef but do not have onions or carrots*

A search like this will certainly find all recipes that have beef, but it will also include any recipe that has any ingredient other than onions or carrots, including *all* the recipes that have beef! Oops. Again, the ingredients for a recipe form a set, so you need to think of solving the problem like this:

> *"Find the recipes whose list of ingredients includes beef, and whose list of ingredients does not include onions, and whose list of ingredients does not include carrots."*

Let's move on now to finding out exactly how to solve these complex "NOT" and "AND" problems.

❖ **Note** I'm going to show you several techniques for solving both "NOT" and "AND" problems without regard to performance. In truth, some methods might perform terribly in one database system but be the best solution in another. You can learn about advanced techniques for discovering performance problems in *Effective SQL: 61 Specific Ways to Write Better SQL* (Addison-Wesley, ISBN 978-0134578897) that I wrote with Ben Clothier and Doug Steele. Having said that, I do comment when appropriate where I think one technique is more likely to run faster than another.

Finding Out the "Not" Case

You might recall that you've already learned how to solve simple "not" cases. In Chapter 9, "OUTER JOINs," I showed you, for example, how to find any ingredients not used in any recipe (CH09_Ingredients_Not_Used), customers who haven't ordered a helmet (CH09_Customers_No_Helmets), and any agents who have no contracts (CH09_Agents_No_Contracts). In Chapter 11, "Subqueries," I showed you how to find students who have never withdrawn (CH11_Students_Never_Withdrawn) and products not ordered (CH11_Products_Not_Ordered). Now let's learn how to handle multiple "not" criteria using four different techniques:

- OUTER JOIN

- NOT IN

- NOT EXISTS

- GROUP BY/HAVING

> ❖ **Note** Throughout this chapter, I use the "Request/Translation/ Clean Up/SQL" technique introduced in Chapter 4, "Creating a Simple Query." Because this process should now be very familiar to you, I have combined the Translation/Clean Up steps for all the following examples to simplify the process.

Using OUTER JOIN

In Chapter 9, you learned that you can use an OUTER JOIN with an IS NULL test to find rows in one table that do not have a matching row in another table. An example is the query to find ingredients that are not used:

"List ingredients not used in any recipe yet."

Translation/ Clean Up	Select ingredient name from ~~the~~ ingredients ~~table~~ left outer join~~ed with the~~ recipe ingredients ~~table~~ on ingredients.ingredient ID ~~in the ingredients table matches~~ = recipe_ingredients.ingredient ID ~~in the recipe ingredients table~~ where recipe ID is null

SQL	SELECT Ingredients.IngredientName
	
	FROM Ingredients LEFT OUTER JOIN
	    Recipe_Ingredients
	
	  ON Ingredients.IngredientID =
	    Recipe_Ingredients.IngredientID
	
	WHERE Recipe_Ingredients.RecipeID IS NULL

CH09_Ingredients_Not_Used (20 rows)

IngredientName
Halibut
Chicken, Fryer
Bacon
Iceberg Lettuce
Butterhead Lettuce
Scallop
Vinegar
Red Wine
<< more rows here >>

Notice that this works because where there is no match in the second table, your database engine returns a Null value for any column in that table. You can use the same technique to exclude rows from the second table that match certain criteria, but you must combine the OUTER JOIN technique that you learned in Chapter 9 with a subquery that you learned how to use in Chapter 11. You must do this because the second "table" that you want to match with must first be filtered by the excluding criteria.

Let's solve the beef, onions, carrots problem using an OUTER JOIN and a subquery:

"Find the recipes that have neither beef, nor onions, nor carrots."

Translation/ Clean Up	Select recipe ID ~~and~~ recipe title from ~~the~~ recipes ~~table~~ left outer join~~ed with the~~ (selection~~ of~~ recipe IDs from ~~the~~ recipe ingredients ~~table~~ inner join~~ed with the~~ ingredients ~~table~~ on Recipe_Ingredients.recipe ID ~~in the recipe ingredients table matches~~ = Ingredients.recipe ID ~~in the ingredients table~~ where ingredient name is in ~~the values~~ ('Beef', 'Onion', ~~or~~ 'Carrot')) where ~~the~~ recipe ID ~~in the selection~~ is NULL ~~empty~~

SQL	SELECT Recipes.RecipeID, Recipes.RecipeTitle
	
	FROM Recipes LEFT JOIN
	
	  (SELECT Recipe_Ingredients.RecipeID
	
	  FROM Recipe_Ingredients INNER JOIN Ingredients
	
	    ON Recipe_Ingredients.IngredientID =
	
	    Ingredients.IngredientID
	
	  WHERE Ingredients.IngredientName
	
	    IN ('Beef', 'Onion', 'Carrot'))
	
	  AS RBeefCarrotOnion
	
	  ON Recipes.RecipeID = RBeefCarrotOnion.RecipeID
	
	WHERE RBeefCarrotOnion.RecipeID Is Null;

CH18_Recipes_NOT_Beef_Onion_Carrot_OUTERJOIN (8 rows)

RecipeID	RecipeTitle
4	Garlic Green Beans
5	Fettuccini Alfredo
6	Pollo Picoso
7	Mike's Summer Salad
8	Trifle
10	Yorkshire Pudding
12	Asparagus
15	Coupe Colonel

What is happening is the query to the right of the OUTER JOIN is finding the recipe ID for all recipes that have beef, onions, or carrots, then the OUTER JOIN with an IS NULL test eliminates all those recipe IDs from consideration—including only the recipes that do not match. You might be tempted to directly do a join on the recipe ingredients table and ingredients table and put the criteria for beef, onion, and carrot in the final WHERE clause. However, as I explained in Chapter 9, applying a filter to the "right" side of a "left" join (or vice-versa) effectively nullifies the "outer" part of the join. The result will be as though you had asked for an INNER JOIN, which won't solve the problem.

Using NOT IN

You have already seen in Chapter 11 how to use NOT IN to solve simple "not" queries. For example, in the Sales Orders database, you can find a query to discover which products have never been ordered (CH11_Products_Not_Ordered). In the Entertainment database, there is a query to list agents who haven't booked anything (CH11_Bad_Agents). But as you might suspect, it gets a bit tricky when you want to find rows using multiple "not" criteria.

Let's solve our old friend in the Recipes database using NOT IN. First, let's do it the hard way using three separate NOT IN clauses.

"Find the recipes that have neither beef, nor onions, nor carrots."

| Translation/
Clean Up | Select recipe ID ~~and~~ recipe title from ~~the~~ recipes ~~table~~ where ~~the~~ recipe ID is not in ~~the~~ (selection of recipe IDs from ~~the~~ recipe ingredients ~~table~~ inner joined ~~with the~~ ingredients ~~table~~ on Recipe_Ingredients.recipe ID ~~in the recipe ingredients table matches~~ = Ingredients.recipe ID ~~in the ingredients table~~ where ingredient name ~~is~~ = 'Beef') and ~~the~~ recipe ID ~~is~~ not in ~~the~~ (selection of recipe IDs from ~~the~~ recipe ingredients ~~table~~ inner joined ~~with the~~ ingredients ~~table~~ on Recipe_Ingredients.recipe ID ~~in the recipe ingredients table matches~~ = Ingredients.recipe ID ~~in the ingredients table~~ where ingredient name ~~is~~ = 'Onion') and the recipe ID is not in ~~the~~ (selection of recipe IDs from ~~the~~ recipe ingredients ~~table~~ inner joined ~~with the~~ ingredients ~~table~~ on Recipe_Ingredients.recipe ID ~~in the recipe ingredients table matches~~ = Ingredients.recipe ID ~~in the ingredients table~~ where ingredient name ~~is~~ = 'Carrot') |

| SQL | ```
SELECT Recipes.RecipeID, Recipes.RecipeTitle
FROM Recipes
WHERE Recipes.RecipeID NOT IN
  (SELECT Recipe_Ingredients.RecipeID
   FROM Recipe_Ingredients
     INNER JOIN Ingredients
     ON Recipe_Ingredients.IngredientID =
     Ingredients.IngredientID
     WHERE Ingredients.IngredientName = 'Beef')
  AND Recipes.RecipeID NOT IN
  (SELECT Recipe_Ingredients.RecipeID
   FROM Recipe_Ingredients
     INNER JOIN Ingredients
     ON Recipe_Ingredients.IngredientID =
     Ingredients.IngredientID
     WHERE Ingredients.IngredientName = 'Onion')
  AND Recipes.RecipeID NOT IN
  (SELECT Recipe_Ingredients.RecipeID
   FROM Recipe_Ingredients
     INNER JOIN Ingredients
     ON Recipe_Ingredients.IngredientID =
     Ingredients.IngredientID
     WHERE Ingredients.IngredientName = 'Carrot');
``` |

Whew! This query is doing three eliminations, first eliminating all recipes that have beef, then eliminating all recipes that have onions, and finally eliminating all recipes that have carrots. (You can find this query saved as CH18_Recipes_NOT_Beef_Onion_Carrot_NOTIN_1.) But if you think about it, if you can collect all the recipes that have neither beef nor onions nor carrots in one subquery, you can do a single elimination like this:

"Find the recipes that have neither beef, nor onions, nor carrots."

Translation/ Clean Up	Select recipe ID ~~and~~ recipe title from ~~the~~ recipes ~~table~~ where ~~the~~ recipe ID is not in ~~the~~ (selection ~~of~~ recipe IDs from ~~the~~ recipe ingredients ~~table~~ inner join~~ed with the~~ ingredients ~~table~~ on Recipe_Ingredients.recipe ID ~~in the recipe ingredients table matches~~ = Ingredients.recipe ID ~~in the ingredients table~~ where ingredient name ~~is~~ in ~~the values~~ ('Beef', 'Onion', ~~or~~ 'Carrots'))
```

| SQL | ```
SELECT Recipes.RecipeID, Recipes.RecipeTitle
FROM Recipes
WHERE Recipes.RecipeID NOT IN
   (SELECT Recipe_Ingredients.RecipeID
    FROM Recipe_Ingredients
    INNER JOIN Ingredients
      ON Recipe_Ingredients.IngredientID =
        Ingredients.IngredientID
    WHERE Ingredients.IngredientName
      IN ('Beef', 'Onion', 'Carrot'));
``` |
| --- | --- |

That's really lots simpler, and, in fact, this is arguably the simplest way to solve a multiple "not" problem. It's also very efficient because your database system will run the subquery once then use the result from that to eliminate recipes that match. You can find this query saved in the Recipes sample database as CH18_Recipes_NOT_Beef_Onion_Carrot_NOTIN_2.

Using NOT EXISTS

In Chapter 11, you also learned about using EXISTS and a subquery to search for related data on a single criterion. You can imagine how this can be expanded to handle multiple criteria. And it's a simple matter to use NOT EXISTS to handle the "not" case. Let's solve our trusty not beef-onions-carrots again using NOT EXISTS.

"Find the recipes that have neither beef, nor onions, nor carrots."

Translation/ Clean Up	Select recipe ID ~~and~~ recipe title from ~~the~~ recipes ~~table~~ where ~~does~~ not exist ~~the~~ (selecti~~on of~~ recipe IDs from ~~the~~ recipe ingredients ~~table~~ inner join~~ed with the~~ ingredients ~~table~~ on Recipe_Ingredients.recipe ID ~~in the recipe ingredients table matches~~ = Ingredients.recipe ID ~~in the ingredients table~~ where ingredient name ~~is~~ in ~~the values~~ ('Beef', 'Onion', ~~or~~ 'Carrot') and ~~the~~ Recipe_Ingredients.recipe ID ~~from the recipe ingredients table matches the~~ = Recipes.recipe ID ~~from the recipes table~~)
```

SQL

```
SELECT Recipes.RecipeID, Recipes.RecipeTitle
FROM Recipes
WHERE NOT EXISTS
    (SELECT Recipe_Ingredients.RecipeID
     FROM Recipe_Ingredients
        INNER JOIN Ingredients
          ON Recipe_Ingredients.IngredientID =
             Ingredients.IngredientID
        WHERE Ingredients.IngredientName
          IN ('Beef', 'Onion', 'Carrot')
        AND Recipe_Ingredients.RecipeID =
            Recipes.RecipeID);
```

This operates similarly to the principles behind the NOT IN solution. You first find all the recipes that include beef, onions, or carrots, and then eliminate them by matching on recipe ID and using NOT EXISTS. The one drawback to this approach is the subquery must make a reference to a field in the main query. This means that your database system must execute the subquery once for every row it finds in the Recipes table— once for each unique RecipeID value. (In some more advanced books, you will find this sort of subquery called a "correlated" subquery because the subquery is, in effect, co-dependent on each row in the outer query.) You can find this query saved as CH18_Recipes_NOT_Beef_Onion_Carrot_NOTEXISTS in the Recipes sample database.

Using GROUP BY/HAVING

In Chapter 14 you learned how to find out if there are "n" or more rows that qualify for one or more criteria. For example, in the Entertainment database, you can find a query to show you the entertainers who play jazz and have three or more members (CH14_Jazz_Entertainers_More_Than_3).

Did it occur to you that you could test for a count of zero to find sets of data that do not qualify? Sure you can! Let's solve our handy, not beef-onions-carrots using GROUP BY and HAVING COUNT = 0.

"Find the recipes that have neither beef, nor onions, nor carrots."

Translation/ Clean Up	Select recipe ID ~~and~~ recipe title from ~~the~~ recipes ~~table~~ left join~~ed with the~~ (~~selection of~~ recipe ID from ~~the~~ recipe ingredients ~~table~~ inner join~~ed with the~~ ingredients ~~table~~ on Ingredients.ingredient ID ~~in the ingredients table equals matches~~ = Recipe_Ingredients.ingredient ID ~~in the recipe ingredients~~ table where ingredient name ~~is in the values~~ ('beef', 'onion', ~~or~~ 'carrot')) AS RIBOC on Recipes. recipe ID ~~in the recipes table equals matches~~ = RIBOC. recipe ID ~~in the selection~~ where RIBOC.recipe ID ~~in the selection~~ is NULL ~~empty, then~~ grouped by recipe ID ~~and~~ recipe title ~~and~~ having ~~the~~ count ~~of~~ RIBOC.recipe ID ~~in the selection equals zero~~ = 0
| SQL | ```
SELECT Recipes.RecipeID, Recipes.RecipeTitle
FROM Recipes LEFT JOIN
    (SELECT Recipe_Ingredients.RecipeID
    FROM Recipe_Ingredients
      INNER JOIN Ingredients
        ON Ingredients.IngredientID =
            Recipe_Ingredients.IngredientID
      WHERE Ingredients.IngredientName
        IN ('Beef', 'Onion', 'Carrot')) AS RIBOC
    ON Recipes.RecipeID = RIBOC.RecipeID
WHERE RIBOC.RecipeID IS NULL
GROUP BY Recipes.RecipeID, Recipes.RecipeTitle
HAVING COUNT(RIBOC.RecipeID) = 0;
``` |

If you noticed that this looks a lot like the LEFT JOIN solution, you're absolutely correct! In fact, the LEFT JOIN solution for a single table is the better method because it avoids the overhead of grouping the rows. If you want to do this sort of exclusion on a JOIN of two or more tables and some other criteria, however, using GROUP BY and COUNT is a good way to do it. Remember that you learned in Chapter 13, "Grouping Data," that when you use COUNT (or, for that matter, any aggregate function) on a column and that column contains a Null value in some rows, the aggregate function ignores the Null values. This is why, when the LEFT JOIN returns no rows from the subquery, COUNT(RIBOC.RecipeID) = 0 works. When a recipe has no rows matching in the set of recipes that have beef, onions, or carrots, the COUNT is zero. (You can find this query saved as CH18_Recipes_NOT_Beef_Onion_Carrot_GROUPBY in the Recipes sample database.)
```

Let's look at an example where the GROUP BY and HAVING make more sense:

"Find the recipes that have butter but have neither beef, nor onions, nor carrots."

Translation/ Clean Up	Select recipe ID ~~and~~ recipe title from ~~the~~ recipes ~~table~~ inner join~~ed with the~~ recipe ingredients ~~table on~~ Recipes.recipe ID ~~in the recipes table equals~~ = Recipe_ Ingredients.recipe ID ~~in the recipe ingredients table, then~~ inner join~~ed with the~~ ingredients ~~table~~ on Ingredients. ingredient ID ~~in the ingredients table equals~~ = Recipe_ Ingredients.ingredient ID ~~in the recipe ingredients table, then~~ left join~~ed with the~~ (selecti~~on of~~ recipe ID from ~~the~~ recipe ingredients ~~table~~ inner join~~ed with the~~ ingredients table on Ingredients.ingredient ID ~~in the ingredients table equals~~ = Recipe_Ingredients.ingredient ID ~~in the recipe ingredients table~~ where ingredient name ~~is~~ in ~~the values~~ ('beef', 'onion', ~~or~~ 'carrot')) AS RIBOC on Recipes. recipe ID ~~in the recipes table equals~~ RIBOC.recipe ID~~in the selection~~ where ingredient name ~~in the ingredients table equals~~ = 'Butter' and RIBOC.recipe ID ~~in the selection~~ is NULL ~~empty, then~~ grouped by recipe ID ~~and~~ recipe title ~~and~~ having ~~the~~ count ~~of~~ RIBOC.recipe ID ~~in the selection equals zero~~ = 0
| SQL | ```
SELECT Recipes.RecipeID, Recipes.RecipeTitle
FROM ((Recipes INNER JOIN Recipe_Ingredients
  ON Recipes.RecipeID
     = Recipe_Ingredients.RecipeID)
INNER JOIN Ingredients
  ON Ingredients.IngredientID =
     Recipe_Ingredients.IngredientID)
LEFT JOIN
   (SELECT Recipe_Ingredients.RecipeID
   FROM Recipe_Ingredients
     INNER JOIN Ingredients
       ON Ingredients.IngredientID =
          Recipe_Ingredients.IngredientID
``` |
```

```
         WHERE Ingredients.IngredientName IN
             ('Beef', 'Onion', 'Carrot')) AS RIBOC
      ON Recipes.RecipeID=RIBOC.RecipeID
   WHERE Ingredients.IngredientName = 'Butter'
      AND RIBOC.RecipeID IS NULL
   GROUP BY Recipes.RecipeID, Recipes.RecipeTitle
   HAVING COUNT(RIBOC.RecipeID) = 0;
```

CH18_Recipes_Butter_NOT_Beef_Onion_Carrot_GROUPBY (2 rows)

RecipeID	RecipeTitle
5	Fettuccini Alfredo
12	Asparagus

Now, this makes more sense because the JOIN between Recipes, Recipe_ Ingredients, and Ingredients will certainly return multiple rows, but I want only one row per recipe to appear in the final result. The GROUP BY accomplishes returning one row per recipe, and the HAVING eliminates all recipes that have beef, onions, or carrots in the ingredients.

That pretty much covers the different ways to solve "not" problems that have multiple criteria. I'll show you some more sample statements and challenge you with some problems later in the chapter.

Finding Multiple Matches in the Same Table

Now, let's look at the other side of the coin—queries that need to find matches on multiple criteria. You had a taste of this in Chapter 8 when you learned how to find customers who have ordered both a bike and a helmet in the Sales Orders Database (*CH08_Customers_Both_Bikes_And_Helmets*), *and in the Entertainment database to discover entertainers who played for* both Berg and Hallmark (CH08_Entertainers_Berg_AND_Hallmark). Let's explore the many ways to solve this type of problem in more detail:

- INNER JOIN

- IN

- EXISTS

- GROUP BY/HAVING

Using INNER JOIN

Remember from Chapter 7 that you can find matching items in two sets by performing an intersection of the two sets. I also told you that it's most common when working in SQL to perform an intersection on key values using an INNER JOIN. Because the Primary Key of each row in a table uniquely identifies each row, an intersection on Primary Key values will show you the rows that are common to two sets.

So, one way to find rows that match multiple criteria is to create a set of data (using a subquery) for each criterion and then JOIN the multiple sets on Primary Key values. Let's work through an example from the Entertainment database:

"List the customers who have booked Carol Peacock Trio, Caroline Coie Cuartet, and Jazz Persuasion."

| Translation/ Clean Up | Select ~~the unique~~ DISTINCT CPT.customer ID, CPT.cust omer first name, ~~and~~ CPT.customer last name from ~~the~~ (~~selection of~~ customer id, customer first name, customer last name from ~~the~~ customers ~~table~~ inner joined ~~with the~~ engagements ~~table~~ on Customers.customer ID ~~in the customers table equals~~ = Engagements.customer ID ~~in the engagements table then~~ inner joined ~~with the~~ entertainers ~~table~~ on Engagements.entertainer ID ~~in the engagements table equals~~ = Entertainers.entertainer ID ~~in the entertainers table~~ where Entertainers.entertainer stage name ~~in the entertainers table equals~~ = 'Carol Peacock Trio') AS CPT inner joined ~~with the~~ (~~selection of~~ customer id from ~~the~~ customers ~~table~~ inner joined ~~with the~~ engagements ~~table~~ on Customers.customer ID ~~in the customers table equals~~ = Engagements.customer ID ~~in the engagements table then~~ inner joined ~~with the~~ entertainers ~~table~~ on Engagements.entertainer ID ~~in the engagements table equals~~ = Entertainers.entertainer ID ~~in the entertainers table~~ where Entertainers.entertainer stage name ~~in the~~ |

~~entertainers table equals~~ = 'Caroline Coie Cuartet') AS CCC on CPT.customer ID ~~in the first selection equals~~ = CCC. customer ID ~~in the second selection~~ inner joined ~~with the~~ (~~selection of~~ customer id from ~~the~~ customers ~~table~~ inner joined ~~with the~~ engagements ~~table~~ on Customers.customer ID ~~in the customers table equals~~ = Engagements.customer ID ~~in the engagements table then~~ inner joined ~~with the~~ entertainers ~~table~~ on Engagements.entertainer ID ~~in the engagements table equals~~ = Entertainers.entertainer ID ~~in the entertainers table~~ where Entertainers.entertainer stage name ~~in the entertainers table equals~~ = 'Jazz Persuasion') AS JP on CCC.customer ID ~~in the second selection equals~~ = JP.customer ID ~~in the third selection~~

SQL	`SELECT DISTINCT CPT.CustomerID, CPT.CustFirstName,`
	`    CPT.CustLastName`
	`FROM ((SELECT Customers.CustomerID,`
	`    Customers.CustFirstName, Customers.CustLastName`
	`        FROM (Customers INNER JOIN Engagements`
	`            ON Customers.CustomerID =`
	`                Engagements.CustomerID)`
	`            INNER JOIN Entertainers`
	`                ON Engagements.EntertainerID =`
	`                    Entertainers.EntertainerID`
	`            WHERE Entertainers.EntStageName =`
	`            'Carol Peacock Trio') As CPT`
	`    INNER JOIN`
	`        (SELECT Customers.CustomerID`
	`        FROM (Customers INNER JOIN Engagements`
	`            ON Customers.CustomerID =`
	`                Engagements.CustomerID)`
	`            INNER JOIN Entertainers`
	`                ON Engagements.EntertainerID =`
	`                    Entertainers.EntertainerID`
	`            WHERE Entertainers.EntStageName =`
	`            'Caroline Coie Cuartet') As CCC`
	`        ON CPT.CustomerID = CCC.CustomerID)`
	`    INNER JOIN`
	`        (SELECT Customers.CustomerID`
	`        FROM (Customers INNER JOIN Engagements`

```
                          ON Customers.CustomerID =
                              Engagements.CustomerID)
                      INNER JOIN Entertainers
                          ON Engagements.EntertainerID =
                              Entertainers.EntertainerID
                      WHERE Entertainers.EntStageName =
                          'Jazz Persuasion') As JP
                  ON CCC.CustomerID = JP.CustomerID;
```

CH18_Customers_Peacock_Coie_Jazz_INNERJOIN (2 rows)

CustomerID	CustFirstName	CustLastName
10004	Dean	McCrae
10010	Zachary	Ehrlich

The three SELECT expressions in the FROM clause fetch the three sets I want—one for customers who booked Carol Peacock Trio; one for customers who booked Caroline Coie Cuartet; and one for customers who booked Jazz Persuasion. I included the customer name fields in the first query so that I can display those fields in the final result, but all I need in the second and third queries is the CustomerID field (the Primary Key of the Customers table) to perform the JOIN to find out who booked all three groups. Finally, I used the DISTINCT keyword to eliminate any duplicate rows produced when a customer booked one of the entertainers multiple times.

If you look back in Chapter 8, you'll find I use the same technique to solve CH08_Entertainers_Berg_AND_Hallmark. The only difference is that I used DISTINCT in each of the subqueries instead of in the outer SELECT statement.

Using IN

Let's solve our customers booking three entertainment groups problem using IN. When you want to find a match on multiple criteria using IN, you might be tempted to do it this simple way:

```
SELECT Customers.CustomerID, Customers.CustFirstName,
   Customers.CustLastName
FROM Customers
WHERE Customers.CustomerID IN
```

```
 (SELECT Customers.CustomerID
   FROM (Customers INNER JOIN Engagements
     ON Customers.CustomerID = Engagements.CustomerID)
   INNER JOIN Entertainers
     ON Engagements.EntertainerID = Entertainers.
       EntertainerID
WHERE Entertainers.EntStageName IN
  ('Carol Peacock Trio', 'Caroline Coie Cuartet',
     'Jazz Persuasion'))
```

Why won't this work? The answer is you'll get *any* customer who booked any of the three groups. You won't get only the customers who booked *all three* groups! You can find this query saved as CH18_Customers_Peacock_Coie_Jazz_IN_WRONG in the Entertainment sample database.

Remember that to find the customers who booked all three, you need an intersection of three sets: one for the customers who booked Carol Peacock Trio; one for the customers who booked Caroline Coie Cuartet; and one for customers who booked Jazz Persuasion. To solve this with IN, you need *three* IN clauses, and you must find the customers who are IN the first set AND IN the second set AND IN the third set. Let's take a whack at it:

"List the customers who have booked Carol Peacock Trio, Caroline Coie Cuartet, and Jazz Persuasion."

Translation/ Clean Up	Select customer ID, ~~customer~~ first name, ~~and~~ ~~customer~~ last name from ~~the~~ customers ~~table~~ where customerID ~~is~~ in ~~the~~ (~~selection of~~ customer id from ~~the~~ engagements ~~table~~ inner join~~ed with the~~ entertainers ~~table~~ on Engagements.entertainer ID ~~in the engagements table equals~~ = Entertainers.entertainer ID ~~in the entertainers table~~ where Entertainers.en~~tertainer~~ stage name ~~in the entertainers table equals~~ = 'Carol Peacock Trio') and customer id ~~is~~ in ~~the~~ (~~selection of~~ customer id from ~~the~~ engagements ~~table~~ inner join~~ed with the~~ entertainers ~~table~~ on Engagements.entertainer ID ~~in the engagements table equals~~ = Entertainers.entertainer ID ~~in the entertainers table~~ where Entertainers.en~~tertainer~~ stage name ~~in the enter-tainers table equals~~ = 'Caroline Coie Cuartet') and customer id ~~is~~ in ~~the~~ (~~selection of~~ customer id from ~~the~~ engagements ~~table~~ inner join~~ed with the~~ entertainers ~~table~~ on Engagements.entertainer ID ~~in the engagements table equals~~ = Entertainers.entertainer ID ~~in the entertainers table~~ where Entertainers.en~~tertainer~~ stage name ~~in the entertainers table equals~~ = 'Jazz Persuasion')

```
SQL        SELECT Customers.CustomerID,
              Customers.CustFirstName,
              Customers.CustLastName
           FROM Customers
           WHERE Customers.CustomerID IN
              (SELECT Engagements.CustomerID
               FROM Engagements INNER JOIN Entertainers
                  ON Engagements.EntertainerID =
                     Entertainers.EntertainerID
               WHERE Entertainers.EntStageName =
                  'Carol Peacock Trio')
           AND Customers.CustomerID IN
              (SELECT Engagements.CustomerID
               FROM Engagements INNER JOIN Entertainers
                  ON Engagements.EntertainerID =
                     Entertainers.EntertainerID
               WHERE Entertainers.EntStageName =
                  'Caroline Coie Cuartet')
           AND Customers.CustomerID IN
              (SELECT Engagements.CustomerID
               FROM Engagements INNER JOIN Entertainers
                  ON Engagements.EntertainerID =
                     Entertainers.EntertainerID
               WHERE Entertainers.EntStageName =
                  'Jazz Persuasion');
```

You should get the same two rows that you found in the solution for INNER JOIN. I have specifically spaced out the three subqueries in the preceding SQL so that you can clearly see how to fetch the three sets. You can find this query in the Entertainment sample database saved as CH18_Customers_Peacock_Coie_Jazz_IN_RIGHT.

Using EXISTS

To solve our customers who booked three specific groups problem using EXISTS, you'll use a technique similar to the one you used to solve the problem using IN. The key difference is that each of your subqueries must also match on customer ID. Because you're testing for the existence of each set, each set must match the customer ID being examined in the current row. Here's how to do it:

"List the customers who have booked Carol Peacock Trio, Caroline Coie Cuartet, and Jazz Persuasion."

Translation/ Clean Up	Select customer ID, ~~customer~~ first name, ~~and~~ ~~customer~~ last name from ~~the~~ customers ~~table~~ where ~~there~~ exists ~~the~~ (~~selection of~~ customer id from ~~the~~ engagements ~~table~~ inner joined ~~with the~~ entertainers ~~table~~ on Engagements.entertainer ID ~~in the engagements table equals~~ = Entertainers.entertainer ID ~~in the entertainers table~~ where Entertainers.~~entertainer~~ stage name ~~in the entertainers table equals~~ = 'Carol Peacock Trio' and ~~the~~ Engagements.customer ID ~~in the engagements table equals the~~ = Customers.customer ID ~~in the customers table~~) and ~~there~~ exists ~~the~~ (~~selection of~~ customer id from ~~the~~ engagements ~~table~~ inner joined ~~with the~~ entertainers ~~table~~ on Engagements.entertainer ID ~~in the engagements table equals~~ = Entertainers.entertainer ID ~~in the entertainers table~~ where Entertainers.~~entertainer~~ stage name ~~in the entertainers table equals~~ = 'Caroline Coie Cuartet' and ~~the~~ Engagements.customer ID ~~in the engagements table equals the~~ = Customers.customer ID ~~in the customers table~~) and ~~there~~ exists ~~the~~ (~~selection of~~ customer id from ~~the~~ engagements ~~table~~ inner joined ~~with the~~ entertainers ~~table~~ on Engagements.entertainer ID ~~in the engagements table equals~~ = Entertainers.entertainer ID ~~in the entertainers table~~ where Entertainers.~~entertainer~~ stage name ~~in the entertainers table equals~~ = 'Jazz Persuasion' and ~~the~~ Engagements.customer ID ~~in the engagements table equals the~~ = Customers.customer ID ~~in the customers table~~)
SQL	```SELECT Customers.CustomerID,
Customers.CustFirstName, Customers.CustLastName
FROM Customers
WHERE EXISTS
(SELECT Engagements.CustomerID
FROM Engagements INNER JOIN Entertainers
ON Engagements.EntertainerID =
Entertainers.EntertainerID
WHERE Entertainers.EntStageName =
'Carol Peacock Trio'```

```
                AND Engagements.CustomerID =
                    Customers.CustomerID)
          AND EXISTS
             (SELECT Engagements.CustomerID
              FROM Enqaqements INNER JOIN Entertainers
                ON Engagements.EntertainerID =
                    Entertainers.EntertainerID
              WHERE Entertainers.EntStageName =
                    'Caroline Coie Cuartet'
                AND Engagements.CustomerID =
                    Customers.CustomerID)
          AND EXISTS
             (SELECT Engagements.CustomerID
              FROM Engagements INNER JOIN Entertainers
                ON Engagements.EntertainerID =
                    Entertainers.EntertainerID
              WHERE Entertainers.EntStageName =
                    'Jazz Persuasion'
                AND Engagements.CustomerID =
                    Customers.CustomerID);
```

This operates similarly to the principles behind the IN solution. You find the three sets of customers who have booked each of the groups and test using EXISTS. The one drawback to this approach is that the subqueries must make a reference to a field in the main query. This means that your database system must execute each of the subqueries once for every row it finds in the Customers table—once for each unique CustomerID value. (In some more advanced books, you will find this sort of subquery called a "correlated" subquery because the subquery is, in effect, co-dependent on each row in the outer query.) You can find this query saved as CH18_Customers_Peacock_Coie_Jazz_EXISTS in the Entertainment sample database.

Using GROUP BY/HAVING

You could try to solve your customers who booked three specific entertainers using GROUP BY and HAVING, but it would be difficult. When I did it for recipes and ingredients, I knew that any one ingredient appears only once in the Recipe_Ingredients table. That's not the case for customers and entertainers because a customer can choose to book an entertainer more than once. Sure, I could do something with groupings on SELECT DISTINCT, but why bother when there are several other ways to solve the problem?

Instead, let's tackle an interesting problem in the Entertainment sample database that is really best solved with GROUP BY and HAVING. Here's the problem:

> *"Display customers and groups where the musical styles of the group match all of the musical styles preferred by the customer."*

This is a "match many" problem because each customer potentially has told the agency that there are several styles that they prefer. The difficulty is the "many" isn't a fixed list—the list of potential matches changes with each customer!

Let's take a look at the tables you need to see how you might begin to construct the request. Figure 18-4 shows the tables you need to find entertainers and all the styles they play, and Figure 18-5 shows the tables you need to find customers and all the styles they prefer.

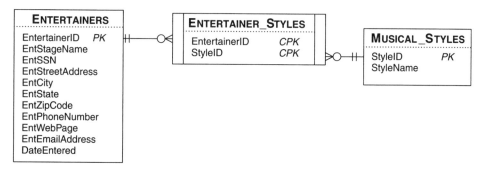

Figure 18-4 *Tables to list all entertainers and the styles that they play*

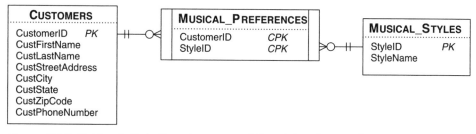

Figure 18-5 *Tables to list all customers and the styles they prefer*

Do you see any column that is common in the two sets of tables? How about the StyleID column? In fact, you probably don't need the Musical_Styles table at all unless you also want to list the matching style. If you look at the full diagram for the Entertainment Agency sample database, you won't see a direct relationship between StyleID in the Musical_Preferences table and StyleID in the Entertainer_Styles table. However, it's perfectly legal to ask for a JOIN between those two tables on StyleID because the columns in both tables are the same data type. It's also logical to do a JOIN this way because the columns you need to use in the JOIN have the same meaning. You want to find all styles that match between customers and entertainers, and you specifically want to find the matches where the number (COUNT) of matches between the two equals the total number of styles preferred by the customer. Let's get started:

"Display customers and groups where the musical styles of the group match all of the musical styles preferred by the customer."

Translation/ Clean Up	Select customer ID, cust~~omer~~ first name, cust~~omer~~ last name, entertainer ID, enter~~tainer~~ stage name, ~~and the~~ count ~~of~~ (style ID) from ~~the~~ customers ~~table~~ inner join~~ed with the~~ musical preferences ~~table~~ on Customers. customer ID ~~in the customers table matches~~ = Musical_Styles.customer ID ~~in the musical styles table then~~ inner join~~ed with the~~ entertainer styles ~~table~~ on Musical_Styles.style ID ~~in the musical styles table matches~~ = Entertainer_Styles.style ID ~~in the entertainer styles table and finally~~ inner join~~ed with the~~ entertainers ~~table~~ on Entertainers.entertainer ID ~~in the entertainers table matches~~ = Entertainer_Styles.entertainer ID ~~in the entertainer styles table~~ grouped by customer ID, cust~~omer~~ first name, cust~~omer~~ last name, entertainer ID, ~~and~~ ent~~ertainer~~ stage name ~~and~~ having ~~the~~ count ~~of~~ (style ID) = ~~equal to the~~ (select~~ion of the~~ count(*) ~~of all rows~~ from ~~the~~ musical preferences ~~table~~ where ~~the~~ Musical_Preferences. customer ID ~~in the musical preferences table matches the~~ = Customers.customer ID ~~in the customers table~~)

SQL	SELECT Customers.CustomerID,
	    Customers.CustFirstName,
	    Customers.CustLastName,
	    Entertainers.EntertainerID,
	    Entertainers.EntStageName,
	    Count(Musical_Preferences.StyleID) AS
	    CountOfStyleID

```
FROM ((Customers INNER JOIN Musical_Preferences
    ON Customers.CustomerID =
        Musical_Preferences.CustomerID)
    INNER JOIN Entertainer_Styles
    ON Musical_Preferences.StyleID =
        Entertainer_Styles.StyleID)
    INNER JOIN Entertainers
    ON Entertainers.EntertainerID =
        Entertainer_Styles.EntertainerID
    GROUP BY Customers.CustomerID,
        Customers.CustFirstName,
        Customers.CustLastName,
        Entertainers.EntertainerID,
        Entertainers.EntStageName
    HAVING Count(Musical_Preferences.StyleID) =
        (SELECT Count(*)
        FROM Musical_Preferences
        WHERE Musical_Preferences.CustomerID =
            Customers.CustomerID);
```

❖ **Note** You could get the same result by doing:

```
HAVING Count(Musical_Preferences.StyleID) =
    (SELECT Count(*)
    FROM Entertainer_Styles
    WHERE Entertainer_Styles.EntertainerID =
        Entertainers.EntertainerID)
```

CH18_Entertainers_Fully_Match_Customers_Style (8 rows)

CustomerID	CustFirstName	CustLastName	EntertainerID	EntStageName	CountOfStyleID
10002	Deb	Waldal	1003	JV & the Deep Six	2
10003	Peter	Brehm	1002	Topazz	2
10005	Elizabeth	Hallmark	1009	Katherine Ehrlich	2

CustomerID	CustFirstName	CustLastName	EntertainerID	EntStageName	CountOfStyleID
10005	Elizabeth	Hallmark	1011	Julia Schnebly	2
10008	Darren	Gehring	1001	Carol Peacock Trio	2
10010	Zachary	Ehrlich	1005	Jazz Persuasion	3
10012	Kerry	Patterson	1001	Carol Peacock Trio	2
10013	Estella	Pundt	1005	Jazz Persuasion	2

This works because each customer or entertainer has a style listed only once. Note that you don't need to know how many styles you have to match on—the query does that for you. I included the CountOfStyleID column only to demonstrate that the number of style preferences varies from customer to customer. Imagine what a sales tool this would be when one of the customers in the list calls up asking for a group recommendation. The agent can confidently recommend at least one group per customer where the group plays *all* the styles the customer prefers.

Sample Statements

You now know the mechanics of constructing queries that solve complex "not" and "and" questions and have seen some of the types of requests you can answer. Let's take a look at a fairly robust set of samples that solve a variety of "not" and "and" problems. These examples come from each of the sample databases, and they illustrate the use of the JOINs, IN, EXISTS, and grouping to find answers requiring multiple search criteria.

> ❖ **Note** Remember in the Introduction that I warned you that results from each database system won't necessarily match the sort order you see in examples in this book unless you include an ORDER BY clause.

Even when you include that specification, the system might return results in columns not included in the ORDER BY clause in a different sequence because of different optimization techniques.

If you're running the examples in Microsoft SQL Server, simply selecting the rows from the view docs not honor any ORDER BY clause specified in the view. You must open the design of the view and execute it from there to see the ORDER BY clause honored.

Also, when you use GROUP BY, you'll often see the results returned by your database system as though the rows are sorted by the columns you specified. This happens because some optimizers first sort the data internally to make it faster to process your GROUP BY. Keep in mind that if you want a specific sort order, you must also include an ORDER BY clause.

I've also included sample result sets that would be returned by these operations and placed them immediately after the SQL syntax line. The name that appears immediately above a result set is the name I gave each query in the sample data on the companion website for the book, www.informit.com/title/9780134858333. I stored each query in the appropriate sample database (as indicated within the example), using "CH18" as the leading part of the query or view name. You can follow the instructions at the beginning of this book to load the samples onto your computer and try them out.

❖ **Note** Remember that all of the field names and table names used in these examples are drawn from the sample database structures shown in Appendix B, "Schema for the Sample Databases."

Because many of these examples use complex joins, the optimizer for your database system may choose a different way to solve these queries. For this reason, the first few rows I show you may not exactly match the result you obtain, but the total number of rows should be the same.

Sales Order Database

"Find all the customers who ordered a bicycle and also ordered a helmet."

❖ **Note** In Chapter 8, I solved this problem using an INNER JOIN of two SELECT DISTINCT subqueries. Here, I solve it using EXISTS.

Translation/ Clean Up	Select customer ID, ~~customer~~ first name, ~~and customer~~ last name from ~~the~~ customers ~~table~~ where ~~there~~ exists ~~some row in~~ (SELECT * FROM ~~the~~ orders ~~table~~ inner join~~ed with the~~ order details ~~table~~ on orders.order number ~~in the orders table equals~~ = order_details.order number ~~in the order details table, and then~~ inner join~~ed with the~~ products ~~table~~ on products.product ID ~~in the products table equals~~ = order_details.product ID ~~in the order details table~~ where product name ~~contains~~ LIKE '%Bike' and Orders.customer ID ~~in the orders table equals~~ = ~~the~~ Customers.customer ID ~~in the customers table)~~, and ~~there also~~ exists ~~some row in~~ (SELECT * FROM ~~the~~ orders ~~table~~ inner join~~ed with the~~ order details ~~table~~ on orders.order ID ~~in the orders table equals~~ = order_details.order ID ~~in the order details table, and then~~ inner join~~ed with the~~ products ~~table~~ on products.product ID ~~in the products table equals~~ = order_details.product ~~ID in the order details table~~ where product name ~~contains~~ LIKE '%Helmet' and ~~the~~ Orders.customer ID ~~in the orders table equals~~ = ~~the~~ Customers.customer ID ~~in the customers table)~~

SQL	<pre>SELECT Customers.CustomerID,
	    Customers.CustFirstName,
	    Customers.CustLastName
	FROM Customers
	WHERE EXISTS
	  (SELECT *
	   FROM (Orders INNER JOIN Order_Details
	     ON Orders.OrderNumber =
	       Order_Details.OrderNumber)
	   INNER JOIN Products
	     ON Products.ProductNumber =
	       Order_Details.ProductNumber
	    WHERE Products.ProductName LIKE '%Bike'
	     AND Orders.CustomerID =
	       Customers.CustomerID)</pre>

```
AND EXISTS
  (SELECT *
   FROM (Orders INNER JOIN Order_Details
     ON Orders.OrderNumber =
        Order_Details.OrderNumber)
   INNER JOIN Products
     ON Products.ProductNumber =
        Order_Details.ProductNumber
   WHERE Products.ProductName LIKE '%Helmet'
     AND Orders.CustomerID =
        Customers.CustomerID)
```

CH18_Cust_Bikes_And_Helmets_EXISTS (21 rows)

CustomerID	CustFirstName	CustLastName
1002	William	Thompson
1004	Robert	Brown
1005	Dean	McCrae
1006	John	Viescas
1007	Mariya	Sergienko
1008	Neil	Patterson
1009	Andrew	Cencini
1010	Angel	Kennedy
1012	Liz	Keyser
1013	Rachel	Patterson

<< more rows here >>

"Find all the customers who have not ordered either bikes or tires."

❖ **Note** I simplified this a bit because I know the category ID for bikes is 2, and the category ID for tires is 6. If I didn't know this, I should have included an additional JOIN to the Categories table and then looked for 'Bikes' and 'Tires'.

Translation/ Clean Up	Select customer ID, cust~~omer~~ first name, ~~and~~ cust~~omer~~ last name from ~~the~~ customers ~~table~~ where customer ID ~~is~~ not in ~~the~~ (select~~ion of~~ customer ID from ~~the~~ orders ~~table~~ inner join~~ed with the~~ order details ~~table~~ on Orders.order number ~~in the orders table equals~~ = Order_Details.order number ~~in the order details table, and then~~ inner joined ~~with the~~ products ~~table~~ on Products.product ID ~~in the products table equals~~ = Order_Details.product ID ~~in the order details table~~ where product category ~~is~~ = 2)~~,~~ and customer ID ~~is~~ not in ~~the~~ (select~~ion of~~ customer ID from ~~the~~ orders ~~table~~ inner join~~ed with the~~ order details ~~table~~ on Orders.order number ~~in the orders table equals~~ = Order_Details.order number ~~in the order details table, and then~~ inner joined ~~with the~~ products ~~table~~ on Products.product ID ~~in the products table equals~~ = Order_Details.product ID ~~in the order details table~~ where product category ID ~~is~~ = 6)

SQL	```SELECT Customers.CustomerID, Customers.CustFirstName,```
	   ```Customers.CustLastName```
	```FROM Customers```
	```WHERE Customers.CustomerID NOT IN```
	  ```(SELECT CustomerID```
	   ```FROM (Orders INNER JOIN Order_Details```
	    ```ON Orders.OrderNumber =```
	     ```Order_Details.OrderNumber)```
	   ```INNER JOIN Products```
	    ```ON Order_Details.ProductNumber =```
	     ```Products.ProductNumber```
	   ```WHERE Products.CategoryID = 2)```
	  ```AND Customers.CustomerID NOT IN```
	  ```(SELECT CustomerID```
	   ```FROM (Orders INNER JOIN Order_Details```
	    ```ON Orders.OrderNumber =```
	     ```Order_Details.OrderNumber)```
	   ```INNER JOIN Products```
	    ```ON Order_Details.ProductNumber =```
	     ```Products.ProductNumber```
	   ```WHERE Products.CategoryID = 6)```

CH18_Customers_Not_Bikes_Or_Tires_NOTIN_2 (2 rows)

CustomerID	CustFirstName	CustLastName
1022	Caleb	Viescas
1028	Jeffrey	Tirekicker

> ❖ **Note** I would expect Jeffrey Tirekicker to show up in any query that asks for customers who haven't bought certain items because this customer has never bought anything! See CH18_Customers_No_Orders_JOIN and CH18_Customers_No_Orders_NOT_IN to verify this.

Entertainment Database

"List the entertainers who played engagements for customers Berg and Hallmark."

> ❖ **Note** I solved this problem in Chapter 8 with a JOIN of two complex table subqueries. This time, I'll use EXISTS.

Translation/ Clean Up	Select entertainer ID, ~~and entertainer~~ stage name from ~~the~~ entertainers ~~table~~ where ~~there~~ exists (SELECT * ~~some row~~ from ~~the~~ customers ~~table~~ inner joined ~~with the~~ engagements ~~table~~ on customers.customer ID ~~in the customers table matches~~ = engagements.customer ID ~~in the engagements table~~ where customer last name ~~is~~ = 'Berg' and ~~the~~ engagements ~~table~~ entertainer ID ~~equals~~ = ~~the~~ Entertainers.entertainer ID ~~in the entertainers table)~~; and ~~there also~~ exists (SELECT * ~~some row~~ from ~~the~~ customers ~~table~~ inner joined ~~with the~~ engagements ~~table~~ on customers.customer ID ~~in the customers table matches~~= engagements.customer ID ~~in the engagements table~~ where customer last name ~~is~~ = 'Hallmark' and ~~the~~ Engagements.entertainer ID ~~in the engagements table equals~~ = ~~the~~ Entertainers.entertainer ID ~~in the entertainers table~~)

SQL	`SELECT Entertainers.EntertainerID,`
	`        Entertainers.EntStageName`
	`FROM Entertainers`
	`WHERE EXISTS`
	`   (SELECT *`

```
              FROM Customers INNER JOIN Engagements
                  ON Customers.CustomerID =
                     Engagements.CustomerID
              WHERE Customers.CustLastName = 'Berg'
                  AND Engagements.EntertainerID =
                     Entertainers.EntertainerID)
          AND EXISTS
              (SELECT *
              FROM Customers INNER JOIN Engagements
                  ON Customers.CustomerID =
                     Engagements.CustomerID
              WHERE Customers.CustLastName = 'Hallmark'
                  AND Engagements.EntertainerID =
                     Entertainers.EntertainerID)
```

CH18_Entertainers_Berg_AND_Hallmark_EXISTS (4 rows)

EntertainerID	EntStageName
1001	Carol Peacock Trio
1003	JV & the Deep Six
1006	Modern Dance
1008	Country Feeling

"Display agents who have never booked a Country or Country Rock group."

Translation/ Clean Up	Select agent ID, ~~agent~~ first name, ~~and~~ ~~agent~~ last name from ~~the~~ agents ~~table~~ where agent ID ~~is~~ not in ~~the~~ (~~selection of~~ agent ID from ~~the~~ engagements ~~table~~ inner joined ~~with the~~ engagements ~~table~~ on Engagements.entertainer ID ~~in the engagements table equals~~ = Entertainers.entertainer ID ~~in the entertainers table, and then~~ inner joined ~~with the~~ entertainer styles ~~table~~ on Entertainers.entertainer ID ~~in the entertainers table equals~~ = Entertainer_Styles.entertainer ID ~~in the entertainer styles table, and then~~ inner joined ~~with the~~ musical styles ~~table~~ on Entertainer_Styles.style ID ~~in the entertainer styles table equals~~ = Musical_Styles.style ID ~~in the musical styles table~~ where style name ~~is~~ in ('Country', ~~or~~ 'Country Rock'))

SQL	SELECT Agents.AgentID, Agents.AgtFirstName,

```
SELECT Agents.AgentID, Agents.AgtFirstName,
      Agents.AgtLastName
FROM Agents
WHERE Agents.AgentID NOT IN
    (SELECT Engagements.AgentID
     FROM ((Engagements INNER JOIN Entertainers
       ON Engagements.EntertainerID =
         Entertainers.EntertainerID)
     INNER JOIN Entertainer_Styles
       ON Entertainers.EntertainerID =
         Entertainer_Styles.EntertainerID)
     INNER JOIN Musical_Styles
       ON Entertainer_Styles.StyleID =
         Musical_Styles.StyleID
     WHERE Musical_Styles.StyleName IN
       ('Country', 'Country Rock'));
```

CH18_Agents_Not_Book_Country_CountryRock (3 rows)

AgentID	AgtFirstName	AgtLastName
2	Scott	Bishop
8	Maria	Patterson
9	Daffy	Dumbwit

❖ **Note** I would expect Daffy Dumbwit to show up in any query that asks for agents who haven't booked certain items because this agent has never booked anything!

School Scheduling Database

"List students who have a grade of 85 or better in both art and computer science."

❖ **Note** I showed you how to solve this problem in Chapter 8 with an INNER JOIN of two DISTINCT subqueries. Here's how to solve it using IN.

Translation/ Clean Up	Select student ID, stud~~ent~~ first name, ~~and~~ stud~~ent~~ last name from ~~the~~ students ~~table~~ where student ID ~~is~~ in ~~the~~ (select~~ion of~~ student ID from ~~the~~ student schedules ~~table~~ inner join~~ed with the~~ classes ~~table~~ on Classes.student ID ~~in the classes table equals~~ = Student_Schedules.student ID ~~in the~~ ~~student schedules table, then~~ inner join~~ed with~~ ~~the~~ subjects ~~table~~ on Subjects.subject ID ~~in the subjects~~ ~~table equals~~ = Classes.subject ID ~~in the classes styles~~ ~~table, and then~~ inner join~~ed with the~~ categories ~~table~~ on Categories.category ID ~~in the categories table equals~~ = Subjects.category ID ~~in the subjects table~~ where category description ~~is equal to~~ = 'art' and grade ~~is greater~~ ~~than or equal to~~ >= 85) and student ID ~~is~~ in ~~the~~ (select~~ion of~~ student ID from ~~the~~ student schedules ~~table~~ inner join~~ed~~ ~~with the~~ classes ~~table~~ on Classes.student ID ~~in the~~ ~~classes table equals~~ = Student_Schedules.student ID ~~in~~ ~~the student schedules table, then~~ inner join~~ed with the~~ subjects ~~table~~ on Subjects.subject ID ~~in the subjects table~~ ~~equals~~ = Classes.subject ID ~~in the classes styles table,~~ ~~and then~~ inner join~~ed with the~~ categories ~~table~~ on Categories.category ID ~~in the categories table equals~~ = Subjects.category ID ~~in the subjects table~~ where category description ~~contains~~ LIKE '%computer%' and grade ~~is greater~~ ~~than or equal to~~ >= 85)

SQL	`SELECT Students.StudentID,`
	    `Students.StudFirstName, Students.StudLastName`
	`FROM Students`
	`WHERE Students.StudentID IN`
	  `(SELECT Student_Schedules.StudentID`
	  `FROM ((Student_Schedules INNER JOIN Classes`
	    `ON Classes.ClassID =`
	      `Student_Schedules.ClassID)`
	  `INNER JOIN Subjects`
	    `ON Subjects.SubjectID = Classes.SubjectID)`
	  `INNER JOIN Categories`
	    `ON Categories.CategoryID = Subjects.`
	      `CategoryID`
	  `WHERE Categories.CategoryDescription = 'Art'`
	    `AND Student_Schedules.Grade >= 85)`

```
AND Students.StudentID IN
    (SELECT Student_Schedules.StudentID
     FROM ((Student_Schedules INNER JOIN Classes
        ON Classes.ClassID =
            Student_Schedules.ClassID)
     INNER JOIN Subjects
        ON Subjects.SubjectID = Classes.SubjectID)
     INNER JOIN Categories
        ON Categories.CategoryID = Subjects.
            CategoryID
     WHERE Categories.CategoryDescription LIKE
            '%Computer%'
     AND Student_Schedules.Grade >= 85);
```

CH18_Good_Art_CS_Students_IN (1 row)

StudentID	StudFirstName	StudLastName
1011	John	Kennedy

"Show me students registered for classes for which they have not completed the prerequisite course."

❖ **Note** This is an interesting combination of "and" and "not." The query needs to compare an unknown number of classes for which a student has registered with an unknown number of those classes that have prerequisites for which the student has not previously registered or completed. (The problem assumes that it's OK if a student is concurrently registered for a prerequisite course.)

Let's restate that so it's a bit clearer how you should solve this problem.

"Show the students and the courses for which they are registered that have prerequisites for which there is not a registration for this student in the prerequisite course (and the student did not withdraw) with a start date of the prerequisite course that is equal to or earlier than the current course."

Translation/ Clean Up	Select student ID, stud~~ent~~ first name, stud~~ent~~ last name start date, subject code, subject name, ~~and~~ subject prereq from ~~the~~ students ~~table~~ inner join~~ed with the~~ student schedules ~~table~~ on Students.student ID ~~in the students table equals~~ = Student_Schedules.student ID ~~in the student schedules table, then~~ inner joined ~~with the~~ classes ~~table~~ on Classes.class ID ~~in the classes table equals~~ = Student_Schedules.class ID ~~in the student schedules table, and then~~ inner joined ~~with the~~ subjects ~~table~~ on Subjects.subject ID ~~in the subjects table equals~~ = Classes.subject ID ~~in the classes table~~ where subject prereq is not null and subject prereq ~~is~~ not in ~~the~~ (selec~~tion of~~ subject code from ~~the~~ subjects ~~table~~ inner join~~ed with the~~ classes ~~table aliased~~ as c2 on Subjects.subject ID ~~in the subjects table equals~~ = C2.subject ID ~~in the c2 aliased table, and then~~ inner join~~ed with the~~ student schedules ~~table~~ on C2.class ID ~~in the c2 aliased table equals~~ = Student_Schedules.class ID ~~in the student schedules table, and then~~ inner joined ~~with the~~ student class status ~~table~~ on Student_Schedules.class status ~~in the student schedules table equals~~ = Student_Class_Status.class status ~~in the student class status table~~ where class status description ~~does not equal~~ <> 'withdrew' and Student_Schedules.student ID ~~in the student schedules table equals~~ = Students.student ID ~~in the students table~~ and C2.start date ~~in the aliased c2 table is less than or equal to~~ <= Classes.start date ~~in the classes table~~)

SQL	```SELECT Students.StudentID,```
	``` Students.StudFirstName,```
	``` Students.StudLastName, Classes.StartDate,```
	``` Subjects.SubjectCode, Subjects.SubjectName,```
	``` Subjects.SubjectPreReq```
	```FROM ((Students INNER JOIN Student_Schedules```
	``` ON Students.StudentID =```
	``` Student_Schedules.StudentID)```
	```INNER JOIN Classes```
	``` ON Classes.ClassID =```
	``` Student_Schedules.ClassID)```
	```INNER JOIN Subjects```
	``` ON Subjects.SubjectID = Classes.SubjectID```
	```WHERE Subjects.SubjectPreReq IS NOT NULL```
	``` AND Subjects.SubjectPreReq NOT IN```

```
                (SELECT Subjects.SubjectCode
        FROM ((Subjects INNER JOIN Classes AS C2
            ON Subjects.SubjectID = C2.SubjectID)
        INNER JOIN Student_Schedules
            ON C2.ClassID = Student_Schedules.ClassID)
            INNER JOIN Student_Class_Status
            ON Student_Schedules.ClassStatus =
                Student_Class_Status.ClassStatus
            WHERE
            Student_Class_Status.ClassStatusDescription
                <> 'Withdrew'
            AND Student_Schedules.StudentID =
                Students.StudentID
            AND C2.StartDate <=  Classes.StartDate);
```

CH18_Students_Missing_Prerequisites (5 rows)

StudentID	StudFirst Name	StudLast Name	StartDate	Subject Code	SubjectName	Prerequisite
1005	Doris	Hartwig	2017-09-11	ENG 102	Composition-Intermediate	ENG 101
1007	Elizabeth	Hallmark	2017-09-11	ENG 102	Composition-Intermediate	ENG 101
1012	Sarah	Thompson	2017-09-11	ENG 102	Composition-Intermediate	ENG 101
1014	Kendra	Bonnicksen	2017-09-11	ENG 102	Composition-Intermediate	ENG 101
1018	Richard	Lum	2017-09-11	ENG 102	Composition-Intermediate	ENG 101

Bowling League Database

"List the bowlers, the match number, the game number, the handicap score, the tournament date, and the tournament location for bowlers who won a game with a handicap score of 190 or less at Thunderbird Lanes, Totem Lanes, and Bolero Lanes."

❖ **Note** You first need to find all bowlers who won a game with a handicap score of 190 or less at one of the three locations, then verify that the bowler ID is also in the list of bowlers who won a game with a handicap score of 190 or less at each of the three locations. (Remember, not in (a, b, c) but in (a) AND in (b), AND in (c).)

Translation/ Clean Up	Select bowler ID, bowler first name, bowler last name, match ID, game number, handicap score, tourney date, ~~and~~ tourney location from ~~the~~ bowlers ~~table~~ inner joined ~~with the~~ bowler scores ~~table~~ on Bowlers.bowler ID ~~in the bowlers table equals~~ = Bowler_Scores.bowler ID ~~in the bowler scores table, then~~ inner joined ~~with the~~ tourney matches ~~table~~ on Bowler_Scores.match ID ~~in the bowler scores table equals~~ = Tourney_Matches.match ID ~~in the tourney matches table, and then~~ inner joined ~~with~~ the tournaments ~~table~~ on Tournaments.tourney ID ~~in the tournaments table equals~~ = Tourney_Matches.tourney ID ~~in the tourney matches table~~ where handicap score ~~is less than or equal to~~ <= 190 and won game ~~equals~~ = 1 and tourney location ~~is in the list~~ ('Thunderbird Lanes', 'Totem Lanes', and 'Bolero Lanes') and bowler ID ~~is in the (selection of~~ bowler ID from ~~the~~ tournaments ~~table~~ inner joined ~~with the~~ tourney matches ~~table~~ on Tournaments.tourney ID ~~in the tournaments table equals~~ = Tourney_Matches.tourney ID ~~in the tourney matches table, and then~~ inner joined ~~with the~~ bowler scores ~~table~~ on Tourney_Matches.match ID ~~in the tourney matches table equals~~ = Bowler_Scores.match ID ~~in the bowler scores table~~ where won game ~~equals~~ = 1 and handicap score ~~is less than or equal to~~ <= 190 and tourney location ~~equals~~ = 'Thunderbird Lanes') and bowler ID ~~is in the (selection of~~ bowler ID from ~~the~~ tournaments ~~table~~ inner joined ~~with the~~ tourney matches ~~table~~ on Tournaments.tourney ID ~~in the tournaments table equals~~ = Tourney_Matches.tourney ID ~~in the tourney matches table, and then~~ inner joined ~~with the~~ bowler scores ~~table~~ on Tourney_Matches.match ID ~~in the tourney matches table equals~~ = Bowler_Scores.match ID ~~in the bowler scores table~~ where won game ~~equals~~ = 1 and handicap score ~~is less than or equal to~~ <= 190 and tourney location ~~equals~~ = 'Totem Lanes') and bowler ID ~~is in the (selection of~~ bowler ID from ~~the~~ tournaments ~~table~~ inner joined ~~with the~~ tourney matches ~~table~~ on Tournaments.tourney ID ~~in the tournaments table equals~~ = Tourney_Matches.tourney ID ~~in the tourney matches table, and then~~ inner joined ~~with the~~ bowler scores ~~table~~ on

Tourney_Matches.match ID ~~in the tourney matches table~~
~~equals~~ = Bowler_Scores.match ID ~~in the bowler scores~~
~~table~~ where won game ~~equals~~ = 1 and handicap score ~~is~~
~~less than or equal to~~ <= 190 and tourney location ~~equals~~
= 'Bolero Lanes')

SQL	SELECT Bowlers.BowlerID, Bowlers.BowlerFirstName,

```
SELECT Bowlers.BowlerID, Bowlers.BowlerFirstName,
    Bowlers.BowlerLastName, Bowler_Scores.MatchID,
    Bowler_Scores.GameNumber,
    Bowler_Scores.HandiCapScore,
    Tournaments.TourneyDate,
    Tournaments.TourneyLocation
FROM ((Bowlers INNER JOIN Bowler_Scores
    ON Bowlers.BowlerID = Bowler_Scores.BowlerID)
INNER JOIN Tourney_Matches
    ON Bowler_Scores.MatchID =
        Tourney_Matches.MatchID)
INNER JOIN Tournaments
    ON Tournaments.TourneyID =
        Tourney_Matches.TourneyID
WHERE (Bowler_Scores.HandiCapScore <= 190)
    AND (Bowler_Scores.WonGame = 1
    AND (Tournaments.TourneyLocation IN
        ('Thunderbird Lanes', 'Totem Lanes',
            'Bolero Lanes'))
    AND (Bowlers.BowlerID  IN
        (SELECT Bowler_Scores.BowlerID
            FROM (Tournaments INNER JOIN Tourney_Matches
                ON Tournaments.TourneyID =
                    Tourney_Matches.TourneyID)
            INNER JOIN Bowler_Scores
                ON Tourney_Matches.MatchID =
                    Bowler_Scores.MatchID
            WHERE Bowler_Scores.WonGame = 1
                AND Bowler_Scores.HandiCapScore <=190
                AND Tournaments.TourneyLocation =
                    'Thunderbird Lanes'))
```

```
                AND (Bowlers.BowlerID IN
                 (SELECT Bowler_Scores.BowlerID
                  FROM (Tournaments INNER JOIN Tourney_Matches
                    ON Tournaments.TourneyID =
                       Tourney_Matches.TourneyID)
                  INNER JOIN Bowler_Scores
                    ON Tourney_Matches.MatchID =
                       Bowler_Scores.MatchID
                  WHERE Bowler_Scores.WonGame = 1
                    AND Bowler_Scores.HandiCapScore <=190
                    AND Tournaments.TourneyLocation =
                      'Totem Lanes'))
                AND (Bowlers.BowlerID IN
                 (SELECT Bowler_Scores.BowlerID
                  FROM (Tournaments INNER JOIN Tourney_Matches
                    ON Tournaments.TourneyID =
                       Tourney_Matches.TourneyID)
                  INNER JOIN Bowler_Scores
                    ON Tourney_Matches.MatchID =
                       Bowler_Scores.MatchID
                  WHERE Bowler_Scores.WonGame = 1
                    AND Bowler_Scores.HandiCapScore <=190
                    AND Tournaments.TourneyLocation =
                      'Bolero Lanes'));
```

CH18_Bowlers_Won_LowScore_TBird_Totem_Bolero_RIGHT (11 rows)

Bowler ID	Bowler FirstName	Bowler LastName	Match ID	Game Number	HandiCap Score	Tourney Date	Tourney Location
13	Elizabeth	Hallmark	10	1	189	2017-09-18	Bolero Lanes
13	Elizabeth	Hallmark	24	3	190	2017-10-09	Totem Lanes
13	Elizabeth	Hallmark	34	1	189	2017-10-30	Thunderbird Lanes
19	John	Viescas	7	3	185	2017-09-11	Thunderbird Lanes

Bowler ID	Bowler FirstName	Bowler LastName	Match ID	Game Number	HandiCap Score	Tourney Date	Tourney Location
19	John	Viescas	12	1	181	2017-09-18	Bolero Lanes
19	John	Viescas	36	1	179	2017-10-30	Thunderbird Lanes
19	John	Viescas	52	2	185	2017-11-27	Totem Lanes
25	Megan	Patterson	7	1	188	2017-09-11	Thunderbird Lanes
25	Megan	Patterson	21	1	189	2017-10-09	Totem Lanes
25	Megan	Patterson	35	1	187	2017-10-30	Thunderbird Lanes
25	Megan	Patterson	39	2	181	2017-11-06	Bolero Lanes

❖ **Note** You can also find the incorrect IN solution saved as CH18_ Bowlers_Won_LowScore_TBird_Totem_Bolero_WRONG in the Bowling League sample database.

"Show me the bowlers who have not bowled a raw score better than 165 at Thunderbird Lanes and Bolero Lanes."

Translation/ Clean Up	Select bowler ID, bowler last name, ~~and~~ bowler first name from ~~the~~ bowlers ~~table~~ where bowler ID ~~is~~ not in ~~the~~ (~~selection of~~ bowler ID from ~~the~~ tournaments ~~table~~ inner join~~ed with the~~ tourney matches ~~table~~ on Tournaments.tourney ID ~~in the tournaments table equals~~ = Tourney_Matches.tourney ID ~~in the tourney matches table, then~~ inner join~~ed with the~~ bowler scores ~~table~~ on Tourney_Matches.match ID ~~in the tourney matches table equals~~ = Bowler_Scores.match ID ~~in the bowler scores table~~ where raw score ~~is greater than~~ > 165 and tourney location ~~is~~ in ~~the list of~~ ('Thunderbird Lanes', ~~and~~ 'Bolero Lanes'))

SQL	`SELECT Bowlers.BowlerID, Bowlers.`
	    `BowlerLastName, Bowlers.BowlerFirstName`
	`FROM Bowlers`
	`WHERE Bowlers.BowlerID NOT IN`
	`(SELECT Bowler_Scores.BowlerID`

```
FROM (Tournaments INNER JOIN Tourney_Matches
      ON Tournaments.TourneyID =
         Tourney_Matches.TourneyID)
      INNER JOIN Bowler_Scores
      ON Tourney_Matches.MatchID =
         Bowler_Scores.MatchID
WHERE (Bowler_Scores.RawScore > 165)
  AND (Tournaments.TourneyLocation IN
      ('Thunderbird Lanes', 'Bolero Lanes')))
```

CH18_Bowlers_LTE_165_Thunderbird_Bolero (15 rows)

BowlerID	BowlerLastName	BowlerFirstName
1	Fournier	Barbara
4	Sheskey	Sara
5	Patterson	Ann
8	Viescas	Stephanie
9	Black	Alastair
12	Viescas	Carol
13	Hallmark	Elizabeth
16	Sheskey	Richard
17	Hernandez	Kendra
20	Viescas	Suzanne

<< *more rows here* >>

Recipes Database

"*Display the ingredients that are not used in the recipes for Irish Stew, Pollo Picoso, and Roast Beef.*"

Translation/ Clean Up	Select ingredient ID, ~~and~~ ingredient name from ~~the~~ ingredients ~~table~~ where ingredient ID ~~is~~ not in ~~the~~ (~~selection of~~ ingredient ID from ~~the~~ recipe ingredients ~~table~~ inner joined ~~with the~~ recipes ~~table~~ on Recipe_Ingredients.recipe ID ~~in the recipe ingredients table equals~~ = Recipes.recipe ID ~~in the recipes table~~ where recipe title ~~is in the list of~~ ('Irish Stew', 'Pollo Picoso', ~~and~~ 'Roast Beef'))

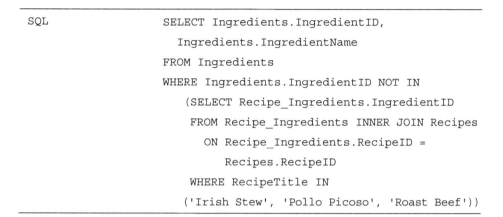

SQL	SELECT Ingredients.IngredientID,
	Ingredients.IngredientName
	FROM Ingredients
	WHERE Ingredients.IngredientID NOT IN
	(SELECT Recipe_Ingredients.IngredientID
	FROM Recipe_Ingredients INNER JOIN Recipes
	ON Recipe_Ingredients.RecipeID =
	Recipes.RecipeID
	WHERE RecipeTitle IN
	('Irish Stew', 'Pollo Picoso', 'Roast Beef'))

CH18_Ingredients_NOTIN_IrishStew_PolloPicoso_RoastBeef (67 rows)

IngredientID	IngredientName
7	Tomato
8	Jalapeno
12	Halibut
13	Chicken, Fryer
14	Bacon
15	Romaine Lettuce
16	Iceberg Lettuce
17	Butterhead Lettuce
18	Scallop
19	Salmon

<< more rows here >>

"List the pairs of recipes where both recipes have at least the same three ingredients."

❖ **Note** This is similar to the query I showed you earlier matching customers and entertainers who play all the customer's preferred styles. Do you suppose you need two copies of the recipes and recipe ingredients tables?

Translation/ Clean Up	Select Recipes.recipe ID ~~and~~ Recipes.recipe title ~~in the first copy of the recipes table and~~ R2.recipe ID AS R2ID ~~and~~ R2.recipe title AS R2Title ~~in the second copy of the recipes table, and the~~ count ~~of~~ (Recipe_Ingredients.recipe ID) AS CountOfRecipeID in ~~the first copy of the recipe ingredients table~~ from the recipes ~~table~~ inner joined ~~with the~~ recipe ingredients ~~table~~ on Recipes.recipe ID ~~in the recipes table equals~~ = Recipe_Ingredients.recipe ID ~~in the recipe ingredients table, then~~ inner joined ~~with the second copy of the~~ recipe ingredients ~~table~~ AS RI2 on Recipe_Ingredients.ingredient ID ~~in the recipe ingredients table equals~~ = RI2.ingredient ID ~~in the second copy of the recipe ingredients table, then~~ inner joined ~~with the second copy of the~~ recipes ~~table~~ AS R2 on R2.recipe ID ~~in the second copy of the recipes table equals~~ = RI2.recipe ID ~~in the second copy of the recipe ingredients table~~ where RI2.recipe ID ~~in the second copy of the recipe ingredients table is greater than~~ > Recipes.recipe ID ~~in the first copy of the recipes table,~~ grouped by Recipes.recipe ID ~~in the first copy of the recipes table~~, Recipes.recipe title ~~in the first copy of the recipes table,~~ R2.recipe ID ~~in the second copy of the recipes table, and~~ R2.recipe title ~~in the second copy of the recipes table, and~~ having ~~the~~ count ~~of matching~~ (Recipe_Ingredients.ingredient ID) ~~in the recipe ingredients table greater than~~ > 3

SQL	<pre>SELECT Recipes.RecipeID, Recipes.RecipeTitle,
	    R2.RecipeID AS R2ID, R2.RecipeTitle AS R2Title,
	    Count(Recipe_Ingredients.RecipeID)
	        AS CountOfRecipeID
	FROM ((Recipes INNER JOIN Recipe_Ingredients
	    ON Recipes.RecipeID =
	        Recipe_Ingredients.RecipeID)
	INNER JOIN Recipe_Ingredients AS RI2
	    ON Recipe_Ingredients.IngredientID =
	        RI2.IngredientID)
	INNER JOIN Recipes AS R2
	    ON R2.RecipeID = RI2.RecipeID
	WHERE RI2.RecipeID > Recipes.RecipeID
	GROUP BY Recipes.RecipeID, Recipes.RecipeTitle,
	    R2.RecipeID, R2.RecipeTitle
	HAVING Count(Recipe_Ingredients.RecipeID) >= 3;</pre>

CH18_Recipes_AtLeast_3_Same_Ingredients (4 rows)

RecipeID	RecipeTitle	R2ID	R2Title	CountOf RecipeID
2	Salsa Buena	11	Huachinango Veracruzana (Red Snapper, Veracruz style	3
2	Salsa Buena	13	Tourtière (French-Canadian Pork Pie)	3
6	Pollo Picoso	9	Roast Beef	3
11	Huachinango Veracruzana (Red Snapper, Veracruz style)	13	Tourtière (French-Canadian Pork Pie)	4

❖ **Note** I threw in the check to make sure the ID of the second recipe is always higher than the ID of the first so that I don't get a pair of recipes listed twice. Following the SQL Standard, I could have put that filter in the JOIN on the two copies of the Recipe_Ingredients tables, but I chose to put the filter in the WHERE clause to ensure compatibility with most database systems.

Summary

I began the chapter with a review of sets to help you get a picture of how you go about solving problems that involve multiple "not" and "and" criteria. I then followed that with an extensive review of four different ways to approach solving problems with multiple "not" criteria, including OUTER JOIN, NOT IN, NOT EXISTS, and GROUP BY/HAVING.

I then covered four different ways to think about solving problems with multiple "and" criteria: INNER JOIN, IN, EXISTS, and GROUP BY/HAVING. To help cement the concepts, I provided five sets of sample statements for each of the sample databases. I was careful to include one "and" example and one "not" example for each sample database.

The following section presents several requests that you can work out on your own.

Problems for You to Solve

Below, I show you the request statement and the name of the solution query in the sample databases. If you want some practice, you can work out the SQL you need for each request and then check your answer with the query I saved in the samples. Don't worry if your syntax doesn't exactly match the syntax of the queries I saved—as long as your Result Set is the same.

Sales Order Database

1. *"Display the customers who have never ordered bikes or tires."*

   I showed you how to solve this earlier using NOT IN on multiple subqueries. Can you figure out a way to solve it more simply using NOT IN? You can find the solution in CH18_Customers_Not_Bikes_Or_Tires_NOTIN_1 (2 rows).

2. *"List the customers who have purchased a bike but not a helmet."*

   First, solve this problem using EXISTS and NOT EXISTS. The solution is in CH18_Cust_Bikes_No_Helmets_EXISTS (2 rows). For extra credit, solve the problem using IN and NOT IN. You can find the solution in CH18_Customer_Bikes_No_Helmets (2 rows).

3. *"Show me the customer orders that have a bike but do not have a helmet."*

   This might seem to be the same as problem 2 above, but it's not. Show me the *orders*, not the customers. Solve it using EXISTS and NOT EXISTS. You can find the solution in CH18_Orders_Bikes_No_Helmet_EXISTS (402 rows).

4. *"Display the customers and their orders that have a bike and a helmet in the same order."*

   Solve this problem using EXISTS. You can find the solution in CH18_Customers_Bikes_And_Helmets_Same_Order (184 rows).

5. *"Show the vendors who sell accessories, car racks, and clothing."*

   Solve this problem using IN. You can find the solution in CH18_Vendors_Accessories_CarRacks_Clothing (3 rows).

Entertainment Database

1. *"List the entertainers who play the Jazz, Rhythm and Blues, and Salsa styles."*

   Solve the problem using IN, but be careful to not take the easy way out! You can find the solution in CH18_Entertainers_Jazz_RhythmBlues_Salsa_IN (1 row). CH18_Entertainers_Jazz_RhythmBlues_Salsa_IN_WRONG shows you the incorrect IN solution (4 rows). For extra credit, solve the problem using GROUP BY and HAVING. You can find the solution in CH18_Entertainers_Jazz_RhythmBlues_Salsa_HAVING (1 row).

2. *"Show the entertainers who did not have a booking in the 90 days preceding May 1, 2018."*

   You can solve this problem using NOT IN, but be careful to use the date and time function appropriate for your database system. You can find the solution in CH18_Entertainers_Not_Booked_90Days_Before_May1_2018 (2 rows).

3. *"Display the customers who have not booked Topazz or Modern Dance."*

   You can solve this problem in a couple of different ways using NOT IN. You can find one solution in CH18_Customers_Not_Booked_Topazz_Or_ModernDance (6 rows).

4. *"List the entertainers who have performed for Hartwig, McCrae, and Rosales."*

   There are several ways to solve this. You can find the solution using EXISTS in CH18_Entertainers_Hartwig_McCrae_AND_Rosales_EXISTS (2 rows).

5. *"Display the customers who have never booked an entertainer."* *"Show the entertainers who have no bookings."*

   You can solve both problems using a simple NOT IN. You can find the solutions in CH18_Customers_No_Bookings_NOT_IN (2 rows), and CH18_Entertainers_Never_Booked_NOT_IN (1 row).

School Scheduling Database

1. *"Show students who have a grade of 85 or better in both Art and Computer Science."*

   I showed you earlier how to solve this problem using IN. Now solve it using EXISTS. You can find the solution in CH18_Good_Art_CS_Students_EXISTS (1 row).

2. *"Display the staff members who are teaching classes for which they are not accredited."*

   The trick is to find rows in the faculty classes table that are not in the faculty subjects table.

   You can find the solution in CH18_Staff_Teaching_NonAccredited_Classes (4 rows).

3. *"List the students who have passed all completed classes with a grade of 80 or better."*

   As you might suspect, this is best done with GROUP BY and HAVING. You can find the solution in CH18_Students_Passed_All_Grade_GTE_80 (3 rows).

4. Solve three of the following simple NOT problems: *"Find classes with no students." "Display staff members not teaching." "Show which students have never withdrawn." "List students not currently enrolled." "Find subjects that have no faculty assigned."*

   You can find the solutions in: CH18_Classes_No_Students_Enrolled_NOT_IN (118 rows), CH18_Staff_Not_Teaching_EXISTS (5 rows), CH18_Students_Never_Withdrawn_EXISTS (16 rows), CH18_Students_Not_Currently_Enrolled_NOT_IN (2 rows), and CH18_Subjects_No_Faculty_NOT_IN (1 row).

Bowling League Database

1. *"Display the bowlers who have never bowled a raw score greater than 150."*

   You can find one way to solve this in CH18_Mediocre_Bowlers (7 rows).

2. *"Show the bowlers who have a raw score greater than 170 at both Thunderbird Lanes and Bolero Lanes."*

   I have shown you how to solve this using an INNER JOIN of SELECT DISTINCT queries. Now solve it using EXISTS. You can find the solution in CH18_Good_Bowlers_TBird_And_Bolero_EXISTS (11 rows).

3. *"List the tournaments that have not yet been played."*

   This is an easy one to solve using NOT IN. You can find the solution in CH18_Tourney_Not_Yet_Played_NOT_IN (6 rows).

Recipes Database

1. *"Show me the recipes that have beef and garlic."*

   Solve the problem this time using EXISTS. You can find the solution in CH18_Recipes_Beef_And_Garlic (1 row).

2. *"List the recipes that have beef, onion, and carrot."*

   This time, solve the problem using IN, but do it carefully! You can find the solution in CH18_Recipes_Beef_Onion_Carrot (1 row).

3. *"Which recipes use no dairy products (cheese, butter, dairy)?"*

   Solve this using NOT IN, but be careful you do it correctly. You can find the correct solution in CH18_Recipes_No_Dairy_RIGHT (10 rows). If you did it incorrectly, your solution might look like CH18_Recipes_No_Dairy_WRONG (15 rows).

4. Solve both of the following using NOT IN: *"Display ingredients not used in any recipe." "Show recipe classes for which there is no recipe."*

   You can find the solution in CH18_Ingredients_No_Recipe (20 rows) and CH18_Recipe_Classes_No_Recipes_NOT_IN (1 row).

Condition Testing

"The only real mistake is the one from which we learn nothing."

—John Powell

Topics Covered in This Chapter

Conditional Expressions (CASE)

Solving Problems with CASE

Sample Statements

Summary

Problems for You to Solve

You might remember that way back in Chapter 4, "Creating a Simple Query," I explained the difference between data and information. You store data in the rows and columns in your tables, but you often need a query to turn that data into useful information. Sometimes, turning data into information requires you to perform complex calculations or transformations of your data to get what you want. It could be something as simple as formatting a salutation for the name line of address labels. Or, you might need to use a complex mathematical expression. When the "calculation" of information you want is based on the values you find in columns not related to your final expression, you need to be able to perform some "If . . . Then . . . Else" sorts of comparisons to create the correct expression. I'll show you how to solve these types of problems in this chapter.

Conditional Expressions (CASE)

When you need to test the data in one column to determine how to handle data in another column, you need to be able to say something like "If the value in column 'a' is 'x', then return expression 'y', else return expression 'z'." The SQL Standard provides a handy syntax to accomplish this: CASE.

Why Use CASE?

Because systems to express a set of values are all man-made and have evolved over time, there are many different way to measure, weigh, or express values in your data. Is the distance measure in feet and inches or in centimeters? Is the temperature expressed as Celsius or Fahrenheit? Is the weight in pounds or kilograms? Some man-invented systems are bizarre, indeed: The Gregorian calendar that most people use to mark the passage of time has 28, 29, 30, or 31 days in a month, and a year can have 365 or 366 days!

You'll also often encounter a case where your table is designed with columns containing code values to represent certain information. A very common example is using "M" or "F" to indicate gender. A database that contains numerical values from multiple different systems might have a column to tell you whether the reading is in Celsius ("C") or Fahrenheit ("F"), or the distance is in meters ("M") or the Imperial inches and feet ("I"). Sometimes, the indication is within the data value itself. For example in a system handling money, a negative number indicates a "debit" whereas a positive number indicates a "credit." Other times, the method to decode a value is embedded in the format of the data itself—any month, day, and year value is, by definition, using the bizarre Gregorian system. Remember that in Chapter 5, "Getting More Than Simple Columns," I showed you a primitive way to calculate years of service that will be correct for most cases. I also promised to show you the accurate way to do it in this chapter. As always, I keep my promises!

All these situations require that you perform some sort of test to discover the correct expression you need to use to fetch the information you want. CASE is the solution for all these problems and more.

Syntax

Let's dig right in and explore the syntax for a CASE expression. First, let's look at where you can use it. Figure 19-1 shows you the diagram for Value Expression, which is the one place where you can use a CASE expression.

That might seem fairly limiting at first glance, but remember that you can use a Value Expression in many places. You can use a Value Expression in the list of items you want returned in the SELECT clause. You can also use it in a predicate in any Search Condition that you can use in the ON clause of a JOIN, a WHERE clause, or a HAVING clause. Now let's examine the syntax of a CASE Expression. Figure 19-2 shows you the diagram.

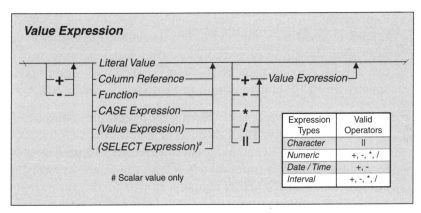

Figure 19-1 *A diagram of a Value Expression*

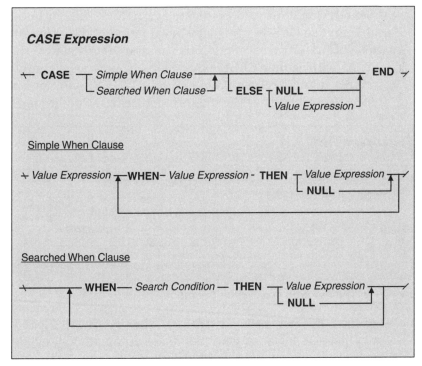

Figure 19-2 *The diagram for the CASE Expression*

A CASE Expression actually has two forms:

- *Simple*: In the Simple version, you use the keyword CASE and immediately follow the keyword with the Value Expression (which can include another CASE Expression) that you want to test. You can then write multiple WHEN/THEN clauses to compare the Value Expression to one or more single values and specify what Value Expression should be returned "when" the value expression in the WHEN clause has a value equal to the Value Expression you specified after the CASE keyword. Note that this is simply an equals test. And if none of your WHEN cases qualify, you can optionally specify an ELSE clause at end to provide a value or NULL.

- *Searched*: If you want to perform a more complex comparison test, such as greater than, less than, IN, BETWEEN, or EXISTS, you must use the Searched form of the CASE Expression. In the Searched form, you immediately follow the CASE keyword with one or more WHEN/THEN clauses. In this form, you can specify a Search Condition after the WHEN keyword to perform any sort of complex comparison of values, including using a subquery to fetch related data from another table. For review, let's take a look at Search Condition and Predicate again. Note that for both Simple and Searched CASE expressions, evaluation of the expression ends when your database system finds the first WHEN clause that is true. As with Simple CASE expressions, you can optionally provide an ELSE value to return if none of your WHEN conditions are true. Figure 19-3 shows you the diagram for Search Condition.

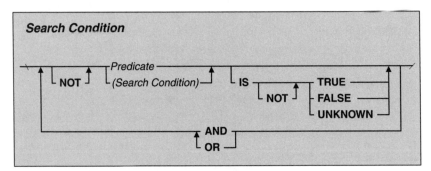

Figure 19-3 *The diagram of a Search Condition*

Note that you do not need to include the IS [NOT] TRUE/FALSE/ UNKNOWN portion because your database automatically evaluates the THEN expression when your Search Condition is true. Figures 19-4 and 19-5 show you the diagrams for a Predicate.

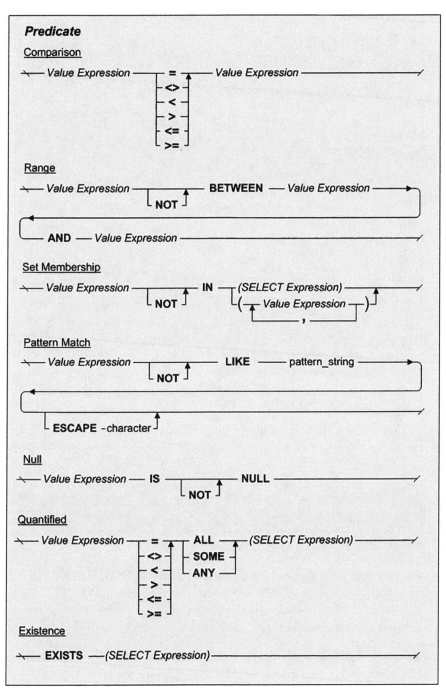

Figure 19-4 *The diagram of a Predicate: Part 1 of 2*

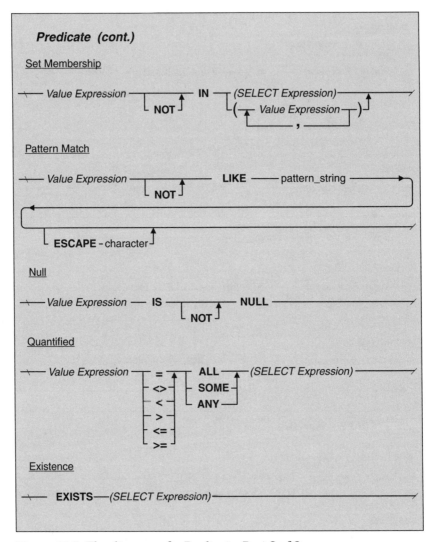

Figure 19-5 *The diagram of a Predicate: Part 2 of 2*

As you can see, the options you can include in a Search Condition that you specify after a WHEN keyword are very extensive. The ability to use a SELECT Expression that returns one or more values from another related table is particularly powerful.

In the following section, I'll explore and explain several examples that show you ways you can use a CASE Expression.

Solving Problems with CASE

Let's take a look at some real-world examples from the School Scheduling sample database. In the following sections, I'll show you how to construct Simple CASE and Searched CASE expressions. In the last section, I'll also show you a simple example of using CASE in a WHERE clause.

> ❖ **Note** Throughout this chapter, I use the "Request/Translation/Clean Up/SQL" technique introduced in Chapter 4, "Creating a Simple Query." Because this process should now be very familiar to you, I have combined the Translation/Clean Up steps for all the following examples to simplify the process.

Solving Problems with Simple CASE

"Simple" CASE is called that because it's, well, very simple. You specify an expression that you want tested, and in the WHEN clauses list values to which you want the expression compared. If the comparison is equal, the CASE Expression returns the expression you specified in the THEN clause. If none of the values are equal, you can also specify an ELSE clause to return an expression.

One common way to use Simple CASE is to examine a code value in a column and transform it into something more meaningful. Suppose you have a column in a table about people that indicates the person's gender. A database designer might define such a column—an efficiently stored single character—to store the values "M" or "F" to indicate Male or Female, respectively. In a report, most people would understand seeing the M or F, but wouldn't it be nice to spell it out? Here's how to do it using CASE and the rows from the Students table:

> "Prepare a list of IDs, student names, and the gender of the student spelled out."

Clearly, you need to use CASE and the name of the Gender column, then compare to the valid codes using WHEN and return out the equivalent word using THEN. Just for safety, let's include an ELSE clause in case I encounter any rows with no value in the Gender column.

Translation/ Clean Up	Select student ID, ~~student~~ first name, ~~student~~ last name, ~~and~~ (CASE gender when ~~the gender code is~~ 'M', then ~~display~~ 'Male', when ~~the gender code is~~ 'F', then ~~display~~ 'Female', ~~and~~ else ~~display~~ 'Not Specified' END) from ~~the~~ students ~~table~~
SQL	``` SELECT StudentID, StudFirstName, StudLastName, (CASE StudGender WHEN 'M' THEN 'Male' WHEN 'F' THEN 'Female' ELSE 'Not Specified' END) AS Gender FROM Students ```

> ❖ **Note** Although the SQL Standard doesn't require parentheses around the CASE expression, I found that both Microsoft SQL Server and MySQL didn't understand the clause without the parentheses. It never hurts to add parentheses to make it crystal clear what you intend, so I added them in all my examples.
>
> Also, Microsoft Office Access does not support CASE at all. Access does have a built-in function (Immediate If or IIf) that serves a similar purpose. If you look at the examples in the Access databases, you'll find I used IIf as a way to solve the problem in a similar fashion. I recommend you reference the examples in Microsoft SQL Server, MySQL, and PostgreSQL to see examples that follow the SQL Standard.

You can find this query in the School Scheduling sample database saved as CH19_Student_Gender.

Now let's look at an example of using Simple CASE that's a bit more complex. In Chapter 15, "Updating Sets of Data," I showed you how to calculate and update each student's current grade point average (GPA) using information from the Classes and Student Schedules tables. I commented at the time that the sample queries use functions specific to each database (NZ in Access, IsNull in SQL Server, IfNull in MySQL, and COALESCE in PostgreSQL) to avoid a divide by zero problem when I encounter a student who has not completed any courses. I noted that I would show you how to avoid this problem using CASE, and, as always, I keep my promises.

Just for review, here's the problem from Chapter 15:

"Modify the students table by setting the grade point average to the sum of the credits times the grade divided by the sum of the credits."

Translation/ Clean Up	Update ~~the~~ students ~~table by~~ setting ~~the~~ student GPA ~~equal to~~ = ~~the~~ (selecti~~on of the~~ sum ~~of~~ (credits ~~times~~ * grade) ~~divided by~~ / ~~the~~ sum ~~of~~ (credits) from ~~the~~ classes ~~table~~ inner join~~ed with the~~ student schedules ~~table~~ on Classes.class ID ~~in the classes table matches~~ = Student_Schedules.class ID ~~in the student schedules table~~ where ~~the~~ class status ~~is~~ = ~~complete~~ 2 and ~~the~~ student schedules ~~table~~ student ID ~~is equal to~~ = ~~the~~ students ~~table~~ student ID)
| SQL | ```
UPDATE Students
SET Students.StudGPA =
    (SELECT ROUND(SUM(Classes.Credits *
        Student_Schedules.Grade) /
      SUM(Classes.Credits), 3)
    FROM Classes
    INNER JOIN Student_Schedules =
    ON Classes.ClassID
     Student_Schedules.ClassID
    WHERE (Student_Schedules.ClassStatus = 2)
     AND (Student_Schedules.StudentID =
       Students.StudentID))
``` |

What I want to do is avoid performing a divide by SUM(Classes.Credits) when the student has completed no classes. The sum would be 0, and a divide by 0 would normally generate an error. Because there is no GPA field in the Students table in the Example database (there is one in the Modify version that allows me to run an UPDATE), let's solve this as a simple query. Figure 19-6 shows you the tables you need.

Just for fun, let's be a little more stringent this time and declare that a student not only has to have completed the class but also must have passed the class with a grade of 67 or better. ("Completed" but with a grade of 50 shouldn't get credit!) I want to list all students, so let's create a subquery on the Classes, Student_Schedules, and Student_Class_Status tables and then OUTER JOIN that with the Students table.
```

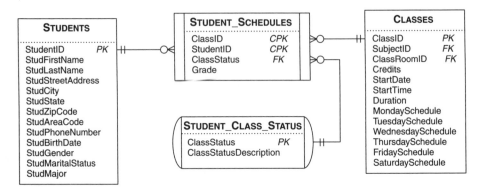

Figure 19-6 *Tables you need to calculate a student's grade point average (GPA)*

Because you need to SUM credits times grade and divide by the sum of credits, you'll need a GROUP BY clause. To avoid a divide by zero, you need to count some field in the subquery (all fields returned by the sub-query will be Null if any student failed to complete and pass any course) and use CASE to see if the result is 0. Let's put the query together:

"Display for all students the Student ID, first name, last name, the number of classes completed, the total credits, and the grade point average for classes that were completed with a grade of 67 or better."

Translation/ Clean Up	Select student ID, student first name, student last name, the count of (student ID), the sum of (credits), and CASE when the count of (student ID) is WHEN 0, then return 0, else return the sum of (credits times the * grade) divided by / the sum of (credits) from the students table left joined with the (selection of student ID, grade, and credits from the student schedules table inner joined with the student class status table on Student_Schedules.class status in the student schedules table matches = Student_Class_Status.class status in the student class status table, then inner joined with the classes table on Student_Schedules.class ID in the student schedules table matches = Classes.class ID in the classes table where the class status description equals = 'Completed' and the grade is greater than or equal to >= 67) AS SClasses on Students.student ID in the students table matches = SClasses.student ID in the selection grouped by student ID, student first name, and student last name

---

```
SQL          SELECT Students.StudentID, Students.StudFirstName,
               Students.StudLastName,
               COUNT(SClasses.StudentID) AS NumberCompleted,
               SUM(SClasses.Credits) AS TotalCredits,
               (CASE COUNT(SClasses.StudentID)
                 WHEN 0 THEN 0
                 ELSE ROUND(SUM(SClasses.Credits * SClasses.Grade)
                       / SUM(SClasses.Credits), 3) END) AS GPA
             FROM Students LEFT OUTER JOIN
               (SELECT Student_Schedules.StudentID,
                   Student_Schedules.Grade, Classes.Credits
                 FROM (Student_Schedules INNER JOIN
                     Student_Class_Status
                     ON Student_Schedules.ClassStatus =
                         Student_Class_Status.ClassStatus)
                     INNER JOIN Classes
                     ON Student_Schedules.ClassID =
                         Classes.ClassID
                 WHERE
                   (Student_Class_Status.ClassStatusDescription =
                         'Completed')
                   AND (Student_Schedules.Grade >= 67))
                     AS SClasses
               ON Students.StudentID = SClasses.StudentID
             GROUP BY Students.StudentID, Students.StudFirstName,
                   Students.StudLastName;
```

Should there be a student who has not completed and passed a class, the number of classes, credits, and grade point average will all be zero for that student. I avoid a divide by zero problem using absolutely standard SQL—I don't have to depend on a non-standard function in the database system. I saved this example in the school scheduling example database as CH19_Student_GPA_Avoid_0_Passed.

Solving Problems with Searched CASE

If you think using Simple CASE is a bit mind twisting, you're in for a whole lot of fun getting familiar with Searched CASE. With Simple CASE, all you can logically perform is simple equal comparisons (maybe that's why they call it "simple"). Searched CASE, on the other hand, lets you perform multiple complex comparisons on different fields and even subqueries. Basically, anything you can specify in a Search Condition in the ON clause of a JOIN, a WHERE clause, or a HAVING clause is fair game. Let's work through a couple of problems that require you to use Searched CASE to solve them.

Remember in Chapter 5 I showed you how to calculate a staff member's full years of service as of a certain date by finding the difference in days between the date hired and the target date and then dividing by 365 days in a year. I warned you that the calculation is imprecise because it doesn't account for the leap years between the two dates. In fact, the answer will be incorrect by one day for each intervening leap year. This matters only when the month and day of the date hired is close to the month and day of the target date, so most of the time, dividing by 365 will give you the correct answer.

I also promised you that I would show you how to perform the calculation exactly using CASE. Basically, you need to subtract the year of the date hired from the year of the target date, then adjust the value by one year if the month and day of the hired date fall later in the year than the month and date of the target date. The idea is you don't want to give a year's credit to a staff member whose anniversary date hasn't occurred yet in the target year. (You want to calculate only full years of service.)

So, you can imagine that you start with the difference between the two years, then subtract 1 if the month of the date hired is greater than the month of the target date or the month of the date hired is equal to the month of the target date but the day of the date hired is later in that month. The calculation looks like the following:

```
Years of service = ((year of target) - (year of date hired)) -
            (If month of date hired < month of target then 0
            If month of date hired > month of target then 1
            If month of date hired = month of target and
                day of date hired > target then 1
            Else 0)
```

What I need to do is convert the "If . . . Then . . . Else" part of the preceding calculation into a Searched CASE statement. Here's how to do it:

"For all staff members, list staff ID, first name, last name, date hired, and length of service in complete years as of October 1, 2017, sorted by last name and first name."

Translation/ Clean Up	Select staff ID, ~~staff~~ first name, ~~staff~~ last name, date hired, ~~and calculate the~~ year ~~of the date~~ (2017-10-1) ~~minus the~~ - year ~~of the~~ (date hired) ~~minus~~ - (CASE when ~~the~~ month ~~of the~~ (date hired) ~~is less than~~ < 10 then 0, when ~~the~~ month ~~of the~~ (date hired) ~~is greater than~~ > 10 then 1, ~~and~~ when ~~the~~ day ~~of the~~ (date hired) ~~is greater than~~ > 1 then 1 else 0 END) as ~~the~~ length of service from ~~the~~ staff ~~table~~ ~~ordered~~ by staff last name, ~~and~~ staff first name

SQL	SELECT StaffID, StfFirstName, StfLastname,
	     YEAR(CAST('2017-10-01' As Date))
	     - YEAR(DateHired) -
	     - CASE WHEN Month(DateHired) < 10
	         THEN 0
	         WHEN Month(DateHired) > 10
	         THEN 1
	         WHEN Day(DateHired) > 1
	         THEN 1
	         ELSE 0 END) AS LengthOfService
	 FROM Staff
	 ORDER BY StfLastName, StfFirstName;

❖ **Note** Nearly all database systems have built-in YEAR, MONTH, and DAY functions (in Oracle use EXTRACT) to obtain the year part of a date, so I decided to use these functions in my example even though they are not specifically defined in the SQL Standard. Also, because I know the "target" date that I want, I directly coded the values 10 and 1 in the CASE statement. If you were using something like today's date from your database system, you would have to extract the month and day parts to do the comparison.

I saved this query as CH19_Length_Of_Service in the School Scheduling sample database. If you open this query and CH05_Length_Of_Service side by side, you'll find that the answer for years of service for Jeffrey Smith is one year less in the accurate CASE example. Jeffrey Smith's date hired is October 6, 1991—five days later than the target date. The error occurs because there were more than six leap years between 1991 and 2017.

You might be wondering why I didn't explicitly test for month equals 10. Remember that your database system keeps evaluating the WHEN clauses until it finds the first one that is true. If month isn't less than 10 and month isn't greater than 10, then obviously month must equal 10. There's no need to test that explicitly.

Now let's look at another example using Searched CASE. Suppose that you want to create a mailing list, and you have gender and marital status information in your table, but you don't have a salutation (Mr., Mrs., and so on). Let's generate one using a CASE test on the fields you do have. Because you need tests on more than one column, you must use a Searched CASE.

> *"Create a student mailing list that includes a generated salutation, first name and last name, the street address, and a city, state, and ZIP code field."*

Translation/ Clean Up	Select (CASE when ~~the~~ gender ~~is male~~ = 'M' then ~~return~~ 'Mr.', when ~~the~~ marital status ~~is single~~ = 'S' then ~~return~~ 'Ms.' else ~~return~~ 'Mrs.' END) ~~concatenated with~~ || student first name ~~concatenated with a space~~ || ' ' ~~and~~ student last name as ~~the~~ name line, student street address as ~~the~~ street line, student city ~~concatenated with a comma and a space~~ || ', ' ~~then concatenated with~~ || student state ~~and two spaces~~ || ' ', ~~then concatenated with~~ || student ZIP code as ~~the~~ city line from ~~the~~ students ~~table~~

SQL	<pre>SELECT
	    (CASE WHEN StudGender = 'M' THEN 'Mr. '
	          WHEN StudMaritalStatus = 'S' THEN 'Ms. '
	          ELSE 'Mrs. ' END)
	    || StudFirstName || ' ' || StudLastName
	        AS NameLine,
	    StudStreetAddress AS StreetLine,
	    StudCity || ', ' || StudState || ' ' ||
	    StudZipCode AS CityLine
	  FROM Students</pre>

All male students will be addressed as "Mr.", so there's no reason to test the marital status of male students. If the student is not male, then there's no reason to test the gender again because the only other value I expect is "F" for female. Finally, if the female student is single, the salutation will be "Ms." Otherwise, use "Mrs." for women who are Married ("M"), Divorced ("D"), or Widowed ("W"). If you construct your WHEN/THEN pairs intelligently, you don't have to test for every possible combination. I saved this query in the Student Scheduling database as CH19_Student_Mailing_List.

Using CASE in a WHERE Clause

Just to cover all the bases, let's take a look at how you might use CASE in a WHERE (or HAVING) clause. Quite frankly, I cannot think of an example where it wouldn't be clearer to simply construct your predicate using all the available predicate expressions. As I've said many times before, just because you can do something doesn't mean you should! Let's give it a shot anyway to see what it might look like:

"List all students who are 'Male'."

Translation/ Clean Up	Select student ID, ~~student~~ first name, ~~student~~ last name, ~~and~~ 'Male' as gender from ~~the~~ students ~~table~~ where 'Male' ~~equals~~ = (CASE when ~~the~~ student gender ~~is~~ 'M' then ~~return~~ 'Male' else ~~return~~ 'Nomatch' END)

SQL	SELECT StudentID, StudFirstName, StudLastName, 'Male' AS Gender
	FROM Students
	WHERE ('Male' = (CASE StudGender
	        WHEN 'M' THEN 'Male'
	        ELSE 'Nomatch' END));

The trick here is the request asked for "Male" students, so I took that literally. To generate a true "Male" value I had to use CASE to return that word when gender is "M". Frankly, it would be much easier to simply say:

```
WHERE Gender = 'M'
```

Not that you'll find it very useful, but you can find this query saved in the School Scheduling sample database as CH19_Male_Students.

Sample Statements

You now know the mechanics of constructing queries using CASE and have seen some of the types of requests you can answer with CASE. Let's take a look at a fairly robust set of samples, all of which use either Simple or Searched CASE. These examples come from each of the sample databases, and they illustrate the use of the CASE to perform logical evaluations in Value Expressions.

❖ **Note** Remember in the Introduction I warned you that results from each database system won't necessarily match the sort order you see in examples in this book unless you include an ORDER BY clause. Even when you include that specification, the system might return results in columns not included in the ORDER BY clause in a different sequence because of different optimization techniques.

If you're running the examples in Microsoft SQL Server, simply selecting the rows from the view does not honor any ORDER BY clause specified in the view. You must open the design of the view and execute it from there to see the ORDER BY clause honored.

Also, when you use GROUP BY, you'll often see the results returned by your database system as though the rows are sorted by the columns you specified. This happens because some optimizers first sort the data internally to make it faster to process your GROUP BY. Keep in mind that if you want a specific sort order, you must also include an ORDER BY clause.

I've also included sample result sets that would be returned by these operations and placed them immediately after the SQL syntax line. The name that appears immediately above a result set is the name I gave each query in the sample data that you'll find on the book's website (www.informit.com/title/9780134858333). I stored each query in the appropriate sample database (as indicated within the example), using "CH19" as the leading part of the query or view name. You can follow the instructions in the Introduction to this book to load the samples onto your computer and try them out.

❖ **Note** Remember that all of the field names and table names used in these examples are drawn from the sample database structures shown in Appendix B, "Schema for the Sample Databases."

Because many of these examples use complex joins, the optimizer for your database system might choose a different way to solve these queries. For this reason, the first few rows I show you may not exactly match the result you obtain, but the total number of rows should be the same. Keep in mind that for any SQL Server View that contains an ORDER BY clause, you must open the view in Design mode first and then execute it to see the specified order. If you SELECT * from the View, SQL Server does not honor the ORDER BY clause.

Sales Order Database

"List all products and display whether the product was sold in December 2017."

Translation/ Clean Up	Select product number, product name, ~~and~~ (CASE when product number ~~is~~ in ~~the~~ (selecti~~on of~~ product number from ~~the~~ order details ~~table inner~~ joi~~ned with the~~ orders ~~table~~ on Orders.order number ~~in the orders table matches~~ = Order_Details.order number ~~in the order details table~~ where ~~the~~ order date ~~is~~ between '2017-12-01 and '2017-12-31') then ~~return~~ 'Ordered' else ~~return~~ 'Not Ordered' END) as product ordered from ~~the~~ products ~~table~~

SQL	```SELECT ProductNumber, ProductName,
	    (CASE WHEN Products.ProductNumber IN
	        (SELECT Order_Details.ProductNumber
	        FROM Order_Details INNER JOIN Orders
	        ON Orders.OrderNumber =
	            Order_Details.OrderNumber
	        WHERE (Orders.OrderDate BETWEEN
	                CAST('2017-12-01' AS Date) AND
	                CAST('2017-12-31' AS Date)))
	        THEN 'Ordered'
	        ELSE 'Not Ordered' END) AS
	        ProductOrdered
	FROM Products;```

CH19_Products_Ordered_Dec_2017 (40 rows)

ProductNumber	ProductName	ProductOrdered
1	Trek 9000 Mountain Bike	Ordered
2	Eagle FS-3 Mountain Bike	Ordered
3	Dog Ear Cyclecomputer	Ordered
4	Victoria Pro All Weather Tires	Not Ordered
5	Dog Ear Helmet Mount Mirrors	Ordered
6	Viscount Mountain Bike	Ordered
7	Viscount C-500 Wireless Bike Computer	Ordered
8	Kryptonite Advanced 2000 U-Lock	Ordered

<< more rows here >>

"Display products and a sale rating based on number sold (poor <= 200 sales, Average > 200 and <= 500, Good > 500 and <= 1000, Excellent > 1000)."

Translation/ Clean Up	Select product number, product name, ~~and~~ (CASE when ~~the~~ (~~selection of the~~ sum ~~of~~ (quantity ordered) from ~~the~~ order details ~~table~~ where ~~the~~ Order_Details.product number ~~in the order details table equals~~ = the Products.product number ~~in the products table~~) ~~is less than or equal to~~ <= 200 then ~~return~~ 'Poor' when ~~the~~ (~~selection of the~~ sum ~~of~~ (quantity ordered) from ~~the~~ order details ~~table~~ where ~~the~~ Order_Details.product number ~~in the order details table equals~~ = the Products.product number ~~in the products table~~) ~~is less than or equal to~~ <= 500 then ~~return~~ 'Average' when ~~the~~ (~~selection of the~~ sum ~~of~~ (quantity ordered) from ~~the~~ order details ~~table~~ where ~~the~~ Order_Details.product number ~~in the order details table equals~~ = the Products.product number ~~in the products table~~) ~~is less than or equal to~~ <= 1000 then ~~return~~ 'Good' else ~~return~~ 'Excellent' END) as sales quality from ~~the~~ products ~~table~~
| SQL | ```
SELECT ProductNumber, ProductName,
    (CASE WHEN
            (SELECT SUM(QuantityOrdered)
            FROM Order_Details
            WHERE (Order_Details.ProductNumber =
                Products.ProductNumber)) <= 200
``` |
```

```
              THEN 'Poor'
              WHEN
                (SELECT SUM(QuantityOrdered)
                 FROM Order_Details
                 WHERE (Order_Details.ProductNumber =
                     Products.ProductNumber)) <= 500
              THEN 'Average'
              WHEN
                (SELECT SUM(QuantityOrdered)
                 FROM Order_Details
                 WHERE (Order_Details.ProductNumber =
                     Products.ProductNumber)) <= 1000
              THEN 'Good'
              ELSE 'Excellent' END) AS SalesQuality
        FROM Products
```

CH19_Products_And_SalesQuality (40 rows)

ProductNumber	ProductName	SalesQuality
1	Trek 9000 Mountain Bike	Excellent
2	Eagle FS-3 Mountain Bike	Poor
3	Dog Ear Cyclecomputer	Poor
4	Victoria Pro All Weather Tires	Excellent
5	Dog Ear Helmet Mount Mirrors	Poor
6	Viscount Mountain Bike	Good
7	Viscount C-500 Wireless Bike Computer	Average
8	Kryptonite Advanced 2000 U-Lock	Poor
<< more rows here >>		

❖ **Note** Even though the request specified criteria such as > 200 and <= 500, you don't need to specify the greater than part in each WHEN because the previous WHEN for <= 200 is already not true. (If the sum is not <= 200, then it is, by definition, greater than 200.) It would be nice to run the subquery only once in a Simple CASE format, but I can't do that because the tests are not strictly for equality. A database system with a smart optimizer will recognize that all three subqueries are the same and execute it just once per row.

Entertainment Database

"List entertainers and display whether the entertainer was booked on Christmas 2017 (December 25)."

Translation/ Clean Up	Select entertainer ID, ~~entertainer~~ stage name ~~and~~ (CASE when entertainer ID ~~is~~ in ~~the~~ (selection of the entertainer ID from ~~the~~ engagements ~~table~~ where '2017-12-25' ~~is~~ between start date and end date) then ~~return~~ 'Booked' else ~~return~~ 'Not Booked' END) as booked Xmas 2017 from ~~the~~ entertainers ~~table~~
| SQL | ```
SELECT  EntertainerID, EntStageName,
      (CASE WHEN EntertainerID IN
              (SELECT  EntertainerID
              FROM      Engagements
              WHERE CAST('2017-12-25' AS Date)
                      BETWEEN StartDate AND
                      EndDate)
            THEN 'Booked'
            ELSE 'Not Booked' END) AS BookedXmas2017
FROM  Entertainers;
``` |

CH19_Entertainers_Booked_Xmas_2017 (13 rows)

EntertainerID	EntStageName	BookedXmas2017
1001	Carol Peacock Trio	Booked
1002	Topazz	Not Booked
1003	JV & the Deep Six	Booked
1004	Jim Glynn	Not Booked
1005	Jazz Persuasion	Booked
1006	Modern Dance	Booked
```

EntertainerID	EntStageName	BookedXmas2017
1007	Coldwater Cattle Company	Not Booked
1008	Country Feeling	Not Booked
	<< more rows here >>	

❖ **Note** Remember that engagements have both a start and an end date, so you want the engagements where December 25, 2017 is anywhere in the span (BETWEEN) those two dates.

"Find customers who like Jazz but not Standards (using Searched CASE in the WHERE clause)."

Translation/ Clean Up	Select customer ID, ~~customer~~ first name ~~and customer~~ last name from ~~the~~ customers ~~table~~ where ~~true~~ 1 ~~equals~~ = (CASE when customer ~~is~~ not in ~~the~~ (selec~~tion of the~~ customer ID from ~~the~~ musical preferences ~~table~~ inner join~~ed~~ ~~with the~~ musical styles ~~table~~ on Musical_Preferences.style ID ~~in the musical preferences table equals~~ = Musical_Styles. style ID ~~in the musical styles table~~ where style name ~~equals~~ = 'Jazz') then ~~return~~ 0 when customer ~~is~~ in ~~the~~ (selec~~tion of the~~ customer ID from ~~the~~ musical preferences ~~table~~ inner join~~ed with the~~ musical styles ~~table~~ on Musical_Preferences. style ID ~~in the musical preferences table equals~~ = Musical_ Styles.style ID ~~in the musical styles table~~ where style name ~~equals~~ = 'Standards') then ~~return~~ 0 else ~~return~~ 1 END)
| SQL | ```
SELECT  CustomerID, CustFirstName, CustLastName
FROM    Customers
WHERE   (1 =
            (CASE WHEN CustomerID NOT IN
                (SELECT CustomerID
                 FROM Musical_Preferences
                 INNER JOIN Musical_Styles
                 ON Musical_Preferences.StyleID =
                    Musical_Styles.StyleID
                 WHERE Musical_Styles.StyleName =
                    'Jazz')
``` |
```

```
                                   THEN 0
                                   WHEN CustomerID IN
                                    (SELECT CustomerID
                                     FROM Musical_Preferences
                                     INNER JOIN Musical_Styles
                                    ON Musical_Preferences.StyleID =
                                        Musical_Styles.StyleID
                                     WHERE Musical_Styles.StyleName =
                                          'Standards')
                                   THEN 0 ELSE 1 END));
```

❖ **Note** Although the request asks for customers that do like Jazz and do not like Standards, keep in mind that evaluation of WHEN/ THEN clauses ends with the first one that is true. Because of that, I coded the tests logically "backward." First, I eliminated the customers who do not like Jazz, and then I eliminated the customers who do like Standards. If I had specified a test for customers who do like Jazz first, that would have selected all Jazz customers without ever testing for those in that set who might not like Standards.

CH19_Customers_Jazz_Not_Standards (2 rows)

CustomerID	CustFirstName	CustLastName
10010	Zachary	Ehrlich
10013	Estella	Pundt

School Scheduling Database

"Show what new salaries for full-time faculty would be if you gave a 5 percent raise to instructors, a 4 percent raise to associate professors, and a 3.5 percent raise to professors."

Translation/ Clean Up	Select staff ID, st~~aff~~ staff first name, st~~aff~~ staff last name, title, status, salary, ~~and~~ (CASE ~~when~~ title ~~is~~ WHEN 'Instructor' then ~~return~~ salary ~~times~~ * 1.05 when 'Associate Professor' then ~~return~~ salary ~~times~~ * 1.04 when 'Professor' then ~~return~~

salary ~~times~~ * 1.035 else ~~return~~ salary END) as new salary from ~~the~~ staff ~~table~~ inner joi~~ned with the~~ faculty ~~table~~ on Staff.staff ID ~~in the staff table equals~~ = Faculty. staff ID ~~in the faculty table~~ where status ~~equals~~ = 'Full Time'

SQL	
| | ```
SELECT  StaffID, StfFirstName, StfLastname, Title,
    Status, Salary,
    (CASE Title
        WHEN 'Instructor'
        THEN ROUND(Salary * 1.05, 0)
        WHEN 'Associate Professor'
        THEN ROUND(Salary * 1.04, 0)
        WHEN 'Professor'
        THEN ROUND(Salary * 1.035, 0)
        ELSE Salary END) AS NewSalary
FROM Staff INNER JOIN Faculty
  ON Staff.StaffID = Faculty.StaffID
WHERE  Faculty.Status = 'Full Time';
``` |

CH19_FullTime_Instructor_Raises (22 rows)

StaffID	StfFirstName	StfLastName	Title	Status	Salary	NewSalary
98005	Suzanne	Viescas	Instructor	Full Time	$44,000.00	$46,200.00
98007	Gary	Hallmark	Associate Professor	Full Time	$53,000.00	$55,120.00
98011	Ann	Patterson	Instructor	Full Time	$45,000.00	$47,250.00
98012	Robert	Brown	Instructor	Full Time	$49,000.00	$51,450.00
98013	Deb	Waldal	Instructor	Full Time	$44,000.00	$46,200.00
98014	Peter	Brehm	Professor	Full Time	$60,000.00	$62,100.00
98019	Mariya	Sergienko	Instructor	Full Time	$45,000.00	$47,250.00
98020	Jim	Glynn	Instructor	Full Time	$45,000.00	$47,250.00

<< more rows here >>
```

"List all students, the classes for which they enrolled, the grade they received, and a conversion of the grade number to a letter."

❖ **Note** I'll use a conversion scheme common to schools in the United States where 97 to 100 is A+, 93 to 96.99 is A, 90 to 92.99 is A-, and so on in 10 point increments down to 60 to 62.99, which is D-, and anything less is failing or F.

Translation/ Clean Up	Select student ID stu~~dent~~ first name, stu~~dent~~ last name, class ID start date, subject code, subject name, grade, ~~and~~ (CASE when the grade is between 97 and 100 then ~~return~~ 'A+',

when ~~the~~ grade ~~is~~ between 93 and 96.99 then ~~return~~ 'A',

when ~~the~~ grade ~~is~~ between 90 and 92.99 then ~~return~~ 'A-',

when ~~the~~ grade ~~is~~ between 87 and 89.99 then ~~return~~ 'B+',

when ~~the~~ grade ~~is~~ between 83 and 86.99 then ~~return~~ 'B',

when ~~the~~ grade ~~is~~ between 80 and 82.99 then ~~return~~ 'B-',

when ~~the~~ grade ~~is~~ between 77 and 79.99 then ~~return~~ 'C+',

when ~~the~~ grade ~~is~~ between 73 and 76.99 then ~~return~~ 'C',

when ~~the~~ grade ~~is~~ between 70 and 72.99 then ~~return~~ 'C-',

when ~~the~~ grade ~~is~~ between 67 and 69.99 then ~~return~~ 'D+',

when ~~the~~ grade ~~is~~ between 63 and 66.99 then ~~return~~ 'D',

when ~~the~~ grade ~~is~~ between 60 and 62.99 then ~~return~~ 'D-',

else ~~return~~ 'F' END) as letter grade from ~~the~~ students ~~table~~ inner join~~ed with the~~ student schedules ~~table~~ on Students.student ID ~~in the students table equals~~ = Student_Schedules.student ID ~~in the student schedules table, then~~ inner join~~ed with~~ ~~the~~ classes ~~table~~ on Student_Schedules.class ID ~~in the student schedules table equals~~ = Classes.class ID ~~in the classes table, then~~ inner join~~ed with the~~ subjects ~~table~~ on Classes.subject ID ~~in the classes table equals~~ = Subjects.subject ID ~~in the subjects table, and then finally~~ inner join~~ed with the~~ student class status ~~table~~ on Student_Schedules.class status ~~in the student schedules table equals~~ = Student_Class_Status.class status ~~in the student class status table~~ where class status description ~~equals~~ = 'Completed'

SQL

```
SELECT Students.StudentID, Students.StudFirstName,
Students.StudLastName, Classes.ClassID,
Classes.StartDate, Subjects.SubjectCode,
Subjects.SubjectName, Student_Schedules.Grade,
       (CASE WHEN Grade BETWEEN 97 AND 100 THEN 'A+'
             WHEN Grade BETWEEN 93 AND 96.99 THEN 'A'
             WHEN Grade BETWEEN 90 AND 92.99 THEN 'A-'
             WHEN Grade BETWEEN 87 AND 89.99 THEN 'B+'
             WHEN Grade BETWEEN 83 AND 86.99 THEN 'B'
             WHEN Grade BETWEEN 80 AND 82.99 THEN 'B-'
             WHEN Grade BETWEEN 77 AND 79.99 THEN 'C+'
             WHEN Grade BETWEEN 73 AND 76.99 THEN 'C'
             WHEN Grade BETWEEN 70 AND 72.99 THEN 'C-'
             WHEN Grade BETWEEN 67 AND 69.99 THEN 'D+'
             WHEN Grade BETWEEN 63 AND 66.99 THEN 'D'
             WHEN Grade BETWEEN 60 AND 62.99 THEN 'D-'
             ELSE 'F' END) AS LetterGrade
FROM (((Students INNER JOIN Student_Schedules
ON Students.StudentID = Student_Schedules.StudentID)
INNER JOIN Classes
ON Student_Schedules.ClassID = Classes.ClassID)
INNER JOIN Subjects
ON Classes.SubjectID = Subjects.SubjectID)
INNER JOIN Student_Class_Status
ON Student_Schedules.ClassStatus =
   Student_Class_Status.ClassStatus
WHERE Student_Class_Status.ClassStatusDescription =
      'Completed';
```

CH19_Students_Classes_Letter_Grades (68 rows)

Student ID	StudFirst Name	StudLast Name	ClassID	StartDate	Subject Code	Subject Name	Grade	Letter Grade
1001	Kerry	Patterson	1000	2017-09-12	ART 100	Introduction to Art	99.83	A+
1001	Kerry	Patterson	1168	2017-09-11	ENG 101	Composition - Fundamentals	70	C-

Student ID	StudFirst Name	StudLast Name	ClassID	StartDate	Subject Code	Subject Name	Grade	Letter Grade
1001	Kerry	Patterson	2907	2017-09-11	MAT 097	Elementary Algebra	67.33	D+
1001	Kerry	Patterson	3085	2017-09-11	HIS 111	U.S. History to 1877	87.14	B+
1002	David	Hamilton	1156	2017-09-11	ENG 101	Composition - Fundamentals	86.33	B
1002	David	Hamilton	1500	2017-09-11	MUS 100	Music in the Western World	85.72	B
1002	David	Hamilton	2889	2017-09-11	MAT 080	Preparatory Mathematics	68.22	D+
1003	Betsy	Stadick	1156	2017-09-11	ENG 101	Composition Fundamentals	71.09	C-

<< more rows here >>

Bowling League Database

> *"List Bowlers and display 'fair' (average < 140), 'average' (average >= 140 and < 160), 'good' (average >= 160 and < 185), 'excellent' (average >= 185)."*

Translation/ Clean Up	Select bowler ID, bowler last name, bowler first name, ~~the average of~~ (raw score), ~~and~~ (CASE when ~~the average of~~ (raw score) ~~is less than~~ < 140, then ~~return~~ 'Fair', when the ~~average of~~ (raw score) ~~is less than~~ < 160, then ~~return~~ 'Average', when ~~the average of~~ (raw score) ~~is less than~~ < 185, then ~~return~~ 'Good', else ~~return~~ 'Excellent' END) as bowler rating from ~~the~~ bowlers ~~table~~ inner join~~ed with the~~ bowler scores ~~table~~ on Bowlers.bowler ID ~~in the bowlers table equals~~ = Bowler_Scores.bowler ID ~~in the bowler scores table~~ grouped ~~by~~ bowler ID, bowler last name, ~~and~~ bowler first name
SQL	SELECT Bowlers.BowlerID, Bowlers.BowlerLastName, Bowlers.BowlerFirstName, CAST(AVG(RawScore) AS Int) AS BowlerAverage, (CASE WHEN CAST(AVG(Bowler_Scores.RawScore) AS Int) < 140

```
      THEN 'Fair'
      WHEN CAST(AVG(Bowler_Scores.RawScore) AS Int)
        < 160
      THEN 'Average'
      WHEN CAST(AVG(Bowler_Scores.RawScore) AS Int)
        < 185
      THEN 'Good'
      ELSE 'Excellent' END) AS BowlerRating
   FROM  Bowlers INNER JOIN Bowler_Scores
   ON Bowlers.BowlerID = Bowler_Scores.BowlerID
   GROUP BY Bowlers.BowlerID, Bowlers.BowlerLastName,
          Bowlers.BowlerFirstName;
```

CH19_Bowler_Ratings (32 rows)

BowlerID	BowlerLastName	BowlerFirstName	BowlerAverage	BowlerRating
1	Fournier	Barbara	148	Average
2	Fournier	David	156	Average
3	Kennedy	John	165	Good
4	Sheskey	Sara	141	Average
5	Patterson	Ann	149	Average
6	Patterson	Neil	158	Average
7	Viescas	David	167	Good
8	Viescas	Stephanie	142	Average

<< more rows here >>

❖ **Note** Remember that your database system stops at the first WHEN/THEN that is true, so you do not need to check for >= as well as <.

"Show all tournaments with either their match details or 'Not Played Yet.'"

Translation/ Clean Up	Select tourney ID, tourney date, tourney location, ~~and~~ (CASE when ~~the~~ match ID is ~~empty~~ NULL then ~~return~~ 'Not Played Yet' else ~~return~~ 'Match: ' ~~concatenated with~~ || match ID ~~concatenated with~~ || ' Lanes: ' ~~concatenated with~~ || lanes ~~concatenated with~~ || ' Odd Lane Team: ' ~~concatenated with~~ || Teams.team name ~~from the teams table concatenated with~~ || ' Even Lane Team: ' ~~concatenated with~~ || Teams_1.team name ~~from the second copy of the teams table~~ from the tourney matches ~~table~~ inner joined ~~with the~~ teams ~~table~~ on Tourney_Matches.odd lane team ID ~~in the tourney matches table equals~~ = Teams.team ID ~~in the teams table, then~~ inner joined ~~with a second copy of the~~ teams ~~table~~ AS Teams_1 on Tourney_Matches.even lane team ~~in the tourney matches table equals~~ = Teams_1.team ID ~~in the second copy of the teams table, then~~ RIGHT outer join~~ed with the tournaments table~~ on Tourney_Matches.tourney ID ~~in the tourney matches table equals~~ = Tournaments.tourney ID ~~in the tournaments table~~

SQL	```SELECT Tournaments.TourneyID,```
	``` Tournaments.TourneyDate,```
	``` Tournaments.TourneyLocation,```
	``` (CASE WHEN Tourney_Matches.MatchID IS NULL```
	``` THEN 'Not Played Yet'```
	``` ELSE 'Match: ' ||```
	``` CAST(Tourney_Matches.MatchID AS char)```
	``` || ' Lanes: ' || Tourney_Matches.Lanes```
	``` || ' Odd Lane Team: '```
	``` || Teams.TeamName || ' Even Lane Team: '```
	``` || Teams_1.TeamName END) AS Match```
	```FROM ((Tourney_Matches INNER JOIN Teams```
	``` ON Tourney_Matches.OddLaneTeamID =```
	``` Teams.TeamID)```
	```INNER JOIN Teams AS Teams_1```
	``` ON Tourney_Matches.EvenLaneTeamID =```
	``` Teams_1.TeamID)```
	```RIGHT OUTER JOIN Tournaments```
	``` ON Tourney_Matches.TourneyID =```
	``` Tournaments.TourneyID;```

CH19_All_Tournaments_Any_Matches (63 rows)

TourneyID	TourneyDate	TourneyLocation	Match
1	2017-09-04	Red Rooster Lanes	Match: 2 Lanes: 03-04 Odd Lane Team: Terrapins Even Lane Team: Barracudas
1	2017-09-04	Red Rooster Lanes	Match: 3 Lanes: 05-06 Odd Lane Team: Dolphins Even Lane Team: Orcas
1	2017-09-04	Red Rooster Lanes	Match: 4 Lanes: 07-08 Odd Lane Team: Manatees Even Lane Team: Swordfish
1	2017-09-04	Red Rooster Lanes	Match: 1 Lanes: 01-02 Odd Lane Team: Marlins Even Lane Team: Sharks
2	2017-09-11	Thunderbird Lanes	Match: 5 Lanes: 21-22 Odd Lane Team: Terrapins Even Lane Team: Marlins
2	2017-09-11	Thunderbird Lanes	Match: 6 Lanes: 23-24 Odd Lane Team: Barracudas Even Lane Team: Sharks
2	2017-09-11	Thunderbird Lanes	Match: 7 Lanes: 25-26 Odd Lane Team: Dolphins Even Lane Team: Manatees
2	2017-09-11	Thunderbird Lanes	Match: 8 Lanes: 27-28 Odd Lane Team: Swordfish Even Lane Team: Orcas

<< more rows here >>

❖ **Note** You should find tournaments 15–20 at the end of the list marked "Not Played Yet."

Summary

I began this chapter with a discussion of why CASE is useful and an examination of the syntax of not only the CASE Expression but also Search Condition and Predicate in which you might use a Value Expression constructed with CASE. Next, I explained how to solve problems using Simple CASE and gave you some examples. I then covered Searched CASE with detailed explanations using examples. I then showed you how to use CASE in a WHERE clause, but I noted that you can often specify what you want more clearly with predicate expressions. Finally, I gave you two examples each from four of the sample databases that showed you other ways to use Simple CASE, Searched CASE, and CASE within a WHERE clause.

The following section presents several requests that you can work out on your own.

Problems for You to Solve

Below, I show you the request statement and the name of the solution query in the sample databases. If you want some practice, you can work out the SQL you need for each request and then check your answer with the query I saved in the samples. Don't worry if your syntax doesn't exactly match the syntax of the queries I saved—as long as your Result Set is the same.

Sales Order Database

1. *"Show all customers and display whether they placed an order in the first week of December 2017."*

   (Hint: Use a Searched CASE and the dates December 1, 2017 and December 7, 2017.)

   You can find the solution in CH19_Customers_Ordered_First-Week_Dec2017 (28 rows).

2. *"List customers and the state they live in spelled out."*

   (Hint: Use a Simple CASE and look for WA, OR, CA, and TX.)

   You can find the solution in CH19_Customers_State_Names (28 rows).

3. *"Display employees and their age as of February 15, 2018."*

   (Be sure to use the functions to extract Year, Month, and Day portions of a date value that are supported by your database system.)

   You can find the solution in CH19_Employee_Age_Feb152018 (8 rows).

Entertainment Database

1. *"Display Customers and their preferred styles, but change 50's, 60's, 70's, and 80's music to 'Oldies'."*

   (Hint: Use a Simple CASE expression.)

   You can find the solution in CH19_Customer_Styles_Oldies (36 rows).

2. *"Find Entertainers who play Jazz but not Contemporary musical styles."*

   (Hint: Use a Searched CASE in the WHERE clause and be careful to think in the negative.)

   You can find the solution in CH19_Entertainers_Jazz_Not_Contemporary (1 row).

School Scheduling Database

1. *"Display student Marital Status based on a code."*

   (Hint: Use Simple CASE in the SELECT clause. M = Married, S = Single, D = Divorced, W = Widowed)

   You can find the solution in CH19_Student_Marital_Status (18 rows).

2. *"Calculate student age as of November 15, 2017."*

   (Be sure to use the functions to extract Year, Month, and Day portions of a date value that are supported by your database system.)

   You can find the solution in CH19_Student_Age_Nov15_2017 (18 rows).

Bowling League Database

1. *"List all bowlers and calculate their averages using the sum of pins divided by games played, but avoid a divide by zero error."*

   (Hint: Use Simple CASE in a query using an OUTER JOIN and GROUP BY.)

   You can find the solution in CH19_Bowler_Averages_Avoid_0_Games (32 rows).

2. *"List tournament date, tournament location, match number, teams on the odd and even lanes, game number, and either the winner or 'Match not played.'"*

(Hint: Use an outer join between tournaments, tourney matches, teams, and a second copy of teams with a subquery using match games and a third copy of teams to indicate the winning team. Use a Searched Case to decide whether to display "not played" or the match results in the SELECT list.)

You can find the solution in CH19_All_Tourney_Matches (169 rows – one row on November 13, 2017 for match number 57 that was not played).

Using Unlinked Data and "Driver" Tables

"If you only have a hammer, you tend to see every problem as a nail."
—ABRAHAM MASLOW

Topics Covered in This Chapter

What Is Unlinked Data?

Solving Problems with Unlinked Data

Solving Problems Using "Driver" Tables

Sample Statements

Summary

Problems for You to Solve

Before you start this chapter, make sure you get a good night's sleep! And while I'm doling out warnings, perhaps you should also make sure your seatbelt is securely fastened. I promised that I would introduce you to concepts that make you think "outside the box." In this chapter, I am going to tackle problems that can be solved using unlinked data— problems where you will use more than one table in your FROM clause, but you won't specify any linking criteria using an ON clause. Let's get started.

> ❖ **Caution** I am going to use the CASE expression extensively in this chapter. If you are not familiar with using CASE, I strongly recommend you work through Chapter 19, "Condition Testing," before tackling this chapter.

What Is Unlinked Data?

As you learned beginning in Chapter 7, "Thinking in Sets," most problems you'll solve using SQL involve gathering data from more than one table. In Chapter 8, "INNER JOINs," I showed you how to fetch information from multiple tables by linking them on matching data in the Primary and Foreign keys where all the values match. In Chapter 9, "OUTER JOINs," I showed you how to fetch all the rows from one table and any matching information from a related table again using matching data in the Primary and Foreign keys. In this chapter, I'll use multiple tables, but I will purposefully not match on key values—I will be using "unlinked" tables.

Let's take a look at the SQL syntax to create unlinked tables. First, Figure 20-1 shows you the syntax for the SELECT Statement.

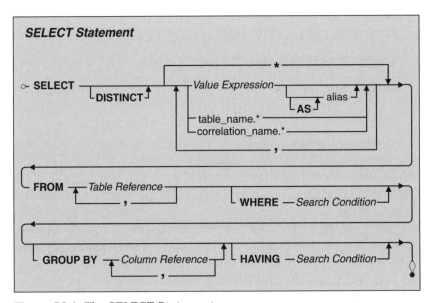

Figure 20-1 *The SELECT Statement*

You need to study the Table Reference to understand how to put unlinked tables in a FROM clause. Figure 20-2 shows you the full diagram for Table Reference.

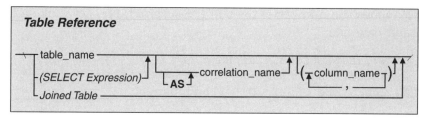

Figure 20-2 *The structure of a Table Reference*

And finally, you need to study the diagram for Joined Table. Even though you really aren't going to "join" unlinked tables, the SQL Standard does show you how to do it in the Joined Table definition, as shown in Figure 20-3.

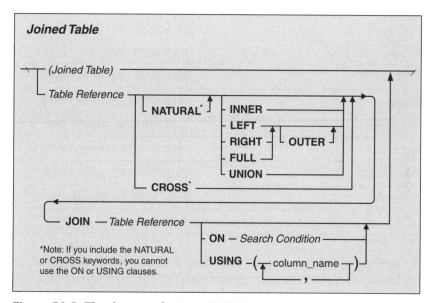

Figure 20-3 *The diagram for Joined Table*

To get unlinked tables, you need to do what the SQL Standard calls a CROSS JOIN. So what do you get when you put two or more tables in the FROM clause of your SQL using a CROSS JOIN? The result is something called a Cartesian Product. You'll get all rows from the first table matched with all rows from the second table, and the total number of rows you will get will be the product of the number of rows in the first table times the number of rows in the second table. Let's take a look at a simple example:

```
SELECT Customers.CustLastName,
   Products.ProductName
FROM Customers CROSS JOIN Products;
```

In the Sales Orders sample database, you can find 28 customers and 40 products, so you'll get 28 times 40 rows or 1,120 rows! The result looks like this:

CustLastName	ProductName
Viescas	Trek 9000 Mountain Bike
Thompson	Trek 9000 Mountain Bike
Hallmark	Trek 9000 Mountain Bike
Brown	Trek 9000 Mountain Bike
McCrae	Trek 9000 Mountain Bike
Viescas	Trek 9000 Mountain Bike
Sergienko	Trek 9000 Mountain Bike
Patterson	Trek 9000 Mountain Bike
Cencini	Trek 9000 Mountain Bike
Kennedy	Trek 9000 Mountain Bike
<< more rows here >>	

You might be asking: Why is this useful? Let's say you need to produce a catalog of all products that is customized for each customer. Your sales department has asked you to create the information to be able to say "Dear Mr. Thompson" or "Dear Mrs. Brown," print a mailing label on the outside cover, and then list all the products available. You could certainly include the Orders and Order_Details tables to fully link Customers with Products, but then you would get only the products that each customer had ever purchased. To solve your problem, you need to use unlinked tables that result in a Cartesian Product to get the information you need. (By the way, I saved the query to produce the list of all customers and products as CH20_Customer_Catalog in the Sales Orders sample database.)

> ❖ **Note** The SQL Standard allows you to simply list tables separated by commas when you want to use unlinked tables (see Figure 20-1 of the SELECT Statement shown previously), and nearly all database systems accept this syntax. However, as you have learned, the SQL Standard also defines the keywords CROSS JOIN to explicitly indicate that you intend to get the Cartesian Product of the table reference on the left with the table reference on the right.
>
> When you save a View in Microsoft SQL Server using only commas to separate the table names, you'll find the view saved with the commas replaced with CROSS JOIN. When you save a View in MySQL using only commas, you'll find the view saved with the commas replaced with JOIN. (CROSS is the default if you don't specify INNER or OUTER and do not include an ON clause.) PostgreSQL leaves the commas but replaces INNER JOIN with just JOIN—the default being INNER when not specified. Go figure! Microsoft Office Access doesn't support CROSS JOIN, so I created all the sample queries using only the lowest common denominator—the comma syntax. I will, however, continue to use CROSS JOIN in the text and in the Clean Up steps to make it clear that's what I am doing. In the SQL statements in the sample databases, I'll use only commas.

Deciding When to Use a CROSS JOIN

Deciding to use a CROSS JOIN isn't easy. You can think of these types of queries in two categories:

- Using data from two or more of the main data tables in your database—the tables that you built to store all the subjects and actions described by your application.

I mentioned Customers and all Products previously in this chapter. The same might apply to all Agents and Entertainers, Students and Courses, or even Teams unlinked with a second copy of the Teams table to list all potential matches.

- Using data from one or more of your main data tables and a "helper" or "driver" table that contains rows, for example, for all dates across a relevant time period.

You certainly have date information in your database, such as the OrderDate in the Orders table. But when you want to look at all dates across a range regardless of whether an order was placed on that date, you need a driver table to supply all the values. You can also use driver tables to supply "lookup" values such as a translation from Gender code to the relevant word or conversion of a grade point to a letter grade defined by a range of grade points.

Solving Problems with Unlinked Data

Normally when you set about solving problems using data in your main data tables, you figure out where the data you want is stored and then gather all the tables required to link that data in some meaningful way. When the data you want is in two or more tables, you think about using a JOIN to link the tables, including any intervening tables necessary to logically link all the tables even if you don't actually need data columns from some of those tables.

Solving problems with unlinked data involves breaking this mold and "thinking outside of the box" to get the answer you want. Let's take a look again at the Customers and Products "catalog" problem, but let's complicate it by flagging any products the customers have already ordered.

> ❖ **Note** Throughout this chapter, I use the "Request/Translation/ Clean Up/SQL" technique introduced in Chapter 4, "Creating a Simple Query." Because this process should now be very familiar to you, I have combined the Translation/Clean Up steps for all the following examples to simplify the process.

> *"Produce a list of all customer names and address and all products that we sell and indicate the products the customer has already purchased."*

From what you learned in Part III, "Working with Multiple Tables," you would look at your table relationships to start to figure out how to proceed. Figure 20-4 shows you the standard way you would link Customers and Products, using the Orders and Order_Details tables as intermediaries.

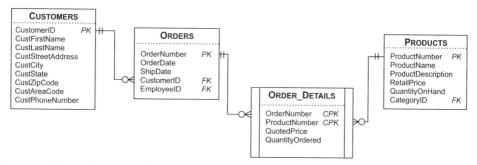

Figure 20-4 *The normal way to connect Customers to Products*

Remember that I want all customers (including those who haven't ordered anything) and all Products (including products never ordered). If you have your thinking cap on, you might come up with using a FULL OUTER JOIN (see Chapter 9), and you are correct—that would be one way to do it. Keep in mind that not all database systems support FULL OUTER JOINs, so that might not be a solution for you. You could also create one query (view) that LEFT JOINs Customers with Orders and Order_Details, and then use that query in another query to RIGHT JOIN with the Products table. When (remember CASE?) a key field in the Order_Details table is not Null, then indicate that the customer has previously ordered the product.

But this chapter is about solving problems with unlinked tables, so let's tackle the problem head-on by using a CROSS JOIN of Customers and Products and a subquery in the SELECT clause to do a lookup to see if the customer ever ordered the product. Just for fun, let's also look up the category description for each product. Here's how to do it:

Translation/ Clean Up	Select customer first name, customer last name, customer street address, customer city, customer state, customer zip code, category description, product number, product name, retail price, and (CASE when the customer ID is in the (selection of customer ID from the orders table inner joined with the order details table on Orders.order number in the orders table equals = Order_Details.order number in the order details table where the Products.product number in the products table equals the = Order_Details.product number in the order details table then display 'You purchased this!'; else ' ' END) display a blank from the customers table and the CROSS JOIN categories table inner joined with the products table on Categories.category ID in the categories table equals = Products.category ID in the products table sorted ORDER BY customer ID, category description, and product number

```
SQL          SELECT Customers.CustomerID, Customers.
             CustFirstName,
                Customers.CustLastName,
                Customers.CustStreetAddress,
                Customers.CustCity, Customers.CustState,
                Customers.CustZipCode,
                Categories.CategoryDescription,
                Products.ProductNumber, Products.ProductName,
                Products.RetailPrice,
                  (CASE WHEN Customers.CustomerID IN
                    (SELECT Orders.CustomerID
                    FROM ORDERS INNER JOIN Order_Details
                    ON Orders.OrderNumber =
                        Order_Details.OrderNumber
                    WHERE Order_Details.ProductNumber =
                          Products.ProductNumber)
                  THEN 'You purchased this! '
                  ELSE ' ' END) AS ProductOrdered
             FROM Customers, Categories INNER JOIN Products
                    ON Categories.CategoryID = Products.CategoryID
             ORDER BY Customers.CustomerID,
                Categories.CategoryDescription,
                Products.ProductNumber;
```

Yes, there is an INNER JOIN to link Categories with Products, but the
key part of the FROM clause is the CROSS JOIN with the Customers
table. You can find this query saved as CH20_Customer_All_Products_
PurchasedStatus in the Sales Orders sample database. As expected, the
query returns 1,120 rows.

> ❖ **Note** Recall from Chapter 19 that Microsoft Office Access does not
> support the CASE expression. In the samples I created in the Access
> databases, you'll find that I used a built-in function called Immediate
> If (IIf) that serves a similar purpose.

Solving Problems Using "Driver" Tables

Let's move on now to solving problems that require you to set up one or more tables containing a list of values that you'll CROSS JOIN with other tables in your database to get your answer. I call this sort of table a "driver" table because the contents of the table "drive" the result you get. (If you also own *Effective SQL* that I wrote with my good friends, Doug Steele and Ben Clothier, we decided to call them "tally" tables in that book, but they're the same thing.) Arguably, the most common type of driver table contains a list of dates or weeks or months that you can CROSS JOIN with your data to list all days or weeks or months and any matching events that occur on those dates.

Another use of a driver table is to define a categorization of values across a set of defined ranges. Examples include assigning a letter grade to a grade point score, rating instructors based on their proficiency rating, evaluating bowlers based on their average score, categorizing product prices, or categorizing the amount spent by a customer.

A really creative use of a driver table lets you "pivot" your data to display a result that looks more like a spreadsheet. A common example would be to display sales or purchases by month, with the months listed across by product or customer.

Setting Up a Driver Table

The SQL Standard defines WITH RECURSIVE that allows you to execute a stated SQL query multiple times in a loop. This can be useful to load a driver table with consecutive dates across a date range. Unfortunately, only a few database systems support this. To load my large driver tables, I resorted to using Visual Basic in Microsoft Office Access to perform the recursion necessary to load hundreds of rows into a date range table. (You can actually find some of the code I used if you dig around in the sample databases that are in Microsoft Office Access format.)

When your driver table is a simple set of ranges to translate to a value, it's easy enough to load the data by hand. For example, here's the list of values I entered into the ztblLetterGrades table you can find in the School Scheduling sample database:

LetterGrade	LowGradePoint	HighGradePoint
A	93	96.99
A-	90	92.99
A+	97	120
B	83	86.99
B-	80	82.99
B+	87	89.99
C	73	76.99
C-	70	72.99
C+	77	79.99
D	63	66.99
D-	60	62.99
D+	67	69.99
F	0	59.99

This should look familiar because it's the same list of ranges that I used in the CH19_Students_Classes_Letter_Grades query in the previous chapter. (By the way, I named all the driver tables using a "ztbl" prefix to clearly separate them from the main data tables in each database.) One clear advantage to setting up a table like this is that you can easily change the range values should the need arise. You don't have to go digging in the CASE clauses in each query that depends on the ranges to obtain the answer.

As I noted previously, a really creative use of a driver table lets you pivot your result to look like a spreadsheet. Quite a few database systems provide nonstandard ways to pivot data, but I'll show you how to create a pivot using standard SQL and a driver table. You can find one such table I created for this purpose in the Sales Orders sample database called ztblMonths. Here is what part of the table looks like:

MonthYear	YearNumber	MonthNumber	MonthStart	MonthEnd
January 2017	2017	1	1/1/2017	1/31/2017
February 2017	2017	2	2/1/2017	2/29/2017

MonthYear	YearNumber	MonthNumber	MonthStart	MonthEnd
March 2017	2017	3	3/1/2017	3/31/2017
April 2017	2017	4	4/1/2017	4/30/2017
May 2017	2017	5	5/1/2017	5/31/2017
June 2017	2017	6	6/1/2017	6/30/2017
July 2017	2017	7	7/1/2017	7/31/2017
August 2017	2017	8	8/1/2017	8/31/2017

<< more rows here >>

Additional columns...

January	February	March	April	May	June
1	0	0	0	0	0
0	1	0	0	0	0
0	0	1	0	0	0
0	0	0	1	0	0
0	0	0	0	1	0
0	0	0	0	0	1
0	0	0	0	0	0
0	0	0	0	0	0

<< more rows here >>

Additional columns...

July	August	September	October	November	December
0	0	0	0	0	0
0	0	0	0	0	0
0	0	0	0	0	0
0	0	0	0	0	0
0	0	0	0	0	0
0	0	0	0	0	0
1	0	0	0	0	0
0	1	0	0	0	0

<< more rows here >>

Looks a bit strange, doesn't it? The little secret is you'll use a WHERE clause to match the rows in this driver table with the date of the order, and then you will build columns by multiplying the total sales times the value found in a particular column to get a total for that month. When the order occurs in January 2017, only the January column on the matching row contains a 1 to result in 1 times quantity times the price. The value won't be added to the columns for the other months because zero times any value is always zero. Another way to think of it is the ones and zeros define the horizontal "buckets" for each value encountered in your query that calculates the values you want to display. When a date matches the range defined by the row in the driver table, the 1 indicates the correct horizontal bucket in which to place the value. So, when a value is in January 2017, that value ends up in the January column by multiplying the column value times the expression that calculates the total.

Using a Driver Table

Let's use the two driver tables described in the previous section to solve problems. First, I want to display a grade letter based on each student's numeric grade received for a class. I solved this problem using CASE in the previous chapter. Now I'll solve it using the driver table.

> *"List all students, the classes for which they enrolled, the grade they received, and a conversion of the grade number to a letter."*

Translation/ Clean UP	Select Students.student ID ~~from the students table~~, Students. student first name ~~from the students table~~, Students.student last name ~~from the students table~~, Classes.class ID ~~from the classes table~~, Classes.start date ~~from the classes table~~, Subjects.subject code ~~from the subjects table~~, Subjects.subject name ~~from the subjects table~~, Student_Schedules.grade ~~from the student_schedules table~~, ~~and~~ ztblLetterGrades.letter grade ~~from the letter grades driver table~~ from ztblLetterGrades ~~the letter grades driver table and~~ CROSS JOIN ~~the~~ students ~~table~~ inner joined ~~with the~~ student schedules ~~table~~ on Students.student ID ~~in the students table equals~~ = Student_Schedules.student ID ~~in the student schedules table, then~~ inner joined ~~with the~~ classes ~~table~~ on Student_Schedules.class ID ~~in the student schedules table equals~~ = Classes.class ID ~~in the classes table, then~~ inner joined ~~with the~~ subjects ~~table~~ on Classes.subject ID ~~in the classes table equals~~ = Subjects.subject ID ~~in the subjects table, then~~ inner joined ~~with the~~ student class status ~~table~~ on

Student_Schedules.class status ~~in the student schedules table~~ equals = Student_Class_Status.class status ~~in the student class status table~~ where Student_Class_Status.class status description ~~in the student class status table equals~~ = 'Completed' and Student_Schedules.grade ~~in the student schedules table is~~ between ztblLetterGrades.low grade point ~~in the letter grades driver table~~ and ztblLetterGrades.high grade point ~~in the letter grades driver table~~

SQL

```
SELECT Students.StudentID, Students.StudFirstName,
    Students.StudLastName, Classes.ClassID,
    Classes.StartDate,
    Subjects.SubjectCode, Subjects.SubjectName,
    Student_Schedules.Grade,
    ztblLetterGrades.LetterGrade
FROM ztblLetterGrades, (((Students
INNER JOIN Student_Schedules
  ON Students.StudentID =
      Student_Schedules.StudentID)
INNER JOIN Classes
  ON Student_Schedules.ClassID = Classes.ClassID)
INNER JOIN Subjects
  ON Classes.SubjectID = Subjects.SubjectID)
INNER JOIN Student_Class_Status
  ON Student_Schedules.ClassStatus =
      Student_Class_Status.ClassStatus
WHERE
  (Student_Class_Status.ClassStatusDescription =
      'Completed')
  AND (Student_Schedules.Grade Between
      ztblLetterGrades.LowGradePoint
      AND ztblLetterGrades.HighGradePoint);
```

You can find this query saved as CH20_Students_Classes_Letter_Grades in the School Scheduling sample database. You'll find that it returns the same 68 rows as the CH19_Student_Classes_Letter_Grades that I showed you in Chapter 19.

Now let's take a look at using the second driver table.

"Show product sales for each product for all months, listing the months as columns."

Translation/ Clean Up	Select Products.product name ~~from the products table~~, ~~the~~ sum ~~of~~ (Order_Details.quoted price ~~from the order details table times~~ * Order_Details.quantity ordered ~~from the order details table times~~ * ztblMonths.January ~~from the months driver table~~) as January, ~~the~~ sum ~~of~~ (Order_Details.quoted price ~~from the order details table times~~ * Order_Details.quantity ordered ~~from the order details table times~~ * ztblMonths.February ~~from the months driver table~~) as February, ~~the~~ sum ~~of~~ (Order_Details. quoted price ~~from the order details table times~~ * Order_ Details.quantity ordered ~~from the order details table times~~ * ztblMonths.March ~~from the months driver table~~) as March, ~~the~~ sum ~~of~~ (Order_Details.quoted price ~~from the order details table times~~ * Order_Details.quantity ordered ~~from the order details table times~~ * ztblMonths.April ~~from the months driver table~~) as April, ~~the~~ sum ~~of~~ (Order_Details.quoted price ~~from the order details table times~~ * Order_Details.quantity ordered ~~from the order details table times~~ * ztblMonths.May ~~from the months driver table~~) as May, ~~the~~ sum ~~of~~ (Order_Details.quoted price ~~from the order details table times~~ * Order_Details.quantity ordered ~~from the order details table times~~ * ztblMonths. June ~~from the months driver table~~) as June, ~~the~~ sum ~~of~~ (Order_Details.quoted price ~~from the order details table times~~ * Order_Details.quantity ordered ~~from the order details table times~~ * ztblMonths.July ~~from the months driver table~~) as July, ~~the~~ sum ~~of~~ (Order_Details.quoted price ~~from the order details table times~~ * Order_Details.quantity ordered ~~from the order details table times~~ * ztblMonths.August ~~from the months driver table~~) as August, ~~the~~ sum ~~of~~ (Order_Details.quoted price ~~from the order details table times~~ * Order_Details.quantity ordered ~~from the order details table times~~ * ztblMonths.September ~~from the months driver table~~) as September, ~~the~~ sum ~~of~~ (Order_ Details.quoted price ~~from the order details table times~~ * Order_ Details.quantity ordered ~~from the order details table times~~ * ztblMonths.October ~~from the months driver table~~) as October, ~~the~~ sum ~~of~~ (Order_Details.quoted price ~~from the order details table times~~ * Order_Details.quantity ordered ~~from the order details table times~~ * ztblMonths.November ~~from the months driver table~~) as November, ~~and the~~ sum ~~of~~ (Order_Details.quoted price ~~from the order details table~~ times * Order_Details.quantity ordered ~~from the order details table times~~ * ztblMonths. December ~~from the months driver table~~) as December from

ztblMonths ~~the months driver table~~ CROSS JOIN ~~and the~~ products ~~table then~~ inner join~~ed with the~~ order details ~~table~~ on Products.product number ~~in the products table equals~~ = Order_Details.product number ~~in the order details table~~ then inner join~~ed with the~~ orders ~~table~~ on Orders.order number ~~in the orders table equals~~ = Order_Details.order number ~~in the order details table~~ where Orders.order date in the orders table is between ztblMonths.month start ~~in the months driver table~~ and ztblMonths.month end ~~in the months driver table~~ group~~ed~~ by Products.product name ~~in the products table~~

SQL

```
SELECT Products.ProductName,
  SUM(Order_Details.QuotedPrice *
    Order_Details.QuantityOrdered *
    ztblMonths.January)
  AS January,
  SUM(Order_Details.QuotedPrice *
    Order_Details.QuantityOrdered *
    ztblMonths.February)
  AS February,
  SUM(Order_Details.QuotedPrice *
    Order_Details.QuantityOrdered *
    ztblMonths.March)
  AS March,
  SUM(Order_Details.QuotedPrice *
    Order_Details.QuantityOrdered *
    ztblMonths.April)
  AS April,
  SUM(Order_Details.QuotedPrice *
    Order_Details.QuantityOrdered *
    ztblMonths.May)
  AS May,
  SUM(Order_Details.QuotedPrice *
    Order_Details.QuantityOrdered *
    ztblMonths.June)
  AS June,
```

```
            SUM(Order_Details.QuotedPrice *
              Order_Details.QuantityOrdered *
              ztblMonths.July)
              AS July,
            SUM(Order_Details.QuotedPrice *
              Order_Details.QuantityOrdered *
              ztblMonths.August)
              AS August,
            SUM(Order_Details.QuotedPrice *
              Order_Details.QuantityOrdered *
              ztblMonths.September)
              AS September,
            SUM(Order_Details.QuotedPrice *
              Order_Details.QuantityOrdered *
              ztblMonths.October)
              AS October,
            SUM(Order_Details.QuotedPrice *
              Order_Details.QuantityOrdered *
              ztblMonths.November)
              AS November,
            SUM(Order_Details.QuotedPrice *
              Order_Details.QuantityOrdered *
              ztblMonths.December)
              AS December
          FROM ztblMonths, (Products
          INNER JOIN Order_Details
            ON Products.ProductNumber =
              Order_Details.ProductNumber)
          INNER JOIN Orders
            ON Orders.OrderNumber = Order_Details.OrderNumber
          WHERE Orders.OrderDate BETWEEN ztblMonths.MonthStart
            AND ztblMonths.MonthEnd
          GROUP BY Products.ProductName;
```

The "magic" happens when you restrict the row returned by the driver table to the month that matches the date in the orders table. When the date falls in January, only the January column has the value 1. That places the amount for that row in January in the correct "bucket" to be finally summed to get your pivoted result. You can find this query saved in the Sales Orders sample database as CH20_Product_Sales_Month_Pivot. The query returns 38 rows, but there are 40 products in the Products table. The two missing rows occur because two of the products have never been sold. (See CH09_Products_Never_Ordered to discover those two products.)

Sample Statements

You now know the mechanics of constructing queries using CROSS JOIN and driver tables and have seen some of the types of requests you can answer with these techniques. Let's take a look at a fairly robust set of samples, all of which use CROSS JOIN between two data tables or with a driver table. These examples come from each of the sample databases, and they illustrate the use of these techniques to solve "thinking outside the box" problems.

> ❖ **Note** Remember in the Introduction that I warned you that results from each database system won't necessarily match the sort order you see in examples in this book unless you include an ORDER BY clause. Even when you include that specification, the system might return results in columns not included in the ORDER BY clause in a different sequence because of different optimization techniques.
>
> If you're running the examples in Microsoft SQL Server, simply selecting the rows from the view does not honor any ORDER BY clause specified in the view. You must open the design of the view and execute it from there to see the ORDER BY clause honored.
>
> Also, when you use GROUP BY, you'll often see the results returned by your database system as though the rows are sorted by the columns you specified. This happens because some optimizers first sort the data internally to make it faster to process your GROUP BY. Keep in mind that if you want a specific sort order, you must also include an ORDER BY clause.

I've also included sample result sets that would be returned by these operations and placed them immediately after the SQL syntax line. The name that appears immediately above a result set is the name I gave each query in the sample data that you'll find on the book's website, www.informit.com/title/9780134858333. I stored each query in the appropriate sample database (as indicated within the example), using "CH20" as the leading part of the query or view name. You can follow the instructions in the Introduction to this book to load the samples onto your computer and try them out.

> ❖ **Note** Remember that all of the field names and table names used in these examples are drawn from the sample database structures shown in Appendix B, "Schema for the Sample Databases."
>
> Because many of these examples use complex joins, the optimizer for your database system may choose a different way to solve these queries. For this reason, the first few rows I show you may not exactly match the result you obtain, but the total number of rows should be the same. Keep in mind that for any SQL Server View that contains an ORDER BY clause, you must open the view in Design mode first and then execute it to see the specified order. If you SELECT * from the View, SQL Server does not honor the ORDER BY clause.

Examples Using Unlinked Tables

This first set of sample statements shows you problems you can solve using unlinked tables. All of them use a CROSS JOIN between two data tables.

Sales Order Database

"List all employees and customers who live in the same state and indicate whether the customer has ever placed an order with the employee."

Translation/ Clean Up	Select employee first name, employee last name, customer first name, customer last name, customer area code, customer phone number, and (CASE when the customer ID in the customers table is in the (selection of Orders. customer ID from the orders table where Orders.employee

ID ~~in the orders table equals~~ = Employees.employee ID) ~~in the employees table~~ then ~~display~~ 'Ordered from you.' else ~~display~~ ' ' END) from employees ~~and~~ CROSS JOIN customers where ~~the~~ Employees.~~employee~~ state ~~in the employees table equals~~ = Customer.cust~~omer~~ state ~~in the customers table~~

SQL	
	SELECT Employees.EmpFirstName,
	Employees.EmpLastName,
	Customers.CustFirstName,
	Customers.CustLastName,
	Customers.CustAreaCode,
	Customers.CustPhoneNumber,
	(CASE WHEN Customers.CustomerID IN
	(SELECT Orders.CustomerID
	FROM Orders
	WHERE Orders.EmployeeID =
	Employees.EmployeeID)
	THEN 'Ordered from you. '
	ELSE ' ' END) AS CustStatus
	FROM Employees, Customers
	WHERE Employees.EmpState = Customers.CustState;

CH20_Employees_Same_State_Customers (83 rows)

Emp FirstName	Emp LastName	Cust FirstName	Cust LastName	Cust AreaCode	Cust PhoneNumber	Cust Status
Ann	Patterson	William	Thompson	425	555-2681	Ordered from you.
Ann	Patterson	Gary	Hallmark	253	555-2676	Ordered from you.
Ann	Patterson	Dean	McCrae	425	555-2506	Ordered from you.
Ann	Patterson	John	Viescas	425	555-2511	Ordered from you.
Ann	Patterson	Andrew	Cencini	206	555-2601	Ordered from you.

Emp FirstName	Emp LastName	Cust FirstName	Cust LastName	Cust AreaCode	Cust PhoneNumber	Cust Status
Ann	Patterson	Liz	Keyser	425	555-2556	Ordered from you.
Ann	Patterson	Julia	Schnebly	206	555-9936	Ordered from you.
Ann	Patterson	Suzanne	Viescas	425	555-2686	Ordered from you.
Ann	Patterson	Jeffrey	Tirekicker	425	555-9999	
Ann	Patterson	Joyce	Bonnicksen	425	555-2726	Ordered from you.

<< more rows here >>

❖ **Note** If you're really sharp, you probably figured out that I could have solved the problem using an INNER JOIN between Employees and Customers ON EmpState = CustState. As I have stated many times before, there's almost always more than one way to solve a problem. Now you know how to solve it using a CROSS JOIN.

Entertainment Database

"List all customer preferences and the count of first, second, and third preferences."

❖ **Note** This is a bit tricky because you first need to "pivot" each customer's first, second, and third preferences (as indicated by the PreferenceSeq column), and then count them. You could use a driver table to help perform the pivot, but with only three unique values to pivot into columns, it's just as easy to do it with CASE.

Translation/ Clean Up	Select Musical_Styles.style ID ~~from the musical styles table~~, Musical_Styles.style name ~~from the musical styles table~~, ~~the~~ count ~~of~~ (RankedPeferences.first style) ~~from the ranked preferences query~~ as first preference, ~~the~~ count ~~of~~ (RankedPreferences.second style) ~~from the ranked preferences query~~ as second preference, ~~and the~~

count of (RankedPreferences.third style) ~~from the ranked prefer-~~ ~~ences query~~ as third preference from ~~the~~ musical styles ~~table and~~ CROSS JOIN ~~the~~ (selection of (CASE when Musical_Preferences. preference sequence ~~in the musical preferences table is~~ = 1 then ~~return the~~ Musical_Preferences.style ID ~~from the musical prefer-~~ ~~ences table~~ else ~~return~~ Null END) as first style, (CASE when Musi- cal_Preferences.preference sequence ~~in the~~ ~~musical preferences~~ ~~table is~~ = 2 then ~~return the~~ Musical_Preferences.style ID ~~from the~~ ~~musical preferences table~~ else ~~return~~ Null END) as second style, (CASE when Musical_Preferences.preference sequence ~~in the musi-~~ ~~cal preferences table is~~ = 3 then ~~return the~~ Musical_Preferences. style ID ~~from the musical preferences table~~ else ~~return~~ Null END) as third style from ~~the~~ musical preferences ~~table~~) as ranked pref- erences where Musical_Styles.style ID ~~in the musical styles table~~ ~~equals~~ = RankedPreferences.first style ~~in the ranked preferences~~ ~~query~~ or Musical_Styles.style ID ~~in the musical styles table~~ equals = RankedPreferences.second style ~~in the ranked preferences query~~ or Musical_Styles.style ID ~~in the musical styles table~~ equals = RankedPreferences.third style ~~in the ranked preferences query~~ grouped by style ID, ~~and~~ style name having ~~the~~ count of (first style) > ~~greater than~~ 0 or ~~the~~ count of (second style) > ~~greater than~~ 0 or ~~the~~ count of (third style) > ~~greater than~~ 0 ordered by first pref- erence descending, second preference descending, third preference descending, ~~and~~ style ID

SQL

```
SELECT Musical_Styles.StyleID,
   Musical_Styles.StyleName,
   COUNT(RankedPreferences.FirstStyle)
     AS FirstPreference,
   COUNT(RankedPreferences.SecondStyle)
     AS SecondPreference,
   COUNT(RankedPreferences.ThirdStyle)
     AS ThirdPreference
FROM Musical_Styles,
  (SELECT (CASE WHEN
     Musical_Preferences.PreferenceSeq = 1
              THEN Musical_Preferences.StyleID
              ELSE Null END) As FirstStyle,
        (CASE WHEN
     Musical_Preferences.PreferenceSeq = 2
              THEN Musical_Preferences.StyleID
              ELSE Null END) As SecondStyle,
```

```
                      (CASE WHEN
           Musical_Preferences.PreferenceSeq = 3
                        THEN Musical_Preferences.StyleID
                        ELSE Null END) AS ThirdStyle
          FROM Musical_Preferences)  AS RankedPreferences
        WHERE Musical_Styles.StyleID =
                  RankedPreferences.FirstStyle
          OR Musical_Styles.StyleID =
                  RankedPreferences.SecondStyle
          OR Musical_Styles.StyleID =
                  RankedPreferences.ThirdStyle
        GROUP BY StyleID, StyleName
        HAVING COUNT(FirstStyle) > 0
             OR      COUNT(SecondStyle) > 0
             OR      COUNT(ThirdStyle) > 0
        ORDER BY FirstPreference DESC,
                  SecondPreference DESC,
                  ThirdPreference DESC, StyleID;
```

CH20_Customer_Style_Preference_Rankings (20 rows)

StyleID	StyleName	FirstPreference	SecondPreference	ThirdPreference
21	Standards	2	2	0
15	Jazz	2	1	0
19	Rhythm and Blues	2	0	1
22	Top 40 Hits	2	0	0
10	Contemporary	1	2	0
8	Classic Rock & Roll	1	1	0
20	Show Tunes	1	1	0
3	60's Music	1	0	0
11	Country Rock	1	0	0
14	Chamber Music	1	0	0
23	Variety	1	0	0

<< more rows here >>

Notice that although there are 25 distinct musical styles defined in the database, the query returns only 20 rows. The styles that are missing aren't ranked first, second, or third by any customer.

School Scheduling Database

"List all students who have completed English courses and rank them by Quintile on the grades they received."

A Quintile divides a group into five equal ranges. When applied to student rankings, a quintile will be 20% of students—those in the top 20 percent are in the first quintile, those in the next 20% are in the second quintile, and so on. To solve this, you need to CROSS JOIN two queries:

1. A query that assigns a ranking number to each student who completed an English course. You can calculate the rank by counting the number of students who have a grade greater than or equal to the current student's grade. The student with the highest grade will be ranked #1, the student with the second highest grade #2, and so on.

2. A query that counts all students who completed an English course. You can use this count times 0.2, 0.4, 0.6, and 0.8 to figure out the quintile. The students whose rank (as calculated by the first query) is less than or equal to 0.2 times the total number of students is in the first quintile.

Translation/ Clean Up	Select S1.subject ID ~~from the first query~~, S1.student first name ~~from the first query~~, S1.student last name ~~from the first query~~, S1.class status ~~from the first query~~, S1.grade ~~from the first query~~, S1.category ID ~~from the first query~~, S1.subject name ~~from the first query~~, S1.rank in category ~~from the first query~~, StudCount.~~number of~~ students ~~from the student count query~~, ~~and~~ (CASE when the rank in category <= ~~is less than or equal to~~ 0.2 * ~~times the~~ ~~number of~~ students then ~~return~~ 'First' when ~~the~~ rank in category <= ~~is less than or equal to~~ 0.4 * ~~times the~~ ~~number of~~ students then ~~return~~ 'Second' when ~~the~~ rank in category <= ~~is less than or equal to~~ 0.6 * ~~times the~~ ~~number of~~ students then ~~return~~ 'Third' when ~~the~~ rank in category <= ~~is less than or equal to~~ 0.8 * ~~times the~~ ~~number of~~ students then ~~return~~ 'Fourth' else ~~return~~ 'Fifth' END) as ~~the~~ quintile from ~~the~~ (~~selection of~~ Subjects.subject ID ~~in the subjects table~~, Students.student first name ~~in the students table~~, Students.student last name ~~in the students table~~, Student_Schedules.class status ~~in the student schedules table~~, Student_Schedules.grade ~~in the student schedules table~~, Subjects.category ID ~~in the subjects table~~, Subjects.subject name ~~in the subjects table~~, ~~and the~~

(selection of the count(*) of all rows from the classes table inner joined with the student schedules table AS SS2 on Classes.class ID in the classes table = equals SS2.class ID in the student schedules table, then inner joined with the subjects table AS S3 on S3.subject ID in the subjects table = equals Classes.subject ID in the classes table where S3.category ID in the subjects table = equals 'ENG' and SS2.grade in the student schedules table >= is greater than or equal to Student_Schedules.grade in the student schedules table) as rank in category) from the subjects table inner joined with the classes table on Subjects.subject ID in the subjects table = equals Classes.subject ID in the classes table, then inner joined with the student schedules table on Student_Schedules.class ID in the student schedules table = equals Classes.class ID in the classes table, then inner joined with the students table on Students.student ID in the students table = equals Student_Schedules.student ID in the student schedules table where Student_Schedules.class status in the student schedules table = equals 2 and Subjects.category ID in the subjects table = equals 'ENG') AS S1 CROSS JOIN and the (selection of the count(*) of all rows as number of students from the classes table AS C2 inner joined with the student schedules table AS SS3 on C2.class id in the classes table = equals SS3.class ID in the student schedules table, then inner joined with the subjects table AS S2 on S2.subject ID in the subjects table = equals C2.subject ID in the classes table where SS3.class status in the student schedules table = equals 2 and S2.category ID in the subjects table = equals 'ENG') As student count ordered by S1.grade in the first query descending

SQL	

```sql
SELECT S1.SubjectID, S1.StudFirstName,
    S1.StudLastName,
    S1.ClassStatus, S1.Grade, S1.CategoryID,
    S1.SubjectName,
    S1.RankInCategory, StudCount.NumStudents,
    (CASE WHEN RankInCategory <= 0.2 * NumStudents
        THEN 'First'
        WHEN RankInCategory <= 0.4 * NumStudents
        THEN 'Second'
        WHEN RankInCategory <= 0.6 * NumStudents
        THEN 'Third'
        WHEN RankInCategory <= 0.8 * NumStudents
        THEN 'Fourth'
        ELSE 'Fifth' END) AS Quintile
```

```
FROM
   (SELECT Subjects.SubjectID,
      Students.StudFirstName,
      Students.StudLastName,
      Student_Schedules.ClassStatus,
      Student_Schedules.Grade, Subjects.CategoryID,
      Subjects.SubjectName,
      (SELECT Count(*)
      FROM (Classes
      INNER JOIN Student_Schedules AS SS2
         ON Classes.ClassID = SS2.ClassID)
      INNER JOIN Subjects As S3
         ON S3.SubjectID = Classes.SubjectID
      WHERE S3.CategoryID = 'ENG'
         AND SS2.Grade >=
            Student_Schedules.Grade)
            AS RankInCategory
   FROM ((Subjects INNER JOIN Classes
      ON Subjects.SubjectID = Classes.SubjectID)
   INNER JOIN Student_Schedules
      ON Student_Schedules.ClassID =
         Classes.ClassID)
   INNER JOIN Students
      ON Students.StudentID =
      Student_Schedules.StudentID
   WHERE Student_Schedules.ClassStatus = 2 AND
      Subjects.CategoryID = 'ENG') AS S1,
   (SELECT Count(*) AS NumStudents
   FROM (Classes AS C2 INNER JOIN
         Student_Schedules AS SS3
         ON C2.ClassID = SS3.ClassID)
      INNER JOIN Subjects AS S2
         ON S2.SubjectID = C2.SubjectID
   WHERE SS3.ClassStatus = 2 And S2.CategoryID = 'ENG')
      AS StudCount
ORDER BY S1.Grade DESC;
```

CH20_English_Student_Quintiles (18 rows)

Subject ID	Stud First Name	Stud Last Name	Class Status	Grade	Category	Subject Name	RankIn Category	Num Students	Quintile
37	Scott	Bishop	2	98.07	ENG	Composition - Fundamentals	1	18	First
37	Sara	Sheskey	2	97.59	ENG	Composition - Fundamentals	2	18	First
37	John	Kennedy	2	93.01	ENG	Composition - Fundamentals	3	18	First
37	Brannon	Jones	2	91.66	ENG	Composition - Fundamentals	4	18	Second
37	Janice	Galvin	2	91.44	ENG	Composition - Fundamentals	5	18	Second
38	Kendra	Bonnicksen	2	88.91	ENG	Composition - Intermediate	6	18	Second
37	George	Chavez	2	88.54	ENG	Composition - Fundamentals	7	18	Second
37	Mari-anne	Wier	2	87.4	ENG	Composition - Fundamentals	8	18	Third

<< more rows here >>

❖ **Note** This query uses the grade from each English class to rank the students, so it is possible to see a student listed more than once if the student has completed more than one English class. To rank students for all English classes taken, you would first have to calculate the average of credits times grade divided by credits for each student and then rank those results.

Bowling League Database

"List all potential matches between teams without duplicating any team pairing."

To solve this problem, you need two copies of the Teams table in your FROM clause. That will give you all combinations of two teams, but you obviously don't want to list a team bowling itself. Think about dealing with each team one at a time. When looking at Team 1, you need to match it with any team that has a higher TeamID value. Looking at

Team 2, you've already matched it with Team 1 on the first pass, but any higher value in TeamID will work. So as long as the TeamID in the second copy of the table has a higher value than the TeamID in the first copy of the table, you're good to go!

Translation/ Clean Up	Select Teams.team ID ~~from the 1st copy of the teams table~~ as team1 ID, Teams.TeamName ~~from the 1st copy of the teams table~~ as team1 name, Teams_1.team ID ~~from the 2nd copy of the teams table~~ as team1 name, and Teams_1.team name ~~from the 2nd copy of the teams table~~ as team2 name from ~~the~~ teams table CROSS JOIN ~~and a 2nd copy of the~~ teams table AS Team_1 where Teams_1.team ID ~~in the 2nd copy of the teams table is greater than~~ > Teams.team ID ~~in the 1st copy of the teams table~~ ordered by Teams.team ID ~~in the 1st copy of the teams table~~, ~~and~~ Teams_1.team ID ~~in the 2nd copy of the teams table~~
| SQL | ```
SELECT Teams.TeamID AS Team1ID,
   Teams.TeamName AS Team1Name,
   Teams_1.TeamID AS Team2ID,
   Teams_1.TeamName AS Team2Name
FROM Teams, Teams AS Teams_1
WHERE Teams_1.TeamID > Teams.TeamID
ORDER BY Teams.TeamID, Teams_1.TeamID;
``` |

CH20_Team_Pairings (45 rows)

Team1ID	Team1Name	Team2ID	Team2Name
1	Marlins	2	Sharks
1	Marlins	3	Terrapins
1	Marlins	4	Barracudas
1	Marlins	5	Dolphins
1	Marlins	6	Orcas
1	Marlins	7	Manatees
1	Marlins	8	Swordfish
1	Marlins	9	Huckleberrys
1	Marlins	10	MintJuleps
2	Sharks	3	Terrapins
2	Sharks	4	Barracudas

<< more rows here >>
```

> ❖ **Note** You might look at this query and ask: "Couldn't I also solve this with an INNER JOIN moving the WHERE clause to an ON clause?" You would be absolutely correct for most database systems that support something other than an equijoin in the ON clause. As usual, there's always more than one way to solve a particular problem using SQL.

Examples Using Driver Tables

Let's move on to solving some problems using driver tables. All the following solutions use driver tables that I've already built for you in the sample databases.

Sales Order Database

"The warehouse manager has asked you to print an identification label for each item in stock."

You can look up the quantity on hand in the Products table. The trick here is to use a driver table that has one column of integers, and each row has a successive value from 1 to the maximum number you might have in stock. You can use ztblSeqNumbers in the sample database for this purpose.

Translation/ Clean Up	Select ztblSeqNumbers.Sequence from ~~the sequence driver table~~, Products.product number ~~from the products table, and~~ Products.product name ~~from the products table~~ from ztblSeqNumbers ~~the sequence driver table~~ CROSS JOIN ~~and the~~ products ~~table~~ where ztblSeqNumbers.sequence ~~in the sequence driver table is less than or equal to~~ <= Products.quantity on hand ~~in the products table~~ ordered by Products.product number ~~from the products table, and~~ ztblSequenceNumbers.sequence ~~from the sequence driver table~~

SQL	SELECT ztblSeqNumbers.Sequence,
	    Products.ProductNumber,
	    Products.ProductName
	FROM ztblSeqNumbers, Products
	WHERE ztblSeqNumbers.Sequence <=
	    Products.QuantityOnHand
	ORDER BY Products.ProductNumber,
	    ztblSeqNumbers.Sequence;

CH20_Product_Stock_Labels (813 rows)

Sequence	ProductNumber	ProductName
1	1	Trek 9000 Mountain Bike
2	1	Trek 9000 Mountain Bike
3	1	Trek 9000 Mountain Bike
4	1	Trek 9000 Mountain Bike
5	1	Trek 9000 Mountain Bike
6	1	Trek 9000 Mountain Bike
1	2	Eagle FS-3 Mountain Bike
2	2	Eagle FS-3 Mountain Bike
	<< more rows here >>	

Entertainment Database

"Produce a booking calendar that lists for all weeks in January 2018 any engagement during that week."

❖ **Note** Remember to find an engagement that occurs in any part of a date span you need to find engagements that begin before or on the end date of the span and end after or on the start date of the span. You need to do a similar thing to find weeks in which any part of the week falls in January 2018.

Translation/ Clean Up	Select ztblWeeks.week start from ~~the weeks driver table~~, ztblWeeks.week end ~~from the weeks driver table~~, Entertainers.entertainer ID ~~from the entertainers table~~, Entertainers.entertainer stage name ~~from the entertainers table~~, Customers.customer first ~~name from the customers table~~, Customers.customer last name ~~from the customers table~~, Engagements.start date ~~from the engagements table~~, ~~and~~ Engagements.end date ~~from the engagements table~~ from ztblWeeks ~~the weeks driver table~~ CROSS JOIN ~~and the~~ customers ~~table~~ inner joined ~~with the~~ engagements ~~table~~ on Customers.customer ID ~~in the customers table equals~~

= Engagements.customer ID ~~in the engagements table,~~ ~~then~~ inner joined ~~with the~~ entertainers table on Entertainers.entertainer ID ~~in the entertainers table equals~~ = Engagements.entertainer ID ~~in the engagements table~~ where ztblWeeks.week start ~~in the weeks driver table is~~ ~~less than or equal to~~ <= '2018-01-31' and ztblWeeks.week end ~~in the weeks driver table is greater than or equal to~~ >= '2018-01-01' and Engagements.start date ~~in the engagements table is less than or equal to~~ <= ztblWeeks.week end ~~in the weeks driver table~~ and Engagements.end date ~~in the engagements table is greater than or equal to~~ >= ztblWeeks.week start ~~in the weeks driver table~~

SQL

```
SELECT ztblWeeks.WeekStart, ztblWeeks.WeekEnd,
    Entertainers.EntertainerID,
    Entertainers.EntStageName,
    Customers.CustFirstName, Customers.
    CustLastName,
    Engagements.StartDate, Engagements.EndDate
FROM ztblWeeks, (Customers INNER JOIN Engagements
    ON Customers.CustomerID =
        Engagements.CustomerID)
INNER JOIN Entertainers
    ON Entertainers.EntertainerID =
        Engagements.EntertainerID
WHERE ztblWeeks.WeekStart <= '2018-01-31' AND
    ztblWeeks.WeekEnd >= '2018-01-01' AND
    Engagements.StartDate <= ztblWeeks.WeekEnd AND
    Engagements.EndDate >= ztblWeeks.WeekStart;
```

CH20_All_Weeks_Jan2018_All_Engagements (50 rows)

Week Start	WeekEnd	Entertainer ID	EntStage Name	CustFirst Name	CustLast Name	Start Date	End Date
2017-12-31	2018-01-05	1001	Carol Peacock Trio	Mark	Rosales	2017-12-30	2018-01-08
2018-01-07	2018-01-12	1001	Carol Peacock Trio	Mark	Rosales	2017-12-30	2018-01-08

Week Start	WeekEnd	Entertainer ID	EntStage Name	CustFirst Name	CustLast Name	Start Date	End Date
2018-01-07	2018-01-12	1001	Carol Peacock Trio	Matt	Berg	2017-01-09	2018-01-09
2018-01-21	2018-01-26	1001	Carol Peacock Trio	Dean	McCrae	2017-01-23	2018-01-31
2018-01-28	2018-02-02	1001	Carol Peacock Trio	Dean	McCrae	2018-01-23	2018-01-31
2017-12-31	2018-01-05	1002	Topazz	Estella	Pundt	2018-01-02	2018-01-10
2018-01-07	2018-01-12	1002	Topazz	Estella	Pundt	2018-01-02	2018-01-10
2017-12-31	2018-01-05	1003	JV & the Deep Six	Carol	Viescas	2017-12-31	2018-01-05
2018-01-07	2018-01-12	1003	JV & the Deep Six	Mark	Rosales	2018-01-09	2018-01-10
2018-01-28	2018-02-02	1003	JV & the Deep Six	Zachary	Ehrlich	2018-01-29	2018-02-02

<< more rows here >>

School Scheduling Database

"Display a list of classes by semester, date, and subject."

❖ **Note** This is a bit tricky because the Classes table has an unnormalized list of days listed as columns. When a class is scheduled for a given day, the value is 1 or "true" for that column. I need to use the ztblSemesterDays driver table and include a class when the semester matches and the day of the week in the driver table has the "flag" turned on in the appropriate day column. Because some database systems use -1 (Microsoft Office Access, for example) and others use 1 for "true," I will test for not equal to 0 to determine whether the column has a "true" value.

Translation/ Clean Up	Select ztblSemesterDays.semester no ~~from the semester driver table~~, ztblSemesterDays.sem~~ester~~ date ~~from the semester driver table~~, Classes.start time ~~from the classes table~~, ztblSemesterDays.sem~~ester~~ day name ~~from the semester driver table~~, Subjects.subject code ~~from the subjects table~~, Subjects.subject name ~~from the subjects table~~, Class_Rooms.building code ~~from the class rooms table~~, Class_Rooms.class room ID ~~from the class rooms table~~ from ztblSemesterDays ~~the semester driver table~~ CROSS JOIN ~~and the~~ subjects ~~table then~~ inner join~~ed with the~~ classes table on Subjects.subject ID ~~in the subjects table equals~~ = Classes.subject ID ~~in the classes table then~~ inner join~~ed with the~~ class rooms ~~table~~ on Class_Rooms.class room ID ~~in the class rooms table equals~~ = Classes.class room ID ~~in the classes table~~ where Classes.semester number ~~in the classes table equals~~ = ztblSemesterDays.semester no ~~in the semester driver table~~ and 1 ~~equals~~ = (CASE when ztblSemesterDays.semester day name ~~in the semester driver table~~ equals = 'Monday' and Classes. Monday schedule ~~in the classes table~~ does not equal <> 0 then return 1 when ztblSemesterDays.sem~~ester~~ day name ~~in the semester driver table equals~~ = 'Tuesday' and Classes.Tuesday schedule ~~in the classes table does not equal~~ <> 0 then ~~return~~ 1 when ztblSemesterDays.sem~~ester~~ day name ~~in the semester driver table equals~~ = 'Wednesday' and Classes.Wednesday schedule ~~in the classes table does not equal~~ <> 0 then ~~return~~ 1 when ztblSemesterDays.sem~~ester~~ day name ~~in the semester driver table equals~~ = 'Thursday' and Classes.Thursday schedule ~~in the classes table does not equal~~ <> 0 then ~~return~~ 1 when ztblSemesterDays.sem~~ester~~ day name ~~in the semester driver table equals~~ = 'Friday' and Classes.Friday schedule ~~in the classes table does not equal~~ <> 0 then ~~return~~ 1 when ztblSemesterDays.sem~~ester~~ day name ~~in the semester driver table equals~~ = 'Saturday' and Classes.Saturday schedule ~~in the classes table does not equal~~ <> 0 then ~~return~~ 1 else ~~return~~ 0 END) order~~ed~~ by ztblSemesterDays.semester no ~~in the semester driver table~~, ztblSemesterDays.semes~~ter~~ date ~~in the semester driver table~~, Subjects.subject code ~~in the subjects table~~, Class_Rooms.building code ~~in the class rooms table~~, Class_Rooms.class room ID ~~in the class rooms table~~, ~~and~~ Classes.start time ~~in the classes table~~

SQL	```
	SELECT ztblSemesterDays.SemesterNo,
	    ztblSemesterDays.SemDate, Classes.StartTime,
	    ztblSemesterDays.SemDayName, Subjects.SubjectCode,
	    Subjects.SubjectName, Class_Rooms.BuildingCode,
	    Class_Rooms.ClassRoomID
	FROM ztblSemesterDays, (Subjects
	INNER JOIN Classes
	    ON Subjects.SubjectID = Classes.SubjectID)
	``

```
      INNER JOIN Class_Rooms
         ON Class_Rooms.ClassRoomID =
            Classes.ClassRoomID
      WHERE Classes.SemesterNumber =
            ztblSemesterDays.SemesterNo
      AND Classes.StartDate <= ztblSemesterDays.SemDate
      AND 1 =
      (CASE WHEN ztblSemesterDays.SemDayName = 'Monday'
                 AND Classes.MondaySchedule <> 0 THEN 1
              WHEN ztblSemesterDays.SemDayName = 'Tuesday'
                 AND Classes.TuesdaySchedule <> 0 THEN 1
              WHEN ztblSemesterDays.SemDayName = 'Wednesday'
                 AND Classes.WednesdaySchedule <> 0 THEN 1
              WHEN ztblSemesterDays.SemDayName = 'Thursday'
                 AND Classes.ThursdaySchedule <> 0 THEN 1
              WHEN ztblSemesterDays.SemDayName = 'Friday'
                 AND Classes.FridaySchedule <> 0 THEN 1
              WHEN ztblSemesterDays.SemDayName = 'Saturday'
                 AND Classes.SaturdaySchedule <> 0 THEN 1
              ELSE 0 END)
      ORDER BY ztblSemesterDays.SemesterNo,
         ztblSemesterDays.SemDate, Subjects.SubjectCode,
         Class_Rooms.BuildingCode,
         Class_Rooms.ClassRoomID,
         Classes.StartTime;
```

CH20_Class_Schedule_Calendar (7,221 rows)

Semester No	SemDate	Start Time	SemDay Name	Subject Code	Subject Name	Building	Class RoomID
1	2018-09-11	16:00	Monday	ACC 210	Financial Accounting Fundamentals I	IB	3305
1	2018-09-11	15:30	Monday	ART 101	Design	AS	1619
1	2018-09-11	8:00	Monday	ART 111	Drawing	AS	1627
1	2018-09-11	9:00	Monday	ART 111	Drawing	AS	1627

Semester No	SemDate	Start Time	SemDay Name	Subject Code	Subject Name	Building	Class RoomID
1	2018-09-11	11:00	Monday	ART 251	Art History	LB	1231
1	2018-09-11	14:00	Monday	ART 251	Art History	LB	1231
1	2018-09-11	10:00	Monday	BIO 100	Biological Principles	AS	1532
1	2018-09-11	12:00	Monday	BIO 101	General Biology	AS	1532
1	2018-09-11	13:30	Monday	BIO 280	Microbiology	AS	1530
1	2018-09-11	7:30	Monday	CHE 101	Chemistry	AS	1519

<< more rows here >>

Bowling League Database

"Print a bowler mailing list, but skip the first three labels on the first page that have already been used."

> ❖ **Note** What you want to do is produce three blank name and address lines to bypass the used labels, and then list all the bowlers and their addresses. You can use ztblSkipLabels in a SELECT statement that substitutes blanks for all the fields and stops when the number in the driver table becomes greater than the number of labels you want to skip. Follow that with a UNION ALL of a SELECT statement to produce the names and addresses for all bowlers. You must use a UNION ALL because a simple UNION would eliminate all the duplicate blank lines you produced in the first query.

Translation / Clean Up	Select ~~blanks~~ ' ' as bowler last name, ~~blanks~~ ' ' as bowler first name, ~~blanks~~ ' ' as bowler address, ~~blanks~~ ' ' as bowler city, ~~blanks~~ ' ' as bowler state, ~~blanks~~ ' ' as bowler zip from ztblSkipLabels ~~the skip labels driver table~~ where ~~the~~ ztblSkipLabels.label count ~~in the skip labels driver table is less than or equal to~~ <= 3 unioned ~~with~~ all ~~rows in~~ select bowler last name, bowler first name, bowler address, bowler city, bowler state, and bowler zip from ~~the~~ bowlers ~~table~~ ordered by bowler zip, ~~and~~ bowler last name

SQL	SELECT ' ' As BowlerLastName, ' ' As BowlerFirstName,
	' ' As BowlerAddress, ' ' As BowlerCity,
	' ' As BowlerState, ' ' As BowlerZip
	FROM ztblSkipLabels
	WHERE ztblSkipLabels.LabelCount <= 3
	UNION ALL
	SELECT BowlerLastName, BowlerFirstName,
	BowlerAddress, BowlerCity, BowlerState,
	BowlerZip
	FROM Bowlers
	ORDER BY BowlerZip, BowlerLastName;

CH20_Bowler_Mailing_Skip_3 (35 rows)

BowlerLast Name	BowlerFirst Name	Bowler Address	Bowler City	Bowler State	Bowler Zip
Patterson	Kathryn	16 Maple Lane	Auburn	WA	98002
Patterson	Rachel	16 Maple Lane	Auburn	WA	98002
Patterson	Ann	16 Maple Lane	Auburn	WA	98002
Patterson	Neil	16 Maple Lane	Auburn	WA	98002
Patterson	Megan	16 Maple Lane	Auburn	WA	98002
Viescas	Carol	16345 NE 32nd Street	Bellevue	WA	98004
Sheskey	Sara	17950 N 59th	Seattle	WA	98011

<< more rows here >>

Summary

I started this chapter with a definition of unlinked data and a discussion of how to use CROSS JOIN to handle unlinked data in your queries. At the end of the first section, I outlined the two cases where a CROSS

JOIN can be useful—linking main data tables with each other and linking main data tables with a "driver" table.

I next covered solving problems using main data tables linked to each other and explained a complex example. After that, I covered using a driver table, showing you how to set one up and discussing another two examples. Finally, I showed you and explained examples from four of the sample databases using both main tables linked to each other and a driver table linked to one or more main tables. I encourage you to try to work out the problems presented in the final section that follows.

Problems for You to Solve

The following problems show you the request statement and the name of the solution query in the sample databases. If you want some practice, you can work out the SQL you need for each request and then check your answer with the query I saved in the samples. Don't worry if your syntax doesn't exactly match the syntax of the queries I saved—as long as your Result Set is the same.

Sales Order Database

1. *"List months and the total sales by products for each month."*

   (Hint: Use the ztblMonths driver table I provided.)

   You can find the solution in CH20_Product_Sales_ByMonth (253 rows).

2. *"Produce a customer mailing list, but skip the five labels already used on the first page of the labels."*

   (Hint: Use the ztblSeqNumbers driver table I provided.)

   You can find the solution in CH20_Customer_Mailing_Skip_5 (33 rows).

3. *"The sales manager wants to send out 10% discount coupons for customers who made large purchases in December 2017. Use the ztblPurchaseCoupons table to determine how many coupons each customer gets based on the total purchases for the month."*

   (Hint: You need to CROSS JOIN the driver table with the Customers table joined with a subquery that calculates the total spend for each customer.)

   You can find the solution in CH20_Customer_Dec_2017_Order_Coupons (27 rows).

4. *"Using the solution to #3 above, print out one 10% off coupon based on the number of coupons each customer earned."*

   (Hint: Use the ztblSeqNumbers driver table that I provided with the query in the above problem.)

   You can find the solution in CH20_Customer_Discount_Coupons_Print (309 rows).

5. *"Display all months in 2017 and 2018, all products, and the total sales (if any) registered for the product in the month."*

   (Hint: Use a CROSS JOIN between the ztblMonths driver table and the Products table and use a subquery to fetch the product sales for each product and month.)

   You can find the solution in CH20_Product_Sales_All_Months_2017_2018 (960 rows).

6. *"Display all products and categorize them from Affordable to Expensive."*

   (Hint: Use a CROSS JOIN with ztblPriceRanges.) You can find the solution in CH20_Product_Price_Ranges (40 rows).

Entertainment Database

1. *"List all agents and any entertainers who haven't had a booking since February 1, 2018."*

   (Hint: Use a CROSS JOIN between Agents and Entertainers and use NOT IN on a subquery in the WHERE clause to find entertainers not booked since February 1, 2018.)

   You can find the solution in CH20_Agents_Entertainers_Unbooked_Feb1_2018 (162 rows).

2. *"Show all entertainer styles and the count of the first, second, and third strengths."*

   (Hint: This is similar to the CH20_Customer_Style_Preference_Rankings query I showed you earlier. Use a CROSS JOIN of the Musical_Styles table with a subquery that "pivots" the strengths into three columns, then count the columns.)

   You can find the solution in CH20_Entertainer_Style_Strength_Rankings (17 rows).

3. *"Display customers and their first, second, and third-ranked preferences along with entertainers and their first, second, and third-ranked strengths, then match customers to entertainers when the first or second preference matches the first or second strength."*

    (Hint: Create a query on musical styles and customers and pivot the first, second, and third strengths using a CASE expression. You will need to use MAX and GROUP BY because the pivot will return Null values for some of the positions. Do the same with entertainers and musical styles, then CROSS JOIN the two subqueries and return the rows where the preferences and strengths match in the first two positions.)

    You can find the solution in CH20_Customers_Match_Entertainers_FirstSecond_PrefStrength (6 rows).

4. *"List all months across and calculate each entertainer's income per month."*

    (Hint: Use the ztblMonths driver table to pivot the amounts per month and use SUM to total the amounts per entertainer.)

    You can find the solution in CH20_Entertainer_BookingAmount_ByMonth (12 rows).

5. *"Display all dates in December 2017 and any entertainers booked on those days."*

    (Hint: Build a subquery using a CROSS JOIN between the ztblDays driver table and a JOIN on entertainers and engagements, then LEFT JOIN that with ztblDays again to get all dates.)

    You can find the solution in CH20_All_December_Days_Any_Bookings (79 rows).

6. *"Produce a customer mailing list, but skip the four labels already used on the first page of labels."*

    You can find the solution in CH20_Customer_Mailing_Skip_4 (19 rows).

School Scheduling Database

1. *"List all students and the classes they could take, excluding the subjects enrolled or already completed. Be sure to list any subject prerequisite."*

    (Hint: Do a CROSS JOIN between students and subjects joined with classes, and use a subquery to eliminate classes found in the student schedules table for the current student where the class status in the student schedules table is not 1 (enrolled) or 2 (completed).)

You can find the solution in CH20_Students_Additional_Courses (1,894 rows).

2. *"Display a count of students by gender and marital status by state of residence in columns across."*

(Hint: Use the ztblGenderMatrix and ztblMaritalStatusMatrix driver tables to pivot your values.)

You can find the solution in CH20_Student_Crosstab_Gender_MaritalStatus (4 rows).

3. *"Calculate an average proficiency rating for all teaching staff across the subjects they teach and show an overall rating based on the values found in the ztblProfRatings driver table."*

You can find the solution in CH20_Staff_Proficiency_Ratings (24 rows).

4. *"Create a mailing list for students, but skip the first two labels already used on the first page."*

You can find the solution in CH20_Student_Mailing_Skip_2 (20 rows).

Bowling League Database

1. *"Show bowlers and a rating of their raw score averages based on the values found in the ztblBowlerRatings driver table."*

You can find the solution in CH20_Bowler_Ratings (32 rows).

2. *"List all weeks from September through December 2017 and the location of any tournament scheduled for those weeks."*

You can find the solution in CH20_Tournament_Week_Schedule_2017 (19 rows).

21

Performing Complex Calculations on Groups

Before a group can enter the open society, it must first close ranks.
STOKELY CARMICHAEL

Topics in this Chapter

Grouping in Sub-Groups

Extending the GROUP BY Clause

Getting Totals in a Hierarchy Using ROLLUP

Calculating Totals on Combinations Using CUBE

Creating a Union of Totals with GROUPING SETS

Variations on Grouping Techniques

Sample Statements

Summary

Problems for You to Solve

In Part IV, I showed you how to summarize and group data. Specifically, in Chapter 12, "Simple Totals," I showed how to calculate totals, counts, and other aggregate functions, in Chapter 13, "Grouping Data," I showed how to group data, and in Chapter 14, "Filtering Grouped Data," I showed both how to filter the grouped data, as well as how to filter the data that gets grouped. However, I've always found that it can be a somewhat limited way to report the data. You can only group one specific way at a time, and sometimes that's just not enough.

Let's see whether we can do a little more with grouping in this chapter.

Grouping in Sub-Groups

In Chapter 13, I showed how to use the GROUP BY clause to specify one or more columns to specify how to group the aggregated data. When you specify more than one column, the aggregation is done for each unique combination of values for all of those columns.

Let's look at our Student Population. Using the techniques I've already shown in Chapter 13, I can build a query to fetch the data summarizing by state, gender, and marital status. Here's the SQL:

SQL	SELECT StudState, StudGender, StudMaritalStatus,
	Count(*) AS Number
	FROM Students
	GROUP BY StudState, StudGender, StudMaritalStatus;

The result looks like the following table. (I saved this request as CH21_ Students_State_Gender_MaritalStatus_Count_GROUP_BY in the School Scheduling Example database.)

StudState	StudGender	StudMaritalStatus	Number
CA	F	W	1
CA	M	S	1
OR	F	M	1
OR	F	S	1
OR	M	S	2
TX	F	S	2
TX	M	S	1
WA	F	D	1
WA	F	M	1
WA	F	S	3
WA	M	S	4

It's a useful way of looking at the data, but what if I also want to know the total number of students by State, or the total number of Female students? I'd have to create one or more additional queries for any other breakdowns I want to see.

What if there were another way to retrieve the data? Perhaps I could return something like the following:

State	Gender	MaritalStatus	Number
Any State	Any Gender	Any Status	18
Any State	Any Gender	D	1
Any State	Any Gender	M	2
Any State	Any Gender	S	14
Any State	Any Gender	W	1
Any State	F	Any Status	10
Any State	F	D	1
Any State	F	M	2
Any State	F	S	6
Any State	F	W	1
Any State	M	Any Status	8
Any State	M	S	8
CA	Any Gender	Any Status	2
CA	Any Gender	S	1
CA	Any Gender	W	1
CA	F	Any Status	1
CA	F	W	1
CA	M	Any Status	1
CA	M	S	1
OR	Any Gender	Any Status	4
OR	Any Gender	M	1
OR	Any Gender	S	3
OR	F	Any Status	2

State	Gender	MaritalStatus	Number
OR	F	M	1
OR	F	S	1
OR	M	Any Status	2
OR	M	S	2
TX	Any Gender	Any Status	3
TX	Any Gender	S	3
TX	F	Any Status	2
TX	F	S	2
TX	M	Any Status	1
TX	M	S	1
WA	Any Gender	Any Status	9
WA	Any Gender	D	1
WA	Any Gender	M	1
WA	Any Gender	S	7
WA	F	Any Status	5
WA	F	D	1
WA	F	M	1
WA	F	S	3
WA	M	Any Status	4
WA	M	S	4

This new table may require some explanation. Look at the shaded rows: they represent the 11 rows of data returned by the first query that give the number of students broken down by the various combination of State, Gender, and Marital Status. However, let's look at some of the other rows in that table. In them, one or more of the columns represents all the values. For instance, the first row represents the total number of students, regardless of the state they're from, their gender, or their marital status (18 in this case). The next row represents the total number of Divorced students, regardless of the state they're from or their gender (one in this case). The sixth row represents the total number of Female students, regardless of the state they're from or their marital status (10 in this case).

Does this look like it might be useful in analyzing the demographics of your student population? I'll show you how to achieve this in the following section. (And if you're curious and want to look at the SQL, I saved the above request as CH21_Students_State_Gender_MaritalStatus_Count_CUBE_No_Nulls in the Student Scheduling sample database.)

Extending the GROUP BY Clause

What I talked about in Chapter 13 applies to the more comprehensive groupings I'm going to talk about in this chapter. In fact, when you look at the syntax for these more comprehensive groupings, you'll see it's almost identical to the diagram shown there.

Syntax

Let's take a close look at the complete GROUP BY clause. Figure 21-1 shows the basic diagram for a SELECT statement with GROUP BY expanded to show the additional features you'll learn about in this chapter. If you compare this figure to Figure 13-1, you can see the difference is the addition of one of three different keywords (ROLLUP, CUBE, or GROUPING SETS), plus the fact that the Column Reference clause for each of these is enclosed in parentheses.

As you might expect, each of the different keywords results in different results being returned.

> ❖ **Note** Because the extensions to GROUP BY are just variations on the GROUP BY syntax, all of the restrictions discussed in Chapter 13 apply equally here. Specifically, any column that's listed in the SELECT clause that's not part of an aggregate expression must be included in the GROUP BY clause, and the GROUP BY clause must refer to columns created by the FROM and WHERE, not by expressions created in the SELECT clause.

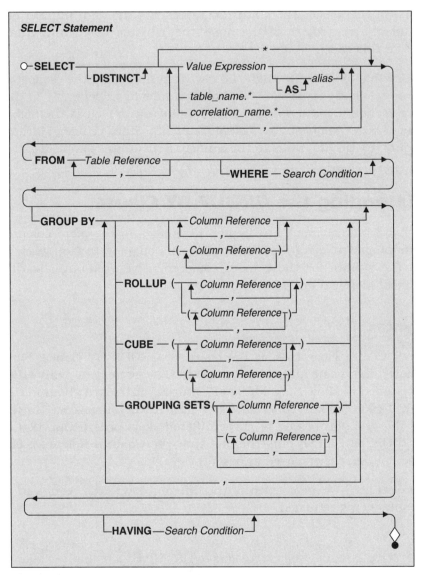

Figure 21-1 *Full syntax for the GROUP BY clause*

Getting Totals in a Hierarchy Using Rollup

As you've already seen, when you use GROUP BY, the results summarize the data for all existing combinations of values that exist for those columns. When you add ROLLUP to the grouping clause, your database system adds new rows to produce group subtotals, plus a grand total. If there are n columns listed in the ROLLUP, there will be n+1 levels of subtotals. Note that the subtotals are added from right to left, so the order in which you list the columns in the clause is important.

> ❖ **Note** You can find all the sample statements and solutions in the respective sample databases—SalesOrdersExample, Entertainment AgencyExample, RecipesExample, SchoolSchedulingExample, and BowlingLeagueExample. Because neither Microsoft Access nor MySQL support grouping sets, you'll find the sample solutions only in the Microsoft SQL Server and PostgreSQL sample databases.

Suppose you wanted a total by student state, student gender, and student marital status, but with subtotals by state and by state and gender. Your request might look like the following:

> ❖ **Note** Throughout this chapter, I use the "Request/Translation/ Clean Up/SQL" technique introduced in Chapter 4, "Creating a Simple Query." Because this process should now be very familiar to you, I have combined the Translation/Clean Up steps for all the following examples to simplify the process.

"Show me the count for all unique combinations of student state, student gender, and student marital status, summarized for each combination of state and gender and the total by state."

Translation/ Clean Up	Select ~~the~~ student state, student gender, student marital status, ~~and the~~ count (*) ~~of rows~~ from ~~the~~ Students ~~table,~~ grouped by ~~and~~ rolled up ~~by~~ student state, student gender, ~~and~~ student marital status

SQL	SELECT StudState, StudGender, StudMaritalStatus,
	    Count(*) AS Number
	 FROM Students
	 GROUP BY ROLLUP
	    (StudState, StudGender, StudMaritalStatus);

> ❖ **Note** When you find yourself using "summarized for each unique combination" of a subset but not all combinations, you should replace that with the ROLLUP keyword.

That request results look like the following table. (I saved this request as CH21_Students_State_Gender_MaritalStatus_Count_ROLLUP_Order1 in the School Scheduling Example database.)

StudState	StudGender	StudMaritalStatus	Number
CA	F	W	1
CA	F	NULL	1
CA	M	S	1
CA	M	NULL	1
CA	NULL	NULL	2
OR	F	M	1
OR	F	S	1
OR	F	NULL	2
OR	M	S	2
OR	M	NULL	2
OR	NULL	NULL	4
TX	F	S	2
TX	F	NULL	2
TX	M	S	1
TX	M	NULL	1
TX	NULL	NULL	3
WA	F	D	1
WA	F	M	1
WA	F	S	3
WA	F	NULL	5
WA	M	S	4

StudState	StudGender	StudMaritalStatus	Number
WA	M	NULL	4
WA	NULL	NULL	9
NULL	NULL	NULL	18

Let's look at those results. When a column on a particular row is Null, you can interpret that to mean that it represents all the values.

> ❖ **Note** Remember in the Introduction that I warned you that results from each database system won't necessarily match the sort order you see in examples in this book unless you include an ORDER BY clause. Even when you include that specification, the system might return results in columns not included in the ORDER BY clause in a different sequence because of different optimization techniques.
>
> If you're running the examples in Microsoft SQL Server, simply selecting the rows from the view does not honor any ORDER BY clause specified in the view. You must open the design of the view and execute it from there to see the ORDER BY clause honored.
>
> Also, when you use GROUP BY, you'll often see the results returned by your database system as though the rows are sorted by the columns you specified. This happens because some optimizers first sort the data internally to make it faster to process your GROUP BY. Keep in mind that if you want a specific sort order, you must also include an ORDER BY clause.

The first row shows that there is one widowed female from California. Because there are no other females from California, the second row summarizes that there is one female from California. (Remember that the Null value in the StudMaritalStatus means "Any Status"). The third row shows that there is one single male from California. Again, because there are no other males from California, the fourth row summarizes that there is one male from California. After covering all the genders and marital statuses recorded in the table, the fifth row summarizes that there are two students from California.

Rows six and seven indicate that there's one married female from Oregon and one single female from Oregon respectively. That's all the females from Oregon, so row eight summarizes that there are two females from Oregon.

This summarization continues to be interspersed with the grouping results until the last row, which summarizes that there are eighteen students in total.

Because there are three columns listed in the ROLLUP clause (Stud-State, StudGender, and StudMaritalStatus, in that order), there are four levels of subtotals:

1. Unique combinations of StudState, StudGender, and StudMaritalStatus

2. Unique combinations of StudState and StudGender regardless of StudMaritalStatus values

3. Unique values of StudState regardless of StudGender and StudMaritalStatus values

4. Grand total

> ❖ **Note** The query actually returns Null as the value for the columns that are being rolled up. If you like, you can use the CASE expression or the ISNULL or COALESCE functions (in SQL Server) or the CASE expression or COALESCE function (in PostgreSQL) to convert that Null value to something more meaningful in the results.

Perhaps the user would like to see words instead of Null. This query actually returns Null as the value for the columns that are being rolled up. However, that will not always be the case if the column in your table actually contains NULL values. (None of the columns do in this case.) So, you could use the CASE expression or the ISNULL or COALESCE functions (in SQL Server) or the CASE expression or COALESCE function (in PostgreSQL) to convert that Null value to something more meaningful in the results. But there's a better way. There's a cool function called GROUPING as shown in Figure 21-2.

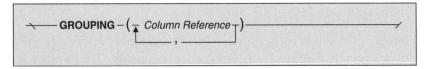

Figure 21-2 *The GROUPING function*

This handy little function—when used on a column that is being grouped using CASE, ROLLUP, or GROUPING SETS—returns a numeric value to indicate the level of grouping. When the value returned is zero, the value is not "rolled up" or "summarized," so you can display the column value. When the value is other than zero, the column is being summarized, so it will definitely contain a Null value. You can use this function in a CASE expression (See Chapter 19, "Condition Testing") to decide whether to display the column value or an "Any" literal.

So, the request could have been like this:

"Show me the count for all unique combinations of student state, student gender, and student marital status, summarized for each combination of state and gender and the total by state. Show 'Any State,' 'Any Gender,' or 'Any Status' for the subtotaled rows."

Translation/ Clean Up	Select ~~when~~ (CASE WHEN ~~the grouping level of~~ GROUPING(student state) ~~is~~ = 0 then ~~display~~ student state else 'Any State' END), ~~when~~ (CASE WHEN ~~the grouping level of~~ GROUPING(student gender) ~~is~~ = 0 then ~~display~~ student gender else 'Any Gender' END), ~~when~~ (CASE WHEN ~~the grouping level of~~ GROUPING(student marital status) ~~is~~ = 0 then ~~display~~ student marital status else 'Any Status' END), ~~and the~~ count (*) ~~of rows~~ from ~~the~~ Students ~~table~~, grouped by ~~and~~ rolled up ~~by~~ student state, student gender, ~~and~~ student marital status
| SQL | ```
SELECT (CASE WHEN GROUPING(StudState) = 0
            THEN StudState
            ELSE 'Any State' END) AS State,
       (CASE WHEN GROUPING(StudGender) = 0
            THEN StudGender
            ELSE 'Any Gender') AS Gender,
       (CASE WHEN GROUPING(StudMaritalStatus) = 0
            THEN StudMaritalStatus
            ELSE 'Any Status') AS MaritalStatus,
    Count(*) AS Number
FROM Students
GROUP BY ROLLUP (StudState, StudGender,
    StudMaritalStatus);
``` |
```

That query returns the following table (I saved this request as CH21_Students_State_Gender_MaritalStatus_Count_ROLLUP_No_Nulls in the School Scheduling Example database.):

State	Gender	MaritalStatus	Number
CA	F	W	1
CA	F	Any Status	1
CA	M	S	1
CA	M	Any Status	1
CA	Any Gender	Any Status	2
OR	F	M	1
OR	F	S	1
OR	F	Any Status	2
OR	M	S	2
OR	M	Any Status	2
OR	Any Gender	Any Status	4
TX	F	S	2
TX	F	Any Status	2
TX	M	S	1
TX	M	Any Status	1
TX	Any Gender	Any Status	3
WA	F	D	1
WA	F	M	1
WA	F	S	3
WA	F	Any Status	5
WA	M	S	4
WA	M	Any Status	4
WA	Any Gender	Any Status	9
Any State	Any Gender	Any Status	18

The above request returns four levels of subtotals:

1. Unique combinations of StudState, StudGender, and StudMaritalStatus

2. Unique combinations of StudState and StudGender regardless of StudMaritalStatus values

3. Unique values of StudState regardless of StudGender and StudMaritalStatus values

4. Grand total

> ❖ **Note** The query above illustrates the rule that the GROUP BY clause must refer to columns created by the FROM and WHERE, not by expressions created in the SELECT clause. You can see that the columns have been assigned aliases in the SELECT clause, but the GROUP BY clause cannot use those aliases: it must use the original names of the columns.

Let's take a look at what happens when you use a different column sequence in ROLLUP. Consider the following request:

"Show me the count for all unique combinations of student marital status, student gender, and student state, summarized for each combination of marital status with gender and a total by marital status."

Translation/ Clean Up	Select ~~the~~ student marital status, student gender, ~~student~~ state, ~~and the~~ count (*) ~~of rows~~ from ~~the~~ Students ~~table,~~ grouped ~~by and~~ rolled up ~~by~~ student marital status, student gender, and student state

SQL	SELECT StudMaritalStatus, StudGender, StudState,
	    Count(*) AS Number
	FROM Students
	GROUP BY ROLLUP
	    (StudMaritalStatus, StudGender, StudState);

The result returned looks like the following table. (I saved this request as CH21_Students_State_Gender_MaritalStatus_Count_ROLLUP_Order2 in the School Scheduling Example database.)

StudMaritalStatus	StudGender	StudState	Number
D	F	WA	1
D	F	NULL	1
D	NULL	NULL	1
M	F	OR	1
M	F	WA	1
M	F	NULL	2
M	NULL	NULL	2
S	F	OR	1
S	F	TX	2
S	F	WA	3
S	F	NULL	6
S	M	CA	1
S	M	OR	2
S	M	TX	1
S	M	WA	4
S	M	NULL	8
S	NULL	NULL	14
W	F	CA	1
W	F	NULL	1
W	NULL	NULL	1
NULL	NULL	NULL	18

Rather than 24 rows returned by the first query, there are now only 21 rows returned. Whereas before it was easy to see that there are two students from California, four students from Oregon, three students from Texas, and nine students from Washington making up the 18 students at the school, now it's easy to see that there is one divorced student, two married students, fourteen single students, and one widowed student.

And because the three columns listed in the ROLLUP clause are Stud-MaritalStatus, StudGender, and StudState, in that order, the four levels of subtotals are:

1. Unique combinations of StudMaritalStatus, StudGender, and StudState

2. Unique combinations of StudMaritalStatus and StudGender regardless of StudState values

3. Unique values of StudMaritalStatus regardless of StudGender and StudState values

4. Grand total

Notice that the focus is now on marital status, so that is the first column in the ROLLUP. Putting gender second generates a subtotal for each combination of marital status and gender, and finally adding state creates totals for each combination of marital status, gender, and state. The totals are "rolled up" first into gender and then into marital status, with a final "rolled up" grand total of the count of all rows.

If the request is as follows:

"Show me the count for all unique combinations of student state, student gender, and student marital status, summarized for each combination of marital status with gender and a total by marital status."

Translation/ Clean Up	Select ~~the~~ student state, ~~student~~ gender, ~~student~~ marital status, ~~and the~~ count (*) ~~of rows~~ from ~~the~~ Students ~~table,~~ grouped by ~~and~~ rolled up ~~by~~ student marital status, student gender, and student state
SQL	SELECT StudState, StudGender, StudMaritalStatus, Count(*) AS Number FROM Students GROUP BY ROLLUP (StudMaritalStatus, StudGender, StudState);

All I did was change the order of the columns in the SELECT clause. The result returned looks like the following table. (I saved this request as CH21_Students_State_Gender_MaritalStatus_Count_ROLLUP_Order3 in the School Scheduling Example database.)

StudState	StudGender	StudMaritalStatus	Number
WA	F	D	1
NULL	F	D	1
NULL	NULL	D	1
OR	F	M	1
WA	F	M	1
NULL	F	M	2
NULL	NULL	M	2
OR	F	S	1
TX	F	S	2
WA	F	S	3
NULL	F	S	6
CA	M	S	1
OR	M	S	2
TX	M	S	1
WA	M	S	4
NULL	M	S	8
NULL	NULL	S	14
CA	F	W	1
NULL	F	W	1
NULL	NULL	W	1
NULL	NULL	NULL	18

There are still 21 rows returned, and you still get the following sets of totals:

1. Unique combinations of StudMaritalStatus, StudGender, and StudState

2. Unique combinations of StudMaritalStatus and StudGender regardless of StudState values

3. Unique values of StudMaritalStatus regardless of StudGender and StudState values

4. Grand total

However, because I listed the StudState column first, it appears first in the output.

> ❖ **Note** It should be noted that MySQL does, in fact, support the ROLLUP extension. However, the syntax for using it is different, which is why I chose to omit it from the examples. Check your MySQL documentation for more information. (MySQL does not, however, support either the CUBE or GROUPING SETS extensions.)

Calculating Totals on Combinations Using CUBE

You saw how using ROLLUP results in group subtotals from right to left, plus a grand total. The CUBE extension will generate those same group subtotals, but will also produce subtotals for all combinations of the columns specified in the CUBE clause. If there are n columns listed in the CUBE, there will be 2^n subtotal combinations generated.

You've already seen the results of using the CUBE extension as the second table of results above, although I will admit that I cheated and added an ORDER BY clause to make the different subtotal rows stand out.

If the request were as follows:

> *"Show me the count for all combinations of student state, student gender, and student marital status, with summarized sets for each combination of state, gender, and marital status, for each combination of state and gender, state and marital status, gender and marital status, and for each state, gender, and marital status on its own."*

Translation / Clean Up	Select ~~the~~ student state, ~~student~~ gender, ~~student~~ marital status, ~~and the~~ count (*) ~~of rows~~ from ~~the~~ Students ~~table,~~ ~~summarized in sets~~ GROUP BY CUBE student state, student gender, ~~and~~ student marital status ~~and by all~~ ~~combinations of pairs of student state, student gender~~ ~~and student marital status~~

```
SQL                    SELECT StudState, StudGender, StudMaritalStatus,
                           Count(*) AS Number
                       FROM Students
                       GROUP BY CUBE
                           (StudState, StudGender, StudMaritalStatus);
```

> ❖ **Note** When you find yourself using "and each combination of …
> every combination" or "summarized in sets," you should replace that
> with the CUBE keyword.

The results look like the following table. (I saved this request as
CH21_Students_State_Gender_MaritalStatus_Count_CUBE_Order1 in the
School Scheduling Example database.)

StudState	StudGender	StudMaritalStatus	Number
WA	F	D	1
NULL	F	D	1
NULL	NULL	D	1
OR	F	M	1
WA	F	M	1
NULL	F	M	2
NULL	NULL	M	2
OR	F	S	1
TX	F	S	2
WA	F	S	3
NULL	F	S	6
CA	M	S	1
OR	M	S	2
TX	M	S	1
WA	M	S	4
NULL	M	S	8

StudState	StudGender	StudMaritalStatus	Number
NULL	NULL	S	14
CA	F	W	1
NULL	F	W	1
NULL	NULL	W	1
NULL	NULL	NULL	18
CA	NULL	S	1
CA	NULL	W	1
CA	NULL	NULL	2
OR	NULL	M	1
OR	NULL	S	3
OR	NULL	NULL	4
TX	NULL	S	3
TX	NULL	NULL	3
WA	NULL	D	1
WA	NULL	M	1
WA	NULL	S	7
WA	NULL	NULL	9
CA	F	NULL	1
OR	F	NULL	2
TX	F	NULL	2
WA	F	NULL	5
NULL	F	NULL	10
CA	M	NULL	1
OR	M	NULL	2
TX	M	NULL	1
WA	M	NULL	4
NULL	M	NULL	8

There are three columns listed in the CUBE, so your database system generates 2^3, or 8, subtotals:

1. Unique combinations of StudState, StudGender, and StudMaritalStatus

2. Unique combinations of StudState and StudGender regardless of StudMaritalStatus values

3. Unique combinations of StudState and StudMaritalStatus regardless of StudGender values

4. Unique combinations of StudGender and StudMaritalStatus regardless of StudState values

5. Unique values of StudState regardless of StudGender and StudMaritalStatus values

6. Unique values of StudGender regardless of StudState and StudMaritalStatus values

7. Unique values of StudMaritalStatus regardless of StudState and StudGender combinations

8. Grand total

As you might expect from the fact that a CUBE produces subtotals for all combinations of the columns specified in the GROUP BY CUBE clause, changing the order of the columns in the SQL statement doesn't affect the results (other than the order).

If instead, the request was as follows:

> *"Show me the count for all combinations of student marital status, student gender, and student state, with summarized sets for each combination of marital status, gender, and state, for each combination of state and gender, state and marital status, gender and marital status, and for each state, gender, and marital status on its own."*

Translation/ Clean Up	Select ~~the~~ student marital status, stu~~dent~~ gender, stu~~dent~~ state, ~~and the~~ count (*) ~~of rows~~ from ~~the~~ Students ~~table, summarized in sets~~ GROUP BY CUBE student marital status, stu~~dent~~ gender, ~~and~~ student state ~~and by all combinations of pairs of student marital status, student gender and student state~~

SQL	`SELECT StudMaritalStatus, StudGender, StudState,`
	`  Count(*) AS Number`
	`FROM Students`
	`GROUP BY CUBE`
	`  (StudMaritalStatus, StudGender, StudState);`

You will see results as shown in the following table. (I saved this request as CH21_Students_State_Gender_MaritalStatus_Count_CUBE_Order2 in the School Scheduling Example database.)

StudMaritalStatus	StudGender	StudState	Number
W	F	CA	1
NULL	F	CA	1
S	M	CA	1
NULL	M	CA	1
NULL	NULL	CA	2
M	F	OR	1
S	F	OR	1
NULL	F	OR	2
S	M	OR	2
NULL	M	OR	2
NULL	NULL	OR	4
S	F	TX	2
NULL	F	TX	2
S	M	TX	1
NULL	M	TX	1
NULL	NULL	TX	3
D	F	WA	1
M	F	WA	1
S	F	WA	3

StudMaritalStatus	StudGender	StudState	Number
NULL	F	WA	5
S	M	WA	4
NULL	M	WA	4
NULL	NULL	WA	9
NULL	NULL	NULL	18
D	NULL	WA	1
D	NULL	NULL	1
M	NULL	OR	1
M	NULL	WA	1
M	NULL	NULL	2
S	NULL	CA	1
S	NULL	OR	3
S	NULL	TX	3
S	NULL	WA	7
S	NULL	NULL	14
W	NULL	CA	1
W	NULL	NULL	1
D	F	NULL	1
M	F	NULL	2
S	F	NULL	6
W	F	NULL	1
NULL	F	NULL	10
S	M	NULL	8
NULL	M	NULL	8

If you look closely at the two sets of results, you'll see that the 43 rows in both represent the same results. The changes are the order of the columns, and the order of the rows is different.

Creating a Union of Totals with GROUPING SETS

The third possible extension for GROUP BY is GROUPING SETS. As you can probably imagine, calculating all of the possible subtotals in a cube can require a lot of resources, particularly when there are many dimensions in the data, and not all of the subtotals may be of interest to you. If you don't need all of the subtotals, but want more than either GROUP BY alone or GROUP BY ROLLUP can provide, GROUPING SETS may be the answer for you.

Using GROUPING SETS is similar to having several different GROUP BY queries combined by a UNION statement.

On the simplest level, the request might be as follows:

"Show me the count for all combinations of student state, student gender, and student marital status, with subtotals for each of student state, student gender, and student marital status."

Translation / Clean Up	Select ~~the~~ student state, student gender, student marital status, ~~and the~~ count (*) ~~of rows~~ from ~~the~~ Students ~~table,~~ grouped by ~~and in~~ GROUPING SETS ~~of~~ student state, student gender, ~~and~~ student marital status

SQL	SELECT StudState, StudGender, StudMaritalStatus,
	    Count(*) AS Number
	FROM Students
	GROUP BY GROUPING SETS
	    (StudState, StudGender, StudMaritalStatus);

This will return results shown the following table. (I saved this request as CH21_Students_State_Gender_MaritalStatus_Count_GROUPING_SETS in the School Scheduling Example database.)

StudState	StudGender	StudMaritalStatus	Number
NULL	NULL	D	1
NULL	NULL	M	2
NULL	NULL	S	14

StudState	StudGender	StudMaritalStatus	Number
NULL	NULL	W	1
NULL	F	NULL	10
NULL	M	NULL	8
CA	NULL	NULL	2
OR	NULL	NULL	4
TX	NULL	NULL	3
WA	NULL	NULL	9

Yes, if your database system doesn't support the GROUPING SETS syntax, you can obtain the same results by using the UNION operator on three separate GROUP BY queries, as follows:

```
SQL        SELECT NULL AS StudState, NULL AS StudGender,
               StudMaritalStatus, Count(*) AS Number
           FROM Students
           GROUP BY StudMaritalStatus
           UNION
           SELECT NULL, StudGender, NULL, Count(*)
           FROM Students
           GROUP BY StudGender
           UNION
           SELECT StudState, NULL, NULL, Count(*)
           FROM Students
           GROUP BY StudState;
```

(I saved this request as CH21_Students_State_Gender_MaritalStatus_ Count_GROUP_BY_UNION in the School Scheduling Example database.)

Where the power of GROUPING SETS comes in is that they give you the flexibility to choose which subtotals you wish to see.

Let's examine the following request.

"Show me the count for all combinations of student state, student gender, and student marital status, with subtotals for student state, for the combination of student state and student gender and for the combination of student state and student marital status, but no grand total by student state, student gender, and student marital status."

> ❖ **Note** When you find yourself asking for a subtotal on the combination as well as the individual columns and some but not all combinations of columns, you should replace that with the sets of GROUPING SETS. This is particularly true if you do not need a grand total across all the grouped columns because CUBE and ROLLUP do return a grand total, but GROUPING SETS does not return a grand total unless you include an empty set in the GROUPING SETS list.

Translation/ Clean Up	Select ~~the~~ student state, student gender, student marital status, ~~and the~~ count (*) ~~of rows~~ from ~~the~~ Students ~~table,~~ grouped by ~~and in~~ GROUPING SETS ~~of the combination of~~ student state ~~and~~ student gender, ~~and by the combination of~~ student state ~~and~~ student marital status

SQL	```SELECT StudState, StudGender, StudMaritalStatus,```
	    ```Count(*) AS Number```
	```FROM Students```
	```GROUP BY GROUPING SETS```
	    ```(StudState,```
	      ```(StudState, StudGender),```
	      ```(StudState, StudMaritalStatus));```

This will return results as shown in the following table. (I saved this request as CH21_Students_State_Gender_MaritalStatus_Count_GROUPING_SETS_1 in the School Scheduling Example database.)

StudState	StudGender	StudMaritalStatus	Number
CA	NULL	S	1
CA	NULL	W	1
CA	NULL	NULL	2
OR	NULL	M	1

StudState	StudGender	StudMaritalStatus	Number
OR	NULL	S	3
OR	NULL	NULL	4
TX	NULL	S	3
TX	NULL	NULL	3
WA	NULL	D	1
WA	NULL	M	1
WA	NULL	S	7
WA	NULL	NULL	9
CA	F	NULL	1
OR	F	NULL	2
TX	F	NULL	2
WA	F	NULL	5
CA	M	NULL	1
OR	M	NULL	2
TX	M	NULL	1
WA	M	NULL	4

If you look carefully at those results, you'll see three different sets of subtotals:

1. Unique values of StudState, regardless of values of StudGender or StudMaritalStatus

2. Unique combinations of StudState and StudGender, regardless of values of StudMaritalStatus

3. Unique combinations of StudState and StudMaritalStatus, regardless of values of StudGender

Notice that unlike ROLLUP that asks for subtotals to be "rolled up" right to left or CUBE that asks for subtotals of all combinations, you can exactly specify the combinations of columns on which you want subtotals.

You can get a nearly identical result by using a GROUP BY column followed by a CUBE on the remaining columns. I'll show you how to do that in the following section.

Variations on Grouping Techniques

If you take a closer look at Figure 21-1, you should be able to figure out that it's perfectly legal to use combinations of simple grouping columns, ROLLUP, CUBE, and GROUPING SETS in a GROUP BY clause. You can also list combinations of columns in the list of columns you pass to ROLLUP, CUBE, or GROUPING SETS. Quite frankly, I'm hard-pressed to think of a case in which you would want to use a combination of ROLLUP, CUBE, and/or GROUPING SETS, but it is reasonable to "promote" one or more columns to simple grouping columns or to specify sub-groups of columns within a grouped set. Let's take a look at a couple of examples.

Suppose you don't need all the subtotals; your request could be as follows:

> *"Show me the count for all combinations of student state, student gender, and student marital status. Summarize by student state and by the combination of student state and student marital status."*

Translation/ Clean Up	Select ~~the~~ student state, student gender, student marital status, ~~and the~~ count (*) ~~of rows~~ from ~~the~~ Students ~~table,~~ grouped by ~~and in a~~ GROUPING SETS ~~set of~~ student state, student gender, ~~and~~ student marital status

SQL	SELECT StudState, StudGender, StudMaritalStatus,
	    Count(*) AS Number
	FROM Students
	GROUP BY GROUPING SETS (StudState,
	    (StudGender, StudMaritalStatus));

The returned results look like the following table. (I saved this request as CH21_Students_State_Gender_MaritalStatus_Count_GROUPING_SETS_2 in the School Scheduling Example database.)

StudState	StudGender	StudMaritalStatus	Number
NULL	F	D	1
NULL	F	M	2
NULL	F	S	6
NULL	M	S	8
NULL	F	W	1
CA	NULL	NULL	2
OR	NULL	NULL	4
TX	NULL	NULL	3
WA	NULL	NULL	9

There are only two different sets of subtotals:

1. Unique values of StudState, regardless of values of StudGender or StudMaritalStatus

2. Unique combinations of StudGender and StudMaritalStatus, regardless of values of StudState

"Show me the count for all combinations of student state, student gender, and student marital status, with subtotals for each state and for each combination of gender and marital status."

The database system returned this result because I specified two different sets of columns in the GROUPING SETS list: StudState by itself and StudGender and StudMaritalStatus in a group. You can see that the result is a total for each of the states and a total for each of the combinations of gender and marital status.

Now, let's see what happens when you "promote" one of the columns by moving it out of the grouping sets clause and using it as a simple grouped column. Take a look at the following request.

Translation/ Clean Up	Select ~~the~~ student state, student gender, student marital status, ~~and the~~ count (*) ~~of rows~~ from ~~the~~ Students ~~table,~~ grouped by student state ~~and~~ rolled up ~~by~~ student gender ~~and~~ student marital status

	SELECT StudState, StudGender, StudMaritalStatus,
SQL	Count(*) AS Number
	FROM Students
	GROUP BY StudState,
	ROLLUP (StudMaritalStatus, StudGender);

In that case, the results look like the following table. (I saved this request as CH21_Students_State_Gender_MaritalStatus_Count_ROLLUP_Partial in the School Scheduling Example database.)

StudState	StudGender	StudMaritalStatus	Number
CA	F	W	1
CA	F	NULL	1
CA	M	S	1
CA	M	NULL	1
CA	NULL	NULL	2
OR	F	M	1
OR	F	S	1
OR	F	NULL	2
OR	M	S	2
OR	M	NULL	2
OR	NULL	NULL	4
TX	F	S	2
TX	F	NULL	2
TX	M	S	1
TX	M	NULL	1
TX	NULL	NULL	3
WA	F	D	1
WA	F	M	1
WA	F	S	3
WA	F	NULL	5

StudState	StudGender	StudMaritalStatus	Number
WA	M	S	4
WA	M	NULL	4
WA	NULL	NULL	9

You can see that it groups by StudState, but does a ROLLUP on the combination of StudGender and StudMaritalStatus, resulting in three levels of subtotals:

1. StudState and unique combinations of StudGender and StudMaritalStatus

2. StudState and unique values of StudGender regardless of StudMaritalStatus values

3. StudState, regardless of StudGender and StudMaritalStatus values

By moving StudState outside the GROUPING SETS, I get the same results as you saw in CH21_Students_State_Gender_MaritalStatus_Count_CUBE_Order1 earlier, but without the grand totals row.

Let's try that again, but this time use CUBE instead of GROUPING SETS and sort the results to make it easier to see what's happening. I'll skip the request and Translation/Cleanup and go straight to the SQL.

```
SQL          SELECT StudState, StudGender, StudMaritalStatus,
                  Count(*) AS Number
             FROM Students
             GROUP BY StudState,
                CUBE (StudMaritalStatus, StudGender)
             ORDER BY StudState, StudGender, StudMaritalStatus
```

That gives you in the following result:

StudState	StudGender	StudMaritalStatus	Number
CA	NULL	NULL	2
CA	NULL	S	1
CA	NULL	W	1

StudState	StudGender	StudMaritalStatus	Number
CA	F	NULL	1
CA	F	W	1
CA	M	NULL	1
CA	M	S	1
OR	NULL	NULL	4
OR	NULL	M	1
OR	NULL	S	3
OR	F	NULL	2
OR	F	M	1
OR	F	S	1
OR	M	NULL	2
OR	M	S	2
TX	NULL	NULL	3
TX	NULL	S	3
TX	F	NULL	2
TX	F	S	2
TX	M	NULL	1
TX	M	S	1
WA	NULL	NULL	9
WA	NULL	D	1
WA	NULL	M	1
WA	NULL	S	7
WA	F	NULL	5
WA	F	D	1
WA	F	M	1
WA	F	S	3
WA	M	NULL	4
WA	M	S	4

I saved this example as CH21_Students_State_Gender_MaritalStatus_ CUBE_Partial in the School Scheduling sample database.

Because StudState is now outside the CUBE, it doesn't participate directly in the cubing action, but you do get a total for all states and all combinations of gender and marital status. Notice that moving one column out now avoids the grand total column—a result similar to what you would get with GROUPING SETS and multiple combinations of columns. Does your head hurt yet?

Feel free to play with other variations or combinations using my sample databases. You can simply copy the SQL from one of the Views and tinker with it to see what happens.

Sample Statements

You now know the mechanics of constructing queries using grouping sets and have seen some of the types of requests you can answer with grouping sets. Let's stop worrying about the gender or marital status of students and take a look at a fairly robust set of samples, all of which use one or more grouping set specifications. These examples come from each of the sample databases, and they illustrate the use of the grouping sets to generate subtotals in various ways.

I've also included sample result sets that would be returned by these operations and placed them immediately after the SQL syntax line. The name that appears immediately above a result set is the name I gave each query in the sample data on the companion website for this book, www.informit.com/title/9780134858333. I stored each query in the appropriate sample database (as indicated within the example), and I prefixed the names of the queries relevant to this chapter with "CH21." You can follow the instructions in the Introduction of this book to load the samples onto your computer and try them.

❖ **Note** Remember that all the column names and table names used in these examples are drawn from the sample database structures shown in Appendix B, "Schema for the Sample Databases." Because many of these examples use complex JOINs, your database system might choose a different way to solve these queries. For this reason, the first few rows might not exactly match the result you obtain, but the total number of rows should be the same. To simplify the process, I have combined the Translation and Clean Up steps for all the following examples.

Examples using ROLLUP

Sales Orders Database

"For each category of product, show me, by state, the count of orders and how much revenue the customers have generated. Give me a subtotal for each category plus a grand total."

Translation/ Clean Up	Select CategoryDescription, CustState, ~~the~~ count ~~of~~ DISTINCT orders.OrderNumber, ~~and the~~ sum ~~of~~ (QuotedPrice ~~times~~ * QuantityOrdered) as Price from ~~the~~ Order_Details ~~table~~ inner join~~ed with the~~ Orders ~~table~~ on Orders.OrderNumber = Order_Details.OrderNumber inner join~~ed with the~~ Customers ~~table~~ on Customers.CustomerID = Orders.CustomerID inner join~~ed with the~~ Products ~~table~~ on Products.ProductNumber = Order_Details.ProductNumber inner join~~ed with the~~ Categories ~~table~~ on Categories.CategoryID = Products.Category ID ~~summarized by~~ GROUP BY ROLLUP (CategoryDescription ~~and~~ CustState)

talSQL	```SELECT PC.CategoryDescription, C.CustState,```
	 ``` COUNT(DISTINCT O.OrderNumber) AS OrderCount,```
	 ``` SUM(OD.QuotedPrice * QuantityOrdered) AS Revenue```
	 ```FROM Order_Details AS OD```
	 ``` INNER JOIN Orders AS O```
	 ``` ON O.OrderNumber = OD.OrderNumber```
	 ``` INNER JOIN Customers AS C```
	 ``` ON C.CustomerID = O.CustomerID```
	 ``` INNER JOIN Products AS P```
	 ``` ON P.ProductNumber = OD.ProductNumber```
	 ``` INNER JOIN Categories AS PC```
	 ``` ON PC.CategoryID = P.CategoryID```
	 ```GROUP BY ROLLUP```
	 ``` (PC.CategoryDescription, C.CustState)```

CH21_ProductCategory_CustomerState_Revenue_ROLLUP (31 rows)

CategoryDescription	CustState	OrderCount	Price
Accessories	CA	174	$85,201.52
Accessories	OR	122	$56,551.79
Accessories	TX	112	$89,104.78
Accessories	WA	37	$141,212.93
Accessories	NULL	94	$372,071.02
Bikes	CA	69	$729,481.45
<< more rows here >>			
Tires	NULL	257	$25,249.24
Components	NULL	586	$244242.53
NULL	NULL	933	$4,630,731.37

Just for comparison, if you GROUP BY the two columns, you get one total for each combination of category description and state, with no grand total. If you CUBE the two columns, you get a total for each combination of category description and state, subtotals by category, subtotals by state, and a grand total. Because the request asked for a subtotal only by category, I used ROLLUP.

School Scheduling Database

> *"Show me how many sessions are scheduled for each classroom over the next two semesters. Give me subtotals by building, by classroom, by semester, and by subject, plus a grand total."*

Because this involves a rather tricky bit of SQL due to the unnormalized list of days in the Classes table, I'm going to use the solution presented in CH20_Class_Schedule_Calendar, which returns one row for each individual class session, as a starting point. You might wish to review that example in the previous chapter if you're uncertain.

Translation/ Clean Up	Select BuildingCode, ClassRoomID, SemesterNo, SubjectCode, ~~and the count of classes~~ Count(*) from ~~the~~ CH20_Class_Schedule_Calendar ~~view summarized by~~ GROUP BY ROLLUP (BuildingCode, ClassRoomID, SemesterNo, SubjectCode)

talSQL	SELECT BuildingCode, ClassRoomID, SemesterNo, SubjectCode, Count(*) AS NumberOfSessions FROM CH20_Class_Schedule_Calendar GROUP BY ROLLUP(BuildingCode, ClassRoomID, SemesterNo, SubjectCode);

CH21_Building_ClassRoom_Semester_Subject_Count_ROLLUP (212 rows)

BuildingCode	ClassRoomID	SemesterNo	SubjectCode	NumberOfSessions
AS	1514	1	JRN 104	29
AS	1514	1	NULL	29
AS	1514	2	JRN 104	29
AS	1514	2	NULL	29
AS	1514	NULL	NULL	58
		<< more rows here >>		
TB	1642	2	CIS 114	58
TB	1642	2	NULL	58
TB	1642	NULL	NULL	117
TB	NULL	NULL	NULL	439
NULL	NULL	NULL	NULL	7221

Examples using CUBE

Bowling League Database

"I want to know the average handicap score for each bowler by team and city. Give me subtotals for each combination of team and city, for each team, for each city, plus a grand total."

Translation/ Clean Up	Select TeamName, BowlerCity, ~~and the average of~~ Avg(HandicapScore) as AvgHandicap from ~~the~~ Teams ~~table~~ inner join~~ed with the~~ Bowlers ~~table~~ on Bowlers. TeamID = Teams.TeamID inner join~~ed with the~~ Bowler_ Scores ~~table~~ on Bowler_Scores.BowlerID = Bowlers. BowlerID ~~summarized in sets by~~ GROUP BY CUBE (TeamName, ~~and~~ BowlerState)

SQL	SELECT T.TeamName, B.BowlerCity,
	Avg(BS.HandicapScore) AS AvgHandicap
	FROM Teams AS T
	INNER JOIN Bowlers AS B
	ON B.TeamID = T.TeamID
	INNER JOIN Bowler_Scores AS BS
	ON BS.BowlerID = B.BowlerID
	GROUP BY CUBE (T.TeamName, B.BowlerCity);

The clue here is the request asks not only for the average for each combination of team and city and for subtotals by all individual columns. This calls for CUBE.

CH21_Team_City_AverageHandicapScore_CUBE (44 rows)

TeamName	BowlerCity	AvgHandicap
Barracudas	Auburn	197
Manatees	Auburn	196
Sharks	Auburn	196
Swordfish	Auburn	193
NULL	Auburn	196
Marlins	Ballard	196
Terrapins	Ballard	195
NULL	Ballard	196
Terrapins	Bellevue	194
<< more rows here >>		

Sales Orders Database

"For each category of product, show me, by state, how much quantity the vendors have on hand. Give me subtotals for each category, for each state, plus a grand total."

Translation/ Clean Up	Select CategoryDescription, VendState, ~~and the~~ sum ~~of~~ (QuantityOfHand) as Price from ~~the~~ Products ~~table~~ inner join~~ed with the~~ Categories ~~table~~ on Orders.Order-Number = Categories.CategoryID = Products.CategoryID inner join~~ed with the~~ Product_Vendors ~~table~~ on Product_Vendors.ProductNumber = Products.ProductNumber inner join~~ed with the~~ Vendors ~~table~~ on Vendors.VendorID = Product_Vendors.VendorID ~~summarized in sets by~~ GROUP BY CUBE (CategoryDescription, ~~and~~ VendState)
| SQL | ```
SELECT PC.CategoryDescription, V.VendState,
   SUM(P.QuantityOnHand) AS QOH
FROM Products AS P
  INNER JOIN Categories AS PC
    ON PC.CategoryID = P.CategoryID
  INNER JOIN Product_Vendors AS PV
    ON PV.ProductNumber = P.ProductNumber
  INNER JOIN Vendors AS V
    ON V.VendorID = PV.VendorID
  GROUP BY CUBE (PC.CategoryDescription,
    V.VendState)
``` |

CH21_ProductCategory_VendorState_QOH_CUBE (39 rows)

CategoryDescription	VendState	QOH
Accessories	AK	48
Bikes	AK	8
Car racks	AK	14
Clothing	AK	94
Components	AK	278
Tires	AK	60
NULL	AK	502
Accessories	CA	54
NULL	NULL	1914
```

CategoryDescription	VendState	QOH
Accessories	NULL	642
Bikes	NULL	48
Car racks	NULL	28
Clothing	NULL	222
Components	NULL	794
Tires	NULL	180

<< more rows here >>

Examples using GROUPING SETS

Bowling League Database

"Show me how many games each bowler has participated in, summarized by both team and city."

Translation/ Clean Up	Select TeamName, BowlerCity, ~~and the count~~ count(*) ~~of~~ from ~~the~~ Teams ~~table~~ inner join~~ed with the~~ Bowlers ~~table~~ on Bowlers.TeamID = Teams.TeamID inner join~~ed with~~ ~~the~~ Bowler_Scores ~~table~~ on Bowler_Scores.BowlerID = Bowlers.BowlerID ~~summarized both by~~ GROUP BY GROUPING SETS (TeamName, ~~and~~ BowlerCity)
SQL	``` SELECT T.TeamName, B.BowlerCity, Count(*) AS GamesBowled FROM Teams AS T INNER JOIN Bowlers AS B ON B.TeamID = T.TeamID INNER JOIN Bowler_Scores AS BS ON BS.BowlerID = B.BowlerID GROUP BY GROUPING SETS (T.TeamName, B.BowlerCity); ```

Notice that I didn't ask for subtotals for each team and city combination. I only want summaries by team and by city, so GROUPING SETS is ideal.

CH21_Team_City_GamesBowled_GROUPING_SETS (18 rows)

TeamName	BowlerCity	GamesBowled
NULL	Auburn	210
NULL	Ballard	84
NULL	Bellevue	42
NULL	Bothell	84
NULL	Duvall	126
NULL	Kirkland	126
NULL	Redmond	294
NULL	Seattle	168
NULL	Tacoma	42
NULL	Woodinville	168
Barracudas	NULL	168
Dolphins	NULL	168
Manatees	NULL	168
Marlins	NULL	168
Orcas	NULL	168
Sharks	NULL	168
Swordfish	NULL	168
Terrapins	NULL	168

Entertainment Agency Database

"Show me counts of our customers summarized by both style and zip code."

Translation/ Clean Up	Select StyleName, CustZipCode, ~~and the count~~ count(*) ~~of~~ from ~~the~~ Customers ~~table~~ inner joined ~~with the~~ Musical_Preferences ~~table~~ on Musical_Preferences.CustomerID = Customers.CustomerID inner joined ~~with the~~ Musical_Styles ~~table~~ on Musical_Styles.StyleID = Musical_Styles.Style ~~summarized both by~~ GROUP BY GROUPING SETS (StyleName, ~~and~~ CustZipCode)

```
talSQL          SELECT MS.StyleName, C.CustZipCode, Count(*) AS
                   Instances
                FROM Customers AS C
                   INNER JOIN Musical_Preferences AS MP
                      ON MP.CustomerID = C.CustomerID
                   INNER JOIN Musical_Styles AS MS
                      ON MS.StyleID = MP.StyleID
                GROUP BY GROUPING SETS (MS.StyleName,
                   C.CustZipCode)
```

CH21_Style_CustomerZipCode_Count_GROUPING_SETS (27 rows)

StyleName	CustZipCode	Instances
NULL	98002	2
NULL	98006	14
NULL	98033	7
NULL	98052	4
NULL	98105	2
NULL	98115	3
NULL	98413	4
40's Ballroom Music	NULL	2
60's Music	NULL	1
70's Music	NULL	1
80's Music	NULL	1
<< more rows here >>		

Summary

I began the chapter by describing to you why you might need to group data differently from how you were shown in Chapter 13. This included an example illustrating one possibility.

I went on to explain the difference between the three extensions to GROUP BY:

- GROUP BY ROLLUP

- GROUP BY CUBE

- GROUP BY GROUPING SETS

I kept mentioning that the three keywords ROLLUP, CUBE and GROUPING SETS are simply extensions of the GROUP BY syntax I discussed in Chapter 13, so all restrictions from that chapter apply equally here.

I summarized why these extensions to GROUP BY can be useful, and I provided you with examples of how to build requests that require these extensions to the GROUP BY clause.

The following section presents some requests that you can work out on your own.

Problems for You to Solve

Below, I show you the request statement and the name of the solution query in the sample databases. (Hint: the name of the saved query lets you know whether you should use ROLLUP, CUBE, or GROUPING SETS.) If you want some practice, you can work out the SQL you need for each request and then check your answer with the query I saved in the samples. Don't worry if your syntax doesn't exactly match the syntax of the queries I saved—as long as your result set is the same.

Bowling League Database

1. *"Show me how many bowlers live in each city. Give me totals for each combination of Team and City, for each Team, for each City plus a grand total."*

   You can find my solution in CH21_Team_City_Count_CUBE (44 rows).

2. *"Show me the average raw score for each bowler. Give me totals by Team and by City."*

   You can find my solution in CH21_Team_City_AverageRawScore_ GROUPING_SETS (18 rows).

3. *"Show me the average handicap score for each bowler. For each team, give me average for each city in which the bowlers live. Also give me the average for each team, and the overall average for the entire league."*

You can find my solution in CH21_Team_City_AverageHandicap-Score_ROLLUP (34 rows).

Entertainment Agency Database

1. *"For each city where our entertainers live, show me how many different musical styles are represented. Give me totals for each combination of City and Style, for each City plus a grand total."*

You can find my solution in CH21_EntertainerCity_Style_ROLLUP (36 rows).

2. *"For each city where our customers live, show me how many different musical styles they're interested in. Give me total counts by city, total counts by style and total counts for each combination of city and style."*

You can find my solution in CH21_CustomerCity_Style_GROUP-ING_SETS (18 rows).

3. *"Give me an analysis of all the bookings we've had. I want to see the number of bookings and the total charge broken down by the city the agent lives in, the city the customer lives in, and the combination of the two."*

You can find my solution in CH21_AgentCity_CustomerCity_Count_Charge_GROUPING_SETS (34 rows).

Recipes Database

1. *"I want to know how many recipes there are in each of the recipe classes in my cookbook, plus an overall total of all the recipes regardless of recipe class. Make sure to include any recipe classes that don't have any recipes in them."*

You can find my solution in CH21_RecipeClass_Recipe_Counts_ROLLUP (8 rows).

2. *"I want to know the relationship between RecipeClasses and IngredientClasses. For each recipe class, show me how many different ingredient classes are represented, and for each ingredient class, show me how many different recipe classes are represented."*

You can find my solution in CH21_RecipeClass_IngredClass_Counts_GROUPING_SETS (25 rows).

3. *"I want to know even more about the relationship between RecipeClasses and IngredientClasses. Show me how many recipes there are in each combination of recipe class and ingredient class. Also show me how many recipes there are in each ingredient class regardless of the recipe class, how many recipes there are in each recipe class regardless of the ingredient class, and how many recipes there are in total."*

You can find my solution in CH21_RecipeClass_IngredClass_CUBE (61 rows).

Sales Orders Database

1. *"For each category of product, show me, by state, how much revenue the customers have generated. Give me subtotals for each state, for each category, plus a grand total."*

You can find my solution in CH21_ProductCategory_CustomerState_Revenue_CUBE (35 rows).

2. *"For each category of product, show me, by state, how much quantity the vendors have on hand. Give me subtotals for each state within a category, plus a grand total."*

You can find my solution in CH21_ProductCategory_VendorState_QOH_ROLLUP (33 rows).

3. *"For each of our vendors, let me know how many products they supply in each category. I want to see this broken down by state. For each state, show me the number of products in each category. Show me the number of products for all categories and a grand total as well."*

Note that the counts will not represent the number of different products that are sold!

You can find my solution in CH21_VendorState_Category_Count_ROLLUP (43 rows).

School Scheduling Database

1. *"Summarize the number of class sessions scheduled, showing semester, building, classroom, and subject. Give me subtotals for each semester, for each combination of building and classroom and for each subject."*

You can find my solution in CH21_Semester_Building_ClassRoom_Subject_Count_GROUPING_SETS (82 rows).

2. *"For each department, show me the number of courses that could be offered, and whether they're taught by a Professor, an Associate Professor, or an Instructor. Give me total courses per department and total courses overall as well."*

   Note that the number of courses returned will be greater than the number of courses offered by the school because some courses could be taught by more than instructors.

   You can find my solution in CH21_Department_Title_Count_ROLLUP (20 rows).

3. *"I want to know how many courses our students have been in contact with. Give me totals by whether they completed the course, are currently enrolled in it or withdrew. I'd also like to see this broken down by student major. May as well give me the total courses completed, enrolled and withdrawn while you're at it. Don't worry about splitting it up by semester."*

   You can find my solution in CH21_Major_ClassStatus_Count_GROUPING_SETS (26 rows).

22

Partitioning Data into Windows

In my head there are several windows, that I do know, but perhaps it is always the same one, open variously on the parading universe.

SAMUEL BECKETT

Topics in this Chapter

What You Can Do with a "Window" into Your Data

Calculating a Row Number

Ranking Data

Splitting Data into Quintiles

Using Windows with Aggregate Functions

Sample Statements

Summary

Problems for You to Solve

I've shown you several different ways that you can group and aggregate data, but I still haven't shown you everything.

In earlier incarnations of the SQL standards, there really was no ability to work with data where the results depended on adjacent rows. It was always felt that the order of the rows didn't matter, as long as you could match the rows to your filters. While the ability to sort the data using the ORDER BY clause existed, it was seen as being related to presentation, not to data manipulation. This meant that operations such as generating running sums, where the sum on a particular row is dependent on the values of the rows that precede that row, were very difficult (or even impossible) to write using only SQL.

With the introduction of the SQL:2003 Standard, though, this changed. The SQL:2003 Standard introduced the concept of window functions, which are functions that are applied to a set of rows defined by a window descriptor and return a single value for each row from the underlying query.

I intend to delve into the world of window functions in this chapter. Don't worry if you use an Apple computer: window functions have nothing to do with the PC operating system. In fact, Microsoft's SQL Server was late coming to the party with respect to window functions; they weren't introduced until SQL Server 2017, and they still aren't in Microsoft Access!

> ❖ **Note** You can find all the sample statements and solutions for the respective sample databases—SalesOrdersExample, Entertainment-AgencyExample, RecipesExample, SchoolSchedulingExample, and BowlingLeagueExample. Because neither Microsoft Access nor MySQL support window functions, you'll find the sample solutions only in the Microsoft SQL Server and PostgreSQL example databases.

What You Can Do With a "Window" into Your Data

In all the examples I've shown you to aggregate data so far, the aggregated data is replaced by a subtotal row. You lose the actual details of the data that went into the aggregation.

For instance, if you wanted to know how many styles of music each customer prefers, you might use a query like this:

```
SQL          SELECT CustomerID, C.CustFirstName || ' ' || C.CustLastName
                AS Customer,
                COUNT(*) AS Preferences
             FROM Customers AS C
                INNER JOIN Musical_Preferences AS MP
                   ON MP.CustomerID = C.CustomerID
             GROUP BY C.CustFirstName, C.CustLastName;
```

You will obtain results like the following table. (I saved this request as CH22_Customers_PreferredStyles_Count in the Entertainment Agency Example database.)

CustomerID	Customer	Preferences
10001	Doris Hartwig	2
10002	Deb Waldal	2
10003	Peter Brehm	2
10004	Dean McCrae	2
10005	Elizabeth Hallmark	2
10006	Matt Berg	2
10007	Liz Keyser	3
10008	Darren Gehring	2
10009	Sarah Thompson	3
10010	Zachary Ehrlich	3
10011	Joyce Bonnicksen	3
10012	Kerry Patterson	2
10013	Estella Pundt	2
10014	Mark Rosales	3
10015	Carol Viescas	3

Great. This does let you know exactly how many preferences each customer has indicated. However, it doesn't tell you what their preferences are!

What if we could use a window function to figure out the total number of preferences for customers but also return what each of their preferences is? It turns out you can get results like the following table:

CustomerID	Customer	StyleName	Preferences
10001	Doris Hartwig	Contemporary	2
10001	Doris Hartwig	Top 40 Hits	2

CustomerID	Customer	StyleName	Preferences
10002	Deb Waldal	60's Music	2
10002	Deb Waldal	Classic Rock & Roll	2
10003	Peter Brehm	Motown	2
10003	Peter Brehm	Rhythm and Blues	2
10004	Dean McCrae	Jazz	2
10004	Dean McCrae	Standards	2
10005	Elizabeth Hallmark	Classical	2
10005	Elizabeth Hallmark	Chamber Music	2
10006	Matt Berg	Folk	2
10006	Matt Berg	Variety	2
10007	Liz Keyser	70's Music	3
10007	Liz Keyser	Classic Rock & Roll	3
10007	Liz Keyser	Rhythm and Blues	3
10008	Darren Gehring	Contemporary	2
10008	Darren Gehring	Standards	2
10009	Sarah Thompson	Country	3
10009	Sarah Thompson	Country Rock	3
10009	Sarah Thompson	Modern Rock	3
10010	Zachary Ehrlich	Jazz	3
10010	Zachary Ehrlich	Rhythm and Blues	3
10010	Zachary Ehrlich	Salsa	3
10011	Joyce Bonnicksen	40's Ballroom Music	3
10011	Joyce Bonnicksen	Classical	3
10011	Joyce Bonnicksen	Standards	3
10012	Kerry Patterson	Contemporary	2
10012	Kerry Patterson	Show Tunes	2

CustomerID	Customer	StyleName	Preferences
10013	Estella Pundt	Jazz	2
10013	Estella Pundt	Salsa	2
10014	Mark Rosales	80's Music	3
10014	Mark Rosales	Modern Rock	3
10014	Mark Rosales	Top 40 Hits	3
10015	Carol Viescas	40's Ballroom Music	3
10015	Carol Viescas	Show Tunes	3
10015	Carol Viescas	Standards	3

❖ **Note** If you're really on your toes, you would probably tell me, "But, John, I already know how to get that result using a subquery, like this":

```
SELECT CustomerID, CustFirstName || ' ' || CustLastName,
    StyleName, (SELECT COUNT(*)
                FROM Musical_Preferences AS MP
                WHERE MP.CustomerID = Customers.
                CustomerID)
            AS Preferences
FROM Customers INNER JOIN Musical_Preferences
   ON Customers.CustomerID = Musical_Preferences.
      CustomerID
INNER JOIN Musical_Styles
   ON Musical_Styles.StyleID = Musical_Preferences.
      StyleID;
```

And you would be correct! But the focus of this chapter is to show you another, perhaps more efficient, way to get that result.

Now we know not only that Doris Hartwig has specified two preferences, but we also know that the two styles she prefers are Contemporary and Top 40 Hits! I'm sure you can see that these results could be far more useful.

So how do you go about achieving results such as this? You guessed it: you use window functions. So without further ado, let me show you how.

Syntax

Let's take a close look at the syntax for window functions. Figure 22-1 shows the basic diagram. Note that they are only valid in SELECT and ORDER BY clauses. Hmmm, that looks pretty complicated, doesn't it?

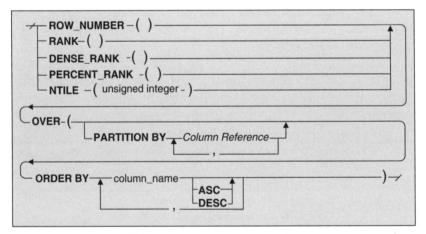

Figure 22-1 *Syntax of the primary Window functions*

But that's not all! (Sounds like a TV game show, doesn't it?) And you can "power up" an Aggregate Function by turning it into a window, as shown in Figure 22-2.

❖ **Note** As you can imagine from how lengthy those lists in Figures 22-1 and 22-2 are, window functions are a huge topic; more than can possibly be covered in a single chapter. As a result, I will be not covering ALL of the window functions, just the ones that I think are most useful. However, you can find syntax for all the window functions in Appendix A.

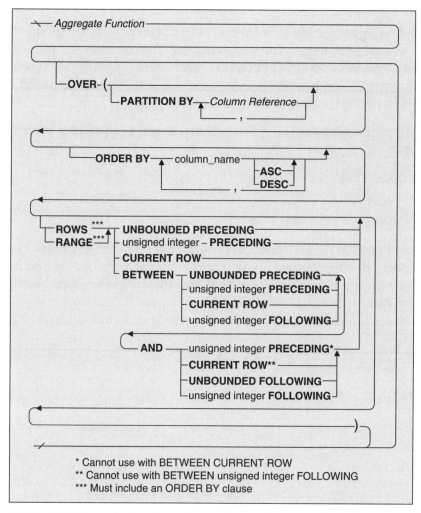

Figure 22-2 *Extended syntax when using an Aggregate Function*

You can see that the Aggregate Functions (COUNT, SUM, AVG, MIN, and MAX) I taught you about in Chapter 12, "Simple Totals," are in those figures, along with several new ones: ROW_NUMBER(), RANK(), DENSE_RANK(), PERCENT_RANK(), and NTILE(), but there seems to be a lot more that can be specified as well.

The clause that allows you to use the windows functions is OVER(). That clause lets you define the range on which the aggregate functions are applied.

The key difference between GROUP BY and OVER() is that GROUP BY applies aggregations across the entire query, rolling up the specified non-aggregate fields, thereby reducing the number of rows returned (usually). With OVER(), however, the same number of rows will be returned as the base query. Any aggregations will be returned for each row in the range identified in the OVER() clause.

Within the OVER() clause, there are several predicates which can be used:

PARTITION BY

ORDER BY

ROWS (or RANGE)

The PARTITION BY predicate specifies how the window should be divided. In the example above, I'm dividing the window by the customer. The SQL for the table above that includes a Preferences column looks like this:

SQL

```
SELECT C.CustomerID,
   C.CustFirstName || ' ' || C.CustLastName AS Customer,
   MS.StyleName,
   COUNT(*) OVER (
     PARTITION BY C.CustomerID
   ) AS Preferences
FROM Customers AS C
   INNER JOIN Musical_Preferences AS MP
     ON MP.CustomerID = C.CustomerID
   INNER JOIN Musical_Styles AS MS
     ON MS.StyleID = MP.StyleID;
```

Now you know how to create that "magical" table I showed you at the beginning of the chapter. I saved this query as CH22_Customers_PreferredStyles_Details_Count in the Entertainment sample database.

If I don't specify anything for the PARTITION BY predicate, the database system applies the function over the entire result set.

❖ **Note** Throughout this chapter, I use the "Request/Translation/ Clean Up/SQL" technique introduced in Chapter 4, "Creating a Simple Query." Because this process should now be very familiar to you, I have combined the Translation/Clean Up steps for all the following examples to simplify the process.

"For each customer, show me the musical preference styles they've selected. Show me a running total of the number of styles selected for all the customers."

Translation/ Clean Up	Select ~~the customer~~ CustomerID, CustFirstName || '' || CustLastName, StyleName, ~~and the~~ count(*) OVER ~~with no partition but~~ ordered by CustomerID from ~~the~~ Customers ~~table,~~ inner join~~ed with the~~ Musical_Preferences ~~table~~ on Musical_Preferences.CustomerID = Customers.Customer ID inner join~~ed with the~~ Musical_Styles ~~table~~ on Musical_ Styles.StyleID = Musical_Preferences.StyleID

SQL	SELECT C.CustomerID,
	   C.CustFirstName || ' ' || C.CustLastName AS Customer,
	   MS.StyleName,
	   COUNT(*) OVER (
	     ORDER BY C.CustomerID
	   ) AS Preferences
	FROM Customers AS C
	  INNER JOIN Musical_Preferences AS MP
	    ON MP.CustomerID = C.CustomerID
	  INNER JOIN Musical_Styles AS MS
	    ON MS.StyleID = MP.StyleID;

That query returns results like the following table. (I saved this request as CH22_Customers_PreferredStyles_Details_NO_PARTITION in the Entertainment Agency Example database.)

CustomerID	Customer	StyleName	Preferences
10001	Doris Hartwig	Contemporary	2
10001	Doris Hartwig	Top 40 Hits	2

CustomerID	Customer	StyleName	Preferences
10002	Deb Waldal	60's Music	4
10002	Deb Waldal	Classic Rock & Roll	4
10003	Peter Brehm	Motown	6
10003	Peter Brehm	Rhythm and Blues	6
10004	Dean McCrae	Jazz	8
10004	Dean McCrae	Standards	8
10005	Elizabeth Hallmark	Classical	10
10005	Elizabeth Hallmark	Chamber Music	10
10006	Matt Berg	Folk	12
10006	Matt Berg	Variety	12
10007	Liz Keyser	70's Music	15
10007	Liz Keyser	Classic Rock & Roll	15
10007	Liz Keyser	Rhythm and Blues	15
10008	Darren Gehring	Contemporary	17
10008	Darren Gehring	Standards	17
10009	Sarah Thompson	Country	20
10009	Sarah Thompson	Country Rock	20
10009	Sarah Thompson	Modern Rock	20
10010	Zachary Ehrlich	Jazz	23
10010	Zachary Ehrlich	Rhythm and Blues	23
10010	Zachary Ehrlich	Salsa	23
10011	Joyce Bonnicksen	40's Ballroom Music	26
10011	Joyce Bonnicksen	Classical	26
10011	Joyce Bonnicksen	Standards	26
10012	Kerry Patterson	Contemporary	28
10012	Kerry Patterson	Show Tunes	28
10013	Estella Pundt	Jazz	30
10013	Estella Pundt	Salsa	30

CustomerID	Customer	StyleName	Preferences
10014	Mark Rosales	80's Music	33
10014	Mark Rosales	Modern Rock	33
10014	Mark Rosales	Top 40 Hits	33
10015	Carol Viescas	40's Ballroom Music	36
10015	Carol Viescas	Show Tunes	36
10015	Carol Viescas	Standards	36

I still get the same data, but the totals are different. Rather than indicating the number of preferences for each customer, I'm now getting a running total. The totals in both rows for Doris Hartwig are still two, corresponding to the two preference styles she's indicated, but now the totals for Deb Waldal are four (her two preference styles added to Doris's two preference styles), the totals for Peter Brehm are six (his two preference styles added to Deb's two preference styles and Doris's two) and so on. Basically, I've generated a running sum of the preferences count.

Note that you can specify a different OVER() clause for each aggregate function. For instance, you can get both counts of preferences per customer plus overall counts of preferences using a query like the following:

"For each customer, show me the musical preference styles they've selected. Show me both the total for each customer plus a running total of the number of styles selected for all the customers."

Translation/ Clean Up	Select ~~the customer~~ CustomerID, CustFirstName || ' ' || CustLastName, StyleName, ~~the~~ count(*) OVER partition by CustomerID ordered by CustomerID ~~and the~~ count(*) OVER ~~with no partition but~~ ordered by CustomerID from ~~the~~ Customers ~~table,~~ inner join~~ed with the~~ Musical_Preferences ~~table~~ on Musical_Preferences.CustomerID = Customers. Customer ID inner join~~ed with the~~ Musical_Styles ~~table~~ on Musical_Styles.StyleID = Musical_Preferences.StyleID

SQL	`SELECT C.CustomerID,`
	
	`    C.CustFirstName || ' ' || C.CustLastName AS`
	`      Customer,`
	
	`    MS.StyleName,`

```
COUNT(*) OVER (
    PARTITION BY C.CustomerID
    ORDER BY C.CustomerID
) AS CustomerPreferences,
COUNT(*) OVER (
    ORDER BY C.CustomerID
) AS TotalPreferences
FROM Customers AS C
    INNER JOIN Musical_Preferences AS MP
        ON MP.CustomerID = C.CustomerID
    INNER JOIN Musical_Styles AS MS
        ON MS.StyleID = MP.StyleID;
```

That will return results like the following table. (I saved this request as CH22_Customers_PreferredStyles_Details_Multiple_Counts in the Entertainment Agency Example database.)

CustomerID	Customer	StyleName	Customer Preferences	Total Preferences
10001	Doris Hartwig	Contemporary	2	2
10001	Doris Hartwig	Top 40 Hits	2	2
10002	Deb Waldal	60's Music	2	4
10002	Deb Waldal	Classic Rock & Roll	2	4
10003	Peter Brehm	Motown	2	6
10003	Peter Brehm	Rhythm and Blues	2	6
10004	Dean McCrae	Jazz	2	8
10004	Dean McCrae	Standards	2	8
10005	Elizabeth Hallmark	Classical	2	10
10005	Elizabeth Hallmark	Chamber Music	2	10
10006	Matt Berg	Folk	2	12
10006	Matt Berg	Variety	2	12
10007	Liz Keyser	70's Music	3	15

CustomerID	Customer	StyleName	Customer Preferences	Total Preferences
10007	Liz Keyser	Classic Rock & Roll	3	15
10007	Liz Keyser	Rhythm and Blues	3	15
10008	Darren Gehring	Contemporary	2	17
10008	Darren Gehring	Standards	2	17
10009	Sarah Thompson	Country	3	20
10009	Sarah Thompson	Country Rock	3	20
10009	Sarah Thompson	Modern Rock	3	20
10010	Zachary Ehrlich	Jazz	3	23
10010	Zachary Ehrlich	Rhythm and Blues	3	23
10010	Zachary Ehrlich	Salsa	3	23
10011	Joyce Bonnicksen	40's Ballroom Music	3	26
10011	Joyce Bonnicksen	Classical	3	26
10011	Joyce Bonnicksen	Standards	3	26
10012	Kerry Patterson	Contemporary	2	28
10012	Kerry Patterson	Show Tunes	2	28
10013	Estella Pundt	Jazz	2	30
10013	Estella Pundt	Salsa	2	30
10014	Mark Rosales	80's Music	3	33
10014	Mark Rosales	Modern Rock	3	33
10014	Mark Rosales	Top 40 Hits	3	33
10015	Carol Viescas	40's Ballroom Music	3	36
10015	Carol Viescas	Show Tunes	3	36
10015	Carol Viescas	Standards	3	36

Note that this now gives me both a total count of preferences by customer as well as a running total over all customers. As its name suggests, the ORDER BY predicate controls the order in which the rows are returned. I could change the ORDER BY predicate in the previous query like this:

> *"For each customer, show me the musical preference styles they've selected. Show me both the total for each customer plus a running total of the number of styles selected for all the customers. I want to see the customers sorted by name."*

Translation/ Clean Up	Select ~~the~~ CustomerID, CustFirstName || ' ' || CustLast-Name, StyleName, ~~the~~ count(*) OVER partition by Custo-merID ~~ordered~~ by CustLastName, CustFirstName ~~and the~~ count(*) OVER ~~with no partition but~~ ordered by CustLast-Name, CustFirstName from ~~the~~ Customers ~~table,~~ inner join~~ed with the~~ Musical_Preferences ~~table~~ on Musical_Pref-erences.CustomerID = Customers.Customer ID inner join~~ed with the~~ Musical_Styles ~~table~~ on Musical_Styles.StyleID = Musical_Preferences.StyleID

SQL	<pre>SELECT C.CustomerID,
	    C.CustFirstName || ' ' || C.CustLastName
	      AS Customer,
	    MS.StyleName,
	    COUNT(*) OVER (
	      PARTITION BY C.CustomerID
	        ORDER BY C.CustLastName, C.CustFirstName
	    ) AS CustomerPreferences,
	    COUNT(*) OVER (
	      ORDER BY C.CustLastName, C.CustFirstName
	    ) AS TotalPreferences
	FROM Customers AS C
	  INNER JOIN Musical_Preferences AS MP
	    ON MP.CustomerID = C.CustomerID
	  INNER JOIN Musical_Styles AS MS
	    ON MS.StyleID = MP.StyleID;</pre>

This returns results like the following table. (I saved this request as CH22_Customers_PreferredStyles_Details_Multiple_Counts_Sort1 in the Entertainment Agency Example database.)

CustomerID	Customer	StyleName	Customer Preferences	Total Preferences
10006	Matt Berg	Folk	2	2
10006	Matt Berg	Variety	2	2
10011	Joyce Bonnicksen	40's Ballroom Music	3	5
10011	Joyce Bonnicksen	Classical	3	5
10011	Joyce Bonnicksen	Standards	3	5
10003	Peter Brehm	Motown	2	7
10003	Peter Brehm	Rhythm and Blues	2	7
10010	Zachary Ehrlich	Jazz	3	10
10010	Zachary Ehrlich	Rhythm and Blues	3	10
10010	Zachary Ehrlich	Salsa	3	10
10008	Darren Gehring	Contemporary	2	12
10008	Darren Gehring	Standards	2	12
10005	Elizabeth Hallmark	Classical	2	14
10005	Elizabeth Hallmark	Chamber Music	2	14
10001	Doris Hartwig	Contemporary	2	16
10001	Doris Hartwig	Top 40 Hits	2	16
10007	Liz Keyser	70's Music	3	19
10007	Liz Keyser	Classic Rock & Roll	3	19
10007	Liz Keyser	Rhythm and Blues	3	19
10004	Dean McCrae	Jazz	2	21
10004	Dean McCrae	Standards	2	21
10012	Kerry Patterson	Contemporary	2	23
10012	Kerry Patterson	Show Tunes	2	23
10013	Estella Pundt	Jazz	2	25
10013	Estella Pundt	Salsa	2	25
10014	Mark Rosales	80's Music	3	28
10014	Mark Rosales	Modern Rock	3	28
10014	Mark Rosales	Top 40 Hits	3	28

CustomerID	Customer	StyleName	Customer Preferences	Total Preferences
10009	Sarah Thompson	Country	3	31
10009	Sarah Thompson	Country Rock	3	31
10009	Sarah Thompson	Modern Rock	3	31
10015	Carol Viescas	40's Ballroom Music	3	34
10015	Carol Viescas	Show Tunes	3	34
10015	Carol Viescas	Standards	3	34
10002	Deb Waldal	60's Music	2	36
10002	Deb Waldal	Classic Rock & Roll	2	36

You can see that the final output is now sorted by customer last name and first name, not by customer ID. Note, however, that ORDER BY clause should be consistent with the PARTITION clause, or the results you get might be confusing.

> *"For each customer, show me the musical preference styles they've selected. Show me both the total for each customer plus a running total of the number of styles selected for all the customers. I want to see the styles sorted by name."*

Translation/ Clean Up	Select ~~the customer~~ CustomerID, CustFirstName || ' ' || CustLastName, StyleName, ~~the~~ count(*) OVER partition by CustomerID ordered by StyleName ~~and the~~ count(*) OVER ~~with no partition but~~ ordered by StyleName from ~~the~~ Customers ~~table,~~ inner joined ~~with the~~ Musical_Preferences ~~table~~ on Musical_Preferences.CustomerID = Customers. Customer ID inner joined ~~with the~~ Musical_Styles ~~table~~ on Musical_Styles.StyleID = Musical_Preferences.StyleID
| SQL | ```
SELECT C.CustomerID,
   C.CustFirstName || ' ' || C.CustLastName AS
      Customer,
   MS.StyleName,
   COUNT(*) OVER (
    PARTITION BY C.CustomerID
    ORDER BY MS.StyleName
   ) AS CustomerPreferences,
``` |
```

```
COUNT(*) OVER (
    ORDER BY MS.StyleName
) AS TotalPreferences
FROM Customers AS C
    INNER JOIN Musical_Preferences AS MP
        ON MP.CustomerID = C.CustomerID
    INNER JOIN Musical_Styles AS MS
        ON MS.StyleID = MP.StyleID;
```

That query would lead to results like the following table. (I saved this request as CH22_Customers_PreferredStyles_Details_Multiple_Counts_Sort2 in the Entertainment Agency Example database.) This time, the output is sorted by style name, as I requested.

CustomerID	Customer	StyleName	Customer Preferences	Total Preferences
10011	Joyce Bonnicksen	40's Ballroom Music	1	2
10015	Carol Viescas	40's Ballroom Music	1	2
10002	Deb Waldal	60's Music	1	3
10007	Liz Keyser	70's Music	1	4
10014	Mark Rosales	80's Music	1	5
10005	Elizabeth Hallmark	Chamber Music	1	6
10007	Liz Keyser	Classic Rock & Roll	2	8
10002	Deb Waldal	Classic Rock & Roll	2	8
10005	Elizabeth Hallmark	Classical	2	10
10011	Joyce Bonnicksen	Classical	2	10
10012	Kerry Patterson	Contemporary	1	13
10008	Darren Gehring	Contemporary	1	13
10001	Doris Hartwig	Contemporary	1	13
10009	Sarah Thompson	Country	1	14
10009	Sarah Thompson	Country Rock	2	15
10006	Matt Berg	Folk	1	16

CustomerID	Customer	StyleName	Customer Preferences	Total Preferences
10004	Dean McCrae	Jazz	1	19
10010	Zachary Ehrlich	Jazz	1	19
10013	Estella Pundt	Jazz	1	19
10014	Mark Rosales	Modern Rock	2	21
10009	Sarah Thompson	Modern Rock	3	21
10003	Peter Brehm	Motown	1	22
10003	Peter Brehm	Rhythm and Blues	2	25
10007	Liz Keyser	Rhythm and Blues	3	25
10010	Zachary Ehrlich	Rhythm and Blues	2	25
10010	Zachary Ehrlich	Salsa	3	27
10013	Estella Pundt	Salsa	2	27
10015	Carol Viescas	Show Tunes	2	29
10012	Kerry Patterson	Show Tunes	2	29
10011	Joyce Bonnicksen	Standards	3	33
10015	Carol Viescas	Standards	3	33
10008	Darren Gehring	Standards	2	33
10004	Dean McCrae	Standards	2	33
10001	Doris Hartwig	Top 40 Hits	2	35
10014	Mark Rosales	Top 40 Hits	3	35
10006	Matt Berg	Variety	2	36

The TotalPreferences counts still look okay (two people like 40's Ballroom Music, so the value for TotalPreferences is 2 for both those rows, one person likes 60's Music, so the value for TotalPreferences for that style is 3. TotalPreferences is a running total—the total for the previous style plus the total for the current style and so on). The CustomerPreferences counts are a little harder to figure out, but they are simply a running sum of the number of preferences specified by each customer. The first row for any given customer shows the value 1, the second row the value 2, and so on.

> ❖ **Note** It is possible to include an OVER() clause with no optional clauses. The result is the aggregate you specified calculated for all the rows returned by the FROM and WHERE clauses and displayed on each row. For example, this query:
>
> ```
> SELECT C.CustomerID,
>   C.CustFirstName || ' ' || C.CustLastName AS Customer,
>   MS.StyleName,
>   COUNT(*) OVER () AS NumRows
> FROM Customers AS C
>   INNER JOIN Musical_Preferences AS MP
>     ON MP.CustomerID = C.CustomerID
>   INNER JOIN Musical_Styles AS MS
>     ON MS.StyleID = MP.StyleID;
> ```
>
> . . . returns the count of all rows in the NumRows column. You can think of it as a way to display all rows and get a grand total without having to include a GROUP BY clause.

The ROWS (or RANGE) predicate allows you to further limit the rows of data that are included within the partition. It does this by letting you specify a range of rows with respect to the current row.

The ROWS clause lets you specify the range physically by specifying a fixed number of rows preceding or following the current row. For instance, you can specify ROWS BETWEEN CURRENT ROW AND 1 FOLLOWING, which would mean that the rows to be considered are simply this row and the one right after it.

The RANGE clause lets you specify the range logically by specifying a range of values with respect to the value in the current row.

> ❖ **Note** Both the ROWS and RANGE clauses require that the ORDER BY clause be specified. If ORDER BY specifies multiple columns, CURRENT ROW FOR RANGE considers all columns in the ORDER BY list when determining what constitutes the range.

Let's look at an example to see the difference between using ROWS and RANGES when calculating the total number of preferences. (Don't worry,

I'll be talking more about using aggregate functions like SUM with the OVER() clause in a little bit.) Let's just go straight to the SQL, asking for a SUM of the COUNT OVER ROWS and a SUM of the COUNT OVER RANGE to see the difference.

"For each city where we have customers, show me the customer and the number of musical preference styles they've selected. Also give me a running total by city, both for each customer in the city as well as for the city overall."

```
SQL        SELECT C.CustCity,
              C.CustFirstName || ' ' || C.CustLastName AS Customer,
              COUNT(*) AS Preferences,
              SUM(COUNT(*)) OVER (
                ORDER BY C.CustCity
                  ROWS BETWEEN UNBOUNDED PRECEDING AND CURRENT ROW
              ) AS TotalUsingRows,
              SUM(COUNT(*)) OVER (
                ORDER BY C.CustCity
                RANGE BETWEEN UNBOUNDED PRECEDING AND CURRENT ROW
              ) AS TotalUsingRange
            FROM Customers AS C
              INNER JOIN Musical_Preferences AS MP
                ON MP.CustomerID = C.CustomerID
            GROUP BY C.CustCity, C.CustFirstName, C.CustLastName;
```

That query would lead to results like the following table. (I saved this request as CH22_Customer_ByCity_PreferredStyles_Sums in the Entertainment Agency Example database.)

CustCity	Customer	Preferences	Total UsingRows	Total UsingRange
Auburn	Elizabeth Hallmark	2	2	2
Bellevue	Estella Pundt	2	4	16
Bellevue	Joyce Bonnicksen	3	7	16
Bellevue	Liz Keyser	3	10	16

CustCity	Customer	Preferences	Total UsingRows	Total UsingRange
Bellevue	Mark Rosales	3	13	16
Bellevue	Sarah Thompson	3	16	16
Kirkland	Darren Gehring	2	18	23
Kirkland	Peter Brehm	2	20	23
Kirkland	Zachary Ehrlich	3	23	23
Redmond	Dean McCrae	2	25	27
Redmond	Kerry Patterson	2	27	27
Seattle	Carol Viescas	3	30	32
Seattle	Doris Hartwig	2	32	32
Tacoma	Deb Waldal	2	34	36
Tacoma	Matt Berg	2	36	36

Look at the two calculated SUM fields. The first (TotalUsingRows) included a ROWS predicate ROWS BETWEEN UNBOUNDED PRECEDING AND CURRENT ROW, while the second (TotalUsingRange) included a RANGE predicate RANGE BETWEEN UNBOUNDED PRECEDING AND CURRENT ROW.

Each value in the TotalUsingRows column is the value in the Preferences column for that row added to the value in the TotalUsingRows column for the preceding row. In other words, using the SUM aggregate function with the ROWS BETWEEN UNBOUNDED PRECEDING AND CURRENT ROW predicate results in a running total.

The values in the TotalUsingRange column are quite different (although the values on the first and last rows are the same). The RANGE predicate creates a range of all rows with the same value for the column specified in the ORDER BY predicate (CustCity) as the current row. In other words, the first row is the sum of Preferences for all rows corresponding to the city of the first row (Auburn). There are five rows for Bellevue, with preferences 2, 3, 3, 3, 3, respectively. Those five values result in 14 when added together. That value is added to the value for the previous range so that the TotalUsingRange column shows 16 for the five Bellevue rows. Similarly, there are three rows for Kirkland, which total 7.

That total for Kirkland is added to the value for the previous range (16), resulting in the TotalUsingRange column showing 23 for the range consisting of the three Kirkland rows. You can still call it a running total, but the running total for each row in the range is the same. Looking at it another way, the value in the TotalUsingRange column for any city matches the last row for that city in the TotalUsingRows column (Auburn, Elizabeth Hallmark; Bellevue, Sarah Thompson; Kirkland, Zachary Ehrlich; and so on).

One thing that should be pointed out is that it's only possible to use the ROWS (or RANGE) predicate with aggregate functions. Figure 22-3 summarizes the rules.

Function	OVER clause	PARTITION BY	ORDER BY	ROWS or RANGE
ROW_NUMBER()	Required	Optional	Required	Not allowed
RANK()	Required	Optional	Required	Not allowed
DENSE_RANK()	Required	Optional	Required	Not allowed
PERCENT_RANK()	Required	Optional	Required	Not allowed
NTILE(n)	Required	Optional	Required	Not allowed
Aggregate Function	Optional	Optional	Optional	Optional

Figure 22-3 *The clauses that are required and optional for each window function*

Calculating a Row Number

One of the new functions introduced in Figure 22-1 is ROW_NUMBER(). As you might expect from the name, this allows you to assign unique numbers to each row.

"Assign a number for each customer. Show me their CustomerID, their name and their state. Return the customers in alphabetic order."

Translation/ Clean Up	Select ~~the~~ ROW_NUMBER (*) OVER ordere~~d~~ by CustLast-Name, CustFirstName, ~~the customer and state~~ CustomerID, CustFirstName || ' ' || CustLastName, CustState from ~~the~~ Customers ~~table~~

SQL	``SELECT ROW_NUMBER() OVER (``
	`    ORDER BY CustLastName, CustFirstName`
	`) AS RowNumber,`
	`    C.CustomerID,`

```
C.CustFirstName || ' ' || C.CustLastName
   AS CustomerName,
C.CustState
FROM Customers AS C;
```

That query would lead to results like the following table. (I saved this
request as CH22_Customers_Numbering in the Sales Orders Example
database.)

RowNumber	CustomerID	CustomerName	CustState
1	1014	Sam Abolrous	CA
2	1020	Joyce Bonnicksen	WA
3	1004	Robert Brown	TX
4	1009	Andrew Cencini	WA
5	1026	Kirk DeGrasse	TX
6	1019	Zachary Ehrlich	CA
7	1015	Darren Gehring	CA
8	1011	Alaina Hallmark	WA
9	1003	Gary Hallmark	WA
10	1010	Angel Kennedy	TX
11	1012	Liz Keyser	WA
12	1005	Dean McCrae	WA
13	1027	Luke Patterson	OR
14	1025	Maria Patterson	TX
15	1008	Neil Patterson	CA
16	1013	Rachel Patterson	CA
17	1021	Estella Pundt	TX
18	1024	Mark Rosales	TX
19	1023	Julia Schnebly	WA

RowNumber	CustomerID	CustomerName	CustState
20	1017	Manuela Seidel	OR
21	1007	Mariya Sergienko	OR
22	1018	David Smith	CA
23	1002	William Thompson	WA
24	1028	Jeffrey Tirekicker	WA
25	1022	Caleb Viescas	CA
26	1006	John Viescas	WA
27	1001	Suzanne Viescas	WA
28	1016	Jim Wilson	OR

Of course, because ROW_NUMBER is a window function, we can use the OVER clause to partition the table differently.

> *"Assign a number for each customer within their state. Show me their CustomerID, their name, and their state. Return the customers in alphabetic order."*

Translation/ Clean Up	Select ~~the~~ ROW_NUMBER() OVER partition by CustState, ~~ordered~~ by CustLastName, CustFirstName, ~~the~~ CustomerID, CustFirstName || ' ' || CustLastName, ~~and~~ CustState from ~~the~~ Customers ~~table~~
SQL	```SELECT ROW_NUMBER() OVER (PARTITION BY CustState ORDER BY CustLastName, CustFirstName) AS RowNumber, C.CustomerID, C.CustFirstName || ' ' || C.CustLastName AS CustomerName, C.CustState FROM Customers AS C;```

That query would lead to results like the following table. (I saved this request as CH22_Customers_Numbering_By_State in the Sales Orders Example database.)

RowNumber	CustomerID	CustomerName	CustState
1	1014	Sam Abolrous	CA
2	1019	Zachary Ehrlich	CA
3	1015	Darren Gehring	CA
4	1008	Neil Patterson	CA
5	1013	Rachel Patterson	CA
6	1018	David Smith	CA
7	1022	Caleb Viescas	CA
1	1027	Luke Patterson	OR
2	1017	Manuela Seidel	OR
3	1007	Mariya Sergienko	OR
4	1016	Jim Wilson	OR
1	1004	Robert Brown	TX
2	1026	Kirk DeGrasse	TX
3	1010	Angel Kennedy	TX
4	1025	Maria Patterson	TX
5	1021	Estella Pundt	TX
6	1024	Mark Rosales	TX
1	1020	Joyce Bonnicksen	WA
2	1009	Andrew Cencini	WA
3	1011	Alaina Hallmark	WA
4	1003	Gary Hallmark	WA
5	1012	Liz Keyser	WA
6	1005	Dean McCrae	WA
7	1023	Julia Schnebly	WA
8	1002	William Thompson	WA
9	1028	Jeffrey Tirekicker	WA
10	1006	John Viescas	WA
11	1001	Suzanne Viescas	WA

Because I asked for a partition by state, the RowNumber column restarts at 1 for each different state, and the rows are sorted by customer last name and first name within each state.

Ranking Data

Another one of the new functions introduced in Figure 22-1 is RANK(). As you might expect from the name, this allows you to rank rows of data relative to one another.

"List all students who have completed English courses and rank them by the grade they received."

Translation/ Clean Up	Select ~~the~~ SubjectID, StudFirstName, StudLastName, SubjectName, Grade, ~~and~~ RANK() OVER ordered by Grade DESC from ~~the~~ Students ~~table~~ inner joined ~~with the~~ Student_Schedules ~~table~~ on Students.StudentID = Student_Schedules.StudentID inner join~~ed with the~~ Classes ~~table~~ on Classes.ClassID = Student_Schedules.ClassID inner join~~ed with the~~ Subjects ~~table~~ on Subjects.SubjectID = Classes.SubjectID where ClassStatus = 2 and CategoryID = 'ENG'

SQL	SELECT Su.SubjectID, St.StudFirstName,
	   St.StudLastName, Su.SubjectName,
	   SS.Grade,
	   RANK() OVER (
	     ORDER BY SS.Grade DESC
	   ) AS Rank
	FROM Students AS St
	  INNER JOIN Student_Schedules AS SS
	    ON SS.StudentID = St.StudentID
	  INNER JOIN Classes AS C
	    ON C.ClassID = SS.ClassID
	  INNER JOIN Subjects AS Su
	    ON Su.SubjectID = C.SubjectID
	  WHERE SS.ClassStatus = 2
	    AND Su.CategoryID = 'ENG';

That query would lead to results like the following table. (I saved this request as CH22_English_Students_Rank in the School Scheduling Example database.)

SubjectID	Stud FirstName	Stud LastName	SubjectName	Grade	Rank
37	Scott	Bishop	Composition - Fundamentals	98.07	1
37	Sara	Sheskey	Composition - Fundamentals	97.59	2
37	John	Kennedy	Composition - Fundamentals	93.01	3
37	Brannon	Jones	Composition - Fundamentals	91.66	4
37	Janice	Galvin	Composition - Fundamentals	91.44	5
38	Kendra	Bonnicksen	Composition - Intermediate	88.91	6
37	George	Chavez	Composition - Fundamentals	88.54	7
37	Marianne	Wier	Composition - Fundamentals	87.4	8
37	David	Hamilton	Composition - Fundamentals	86.33	9
37	Steve	Pundt	Composition - Fundamentals	82.58	10
38	Doris	Hartwig	Composition - Intermediate	81.66	11
37	Michael	Viescas	Composition - Fundamentals	77.59	12
38	Elizabeth	Hallmark	Composition - Intermediate	72.88	13
37	Karen	Smith	Composition - Fundamentals	72.05	14
37	Betsy	Stadick	Composition - Fundamentals	71.09	15
37	Kerry	Patterson	Composition - Fundamentals	70	16
38	Sarah	Thompson	Composition - Intermediate	67.6	17
38	Richard	Lum	Composition - Intermediate	67.19	18

In this case, there are no duplicate grade values, so the ranking is simply the grades in descending order.

If two or more rows tie for a rank in the same partition, each of the tied rows receives the same rank. If we take the above table and give both Brannon Jones and Janice Galvin a grade of 91.66 for Composition – Fundamentals, both Brannon and Janice would be listed at rank value 4, and Kendra Bonnicksen would still have rank 6, with the value 5 skipped. Like this:

SubjectID	StudFirstName	StudLastName	SubjectName	Grade	Rank
37	Scott	Bishop	Composition - Fundamentals	98.07	1
37	Sara	Sheskey	Composition - Fundamentals	97.59	2
37	John	Kennedy	Composition - Fundamentals	93.01	3
37	Brannon	Jones	Composition - Fundamentals	91.66	4
37	Janice	Galvin	Composition - Fundamentals	91.66	4
38	Kendra	Bonnicksen	Composition - Intermediate	88.91	6

<< more rows here >>

Figure 22-1 also included the DENSE_RANK() and PERCENT_RANK() functions. The difference between those two functions and RANK() is straightforward. Because there is only one distinct value that precedes the row, the DENSE_RANK() function would not skip a value. It would return the value 5 for Kendra Bonnicksen. This is one more than the number of distinct rows that come before the current row. The numbers returned by the DENSE_RANK function do not have gaps and always have consecutive ranks.

The PERCENT_RANK() function, however, returns a number that represents the percentage of values less than the current value in the group, excluding the highest value. In the absence of ties, the PERCENT_RANK() function will always return 0 for the first value in the group, and 1 for the last value in a group. For the remaining rows in the partition, the PERCENT_RANK function ranks a value by calculating its rank minus 1 (rk – 1), and dividing that value by the number of rows in the partition minus 1 (nr – 1). Here's the formula:

$$PERCENT\_RANK = \frac{(rk - 1)}{(nr - 1)}$$

Let's take a look at an example.

"List all bowlers in the league, ranking them by their average handi-capped score. Show all three of RANK(), DENSE_RANK(), and PER-CENT_RANK() to show the difference. (Remember that bowling scores are reported as rounded integer values.)"

Translation/ Clean Up	Select ~~the~~ BowlerID, BowlerName, ROUND(AVG(HandiCapScore), 0), RANK() OVER ~~ordered~~ by ROUND(AVG(HandiCapScore), 0) DESC AS Rank, DENSE_RANK () OVER ~~ordered~~ by ROUND(AVG(Handi-CapScore), 0) DESC AS DenseRank ~~and~~ PERCENT_RANK () OVER ~~ordered~~ by ROUND(AVG(HandiCapScore), 0) DESC AS PercentRank from ~~table~~ Bowlers inner ~~joined with the~~ Bowler_Scores ~~table~~ ON Bowler_Scores.BowlerID = Bowlers.BowlerID, ~~grouped~~ by BowlerID, BowlerFirstName ~~and~~ BowlerLastName

SQL	<pre>SELECT B.BowlerID,
	   B.BowlerFirstName || ' ' || B.BowlerLastName
	     AS BowlerName,
	   ROUND(AVG(BS.HandiCapScore), 0) AS AvgHandicap,
	   RANK () OVER (
	     ORDER BY ROUND(AVG(BS.HandiCapScore), 0) DESC)
	       AS Rank,
	   DENSE_RANK () OVER (
	     ORDER BY ROUND(AVG(BS.HandiCapScore), 0) DESC)
	       AS DenseRank,
	   PERCENT_RANK () OVER (
	     ORDER BY ROUND(AVG(BS.HandiCapScore), 0) DESC)
	       AS PercentRank
	FROM Bowlers AS B
	   INNER JOIN Bowler_Scores AS BS
	     ON BS.BowlerID = B.BowlerID
	GROUP BY B.BowlerID, B.BowlerFirstName,
	   B.BowlerLastName;</pre>

> ❖ **Note** I rounded the averages because that's what a real bowling league does. You need a rounded integer value to be able to calculate the handicap. I had to include the rounded expression in each of the ORDER BY clauses to get the correct answer. And if you look at the code I had to use in Microsoft SQL Server, I also CAST the Handi-CapScore column AS FLOAT because, if I don't do that, the database system returns a truncated, not rounded, average value.

That query would lead to results like the following table. (I saved this request as CH22_Bowlers_Average_Score_Rankings in the Bowling League Example database.)

BowlerID	BowlerName	Avg Handicap	Rank	Dense Rank	Percent Rank
15	Kathryn Patterson	198	1	1	0
6	Neil Patterson	198	1	1	0
27	William Thompson	198	1	1	0
19	John Viescas	198	1	1	0
25	Megan Patterson	197	5	2	0.129032258064516
3	John Kennedy	197	5	2	0.129032258064516
29	Bailey Hallmark	197	5	2	0.129032258064516
14	Gary Hallmark	197	5	2	0.129032258064516
2	David Fournier	196	9	3	0.258064516129032
31	Ben Clothier	196	9	3	0.258064516129032
11	Angel Kennedy	196	9	3	0.258064516129032
26	Mary Thompson	196	9	3	0.258064516129032
7	David Viescas	196	9	3	0.258064516129032
1	Barbara Fournier	196	9	3	0.258064516129032
24	Sarah Thompson	196	9	3	0.258064516129032
18	Michael Hernandez	195	16	4	0.483870967741936
10	Doug Steele	195	16	4	0.483870967741936

BowlerID	BowlerName	Avg Handicap	Rank	Dense Rank	Percent Rank
12	Carol Viescas	195	16	4	0.483870967741936
9	Alastair Black	195	16	4	0.483870967741936
5	Ann Patterson	195	16	4	0.483870967741936
22	Alaina Hallmark	195	16	4	0.483870967741936
16	Richard Sheskey	194	22	5	0.67741935483871
20	Suzanne Viescas	194	22	5	0.67741935483871
28	Michael Viescas	194	22	5	0.67741935483871
23	Caleb Viescas	194	22	5	0.67741935483871
21	Zachary Ehrlich	194	22	5	0.67741935483871
4	Sara Sheskey	194	22	5	0.67741935483871
13	Elizabeth Hallmark	194	22	5	0.67741935483871
30	Rachel Patterson	194	22	5	0.67741935483871
32	Joe Rosales	193	30	6	0.935483870967742
8	Stephanie Viescas	193	30	6	0.935483870967742
17	Kendra Hernandez	193	30	6	0.935483870967742

You can see the difference between the values in the Rank and Dense-Rank columns. The first four bowlers (Kathryn Patterson, Neil Patterson, William Thompson, and John Viescas) all have the same highest average score (198), so they're each ranked 1 by both functions. The next four people (Megan Patterson, John Kennedy, Bailey Hallmark, and Gary Hallmark) also have the same average score (197), so the values in the Rank and DenseRank columns are the same for all of them as well. Since four bowlers have been ranked before them, the RANK() function returns a value of 5, one more than the number already ranked. However, there's only one distinct value ahead of them (198), so the DENSE_RANK() function returns a value of 2, one more than the number of distinct values.

Ranking continues in this manner. The next seven bowlers (David Fournier, Ben Clothier, Angel Kennedy, Mary Thompson, David Viescas, Barbara Fournier, and Sarah Thompson) have the same average score (196). Since eight bowlers have already been ranked ahead of them, the

RANK() function returns 9 for each of them. However, there are only two distinct values ahead of them (198 and 197), so the DENSE_RANK() function returns 3. Finally, Joe Rosales, Stephanie Viescas, and Kendra Hernandez all get a rank of 30 (because twenty-nine bowlers have already been ranked ahead of them) and a dense rank of 6 (because there are only five distinct values ahead of theirs)

Look, too, at the PercentRank column. Once again, since Kathryn Patterson, Neil Patterson, William Thompson, and John Viescas have the highest average score, the PERCENT_RANK() function returns 0 for their rows. The next four bowlers (Megan Patterson, John Kennedy, Bailey Hallmark, and Gary Hallmark) are all ranked as 5, and there are 32 rows in the partition. As explained above, that means the PERCENT_RANK function returns

$$\frac{(rk-1)}{(nr-1)} = \frac{(5-1)}{(32-1)} = 0.129032258064516$$

Similarly, the next seven bowlers (David Fournier, Ben Clothier, Angel Kennedy, Mary Thompson, David Viescas, Barbara Fournier, and Sarah Thompson) are all ranked and 9, so the PERCENT_RANK function returns

$$\frac{(rk-1)}{(nr-1)} = \frac{(9-1)}{(32-1)} = 0.258064516129032$$

One thing that doesn't show up in this example is the fact that, should the last row represent a single individual, the PERCENT_RANK function would return 1 for that row. Because Joe Rosales, Stephanie Viescas, and Kendra Hernandez are tied for last place, the PERCENT_RANK function returns the same value for all three of them:

$$\frac{(rk-1)}{(nr-1)} = \frac{(30-1)}{(32-1)} = 0.935483870967742$$

Splitting Data into Quintiles

You may remember that I showed you how to calculate quintiles in Chapter 20, "Using Unlinked Data and 'Driver' Tables." You may also recall that you needed to CROSS JOIN two separate queries (one that assigned a ranking number to each student who completed an English course and one that counted all students who completed an English course). That's a lot of data retrieval that can be prevented through the use of window functions! In fact, one of the aggregate functions introduced along with window functions is NTILE, which lets you divide the data into as many different ranges as you want.

"List all students who have completed English courses, rank them by the grades they received, and indicate the Quintile into which they fall."

Translation/ Clean Up	Select ~~the~~ SubjectID, StudFirstName, StudLastName, SubjectName, Grade, RANK() OVER ordered by Grade DESC ~~and~~ NTILE (5) OVER ordered by Grade DESC from ~~the~~ Students ~~table~~ inner joined ~~with the~~ Student_Schedules ~~table~~ on Students.StudentID = Student_Schedules.StudentID inner joined ~~with the~~ Classes ~~table~~ on Classes.ClassID = Student_Schedules.ClassID inner joined ~~with the~~ Subjects ~~table~~ on Subjects.SubjectID = Classes.SubjectID where ClassStatus = 2 and CategoryID = 'ENG'
| SQL | ```
SELECT Su.SubjectID, St.StudFirstName,
       St.StudLastName,
       SS.ClassStatus,
       SS.Grade, Su.CategoryID,
       Su.SubjectName,
       RANK() OVER (ORDER BY Grade DESC) AS Rank,
       NTILE(5) OVER(ORDER BY Grade DESC) AS Quintile
FROM Subjects AS Su
  INNER JOIN Classes AS C
    ON C.SubjectID = S.SubjectID
  INNER JOIN Student_Schedules AS SS
    ON SS.ClassID = C.ClassID)
  INNER JOIN Students AS St
  ON St.StudentID = SS.StudentID
WHERE SS.ClassStatus = 2
  AND Su.CategoryID = 'ENG';
``` |

That query would lead to results like the following table. (I saved this request as CH22_English_Students_Quintiles in the School Scheduling Example database.)
```

Subject ID	Stud FirstName	Stud LastName	Subject Name	Grade	Rank	Quintile
37	Scott	Bishop	Composition - Fundamentals	98.07	1	1
37	Sara	Sheskey	Composition - Fundamentals	97.59	2	1
37	John	Kennedy	Composition - Fundamentals	93.01	3	1
37	Brannon	Jones	Composition - Fundamentals	91.66	4	1
37	Janice	Galvin	Composition - Fundamentals	91.44	5	2
38	Kendra	Bonnicksen	Composition - Intermediate	88.91	6	2
37	George	Chavez	Composition - Fundamentals	88.54	7	2
37	Marianne	Wier	Composition - Fundamentals	87.4	8	2
37	David	Hamilton	Composition - Fundamentals	86.33	9	3
37	Steve	Pundt	Composition - Fundamentals	82.58	10	3
38	Doris	Hartwig	Composition - Intermediate	81.66	11	3
37	Michael	Viescas	Composition - Fundamentals	77.59	12	3
38	Elizabeth	Hallmark	Composition - Intermediate	72.88	13	4
37	Karen	Smith	Composition - Fundamentals	72.05	14	4
37	Betsy	Stadick	Composition - Fundamentals	71.09	15	4
37	Kerry	Patterson	Composition - Fundamentals	70	16	5

Subject ID	Stud FirstName	Stud LastName	Subject Name	Grade	Rank	Quintile
38	Sarah	Thompson	Composition - Intermediate	67.6	17	5
38	Richard	Lum	Composition - Intermediate	67.19	18	5

❖ **Note** The more astute of you might notice that the quintiles returned are slightly different in this example from those returned by the example in Chapter 20, CH20_English_Student_Quintiles.

The NTILE() function is used to distribute rows into a specified number of groups, When the number of rows is not divisible equally by the number of groups, larger groups will come before smaller groups. For instance, if you have 10 rows of data, NTILE(2) can divide the rows into two equal size groups, but NTILE(3) will put 4 in the first group, and 3 in each of the second and third groups. That's what happened in this case: there were 18 rows being divided into five groups, so the groups were 4, 4, 4, 3 and 3. That's different from the algorithm used to distribute the rows among the five groups in the CH20_English_Student_Quintiles.

One approach is not necessarily better or worse than the other. If there had been twenty students, the quintiles would have been the same.

Using Windows with Aggregate Functions

As I already pointed out, you can use any of the Aggregate Functions I showed you in Chapter 12 with the OVER() clause. You saw the full diagram earlier as Figure 22–2. I've already shown the use of the COUNT(*) function and SUM(COUNT(*)), but let's take a quick look at it again in conjunction with the ROWS and RANGE predicates.

Remember that both the ROWS and RANGE predicates limit the data on which the aggregate function will work. Using the same ROWS BETWEEN UNBOUNDED PRECEDING AND CURRENT ROW predicate in conjunction with the COUNT(*) function really doesn't provide much. It'll let you count all the rows "in front" of the current row: in other words, it'll simply provide you with the same values as the ROW_ NUMBER() function you've already seen. Using RANGE BETWEEN UNBOUNDED PRECEDING AND CURRENT ROW potentially is more useful: it'll give you a running total by range.

"Give a count of how many detail lines are associated with each order placed. I want to see the order number, the product purchased and a count of how many items are on the invoice. I'd also like to see how many detail lines there are in total."

Translation/ Clean Up	Select ~~the~~ OrderNumber, ProductName, COUNT(*) OVER partition by OrderNumber, COUNT(*) OVER order by Order-Number rows between unbounded preceding and current row, COUNT(*) OVER order by OrderNumber ranges between unbounded preceding and current row from ~~the~~ Orders ~~table~~ inner join~~ed with the~~ Order_Details ~~table~~ on Order_Details. OrderNumber = Orders.OrderNumber inner join~~ed with the~~ Products ~~table~~ on Products.ProductNumber = OrderDetails. ProductNumber
SQL	

```
SELECT O.OrderNumber AS OrderNo, P.ProductName,
    COUNT(*) OVER (
        PARTITION BY O.OrderNumber
    ) AS Total,
    COUNT(*) OVER (
        ORDER BY O.OrderNumber
        ROWS BETWEEN UNBOUNDED PRECEDING AND CURRENT
            ROW
    ) AS TotalUsingRows,
    COUNT(*) OVER (
        ORDER BY O.OrderNumber
        RANGE BETWEEN UNBOUNDED PRECEDING AND CURRENT
            ROW
    ) AS TotalUsingRange
FROM Orders AS O
    INNER JOIN Order_Details AS OD
        ON OD.OrderNumber = O.OrderNumber
    INNER JOIN Products AS P
        ON P.ProductNumber = OD.ProductNumber;
```

That query would lead to results like the following table. (I saved this request as CH22_Order_Counts_ByInvoice_ROWS_RANGE in the Sales Orders Example database.)

OrderNo	ProductName	Total	Total UsingRows	Total UsingRange
1	Trek 9000 Mountain Bike	7	1	7
1	Viscount Mountain Bike	7	2	7
1	GT RTS-2 Mountain Bike	7	3	7
1	ProFormance ATB All-Terrain Pedal	7	4	7
1	Dog Ear Aero-Flow Floor Pump	7	5	7
1	Glide-O-Matic Cycling Helmet	7	6	7
1	Ultimate Export 2G Car Rack	7	7	7
2	X-Pro All Weather Tires	2	8	9
2	Ultimate Export 2G Car Rack	2	9	9
3	Trek 9000 Mountain Bike	8	10	17
3	Viscount Mountain Bike	8	11	17

<< more rows here >>

You can see that there are seven separate products associated with order 1, so the Total column contains 7 for each of the rows. Similarly, the two separate rows associated with order 2 both have 2 for Total associated with them. (Only part of order 3 is shown, but you can see that the two rows that are shown both have the same value associated with them as well.)

As mentioned, the TotalUsingRows column is simply consecutive numbers, the same as the ROW_NUMBER() function would provide.

Finally, the TotalUsingRange column shows the total number of products by order. In other words, it shows 7 for all seven rows in order 1, then 9 for both rows in order 2 (corresponding to the seven rows from order 1 plus the two rows from order 2). You can see that the Total column indicates that there are eight rows in order 3, so the Total-UsingRange column contains 17 (7 + 2 + 8) for the rows associated with order 3.

Of course, other aggregate functions can be useful. For instance, perhaps you want to see the details of all the orders your customers have placed, and you'd like to see the Order total associated with each.

"List all orders placed, including the customer name, the order number, the product name, the quantity ordered, the quoted price and the total price per order."

Translation/ Clean Up	Select ~~the~~ CustFirstName || ' ' ||, CustLastName, Order-Number, ProductName, QuantityOrdered, QuotedPrice, ~~and~~ SUM(QuotedPrice) OVER partition by OrderNumber from ~~the~~ Orders ~~table~~ inner join~~ed with the~~ Order_Details ~~table~~ on Order_Details.OrderNumber = Orders.OrderNumber inner join~~ed with the~~ Customers ~~table~~ on Customers.CustomerID = Orders.CustomerID inner join~~ed with the~~ Products ~~table~~ on Products.ProductNumber = OrderDetails.ProductNumber
SQL	``` SELECT C.CustFirstName || ' ' || C.CustLastName AS Customer, O.OrderNumber AS Order, P.ProductName, OD.QuantityOrdered AS Quantity, OD.QuotedPrice AS Price, SUM(OD.QuotedPrice) OVER (PARTITION BY O.OrderNumber) AS OrderTotal FROM Orders AS O INNER JOIN Order_Details AS OD ON OD.OrderNumber = O.OrderNumber INNER JOIN Customers AS C ON C.CustomerID = O.CustomerID INNER JOIN Products AS P ON P.ProductNumber = OD.ProductNumber; ```

That query would lead to results like the following table. (I saved this request as CH22_Order_Totals_ByInvoice in the Sales Orders Example database.)

Customer	Order	ProductName	Quantity	Price	OrderTotal
David Smith	1	Trek 9000 Mountain Bike	2	1200.00	3863.85
David Smith	1	Viscount Mountain Bike	3	635.00	3863.85
David Smith	1	GT RTS-2 Mountain Bike	4	1650.00	3863.85
David Smith	1	ProFormance ATB All-Terrain Pedal	1	28.00	3863.85
David Smith	1	Dog Ear Aero-Flow Floor Pump	3	55.00	3863.85
David Smith	1	Glide-O-Matic Cycling Helmet	5	121.25	3863.85
David Smith	1	Ultimate Export 2G Car Rack	6	174.60	3863.85
Suzanne Viescas	2	X-Pro All Weather Tires	4	24.00	204.00
Suzanne Viescas	2	Ultimate Export 2G Car Rack	4	180.00	204.00
William Thompson	3	Trek 9000 Mountain Bike	5	1164.00	3824.29
William Thompson	3	Viscount Mountain Bike	5	615.95	3824.29

<< more rows here >>

You can see that the seven separate rows associated with order 1 all have the same OrderTotal associated with them, while the two separate rows associated with order 2 all have the same OrderTotal associated with them. (Only part of order 3 is shown, but you can see that the two rows that are shown both have the same value associated with them as well.)

Let's look at one more example of using the ROWS predicate. (Although I can't see a legitimate use for this example, hopefully, it'll give you a little more insight into how the ROWS predicate works!)

> *"List all engagements booked, showing the customer, the start date, the contract price and the sum of the current row plus the row before and after. Also, show the sum of the current row plus the row before and after partitioned by customer."*

Translation/ Clean Up	Select ~~the~~ CustFirstName || ' ' ||, CustLastName, StartDate, ContractPrice, SUM(ContractPrice) OVER order by CustLastName, CustFirstName rows between 1 preceding and 1 following ~~and~~ SUM(ContractPrice) OVER partition by CustLastName, CustFirstName order by CustLastName, CustFirstName rows between 1 preceding and 1 following from ~~the~~ Engagements ~~table~~ inner joined ~~with the~~ Customers ~~table~~ on Customers.CustomerID = Engagements.CustomerID = Orders.CustomerID

SQL	```SELECT C.CustFirstName || ' ' || C.CustLastName AS Customer,```
	 ``` E.StartDate, E.ContractPrice,```
	 ``` SUM(E.ContractPrice) OVER (```
	 ``` ORDER BY C.CustLastName, C.CustFirstName```
	 ``` ROWS BETWEEN 1 PRECEDING AND 1 FOLLOWING```
	 ```) AS SumOf3,```
	 ``` SUM(E.ContractPrice) OVER (```
	 ``` PARTITION BY C.CustLastName, C.CustFirstName```
	 ``` ORDER BY C.CustLastName, C.CustFirstName```
	 ``` ROWS BETWEEN 1 PRECEDING AND 1 FOLLOWING```
	 ```) AS PartitionedSumOf3```
	 ```FROM Engagements AS E```
	 ``` INNER JOIN Customers AS C```
	 ``` ON C.CustomerID = E.CustomerID;```

That query would lead to results like the following table. (I saved this request as CH22_Odd_Contract_Sums in the Entertainment Agency Example database.)

Customer	StartDate	ContractPrice	SumOf3	PartitionedSumOf3
Matt Berg	2017-09-02	200.00	1330.00	1330.00
Matt Berg	2017-09-12	1130.00	3180.00	3180.00
Matt Berg	2017-09-19	1850.00	5655.00	5655.00
Matt Berg	2017-10-14	2675.00	6450.00	6450.00
Matt Berg	2017-10-23	1925.00	6150.00	6150.00
Matt Berg	2017-12-31	1550.00	3795.00	3795.00
Matt Berg	2018-01-09	320.00	3540.00	3540.00

Customer	StartDate	ContractPrice	SumOf3	PartitionedSumOf3
Matt Berg	2018-02-12	1670.00	3840.00	3840.00
Matt Berg	2018-02-24	1850.00	4320.00	3520.00
Peter Brehm	2018-02-17	800.00	2940.00	1090.00
Peter Brehm	2018-01-07	290.00	1860.00	1860.00
Peter Brehm	2018-01-30	770.00	1380.00	1380.00
Peter Brehm	2018-02-27	320.00	1590.00	1590.00
Peter Brehm	2017-12-10	500.00	4620.00	4620.00
Peter Brehm	2017-10-07	3800.00	5070.00	5070.00
Peter Brehm	2017-09-18	770.00	6120.00	4570.00
Zachary Ehrlich	2017-10-03	1550.00	3690.00	2920.00
Zachary Ehrlich	2017-09-19	1370.00	4170.00	4170.00
Zachary Ehrlich	2017-10-08	1250.00	3030.00	3030.00

<< more rows here >>

The column labeled SumOf3 represents the sum of the ContractPrice for the current row, plus the ContractPrice on the previous row and the following row. Look at the first row, where it's 1330.00. There is no previous row, the ContractPrice on that row is 200.00, and the ContractPrice on the next row is 1130.00, so the sum is indeed 1330.00. For the second row, the ContractPrice on the previous row is 200.00, the ContractPrice on the current row is 1130.00, and the ContractPrice on the following row is 1850.00, so the value in the SumOf3 column is 200.00 + 1130.00 + 1850.00, or 3180.00. Look down to the tenth row (the first row for Peter Brehm). Even though it's for a different customer, there is a previous row (remember, I only specified ORDER BY, not PARTITION BY!), with a ContractPrice of 1850.00. The ContractPrice on the current row is 800.00, and on the next row it is 290.00, so the SumOf3 value for that row is 1850.00 + 800.00 + 290.00, or 2940.00.

The first eight rows are all for the same customer (Matt Berg), so there's no difference between the value in the SumOf3 and the Partitioned-SumOf3 columns. However, the ninth row is the last row for Matt, so there isn't a following row. That means that the value in PartitionedSumOf3 is simply the value of the ContractPrice on the previous row (1670.00) plus the value of the ContractPrice on the current row (1850.00), or 3520.00. Now, there's no previous row for the tenth row (the first row for Peter Brehm), so the PartitionedSumOf3 is the value of the ContractPrice for the current row (800.00) plus the value of the ContractPrice for the following row (290.00), or 1090.00.

Sample Statements

You now know the mechanics of constructing queries using window functions and have seen some of the types of requests you can answer with window functions. Let's take a look at a fairly robust set of samples, all of which use one or more window functions. These examples come from each of the sample databases, and they illustrate the use of the window functions.

> ❖ **Note** Remember in the Introduction that I warned you that results from each database system won't necessarily match the sort order you see in examples in this book unless you include an ORDER BY clause. Even when you include that specification, the system might return results in columns not included in the ORDER BY clause in a different sequence because of different optimization techniques.
>
> If you're running the examples in Microsoft SQL Server, simply selecting the rows from the view does not honor any ORDER BY clause specified in the view. You must open the design of the view and execute it from there to see the ORDER BY clause honored.
>
> Also, when you use GROUP BY, you'll often see the results returned by your database system as though the rows are sorted by the columns you specified. This happens because some optimizers first sort the data internally to make it faster to process your GROUP BY. Keep in mind that if you want a specific sort order, you must also include an ORDER BY clause.

I've also included sample result sets that would be returned by these operations and placed them immediately after the SQL syntax line. The name that appears immediately above a result set is the name I gave each query in the sample data on the companion website for this book, www.informit.com/title/9780134858333. I stored each query in the appropriate sample database (as indicated within the example), and I prefixed the names of the queries relevant to this chapter with "CH22." You can follow the instructions in the Introduction of this book to load the samples onto your computer and try them.

> ❖ **Note** Remember that all the column names and table names used in these examples are drawn from the sample database structures shown in Appendix B, "Schema for the Sample Databases." Because many of these examples use complex JOINs, your database system might choose a different way to solve these queries. For this reason, the first few rows might not exactly match the result you obtain, but the total number of rows should be the same. To simplify the process, I have combined the Translation and Clean Up steps for all the following examples.

Examples Using ROW_NUMBER

Entertainment Agency Database

"I'd like a list of all of the engagements. Show me the start date for each engagement, the name of the customer, and the entertainer. Number the engagements overall, plus number the engagements within each start date."

Translation/ Clean Up	Select ~~the~~ StartDate, CustFirstName || ' ' || CustLast-Name AS Customer, EntStartName AS Entertaine,~~the~~ ROW_NUMBER() order~~ed~~ by StartDate AS Number ~~and the~~ ROW_NUMBER() partition~~ed~~ by StartDate ~~and~~ order~~ed~~ by StartDate AS NumberByDate from ~~the~~ Engagements ~~table~~ inner join~~ed with the~~ Entertainers ~~table~~ on Entertainers.EntertainerID = Engagements.EntertainerID inner join~~ed with the~~ Customers ~~table~~ on Customers.CustomerID = Engagements.CustomerID
| SQL | ```
SELECT ROW_NUMBER() OVER (
    ORDER BY Engagements.StartDate
) AS Number,
Engagements.StartDate,
``` |
```

```
        ROW_NUMBER() OVER (
          PARTITION BY Engagements.StartDate
          ORDER BY Engagements.StartDate
        ) AS NumberByDate,
      Customers.CustFirstName || ' ' ||
        Customers.CustLastName AS Customer,
      Entertainers.EntStageName AS Entertainer
    FROM Engagements
      INNER JOIN Entertainers
        ON Entertainers.EntertainerID =
          Engagements.EntertainerID
      INNER JOIN Customers
        ON Customers.CustomerID =
          Engagements.CustomerID;
```

CH22_Engagements_Numbered (111 rows)

Number	StartDate	Number ByDate	Customer	Entertainer
1	2017-09-02	1	Matt Berg	Jim Glynn
2	2017-09-11	1	Doris Hartwig	Jazz Persuasion
3	2017-09-11	2	Mark Rosales	Country Feeling
4	2017-09-12	1	Dean McCrae	Topazz
5	2017-09-12	2	Liz Keyser	Jim Glynn
6	2017-09-12	3	Matt Berg	JV & the Deep Six
7	2017-09-16	1	Elizabeth Hallmark	Country Feeling
8	2017-09-18	1	Elizabeth Hallmark	JV & the Deep Six
9	2017-09-18	2	Peter Brehm	Modern Dance
10	2017-09-19	1	Matt Berg	Coldwater Cattle Company
11	2017-09-19	2	Zachary Ehrlich	Saturday Revue
12	2017-09-19	3	Mark Rosales	Carol Peacock Trio
13	2017-09-25	1	Doris Hartwig	Country Feeling

Number	StartDate	Number ByDate	Customer	Entertainer
14	2017-09-25	2	Liz Keyser	Caroline Coie Cuartet
15	2017-09-30	1	Deb Waldal	Saturday Revue
16	2017-09-30	2	Sarah Thompson	Jim Glynn
			<< more rows here >>	
110	2018-02-27	1	Peter Brehm	Julia Schnebly
111	2018-03-04	1	Mark Rosales	JV & the Deep Six

Recipes Database

"I'd like a numbered list of all of the recipes. Number the recipes over-all, plus number each recipe within its recipe class. Sort the lists alphabetically by recipe name within recipe class. Don't forget to include any recipe classes that don't have any recipes in them."

Translation/ Clean Up	Select ~~the~~ RecipeClassDescription, ~~the~~ RecipeTitle, ~~the~~ ROW_NUMBER() ~~ordered~~ by RecipeClassDescription, RecipeTitle AS OverallNumber ~~and the~~ ROW_NUMBER() ~~partitioned~~ by RecipeClassDescription ~~and~~ ordered by RecipeTitle AS ClassNumber from ~~the~~ Recipe_Classes ~~table~~ inner ~~joined with the~~ Recipes ~~table~~ on Recipes.RecipeClass ID = Recipe_Classes.RecipeClassID

SQL	<pre>SELECT ROW_NUMBER() OVER (
	        ORDER BY RC.RecipeClassDescription,
	                R.RecipeTitle
	    ) AS OverallNumber,
	    RC.RecipeClassDescription,
	    ROW_NUMBER() OVER (
	      PARTITION BY RC.RecipeClassDescription
	      ORDER BY R.RecipeTitle
	    ) AS NumberInClass,
	    R.RecipeTitle
	FROM Recipe_Classes AS RC
	    LEFT JOIN Recipes AS R
	        ON R.RecipeClassID = RC.RecipeClassID;</pre>

CH22_Recipe_Classes_Numbered (16 rows)

Overall Number	RecipeClass Description	Number InClass	RecipeTitle
1	Dessert	1	Coupe Colonel
2	Dessert	2	Trifle
3	Hors d'oeuvres	1	Machos Nachos
4	Hors d'oeuvres	2	Salsa Buena
5	Main course	1	Fettuccini Alfredo
6	Main course	2	Huachinango Veracruzana (Red Snapper, Veracruz style)
7	Main course	3	Irish Stew
8	Main course	4	Pollo Picoso
9	Main course	5	Roast Beef
10	Main course	6	Salmon Filets in Parchment Paper
11	Main course	7	Tourtière (French-Canadian Pork Pie)
12	Salad	1	Mike's Summer Salad
13	Soup	1	NULL
14	Starch	1	Yorkshire Pudding
15	Vegetable	1	Asparagus
16	Vegetable	2	Garlic Green Beans

Examples Using RANK, DENSE_RANK, and PERCENT_RANK

Sales Orders Database

"Rank all employees by the number of orders with which they're associated."

Translation/ Clean Up	Select ~~the~~ EmployeeID, EmpFirstName || ' ' || EmpLastName AS EmployeeName, COUNT(DISTINCT OrderNumber) AS OrdersReceived and RANK() OVER order~~ed~~ by COUNT(DISTINCT OrderNumber DESC from ~~the~~ Employees ~~table~~ inner join~~ed with the~~ Orders ~~table~~ ON Orders.EmployeeID = Employees.EmployeeID inner join~~ed with the~~ Order_Details ~~table~~ on OrderDetails.OrderNumber = Orders.OrderNumber, group~~ed~~ by EmployeeID, EmpFirstName ~~and~~ EmpLastName

SQL	`SELECT E.EmployeeID, E.EmpFirstName || ' ' ||`
	`  E.EmpLastName AS Employee,`
	`  COUNT(DISTINCT O.OrderNumber) AS OrdersReceived,`
	`  RANK() OVER (`
	`    ORDER BY COUNT(DISTINCT O.OrderNumber) DESC`
	`  ) AS Rank`
	`FROM Employees AS E`
	`  INNER JOIN Orders AS O`
	`    ON O.EmployeeID = E.EmployeeID`
	`  INNER JOIN Order_Details AS OD`
	`    ON OD.OrderNumber = O.OrderNumber`
	`GROUP BY E.EmployeeID, E.EmpFirstName,`
	`  E.EmpLastName;`

CH22_Employee_Sales_Ranked (8 rows)

EmployeeID	Employee	OrdersReceived	Rank
707	Kathryn Patterson	138	1
708	Susan McLain	129	2
702	Mary Thompson	117	3
704	Carol Viescas	117	3
705	Kirk DeGrasse	115	5
701	Ann Patterson	109	6
706	David Viescas	104	7
703	Matt Berg	104	7

If you're wondering why I included the Order_Details table in the above SQL, the answer is that I know there are some rows in the Orders table that do not have any matching rows in the Order_Details table. I don't want to include orders that have no items specified, so including the Order_Details in an INNER JOIN with the Orders table eliminates those "empty" orders.

School Scheduling Database

"Rank the staff by how long they've been with us as of January 1, 2018. I don't want to see any gaps in the rank numbers."

(Remember that I showed you how to calculate the years of service in CH19_Length_Of_Service)

Translation/ Clean Up	Select ~~the~~ StaffID, StfFirstName || ' ' || StfLastName AS StaffName, LengthOfService, ~~and~~ DENSE_ RANK() OVER ~~ordered~~ by LengthOfService DESC from ~~table~~ Staff
SQL	```SELECT StaffID, StfFirstName || ' ' || StfLastname AS StaffName, YEAR(CAST('2018-01-01' As Date)) - YEAR(DateHired) - (CASE WHEN Month(DateHired) < 10 THEN 0 WHEN Month(DateHired) > 10 THEN 1 WHEN Day(DateHired) > 1 THEN 1 ELSE 0 END) AS LengthOfService, DENSE_RANK() OVER (ORDER BY YEAR (CAST('2018-01-01' As Date)) - YEAR(DateHired) - (CASE WHEN Month(DateHired) < 10 THEN 0 WHEN Month(DateHired) > 10 THEN 1 WHEN Day(DateHired) > 1 THEN 1 ELSE 0 END) DESC) AS Rank FROM Staff;```

CH22_Staff_Service_Ranked (27 rows)

StaffID	StaffName	LengthOfService	Rank
98036	Sam Abolrous	27	1
98062	Caroline Coie	27	1
98025	Carol Viescas	26	2
98028	Alaina Hallmark	26	2
98010	Jeffrey Smith	26	2
98011	Ann Patterson	26	2
98007	Gary Hallmark	25	3
98020	Jim Glynn	25	3
98043	Kathryn Patterson	25	3
98052	Katherine Ehrlich	25	3
98013	Deb Waldal	24	4
98014	Peter Brehm	24	4
98005	Suzanne Viescas	24	4
98048	Joyce Bonnicksen	24	4
98059	Maria Patterson	24	4
98040	Jim Wilson	23	5
98030	Liz Keyser	22	6
98063	Kirk DeGrasse	22	6
98064	Luke Patterson	21	7
98055	Alastair Black	21	7
98057	Joe Rosales III	21	7
98012	Robert Brown	21	7
98021	Tim Smith	21	7
98019	Mariya Sergienko	20	8
98045	Michael Hernandez	20	8
98053	Caleb Viescas	18	9
98042	David Smith	18	9

Examples Using NTILE

Bowling League Database

"Rank all the teams from best to worst based on the average handicap score of all the players. Arrange the teams into four quartiles."

Translation/ Clean Up	Select ~~the~~ TeamName, AVG(HandiCapScore) ~~and~~ NTILE(4) OVER ordered by AVG(HandiCapScore) DESC from ~~the~~ Teams ~~table~~ inner join~~ed with the~~ Bowlers ~~table~~ ON Bowlers.TeamID = Teams.TeamID inner join~~ed with the~~ Bowler_ Scores ~~table~~ on BowlerScores.BowlerID = Bowlers.BowerID, group~~ed~~ by TeamName

SQL	`SELECT Teams.TeamName,`
	`    ROUND(AVG(Bowler_Scores.HandiCapScore), 0)`
	`        AS AvgTeamHandicap,`
	`    NTILE(4) OVER (`
	`        ORDER BY ROUND(AVG(Bowler_Scores.HandiCap-`
	`                Score), 0)`
	`        DESC) AS Quartile`
	`FROM Teams INNER JOIN Bowlers`
	`    ON Bowlers.TeamID = Teams.TeamID`
	`    INNER JOIN Bowler_Scores`
	`        ON Bowler_Scores.BowlerID = Bowlers.BowlerID`
	`    GROUP BY Teams.TeamName;`

CH22_Teams_In_Quartiles (8 rows)

TeamName	AvgTeamHandicap	Quartile
Marlins	196	1
Barracudas	196	1
Manatees	196	2
Swordfish	195	2
Orcas	195	3
Dolphins	195	3
Sharks	195	4
Terrapins	195	4

I bet you're wondering what's going on here. Because there's so little difference between the team handicaps, the database system sorts the teams by average handicap and then applies the value 1 to the first two rows, 2 to the second two rows, 3 to the fifth and sixth rows, and 4 to the remaining ones. In fact, the sorting within an equal is arbitrary and can vary from system to system. If you run both the Microsoft SQL Server and PostgreSQL examples, you'll find that the choice of "top two" is entirely different.

Entertainment Agency Database

"Rank all the entertainers based on the number of engagements booked for each. Arrange the entertainers into three groups. Remember to include any entertainers who haven't been booked for any engagements."

Translation/ Clean Up	Select ~~the~~ EntStageName, COUNT(Engagements.EntertainerID), ~~and~~ NTILE(3) OVER ordered by COUNT(Engagements.EntertainerID) DESC from ~~the~~ Entertainers ~~table~~ left join ~~with the~~ Engagements ~~table~~ ON Engagements.EntertainerID = Entertainers.EntertainerID, grouped by EntStageName
SQL	```SELECT Entertainers.EntStageName AS Entertainer,` ` COUNT(Engagements.EntertainerID) AS Gigs,` ` NTILE(3) OVER (` ` ORDER BY COUNT(Engagements.EntertainerID) DESC` `) AS [Group]` `FROM Entertainers` ` LEFT JOIN Engagements` ` ON Engagements.EntertainerID = Entertainers.` ` EntertainerID` `GROUP BY Entertainers.EntStageName;```

CH22_Entertainer_3_Groups (13 rows)

Entertainer	Gigs	Group
Country Feeling	15	1
Carol Peacock Trio	11	1
Caroline Coie Cuartet	11	1
JV & the Deep Six	10	1

Entertainer	Gigs	Group
Modern Dance	10	1
Saturday Revue	9	2
Jim Glynn	9	2
Julia Schnebly	8	2
Coldwater Cattle Company	8	2
Jazz Persuasion	7	3
Topazz	7	3
Susan McLain	6	3
Katherine Ehrlich	0	3

Examples Using Aggregate Functions

Bowling League Database

"For each team, show me the details of all of the games bowled by the team captains. Include the date and location for each tournament, their handicap score, whether or not they won the game. Include counts for how many games they won and their average handicap score."

Translation/ Clean Up	Select ~~the~~ TeamName, BowlerFirstName || ' ' || BowlerLastName AS Captain, TourneyDate, TourneyLocation, HandiCapScore, CASE WonGame WHEN 1 THEN 'Won' ELSE 'Lost' END As WonGame, SUM(CAST(WonGame AS INT) OVER partition~~ed by~~ TeamName AS TotalWindws, AVG(HandiCapScore) OVER (partition~~ed by~~ TeamName) AS AvgHandicap from ~~table~~ Teams inner join~~ed with the~~ Bowlers ~~table~~ ON Bowler.BowlerID = Teams.CaptainID inner join~~ed with the~~ Bowler_Scores ~~table~~ on Bowler_Scores.BowlerID = Teams.CaptainID inner join~~ed with the~~ Match_Games ~~table~~ on MatchGames.MatchID = Bowler_Scores.MatchID and MatchGames.GameNumber = Bowler_Scores.GameNumber inner join~~ed with the~~ Tourney_Matches ~~table~~ on Tourney_Matches.MatchID = Match_Games.MatchID inner join~~ed with the~~ Tournaments ~~table~~ on Tournaments.TourneyID = Tourney_Matches.TourneyID

SQL	```SELECT Teams.TeamName,```
	``` B.BowlerFirstName || ' ' || B.BowlerLastName```
	``` AS Captain,```
	``` T.TourneyDate, T.TourneyLocation,```
	``` BS.HandiCapScore,```
	``` CASE BS.WonGame```
	``` WHEN 1 THEN 'Won'```
	``` ELSE 'Lost'```
	``` END AS WonGame,```
	``` SUM(CAST(BS.WonGame AS INT)) OVER (```
	``` PARTITION BY Teams.TeamName```
	```) AS TotalWins,```
	``` AVG(BS.HandiCapScore) OVER (```
	``` PARTITION BY Teams.TeamName```
	```) AS AvgHandicap```
	``` FROM Teams```
	``` INNER JOIN Bowlers AS B```
	``` ON B.BowlerID = Teams.CaptainID```
	``` INNER JOIN Bowler_Scores AS BS```
	``` ON BS.BowlerID = B.BowlerID```
	``` INNER JOIN Match_Games AS MG```
	``` ON MG.MatchID = BS.MatchID```
	``` AND MG.GameNumber = BS.GameNumber```
	``` INNER JOIN Tourney_Matches AS TM```
	``` ON TM.MatchID = MG.MatchID```
	``` INNER JOIN Tournaments AS T```
	``` ON T.TourneyID = TM.TourneyID;```

CH22_Comparing_Team_Captains (420 rows)

TeamName	Captain	Tourney Date	Tourney Location	HandiCap Score	Won Game	Total Wins	Avg Handicap
Barracudas	Richard Sheskey	2017-09-04	Red Rooster Lanes	195	Won	25	194
Barracudas	Richard Sheskey	2017-09-04	Red Rooster Lanes	191	Lost	25	194
Barracudas	Richard Sheskey	2017-09-04	Red Rooster Lanes	195	Won	25	194

TeamName	Captain	Tourney Date	Tourney Location	HandiCap Score	Won Game	Total Wins	Avg Handicap
Barracudas	Richard Sheskey	2017-09-11	Thunderbird Lanes	201	Won	25	194
Barracudas	Richard Sheskey	2017-09-11	Thunderbird Lanes	201	Won	25	194
Barracudas	Richard Sheskey	2017-09-11	Thunderbird Lanes	188	Won	25	194
Barracudas	Richard Sheskey	2017-09-18	Bolero Lanes	196	Won	25	194
Barracudas	Richard Sheskey	2017-09-18	Bolero Lanes	189	Lost	25	194
Barracudas	Richard Sheskey	2017-09-18	Bolero Lanes	193	Won	25	194
Barracudas	Richard Sheskey	2017-09-25	Imperial Lanes	190	Lost	25	194
Barracudas	Richard Sheskey	2017-09-25	Imperial Lanes	188	Lost	25	194
Barracudas	Richard Sheskey	2017-09-25	Imperial Lanes	198	Won	25	194
Barracudas	Richard Sheskey	2017-10-02	Sports World Lanes	195	Lost	25	194
Barracudas	Richard Sheskey	2017-10-02	Sports World Lanes	189	Won	25	194
Barracudas	Richard Sheskey	2017-10-02	Sports World Lanes	190	Lost	25	194
Barracudas	Richard Sheskey	2017-10-09	Totem Lanes	191	Lost	25	194
Barracudas	Richard Sheskey	2017-10-09	Totem Lanes	200	Won	25	194
Barracudas	Richard Sheskey	2017-10-09	Totem Lanes	191	Lost	25	194
Barracudas	Richard Sheskey	2017-10-16	Acapulco Lanes	190	Won	25	194
Barracudas	Richard Sheskey	2017-10-16	Acapulco Lanes	200	Won	25	194
Barracudas	Richard Sheskey	2017-10-16	Acapulco Lanes	187	Lost	25	194

<< *more rows here* >>

> ❖ **Note** I could have just as easily partitioned by BowlerFirstName, BowlerLastName rather than by TeamName, but I feel it's usually a good idea not to group (or partition) by people names, since they're often not unique. Other possibilities would have been BowlerID or CaptainID.

Sales Orders Database

I'll confess that this is yet another somewhat artificial example of using ROWS to try and give you another example of how it works.

> *"For each order, give me a list of the customer, the product, and the quantity ordered. Give me the total quantity of products for each order. As well, for every group of three products on the invoice, show me their total and the highest and lowest value."*

Translation/ Clean Up	Select ~~the~~ CustFirstName || ' ' || CustLastName, Order-Number, ProductName, QuantityOrders, SUM(Quantity-Ordered) OVER (partitioned by OrderNumber) AS TotalQuantity, SUM(QuantityOrdered) OVER (partitioned by OrderNumber ordered by OrderNumber ROWS BETWEEN 1 PRECEDING AND 1 FOLLOWING) AS Quantity3, MIN(Quan-tityOrdered) OVER (partitioned by OrderNumber ordered by OrderNumber ROWS BETWEEN 1 PRECEDING AND 1 FOLLOWING) AS Minimum3, MAX(QuantityOrdered) OVER (partitioned by OrderNumber ordered by OrderNum-ber ROWS BETWEEN 1 PRECEDING AND 1 FOLLOWING) AS Maximum3 from ~~the~~ Orders ~~table~~ inner joined ~~with the~~ Order_Details ~~table~~ ON Order_Details.OrderNumber = Orders.OrderNumber inner joined ~~with the~~ Customers ~~table~~ on Customers.CustomerID = Orders.CustomerID inner joined ~~with the~~ Products ~~table~~ on Products.ProductNumber = Order_Details.ProductNumber
SQL	```SELECT O.OrderNumber,```

```
SELECT O.OrderNumber,

    C.CustFirstName || ' ' || C.CustLastName AS
Customer,

    O.OrderNumber,

    P.ProductName,

    OD.QuantityOrdered,

    SUM(OD.QuantityOrdered) OVER (

        PARTITION BY O.OrderNumber

    ) AS TotalQuantity,
```

```
        SUM(OD.QuantityOrdered) OVER (
          PARTITION BY O.OrderNumber
          ORDER BY O.OrderNumber
          ROWS BETWEEN 1 PRECEDING AND 1 FOLLOWING
        ) AS Quantity3,
        MIN(OD.QuantityOrdered) OVER (
          PARTITION BY O.OrderNumber
          ORDER BY O.OrderNumber
          ROWS BETWEEN 1 PRECEDING AND 1 FOLLOWING
        ) AS Minimum3,
        MAX(OD.QuantityOrdered) OVER (
          PARTITION BY O.OrderNumber
          ORDER BY O.OrderNumber
          ROWS BETWEEN 1 PRECEDING AND 1 FOLLOWING
        ) AS Maximum3
      FROM Orders AS O
        INNER JOIN Order_Details AS OD
          ON OD.OrderNumber = O.OrderNumber
        INNER JOIN Customers AS C
          ON C.CustomerID = O.CustomerID
        INNER JOIN Products AS P
          ON P.ProductNumber  = OD.ProductNumber;
```

CH22_Orders_Min_Max (3973 rows)

Order Number	Customer	Product Name	Quantity Ordered	Total Quantity	Quantity3	Minimum3	Maximum3
1	David Smith	Trek 9000 Mountain Bike	2	24	5	2	3
1	David Smith	Viscount Mountain Bike	3	24	9	2	4
1	David Smith	GT RTS-2 Mountain Bike	4	24	8	1	4
1	David Smith	ProFormance ATB All-Terrain Pedal	1	24	8	1	4

Order Number	Customer	Product Name	Quantity Ordered	Total Quantity	Quantity3	Minimum3	Maximum3
1	David Smith	Dog Ear Aero-Flow Floor Pump	3	24	9	1	5
1	David Smith	Glide-O-Matic Cycling Helmet	5	24	14	3	6
1	David Smith	Ultimate Export 2G Car Rack	6	24	11	5	6
2	Suzanne Viescas	X-Pro All Weather Tires	4	8	8	4	4
2	Suzanne Viescas	Ultimate Export 2G Car Rack	4	8	8	4	4
3	William Thompson	Trek 9000 Mountain Bike	5	28	10	5	5
3	William Thompson	Viscount Mountain Bike	5	28	11	1	5
3	William Thompson	GT RTS-2 Mountain Bike	1	28	8	1	5
3	William Thompson	ProFormance ATB All-Terrain Pedal	2	28	6	1	3
3	William Thompson	Dog Ear Aero-Flow Floor Pump	3	28	8	2	3
3	William Thompson	Glide-O-Matic Cycling Helmet	3	28	11	3	5
3	William Thompson	True Grip Competition Gloves	5	28	12	3	5
3	William Thompson	Cosmic Elite Road Warrior Wheels	4	28	9	4	5
4	Andrew Cencini	Trek 9000 Mountain Bike	4	19	7	3	4

<< more rows here >>

The QuantityOrdered column is hopefully straightforward to understand. The first order (number 1, ordered by David Smith) consisted of seven products. David ordered 2 Trek 9000 Mountain Bikes, 3 Viscount Mountain Bikes, 4 GT RTS-2 Mountain Bikes, 1 ProFormance ATB All-Terrain Pedal, 3 Dog Ear Aero-Flow Floor Pumps, 5 Glide-O-Matic Cycling Helmets, and 6 Ultimate Export 2G Car Racks, for a total of 24 items. The second order (number 2, ordered by Suzanne Viescas) consisted of 4 X-Pro All Weather Tires and 4 Ultimate Export 2G Car Racks for a total of 8 items. That's pretty standard.

The other three columns are the off-beat ones. I asked for the products on each invoice to be divided into groups of three, and for the sum, the minimum and the maximum of each of those groups. Remember how ROWS BETWEEN 1 PRECEDING AND 1 FOLLOWING works. Because I'm partitioning on Order, there is no preceding row for the first product on the first order (Trek 9000 Mountain Bike), so only the current row (with a quantity of 2) and the following row (with a quantity of 3) are considered. The total of those quantities is 5, the minimum is 2, and the maximum is 3. The next row (Viscount Mountain Bike) does have a preceding row, so there are three quantities to be considered: 2 (the preceding row), 3 (the current row), and 4 (the following row). The sum of those quantities is 9, the minimum is 2, and the maximum is 4. Skip down to the seventh row (Ultimate Export 2G Car Rack). Again, because I'm partitioning on Order, there is no following row, so only the preceding row (with a quantity of 5) and the current row (with a quantity of 6) are considered. The total of those two quantities is 11, the minimum is 5, and the maximum is 6.

Because the second order consists of only two rows, those two rows (both with quantities of 4) are the only ones considered in both cases. The sum of the quantities of those two rows is 8, the minimum is 4, and the maximum is 4.

For the third order, there is no preceding row for the Trek 9000 Mountain Bike row, so only it and the following Viscount Mountain Bike row are considered for the first calculation. Similarly, there is no following row for the Cosmic Elite Road Warrior Wheels row, so only it and the preceding True Grip Competition Gloves row are considered for the last calculation.

School Scheduling Database

"For each subject, give me the highest mark that's been received. Also, show me the highest mark that's been received for each category of subjects, as well as the highest mark that's been received overall."

Translation/ Clean Up	Select ~~the~~ CategoryID, SubjectCode, SubjectName, MAX(Grade) OVER (partioned by SubjectID) AS SubjectMax, MAX(Grade) OVER (partitioned by CategoryID) AS CategoryMax, MAX(Grade) OVER() AS OverallMax from ~~the~~ Subjects ~~table~~ inner joined ~~with the~~ Classes ~~table~~ ON Classes.ClassID = Subjects.ClassID inner joined ~~with the~~ Student_Schedules ~~table~~ on Student_Schedules.ClassID = Classes.ClassID where ClassStatus = 2

SQL	<pre>SELECT DISTINCT Subjects.CategoryID,
	    Subjects.SubjectCode, Subjects.SubjectName,
	    MAX(Student_Schedules.Grade) OVER (
	       PARTITION BY Subjects.SubjectID
	    ) AS SubjectMax,
	    MAX(Student_Schedules.Grade) OVER (
	       PARTITION BY Subjects.CategoryID
	    ) AS CategoryMax,
	    MAX(Student_Schedules.Grade) OVER (
	    ) AS OverallMax
	FROM Subjects
	  INNER JOIN Classes
	    ON Classes.SubjectID = Subjects.SubjectID
	  INNER JOIN Student_Schedules
	    ON Student_Schedules.ClassID = Classes.ClassID
	WHERE Student_Schedules.ClassStatus = 2;</pre>

CH22_Top_Marks (14 rows)

CategoryID	SubjectCode	SubjectName	Subject Max	Category Max	Overall Max
ACC	ACC 210	Financial Accounting Fundamentals I	91.12	91.12	99.83
ART	ART 100	Introduction to Art	99.83	99.83	99.83

CategoryID	SubjectCode	SubjectName	Subject Max	Category Max	Overall Max
ART	ART 210	Computer Art	87.65	99.83	99.83
ART	ART 251	Art History	97.81	99.83	99.83
BIO	BIO 101	General Biology	94.54	94.54	99.83
CHE	CHE 139	Fundamentals of Chemistry	98.31	98.31	99.83
CIS	CIS 101	Microcomputer Applications	98.01	98.01	99.83
ENG	ENG 101	Composition - Fundamentals	98.07	98.07	99.83
ENG	ENG 102	Composition - Intermediate	88.91	98.07	99.83
HIS	HIS 111	U.S. History to 1877	87.14	87.14	99.83
MAT	MAT 080	Preparatory Mathematics	93.19	94.33	99.83
MAT	MAT 097	Elementary Algebra	94.33	94.33	99.83
MUS	MUS 100	Music in the Western World	97.84	97.84	99.83
MUS	MUS 101	First Year Theory and Ear Training	86.57	97.84	99.83

Summary

I began the chapter by describing to you why you might want to aggregate data differently from how you were shown in previous chapters and included an example to show one possibility.

I then explored ways to use "windows" into your data and talked about how the OVER() clause is the key to using window functions, and I explained the difference between GROUP BY and OVER().

I showed you how PARTITION BY, ORDER BY, and ROWS or RANGE influence your results.

- The PARTITION BY predicate divides the result set from the query into data subsets.

- The ORDER BY predicate controls the order that the rows are evaluated.

- The ROWS or RANGE predicate determines the subset of rows within the partition that are to be applied (and can only be used with aggregate functions).

I went on to show that window functions include all of the aggregate functions I'd already shown you, plus several others: ROW_NUMBER, RANK, DENSE_RANK, PERCENT_RANK and NTILE. Then I described the use of both the PARTITION BY and ORDER BY predicates with the OVER() clause. Finally, I gave several examples of how to use window functions to solve real-world problems.

The following section presents some requests that you can work out on your own.

Problems for You to Solve

Bowling League Database

1. *"Divide the teams into quartiles based on the best raw score bowled by any member of the team."*

   You can find my solution in CH22_Team_Quartiles_Best_Raw-Score (8 rows).

2. *"Give me a list of all of the bowlers in the league. Number the bowlers overall, plus number them within their teams, sorting their names by LastName then FirstName."*

   You can find my solution in CH22_Bowler_Numbers (32 rows).

3. *"Rank all of the bowlers in the league by their average handicap score. Show me the "standard" ranking, but also show me the ranking with no gaps."*

   You can find my solution in CH22_Bowler_Ranks (32 rows).

Entertainment Agency Database

1. *"Rank all the agents based on the total dollars associated with the engagements that they've booked. Make sure to include any agents that haven't booked any acts."*

   You can find my solution in CH22_Agent_Ranks (9 rows).

2. *"Give me a list of all of the engagements our entertainers are booked for. Show me the entertainer's stage name, the customer's name, and the start date for each engagements, as well as the total number of engagements booked for each entertainer."*

   You can find my solution in CH22_Entertainer_Engagements (111 rows).

3. *"Give me a list of all of the Entertainers and their members. Number each member within a group."*

   You can find my solution in CH22_Entertainer_Lists (40 rows).

Recipes Database

1. *"Give me a list of all of the recipes I've got. For each recipe, I want to see all of the ingredients in the recipe, plus a count of how many different ingredients there are."*

   You can find my solution in CH22_Recipe_Ingredient_Counts (88 rows).

2. *"I'd like a list of all the different ingredients, with each recipe that contains that ingredient. While you're at it, give me a count of how many recipes there are that use each ingredient."*

   You can find my solution in CH22_Ingredient_Recipe_Counts (88 rows).

3. *"I want a numbered list of all of the ingredients. Number the ingredients overall, plus number each ingredient within its ingredient class. Sort the lists alphabetically by ingredient within ingredient class. Don't forget to include any ingredient classes that don't have any ingredients in them."*

   You can find my solution in CH22_Ingredients_By_Ingredient_Class (83 rows, including four classes with no ingredients in them).

Sales Orders Database

1. *"Show totals for each invoice, ranking them from highest purchase value to lowest."*

   You can find my solution in CH22_Order_Totals_RankedBy-InvoiceTotal (933 rows).

2. *"Produce a list of each category and the total purchase price of all products in each category. Include a column showing the total purchase price regardless of category as well."*

    You can find my solution in CH22_Sales_Totals (6 rows).

    How would you write this differently if you knew there were categories that had no sales in them? (The sample database does have sales in each category, but you can always add a new category with no sales to see whether your query works!) My solution is CH22_Sales_Totals_Handle_Nulls. If you didn't add a new category, it would return the same as CH22_Sales_Totals (6 rows). If you did add a new category, it would return seven rows.

3. *"Rank each customer by the number of orders which they've placed. Be sure to include customers that haven't placed any orders yet."*

    You can find my solution in CH22_Customer_Order_Counts_Ranked (28 rows, including Jeffrey Tirekicker having placed no orders).

School Scheduling Database

1. *"Rank the students in terms of the number of classes they've completed."*

    You can find my solution in CH22_Student_Class_Totals_Rank (18 rows). (Pretty homogenous class, isn't it?)

2. *"Rank the faculty in terms of the number of classes they're teaching."*

    You can find my solution in CH22_Staff_Class_Totals_Rank (22 rows).

3. *"Arrange the students into 3 groups depending on their average grade for each of the classes they've completed."*

    You can find my solution in CH22_Student_AverageGrade_Groups (18 rows).

4. *"For each student, give me a list of each course he or she has completed and the mark he or she got in that course. Show me their overall average for all the completed courses, plus, for every group of three courses, show me their average and the highest and lowest marks of the three highest marks that have been received."*

    You can find my solution in CH22_Marks_Min_Max (68 rows).

In Closing

"That is what learning is. You suddenly understand something you've understood all your life, but in a new way."

—Doris Lessing

You now have all the tools you need to query or change data in a database successfully. You've learned how to create both simple and complex SELECT statements and how to work with various types of data. You've also learned how to filter data with search conditions, work with multiple tables using JOINs, and produce statistical information by grouping data. You learned how to update, add, and delete data in your tables. And finally, you learned to "think out of the box" to build solutions to "NOT" and "AND" problems, use condition testing, work with unlinked tables, perform complex grouping, and look at "windows" into your data.

As with any new endeavor, there's always more to learn. Your next task is to take the techniques you've learned in this book and apply them within your database system. Be sure to refer to your database system's documentation to determine whether there are any differences between standard SQL syntax and the SQL syntax your database uses. If your database allows you to create queries using a graphical interface, you'll probably find that the interface now makes more sense and is much easier to use.

Also remember that I focused only on the data manipulation portion of SQL—there are still many parts to SQL that you can delve into should you be so inspired. For example, you could learn how to create data structures; incorporate several tables and commands into a single view, function, or stored procedure; or embed SQL statements within an application program. If you want to learn more about SQL, I suggest you start with any of the books I've listed in Appendix D, "Suggested Reading."

I hope you've enjoyed reading this book as much as I've enjoyed writing it. I know that books on this subject tend to be rather dry, so I decided to have a little fun and inject some humor wherever I could. There's absolutely no reason why learning should be boring and tedious. On the contrary, you should look forward to learning something new each day.

Writing a book is always a humbling experience. It makes you realize just how much more there is to learn about the subject at hand. And as you work through the writing process, it is inevitable that you'll see things from a fresh perspective and in a different light. I found out just how much Doris Lessing's statement rings true.

I hope you will, too.

Part VII
Appendices

A

SQL Standard Diagrams

Here are the complete diagrams for all the SQL grammar and syntax we've covered throughout the book.

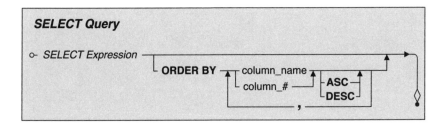

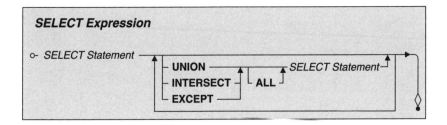

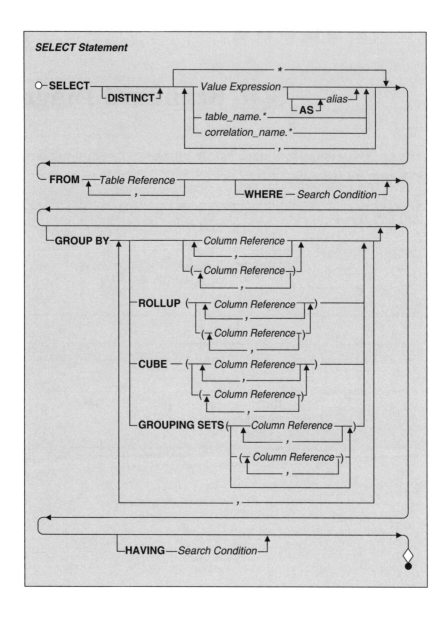

Column Reference

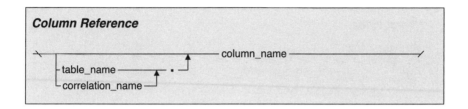

Value Expression

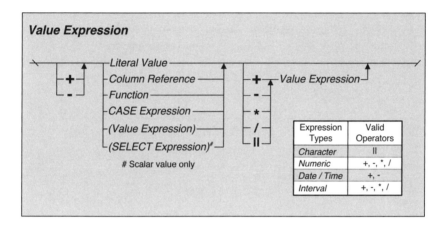

Scalar value only

Expression Types	Valid Operators
Character	||
Numeric	+, -, *, /
Date / Time	+, -
Interval	+, -, *, /

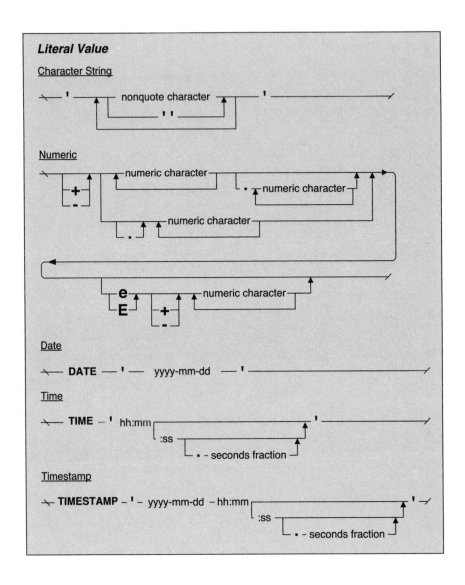

Literal Value (cont.)

Interval

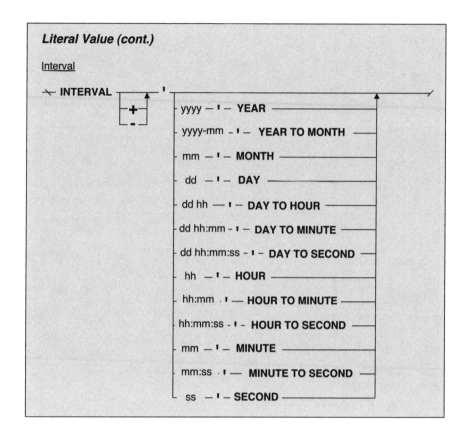

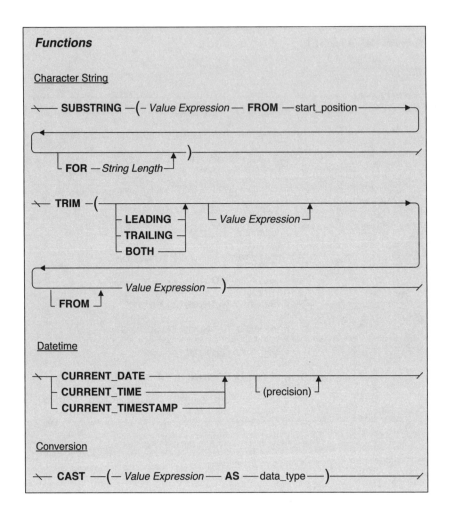

Functions

<u>Character String</u>

SUBSTRING —(— *Value Expression* — **FROM** —start_position

FOR —*String Length*—)

TRIM —(
— **LEADING** —
— **TRAILING** —
— **BOTH** —
— *Value Expression*—

— *Value Expression* —)
FROM

<u>Datetime</u>

— **CURRENT_DATE**
— **CURRENT_TIME**
— **CURRENT_TIMESTAMP**
— (precision)

<u>Conversion</u>

— **CAST** —(— *Value Expression* — **AS** — data_type —)

Functions (cont.)

Set (*Aggregate Functions*)

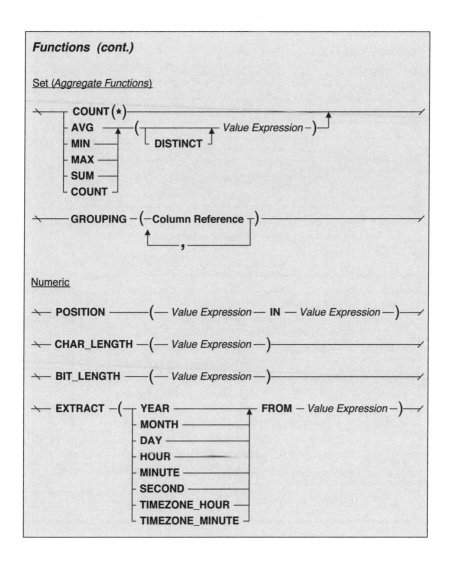

Numeric

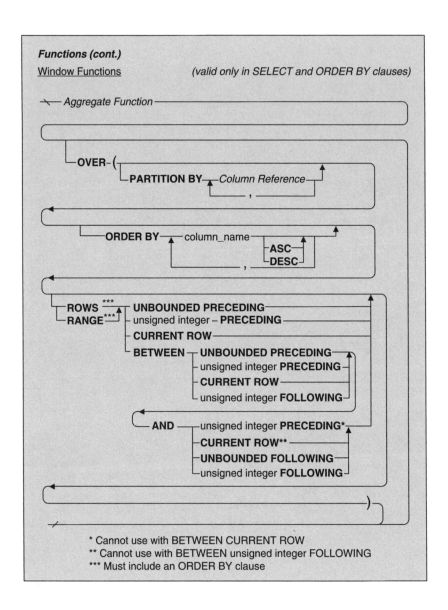

Functions (cont.)

Window Functions   *(valid only in SELECT and ORDER BY clauses)*

Aggregate Function

OVER (

  PARTITION BY — *Column Reference*

  ,

ORDER BY — column_name

  ASC
  DESC

  ,

ROWS ***
RANGE ***

UNBOUNDED PRECEDING
unsigned integer – **PRECEDING**
CURRENT ROW
BETWEEN — **UNBOUNDED PRECEDING**
  unsigned integer **PRECEDING**
  CURRENT ROW
  unsigned integer **FOLLOWING**

AND — unsigned integer **PRECEDING***
  CURRENT ROW**
  UNBOUNDED FOLLOWING
  unsigned integer **FOLLOWING**

)

* Cannot use with BETWEEN CURRENT ROW
** Cannot use with BETWEEN unsigned integer FOLLOWING
*** Must include an ORDER BY clause

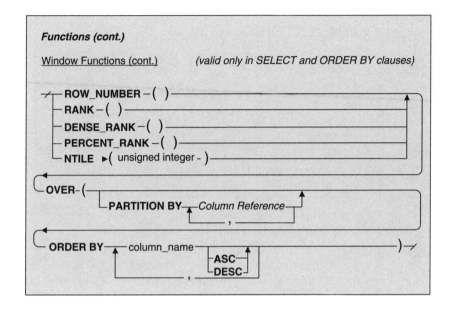

Functions (cont.)

<u>Window Functions (cont.)</u>   *(valid only in SELECT and ORDER BY clauses)*

- **ROW_NUMBER** – ( )
- **RANK** – ( )
- **DENSE_RANK** – ( )
- **PERCENT_RANK** – ( )
- **NTILE** ►(unsigned integer -)

OVER–(
  └**PARTITION BY**─Column Reference
                ,

ORDER BY──column_name
                       ┌**ASC**┐
              , ──────└**DESC**┘)

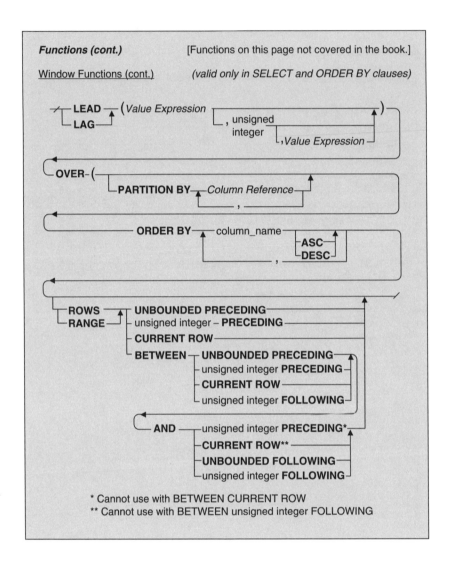

Functions (cont.)   [Functions on this page not covered in the book.]

<u>Window Functions (cont.)</u>   *(valid only in SELECT and ORDER BY clauses)*

LEAD / **LAG** (*Value Expression* , unsigned integer , *Value Expression*)

OVER– (**PARTITION BY** *Column Reference* ,)

ORDER BY column_name **ASC** **DESC** ,

ROWS / **RANGE**
- **UNBOUNDED PRECEDING**
- unsigned integer – **PRECEDING**
- **CURRENT ROW**
- **BETWEEN**
  - **UNBOUNDED PRECEDING**
  - unsigned integer **PRECEDING**
  - **CURRENT ROW**
  - unsigned integer **FOLLOWING**

AND
- unsigned integer **PRECEDING***
- **CURRENT ROW****
- **UNBOUNDED FOLLOWING**
- unsigned integer **FOLLOWING**

* Cannot use with BETWEEN CURRENT ROW
** Cannot use with BETWEEN unsigned integer FOLLOWING

Functions (cont.)   [Functions on this page not covered in the book.]

<u>Window Functions (cont.)</u>   *(valid only in SELECT and ORDER BY clauses)*

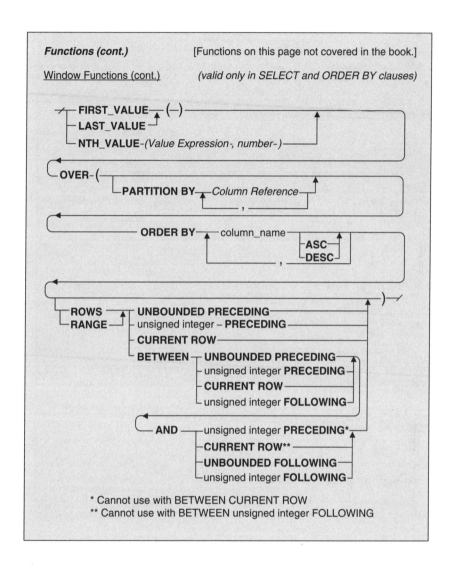

* Cannot use with BETWEEN CURRENT ROW
** Cannot use with BETWEEN unsigned integer FOLLOWING

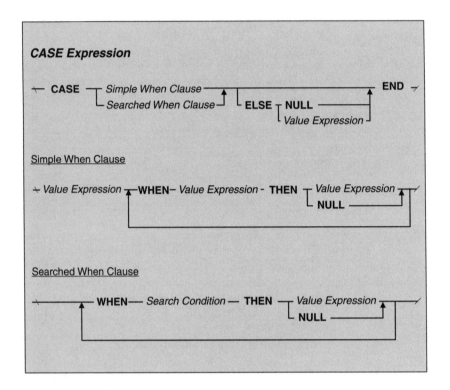

CASE Expression

CASE ─┬─ Simple When Clause ──┬─────────────────────── END
      └─ Searched When Clause ─┘ └─ ELSE ─┬─ NULL ──────┤
                                           └─ Value Expression ─┘

Simple When Clause

Value Expression ─┬─ WHEN ─ Value Expression ─ THEN ─┬─ Value Expression ─┬─
                                                      └─ NULL ─────────────┘

Searched When Clause

─┬───── WHEN ── Search Condition ── THEN ─┬─ Value Expression ─┬──
                                          └─ NULL ─────────────┘

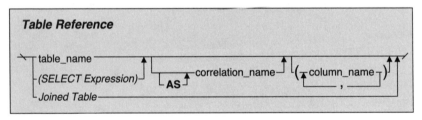

Table Reference

─┬─ table_name ───────────┬─────────────────────┬─────────────────────
 ├─ (SELECT Expression) ─┘ └─ AS ─┬─ correlation_name ─┘ (─┬─ column_name ─┬─)
 └─ Joined Table ─── , ──────

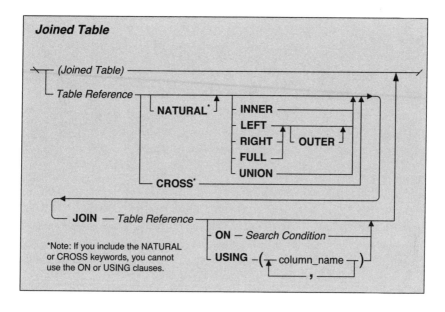

Joined Table

*Note: If you include the NATURAL or CROSS keywords, you cannot use the ON or USING clauses.

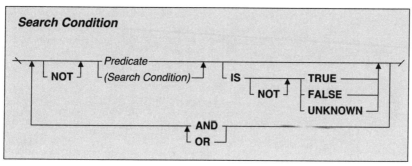

Search Condition

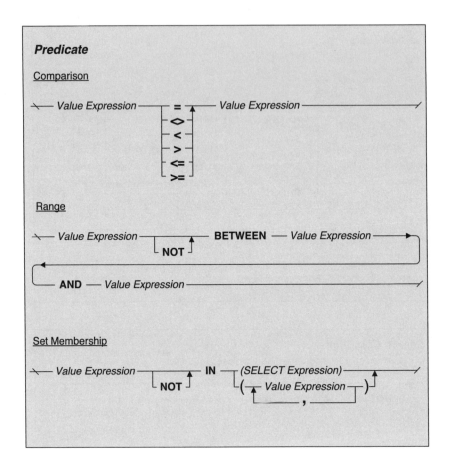

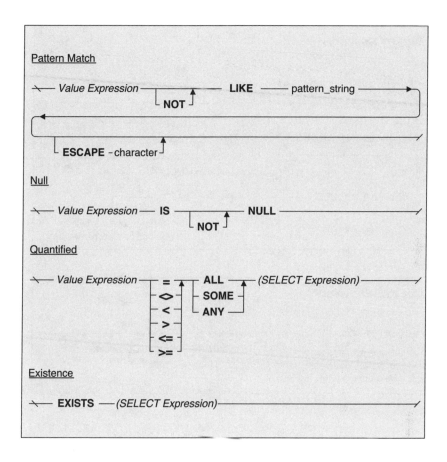

Pattern Match

Null

Quantified

Existence

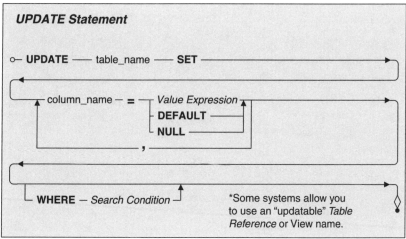

UPDATE Statement

*Some systems allow you to use an "updatable" Table Reference or View name.

INSERT Statement

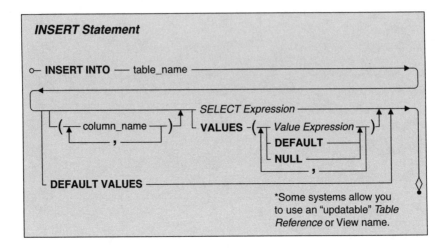

*Some systems allow you to use an "updatable" *Table Reference* or View name.

DELETE Statement

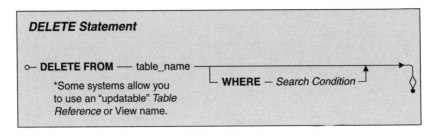

*Some systems allow you to use an "updatable" *Table Reference* or View name.

B

Schema for the Sample Databases

Sales Orders Example Database

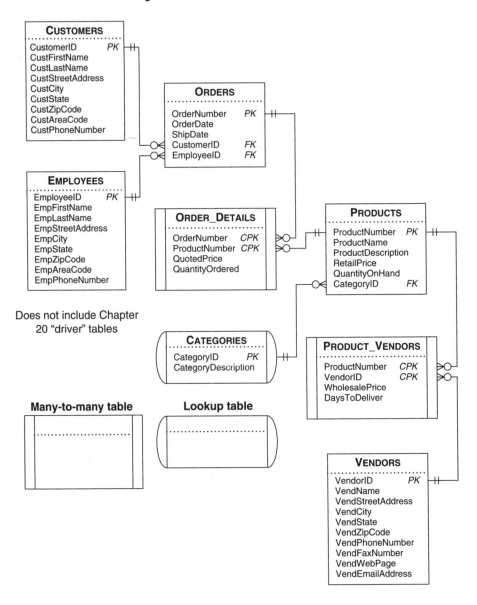

Sales Orders Modify Database

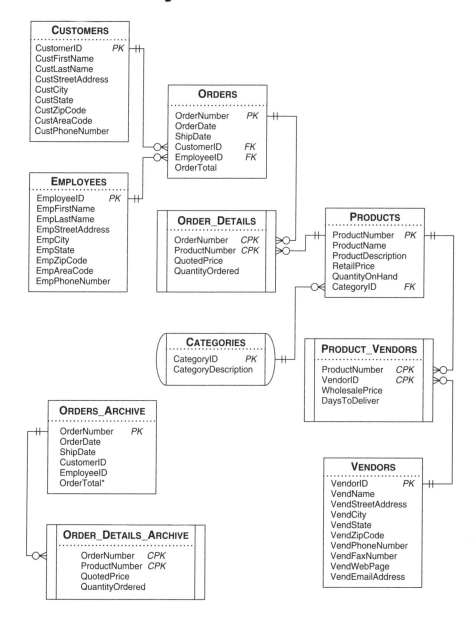

Entertainment Agency Example Database

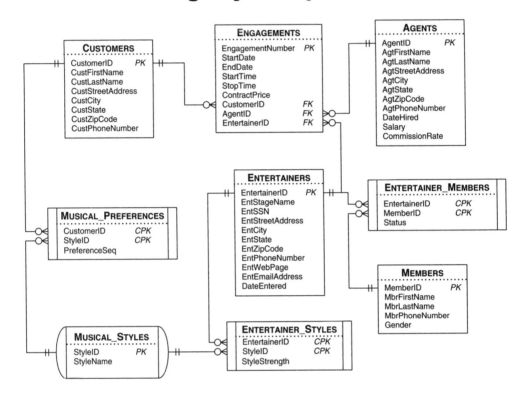

Does not include Chapter
20 "driver" tables

Entertainment Agency Modify Database

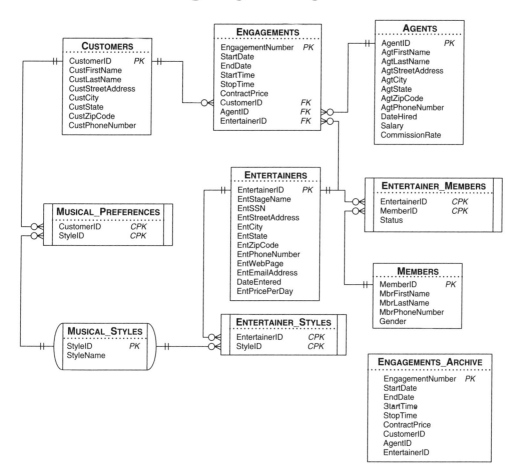

School Scheduling Example Database

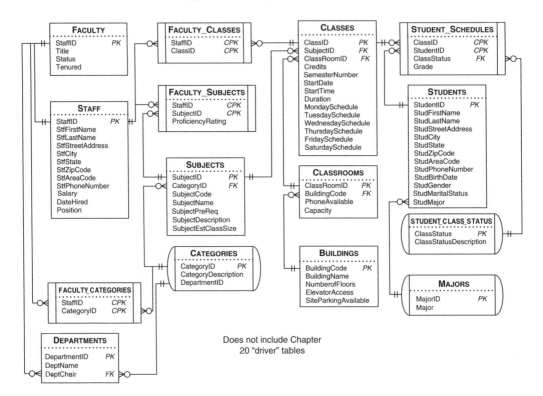

Does not include Chapter
20 "driver" tables

School Scheduling Modify Database

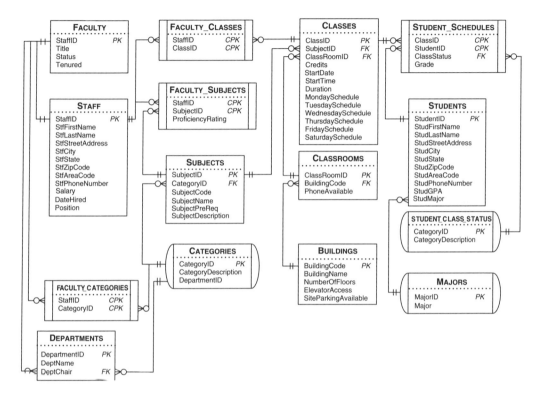

Bowling League Example Database

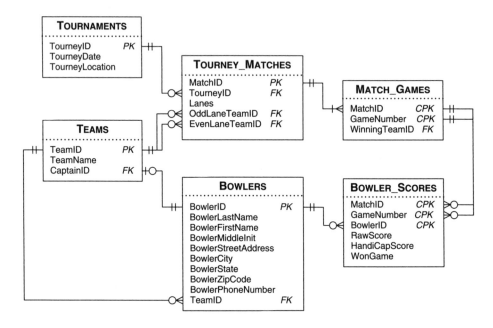

Does not include Chapter
20 "driver" tables

Bowling League Modify Database

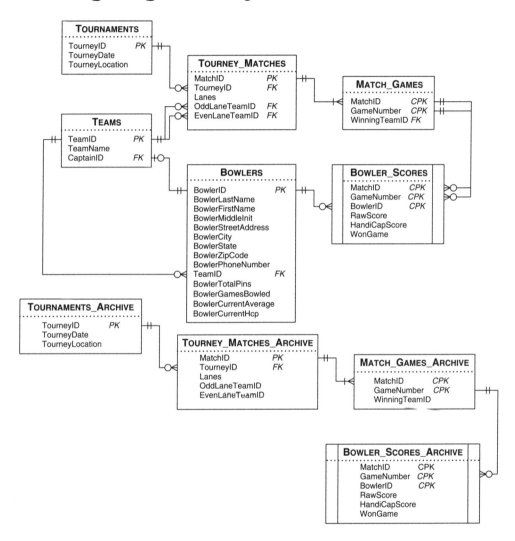

Recipes Database

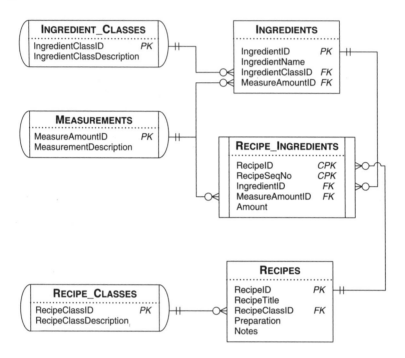

"Driver" Tables

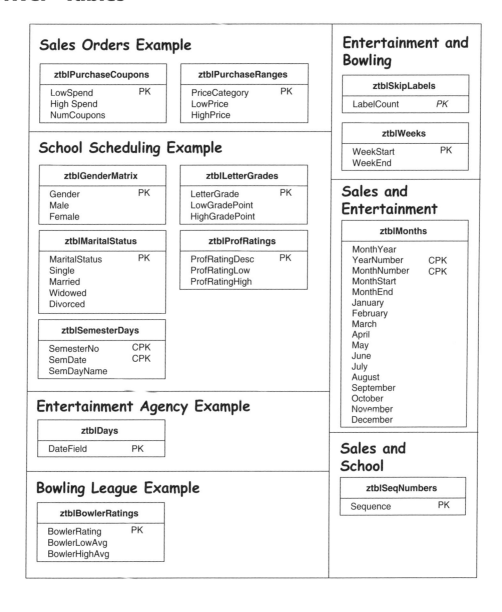

Sales Orders Example

ztblPurchaseCoupons

LowSpend	PK
High Spend	
NumCoupons	

ztblPurchaseRanges

PriceCategory	PK
LowPrice	
HighPrice	

School Scheduling Example

ztblGenderMatrix

Gender	PK
Male	
Female	

ztblLetterGrades

LetterGrade	PK
LowGradePoint	
HighGradePoint	

ztblMaritalStatus

MaritalStatus	PK
Single	
Married	
Widowed	
Divorced	

ztblProfRatings

ProfRatingDesc	PK
ProfRatingLow	
ProfRatingHigh	

ztblSemesterDays

SemesterNo	CPK
SemDate	CPK
SemDayName	

Entertainment Agency Example

ztblDays

DateField	PK

Bowling League Example

ztblBowlerRatings

BowlerRating	PK
BowlerLowAvg	
BowlerHighAvg	

Entertainment and Bowling

ztblSkipLabels

LabelCount	*PK*

ztblWeeks

WeekStart	PK
WeekEnd	

Sales and Entertainment

ztblMonths

MonthYear	
YearNumber	CPK
MonthNumber	CPK
MonthStart	
MonthEnd	
January	
February	
March	
April	
May	
June	
July	
August	
September	
October	
November	
December	

Sales and School

ztblSeqNumbers

Sequence	PK

Date and Time Types, Operations, and Functions

As mentioned in Chapter 5, "Getting More Than Simple Columns," each database system has a variety of functions that you can use to fetch or manipulate date and time values. Each database system also has its own rules regarding data types and date and time arithmetic. The SQL Standard specifically defines three functions, CURRENT_DATE, CURRENT_TIME, and CURRENT_TIMESTAMP, but not all commercial database systems support all three function calls. To help you work with date and time values in your database system, we provide a summary of the data types and arithmetic operations supported. Following that, we've compiled a list of functions for five of the major database systems that you can use to work with date and time values. The lists in this appendix include the function name and a brief description of its use. Consult your database documentation for the specific syntax to use with each function.

IBM DB2

Data Types Supported

> DATE
>
> TIME
>
> TIMESTAMP

Arithmetic Operations Supported

> DATE + <year, month, or day duration or date duration> = DATE
>
> DATE +/- TIME = TIMESTAMP
>
> TIME + <hour, minute, or second duration or time duration> = TIME

TIMESTAMP + <date, or time, or date and time duration> = TIMESTAMP

DATE – DATE = date duration (DECIMAL(8,0) value containing yyyymmdd)

DATE – <year, month, or day duration or date duration> = DATE

TIME – TIME = time duration (DECIMAL(6,0) value containing hhmmss)

TIME – <hour, minute, or second duration or time duration> = TIME

TIMESTAMP – TIMESTAMP = time duration (DECIMAL(20,6) value containing yyyymmddhhmmss.microseconds)

TIMESTAMP – <date, or time, or date and time duration> = TIMESTAMP

Functions

Function Name	Description
ADD_MONTHS (<*expression*>, <*number*>)	Adds a specified number of months to a date or timestamp value.
CURDATE	Obtains the current date value.
CURRENT_DATE	Obtains the current date value.
CURRENT_TIME	Obtains the current time value in the local time zone.
CURRENT_TIMESTAMP	Obtains the current date and time in the local time zone.
CURTIME	Obtains the current time value in the local time zone.
DATE(<*expression*>)	Evaluates the expression and returns a date.
DAY(<*expression*>)	Evaluates the expression and returns the day part of a date, timestamp, or date interval.
DAYNAME(<*expression*>)	Evaluates the expression and returns the name of the day of a date, timestamp, or date interval.
DAYOFMONTH (<*expression*>)	Evaluates the expression and returns the day part (value between 1 and 31) of a date or timestamp.
DAYOFWEEK (<*expression*>)	Evaluates the expression and returns the day number of the week, where 1 = Sunday.

Function Name	Description
DAYOFWEEK_ISO (*<expression>*)	Evaluates the expression and returns the day number of the week, where 1 = Monday.
DAYOFYEAR (*<expression>*)	Evaluates the expression and returns the day number (value between 1 and 366) of the year.
DAYS(*<expression>*)	Evaluates the expression and returns the number of days since January 1, 0001, plus 1.
HOUR(*<expression>*)	Evaluates the expression and returns the hour part of a time or timestamp.
JULIAN_DAY (*<expression>*)	Evaluates the expression and returns the number of days from January 1, 4713 B.C., to the date specified in the expression.
LAST_DAY(*<expression>*)	Returns the last day of the month indicated by the date in the expression.
MICROSECOND (*<expression>*)	Evaluates the timestamp or duration in the expression and returns the microsecond part.
MIDNIGHT_SECONDS (*<expression>*)	Evaluates the time or timestamp and returns the number of seconds between midnight and the time in the expression.
MINUTE (*<expression>*)	Evaluates the expression and returns the minute part of a time, timestamp, or time interval.
MONTH (*<expression>*)	Evaluates the expression and returns the month part of a date, timestamp, or date interval.
MONTHNAME (*<expression>*)	Evaluates the expression and returns the name of the month of a date, timestamp, or date interval.
MONTHS_BETWEEN (*<expression1>*, *<expression2>*)	Evaluates both expressions as a date or timestamp and returns the approximate number of months between the two values. If expression1 is later than expression2, the value is positive.
NEXT_DAY (*<expression>*, *<dayname>*)	Evaluates the expression and returns as a timestamp the date of the first day specified in *<dayname>* (a string containing "MON", "TUE", etc.) following the date in the expression.
NOW	Obtains the current date and time in the local time zone.
QUARTER (*<expression>*)	Evaluates the expression and returns the number of the quarter part of a year in which the date in the expression occurs.

Function Name	Description
ROUND_TIMESTAMP (*<expression>*, *<format string>*)	Evaluates the expression and rounds it to the nearest interval specified in the format string.
SECOND(*<expression>*)	Evaluates the expression and returns the seconds part of a time, timestamp, or time interval.
TIME(*<expression>*)	Evaluates the expression and returns the time part of a time or timestamp value.
TIMESTAMP (*<expression1>*, [*<expression2>*])	Converts separate date or datetime (expression1) and time (expression2) values into a timestamp.
TIMESTAMP_FORMAT (*<expression1>*, *<expression2>*)	Returns a timestamp by formatting the string in expression1 using the format string in expression2.
TIMESTAMP_ISO (*<expression>*)	Evaluates the date, time, or timestamp in the expression and returns a timestamp. If the expression contains only a date, the timestamp contains that date and zero for the time. If the expression contains only a time, the timestamp contains the current date and the time specified.
TIMESTAMPDIFF (*<numeric expression>*, *<string expression>*)	The numeric expression must contain a code numeric value where 1 = microseconds, 2 = seconds, 4 = minutes, 8 = hours, 16 = days, 32 = weeks, 64 = months, 128 = quarters, and 256 = years. The string expression must be the result of subtracting two timestamps and converting the result to a string. The function returns the estimated number of requested intervals represented by the string.
TRUNC_TIMESTAMP (*<expression>*, *<format string>*)	Evaluates the expression and truncates it to the nearest interval specified in the format string.
WEEK(*<expression>*)	Evaluates the expression and returns the week number of the date part of the value, where January 1 starts the first week.
WEEK_ISO(*<expression>*)	Evaluates the expression and returns the week number of the date part of the value, where the first week of the year is the first week containing a Thursday.
YEAR(*<expression>*)	Evaluates the expression and returns the year part of a date or timestamp.

Microsoft Access

Data Types Supported

Date/Time

Arithmetic Operations Supported

Date/Time + Date/Time = Date/Time

(Value is the result of adding the number of days and fractions of a day in each value. December 31, 1899 is day 0.)

Date/Time – Date/Time = number of days and fractions of days between the two values

Date/Time +/– integer = Date/Time

(Adds or subtracts the number of days in the integer)

Date/Time +/– fraction = Date/Time

(Adds or subtracts the time represented by the fraction – 0.5 = 12 hours)

Date/Time +/– integer.fraction = Date/Time

Functions

Function Name	Description
CDate(*<expression>*)	Converts the expression to a date value.
Date	Obtains the current date value.
DateAdd(*<interval>*, *<number>*, *<expression>*)	Adds the specified number of the interval to the date or Date/Time expression.
DateDiff(*<interval>*, *<expression1>*, *<expression2>*, *<firstdayofweek>*, *<firstdayofyear>*)	Returns the specified number of intervals between the Date/Time in expression1 and the Date/Time in expression2. You can optionally specify a first day of the week other than Sunday and a first week of the year to start on January 1, the first week that has at least four days, or the first full week.
DatePart(*<interval>*, *<expression>*, *<firstdayofweek>*, *<firstdayofyear>*)	Extracts the part of the date or time from the expression as specified by the interval. You can optionally specify a first day of the week other than Sunday and a first week of the year to start on January 1, the first week that has at least four days, or the first full week.

Function Name	Description
DateSerial(<*year*>, <*month*>, <*day*>)	Returns the date value corresponding to the specified year, month, and day.
DateValue(<*expression*>)	Evaluates the expression and returns a Date/Time value.
Day(<*expression*>)	Evaluates the expression and returns the day part of a date.
Hour(<*expression*>)	Evaluates the expression and returns the hour part of a time.
IsDate(<*expression*>)	Evaluates the expression and returns True if the expression is a valid date value.
Minute(<*expression*>)	Evaluates the expression and returns the minute part of a time value.
Month(<*expression*>)	Evaluates the expression and returns the month part of a date value.
MonthName (<*expression*>, <*abbreviate*>)	Evaluates the expression (which must be an integer value from 1 to 12) and returns the equivalent month name. The name is abbreviated if the abbreviated argument is True.
Now	Obtains the current date and time value in the local time zone.
Second(<*expression*>)	Evaluates the expression and returns the seconds part of a time.
Time	Obtains the current time value in the local time zone.
TimeSerial(<*hour*>, <*minute*>, <*second*>)	Returns the time value corresponding to the specified hour, minute, and second.
TimeValue (<*expression*>)	Evaluates the expression and returns the time portion.
WeekDay(<*expression*>, <*firstdayofweek*>)	Evaluates the expression and returns an integer representing the day of the week. Optionally, you can specify a first day of the week other than Sunday.
WeekDayName (<*daynumber*>, <*abbreviate*>, <*firstdayofweek*>)	Returns the day of the week according to the specified day number. Optionally, you can ask to have the name abbreviated, and you can specify a first day of the week other than Sunday.
Year(<*expression*>)	Evaluates the expression and returns the year part of a date.

Microsoft SQL Server

Data Types Supported

date

time

smalldatetime

datetime

datetime2

datetimeoffset

Arithmetic Operations Supported

datetime + datetime = datetime

(Value is the result of adding the number of days and fractions of a day in each value. January 1, 1900 is day 0.)

datetime +/– integer = datetime

(Adds or subtracts the number of days in the integer)

datetime +/– fraction = datetime

(Adds or subtracts the time represented by the fraction – 0.5 = 12 hours)

datetime +/– integer.fraction = datetime

datetime – datetime = number of days and fractions of days between the two values

smalldatetime + smalldatetime = smalldatetime

(Value is the result of adding the number of days and fractions of a day in each value. January 1, 1900 is day 0.)

smalldatetime +/– integer = smalldatetime

(Adds or subtracts the number of days in the integer)

smalldatetime +/– fraction = smalldatetime

(Adds or subtracts the time represented by the fraction – 0.5 = 12 hours)

smalldatetime + integer.fraction = smalldatetime

smalldatetime – smalldatetime = number of days and fractions of days between the two values

Functions

Function Name	Description
CURRENT_TIMESTAMP	Obtains the current date and time in the local time zone.
DATEADD(*<interval>*, *<number>*, *<expression>*)	Adds the specified number of the interval to the date or datetime expression.
DATEDIFF (*<interval>*, *<expression1>*, *<expression2>*)	Returns the specified number of intervals between the datetime in expression1 and the datetime in expression2.
DATEFROMPARTS(*<year>*, *<month>*, *<day>*)	Returns the date value for a specified year, month, and day
DATENAME(*<interval>*, *<expression>*)	Evaluates the expression and returns a string containing the name of the interval specified. If the interval is a month or a day of a week, the name is spelled out.
DATEPART(*<interval>*, *<expression>*)	Extracts as an integer the part of the date or time from the expression as specified by the interval.
DATETIMEFROMPARTS (*<year>*, *<month>*, *<day>*, *<hour>*, *<minute>*, *<second>*, *<millisecond>*)	Returns the datetime value for a specified year, month, day, hour, minute, second, and millisecond.
DATETIME2FROMPARTS (*<year>*, *<month>*, *<day>*, *<hour>*, *<minute>*, *<second>*, *<fraction>*, *<precision>*)	Returns the datetime2 value for a specified year, month, day, hour, minute, second, and fraction with the specified precision.
DAY(*<expression>*)	Evaluates the expression and returns the day part of a date.
EOMONTH(*<date>* [,*<months>*])	Adds the optional number of months to the date specified and returns the last day of that month.
GETDATE()	Obtains the current date as a datetime value.
GETUTCDATE()	Obtains the current UTC (Coordinated Universal Time) date as a datetime value.
ISDATE(*<expression>*)	Evaluates the expression and returns 1 if the expression is a valid date value.

Function Name	Description
MONTH(<*expression*>)	Evaluates the expression and returns the month part of a date value as an integer.
SMALLDATETIMEFROM-PARTS(<*year*>, <*month*>, <*day*>, <*hour*>, <*minute*>, <*second*>)	Returns the smalldatetime value for a specified year, month, day, hour, minute, and second.
SWITCHOFFSET (<*datetimeoffset*>, <*offset*>)	Changes the time zone offset of the date-timeoffset value to the specified offset and returns a datetimeoffset.
SYSDATETIME()	Returns the current date and time as a datetime2 value.
SYSDATETIMEOFFSET()	Returns the current date and time (including time zone offset) as a datetimeoffset value.
SYSUTCDATETIME()	Returns the current UTC date and time as a datetime2 value.
TIMEFROMPARTS(<*hour*>, <*minute*>, <*second*>, <*fraction*>, <*precision*>)	Returns the time value for a specified hour, minute, second, and fraction with the specified precision.
TODATETIMEOFFSET (<*datetime2*>, <*offset*>)	Converts the datetime2 value using the specified time zone offset and returns a date-timeoffset value.
YEAR(<*expression*>)	Evaluates the expression and returns the year part of a date as an integer.

MySQL

Data Types Supported

date

datetime

timestamp

time

year

Arithmetic Operations Supported

date +/– Interval <interval [year/quarter/month/week/day]> = date

datetime +/– Interval <interval [year/quarter/month/week/day/hour/minute/second]> = datetime

timestamp +/– Interval <interval [year/quarter/month/week/day/hour/minute/second]> = timestamp

time +/– Interval <interval [hour/minute/second]> = time

❖ **Note** It is also legal to add or subtract an integer or decimal value to or from any of the date and time data types, but MySQL will first convert the date or time value to a number and then perform the operation. For example, adding 30 to the date value '2017-11-15' yields the number 20171145. Adding 100 to the time value '12:20:00' yields 122100. Be sure to use the INTERVAL keyword when performing date and time arithmetic.

Functions

Function Name	Description
ADDDATE(<*expression*>, <*days*>)	Adds the specified number of days to the date value in the expression.
ADDDATE(<*expression*>, INTERVAL <*amount*> <*units*>)	Adds the specified interval quantity to the date value in the expression.
ADDTIME(<*expression*>, <*time*>)	Adds the specified amount of time to the time or datetime expression value.
CONVERT_TZ(<*datetime*>, <*from tz*>, <*to tz*>)	Converts the datetime value from the specified time zone to the specified time zone.
CURRENT_DATE, CURDATE()	Obtains the current date value.
CURRENT_TIME, CURTIME()	Obtains the current time value in the local time zone.
CURRENT_TIMESTAMP	Obtains the current date and time in the local time zone.
DATE(<*expression*>)	Extracts the date from a datetime expression.

Function Name	Description
DATE_ADD(*<expression>*, INTERVAL *<interval>* *<quantity>*)	Adds the specified interval quantity to the date or datetime value in the expression.
DATE_SUB(*<expression>*, INTERVAL *<interval>* *<quantity>*)	Subtracts the specified interval quantity from the date or datetime value in the expression.
DATEDIFF(*<expression1>*, *<expression2>*)	Subtracts the second datetime expression from the first datetime expression and returns the number of days between the two.
DAY(*<expression>*)	Evaluates the expression and returns the day part of a date as a number from 1 to 31.
DAYNAME(*<expression>*)	Evaluates the expression and returns the day name of the date or datetime value.
DAYOFMONTH (*<expression>*)	Evaluates the expression and returns the day part of a date as a number from 1 to 31.
DAYOFWEEK(*<expression>*)	Evaluates the expression and returns the day number within the week for the date or datetime value, where 1 = Sunday.
DAYOFYEAR(*<expression>*)	Evaluates the expression and returns the day number of the year, a value from 1 to 366.
EXTRACT(*<unit>* FROM *<expression>*)	Evaluates the expression and returns the unit portion (such as year or month) specified.
FROM_DAYS(*<number>*)	Returns the date that is the number of days since December 31, 1 B.C. Day 366 is January 1, 01.
HOUR(*<expression>*)	Evaluates the expression and returns the hour part of a time.
LAST_DAY(*<expression>*)	Returns the last day of the month indicated by the date in the expression.
LOCALTIME, LOCALTIMESTAMP	See the NOW function.
MAKEDATE(*<year>*, *<dayofyear>*)	Returns a date for the specified year and day of year (1–366).
MAKETIME(*<hour>*, *<minute>*, *<second>*)	Returns a time for the specified hour, minute, and second.

Function Name	Description
MICROSECOND (<*expression*>)	Evaluates the expression and returns the microsecond portion of a time or datetime value.
MINUTE(<*expression*>)	Evaluates the expression and returns the minute part of a time or datetime value.
MONTH(<*expression*>)	Evaluates the expression and returns the month part of a date value.
MONTHNAME (<*expression*>)	Evaluates the expression and returns the name of the month of a date or datetime value.
NOW()	Obtains the current date and time value in the local time zone.
QUARTER(<*expression*>)	Evaluates the expression and returns the number of the quarter part of a year in which the date in the expression occurs.
SECOND(<*expression*>)	Evaluates the expression and returns the seconds part of a time or datetime value.
STR_TO_DATE (<*expression*>, <*format*>)	Evaluates the expression according to the format specified and returns a date, datetime, or time value.
SUBDATE(<*expression*>, INTERVAL <*interval*> <*quantity*>)	See the DATE_SUB function.
SUBTIME(<*expression1*>, <*expression2*>)	Subtracts the time in expression2 from the datetime or time in expression1 and returns a time or datetime answer.
TIME(<*expression*>)	Evaluates the expression and returns the time part of a time or datetime value.
TIME_TO_SEC (<*expression*>)	Evaluates the time in the expression and returns the number of seconds.
TIMEDIFF(<*expression1*>, <*expression2*>)	Subtracts the time or datetime value in expression2 from the time or datetime value in expression1 and returns the difference.
TIMESTAMP(<*expression*>)	Evaluates the expression and returns a datetime value.
TIMESTAMP(<*expression1*>, <*expression2*>)	Adds the time in expression2 to the date or datetime in expression1 and returns a datetime value.

Function Name	Description
TIMESTAMPADD (*<interval>*, *<number>*, *<expression>*)	Adds the specified number of the interval to the date or datetime expression.
TIMESTAMPDIFF (*<interval>*, *<expression1>*, *<expression2>*)	Returns the specified number of intervals between the date or datetime in expression1 and the date or datetime in expression2.
TO_DAYS(*<expression>*)	Evaluates the date in the expression and returns the number of days since year 0.
UTC_DATE	Obtains the current UTC (Coordinated Universal Time) date.
UTC_TIME	Obtains the current UTC (Coordinated Universal Time) time.
UTC_TIMESTAMP	Obtains the current UTC (Coordinated Universal Time) date and time.
WEEK(*<expression>*, *<mode>*)	Evaluates the expression and returns the week number of the date part of the value using the mode specified.
WEEKDAY(*<expression>*)	Evaluates the expression and returns an integer representing the day of the week, where 0 is Monday.
WEEKOFYEAR (*<expression>*)	Evaluates the date expression and returns the week number (1–53), assuming the first week has more than three days.
YEAR(*<expression>*)	Evaluates the expression and returns the year part of a date.

Oracle

Data Types Supported

DATE

TIMESTAMP

INTERVAL YEAR TO MONTH

INTERVAL DAY TO SECOND

Arithmetic Operations Supported

DATE + INTERVAL = DATE

DATE + numeric = DATE

DATE – DATE = numeric (days and fraction of a day)

DATE – TIMESTAMP = INTERVAL

DATE – INTERVAL = DATE

DATE – numeric = DATE

INTERVAL + DATE = DATE

INTERVAL + TIMESTAMP = TIMESTAMP

INTERVAL + INTERVAL = INTERVAL

INTERVAL – INTERVAL = INTERVAL

INTERVAL * numeric = INTERVAL

INTERVAL / numeric = INTERVAL

Functions

Function Name	Description
ADD_MONTHS(<*date*>, <*integer*>)	Returns the date plus the specified number of months.
CURRENT_DATE	Obtains the current date value.
CURRENT_TIMESTAMP	Obtains the current date, time, and time-stamp in the local time zone.
DBTIMEZONE	Obtains the time zone of the database.
EXTRACT(<*interval*> FROM <*expression*>)	Evaluates the expression and returns the requested interval (year, month, day, etc.).
LOCALTIMESTAMP	Obtains the current date and time in the local time zone.
MONTHS_BETWEEN (<*expression1*>, <*expression2*>)	Calculates the months and fractions of months between expression2 and expression1.
NEW_TIME(<*expression*>, <*timezone1*>, <*timezone2*>)	Evaluates the date expression as though it is the first time zone and returns the date in the second time zone.

Function Name	Description
NEXT_DAY(<*expression*>, <*dayname*>)	Evaluates the expression and returns the date of the first day specified in <dayname> (a string containing "MONDAY", "TUESDAY", etc.) following the date in the expression.
NUMTODSINTERVAL (<*number*>, <*unit*>)	Converts the number to an interval in the unit specified (DAY, HOUR, MINUTE, SECOND).
NUMTOYMINTERVAL (<*number*>, <*unit*>)	Converts the number to an interval in the unit specified (YEAR, MONTH).
ROUND(<*expression*>, <*interval*>)	Rounds a date value to the interval specified.
SESSIONTIMEZONE	Obtains the time zone of the current session.
SYSDATE	Obtains the current date and time on the database server.
SYSTIMESTAMP	Obtains the current date, time, and time zone on the database server.
TO_DATE(<*expression*>, <*format*>)	Converts the string expression to a date data type using the format specified.
TO_DSINTERVAL (<*expression*>)	Converts the string expression to a days-to-seconds interval.
TO_TIMESTAMP (<*expression*>, <*format*>)	Converts the string expression to a time-stamp data type using the format specified.
TO_TIMESTAMP_TZ (<*expression*>, <*format*>)	Converts the string expression to a timestamp with time zone data type using the format specified.
TO_YMINTERVAL	Converts the string expression to a years-to-months interval.
TRUNC(<*expression*>, <*interval*>)	Truncates a date value to the interval specified.

PostgreSQL

Data Types Supported

DATE

TIME (with or without time zone)

TIMESTAMP (with or without time zone)

INTERVAL

Arithmetic Operations Supported

DATE +/– INTERVAL = TIMESTAMP

DATE +/– numeric = DATE

DATE + TIME = TIMESTAMP

DATE – DATE = integer

TIME +/– INTERVAL = TIME

TIME – TIME = INTERVAL

TIMESTAMP +/– INTERVAL = TIMESTAMP

TIMESTAMP – TIMESTAMP = INTERVAL

INTERVAL +/– INTERVAL = INTERVAL

INTERVAL * numeric = INTERVAL

INTERVAL / numeric = INTERVAL

Functions

Function Name	Description
AGE(\<timestamp>, \<timestamp>)	Subtract arguments, producing a "symbolic" result that uses years and months.
AGE(\<timestamp>)	Subtract from current_date (at midnight).
CLOCK_TIMESTAMP()	Current date and time (changes during statement execution).
CURRENT_DATE	Current date.
CURRENT_TIME	Current time of day.
CURRENT_TIMESTAMP	Current date and time (start of current transaction).

Function Name	Description
DATE_PART(<text>, <timestamp>)	Get subfield specified by <text> ('year', 'month', 'day', etc.) from <timestamp> (equivalent to EXTRACT)
DATE_PART(<text>, <interval>)	Get subfield specified by <text> ('day', 'minute', 'second', and so on) from <interval> (equivalent to EXTRACT)
DATE_TRUNC(<text>, <timestamp>)	Truncate <timestamp> to precision specified by <text> ('microseconds', 'milliseconds', 'minute', and the like)
EXTRACT(<text> FROM <timestamp>)	Get subfield specified by <text> ('year', 'month', 'day', and so on) from <timestamp>
EXTRACT(<text> FROM <interval>)	Get subfield specified by <text> (days, minutes, seconds, and the like) from <interval>
ISFINITE(<date>)	Test for finite date (not +/− infinity)
ISFINITE(<timestamp>)	Test for finite time stamp (not +/− infinity)
ISFINITE(<interval>)	Test for finite interval
JUSTIFY_DAYS (<interval>)	Adjust interval so 30-day time periods are represented as months
JUSTIFY_HOURS (<interval>)	Adjust interval so 24-hour time periods are represented as day
JUSTIFY_INTERVAL (<interval>)	Adjust interval using justify_days and justify_ hours, with additional sign adjustments
LOCALTIME	Current time of day
LOCALTIMESTAMP	Current date and time (start of current transaction)
NOW()	Current date and time (start of current transaction)
STATEMENT_ TIMESTAMP()	Current date and time (start of current statement)
TIMEOFDAY()	Current date and time (like clock_timestamp, but as a text string)
TRANSACTION_ TIMESTAMP()	Current date and time (start of current transaction)

Suggested Reading

These are the books I recommend you read if you want to learn more about database design or expand your knowledge of SQL. Keep in mind that some of these books will be challenging because they are more technical in nature. Also, some authors assume that you have a fairly significant background in computers, databases, and programming.

Database Books

Connolly, Thomas, and Carolyn Begg. *Database Systems: A Practical Approach to Design, Implementation, and Management* (6th ed.). Essex, England: Addison-Wesley, 2014.

Coronel, Carlos and Steven Morris. *Database Systems: Design, Implementation, and Management* (11th ed.). Stamford, CT: Cengage Learning, 2015.

Date, C.J. *An Introduction to Database Systems* (8th ed.). Boston, MA: Addison-Wesley, 2003.

Date, C.J. *Database in Depth: Relational Theory for Practitioners.* Sebastopol, CA: O'Reilly Media, 2005.

Date, C.J. *Database Design and Relational Theory: Normal Forms and All That Jazz.* Sebastopol, CA: O'Reilly Media, 2012.

Hernandez, Michael J. *Database Design for Mere Mortals* (3rd ed.). Boston, MA: Addison-Wesley, 2013.

Books on SQL

Bowman, Judith S., Sandra L. Emerson, and Marcy Darnovsky. *The Practical SQL Handbook: Using SQL Variants* (4th ed.). Boston, MA: Addison-Wesley, 2001.

Celko, Joe. *Joe Celko's SQL for Smarties: Advanced SQL Programming* (5th ed.). Burlington, MA: Morgan Kaufmann Publishers, 2014.

Date, C.J., and Hugh Darwen. *A Guide to the SQL Standard* (4th ed.). Reading, MA: Addison-Wesley, 1996.

Rockoff, Larry. *The Language of SQL* (2nd ed.). Boston, MA: Addison-Wesley, 2016.

Viescas, John L., Douglas J. Steele, and Ben G. Clothier. *Effective SQL: 61 Ways to Write Better SQL*. Boston, MA: Addison-Wesley, 2016.

Index

Symbols

* (asterisk), 195
|| (concatenation operator), 138
> (greater than), 186–188
>= (greater than or equal to), 186
< (less than), 186–188
<= (less than or equal to), 186
() (parentheses), 144, 210–211, 216
    CASE (conditional expressions), 684
% (percent sign), 195
? (question mark), 195
_ (underscore), 195

Numbers

2016 SQL Standard, 4

A

ABS, 142
Access, CASE (conditional expressions), 684
Actian, 74
adding sorting specifications to UNION, 382
aggregate expressions, 445
aggregate functions, 444–446, 798–799
    AVG, calculating mean values, 451–452
    Bowling League Database, 844–846
    COUNT, 406–408, 446
    COUNT (*value expression*), 448–449
    COUNT(*), 446
        counting all the rows, 446–448

in filters, 457–459
grouping data, 477–478
MAX, 406–408
    finding largest values, 452–454
MIN, finding smallest values, 454–455
Null values, 445
OVER(), 803–805
Sales Orders Database, 847–850
sample statements, 459–466
    Bowling League Database, 463–465
    Entertainment Agency Database, 461–462
    Recipes Database, 465–466
    Sales Orders Database, 460–461
    School Scheduling Database, 462–463
School Scheduling Database, 851–852
subqueries, 457–458
SUM, computing totals, 450–451
syntax diagrams, 444
using more than one function, 455–457
windows functions, 827–834
alias names, assigning to tables, INNER JOIN, 282–284
ALL, 371, 375, 417–420
all rows, deleting with DELETE statement, 605–607
alphabetical order, sorting by, 108
American National Standards Institute (ANSI), 2, 75
    evolution of SQL/86, 76–79

Register Your Product at informit.com/register

Access additional benefits and **save 35%** on your next purchase

- Automatically receive a coupon for 35% off your next purchase, valid for 30 days. Look for your code in your InformIT cart or the Manage Codes section of your account page.

- Download available product updates.

- Access bonus material if available.*

- Check the box to hear from us and receive exclusive offers on new editions and related products.

Registration benefits vary by product. Benefits will be listed on your account page under Registered Products.

InformIT.com—The Trusted Technology Learning Source

InformIT is the online home of information technology brands at Pearson, the world's foremost education company. At InformIT.com, you can:
- Shop our books, eBooks, software, and video training
- Take advantage of our special offers and promotions (informit.com/promotions)
- Sign up for special offers and content newsletter (informit.com/newsletters)
- Access thousands of free chapters and video lessons

Connect with InformIT—Visit informit.com/community

the trusted technology learning source

31901062629532